A
BIRD of
PASSAGE

the story of my life

BEST WISHES

Otto Lang

by Otto Lang

LIBRARY OF CONGRESS
CATALOG CARD NO. 94-96154

ISBN 1-57510-026-6

First published by Otto Lang, Seattle Washington,
in cooperation with SkyHouse Publishers,
an imprint of Falcon Press, Helena, Montana.

Second Printing, 1996, by Pictorial Histories Publ. Co., Inc.
Missoula, Montana

Front cover photo: Ray Atkeson
Back cover photo: Otto Lang

PICTORIAL HISTORIES PUBLISHING CO., INC.
713 South Third St. W., Missoula, Montana 59801

I know of no more encouraging fact
than the unquestionable ability of man to elevate
his life by a conscious endeavor.
—Henry David Thoreau, *Man and Nature*

In memory of James F. Parker
who lost his life at the foot of Nanga Parbat in Pakistan
when our camera raft capsized in the turbulent Indus River
during the filming of *Search for Paradise*.
May Jimmie have found his.

Jim Parker playing the flute, Hunza.

CONTENTS

ACKNOWLEDGMENTS

Writing and publishing a book involves many people. Had it not been for my father, Alfred Lang, and for Hannes Schneider, Jerome Hill, Darryl F. Zanuck, and Lowell Thomas, I doubt that this "Ottobiography" ever would have seen the light of day. I owe these men a lot. My father gave love and a guiding hand to a growing boy. Hannes Schneider stood tall as icon and mentor to me in the world of skiing. Jerome Hill helped me immeasurably in appreciating fine painting, music, and literature. Darryl Zanuck took me under his wings and tutored me as an aspiring filmmaker. With Lowell Thomas I shared many adventures—on and off the ski slopes, traveling around the globe—and a close friendship for more than fifty years.

There are many others to whom I offer my gratitude—alas, too many to list here. They know who they are. I do wish to express my thanks to Marnie Hagmann Pavelich, who tackled the formidable task of editing my original manuscript. I remember Marnie as a demure and charming teenager; she happened to be sister of Dale, then married to my son Peter.

Thanks also to Barbara Marinacci in California, who struggled with typing the first one hundred pages of my embryonic memoir, and to Kathy Hinds, in Seattle, who took over when I moved here. Kathy was indispensible in deciphering my handprint hieroglyphics. She typed them out in presentable fashion, deeply absorbed in the story and eagerly awaiting the next chapter.

An especially deep bow to gracious Christy Hill at Vail, Jim and Helen Nassikas at San Fransisco, and George Hunt at La Jolla, who backed me up spontaneously when I needed it most in order to turn over my finished manuscript to the printers.

Also, I shall not forget renowned aerial photographer Robert Cameron's sage advice and introduction into the labyrinthine complexities of selling a book. My thanks, too, to, Emmett Watson, Seattle's journalist emeritus, for his enthusiastic response after reading chapters of my book in progress.

To Ray Atkeson and the many other contributing photographers, I feel much indebted.

Last but not least I wish to thank the group of collaborators at SkyHouse Publishers and Falcon Press for their unstinting support and dedication in bringing this project to fruition. To Rick Newby and Jeff Wincapaw, "pros" in their league, my heartfelt gratitude.

O. L.
Seattle, Washington, 1994

FOREWORD

I first met Otto Lang in the winter of 1940, when I was five years old. With the help of Averell Harriman, my parents had discovered a new pastime to take their minds off the rigors of Hollywood. It was called skiing, and if you had listened to my father enthusiastically speak of it, you would have thought it was his invention. Both he and my mother became instant ski bugs, and the getaway they chose to indulge in this new (for them) activity was Sun Valley, Idaho.

To insure that we were in the best of hands, Averell asked Otto to give our family of five his personal attention and teach us to ski. It was important to him that we carry back to Hollywood good word of mouth about his winter resort. He hoped that more of the Hollywood movie colony would follow in our ski tracks.

So my father, Darryl, and mother, Virginia, took to the slopes of Baldy with Otto, while my two sisters and I headed over to the gentler slopes of Dollar Mountain. We all met downstairs in the ski room at a designated hour, with Otto always on hand to make sure our skis had been properly waxed and tuned the night before and that all the arrangements for the day's outing were in perfect order. I remember him as an imposing and dashing figure in those early days—someone whom you instantly recognized as a man in charge. While he never raised his voice and was always in an affable mood, there was a quiet sense of authority about him at all times. It was his manner and appearance and the way he held himself that set him apart from his peers. Handsome, smiling, confident, intelligent—that was Otto. And there was also something very soothing about his voice that reassured those of us who needed a lot of encouragement to face the ski challenges of the day.

Little did my father suspect, while strapping on his skis each day with his giant cigar jutting from his clenched jaw, that it was he who would be the teacher instead of the pupil. For, you see, Otto, already an accomplished still photographer and published author, was learning the movie business, bit by bit, through association with my father.

My father had come to Hollywood from Wahoo, Nebraska, as an aspiring young writer and had gained early fame and fortune writing scenarios for his favorite canine star, Rin Tin Tin. He had spectacularly risen to the top of the heap by cofounding Twentieth Century Fox and becoming boss of a giant movie operation. Otto, much to his credit, never took advantage of this and was perfectly content to just keep on soaking up as much knowledge about the movie industry as was possible. To this end, after ski school classes, he often sat in on the rushes that my father screened at the Sun Valley Opera House each afternoon, après-ski. Here the two of them would look at the daily output of films that were shot at the studio and around the globe and then shipped to Sun Valley for Darryl F. Zanuck's evaluation. On many occasions, the film editors and producers involved in these shows would be in attendance, and DFZ would make his editorial suggestions and comments and give instructions to be followed. What a learning opportunity it was for Otto to observe this master showman working at his craft in the Sun Valley Opera House, just as though he were in his Hollywood office. A fledgling filmmaker, bound to leave his mark, was born.

So while my father was learning how to transfer his weight from ski to ski and progress from stem turns to stem christies, Otto was learning how to tell stories on celluloid from A to Zanuck. Theirs was a partnership of a rare sort that would eventually result in my father's becoming a pretty good skier—at least far better than any of his fellow moguls—while Otto was transferring *his* weight completely out of his ski boots and into a pair of suede loafers. It was also a partnership based on friendship, admiration, and mutual respect that would continue until my father and, later, my mother, were to pass away. I, of course, became a beneficiary of this partnership, gaining Otto as a lifelong friend and, on a few occasions, a coworker on films.

Through the years, Otto has been recognized as a skilled writer, producer, and director with a keen eye, not only for the visual images his films and photographs exhibit but also for the sensitive and imaginative nature of his stories and subjects. His reputation as one of the finest ski instructors and technical authorities has long since been eclipsed by this reputation as a respected filmmaker. But more importantly, Otto will always be best remembered for his strength of character, his honesty and sincerity, and for his devotion and loyalty to his family and friends. I am very proud to be counted among the latter.

RICHARD ZANUCK
Beverly Hills, California

Otto Lang, ski jumping at Ruud Mountain, Sun Valley, 1940.

BOSNIA

When I was a lad ten years of age, I had already traveled to many far corners of this earth. I had explored the Gobi Desert of Mongolia. I had endured the bone-chilling cold of the arctic winter and trudged through endless wastes of snow and ice, on foot and by dogsled, to reach the North Pole. I had cut through the Strait of Magellan, skirting the wild coastal shores of Tierra del Fuego, exposed to some of the fiercest storms and buffeted by sky-high waves. On the western coast of the North American continent, I fought hordes of Indians and joined men in pursuit of gold. I had been to fabled Samarkand and Constantinople. From Zanzibar and Dar es Salaam I followed the footsteps of Henry Morton Stanley to unravel the whereabouts of David Livingstone, the Scottish missionary who had been missing for over a year. I shall never forget the day we found him in the jungle outpost of Ujiji on the shores of Lake Tanganyika, when Stanley uttered the immortal words: "Dr. Livingstone, I presume."

I had traveled a world of fantasy, mixed with reality, into which my father had led me. My father was an inveterate world explorer, student of science, and dreamer of ever more conquests of the universe—all this while sitting in his armchair, surrounded by books and maps, eager and willing to take me along on wild flights of fancy. He imbued me with a sense of curiosity and a thirst for knowledge that would remain with me my whole life.

My father was not a tall man, but well-built like an athlete, five feet eleven inches or thereabouts, with an erect military posture, clear blue eyes, a high forehead, plenty of hair parted on one side, a trim moustache, good teeth, a ruddy complexion, and a hearty sense of humor. Although he was not a chain smoker, he enjoyed the ritual of smoking a cigarette of the finest Bosnian tobacco, rolled into a square piece of tissue paper and sealed with the tip of his tongue.

At that time, the early years of the twentieth century, we lived in Zenica, a small provincial town in Bosnia, in eastern Europe. It was only a short train ride to Sarajevo, the capital of Bosnia and part of Yugoslavia, a country with a turbulent history.

Occupied and subjugated by the Turks, the region was ruled for over four hundred years by the Ottoman sultans of Constantinople from their exalted but utterly corrupt throne known as the Porte. For some reason the Turks chose Bosnia and Herzegovina to become their stronghold. They proselytized the indigenous population to embrace Islam. They built new mosques and ruthlessly converted most of the existing Christian churches into houses of worship for Allah and Mohammed, his prophet; in the churches, priceless Byzantine frescoes, dating back to the thirteenth century, were brutally gouged with sharp instruments then whitewashed into oblivion with a heavy coat of lime. A string of formidable Turkish fortresses perched on mountaintops to guard strategic entrances to valleys and mountain passes. As builders and architects the conquerors were a talented lot; many bridges they built spanning rivers and deep gorges are still intact today, having withstood the ravages of time, floods, and war.

The hardships imposed by Turk rule on the indigenous Yugoslavian population were enormous. Someone had to pay for the extravagances of the Ottoman invaders, and it was not the intention of the Porte to do so. The tolls were extracted in forced labor, taxes, and a major share of the yearly harvest, feeding a welling undercurrent of rebellion and hatred. It took four hundred years of tyranny and oppression before the Turks were thrown out. Then others moved in, namely the ruler of the vast Austro-Hungarian Empire, Franz Joseph I.

Kaiser Franz Joseph I first grasped onto the country in 1878, when a long-overdue peace treaty was hammered out in Berlin after the Franco-Prussian War. Countries were doled out to the ruling powers of that era:

Austria, Germany, Russia, France, and Great Britain. The territories of Bosnia and Herzegovina were put into the trusteeship of the Austrian Hapsburg dynasty. Two of the largest and most productive provinces of that splintered region, Croatia and Slovenia, were already part of the Austro-Hungarian domain. Bosnia and Herzegovina were soon to feel the impact of Austrian culture and mores. Two decades later, Franz Joseph I decided to officially "annex" these territories and make them part of his empire. In 1908 his troops marched in and took over.

A graduate of a military academy near Vienna, my father, Alfred Lang, had been part of the Austrian administrative cadre for some years before the actual annexation of Bosnia took place. He liked where he was, and he liked the people. One of his inherent qualities was an ability to make friends, and he did so even in the adverse political climate. He fell in love with Olga Spazinska, a young woman of Croatian origin, and wooed her into marriage. With her high Slavic cheekbones, blooming complexion, and svelte figure, my mother could not help but attract attention.

Nelly, my oldest sister, was born in 1906. I followed in 1908, and Elsa and Erna followed in two-year intervals. Nelly was by far the brightest intellectually. Elsa was the prettiest and blessed with a sunny disposition. Erna, as a baby, was the most endearing of all.

Alas, during my mother's pregnancy with Erna, she contracted German measles, which affected the fetus. Little was known at that time about the devastating effects of this seemingly harmless disease on unborn infants. After two years or so, it became apparent that Erna, although physically normal, was mentally handicapped.

We were a tightly knit family; as children we were enveloped by parental love. My mother dispelled her occasional indigo moods, part of her Slavic heritage and temperament, with cheerfulness. She was a superb cook and most efficient housekeeper. Our home was adjacent to the railroad station, a hub of activity. Passenger trains arrived and left with a perfunctory stop, the daily express roared through unrelentingly, and freight trains crawled by at a leisurely pace, laden with coal, mineral ore, livestock, and timber. There was always something to see, something to stimulate one's imagination.

The entire lower portion of the building in which we lived was taken up by the post office, which was under the jurisdiction of my father. Our living quarters occupied the second story. I remember them as spacious and bathed in light. Windows on one side looked out over the railroad tracks, and those on the opposite side opened onto a busy street. A small, triangular, fenced-in garden with a billowing tree that had a bench around its trunk was reserved for us children and provided a welcome, green enclave to play in. Growing up in these surroundings was idyllic.

THE PLANTING OF SEEDS

The mixture of so many nationalities, minorities, and cultures, the blending (or clashing) of ancient Slavic tradition with Turkish influence, and the superimposition of Austrian civilization made for an almost exotic environment. It was a challenge for me and my friends to sneak into one of the mosques and furtively climb the tightly winding spiral staircase leading up to the high, narrow minaret balcony without being caught by the Turkish mullah. Five times a day the muezzin would appear on this balcony to sing out his mournful call to prayer. Before entering the mosque, followers had to perform certain ritual ablutions at a fountain in the courtyard. Leaving footgear outside before stepping onto the heavily carpeted floor indoors, they began a sequence of meticulously choreographed movements: bending forward, kneeling down, touching the floor with the forehead, rising back to the knees, and standing up again, then repeating the same obeisances while reciting passages from the Koran.

Since a minority of Sephardic Jews also lived in Zenica, there was also a synagogue in our city. Sneaking into the synagogue was taboo—*verboten!* We had been warned that, if caught, a certain vital organ of our reproductive anatomy would be cut off summarily by the rabbi, a bearded, biblical-looking man with silver ringlets dangling from under his yarmulke. This fearsome threat was enough of a deterrent for us to never attempt such an intrusion.

Catholicism was our family's predestined religion, and in due time my siblings and I were enrolled in a Catholic school, run by nuns, adjacent to the imposing church. We were taught in the Serbo-Croatian language. Only at home did we communicate in German, the Austrian idiom.

Whenever my mother was about to give birth to a child, we were taken to our grandparents' home. They lived in Tešanj, a short train ride from Zenica. Our hometown was a bustling cosmopolitan city compared with Tešanj, a typical country village with a pronounced Turkish flavor and large Moslem population. My grandfather was an official in the judicial department of the government. With his white handlebar moustache, muttonchops, and fringe of hair, he cut a benign, grandfatherly figure and had a kindness to match.

We also spent our summer vacations in Tešanj, looking forward to it with much anticipation. Though the village was small, there were so many places to explore. Above all was a crumbling Turkish fortress overlooking the village. There one could climb over bastions into hidden chambers and scale walls by using large blocks of stone as a staircase. Adjoining the backside of my grandparents' house was a Turkish cemetery. Crossing it in darkness was an eerie experience, with its ornate gravestones topped by turbans wound intricately around conical fezzes and tilted at helter-skelter angles.

The weekly market day in Tešanj was always a big and colorful event. Farmers from nearby villages brought produce, livestock, and handicrafts to sell. It was a vibrant tableau bursting with color and excitement—and a distinct smell of humanity, animals, and spicy cooking. Most peasants wore traditional costumes. Ladies with baggy pants and richly embroidered bodices welcomed this diversion but rarely showed their faces, since purdah was the custom. Men with chiselled features and bright red fezzes or rakishly piled-up turbans looked like brigands from a fairy tale.

Swimming in a secluded river hole was another favorite pastime of our childhood. In Zenica we had the River Bosna close by. The first order of business was to obtain from the nearby slaughterhouse a pair of bladders from freshly butchered pigs. These, when blown up, tied, and dried in the sun, served as water wings that kept us afloat and bobbing up and down as we dog paddled across the turbulent river. Although we looked upon each crossing as a daring feat, we were never aware of the possibility of drowning.

My father was an avid fisherman, and Bosnia was the El Dorado of stream fishing. Quite often he and I rose long before sunrise to catch a freight train that dropped us off at a small depot where passenger trains hardly ever stopped. Then we walked until we reached our destination: a rushing stream surrounded by dense, primeval forest, virtually untouched by human hands. Occasionally we stayed overnight in a primitive shelter built to store hay. As a special treat, we were frequently invited to spend the night at the country estate of a nobleman, the Count of Montecuccoli.

We used worms exclusively, since fly-casting amid the dense underbrush and overhanging tree limbs would have been very difficult. I was assigned to worm hunting. Threading worms onto a fishhook was a messy affair I did not particularly enjoy. One day as I crouched down preoccupied with baiting my hook, my father turned to me with a concerned look and his face blanched. Calmly he said, "Ottochaka, hold very still. Don't move until I tell you to jump. Then jump forward as far as you can." An ominous pause ensued, which seemed to last forever. Then in a perfectly controlled voice he said, "Jump!" So I did, not knowing what it was all about. I was told I had been squatting right in front of a poisonous viper ready to strike at the slightest provocation. After a tense and sobering moment we watched the dangerous reptile slither away. The snake probably was just as relieved as I was to have gotten out of the predicament unharmed.

Bosnian streams abounded with trout. One species, which we called *Huchen*, was a predator with ferocious courage and stamina. I remember my father latching onto one; rarely had I seen him so excited and determined to land a fish. It was the biggest I had ever seen when it jumped high out of the water. The tip of my father's rod had broken in two and was hanging limply on the line. He instinctively grabbed the line, wound a few loops around his hand, and started climbing, stumbling, and crawling up the steep bank, dragging the fish behind him until he felt he was far enough away from the stream to grab the prize with his hands.

On these forays into the wilderness, my father always brought his military rifle with him. It was bear country, and bears could be quite ornery. Once my father let me fire his heavy-caliber weapon after careful instructions on how to hold and aim it. The recoil nearly threw me flat on my back, but my father told me proudly that I had hit the mark.

During the hot summer months we had wonderful family picnics on a grassy meadow near our swimming hole. A thick rope with a knot to hold onto was attached to the limb of a tree overhanging the water. We would take running starts, clinging to the rope and swinging like a pendulum until we let go to plop into the water with a resounding splash. A whole lamb roasting on a spit was watched by the gathering; families with people of all ages, ethnic backgrounds, and creeds congenially conversed in half a dozen languages. We played games and displayed feats of strength. In his younger years, my father was a gymnast of note, and even in his thirties he could launch himself into a perfectly executed free somersault. I was impressed by this. The afternoon inevitably wound up with a spirited *kolo* dance accompanied by a *gusla*, an ancient stringed instrument. The dancers held hands, forming a circle, moving clockwise and counterclockwise with a graceful combination of steps. At first stately but with the rhythm gradually accelerating, the dance ended with an exhilarating finale and much merriment.

Winters in Bosnia were bitterly cold and snow fell in abundance. With noses running and hands and feet freezing, my sisters and I enjoyed sledding. I remember seeing my first skier. He came down a pristine snow-covered slope in sweeping turns, arms high. With a graceful forward lunge, pushing one ski slightly ahead at an angle, he initiated perfectly rounded turns in rhythmical succession. It was a most astounding sight. The skier was a Norwegian mining engineer, working at one of the local plants, who had brought along his skis and skill. Since he was a friend of my father's, he explained to me when I saw him next that the turn was known as a "telemark," and that skiing was a very popular sport in the Nordic countries. The seed was planted, as I vowed to myself that someday I would have a pair of these long wooden slats.

Our regimen in Catholic school was strict, with much emphasis on religious education. Going to the movies was considered sinful and absolutely forbidden, at the threat of expulsion from school. There was only one place in town where films were shown, under rather primitive conditions. By coincidence, I knew the man who projected the films onto the white screen. One day he invited me into his projection booth to take a look around. It was like entering a sorcerer's laboratory. The whirling projector with a bright light threw a perfectly clear image onto a distant screen. Oddly—or perhaps understandably—it was not the story that interested me as much as the mechanics of this miracle.

The old and timeworn movie prints, having reached the farthest hinterlands of the Austrian realm, broke frequently. At each break, the projector had to be stopped. The lights went on in the hall, accompanied by dismayed and derisive jeers from the audience as the film ends were spliced together. The emergency operation was done in a jiffy by the deft hands of the projectionist, but every time it was performed, two pieces of film had to be snipped off to make the edges and sprocket holes line up properly. Fascinated with such detritus, I collected these celluloid snippets off the floor and put them in my pocket. Naturally, I could not resist showing them off to my friends in school. Naturally, the nuns found out about it, and naturally, I was booted out.

After receiving a severe tongue-lashing and a few whacks across the bottom with a long-handled wooden spoon at home, I was marched back to school by my mother. She explained to the mother superior that the innocence of my soul was untainted since I had not actually watched the film and had only visited my friend in the projection booth. I was reinstated with the proviso that I would serve as an altar boy from then on, an unexpected punishment, indeed. I had to learn by rote all the proper Latin phrases in response to the priest's incantations, cross the altar at given intervals, genuflect and cross myself interminably, smoke up the church with incense, pass the ceremonial wine, and pour it over the priest's fingers. If I made a mistake or spilled a drop of that precious liquid, I was cuffed rudely and had my ears twisted painfully by the priest after Mass. Thus did I atone for my sins. It caused, alas, a distinct cooling off in me toward the Christian faith. Then and there, I fell by the wayside as a believer, and I have never recovered. However, my first encounter with the magic world of films left a deep impact on my fertile juvenile mind. It planted another seed, as I told myself I would someday learn how to make them.

Skiing and films: these would become my all-consuming passions.

EIGHT HORSES OR FORTY MEN

Although we children knew little about politics and cared even less, it was obvious from the conversations of our elders that ominously dark clouds were rising on the political horizon. The major powers of Europe, like voracious foragers, were always trying to acquire new lands, shuffling small kingdoms and principalities like pawns in an intricate game of chess. Consequently, there was seething turmoil and unrest all over Europe. Bosnia was no exception; it was rife with rebellion, stoked by many underground revolutionaries waiting only for the right opportunity to strike. The situation came to a climax on June 28, 1914, at Sarajevo, when the Archduke Ferdinand, Hapsburg heir apparent, and his wife of common birth, Sophie, were assassinated.

Looking back at the chain of events and remembering what my father, who was an eyewitness to this tragic event, told me, the drama unfolded like the plot of a classic Greek tragedy. Archduke Ferdinand should never have gone to Bosnia, where political resentment, permeated with hatred toward the Hapsburgs, was at a fever pitch. His visit was ill-timed; it took place the week of Saint Vitus's Day, a day of national mourning in memory of the Turks' most devastating victory over the Serbs at Kosovo in 1389. Close to 100,000 soldiers were left dead on a battlefield drenched with the blood of both victor and vanquished. Among the dead was the leader of the Ottoman janissaries and regular soldiers, Sultan Murad, who was slain in hand-to-hand combat. This costly victory spelled the beginning of the Turks' four-hundred-year occupation of Bosnia. For Ferdinand to come on such a day and blatantly inspect Austrian troops in warlike maneuvers was like rubbing salt into an old but still festering wound.

Threats of grave consequences, if such a visit took place, were voiced openly, and Austrian intelligence was well aware of the possibility of an *attentat*. Yet security measures taken were ridiculously insufficient—in fact, practically nil. During the official entry into the city of the six-car motorcade en route to the welcoming ceremonies at city hall, a bomb bounced off the folded canvas roof of the archduke's automobile and exploded in front of the following car. A number of people, including Austrian officers, were wounded and rushed to a hospital. Instead of canceling the official program, Archduke Ferdinand and his entourage insisted on proceeding according to the publicized itinerary.

The parade came to a halt at the steps of the ornate city hall. Trembling with rage and indignation, the archduke and his wife were met by a befuddled delegation of local politicians and functionaries, whom he berated with a bitterly sarcastic greeting. Following unbending protocol, he read his prepared speech perfunctorily with ice-cold irony and a few added verbal barbs, expressing his utmost disgust and predicting dire consequences for the guilty.

That was only the prelude to the drama to follow. It would have been perfectly appropriate to call off the remainder of this ceremonial farce and retreat to a safe haven with some semblance of dignity and decorum, but the party decided not to follow the planned route through the center of the city and instead drive directly to the hospital and call on the wounded officers. This seemed sensible and prudent, except that nobody had thought to inform the driver of the lead car nor of the archduke's, third in line, of this change in plans. Automatically, as rehearsed, when the cars came to the street corner where they were supposed to turn, they did so. The others followed. With much consternation and shouting, the drivers were ordered to stop and then back up so that the parade could continue in a straight line along Apel Quay, bordering the River Milačka. Thus the fleet of cars came to a complete halt amidst much confusion. The archduke and his wife were sitting targets, helplessly immobilized in an open car.

Enter Gavrilo Princip, one of seven designated assassins posted at strategic points along the parade route. The assassins were all members of a clandestine organization called Young Bosnia. Their weapons—bombs and revolvers—were provided through Major Tankosič, who was the leader of a revolutionary group known as "Black Hand." Each assassin was also provided with cyanide tablets to commit suicide in the event of capture. Five of the terrorists never went into action. One had a complete and sudden change of mind. Another could not bring himself to possibly also kill Ferdinand's wife. Still another found himself wedged against a policeman. The rest claimed that their opportunity never came.

Nedeljko Cabrinović, one of the seven, tossed the bomb that glanced off the archduke's automobile. Immediately he jumped over the railing and fell down in the riverbed, having swallowed his supposedly lethal cyanide tablet. The pill was ineffective, and he was overwhelmed and arrested. Gavrilo Princip, next in line, heard the sharp thud of an explosion and assumed that the mission had been accomplished by a coconspirator. He melted inconspicuously into the crowd, but found out in a nearby cafe that the *attentat* had failed after all and that he had bungled his assignment by leaving his post prematurely. Knowing that the parade of cars was scheduled to pass in front of him after the conclusion of the reception at city hall, he bided his time. All he had to do when the cavalcade came to a standstill was to take a few steps forward and fire pointblank at the archduke and his wife.

Their wounds were mortal; Sophie died in the archduke's arms in the car. In a moment of touching tenderness, he implored her not to die: "Sopherl, Sopherl, don't die. Live for the sake of our children." Ferdinand expired shortly thereafter; a bullet had torn through one of the main arteries, and he quietly bled to death while repeating in a fading, raspy voice, "It's nothing, it's nothing . . . ."

Princip, after firing his two shots and then trying to kill himself, was pushed to the ground and nearly lynched by a mob until uniformed policemen came to his rescue and arrested him. Within a short time, the other five conspirators were identified and captured. They were brought to trial, and only their youth saved them from being sentenced to death by hanging. The assassination, even though amateurishly executed and almost botched, was the spark that ignited the powder keg. War in the region—eventually involving the world—was inevitable. On July 29, 1914, an official document was handed to the Serbian foreign minister affirming that a state of war existed between the two countries. Austrian troops poured into Serbia through Bosnia.

The first thrust of the Austrian army was unexpectedly blunted by inhospitable terrain and formidable Serbian resistance. The number of lives lost was staggering. A figure of 150,000 dead was estimated during the first year of war. Only after Germany brought in its battalions, with their superior weaponry and a seemingly inexhaustible reservoir of soldiers, was Serbia brought to its knees. The front then moved to the

Italian border, Italy having joined the war against Germany and Austria. In a short time World War I drew all of Europe into its vortex. The fighting dragged on, with some of the fiercest battles fought in deep valleys surrounded by rocky peaks. Supply lines stretched to their limits, and neither side showed much gain in conquered territory.

My father was immediately mobilized and directed to organize the Field Postal Service. It was considered of utmost importance for the morale of the soldiers in the front lines to be in touch with their families. I remember how proud he was that, no matter what, mail would reach soldiers within a few days of posting and vice versa. For the next four years we did not see much of him except for occasional furloughs that lasted a week to ten days at most. These were joyous reunions interrupted far too soon when duty called him back to the front.

During my father's prolonged absence, my mother carried on housewifely duties and looked after our education and well-being with fortitude and patience. Once every week was bathing day. We had the luxury of running water in our home, but it had to be heated in large pots then poured into a small, portable tub. The pecking order worked to my disadvantage: I was always last after my three sisters, based on the assumption that I was the dirtiest of the bunch. I did not relish being immersed, soaped, scrubbed, and rinsed in a tub of water well polluted by the time my turn came, but such was my fate, facing a majority of four females.

We were not in want of food or clothing. I did notice, as the war lingered on, that more and more our meals consisted of dishes made with cornmeal, which had become the staple food in Bosnia. Luckily, with her culinary talents, my mother managed to create quite a variety of tasty meals, including small tarts filled with plum marmalade as a delicious dessert. Letters from Father addressed to Mother were always received with enormous relief and great joy. It reassured us that he was unharmed and thinking of us. She would often share the pertinent parts of the letters with us, omitting the more personal parts, claiming that these were "censored."

As the war continued, I became aware that the trainloads passing through Zenica were of a markedly different nature than they had been before the war. Heavy cars moved troops to the front; flatcars carried artillery pieces and two-wheeled ammunition carts. But there were also long medical convoys with red crosses painted on the tops and sides of cars, bringing back the wounded to be treated in hospitals nearest their hometowns.

The war dragged on and on. Emperor Franz Joseph died in 1916, but his realm had already begun to disintegrate. Karl II was crowned emperor, and he precipitated the final dissolution of the Hapsburg dynasty in spite of his efforts to salvage what was left to be salvaged. When the United States entered the war in 1917, it tilted the scale in favor of the bogged-down Allied forces. Germany and Austria tasted bitter ashes of defeat, and the cost in American lives and wounded men was heart-rending. Russia was in shambles, both politically and economically. The proletariat had risen: the Bolsheviks hit the country with full force. The Czarist regime was doomed, and those members of the Imperial House of Romanov who could not leave the country clandestinely were brutally murdered. Wherever one looked in Europe there were uprisings by working people who had been shackled and exploited. It was the dawn of a new social order, giving the common man his due. These were indeed "days that shook the world" to its foundations.

Suddenly, World War I was over with a general armistice proclaimed on November 11, 1918. The world could begin to pick up the pieces and start all over again, trying to create an atmosphere of peaceful coexistence. It would never happen, at least not in my lifetime. But my family was together again. After the armistice went into effect, my father returned from the Italian front, physically well and luckily a "whole man," looking ahead with some apprehension to the uncertain future.

Serbs had formed a provisional government and reoccupied all of their lost territory, including Bosnia. A peace treaty was to be signed, its cherished goal to lay foundations for a united nation of Slavs to be named "Yugoslavia." To his great surprise, my father was asked if he would stay and work for the new government. It was explained to him that a man of his experience, general background, and proven ability as an organizer would be helpful in the process of reshaping the country. Yet he declined; his patriotic loyalty lay elsewhere. He chose instead to return to Austria, his homeland, and knew it had to be done in a hurry. The sooner the better, he was told, since no one could guarantee safe conduct in those chaotic days. He was allocated a small freight car to move his family and belongings. How long would it take to get back to Austria? No one could answer. Two weeks, maybe three, they said, depending upon the whims of the railroad operators to hook a straggling freight car onto a train going in the right direction or to shunt it onto a siding until the next lucky break.

In a week of frantic activities, all our furniture and personal belongings had to be packed and prepared to stow in our moveable do-micile. Food supplies had to be procured, since we could not count on being able to purchase food along the route. A potbellied iron stove was essential for cooking and warmth, since we were on the threshold of winter. While packing, my father had a brilliant idea that probably saved us from near starvation in days to come. Every piece of wooden furniture that lent itself to the purpose was equipped with a false bottom. The newly created compartment was filled with a commodity that turned out to be priceless—the best brand of Bosnian tobacco, much sought after by cigarette smokers. We even went so far as to stuff some of the upholstered pieces with tobacco by removing most of the cotton padding.

Our freight car was a standard boxcar of the type I had so often seen passing by our house. It was painted a dull, rust red, and on each side was a sliding double door. What caught my imagination was the stenciled inscription in smudged white letters that read "EIGHT HORSES OR FORTY MEN." I figured out that four horses or twenty men could occupy each end of the car, leaving a passage in the middle.

After stowing all furniture and kitchen utensils, we installed the pot-bellied stove with its long stovepipe going through an opening in the roof of the car. At best it was a rickety arrangement, with jostling and bouncing to be expected when traveling on a freight train. Both stove and stovepipe had to be belayed and anchored with wires. Even so, many a meal almost ready to be eaten wound up on the floor because of a sudden jolt. In memory, I can still see an overturned potful of spaghetti wriggling on the floorboards like a stirred-up nest of white worms. This was enough to bring tears of frustration to my mother's eyes.

Improvised curtains divided the car into living and sleeping compart-ments. Most of the activity was in and around the kitchen area. Toilet facilities were, of course, of the most rudimentary nature, and the use of water for bathing and washing was carefully regulated. With all the smoke and soot emanating from the coal-fired engine, we often looked like chimney sweeps. Not being able to bathe didn't bother me too much, knowing as I did that I would be fourth in line for the same tub of water that had cleansed my sisters.

For us children, the journey was one of the greatest adventures of our young lives. Soon our Eight-Horses-or-Forty-Men coach was hitched to an engine and joined to a long line of equally battered freight cars.

We were the only passengers in the convoy. In a most leisurely way, without a set timetable, we began to move. It was farewell to Zenica and a childhood filled with warm memories of happy days. We were most fortunate to leave together as a family, in good health and with most of our belongings. Our future prospects were uncertain, but we had no reason for despair. After all, we were going to our "homeland," which, except for father, none of us had ever seen.

Vienna, the once glamorous capital of Austria, was our primary destination. There my father would report to his administrative authorities and receive orders for his next assignment. If given a choice, his preference was to return to Salzburg. Our journey took us through northern Bosnia to Bosanski Brod where we were switched onto the mainline track coming from Belgrade. We hoped our new route would take us to Zagreb, the capital of Croatia, where my mother had been born.

After a few days of traveling, we fell into a routine, all of us having certain chores to perform. The car had to be swept every morning, dishes washed after every meal, kerosene lamps cleaned and refilled, the stove emptied of ashes. We had an ample supply of hard coal and enough wood to last us for at least one month. Often one of our parents read us stories while we sat in a circle. We talked about the cities we passed or were about to see. Tacked on the wall was a large map marked with the progress of our journey in heavy red pencil. Even though we were frequently laid off in some of the larger cities, we dared not venture on a sightseeing excursion for fear that we might miss being hitched onto the next train. At every enforced layover, the very first order of business was for my father to call on the local stationmaster in an effort to expedite our progress.

From Zagreb we moved on to Graz, the capital of Styria, one of the most beautiful provinces of old Austria, and from there we proceeded to Vienna. Our first sight of the city had us on tiptoes, craning our necks. In the distance we could spot the majestic spire of Saint Stephen's Cathedral, one of the great landmarks of Europe, dominating the skyline. It was an inspiring and emotional sight. But sadly, this distant view was all we saw of Vienna. Winter had come to Austria, and time was running short. Our paramount objective was finding suitable living quarters and settling down to celebrate our first Christmas in Austria. As my parents had hoped all along, Salzburg was to be the end of our journey. Getting there could take only a few more days.

SALZBURG

Travelers and poets have long acclaimed Salzburg as one of the most beautiful cities in the world. Covered with a blanket of freshly fallen snow it is a sight not easily forgotten. Such was my first impression of Salzburg, the city that was to be our family's home. On a sparkling, clear, sunny day, all bundled up against the cold and with snow crunching under our boots, we took our first exploratory steps into the heart of the city.

Salzburg was a large city, larger than any in which we had ever been. We crossed a bridge over the wide Salzach River, which bisected the city into two distinctly different entities. Rushing by at considerable speed, the river was a pale, jade green, fed by mountain springs and melting snow from glaciers in the surrounding Alps. On the river's left bank stood the oldest, historic section of the town. There the archbishops and rulers of bygone days lived in baronial splendor in sumptuous palaces. The narrow streets running haphazardly in odd directions reminded me of congested medieval cities I had seen in books and magazines. The pièce de résistance was undoubtedly the imposing castle-fortress of Hohensalzburg, majestically overlooking the city. Surprisingly well-preserved, its living quarters, reception halls, kitchen, torture chambers, and dungeons were still intact.

During a prolonged siege in an obscure war, the Hohensalzburg castle was completely surrounded by enemy forces. It remained impervious to assault, and its defenders refused to surrender. The enemy's only alternative was to starve the stubborn occupants into submission. In a show of ingenious deception, the defenders paraded their one and only ox along the parapet, as though leading it to be slaughtered. But before each appearance, the animal was first scrubbed clean and then painted a different color and pattern; to the invaders, it looked like a new ox was brought forth every week or so. After a while, the siege was declared hopeless, the enemy retreated, and the Salzburg citizenry lived happily ever after, having acquired the well-deserved sobriquet *Stierwaschers*, or "steer washers."

At the time we arrived there, Salzburg was, like Vienna and the rest of Austria, in dire straits economically. Inflation ran rampant, depression and unemployment shot to a zenith. The stores were empty, and those with anything left to sell had goods people were unable to afford. Money was virtually worthless, its buying power tantamount to the paper it was printed on. The poverty among the majority of the populace was abysmal. All around it was a matter of survival on a day-to-day basis.

The Hapsburg dynasty had reached the end of its reign. Karl II was urged to abdicate or else be prepared for more radical measures. He flatly refused, and was exiled with the rest of the Hapsburg family. Austria had shrunk considerably, and the once immense Hapsburg fortune had diminished accordingly. What was left—which was still plenty—was funneled into the treasury of the newly founded Republic of Austria. The country was to be governed by a representative parliament and president elected by the Austrian people.

My father was to be director of the main post office as soon as he got settled with his family and found living quarters. But there was the rub: the city was overcrowded and the housing shortage acute. Eventually, we found temporary shelter in one half of a former military barracks, the other half occupied by a family in the same predicament. It was somewhat larger than our boxcar, and at least we were no longer moving. Again the space was divided into compartments by curtains strung on wires. This afforded a modicum of privacy, but of course every word was heard by and shared with everyone else. This turned into a true test of family togetherness, but we passed it. The love of our parents and their determination to pull us out of that situation were the glues that bonded us to each other.

Life was not easy. Food was scarce and money could not buy it. Bread, potatoes, milk, and sugar were rationed. Meat of any kind was a luxury. Our cache of Bosnian tobacco came to our rescue. It was worth its weight in gold and could be bartered for almost anything—but most importantly, food. We organized regular foraging trips into the countryside, hiking to farms in the vicinity and trading tobacco for dairy products and sometimes, if we were fortunate, a chicken or some smoked bacon. Each of us children had a designated day every week to head for the countryside, a knapsack strapped to our back. In time we established close relationships with our farming friends, and as long as the tobacco supply lasted, we ate sufficiently well to survive and stay healthy.

Finally we found an apartment on the right bank of the river. It was an old, old house in a narrow street named Steingasse that was paved with cobblestones. A staircase also made it accessible from the quay along the riverfront. To us it was like moving into a palace. There was a full-size kitchen with a large stove, a sunny living room, and enough bedroom space to accommodate our family of six. At last my parents had a room of their own and the privacy they so deserved.

From the kitchen one stepped out onto an imposing Italianate loggia with four graceful arches supported by five columns. The view from this balcony and all the rooms, including the privy, was spectacular. Directly below, the Salzach River flowed by. The opposite riverbank was lined with houses showing the patina of age. From our new home we could see a picture-postcard panorama: the fortress of Hohensalzburg towering above the city, along with twin bell towers of the cathedral and the spires of the other churches. Far in the distance beckoned the peak of the Untersberg with its characteristic angular shape.

Behind our loggia was a large workshop occupied by a renowned master woodcarver and his highly talented craftsmen. His name was Herr Professor Zwerger, who with his artisans carved likenesses of people and animals in admirable detail. The workshop's main output was religious figures, such as agonizing crucifixes or radiantly beautiful Madonnas. Most popular with the buying public were plump, rosy-cheeked little angels with beatific smiles and tiny wings attached to their shoulder blades. What intrigued me most were lifelike character studies of grizzled mountain men with long beards and pipes. I spent a good deal of my free time in this workshop and occasionally was permitted to whittle on a discarded piece of fruitwood. It gave me an inkling of what an absorbing vocation woodcarving could be.

A few houses up the street from ours was the official city bordello, licensed by the authorities and under strictest sanitary control—so I was told. Every day on my way to and from school, I had to pass this house of hidden pleasures. At first I kept my eyes modestly lowered or straight ahead, and only occasionally, when I was certain no one could see me, I turned my head for a quick glance at the windows of the narrow three-story house. As time went on, I became bolder and would look quite openly to see what was going on, who was busy and who was idle. There was a dark-haired plump woman with enormous bosoms. Then there was the skinny blonde without any visible physical attributes to attract a gent—but then how would I know? Gradually, I recognized all of the bordello's occupants by sight to the point of a nodding acquaintance and an occasional wave. Of course, at my tender age of eleven or so, my relationships with the ladies were platonic. In some instances I found it slightly embarrassing when I was asked, "And where do you live?" I would answer, "Steingasse Eighteen," knowing that most people knew the local whorehouse was practically next door. It gave me an undeserved aura of sophistication.

As a student I did not earn any laurels. I had a language problem, since German grammar and syntax had been sorely neglected in Bosnia. Furthermore, I spoke German with a Slavic accent, inviting the ridicule of my classmates. Youngsters of that age, without meaning to be, can be very cruel, and I was the butt of much of their amusement as they imitated my fractured German. My sisters managed to overcome this problem much more rapidly than I did. Erna was enrolled in a school especially designed to teach children with similar handicaps. Through the years she did master the three "Rs" and assumed responsibilities far beyond anyone's expectations.

One redeeming aspect of going to school was the free lunch given us every day through a program initiated by the American Red Cross. While the menu offered to us was unfailingly the same—a large scoop of rice boiled in a bluish grey liquid (supposedly milk) with a spoon of cocoa powder sprinkled on top—it was hot, sweet, and filling. Still, after a steady diet of boiled rice day after day, one can lose one's liking for this nutritious staple. For many years I could not even look at a bowl of rice, and only much later did I learn to appreciate it again, when I became acquainted with Chinese cuisine.

Moving into the new apartment vastly improved our family's living conditions, but luxurious they were not. While our privy offered an unsurpassed view, it had only that. It had no flushing system and was only a short step ahead of the better-known outdoor type of "one-holer." The house had cold water only, drawn from a faucet outside the kitchen door. To have hot water, we had to heat every drop on the kitchen stove. No longer did we children share a communal bathtub, however. We went to a public bath, as did the majority of people. We brought towels and soap, paid a nominal fee, grabbed the first available stalls, and luxuriated under a hot shower until the attendant called out that our time was up. We did this once a week and in between kept reasonably clean by taking a so-called "French bath" in chilling water from the faucet.

For my mother, the biweekly washday was grueling. In the hallway between the front entrance to the house and our kitchen, she set up her tubs and washboards. We could not send soiled linens to a laundry, and even if there had been one, it would have been prohibitively expensive. Therefore all sheets, pillowcases, towels, shirts, and so forth had to be hand washed. In a tedious and physically exhausting process, the laundry was first boiled in a large cauldron on the stove, and then soaped, scrubbed, pummeled, and squeezed over the washboard before being rinsed and finally hauled to the attic three floors up and hung to dry. We all pitched in, but the main burden rested on our mother's shoulders, as it would until advancing age and an improved financial status permitted her to spare herself such physical exertion.

Clothing had to be patched up and used until past the point of respectability. My father acquired the necessary tools, wooden nails, and leather soles to repair shoes and build new heels for all our footwear. As always, I was his willing apprentice, cobbling away merrily as he hummed a famous tune from Richard Wagner's *Die Meistersinger*. We children went to a school of practical learning if ever there was one. It would stand us in good stead for the rest of our lives. I became proficient in ironing men's shirts and even some of the more delicate items of ladies' wear. I learned how to expertly darn holes in socks and remend the same hole again after it had worn through.

One took for granted that every family had to eliminate all possible expenses in order to survive the depression brought on by World War I. Of course, in times like these, there were always people who became rich. Very rich. These men, elegantly attired in tailor-made suits and overcoats with beaver fur collars, and their bejeweled spouses—or more likely kept mistresses—dressed according to the latest Paris fashions, were much in evidence. Commonly know as *Schiebers* (pushers), they dealt in every possible commodity and generated huge profits from their shady if not illegal transactions. As long as they were not caught, life had a rosy hue for them, even though they were despised by those who had naught. Little did it matter to them.

A WANDER BIRD

Hauntingly beautiful as Salzburg could be on any day with the sun shining, the bluest of skies, and the air incandescently sparkling, it could be equally miserable when one of many prolonged rainy spells hit town. The rain came down in sheets, as though a never-ending fabric were rolling off looms in a factory. Hence the name for this sort of weather— *Schnürlregen*. It could occur in the middle of the summer or in May or October and last for weeks at a time. Our lives became severely restricted, since we were forced to stay indoors most of the time or be drenched to the skin. This was frustrating because part of the pleasure of living in this environment was the long walks one could take along the riverbanks, crossing one of the bridges and returning on the opposite bank to one's starting point. Walking was free, healthy, and invigorating.

To pass the time during the rainy spells, my sisters and I built a small theater in our kitchen. Our parents had given us a kit that consisted of a miniature stage and a proscenium, approximately three by five feet, plus all the necessary paraphernalia to put on a show. The cardboard figures were guided from above the stage by strings attached to our fingers. The stage was set up on our kitchen stove, which jutted out like the prow of a ship, leaving ample working room on both sides. Curtains, hung from the ceiling, shut off the backstage activities. Chairs were set up to accommodate our audience of friends and their often unwilling parents. We improvised plays based on a vague story line with a changeable dialogue to progress the epic to its dramatic climax. We designed our own sets and lighting effects, such as the moon floating across the night sky as the star-crossed lovers declaimed vows of eternal devotion. More than just a diverting pastime, our theatrical venture became an absorbing challenge and undoubtedly contributed very much to my lifelong interest in the performing arts, as it did for my sister Nelly.

I discovered another diversion. During one of the rainy deluges, the Salzach River overflowed its stone embankments and flooded sections of the town. Among the buildings partially inundated was a military warehouse containing obsolete matériel left over from World War I. An assortment of skis used by the decommissioned mountain troops, who had guarded the Alpine peaks and valleys along the border between Austria and Italy, were part of the water-logged inventory. Word spread that these skis would be given away free for the asking. They could be picked up at the military depot as soon as the water subsided, first come, first go. When the day came, I lined up with the early birds and was handed a pair of skis and poles. As simple as that, my long-dreamed-of wish was fulfilled. As it turned out, the skis were far too long for a lad of my height and physique. Also, having been underwater, they had warped slightly out of shape. No matter, they were mine. The poles, also much too long, could be cut down to size. Now it became a matter of scrounging warm clothing, a pair of gloves, and boots that could be fitted to the bindings.

The bindings I had were invented and perfected by an Austrian army colonel named Bilgeri, who was in charge of training Alpine troops during Franz Joseph's reign. Bilgeri's contraption was a rudimentary forerunner of the adjustable metal bindings used today. The metal foot plate could be adjusted to fit the length of the boot, as could the toe irons that held the boot firmly in place. With a leather strap over the toes and another around the ankle, tied at the heel of the foot plate, the boot was almost inseparable from the binding. The most important and innovative part of the binding was a strong, coiled spring made of steel enclosed in a metal casing, attached to the binding and screwed onto the top of the ski at the tip of the boot. This made it possible to raise one's heel freely to the almost vertical position necessary to execute the classic telemark turn, which at that time was still the predominate mode of changing directions.

With the first snow of winter covering the ground, I headed for the nearest mountain, which was the Gaisberg, about one hour and a half of climbing uphill with skis and poles slung over the shoulders. Learning to ski was done by observing and imitating others with more experience; we had no teachers nor any kind of instruction manuals. Occasionally an "expert" would deign to throw us a few measly hints. It was learning to ski the hard way, and the results were not exactly encouraging.

As it turned out, it was almost impossible for me to make any kind of a turn because of the length of my skis. I did not have the skill nor the physical strength to guide them with any semblance of control. Without turns, skiing spelled doom and disaster. The continuous falling and struggle to get up again was exhausting—and cold. My mother, who was always very handy with proverbs, had one for this occasion: "*Einem geschenkten Gaul schaut man nicht in's Maul*," or, in English, "Never look a gift horse in the mouth."

I had attached myself to a group of youngsters on the ski slopes, some of whom would become close friends later in my life. We all had one problem in common: a pair of uncooperative, heavy wooden slats strapped to our feet. But the mere fact of gliding over these snow-covered slopes was exciting and exhilarating. If only . . . . We came up with a solution of our own that required no turns. Ski jumping! By building a small take-off platform with a suitably inclined landing slope below and a flat area farther down, we could diminish our speed gradually and come to a complete stop. Now we had all the fun and excitement of skiing without having to make turns. An added thrill was the spine-tingling feeling of being airborne, if only for a few seconds, depending on the size of the hill.

I joined a popular youth organization named Wandervögel, meaning "wander birds," that was oriented to both summer and winter outdoor activities. The city fathers of Salzburg had given us for our use an abandoned structure, built solidly of stone. It was an impressive square tower with a metal roof and was used as far back as medieval times as a repository for gunpowder and weapons. Inside was nothing but bare walls and years of accumulated debris and filth. After school and during weekends, supervised and helped by the elders of the club, we cleaned it out to make a comfortable clubhouse within the stone shell of the fortresslike tower. A newly installed floor divided the building into two stories connected by a staircase of hand-hewn timbers. The furniture consisted principally of a large square table with a bench surrounding it, and most was handmade.

During the summer months we wander birds frequently embarked on long hikes into the surrounding countryside. When winter came, the challenge was considerably more stringent. Ill-equipped as most of us were, and lacking balanced diets, we used will power, stamina, and enthusiasm to arrive at our destination of a chosen mountain peak. Usually we left on a Saturday, shortly after school was out at noon and the older members who acted as our guardians got off their jobs. On some occasions a short train ride brought us closer to the foot of the mountain we were to ascend. Then it meant climbing for hours, often wallowing waist deep through freshly fallen snow, following the tracks made by our experienced leaders. It was strenuous, at times to the point of exhaustion, especially if the weather was bad.

Often we climbed in raging snowstorms, with numb fingers and frozen feet. Fortunately, now and then a Good Samaritan among our guides would grab the skis of one of us struggling, straggling youngsters and carry them for a while to help us catch our breath. What a relief that was, even though it was only of short duration. Then, as if by a miracle, the storm would subside. The clouds would part and the black night sky would light up with a myriad of twinkling stars. The Milky Way meandered haphazardly across the endless firmament. Straight above was the Big Dipper, and over there the Little Dipper. Cassiopeia, Orion, and the North Star presented as spectacular a galactic display as one could ever hope to see. One couldn't help but wonder how this universe came about. From whence did we come, and where were we headed?

Eventually, late at night, after two or three hours of continuous climbing, we would arrive at one of the primitive mountain huts used by shepherds during the summer months. There was always enough hay to bed down in for the night. Burrowing as deeply as we could and bundling up in every available garment, we found sleep was not long in coming. Sleeping bags and blankets were not included in our gear, alas.

The next morning, if the sun shone, a gradual thawing-out process revived our spirits. After a breakfast of hot tea, black bread, and smoked bacon, with an apple or a piece of chocolate—the menu rarely varied for any meal—we began our skiing activities, climbing up a nearby slope and skiing down, again and again, until our legs gave out. After a short break for lunch, the time came for the descent to the valley floor. It had taken us hours to climb up, and it took us less than half an hour for the descent, depending on the quality of the snow. Being utterly tired but exhilarated and enjoying a sense of accomplishment was our reward, and this was the general pattern of our weekend outings. Each trip was a character builder, a matter of sinking or swimming. Swim we did, thereby learning to ski. For me, it was the foundation laid for a lasting covenant between the mountains and myself.

My close association with the wander birds came to an abrupt and dramatic end. All along, my father had looked somewhat askance at my involvement with this group, suspecting it to be a hotbed of homosexuality. I never had any reason to believe this allegation, nor did I have any way to prove that it was not so. One balmy summer evening I was invited to join the group in a nocturnal frog hunt. My father forbade me to go. I disobeyed his orders and snuck out of our apartment as soon as it was dark. We were in pursuit of these croaking creatures when my father appeared, livid with rage. Normally he was a gentle and fairly self-contained man. But for some reason, he descended upon the suspect leader of our group like the wrath of God. It was an ugly scene, stopping just short of physical blows. The potential violence was surpassed by the ferocity of the verbal abuse hurled against the man. I was hauled back home and given the worst drubbing I remember having ever received from my father.

The result of this unpleasant incident was a lawsuit filed against my father for defamation of character, and of course it also terminated my tenure with the club. The case went to court and came to trial. My father lost and was sentenced to pay a nominal fine and the cost of litigation. But what hurt most was the demand for a public retraction and apology published in one of the daily newspapers. I felt sad to see this proud, decent, and totally honorable man subjected to this humiliation for a "crime of passion" committed on account of my behavior. In retrospect, he may not have been all that wrong. Undoubtedly, he was oversensitive in this regard, but he was well aware that Austria was heavily populated with closet homosexuals. At that time committing a homosexual act was considered a criminal offense subject to severe punishment. Many a time later on I would be accosted by homosexuals, waiting for me after school and offering me all sorts of bribes to come along. I had no interest what-soever. I happened to like girls.

If I can fault my parents for one particular shortcoming, it would have to be their refusal to discuss the subject of sex. It was something that existed but was never talked about. To be caught reading a medical manual that schematically revealed the process of reproduction was considered depraved; sex was sinful or immoral. As young children, we were led to believe the ubiquitous stork brought us into our parents' lives by drop-ping us off conveniently at the doorstep. That fable didn't stand up for long, though, since even in those days there were streetwise kids who hinted darkly that couples coupled, made love, copulated, fornicated, cohabited, and that's how we all originated. Still, there remained a mystique to all this sex business, and it was left to us to grope our way through the dark tunnel. This situation could have easily warped our attitude toward one of the most natural relationships between two human beings of the opposite—or the same—sex.

Nevertheless, sometime along these years of my middle teens I lost my innocence. It was an unmemorable event. I don't remember how we met. I don't remember her face or name or physical appearance. It was simply a basic bodily connection of two human beings, subject to primeval forces of the human libido, needing desperate relief. I recall vaguely that it happened on a late summer night on an isolated park bench. We never saw each other again. I hate to admit this, but it reminded me of two dogs meeting unexpectedly and, on the shortest of notice, indulging in a brief and insignificant session of intercourse. So much for the romantic aspects of losing my virginity. Embarrassing!

In spite of having been removed from the Wandervögels, I continued to ski. Having made good progress as a junior ski jumper, I started to receive invitations to participate in local competitions. It was the beginning of my association with sports; I recognized that through such activities one could widen one's sphere of interest, meet influential people, and find doors open that were quite obviously closed to other youngsters. By joining another ski club as a junior member, I was provided free transportation and additional perks, such as an occasional free meal in one of the popular country inns. Sometimes such a trip required spending a night away from home. It all added up to a novel adventure and a way to build ego. Most importantly, coaching was available. This led inevitably to improvements in our equipment, donated by club members who were upgrading their old equipment. Thus we became heirs to a pair of used skis or boots, poles, and assorted items of clothing. We eagerly snapped up these much-needed hand-me-downs.

During the summer months, soccer, or *fussball,* was my favorite sport. Here again, the initial outlay for equipment was minimal, and by joining a club, I had the use of a playing field and a regulation soccer ball. I started out as a goalkeeper and played this position throughout my entire soccer career, which climaxed when I was selected a member of the senior team representing Salzburg. We played other Austrian teams and a number of international matches. As it happened, I was the youngest member of the team by many years, which provided a human interest angle to sportswriters. It was a pleasant surprise to see my name in the newspapers on Monday after our match on Sunday.

Although we were strictly amateurs, according to the prevailing interpretation of the rules, the rewards were most gratifying. Other than the fulfillment of hard physical exertion flowing with competitive adrenaline, there was the heady elation of having won an important match. Such effort created a feeling of camaraderie among the eleven men forming a soccer team. Of course, the despondency after losing a match was painful, but fortunately it did not last long. There was always the next game to think about. It was all part of growing up and maturing.

The playing fields we used would have been unacceptable by today's standards, and equally rudimentary were the so-called "clubhouse facilities." In fact, there rarely was anything resembling a clubhouse. An empty space in a nearby farmhouse or country inn provided us with enough privacy to change our clothes. Shower facilities were nonexistent, but if we were lucky there would be a cold water faucet at our disposal to rinse off the sweat and grime. Often the field was muddy and slippery, and we players were a sight to behold, caked with mud. I remember one situation when we had a hand pump with a large trough in front of a stable to wash up in. The trough filled with water was a bath alfresco—cold but invigorating. Next to mountain climbing and skiing, soccer was the most popular sport in Austria.

Sports came after classwork, of course. Having squeaked through grade school and received my graduation certificate, I was enrolled in an institution of learning called Realschule. The alternative, the Gymnasium, was geared for a more esoteric education, with Greek and Latin required subjects. In the Realschule, French and English were required, and this suited me as I felt that the knowledge of these two languages might be advantageous for my future, whatever career I chose. I think I made the right decision.

I never considered myself an especially dedicated or gifted student, and my grades proved it. Other than physical education and arts, in which I rated As, my other grades were average, certainly nothing to brag about. Painful as my struggle often was to improve my grades, if for no other reason than to please my parents, it did result in giving me a desire for more knowledge. I have always been an avid reader of books, magazines, and newspapers. The traditional Austrian coffeehouse was a wonderful resource. One would sit down at a little round marble-topped table and order a cup of *kaffee mit schlag*. This entitled one to stay for hours and peruse a variety of magazines and newspapers printed in every major European language. Thus I kept abreast of world affairs and increased my vocabulary in foreign languages.

Of course my preference in books did not always veer toward what was considered required reading. Goethe, Schiller, Grillparzer, Heine, and Shakespeare one had to live with and learn to like. Karl May, a German author of adventure tales that were often set in the American West as well as other foreign lands, did not fit into this illustrious company of literary giants. Reading May was considered a waste of time, yet I loved his books, and so did many other kindred souls. It would be half a century after May's death that many of his books would be made into successful films, shot in Germany with American actors, such as the handsome Lex Barker portraying Chief Winnetu, the bravest of Indian braves.

While I was attending the Realschule, which was sort of a combination high school and junior college, it was a status symbol to belong to one of the student fraternities. Quite different from the American college fraternity, a *Burschenschaft,* or brotherhood, met once a week in a reserved room of a *Gasthof.* Here we would sit at a long wooden table, our characteristic pancake-shaped student caps each with a short visor perched on top of our heads and a narrow, multicolored band showing the insignia and color scheme of the fraternity draped across our chests.

Presiding over the gathering and seated at the head of the table was our chosen leader. With a whack of his saber on the heavy wooden planks of the table and the shouted command "*Silentium,*" he would call the meeting to order. It was all very Teutonic and pompous. Each of us had an assigned name, culled from German mythology. There was Siegfried and Sigmund, Wotan, Tristan, and Lohengrin. My name was Allarich, from one of the fairer heroes in the saga of the Nibelungen. Each of us had a large stein of beer within reach. Many a toast and prosit led to a progressive state of inebriation so that by the time the meeting adjourned, around midnight, we had all had more than enough to drink. At frequent intervals a song would be called for, such as the classic "Gaudeamus Igitur" or something from the vast repertory of German student songs. This camaraderie, although somewhat forced and artificial, nevertheless gave one a feeling of exhilaration in belonging to a body of young men.

Another weekly highlight was the *Bummel,* or walkabout, when on Friday evening all the fraternities in their colorful caps walked along a designated route through the center of town, across the bridge, and back again, like strutting peacocks. Saber practice and dueling were also an integral part of a *Burschenschaft.* I didn't mind the practice sessions, when one wore a protective wire mask and helmet, but I had little use for the actual dueling with sharply honed sabers that could inflict considerable damage and scar one for life. Precautions were taken to protect the eyes with metal goggles and the jugular veins with heavy bandages around the neck. Cheeks, mouth, nose, arms, and the torso, naked from the waist up, remained unprotected. Somehow I escaped being marked with this stigma of Teutonic student life. It seemed utterly idiotic to me to disfigure oneself in such a barbaric manner. Often these duels were arranged as competitive events between two feuding fraternities. Quite frequently, they were duels of honor, to avenge a personal insult or the besmirching of a fair maiden's reputation. Diligently I refrained from such provocations. Admittedly, I was a coward and minded my tongue.

Much later, to my dismay, I realized that these so-called brotherhoods were notorious breeding grounds for anti-Semitism. To me there was no reason nor justice in segregating human beings based upon their race or religious affiliation. After a short tenure, I withdrew with a lame excuse.

MARIANNA

Girls, sports, and final exams were the main preoccupations in my life going on nineteen. Falling in love madly and out of love again happened frequently. These were the typical infatuations of this age. Sex had a lot to do with it. Then one day a very special young woman entered my life. She was lithesome, vivacious, and exotic-looking with large brown eyes and dark hair cascading over her shoulders. Her velvet-smooth complexion had an unusual golden hue, as though she was of Eurasian origin, which definitely she was not. Marianna came from an old Austrian family with an aristocratic heritage, entitling her to use "von" with her surname.

Marianna's father was a retired military officer. Unfortunately, in his old age he was afflicted with Parkinson's disease. To see the old general sitting bent over in a wheelchair with a constant stream of spittle trickling from the corners of his mouth, his hands fiercely trembling, and his head bobbing to one side or the other was a pitiful sight. Naturally, it was embarrassing for Marianna to have me see her father in such an unfortunate condition, since everyone wants to take pride in one's parents. What her father could not deliver in this respect, her mother made up for in many ways. She was a remarkable woman of indomitable courage, compassion, and humor, with a gift for minimizing this misfortune for the whole family.

Marianna's family lived in a small villa on the outskirts of town and also owned a very authentic peasant cottage on the shore of a lake about an hour's ride by postal bus from Salzburg. With loving care and much good taste, their little cottage had been transformed into a most attractive country home. Inside was a collection of old and painted armoires, tables, chairs, and benches. It was a little gem.

Marianna had two older brothers, both very athletic, with whom I established an immediate rapport based on our common interests. Frequently there would be improvised athletic competitions in such events as sprinting, jumping, pole vaulting, swimming and diving, and of course, mountaineering and skiing. It was an idyllic life, to be very much in love and to be accepted and treated like a member of the family.

Herbert, the younger of the brothers, quite possibly saved my life at one time. The long winter had given way at last to spring, but our passion for skiing remained insatiable. The snow had melted and receded to higher elevations, but we didn't mind the long climb and looked forward to one last fling on skis before summer. With skis slung over one shoulder and poles over the other, we climbed until we reached the snow line. It was obvious that there wasn't much chance of getting a downhill run of any length, so we decided to build a small ski jump.

Building a takeoff platform didn't take much time. Using the tail end of a ski as a cutting tool and shovel, we piled square-shaped blocks of snow on top of each other, like building an Eskimo igloo, and molded it with hands and skis into the required shape. More physical effort was required in preparing the in-run and landing slope, especially the latter. The slope had to be firmly packed and repeatedly gone over with the skis strapped to the feet. One walked up and down sideways, stomping the snow into a smooth-textured landing slope. Late in the spring, the snow surface could become very treacherous. The warmth of the earth beneath could melt the snow and create dangerous air pockets. If not packed correctly, the crust might break and a skier could fall into a cavity as if dropped through a trapdoor.

Since I was the more experienced jumper, I made the first test jump. Knowing that this was merely an attempt to get the feel of the hill, I did not exert myself in any way. Yet when I landed I felt the snow give way beneath me. With my feet arrested as though clamped in a bear trap, I fell forward with a thud. Hidden under the snow was a tree stump, which I hit with the left side of my chest. The instant I made contact with this object I knew I was hurt. My stomach turned and I felt like vomiting. The pain was so severe that I blacked out for a while. So I was told by Herbert. When I came to, I could barely move, and only with the greatest effort and his help, I managed to get back on my feet. Here we were, the two of us, hours away from civilization or any kind of shelter. Blood was coming out of my mouth, and when I emptied my bladder, there was blood visible on the white snow, indicating internal injuries. I felt as though the left side of my rib cage had been crushed.

There was no alternative but to start walking down the mountain back to where we had come from. Herbert, in the lead, implored me not to give up and to keep moving until we reached a place where I could lie down while he went ahead and mustered some help to carry me the rest of the way down on a stretcher. Walking on snow was not half as bad as walking on the bare ground. Every step was like a sharp knife thrust into my side. By then I was in a daze and moving like a robot, driven by the will to survive. Our progress was snail-like. After taking a few steps I had to stop, slump over, gasp for air, and try to catch my breath. Eventually we reached the promenade path laid out for summer tourists, where a bench overlooked the valley and lake below. Dimly I could see Marianna's house. Herbert improvised a pillow and some covers, telling me to lie down and wait until he came back with friends. I welcomed the opportunity to get off my feet. By this time it was beginning to get dark. I must have blacked out again; I woke when I heard voices and saw a group of men with lighted torches and a stretcher rushing up the path. By the time we arrived at the house, it was pitch dark. An ambulance was waiting, and I was whisked to a hospital in Salzburg.

My own diagnosis proved correct. A number of ribs were broken, and there were some internal injuries, but none of the vital organs was seriously damaged. Luck was with me since one of my jagged broken ribs had not punctured my left lung. Youth and time are the best healers; a few months passed, and the effects of this ill-fated excursion were soon forgotten. Had it not been for Herbert and his determination to get me back, I could not have made it through the ordeal.

I graduated, just barely, from the Realschule. To enter a university was not in the cards for me. I wanted a job and was anxious to make some money. Depression and unemployment were still rampant in Austria in 1927, and I was fortunate in that my father managed to get me a job with the postal service. It was not at all what I had in mind as my future career, but there was no alternative for the moment. I took the job reluctantly, not wanting to hurt my father's feelings.

I was on the night shift. My first assignment was sorting incoming and outgoing mail. The outgoing mail, collected during the day from various post offices around town and mailboxes on street corners, was delivered to the large sorting center at the railroad station. Here a whole platoon of men stood in front of a grid of small boxes similar to pigeon-holes. These were marked with names of cities, foreign countries, and code numbers indicating final destinations. Each piece of mail was sorted by hand and deposited in the appropriate cubicle. Eventually, all the sorted mail was bundled together and dropped into gunnysacks, securely tied up, and delivered to postal freight cars headed in the right direction.

Between the processing of outgoing mail and the arrival of incoming mail, there was usually a break of a few hours when one could lie down on a cot for a brief nap. Then the process was reversed, and the incoming mail sorted for delivery the next day. It was certainly not a stimulating routine. The job became somewhat more interesting when I was assigned to duty at one of the service counters. This at least brought me in contact with people while I processed registered letters, money orders, and packages, franked letters to foreign countries, and attended to the plethora of details required by postal operations.

One of the not-quite kosher side benefits of my job was free transportation to the lakeside cottage owned by Marianna's family. Part of my duties was to sell tickets for the postal buses, which covered quite a network of routes. It so happened that one of the bus lines passed right by the cottage. I knew all the drivers personally and had a pleasant working relationship with them. Hence, there would always be a seat for me on the bus and a quick unscheduled stop to let me off. With a few bounding steps up a short, steep hill, I was there.

The days I spent with Marianna in this cottage and the lovely surrounding meadows, forests, mountains, and lakes of the Salzkammergut were like a continuous, beautiful dream. They made me forget the frustrations and tedium of a job I did not like. For the first time in my life I was deeply in love, and what made it even more fulfilling was that my feelings were wholly reciprocated. It was too good to be true; nothing as beautiful as that could last forever.

It did not. Marianna became pregnant in spite of my haphazard precautions. For a girl her age from a respectable family, this was a catastrophe, considering the Victorian mores of that era. I was devastated and conscience-stricken to have brought this upon her. My feeling of guilt was overwhelming for having broken the trust shown to me by her family. Marianna was frightened—and so was I. Given our economic circumstances, marriage was out of the question. Giving birth to an illegitimate child was also unthinkable, leaving an indelible mark of shame on both mother and child. Marianna and I talked it over for days. Our options were distressingly limited.

In our predominantly Catholic country, abortion was a dreaded word, tainted with disgrace. But it seemed to us that it was the only solution. Our decided course was fraught with dangers: first, no one must know about it, and second, how did one go about finding a responsible doctor?

At that time, anyone connected with such a procedure was prosecuted as a criminal and subject to imprisonment. No respectable doctor, knowing his career might be in jeopardy, would think of performing an abortion, unless it was a matter of life and death for the mother, as officially certified by a quorum of physicians. Underground quacks performed this kind of operation at great risk to the patient, but I would have none of that under any circumstances. Marianna was too precious to me.

Without any alternative, we decided to see her family doctor together. I had never met him before and was surprised to find him a young-looking man in his late thirties. He listened to our story with a sober mien and gave no indication of sympathy for our desperate dilemma. After a long silence, he asked whether we were aware of the immense risk all of us would be taking from a legal point of view. Abortion was considered a crime. The consequences to his medical career could be grave, and the danger of an infection after such an operation was everpresent. We nodded, crestfallen, realizing that the obstacles were insurmountable.

After another long silence, the doctor said, "I'll do it, providing that total secrecy is maintained and a suitable place will be found to perform the procedure." It could not be done in his office. I had a friend who owned a house in the countryside, where I had occasionally spent a few days during previous summers. I thought that I could arrange to have the use of the house for a few days without any detailed explanation. The summer tourist season was over, and the place was unoccupied. Furthermore, the house stood somewhat isolated off the main road before entering the small village. It was unlikely that anyone would notice us coming or leaving. He accepted this proposal and said that he would arrive on his motorcycle on a given evening after dark. Also, he said that a preliminary examination in his office would be required and a step performed to dilate the cervix, imperative for the subsequent operation.

To this day it puzzles me why the doctor would assume such an enormous risk to help us. I understood perfectly that it was not to do me a favor. Money was not an incentive, since I confessed to the doctor that I was financially strapped and whatever his fee would be, I could only pay it off in driblets as I earned the money. This seemed of no importance to him. I can only assume that he decided to undertake it out of kindness and compassion for Marianna and her family. Perhaps he sensed that a tragedy was in the making unless he came to our rescue. Suicide among young people caught in such a vise was not uncommon, especially girls who could not face the disgrace brought upon themselves and the shame on their family.

The day was set. During the examination in the doctor's office, he explained to us that a packing inserted in the cervix would gradually swell and dilate it substantially. After we arrived at the house in the country, we were to wait one night, and the following day after nightfall the doctor would arrive. Feeling indescribable relief, we left as though we had been given a new lease on life. Little did we realize what an ordeal it would be for Marianna.

As the packing swelled, Marianna's pain became excruciating, reminding me of medieval torture. I was in mental agony, helpless to give her any kind of relief. I huddled next to her, holding her in my arms, hoping to give her some comfort. She became feverish, bathed in perspiration and writhing in pain. If I could have taken some of her misery and endured it myself, I would have gladly done so.

As darkness set in on the dreary, rainy day, the doctor arrived as he had promised, black bag in hand, without being seen. If the preliminaries were difficult, the operation was even more harrowing. Without anesthesia and with only a mild sedative, Marianna underwent surgery performed at its most primitive. Unashamedly I wept, holding her hands, which had clenched into tight fists. I realized she was about to faint into unconsciousness, which would have been a blessed relief from her pain. It was so unjust that only the girl of the couple should have to bear such an ordeal.

At last it was done. Exhausted and looking pale as the whitewashed walls of the kitchen, Marianna was completely spent. I carried her to bed, and mercifully she fell almost immediately into a deep sleep. I mourned the thought of what a beautiful child it might have been. I knew instinctively that this loss would haunt me for the remainder of my life, and so it has.

The doctor had asked me to heat up a cauldron of water to clean away all signs of the operation. The silence between us was leaden, neither of us in a mood for polite conversation. What we had done weighed heavily on both of us. We were fully cognizant that creating a life is an awesome responsibility, and to take a life an even greater one. I accompanied the doctor to the door and thanked him from my heart. He tied his black bag to the rack behind the seat of his motorcycle, and with a determined kick of his foot, started the engine. Very quickly the bright red light above the rear wheel diminished to a small speck that disappeared in the mist and pouring rain. I turned to enter the house, depressed and bone weary.

Marianna and I stayed on at the house for another two nights. I took care of her as, gradually, she regained her strength and mental fortitude. Her family never had the slightest inkling of what had happened, nor did anyone else. It remained a secret between the three of us. Yet Marianna and I had been so badly scarred and frightened, that we shied away from any physical contact. We drifted apart rather than clinging together, as one might expect of two lovers who have shared such an emotional experience. I paid off my debt to the doctor, which was surprisingly reasonable considering the risk he had assumed, as expediently as I could.

Marianna later married a handsome and affluent young man. It appeared to be an ideal marriage, but she was widowed early in life when her husband was killed in a freak hunting accident, chasing chamois in the Alps. She married again, but during the waning days of World War II, her second husband fell on the Russian front. I always make it a point to see Marianna when I am in Austria. A talented fashion designer and graphic artist, she managed to support herself and her daughter born of her second marriage. In spite of all the heartache she has endured, she has never lost her infectious smile or glowing warmth and spontaneity. She occupies a very special niche in my heart.

EVERYMAN—THE PLAY

To my parents' chagrin, I resigned from my position with the postal service. I couldn't take it any longer and felt restricted and imprisoned. "But what will you do? How will you support yourself?" my mother asked anxiously. I assured her that I would not depend upon them for financial support; from that time on I would be strictly on my own. Surprisingly, my father understood what was going through my mind, even though he did not wholeheartedly approve of my sudden decision. He was only waiting to reach the years of service required to qualify for a guaranteed pension. It would be considerably less than he would receive if he served out his full term and retired at the age of sixty-five; however, he realized that the only way to improve the family's financial situation was to seek a position in private business to augment his monthly income.

Of course, I had made up my mind as to what I intended to do before I quit my job. During the summer months I would teach swimming, diving, and gymnastics in one of the many popular summer resorts in Austria. During the winter months I would teach skiing. I had some good leads through friends in the sports world, and fortuitously, an opportunity came to me almost immediately. I was to help out as an assistant instructor for a ladies' gym class.

One day one of the women in the gym class asked me, "How would you like to audition for a part in *Jederman* [*Everyman*]?" I was startled, and said I had never had any ambition to become an actor, nor had I had any training in that field. "Never mind," she said, "It's not that sort of part." She explained to me that she was cast as one of the guests in the banquet scene, and she thought I would be well-suited to portray her paramour.

Jederman had been the pièce de résistance of the annual Salzburg Festival since its inception in 1920. Max Reinhardt, the most famous régisseur of that era, had approached the archbishop of Salzburg, Ignatius Rieder, asking for permission to stage this religious drama, based on a medieval morality play, in front of the cathedral. This would entail closing off the entire area surrounding the *duomo* and eliminating the ringing of church bells during each performance. Although a group of influential city fathers vociferously opposed the idea, the archbishop, a churchman of exceptionally wide and worldly vision, acquiesced. I don't think this decision ever has been regretted, not by his eminence the archbishop nor by any of his successors.

Throughout the years the *Jederman* cast has changed many times, and new costumes and techniques of staging have been tried, but the play and the original setting have endured. The production has quite possibly never reached the caliber of the original Reinhardt staging in 1920. Helped by a stellar cast, headed by the incomparable Alexander Moissi in the leading role, it was a theatrical high mark. I had seen the play and rarely had been so impressed and moved by a dramatic presentation. In fact, it was quite shattering. Who could resist the temptation of becoming even an infinitesimal part of such a world-famous extravaganza? Just imagine, making one's stage debut under the direction of Max Reinhardt! I went to the tryout—and passed. On what basis I don't know, but I was in. Rehearsals, fascinating in themselves for an apprentice such as myself, began shortly thereafter.

The play began with an actor rising from the audience and mounting the stairs leading to center stage. In a ringing declamation he announced that what the audience was about to see was *Everyman*, the play of a rich man's life and death. "Lend your ears and listen well," he exclaimed.

Then, from the lofty height of one of the cathedral's bell towers, the sonorous voice of the Lord floated down. With great sorrow, he proclaimed his disappointment in mankind. "Where art thou, Death, my mighty messenger? Step forth." Whereupon the gaunt and skeletal figure of Death, dressed all in black, rose slowly to its full height, awaiting the Lord's orders. "Go thou to Everyman and tell him in my name that he must enter on a pilgrimage from this day and very hour which by no means he can escape. Tell him to bring his reckoning straight away and ask no further tarrying and delay."

Speaking in a chilling, harsh, metallic voice, Death agreed to do the Lord's bidding. As Death vanished, the richly dressed Everyman bounded onto stage with a few light steps. With a clap of his hands, he summoned his retinue of servants, ordering them to prepare for a feast on the morrow to entertain a number of friends and honored guests. Thus the stage was set to dramatically unravel the life of Everyman.

My big moment came in that banquet scene, in which I played one of the honored guests. We formed couples, and to the tune of an ancient melody, went through the motions of a medieval dance. We had been taught to make stiff, jerky movements of our arms and legs, circling each other as though we were figures carved of wood. Although far from graceful, it was effective. After the dance, everybody sat down at a long table laden with food and ale, which had appeared as if by magic. My place was center stage, very close to Alexander Moissi. I marveled at the range of his voice, which he could mold and modulate like the tones of an organ.

Everyman urged his company to enjoy the feast, but when he heard the ominous sound of bells ringing, he abruptly interrupted, saying, "What bells are those? . . . The sound is loud and frightful of death, pressing the anxious heart to pain and sorrow. Why do the bells ring at this time?"

One of the ladies answered that nowhere was there a thing to be heard. Next came my cue for the one line I could not afford to muff. "Has anyone heard a bell?" I asked. I did it with the poise of a seasoned veteran, even though my heart was pounding and crowding right up into my throat.

Then one of most haunting and memorable moments occurred, when voices from near and distant locations began to call, "Everyman, Every-y-y-man, Everyman-n-n-n, EVERY-MAN," some barely audible, others strong and commanding, from a window in the courtyard, from the spires of the nearby churches of Saint Peter and Saint Francis, and even one from the fortress of Hohensalzburg looming above. It was eerie and sobering. No one was supposed to hear these voices except for Everyman.

At the end of the play, when Everyman entered his tomb, not a sound came from the audience. No one dared applaud. Time stood still momentarily. Slowly, people dispersed through the monumental arches on each side of the courtyard, some with tears in their eyes and others visibly shaken by what they had witnessed. It was one of those extraordinary events when all elements—words, action, natural surroundings, the fading light of the sinking sun, music, cast, and staging—fused into one cohesive entity.

The play was a complete success. On rainy days it was moved indoors, still powerful as ever thanks to Reinhardt's consummate mastery. At the end of one matinee, the assistant director rushed over to me and said, "*Herr Lang, man braucht Sie dringend im Stadt Theater für die Vorführung von Don Giovanni. Einer der Schauspieler musste im letzten moment ausfallen. Er ist krank.*" It meant, get to the theater in a hurry to substitute for an actor who had become ill suddenly in *Don Giovanni,* Mozart's opera. There was no point in trying to explain to the man that I was not much of a singer and certainly not qualified for an appearance in Mozart's famous musical drama. It was obviously a dire emergency, so off I went.

When I arrived at the theater, I was led in haste to the costuming department where make-up was applied to me and a wig was plopped on my head. While all this was going on, I was given rapid instructions as to what my part in the opera would be. I was told to carry a lighted lantern and told not to open my mouth or utter a sound. That took care of the operatic part of my role. By this time the overture was already in progress.

As the curtain rose, Don Giovanni's manservant Leporello was pacing the stage, bitterly complaining about his duties, singing "*Notte, giorno faticar . . .*" He no longer cared to be a servant. The hours were long, and life was too hectic; he wanted out. Suddenly, there was a commotion and a man burst out from the palazzo, pursued by another man, the Commendatore, lord of the manor. The man in flight was Don Giovanni, reputed rake and womanizer, who had tried to seduce Donna Anna and thereby brought the wrath of her father down upon him. They drew their swords and a duel to the death ensued.

At this dramatic moment, I was shoved onto the stage unceremoniously, feebly illuminating the scene with my lantern. I had been told to follow the action with greatest concern, realizing that my master's life, that of the aged Commendatore, was at stake. Needless to say, I gave it my all! No servant ever suffered more or writhed in compassion as I did. At last, mortally wounded, the Commendatore fell into my arms. He weighed a ton. It took all my strength to accommodate his bulk. As I sank to my knees he whispered, "Hang on to me and don't you dare drop me." I didn't, and with a last gasp and twitch of his body, he died convincingly in my arms. With a piercing note of dismay, Donna Anna entered and launched into her first aria. Don Giovanni and Leporello fled in haste. Other servants appeared when they heard the ruckus and hauled off the lifeless body of the Commendatore. By then I felt in complete control of the situation and picked up my flickering lantern and followed them.

There never came an opportunity for me to give a repeat performance. When the bedridden fellow was told about the sterling performance given by his substitute, he recovered very quickly. I knew that my performance, entirely in pantomime, would be hard to top.

In the excitement and euphoria of my "operatic debut," I forgot that I had not been in the Stadt Theater for quite a while—in fact, not since my grandmother's death. My father's mother was a widow who had not seen her son Alfred for many years, nor had Mother and we children ever met her. It was therefore a joyous occasion when my father announced he had invited her to visit us. I remember her as a darling, undemanding person, petite, white-haired with cornflower blue eyes, a sharp mind, and regal bearing, notwithstanding her fourscore years. The highlight of her visit was for us all to attend a performance of a Viennese operetta, *The Merry Widow*, in the Stadt Theater.

The theater was a baroque landmark that looked like a finely tooled jewel box inside. It was smallish with red velvet seats and plump, gilded angels along the row of boxes overlooking the orchestra seats. There was a magnificently painted curtain, a festive tableau before the performance on stage even began. We had not been there often as a family, and when I went alone, I always stood in the standing-room area behind the last row of seats. On the special evening in honor of our grandmother, however, my father bought tickets for a center box that accommodated all seven of us.

With much anticipation and excitement we arrived at the theater in good time before the curtain rose. Slowly the house lights dimmed, and the orchestra prepared to begin the overture. With a barely audible sigh, my grandmother slowly sank out of her chair onto the floor. Her eyes were shut tight, but she appeared not to be in pain. She was rushed into the superintendent's private office and a doctor was summoned post-haste. She was declared dead and covered with a sheet. Her life had come to an end by cardiac arrest, surrounded by people she loved, her favorite son and his family.

It was a traumatic experience for all of us and particularly so for my father, who loved her dearly. Still, we realized, as our father explained to us, how fortunate it was for a person of advanced age to part from this earth as though struck by a mortal blow of lightning. Sad as it may be, we understood. She died elegantly with dignity in a milieu quite familiar to her, since her father had been the resident dancing master at the venerable National Theater in Prague, where many of Mozart's operas were first presented, while she was growing up. It took me a while to get over the pall cast on the Stadt Theater by this mournful incident and to attend any performance of a dramatic play, opera, or operetta, all of which I enjoyed immensely.

With my devotion to music, I have been asked frequently whether I play a musical instrument. The answer, alas, is no, for a ludicrous reason. During my days at the Realschule, musical scholarships were offered to interested students to attend the Mozarteum, which is comparable to the Juilliard School in New York, though perhaps on a smaller scale. The instruments offered were: *Waldhorn* (French horn), flute, and tuba. I surmise that this odd selection was based on the availability of instruments. I chose the *Waldhorn*, possibly because the romantic name "forest horn" appealed to me, but also because I liked the mellow sound of the instrument. Diligently I began lessons with a teacher who happened to be an elderly, rheumy-eyed gentleman with a constantly running nose and a drooping walrus mustache, yellowed by age and the stain of to-bacco juice. He had an unnerving habit: whenever I blew a wrong note, he would say, "No, no, let me show you!", whereupon he would grab the horn out of my hands and bury the mouthpiece in the hair of his wet mustache. After he had produced the correct sound, he would hand the instrument back to me and say, "Now, you try it!" He expected me to play without cleaning the brass mouthpiece; to have done so would have insulted him. I could not take this routine for long. Aside from sanitary reasons, such intimate mouth contact offended my sense of aesthetics. It was like sharing another man's wet toothbrush. I quit. Thus, to my great regret, my musical career fell by the wayside.

Music became an integral part of my life, however. I learned to appre-ciate the compositions of Italian, French, German, Finnish, Czech,

Hungarian, and Russian composers, along with a multitude of other nationalities. They provided me with spiritual nourishment. A life without music would be like living in a desert without water. Of course, I love the music of Mozart, Salzburg's native son, its pride and joy. But I have always felt closest to Beethoven. If for some unlikely reason I were banished to a desert island and had the choice of taking along only one composer's life work, it would be Beethoven's music. There is something so monumental, heroic, and exquisitely tender in his compositions. No matter how often I hear them played, they remain fresh, and I am filled with the wonder of new discoveries at every listening.

STARTING
A CAREER

Following an intuitive hunch, I wrote a letter to a Mr. Konrad Galischko, head of the ski school at the Südbahn Hotel on the Semmering near Vienna, to apply for a position as assistant ski instructor. Before World War I, the Semmering had been a summer playground for affluent merchants, aristocrats, and celebrities of the Austro-Hungarian Empire. By the late 1920s, the resort area was primarily known as a place for people with tuberculosis. A string of sanitariums stretched along the mountainside, with balconies for patients to lie in the sun, exposed to unpolluted mountain air. Antibiotics to combat tuberculosis had not been discovered yet, so overcoming the dreaded disease was mostly a matter of one's own constitution, a great deal of rest, and nature's restorative powers. It was much like what Thomas Mann described in *The Magic Mountain*.

Quite understandably, the tubercular patients were not skiing clientele. They needed every ounce of physical strength to fight off fevers and other debilitating effects of their malady. The Semmering was, however, easily accessible by train and only a few hours from Vienna. There was a sizable population of healthy nouveaux riches who looked for ways to spend their money in an environment of prewar luxury.

VIENNA'S PLAYGROUND

Two impressive hotels accommodated the stream of visitors: the Südbahn Hotel, which catered to the more sedate contingent, and the Panhans Hotel, which lured the younger generation, comparable to today's jet set. During the winter months, aside from sleigh-riding, sledding, skating, walking, and the customary indoor activities, there wasn't much to do. Skiing as a popular sport was still in its infancy, but this mountain complex was one of its budding centers, in the process of developing into a year-round resort.

Galischko, a former officer and instructor of the Austrian ski troops, had the bright idea of opening a ski school on the Semmering, using the slopes surrounding the hotels. The only other ski school of any repute was at St. Anton-am-Arlberg in the Tyrol, under the direction of Hannes Schneider, who was on his way to becoming a legend in skiing circles.

Galischko's answer to my letter was affirmative. I was hired for the winter season of 1928-1929 at a salary far beyond my expectations. I was overjoyed and at the same time apprehensive, well aware of my lack of teaching experience.

When I reported for duty shortly before Christmas, I found out that teaching was a matter of telling a class, "Watch me and observe what I am doing, then follow me." There were only the two of us teaching. I was assigned the beginners, while my boss shepherded the intermediate and better skiers; experts we did not have at this stage. As I recall, the terrain was rather gentle and not very challenging, but at the same time the guests were not proficient enough.

We evolved a teaching plan based on the military system used to teach Alpine troops to ski, with certain modifications for civilians skiing strictly for fun. After learning the basic straight running position, beginners progressed through the snowplow turn to the stem turn and eventually to the stem-christiania. The telemark turn was on its way out, since the latest model of bindings restricted the free up-and-down movement of the heel so essential in executing this graceful turn. Ski equipment left much to be desired. Steel edges had not yet been introduced, and our skis were not worth much when the slopes were icy or hard packed. Bindings were flimsy, boots cumbersome, and poles heavy. But since nothing better existed, it did not matter much.

I found teaching most interesting, challenging, and in the end, gratifying. Every student seemed to have a different problem. It became apparent that every requirement of becoming a good skier was in opposition to the natural instinct for self-preservation. Instead of projecting the bulk of one's body forward, sitting back on the heels seems far safer. Leaning into the hill makes one feel rather more secure than standing straight or leaning slightly away from the hill. Therefore, the main objective in teaching a beginner was to defuse these instincts. One amazing discovery I made was that as I taught others, I also learned every day, and my own technique improved by leaps and bounds. Besides, it was fun. I enjoyed teaching and never looked upon it as monotony or drudgery.

My winter at the Semmering was my first Christmas away from home. I would be twenty years old in January, and my parents always had managed to make Christmas a special celebration. When times were bad and food was scarce, my mother scrounged and saved whatever she could, such as flour and sugar, to provide for our family feast. A week before Christmas, activity in her kitchen was at a high pitch as she baked an assortment of delicious cookies, cakes, and pastries that would last us through the holidays. She was a consummate cook and had been well-taught by her mother to carry on this tradition.

The much-anticipated presents were delivered to us by St. Nicholas, and opened on the eve of St. Nicholas Day, which was the sixth of January. For the Christmas celebration itself, a space was shut off, whether a room or a corner partitioned off by a curtain, and complete secrecy as to what went on behind it was maintained. We were not supposed to peek at any time, and suspense built up unbearably until the moment when, at a given signal, the door burst open or the curtain was pulled aside—and there stood a tree ablaze with small candles and sparklers. On top was a little merry-go-round, activated by heat from the candles, with a miniature angel blowing a glass trumpet as it circled. Beneath the tree were presents, neatly wrapped and marked with our names. It was magical. During our years in Bosnia there were toys galore, and after we moved to Salzburg, the gifts became more practical—a pair of socks, a sweater, a shirt, or if we were lucky, a pair of new shoes. The spirit of Christmas prevailed, no matter what.

I missed Christmas at home while living at the Südbahn, where I had my own room with a bath. I ate in the dining room with the guests and often shared their company for meals. The table was covered with immaculate white linen, fine china, glassware, and silver cutlery, with hovering waiters serving a gourmet dinner. All of a sudden, I was engulfed by an overwhelming feeling of homesickness and ready to burst into tears. Never before had I wanted so much to be with my family and share my good fortune and bounty with them.

I admonished myself sternly, and after enumerating my blessings, I realized that the time had simply come to wean myself of those close family ties. However, whenever I returned to Salzburg for a visit, I always headed straight for home, by this time a place on the Getreidegasse, a few doors away from Mozart's *Geburtshaus* (birthplace). Though inconveniently located on the fourth floor of an old building, the apartment was much larger with running water in the kitchen and even a flush toilet, our first in all these years. Uncomfortable and crowded though it might be, I went there because my parents would have been deeply hurt had it been any other way.

Life at the Südbahn Hotel brought a constantly changing parade of fascinating people, which enlivened the daily routine of teaching classes, going to cocktail parties, and enjoying convivial dinners after a day on the ski slopes. For a young man such as myself—of fairly good appearance, in excellent physical condition, and blessed with a bursting vitality—it was pure carnal temptation. I became infatuated with a ballerina of the Vienna Opera corps de ballet, which kept me out of the delicate involvements that could have easily led to complications. Our infatuation lasted through the winter season, then its bloom gently wore off. We parted best of friends, and it always gave me great pleasure to read her name in a review of a ballet in which she had performed.

I had any number of invitations to come to Vienna after the winter season ended. Vienna in the spring is beautiful. One of the invitations was to spend a few days in one of the most renowned and resplendent *palais* in the city, and I could not resist. The count, who had been one of my ski school students, received me and showed me to my quarters. It was a suite of rooms, the likes of which I had never seen before. A retainer in livery unpacked my suitcase and neatly put away its contents, handling each garment as though it were a priceless relic. Looking out the window, I saw a glorious view: beds of flowers in bloom and the spire of Saint Stephen's Cathedral looming above the palatial buildings across a large plaza bearing the same name as the palace in which I stayed.

As it turned out, my amiable host the count was homosexual, and since I could not reciprocate his overtures, I fled after one night and moved to a low-priced pension. Decades later, when I was shooting scenes for a television special on the life of Beethoven, I returned to the

Schwarzenberg Palais, which the young Beethoven had frequented. The Schwarzenberg family, like other members of the Viennese aristocracy, had sponsored the budding composer. My host had long since died, but the *palais* remained as impressive as I remembered it.

STEFAN ZWEIG

One of the more important reasons for my being in Vienna was to become certified as a government-licensed swimming and gymnastics instructor. One had to be able to teach the various strokes, save a person in danger of drowning, administer first aid, and perform resuscitation procedures as well as pass oral and written tests. I passed, and that made it possible for me to apply for a summer job. On my first attempt I was given the position of director of summer activities at the *Strandbad* at Zell-am-See. This attractive small town, not too distant from Salzburg, was a popular summer resort situated on the shore of a large lake, scenically surrounded by high mountains. The water never warmed to a pleasantly relaxing temperature, however, since the lake was fed by melting glaciers. To dive or slowly walk into the water was a bracing if not jolting experience.

Swimming was taught by putting a harness around the chest of the swimmer and dangling him from a rope attached to a stout pole that was supported and moved along a horizontal barrier by the instructor. It makes me smile today to think of this medieval contraption. Only one who has learned to swim this way could fully appreciate the sense of having one's life hanging by a thread.

Twice a day gymnastics classes were held on the beach. The newly introduced medicine ball was popular at that time. About two feet in diameter and solidly stuffed with cotton, it was tossed about, used to pummel a partner's body, or deployed as a counterweight in certain exercises. Also, it lent itself to some social games. All of this activity went well as long as the sun was shining and the sky was blue. But woe to all when one of those long rainy spells settled in. Nothing is more desolate and forlorn than a *Strandbad* in a pelting rain for days on end. Certainly, one could walk in the rain, eat, and sleep, but what one had come for—the nut-brown suntan that proved one could afford and had been on a summer vacation—was sadly unattainable.

One distraction during the rainy spells was a small pavilion on the lakeshore, which became a popular meeting place. Every afternoon a *thé dansant* developed. No orchestra, of course, but there was a Victrola, which had to be wound up by hand every so often. The Argentine tango was in vogue, and I happened to be quite good at it, with all its precision steps, head tosses, dips, and backward bends. Once I was approached by a middle-aged German gentleman, slightly bald-headed and with the pince-nez typical of a respectable minor functionary in a large industrial enterprise. He asked me if I would teach him and his companion how to dance the tango. The companion turned out to be a young woman many years his junior, with pleated blond hair tightly woven against her temples in a most unbecoming coiffure. She had quite obviously made an illicit arrangement for a free summer vacation.

With the need to generate some income to make up for my rained-out lessons at the *Strandbad*, I jumped at the opportunity to start a dance class. As the rain continued, my class grew in size and we branched out into foxtrots, shimmies, and an occasional Viennese waltz. When the sun broke out again, some of the dancing couples decided to learn to swim and others to frolic in the sand by joining my daily gym class. It worked out well for everyone concerned to make a rain-dampened summer vacation pleasant and—for me—remunerative.

Another of my jobs that summer was to attend to the twice-weekly workouts of the renowned Austrian writer Stefan Zweig, who had been a client of mine in Salzburg. He had rented a summer cottage on the lakeshore opposite Zell-am-See to escape an endless stream of visitors. Of all the nonathletes I have ever known, Zweig deserves the highest marks. Sports of any kind were anathema to him. Bending from the waist with his legs straight, he could not touch his kneecaps with the tips of his fingers. His ambition was to touch his toes, looked upon as a standard test of suppleness. As his gymnastics instructor, my job was to help him reach this goal. We never did accomplish it; it appeared that his vertebrae had solidly fused themselves into an unbending column from sitting at his writing desk day in and day out.

In Salzburg Zweig lived in an attractive villa, possibly built as a pleasure dome by an emancipated prince of the church. It stood on top of the Kapuzinerberg, a short but steep climb from the center of the city. Along the broad stone staircase were the twelve stations of the cross, depicting the trail to Calvary and the crucifixion of Jesus Christ in near life-size figures and with all the gory details. The view from the house was breathtaking, a 180-degree panorama encompassing the city below, with Alpine peaks beckoning in the distance. For a writer it was an ideal environment, so close to a city yet removed from its restless hubbub.

Only a short walk away stood the tiny bungalow in which Wolfgang Amadeus Mozart, during the last year of his short life, composed the score for the opera *Die Zauberflöte*. Zweig's home came to be known as Villa Europa among his acquaintances, some of whom he welcomed with open arms and whose lifelong friendship he treasured. To mention only a few, I noticed Bruno Walter, Richard Strauss, Arturo Toscanini, and Hugo von Hoffmannsthal, among his closest friends.

Twice a week or so, I walked up to Zweig's house and led him through his workout, listening to his moans and groans as he contorted his body into unaccustomed positions. Occasionally, after our sessions of physical torture, he invited me to sit in his study and chat. Sometimes we looked at his autograph collection, which covered an impressive range of living and deceased composers, musicians, poets, painters, and sculptors. Our association continued through the summer, when Zweig moved to the rented country house across the lake from Zell-am-See. He was working on a novel that required his full concentration, hence the move to a quiet spot away from Salzburg.

At the time I was experimenting with two small foldboats, one strapped to each foot. The bottom of the floats had a flexible fin that laid flat against the boat's rubber skin while the wearer was gliding forward but opened up when forward motion stopped, preventing one from sliding backwards. A sturdy six-foot pole with paddles attached to each end provided propellant power: one alternately dipped the oars into the water while striding ahead and pushing oneself forward. It was a cumbersome process of walking on water and rowing in an upright stance.

I was intrigued by this novelty, contrived by a German inventor. It seemed like a good idea, but it never reached the degree of popularity it promised at first sight. The physical dangers were considerable. I risked my neck once by striding down the Salzach River under high flood conditions, racing through the center of town at the speed of an express train. It caused quite a sensation, and I remember the mob of spectators looking down at the river from one side of the bridge and then racing across like a stampede of cattle to follow my progress as I emerged on the other side. Fortunately, I did not fall. In the quiet waters of the lake, getting up after a fall required a modicum of dexterity and some acrobatic skill. Falling in the raging whirlpool of a fast-moving river might have been a different story and quite possibly one without a happy ending.

I always looked forward to my visits to Stefan Zweig's lake house. Undoubtedly he got a kick out of seeing me arrive by walking across the lake and parking my floats at the foot of his terrace. He was a rather quiet and shy man but with a delightful sense of humor and infectious twinkle in his brown eyes. I had made it a point to read some of his books, which I mentioned to him with high compliments for the pleasures derived. *Amok*, one of his most successful novellas, was translated into thirty languages. I was also totally absorbed by his biography of Joseph Fouché, the notorious chief of police of Paris during the Napoleonic regime. When summer ended, our association did, too. I moved on to other distant places and returned to Salzburg only infrequently for short visits. Zweig also traveled a great deal, and our paths rarely crossed again.

Because of Zweig, I followed with great apprehension the rise of Adolf Hitler. The political storm clouds were ominous and frightening. The persecution of the Jews, of whom Zweig was one of the leading luminaries, was relentless and barbaric. Once during Zweig's absence his home was invaded and searched ruthlessly for evidence of conspiratory material, weapons, or literature. After that, Zweig realized he could no longer look upon Salzburg nor Austria as his homeland. For him it was by far the bitterest disappointment of his life. His house was put up for sale and he disposed of many of his material possessions—Beethoven's writing desk and violin in a leather case among his most prized—by giving them to museums or selling them. He wandered the globe, but the fact that he was a man without a country to call his own weighed heavily on his psyche. He could not cope with, as he wrote, "the lunacy of mankind seemingly embarked on a course of universal genocide." He was subject to deep depressions and felt a pervading despondency with regard to what the future might hold for him. Eventually, he settled in Brazil in a small house in Petropolis, on the outskirts of Rio de Janeiro.

Carefully and methodically he prepared a pact for the double suicide of himself and his wife, Lotte. He died with her in 1942. When I learned of this tragedy, I was shocked and deeply saddened. The legacy he left to the literary world is considerable. Among his many other works, the two biographies, *Marie Antoinette* and *Maria Stuart*, stand out as towering achievements. Only recently a compendium of some of his best stories was published in the United States under the title *The Royal Game and Other Stories*. It is a book I treasure.

A FLEDGLING SKI INSTRUCTOR

My tenure at Zell-am-See proved to be a turning point in my professional career. That summer, I met a young man approximately my age who worked in a bank and came every day during the noon hours to the bathing facilities, if the weather was halfway decent. Benno Rybizka was very athletic. He loved to swim, dive from the three-meter springboard, and enjoy a session of vigorous gymnastics. We became friends, sharing many interests, since we were both dedicated outdoor men and athletes. His intelligence and his scholastic background were equal if not superior to mine. His family lived at St. Anton-am-Arlberg, where his father was the resident doctor. Benno taught skiing during the winter as a member of the prestigious Hannes Schneider Ski School.

Naturally, I told Benno that the dream of my life was to join Schneider's school as an instructor. Benno's reaction was not encouraging. He explained that Schneider had a strict policy of hiring only local boys from St. Anton or Stuben (where Schneider was born and grew up) and a few from the nearby villages of Zürs and Lech, accessible through Arlberg Pass, across the mountain range facing St. Anton. However, Benno assured me that no harm could possibly come from my writing a letter to Schneider and applying for a job.

One factor very much in my favor was the increasing need for instructors with a knowledge of foreign languages, especially French, English, and Italian. My command of English and French, which had been obligatory subjects in the Realschule, was adequate. I could get by in Italian and could certainly acquire the necessary phrases to teach Italian skiers. I wrote the letter, using Benno's name as a reference, which undoubtedly was helpful since, I found out later, he was highly thought of in his hometown.

I realized it could be a long time before I received a reply. Hannes Schneider, already internationally known, was a busy man, starring in films, writing magazine articles, and making personal appearances in many cities and foreign countries. So, in the meantime, I made plans to take the exam required to become a government-licensed ski instructor and mountain guide.

To qualify as an expert skier was the least difficult part of this exam. One's ability to communicate with a student and make him understand the basic principles and finer points of skiing technique would be scrutinized in depth. It was a far more demanding test than the one I had taken in Vienna to qualify as a licensed swimming and gymnastics

instructor. I was not at all sure I could succeed on the first try. I immersed myself in technical books about mountain climbing, navigating
in unknown terrain, first aid, survival tactics, protection from ultraviolet
sun rays, the acute danger of snow blindness, nutritional problems, and
many other factors in hope that I would pass.

It was with some trepidation that I reported for the test in early
November after the first snow had fallen high up in the mountains. The
test took place at the Mitterberg Alpe-am-Hochkönig, near Salzburg,
home of the Radachers, a family of competitive skiers. The dozen or so
of us taking the test lived in a rather primitive mountain refuge lacking
the customary amenities. The test consumed the better part of three days,
with on-slope sessions during the day and oral and written tests held in
the evening. I passed—and what a relief it was. I felt a sense of pride and
accomplishment knowing I had become part of a select brotherhood.
Unbeknownst to me, Hannes Schneider had sent an observer to watch
the proceedings and possibly recruit future instructors for his school.
One of his orders was to particularly keep an eye on a fellow by the name
of Otto Lang.

The man sent by Schneider was Luggi Föger, Schneider's number one
instructor and confidant. He left as soon as the examination was over,
without giving me much of an opportunity to ski with him or talk to
him. When I arrived back home again in Salzburg, there was a letter
from Hannes Schneider awaiting me. The long-looked-forward-to
answer at last. But what would it be—yes or no? I tore the envelope open
and my eyes fairly flew over the contents of the letter. I was in and hired.
Much later I found out that Luggi had given me a favorable evaluation
and character reference: "A good skier with an elegant style of his own.
Also a nice guy, from all appearances—but he still has a lot to learn."
How right he was.

To join the Hannes Schneider Ski School at St. Anton, the most prestigious in existence at that time, was intimidating and somewhat awesome. Therefore, during the few weeks remaining before I reported for
duty, I wanted to devote as much time as possible to physical conditioning and polishing the rough edges of my skiing technique. Fortunately,
there was snow on the Gaisberg, the ski mountain of my boyhood.

I remembered how, after school ended on Saturday, I used to spend
weekends with the Hauser family at their farm, called Zistelalm, halfway
up the Gaisberg. The widow Hauser, mother of my friends Hans and
Max, took a liking to me and treated me as though I were a member of

the family. This was fortunate for me. Food was plentiful there and of the most nourishing kind: dark home-baked bread, butter, eggs, bacon, roast chicken, and Austrian doughnuts. I ate shamelessly and couldn't get enough during those postwar days of food shortages. With a bemused smile, Frau Hauser once asked me, "Otto, are you sure you are not feeding a tapeworm with your voracious appetite?" Tapeworms were not uncommon, but not to worry, I was clean. Frau Hauser always slipped some goodies into my haversack to take home to the family.

She was an imposing person. Though of peasant stock, dark-haired with her tresses wound on top of her head like a crown, slender and six feet tall, she had the bearing, poise, and inherent dignity of any wellbred aristocrat. Her husband was killed in the war, but she took over the farm and ran it with a firm grip and only a few hired hands to help her. I looked up to Frau Hauser as a symbol of strength and fortitude.

Hans Hauser and I were approximately the same age; his brother Max was a few years younger. Both were excellent skiers, and all three of us competed in many junior races, downhill and ski jumping. When skiing conditions were good, the three of us, joined by other youngsters our age, skied from early morning until darkness fell, with time out for big slices of heavily buttered peasant bread and bowls of thick lentil soup with square pieces of fat bacon floating on it that would melt in one's mouth.

Based on the memory of those days, I moved up to the Zistelalm to pursue my training. Hans and I had remained close friends through the years. We had reached the onescore milepost in our lives and had become men. The great advantage for me was skiing with Hans and Max, who by now had developed into superb skiers and ran their own ski school on the slopes of the Gaisberg. It was a happy reunion. We had good skiing, with evenings sitting around the table next to the huge tile stove, reminiscing and dreaming of the days ahead. We shared a desire to use skiing as a springboard to recognition and possible riches.

On the last run of a waning Sunday afternoon, Hans and I collided. It wasn't much of a collision, but it was enough to upend us both into a pile of two bodies and entangled skis and poles. I emerged with a pain in my left ankle. I thought it would go away as soon as I moved around a bit, but I was wrong. Hans was unscathed, but my ankle swelled and I was in severe pain shortly thereafter. I skied uncomfortably down the mountain and walked the few kilometers to my home. Consulting a doctor immediately would have been smart. I preferred not to be smart. I didn't want my parents to know about my injury and have them worry. A swollen ankle was nothing new to me, and I was determined to leave by train for St. Anton whenever I was notified to report.

Snow was late in coming that winter in the Tyrol, which gave me some additional time to recover. A few days before Christmas I arrived at St. Anton. Benno met me at the station and took me to my quarters. It was my first sight of that small town with only one long main street with houses and shops scattered along either side. The town surprised me because it was so small and unglamorous. Hannes Schneider, on the contrary, loomed larger than life.

"So, this is Otto Lang," he said when I was introduced to him. "Welcome. I hope you like it here." While shaking my hand, he gave me a penetrating look with his dark brown eyes. A shock of black curls fell over the right side of his forehead. His face, with its high cheekbones, looked gaunt and was dominated by a large, gracefully curved nose. Looking at his head and facial expression, I was immediately reminded of the character studies of Herr Professor Zwerger, the master woodcarver whose workshop I had haunted as a boy in Salzburg. Not only was I impressed, I was also rather overwhelmed to find myself standing face-to-face with a legend who, only the winter before, had made a most successful trip to Japan at the invitation of the government to demonstrate his Arlberg skiing technique and teaching method. I hoped he would be my mentor and employer for many winters to come.

I took an immediate liking to Hannes and we became friends and remained so for the rest of our lives. There was a definite charisma about this man, who from a simple peasant boy had risen to worldwide fame. Not even in my wildest dreams could I have foreseen how profound his influence would be in shaping my future.

ST. ANTON
AM
ARLBERG

In June 1890, Stuben, Austria, was an Alpine village with a population of fifty-six, counting its newest arrival, Johannes Schneider, his name later abbreviated to Hannes. Hannes's parents were farmers. They grew potatoes and owned a few cows that provided fresh milk, the makings of butter and the local cheese.

Hannes's father also worked as road supervisor, a demanding job. At that time Stuben was an important link connecting the province of Vorarlberg, bordering on Switzerland, with St. Anton and Vienna via the Arlberg Pass. In those pre-Arlberg-Tunnel days, a winding, narrow, primitive dirt road led over the pass, and it was Papa Schneider's responsibility to keep it clear, at least to St. Christoph at the crest. On the other side the road dropped into the Rosanna Valley and was attended to by a family named Seeberger, friends of the Schneider clan whose daughter, Ludwina, Hannes would later marry. In summer, long hours and brute physical strength were required to repair washouts and damaged bridges and to remove boulders and debris from rock slides. During snowy winter months, the job was herculean. It required a dozen or so seasoned mountain men to stomp down the fresh snow by foot until a hard-packed surface made it possible for the traffic of horse-drawn sleighs to move in both directions. Minuscule though it was, the road was an important artery.

The road job was a welcome financial supplement for the Schneiders, what with five children to feed, clothe, and raise: Hannes, his sister Eulalia, and brothers Alois, Anton, and Friedrich, in order of birth. Like most children up to the age of fourteen, Hannes was enrolled in the parish school. Hannes's destiny, according to his parents, was to become an expert cheese maker. Somehow, along the way, the honorable brotherhood of cheese makers lost a capable candidate, but the ski world gained a hero in the making.

HANNES SCHNEIDER'S SKIING TECHNIQUE

It began with a casual visit by one Victor Sohm, an affluent young man from an established mercantile family in an industrial city in Vorarlberg. Sohm brought a pair of skis to Stuben and demonstrated his limited prowess, mostly heading straight down a slope, preferably one with a flat run-out at the bottom that would allow him to slow down gradually and come to a complete stop.

To Hannes this was a dazzling sight, something he longed to try himself. He knew Sohm kept his skis in the basement of the inn; there could be nothing wrong in giving them a closer inspection. This he did. He also took careful measurements and on a piece of cardboard made detailed drawings of the curvature of the tips, the thickness of the wood, and the flair of the tails. Whenever Sohm started off on his skis, Hannes followed him on foot as far as he could, often sinking to his waist in deep snow. The gentleman was impressed by the lad. They struck up a conversation and became friends. Sohm told Hannes that the Scandinavians, who had been at it a long time, were superior skiers, and that a Norwegian friend had brought him a pair of skis and started him off. When Sohm left, he promised he would come back soon and bring his Norwegian companion.

Young Hannes had perseverance, a character trait that would become dominant in him in the years ahead. Luckily, the village wheelwright-barrel maker-carpenter was captivated by the boy's enthusiasm and determination to have a pair of skis. He studied the specifications Hannes gave him and agreed to make the skis. By instinct the wheelwright decided that the inordinate length of the skis used by Sohm, seven feet, would have to be shortened considerably and tailored to fit young Hannes's smaller frame. As promised, Hannes got his first pair of skis in this way— which negates the touching tale that Hannes learned to ski on a pair of discarded barrel staves. His were finely tooled skis made of beechwood by a master craftsman.

Improvising a workable binding was Hannes's next problem. It was important to have one's boots firmly attached to the skis in order to have a modicum of control when sliding downhill. By a process of trial and error, resulting in a number of punishing falls, Hannes and his father at last developed a workable binding.

Keeping his promise, Victor Sohm and his Norwegian friend returned to Stuben. To his amazement, he was welcomed by young Hannes, showing off with great pride his new skis. Touched and thrilled by the youngster's enthusiasm, from that day on Sohm took him under his wing, becoming in the process an influential force in Hannes's life and in his decision to build a career. Whatever Sohm knew about skiing he imparted to Hannes. They became inseparable skiing companions, exploring the high mountains surrounding Stuben and often venturing as far as Zürs and Lech. Hannes learned fast—in fact, too fast, as his mentor, who often found himself lagging behind, acknowledged magnanimously. Hannes's ambition was to go faster yet, faster than anyone else, and at the same time remain in complete control of his skis.

The Scandinavians had developed their own form of skiing and were superb skiers in their own terrain. Their method was to follow a winding trail, or *loipe*, through the woods and over gently rolling hills, leaving untouched the higher mountains along the way. They came up with the graceful telemark turn and raised cross-country skiing into a most popular recreational and competitive endeavor.

The Norwegians had another turn well suited to their terrain called the "Christiania," due to its origin near the city of the same name. It was a turn with skis held more or less parallel with the skier sitting back on his heels, thereby enabling him to steer the unweighted front of the skis into the desired direction or force them to a complete standstill. While a promising step, the turn had its drawback: the required sitting-back part. In the steep Alps, this was not suitable. On steep downhills, a skier had to be ahead of his skis with his body to be in control of his movements.

There was at that time only one method of Alpine skiing and teaching, propagated by the Austrian Mathias Zdarsky. He wrote a book explaining his technique, which was based upon the snowplow position in which one kept one's ski tips almost touching while spreading the tail ends far apart in a position resembling the letter "V." This provided not only a means to check speed but also the stance to initiate a turn by shifting the body's weight to one or the other ski, consequently producing a turn to the left or right. To facilitate this change of direction, Zdarsky advocated use of a long pole, similar to an alpenstock, almost eight feet long. It was like having a third leg to lean on and could be used as an emergency brake by planting the pole between one's legs and sitting on it. Graceful it was not; cumbersome and awkward it was indeed, requiring a skier to switch the alpenstock from one side to the other after every completed turn. More advanced was the stem turn, as advocated by Zdarsky, in which the skier traversed the slope at an angle, then slowed down by stemming, or sliding the heels of the skis apart, and initiated the turn with the help of the alpenstock. Thus, gradually, the skier lost altitude with each turn and subsequent traverse.

Sohm decided to try Zdarsky's methods using two poles instead, one for each hand, and Hannes naturally followed suit. Between themselves, by practical experimentation and using some of Zdarsky's stratagems, they found a way to ski that would eventually become the framework of Hannes Schneider's Arlberg technique. It was based on the linkage of the snowplow to the snowplow turn, stem turn, stem christiania, and finally the high-speed christiania, which required a minimum of preliminary stemming. It worked. When Hannes entered a few races locally as a junior, his superiority in speed and stability was so marked that word spread quickly that the young man appeared unbeatable.

Hannes had a natural affinity for all matters concerning snow and skiing. In spite of his slight physical build, his strenuous outdoor activities in tending to the family farm developed his leg muscles and stamina beyond the ordinary fitness of a young man his age. He thrived on it and when winter came around he was fit and ready to go. Above all, he had an analytical mind and an insatiable curiosity as to what would make him go faster on skis, make it easier to turn going down a steep slope at full speed, and allow him to remain in full control of his skis and relatively safe from dangerous high-speed tumbles.

By trial and error Hannes developed a turn of his own, which became known as the stem christie and would in time mature into the sophisticated parallel christie, in which it appeared that the skis were held parallel throughout the turn. On close scrutiny, such as in a slow-motion film of the turn, the vestiges of a stem position could be detected. This came as a surprise to many expert skiers, who were convinced that their skis did not budge a fraction of an inch out of line.

Sohm, with his group of skiing devotees in tow, was instrumental in helping Hannes in his experimental sessions on the slopes. They served as his guinea pigs, as did a few of the youngsters who had taken up skiing at Stuben. The evenings were absorbed with theoretical discussions in evolving a technique suitable for every aspiring skier. When the weather was bad and visibility too poor to ski in the high country, the group built a ski jump and amused themselves by practicing jumping. In no time Hannes excelled in this field also. His jumps would be longer, his form more elegant, and his landing smoother than any of the others'.

Word spread that a veritable skiing prodigy was emerging in sleepy Stuben. Invitations soon arrived, asking Hannes to compete against other skiers under the auspices of Victor Sohm and his friends. This would be Hannes's first opportunity to travel to distant places and discover the outside world, of which he had heard much but seen little thus far. Wherever he entered a competition he won the downhill race hands down. He placed first or respectably near the top in ski jumping, a venue which the Scandinavian jumpers, who had been at it much longer, dominated. Also, since Hannes was too good to compete in the junior class and in order to test his mettle, he chose to challenge the jumpers in the senior class. Although he did not win he was recognized as a most promising talent and threat to reckon with in the future.

The Schneiders could not help but be proud of their son's success. However, they also knew a decision had to be made in regard to the young man's future. An opening was awaiting Hannes to serve as apprentice to a respected cheese maker in the nearby town of Dornbirn. Quite obviously there was no steady income nor financial security in being a skier. The decision was made for Hannes in a circuitous way. One of the skiers in Sohm's group, a Mr. Ickly, was impressed by Hannes's prowess and also had good connections with a prominent hotel owner in Les Avant, Switzerland. The hotel was extremely popular during the summer months, but when winter came, the rate of occupancy dropped to nothing. Ickly's idea was to bring Hannes Schneider to Les Avant and promote it as a ski resort, with Hannes teaching guests how to ski. There was no shortage of snow, and the terrain was ideal for a ski center. This proposal appealed very much to the enterprising hotelier. A letter with a contract enclosed was posted to Hannes Schneider, offering him free board and lodging plus the princely sum of three francs per day for the season, as long as the snow lasted. Hannes and his parents were flabbergasted. Maybe there was a living to be earned in skiing after all, by teaching people how to ski. Since the vocation of professional ski instructor was unknown to them, his parents had no way of judging. Hannes's mind was made up instantly, but being a good son, he gave his parents time to think it over carefully.

Before Hannes answered the letter, he received an invitation to attend a meeting of the recently formed Arlberg Ski Club at St. Anton. The news of the offer made to Hannes from Les Avant had traveled fast from one village to the next until it reached the ears of Karl Schuler, one of the founders of the club, whose family owned the Hotel Post at St. Anton. Schuler realized it would be foolish to let Hannes go to Switzerland when right here at his doorstep was an opportunity to put St. Anton on the map as a premier ski resort. Schuler matched the offer made by Les Avant and pointed out the further advantage that Hannes would be near his family and surrounded by people he knew. The offer was irresistible. Hannes accepted, knowing that this would convince his father of the soundness of his decision. After the autumn's work on the farm was finished and with the first snow falling, he moved to St. Anton to open his ski school. It was December 1907.

The beginning of the newly established ski school was inauspicious; people were not in the habit of leaving their homes during the traditional Christmas celebrations. Undaunted, Hannes skied by himself or with some local youngsters in hot but futile pursuit. Their technique simply could not match his. With the holidays over, a trickle of guests began to drift in, and gradually the daily house count of the Hotel Post grew. By its end, the season was an unequivocal success.

After such a show, Karl Schuler called Hannes into his office and asked him to sit down. He then handed him an envelope containing one hundred kronen for his winter's work. Hannes was overcome with joy. There was no other way that a young man of his background could have earned such a sum of money. He could hardly wait to see his father's surprise when he showed him the ten crisp bills. Furthermore, Schuler asked him to return the following winter. He would still have his board and room free, and as an additional bonus, the entire revenue from the ski school would be his. This was a most generous offer.

When the excitement of the winter's success had died down, Hannes realized that he was faced with two serious shortcomings. One was the lack of a clearly defined teaching curriculum. It was not sufficient for either teacher or pupil to say, "Just watch what I am doing, then you do it. Now follow me." It worked in some cases but not all. The other was a lack of words to explain, for example, how to initiate a turn and how to make it all work in unison. Hannes's vocabulary was limited and the local Stuben dialect he spoke was virtually incomprehensible to anyone from outside his village. Even the people of St. Anton, only a few miles away, had difficulty understanding it.

A solution to Hannes's problems arrived at the close of the winter season in the form of Baron Josef Bliss. Even though spring was at the threshold, snow was still plentiful, and the baron, who was of noble birth and a veteran of Austria's diplomatic corps, proposed to engage Hannes as his private instructor. Spending so much time with Hannes, the baron readily sized him up as an exceptionally worthwhile young man. Hannes gained confidence and opened up when he found a sympathetic ear to listen to his problems of organizing his ski school for the next winter.

Baron Bliss was a man of the world. A connoisseur of the arts and music and a linguist who could converse in many tongues, he had held posts in the embassies of Paris, London, Vienna, and other capitals of Europe. He related the wonders of this world and described the places Hannes more than likely would see in good time. In a very subtle way, he began to correct Hannes's diction, syntax, and choice of words. He was pleased to find such a responsive pupil and to be given the opportunity to reciprocate as a teacher. Hannes knew that he needed instruction and ate it up with the eagerness of a grade school student. The baron also helped Hannes to formulate a teaching concept for his ski school that he would implement next winter. It turned out to be a fruitful association. When Hannes made a friend or was accepted as a friend, the bond was one of lasting duration, not just a superficial acquaintance. Hannes would put all he had learned to good use, and he would be forever grateful to Baron Bliss.

With the first heavy snowfall in early December 1908, Hannes assembled as many local skiers as he could muster—youngsters, beginners, intermediate, and advanced skiers—and put them through a crash course, using his newly evolved teaching plan. The system worked. The "Hannes Schneider Arlberg Ski Technique and Method of Teaching" was thus established and would thrive for decades to come. It would be modified, simplified, and refined in many ways; it would even be attacked and denigrated by some who were jealous of his success or thought they knew better. But in the end it always prevailed. The method has remained basically the same and is still being taught today in its cradle of origin, St. Anton, and the world over.

With teaching success at hand, Hannes soon realized that he would no longer be able to carry the load all by himself. So from among the best skiers in his experimental classes, he selected a few of the most promising to train as future ski instructors. His system required a body of instructors, each one teaching a class with students of equal ability. As a student progressed, he would be advanced to the next higher class and thereby not hold up anybody. Hannes's decision to train an instructor's corps was a wise one, as the subsequent winter season surpassed the fondest expectations of the ski school, hotels, innkeepers, and merchants of the small town. Karl Schuler's face was bathed in a smile when he calculated the revenue and realized what he had wrought by his insistence on keeping Hannes at home. Together, they had indeed put St. Anton on the map as a budding ski resort. And that was only the beginning.

Then, suddenly, it seemed like a false start. In those days, when a man reached the age of twenty-one, he was obligated to three years of military service, providing he passed his physical examination. Hannes's coming of age could not have come at a worse time. The thought of abandoning his ski school for three winters, after having launched it so successfully, was painful, but the law was the law. He reported to the nearest military recruiting center, passed the physical examination, and was told that the quota for new recruits was filled and that he would not be inducted until October.

This respite gave Hannes the opportunity to accept a long-standing invitation from a family in Vienna whose various members had been enrolled in his ski school during the past winter. They took him in as one of their own and introduced him to the rich cultural offerings of that ancient city. This exposure to Vienna with its broad boulevards, imposing palaces, and monumental government buildings broadened his ever-expanding horizons and sparked his desire to learn more about this world. He came to appreciate the comforts of the typical Viennese coffeehouse. He loved to roam the narrow and crooked streets of the older part of the city and wander through the city's many museums.

After his glorious visit to Vienna, Hannes decided to use the remainder of the summer to pass the test for a certificate as a licensed mountain guide and rock climber. He would be the youngest in Austria to hold such a diploma.

October came much too fast, and Hannes was duly sworn in as a soldier and assigned to artillery school, which meant shoveling manure deposited by the ton by the mules and horses trained to pull the heavy carts mounted with cannons. It also meant endless polishing of brass and equipment, a job assigned to the lowliest recruits. After two months of basic training he was transferred to the Fourth Battery of the Fourth Regiment of the mountain artillery. This in no way reflected his background as a licensed mountain guide and elite skier. Any recruit from the province of Tyrol was automatically assigned to this particular regiment. A few weeks before the skiing season opened at St. Anton, Hannes found himself bogged down in military drudgery. His heart simply wasn't in it, and his obvious lack of interest did not escape the notice of his superiors. Thus, one morning when his name was called out and he was ordered to report to the commanding officer, his conscience was uneasy.

To his surprise, the captain greeted him in the friendliest way and informed him that upon orders from higher up, he had been put on the reserve list and was free to return to his hometown as of that moment. Hannes was puzzled by this sudden turn of events and without delay left for St. Anton. Only after he met with Karl Schuler in a happy reunion did he realize that a group of influential citizens under the leadership of Herr Schuler had pulled strings to liberate him, claiming that he was an economic necessity to St. Anton and the surrounding villages and in fact for all of the Tyrol, since ski mania was breaking out all over Europe.

MY YEARS AT ST. ANTON

When I joined Hannes Schneider's ski school I was the lowest man in rank assigned to teach beginners, starting out with the rudimentary exercises of how to walk on skis, climb a slope, and get up after a tumble. Classes started every morning at ten, broke at twelve for lunch, then resumed again at two for the two-hour afternoon session. Each class consisted of ten to fifteen pupils. Twelve was just about the right number for a workable class; more than that was not desirable. Those students who progressed faster than others were rapidly advanced to the next higher class to keep the proficiency of each group balanced. We were allowed to give private lessons during our lunch break to augment our incomes, and Sundays were also free for private lessons.

The immediate goal was to teach beginners how to walk on skis and make a snowplow turn. With skis in the snowplow position, the turn was initiated by shifting the body's weight to one or the other ski, synchronized with an appropriate movement of the upper body. The snowplow position I could manage somehow with my still painful ankle. However, when I had to demonstrate the mechanics of the turn in slow motion, it was sheer agony, especially when I had to put all my weight on the left foot and twist my ankle to guide the skis around. Yet I could not and would not let anyone know about my impediment. Day after day, I gritted my teeth while performing my duties. The stiff leather ski boot was helpful, acting, to some extent, as a support. I was relieved when another day was over and I could get out of my ski boots to soak my poor foot in a tub of hot water and gently massage my ankle. Ever so slowly the swelling subsided, the pain diminished, and the mobility of the injured joint improved. After six weeks or so, I could maneuver fairly well.

What compensated for all this temporary misery was the satisfaction of teaching in the most prestigious ski school in existence. Also, the camaraderie among the instructors was uplifting. Some were true characters, with an innate sense of humor based on the earthy wisdom of peasant folk. Most spoke in their native dialect, which caused much laughter and occasional confusion in a class. Luggi Föger was unquestionably the star instructor and very popular with students. Rudi Matt, due to his ability and aura as a successful racer, stood a close second in popularity.

Hannes was strict with his instructors and equally strict with students, demanding discipline and punctuality. He was not above raising his voice to a bellow when someone misbehaved. He would have none of it. Whether his pupils were rich, titled celebrities, movie stars, or just ordinary people, he treated them all alike. Once enrolled in his ski school, there was no class distinction.

Après-ski life was considerably restricted, since Schneider frowned on his instructors becoming socially involved with guests. To his way of thinking, the various temptations could lead to complications for simple country boys. Gradually, however, the restrictions were loosened, as the guests persevered in wanting to mingle with their instructors for a glass of *glühwein* or cold beer. It was a fitting reward to wind up a hard day's work by relaxing in each other's company. This quite naturally paved the way for further entanglements, and Hannes realized that there was no way of stopping it, as long as discretion prevailed.

Some of the instructors, handsome by nature and bronzed by the sun, developed an amazing aptitude for sexual encounters, according to tales that spread through the school. But woe to those instructors who were reported to Hannes for their nocturnal activities! Other instructors were too busy for such goings-on. After a day of teaching, they had chores to do. Every afternoon at precisely 5:30, one of them would rise infallibly and bid adieu to the gathered company. One day, my curiosity aroused after observing his never-changing ritual, I asked him why he had to leave every day at 5:30 on the dot. "Oh," he said, "I've got to go home to milk my cows. If I'm not on time, they become irascible and uncooperative."

The life of an instructor was fascinating. I met people of many social strata, often from faraway countries. St. Anton had truly become a skier's mecca. In my class at one time was a famous Italian automobile race driver, Piero Taruffi. Another was a prince of the ancient Roman Ruspoli clan. His sister was also with us, accompanied by her spouse, a French nobleman, the Compte de Chambrun. The Marchioness of Londonderry came, though along in years, with her entourage. Among them was a dashing young man, the Duke of Hamilton, who in later years would encounter Rudolf Hess just after his parachute landing near the Duke's estate in his futile attempt as self-appointed "secret emissary" for Hitler to initiate peace talks with England.

When I was invited for dinner by the Marchioness, it was always quite formal, black tie and protocol de rigueur. It was heady company, since members of European royalty, such as Prince Nicholas of Romania or the King or Queen of Belgium, might be guests of honor. Invariably I would find myself seated at the very end of the table. Many an invitation was extended to me to come visit, but I never took advantage of these invitations. I knew how out of place I would feel in such a feudal environment.

Right from the beginning I felt most comfortable with Americans. Their cheerful, freewheeling, and congenial attitude appealed to me immensely. Also, I was able to communicate in their language, though not exactly fluently. It was a marvelous learning process as we exchanged words in German and English. More and more I felt that my ultimate goal would be to pursue an opportunity to visit America and hopefully settle there in good time.

Occasionally on Sunday mornings a group of instructors headed for the mountains to ski for their own enjoyment. These outings also provided opportunities to explore technical refinements and improve teaching methods. On one such beautiful sunny morning, with a heavy layer of fresh snow covering the terrain, I decided to join the group. Benno Rybizka, who was so instrumental in bringing me to St. Anton, led the party toward the peak we had chosen as our destination. When we arrived at the summit of the Galzig, we settled down for a bite to eat from provisions brought along in our rucksacks.

We then proceeded with a bull session on skis, with Benno assuming the role of teacher and the rest of us acting as pupils. It turned out to be one of the most frustrating and humiliating days of my life. Nothing seemed to work for me. I thought my ankle had healed sufficiently, but found out that it hadn't. The long climb had been tiring and the deep snow was an additional handicap. I struggled and floundered around in dismay. At last I told Benno of my problem. He lit into me with a verbal barrage for being such a fool and not having consulted a doctor. He also told me how disappointed he had been in my skiing ability, which had been highly touted to him. He was acutely embarrassed for having sponsored me. I felt destroyed and at one of the lowest ebbs I can remember. To give such a poor account of my skiing ability in front of my colleagues put me to the utmost shame. I was boiling mad—furious with myself and also with Benno for his tactless remarks.

However, some good came of it. I resolved then and there to see a doctor. I also decided to concentrate all my efforts on becoming as good a technician and ski stylist as was humanly possible. I would show my true potential to Benno and the others. I was obsessed with mastering the technical aspects of skiing to perfection. This was my goal.

The doctor who examined my foot diagnosed that indeed a small bone had been cracked but that nature had done its work of healing the hairline fissure. There was nothing to be done except to keep doing what I had already been doing. He suggested that I use my judgment and a reasonable amount of caution until I felt one hundred percent rehabilitated. Next was a matter of restoring my badly bruised self-confidence.

Part of Hannes Schneider's daily routine was to visit with every class and dispense timely advice to struggling students. Often he would select an arcane vantage point from which to observe the progress of a class and the instructor's ability in handling the group. Once, after a brief inspection, he nudged me with his elbow and said, "You are doing just fine. Keep it up." As he pushed off to leave, he added, "Oh, by the way, tomorrow I want you to take over Pepi's class. They are about to get into stem christies." This was the first sign of recognition, and I needed it badly. Hannes may have heard about my predicament. I was elated and more determined than ever to follow through with my resolution.

My first winter in St. Anton passed far too quickly. As the season came to an end, I was fortunate to be hired by a widowed mother and her son, both devoted skiers, to guide them on a tour of the Alps, crossing from Austria into Switzerland. This was one of the popular tours through the Silvretta massif of towering peaks and miles of glaciers. It was my first such assignment, and I was looking forward to it, since it meant exploring new terrain with map and compass. The route was laid out in stages so that one proceeded from one alpine hut to the next. Each hut was strategically placed to be within easy reach: after a day's climb of one peak, it was an easy ski and glide toward the next refuge. Primitive as these huts were, one appreciated their amenities as a shelter and haven, especially when the weather turned bad.

The beds were wooden bunks with hard mattresses, a coarse woolen blanket for a cover, no sheets, and rarely a pillow. Toilet facilities were of the most primitive kind. So were cooking means. Water had to be heated in large pots on a wood-burning stove. We used the hot water mainly to make tea and coffee, which we consumed in large quantities. Each touring party had to bring along their own provisions. Space was limited, and there was no way of making reservations in advance since postal service was haphazard at best, and there were no telephones or other means of communication. If a place became overcrowded, there was nothing to do but squeeze together and bed down wherever space was available.

"Roughing it" this way, getting up at the crack of dawn to climb the next peak, weather permitting, and continue on to the next hut was a physical and mental challenge. The reward was of an esoteric kind. It gave one a feeling of accomplishment, at the end of each day, having taxed one's mind and body and come out on top. And there was majestic alpine scenery.

We lived in this isolated stillness of ice and snow for ten days, with toes and fingers often numb from the cold; we hardly ever got warm enough in the poorly heated huts. Descending into Switzerland was like approaching a wonderland. The meadows were already covered with wild flowers and spring was bursting out. A long, hot bath and a meal served on a table covered with white linen and a bottle of local wine seemed the height of luxury.

The widowed mother I was hired to guide, Mrs. Glasersfeld, was a woman in her fifties. She and her son, who was in his late teens, turned out to be seasoned alpinists and delightful companions. We hated to part. "Well," said Mrs. Glaserfeld, "why don't we just go on to our home in Merano? We'll pick up our automobile and, after a rest, drive on south." I jumped at this enticing invitation, longing for a change of scenery.

Merano was a small town once belonging to Austria's southern Tyrol, a region that had been handed over to Italy after World War I. It had the reputation of being a beauty spot. Mrs. Glaserfeld's home was spacious, comfortable, and unpretentious, and overlooked the city. Into the car we packed our summer gear, which included two tents and the housekeeping paraphernalia necessary should we decide to camp out along the way. We headed for Lago di Garda. There are few lakes in this world, I was told, that can compete with the scenery and charm of the villages and villas strung along the shores of this beautiful lake. None of these claims fell short. With its salubrious climate and the fragrance of the burgeoning spring, it was an intoxicating experience for one who had never ventured so far south, a glorious finale to an eventful winter. Plus, I returned to St. Anton with a nice sum of money in my pocket; combined with the savings from my instructor's salary, this made me flush. I felt relatively rich. In St. Anton, it pleased me to see that the snow had receded to the higher slopes, and spring, always late in coming to this narrow valley, was arriving with an explosion of greenery. I decided to stay for a while, hoping to find work to keep me busy and to preserve my nest egg.

I was put in charge of managing and maintaining St. Anton's one and only tennis court. The surface was a mixture of red clay and fine-grained sand, which every day needed to be brushed with a wide broom, watered, and rolled over, back and forth the full length of the court, with a large metal drum filled with water. The white chalk lines had to be repainted frequently. It kept me busy, all right. Even though I had learned to play tennis and had become adept at the game, I did not consider myself qualified to teach. However, I was good enough to feed balls to players in need of a workout and could give them pointers on how to improve their basic ground strokes. All this at a moderate hourly fee— enough to make it worth my time and give me invaluable experience in teaching another sport.

Since the court belonged to the Hotel Post, I was provided with additional perquisites in the form of free meals. From its inception, the hotel was the domain of the Schuler family. It was Karl Schuler who had taken Hannes Schneider under his wing and, between the two of them, launched the originally sleepy village into worldwide fame. When Karl died, Walter, his son, took over, and with the help of his charming wife, made the Hotel Post into a showcase for high society, aristocrats, business moguls, and ordinary mortals who could afford the tariff. Since Walter and Hannes had grown up together, they were lifelong friends. The Schulers made me feel at home and treated me accordingly.

I ate with members of the family at a long table set apart in the dining room. Occasionally one of their guests would be invited to join us. One such guest was an Englishwoman named Phyllis. The moment I saw her, I was attracted to her. She was small and well proportioned, with a cherubic face and the peaches-and-cream complexion so characteristic of her countrywomen. More than that, she had a pixyish sense of humor. In the lilting English idiom, her choice of words was captivating. Her knowledge of German was rudimentary, and this was one of the reasons, among many others, that she had come to Austria. Naturally, I immediately thought I would be the ideal man to enlarge her German vocabulary. I considered it a challenge sent by fate.

I fell head over heels in love with Phyllis, but could not expect my feelings to be reciprocated as spontaneously as I wished. It took gentle and patient courting on my part to break through her initial reserve. She was in the final stages of a divorce from her English husband, who had put her through two miserable years of wedlock. Money was scarce and she had had to take any sort of job available. She tried to make it as a salesgirl in a well-known London department store, but did not like it. A position as a governess was more stimulating but very tiring. She told me that she frequently found herself in demand as a model for her artist friends. She once posed nude for a famous sculptor who needed a female figure to adorn a public fountain in London. In fact, she showed me a photograph of the finished fountain, with water cascading over the sculpture of her naked body, gleaming in polished white marble. It was a charming tableau; no one could possibly take umbrage at the purity and beauty of this artistic creation. Yet, seeing this photograph made me jealous. Just the thought of so many people sharing the sight of her naked body made me unhappy—a body, I might add, that I had only seen fully clothed at that point.

To my surprise, Phyllis showed up frequently at the tennis court. There were times when I was free and we could sit and talk. The more I saw of her, the more I realized what an exceptionally likable person she was, with a fine sense of values and appreciation of nature, literature, art, and music. The first time I had any physical contact with her was during lunch, sitting opposite her. I slipped off my sandals and with my bare feet searched for her feet to make contact under the table. Whereupon she shed her shoes, and our toes began to caress and entwine. Never before had I experienced the sensitivity of this part of the human anatomy. It was a delicious game of hide-and-seek, and it indicated that we liked each other very much.

We became lovers, though we didn't find it easy to arrange our clandestine trysts, while pretending to be just good friends. Fortunately one could escape into the nearby forest or make a nest in the high grass of a meadow surrounded by wildflowers and the buzzing of bees. Not thinking of the future and blocking out any unpleasant memories of the past, we were blissful lovers and shared an idyllic life. I was happy and felt fortunate to have found such a lovely lady.

Phyllis was not addicted to any sports but did enjoy long walks away from the crowd of summer guests and tourists. I was most anxious to show her one of the eyries frequented by skiers during the winter months. While the snow was virtually gone everywhere else, there remained a mantle of snow at the very summit of each mountain. I selected one that would be fairly easy to ascend without previous climbing experience and that would provide a panoramic view from the peak.

We started off early in the morning with the sun spreading a rosy glow over the mountain toward which we were headed. All went well, and we made good progress. Phyllis proved to be a sturdy mountain hiker. We decided to take a rest at a selected spot and have a traditional morning repast. After a few hours' climb we reached a snowfield at the foot of the summit, and as we laboriously approached the peak, I could sense a certain uneasiness and tension in my friend. In a few minutes there would be nothing ahead of us but the sheer drop into the valley below and an ocean of space as far as the eye could see. We reached the top and sat down, breathing heavily. As I pointed out the towering mountains in the distance, Phyllis's face froze into a mask, and she folded into a fetal position. "I cannot look," she said. "I cannot move. I am petrified and mortally afraid. I think I am going to die here."

I had never been faced with a dramatic situation of this kind. I had heard of people who were afflicted with certain phobias, be these the fear of heights, getting into an elevator, or being pushed into a large crowd of people. How to deal with Phyllis's was now my immediate concern. I knew that the first step was to get her off the mountain. I talked to her gently, assuring her of my protective presence and telling her she was completely safe. I begged her to get up, to hold on to me, and I would guide her to safety down the path we had just climbed. She would not move or respond to my pleas.

Then I took a different approach: sternly explaining to her that we could not stay here forever. We would freeze to death when night fell upon us. We had to get off the mountain without further delay. All this was to no avail. She was catatonic, unable to move a limb. It was a frightening predicament since I was totally unfamiliar with the symptoms I had to deal with. I decided to carry her down the mountain. With her eyes closed, she implored me to leave her and go home alone. She was so frightened, she preferred, she said, to die right there. I held her tightly as I struggled to keep my balance and avoid tumbling down the snowfield. Ever so cautiously, I retraced my steps down the steep slope.

As dearly as I loved Phyllis, she was heavy to carry, and my breath was short and labored, caused by the shortage of oxygen at such high altitude. In desperation, I came up with a solution. I sat her down in the snow and stuffed every garment that could be spared into my rucksack, improvising a sort of sled, strapping her down on it safely with the rucksack's leather thongs. Then I grabbed her by the ankles and simply dragged her down the snowfield until we reached bare earth. I got her back on her feet, and by the time we reached the spot of our last snack, her spirits had revived. She came to as though she had been in a hypnotic trance, barely remembering what had happened. We rested a while, ate what food was left, and then walked home, hand in hand. Sharing such an extraordinary experience was bound to bring us even closer.

As summer faded, I suggested to Phyllis that we move to Salzburg for the remainder of her stay in Austria. I wanted her to meet my parents and, above all, my sister Nelly. There was little doubt in my mind that the whole family would welcome her with open arms. It turned out exactly as I expected. My father and mother took to her lovingly, as though she were one of their own brood. Nelly found a long-looked-for soul mate in her; they hit it off beautifully. Nelly's superior fluency in the English language put me at a slight disadvantage, but at the same time created a powerful incentive for me to improve my English.

The first order of business upon arriving in Salzburg was to find suitable living quarters for Phyllis, since it would have been considered highly immoral for us to live together without being married. A place was found in a villa on the outskirts of the town, and I moved in with my parents at their insistence. How could I resist my mother's pleas when she said, "Ottoshaka, we see so little of you these days, and soon you'll be gone again. God only knows to which faraway country that might be?" In a way she was quite prescient.

The thought of marrying Phyllis was uppermost in my mind, but I realized that I would have to wait. Her divorce was not final, and my prospects as a reliable provider were still unstable. I was just beginning to establish myself as a professional sports instructor and could not count on the steady income so essential to keeping a marriage intact. I knew that my job with Hannes Schneider was secure for the coming winter, but beyond that I had no idea what would be in store for me. Phyllis understood and reluctantly agreed that we should wait and see what happened to both of us. When I put her on the train for her return trip to London, our parting was sad and tearful. Foggy, grey, and cold as London was apt to be that late in the year, and without a job in sight, her prospects were grim, to put it mildly. I was quite desolate, hoping a miracle would bring us together again.

It was not to happen. Phyllis met an English journalist who could provide for her security and the home she wanted so desperately. They married shortly thereafter, and our paths never crossed again. I hope that her life was one filled with the happiness she so very much deserved.

AN INSTRUCTOR'S LIFE

Every winter I spent at St. Anton was a continuous adventure. Every day brought new surprises and discoveries. I loved to teach and couldn't wait to find out who my new pupils would be. The cross section of people I came in contact with was intriguing in its variety. My circle of friends grew steadily, and invitations to visit them at home came frequently. Some of these were heartfelt and sincere; others, I realized, were merely gestures of social grace. I would have hesitated to put them to an actual test. When I had time during the transitions between winter and summer seasons, I did accept a few of the sincere ones.

One such journey took me to London for the first time. My host was a retired British army colonel, proud and erect in bearing. He had digs in a private boarding house at Halfmoon Street, near the venerable Brown's Hotel. He had made arrangements for me to stay in an attic room, with a view of the nearby roofs and a myriad of chimneys dominating the London cityscape. Looking out of the window, I felt transposed to the times of Charles Dickens. To me London was an inspiration. I fell in love with the city and its people.

To this day I think England is the most civilized nation on this earth. My friend, Stanley Crabbe, Esquire, was a member of a sedate London club. To be introduced to the mores of English club life was an experience in itself. Everything was so regulated and orderly. At Halfmoon Street every morning at exactly 7:30 there would be a knock at my door and a manservant would appear with a breakfast tray and a pitcher of scalding hot water. He would slide open the heavy velvet curtains with a whoosh and proclaim, "A jolly good day, sir. Right fit for walking." That meant the sun was shining. Or he might say, "You had better be prepared to wear your galoshes and have your umbrella handy," meaning rain was in the offing. And rain in London could be as bad and as persistent as what I had learned to live with in Salzburg.

I couldn't have wished for a more gentlemanly and considerate host than Colonel Crabbe. He made my ten-day stay in London a memorable pleasure and the prelude to many future return visits long after he died. My only disappointment was that I could not reach Phyllis. I rang her phone number repeatedly. There was no answer. One day during my roaming walks about town, I chanced to pass the house where she lived in a flat. A man, busy with some chore at the front door, volunteered the information upon my inquiry that she and her husband spent a good deal of time abroad, required by his profession as a political analyst and magazine columnist.

Another invitation I accepted was to visit a couple whom I had taught to swim during my tenure in a summer resort. He was an executive with the Phillips Company, one of the largest manufacturers and worldwide distributors of electric equipment and appliances. They had been married for many years but remained childless. Their home was in Eindhoven, a provincial town in Holland. The house was beautifully furnished and immaculately kept, as one might expect of a home in Holland, a country noted for its neatness.

The purpose of my visit was to be exposed to a qualified golf pro. I had told my hosts how, after browsing through a mail-order catalog, I had sent off to Scotland for a matched set of golf clubs, a bag to carry them in, a dozen balls, and a book of instructions. At that time I was still living in Salzburg, and there were no golf courses in existence, not in all of Austria. Somehow I had become fascinated with the game, perhaps a bit out of snobbism, since I knew no other golfer. The soccer field became my improvised links.

My Dutch friends were ardent golfers, and the eighteen-hole layout at Eindhoven was rated among the best in Europe. It was long and demanding at seventy-two par for the course. My self-taught swing needed a lot of work to be smoothed out. Whacking the ball with all my strength did not necessarily achieve the anticipated distance, and above all, the direction of the ball in flight (if it rose to fly) was rather haphazard. The pro had his work cut out for him. With his patience and perseverance, I mastered the basic rudiments of the golf swing.

When not at the golf links having a lesson, practicing on my own, or playing in a foursome with my host, I spent my time at the adjacent riding stables. My hosts also arranged for me to take riding lessons. I had never ridden a horse before, so there were no bad habits to be corrected. I learned from scratch to ride like a proper gentleman in an English saddle on a fine horse. This too would serve me well in years to come.

After a lengthy stay of one month and having been pampered like a prince, I left, much beholden to my generous hosts. We corresponded for many years and our paths crossed occasionally. In fact, for a while they took my sister Elsa into their household as an *au pair* until she moved on to another job as a governess, the profession for which she had been trained.

These visits abroad did not distract me from my vocation in Austria, which I strove to improve. For quite some time I had been aware that most of the students joining the ski classes were not in physical condition to cope with the demands of the sport. I toyed with the idea of initiating a program of preparatory gym classes oriented toward developing the muscles most actively involved in skiing, improving a person's stamina, and practicing proper breathing techniques during strenuous exercise. I discussed this idea with Hannes Schneider, and he agreed that it was an excellent one and suggested I go ahead with my plan. In fact, he hoped to join me for a short visit wherever I decided to open shop. People at that time were not exercise conscious as they would be in decades to come. There were no Jane Fondas or Jack LaLanes or personal trainers with aerobics and machines to build up the human body. In a sense, it was virgin territory.

Since I had made a number of friends among the French students enrolled in my classes during the winter season, I proposed my idea to some of them and found their response most encouraging. They would gladly subscribe to such a course if it were available to them in Paris. So I chose Paris as the venue for my first experimental gym class.

I had never been in Paris before and knew very little about that sprawling metropolis. Fortunately, a Monsieur Roger Lyon, a tall and lanky gentleman with a nose like a hawk's beak and a mordant sense of Gallic humor, was one of my devoted students. He also happened to be the general director of La Salle Pleyel, the newest symphony hall and conservatory for musicians and ballet dancers. He assured me that he would be able to make a studio available to me at a rock-bottom rental fee. It was certainly a most prestigious location on the Faubourg St. Honoré, considered one of the classiest streets in all of Paris. I grabbed his offer without hesitation. Also, I had contacted some prospective participants in advance, and on the basis of their verbal commitment, packed my bags and headed by train for the city of lights.

I had bought myself a guidebook to Paris that listed all the hotels and their rates. The hotel I selected seemed to suit my requirements. It advertised a fairly large number of rooms in a central location and in a price range I could afford. When I arrived with three suitcases to check in at the concierge's desk, I noticed a somewhat quizzical look on his face, for reasons I could not fathom. Upon being shown to my room, I found it small and compact but with a large bed far out of proportion with the rest of the furnishings. The bathroom was equally small but was equipped with the obligatory bidet, always a source of amusement for those of the more laid-back European nationalities. "*Tant pis,*" was my attitude; when in France, do as they do.

It didn't take me long to notice that the flow of traffic through the hotel and the checking in and out of couples at the desk were inordinately brisk. At last it dawned on me that I had selected one of the more popular short-term occupancy hotels with rooms most frequently booked for one hour or perhaps two but rarely for an entire night. It was one of those convenient French institutions paying homage to the Goddess of Sex, so important in the lives of its citizens. No wonder the concierge was baffled when I registered with my luggage and announced that my stay would be of indefinite length. I had no choice but to move out after a frantic search for a private apartment with a more reputable address in the Rue Balzac.

Prior to my arrival, I had placed an ad in the one and only French magazine dedicated to skiing and other winter sports. Its name was *Neige et Glace.* I had contributed some technical pieces for this publication, which gave me something of an entrée with the skiing fraternity. Also, *Le Figaro* ran a diminutive blurb in their anemic sports section commenting upon my arrival, giving the purpose of my visit.

The studio assigned to me was handsome and large. Actually, it was one of the studios used by Serge Lifar, the then-reigning male superstar of the Russian ballet, for his rehearsals and student classes. It had the required barre running the length of an entire mirrored wall. There was, however, one incredible shortcoming: a total lack of shower facilities except for one stall adjoining the symphony maestro's suite that was not available to ordinary mortals. As a special favor, I could use it if I wished. This was devastating to me and rather uncivilized. After my students worked up a lathery sweat, they would have to dry off with a towel and get back into their street clothes to go home and take a bath or shower. I could never reconcile myself to this arrangement, but somehow they put up with this embarrassing situation.

Occasionally Serge Lifar walked through the studio with a faint smile on his face, obviously wondering what this prostrate and sweaty group of humanity rolling on the floor was all about. It was a far cry from the gracefully elegant and regimented exercises of his ballet dancers.

Altogether it was a successful experiment. I had about twenty-five pupils, mostly men. One of my students, Baron Robert de Rothschild, insisted that I come to his home to put him through his paces. Twice a week I would appear at the Rothschild *palais* where Monsieur le Baron awaited me attired in full-length long johns, trap and all. He wore a tight-fitting hairnet like a skullcap to keep every sparse strand of hair in its proper place. To me he looked deceptively like a caricature drawn by the inimitable Honoré Daumier. Naturally, for the Baron it was not something out of the ordinary to have me come to his home; it was like having a barber come to shave him or a pedicurist to do his toenails. For me it was a rather cursory glimpse of how the very, very rich lived. The opulence of the rooms with their elaborate furnishings, paintings by well-known masters, brocades, Gobelin tapestries, and profusion of crystal chandeliers and priceless artifacts was quite a display. It reeked of immense wealth.

To live in Paris for six weeks was an adventure. It's another city designed for walking about, which was one of my favorite pastimes. I saw the wonders of the Louvre and was duly impressed by the soaring elegance of the Eiffel Tower. I gazed at the vast expanse of Versailles and joined a herd of tourists led by a guide through the historical rooms occupied by so many of the imperial kings named Louis. I vicariously followed the footsteps of a lady dear to my heart since she was of Austrian ancestry: Marie Antoinette. Her life at the French court started out like a fairy tale, only to end in stark tragedy when her head was lopped off by the guillotine.

I was graciously entertained and frequently asked to dine in family homes or in popular bistros. Some of the restaurants were rather fancy, such as Maxim's or Le Tour d'Argent near Notre Dame. I shall never forget and forever cringe with embarrassment at the thought of the occasion when I committed a most unpardonable faux pas. Pierre Farman, a delightful young man and pupil of mine, had taken me to one of the finer restaurants in Paris. A scion of the well-known Farman aviation family, he knew about the best food and choicest wines. He ordered a bottle of red wine of renowned vintage. Not knowing any better and not being much of an imbiber of spirits, I proceeded to dilute my glass of wine with a dash of cold drinking water after it had been poured with much ceremony by the dignified sommelier. By the astonished faces of both of these gentlemen, I could tell that I was regarded, if not as a savage, then most certainly as a country bumpkin of the lowest order. Thinking of this incident now, I can't blame them. It was a desecration of one of their proudest heritages. One simply doesn't mess around with a vintage bottle of French wine.

Returning to St. Anton after my Paris interlude, I noticed that my reputation had risen considerably. I had done something daring and innovative.

MEETING THE
HILL CLAN

By the winter of 1934-1935, my fifth season at St. Anton, I had climbed up the ladder to be considered one of the top instructors in the ski school—although not quite on the elevated plateau of the popular Luggi Föger, who always had the number one class with the fastest and most expert skiers. It was a delight to see Föger's class coming down the mountainside, swooping left and right like a flock of birds in flight. Also near the top of the pecking order was Rudi Matt, a superb skier and teacher and one of the most successful competitors of that era. I could not compete with these stars, but it was gratifying to me that Hannes Schneider treated me like a friend. I had gained his respect. Many a time we shared personal confidences beyond the daily business of ski school matters.

In more than one way that winter would be a fateful one for me. It began with an encounter, under circumstances not uncommon for a ski instructor, that veered my life into a direction I never anticipated. Near the end of one day, I was leading my class down a steep gully bisected by a narrow trail when I found a man sprawled across the path, obviously in great pain. He blocked the passage for the group of onrushing skiers following me; I managed to alert them just in time to slow down and thus avoid a collision with the prostrate skier. I asked them to wait until

I had sized up the man's condition. He pointed to his left knee as he lay there, writhing. A lady was with him, showing great concern while mopping his brow and brushing snow from his face. Judging by the imprint left in the snow, he must have taken a nasty spill.

I took his skis off as gently as I could in case his leg might be broken. My primary objective was to make him as comfortable as possible, keep him warm, and get him to a doctor quickly. In those days we had no organized ski patrol, so it was the instructor who functioned in this capacity, using extensive training in first aid and emergency situations. I selected the best skier in the class to lead the group home to the village, which was not too far away. I knew if I could get the injured man to a nearby farm, I would be able to borrow a sled and transport him expediently to the doctor. We had practiced how to improvise a sled by hitching two pairs of skis together at the bindings and tips. This I did, and with me pulling and the lady pushing, we made good progress down the hard-packed chute.

When we arrived at the farmhouse, I asked to borrow a two-horned sled, the type used to transport cut timber, milk cans, and manure down the mountain roads during winter, and a heavy blanket to cover the injured skier. To operate the sled, one stood upright between the horns and pulled, or dug one's heels into the snow as brakes. It was a hazardous undertaking, especially if the load was a live person in acute pain and shivering from cold and shock. I asked one of the boys at the farm to give me a hand in getting the man to the doctor; relieving his agony was of paramount importance.

We got him to the doctor's office in relatively short time. The diagnosis was that the ligaments in one knee had been stretched beyond their functional design, which is a painful injury, as any sportsman who has been subjected to it can attest. "Six weeks in a plaster cast and two months of rehabilitation after the cast has been removed will make the knee as good as new," said the doctor. Eventually, Larry Dorcy—the man's name, as I found out—was returned to his room at the Hotel Post. He was an American, a medical school graduate of Stanford University in California and at one time had been a football player of some repute. The woman with him, Maud, was his wife, as I had surmised.

Maud Dorcy was a descendant of the legendary James Jerome Hill, the famous railroad tycoon who in the previous century had promoted the building of the Great Northern Railway, connecting the American Midwest with the Pacific Northwest. The family resided in St. Paul,

Minnesota, and among other business ventures, J. J. Hill amassed a fortune in money, real estate holdings, timber, and mining claims. His son Louis Hill married Maud van Cortland Taylor, who may not have been an heiress but who did have the credentials of American aristocracy. When I met her later, she turned out to be one of the dearest and kindest ladies I have ever known. She and Louis had four children: three boys—Louis, Jerome, and Cortland—and their sister, Maud. In time, I got to know them all very well. Never were there four people more different from each other.

Maud Hill Dorcy had come to St. Anton with her husband Larry, her brothers Jerome and Louis, and Louis's wife Dorothy and her sister Lucille for a skiing holiday. Their vacation was marred by Larry's accident, which brought us together. The Hill family was grateful and appreciative of the way I had transported Larry to the doctor—especially Maud, who has described to her friends many times since, in my presence, how I came flying down the trail out of nowhere to rescue her in her moment of need. To my embarrassment, she remembers every detail to this day, such as what I was wearing (a dark blue knit jacket with antique silver coin buttons and a Schiaparelli shocking pink woolen scarf). We became good friends. From then on my life became closely intertwined with the Hill family, as though I had known them from the time I was born.

Of the four Hills, Jerome and I had the closest personal affinity. Louis, the oldest, was a happy-go-lucky extrovert. Maud was striking, not beautiful in the conventional sense, but most attractive. She was an interesting storyteller in the vein of Isak Dinesen. Next to Jerome, she was my favorite, and our friendship will continue until the ends of our lives. Cortland, known as Corty, I met later. He was an elegant and impeccable dresser—lively, witty, and handsome. He could create a rapport with any group of people.

Jerome, or Romie as we called him, was the epitome of the Renaissance man. Having graduated from Yale, he had a diverse artistic background. He was an accomplished pianist and composer. He spoke French without a trace of accent, and also spoke German and Italian, eventually mastering the rudiments of even Chinese and Russian. Painting was his passionate avocation, and he made himself quite a name with numerous one-man shows in highly reputable galleries. His style was influenced by the French painters Paul Cézanne and Henri Matisse. Othon Fries was his teacher during his formative years in Paris. Theater, opera, cinema, and concerts were the manna of his life. He was a voracious reader, covering the gamut of literature in various languages.

With Jerome, I was a porous sponge sopping up his vast knowledge on so many subjects. He had an enormous influence in developing my appreciation of music, literature, painting, sculpture, theater, and films. As for sports, Romie was not particularly interested—except for skiing, which had captivated his imagination. He loved the pristine beauty of mountains and meadows covered with snow. The flowing movements of a skier and the mastery of an otherwise inaccessible terrain, while leaving a pure geometrical design in the freshly fallen snow, intrigued him no end. Skiing bound us together.

Sharing days with the Hills, on and off the ski slopes, I had rarely a dull moment. The clan was full of spontaneous fun and joie de vivre. We often ate lunches on a sunny terrace while we watched Jerome sculpt life-size statues out of snow. These were works of art in their medium: Queen Victoria on her throne, or the dramatic *Rape of the Sabine Women*, depicting a heavily muscled Roman centurion hefting a struggling, voluptuous maiden above his shoulders. There were small family dinners and frequent larger ones that made for a stimulating mix of the people the Hills seemed to readily attract. Congeniality, mirth, and laughter came easily in the ambiance of our favorite, intimate, wood-paneled dining room. The food was always good, and the wine flowed freely.

One incident with the Hills disturbed me and showed me the difference between American and Austrian cultures. In the course of a dinner, when spirits were running high, some of the American guests, including my hosts, kneaded the soft, Austrian peasant bread into thumbnail-size balls, which they proceeded to throw at each other. It bothered me and I pleaded for them to stop, to not denigrate our bread by throwing it around like that. I blurted out that, for Austrians, bread was a precious commodity and the staple food for many people. It was painful to see it misused. For a moment, I felt rather awkward and sanctimonious and wished that I had kept my mouth shut. But, without any hesitation, the bombardment stopped. There were no ill feelings. On the contrary, I believe my reputation rose a notch higher for having had the courage to speak up.

One of the more fascinating young women who had come to St. Anton with the Hills was Marina Chaliapin. Russian by birth, she was the daughter of Feodor Chaliapin, the renowned basso profundo of that era. Chaliapin was an operatic phenomenon who rose from a humble background to become one of the great opera stars of all time.

Maud was supposed to chaperon Marina, and she had her hands full in trying to do so. With her stunning Russian features, pale complexion, and luminous grey-green eyes, Marina was beleaguered by suitors, all trying without notable success to lure her into bed. Even a devoted family man such as Hannes Schneider—married, with two children—fell under her spell. I also was smitten with her. Clandestinely, we spent a good deal of time together, knowing full well that ours was not an "immortal commitment" but an infatuation that quite likely would not pass the test of time. I felt bothered when I had to lie to Hannes to cover up my whereabouts at certain times.

Another lady who joined the Hill entourage was Katherine Peckett from Franconia, New Hampshire. She was a New Englander through and through in looks, accent, and prim attitude. Her family owned a country inn called Pecketts on Sugar Hill, which was an exclusive retreat and vacation spot. The place was normally shut tight during the winter months, but Katherine had convinced her parents that the time had come to open the inn for the winter, since skiing was gaining popularity with Americans. She had come to Austria to observe the operations of a ski resort, and St. Anton was the place recommended to her, due to Hannes Schneider's enormous reputation. Her secondary objective was to hire one or two ski instructors. I had the advantage of close contact with Kate through the Hill family. She joined my ski class and so could evaluate my potential as a prospective candidate.

I was more than willing to go to America. To do so would fulfill a long-held dream of mine. So when Kate asked me whether I would be interested in teaching at her family's place, I jumped at the chance and accepted her offer. Obtaining Hannes's permission and blessing was not an obstacle, since he appreciated it whenever one of his protégés was singled out for a special assignment. When I told him about Katherine's offer, he said, "*Das ist wunderbar für Dich. Eine grosse Zukunft steht dir da vor. Alles gute und viel Glück. Ich komme Dich besuchen.*"

Kate told me that the financial details, length of my required service, transportation, and permit to work in America would all be prepared and mailed to me by their legal department in New York. I was to be in New York on or about December 10 to work for a week or so at B. Altman and Company, one of the city's fine old department stores, before moving on to the inn. Katherine had been hired by B. Altman as a technical advisor and buyer of winter apparel and ski equipment. The store was competing with Saks Fifth Avenue for a slice of the burgeoning ski-mania pie. Saks had built a ski slide on the floor of a spacious show-room, which would be an enormous attraction to show neophytes what skiing was all about.

I had only one specific request: Under no circumstances would I appear in a circuslike exhibit, skiing on an indoor slide on a chemical substance simulating snow. It would violate my aesthetic sense and would be contrary to my attitude that skiing is the purest of sports. I told Kate that I could not possibly consent to be a party to such crass commercial-ism and exhibit myself like a carnival performer. She assured me that it would not be necessary for me to do so and that there were no plans afoot to build such a slide at B. Altman. Kate left and I stayed on, look-ing forward to finishing the winter season at St. Anton.

A SHATTERED DREAM

Jerome had spoken to me about making a film on skiing, a documen-tary about the step-by-step progression of the Arlberg technique of skiing, as developed by Hannes Schneider. Jerome would function as director, producer, and cameraman. He would also write the narration and compose the musical score. Having been a dedicated student of films for many years, he was well qualified to wear all those hats. The docu-mentary would be shot in 16 mm black and white, since color film was not available in 1935. I would be the sole performer in front of the cam-era and would also help select locations, serve as technical advisor, and organize the physical movement of all camera equipment from one location to another. Much of the footage would be shot in untracked virgin powder snow for graphic and aesthetic reasons. On the other hand, some of the slopes would have to be packed down in order to clearly show the action of legs and skis above the snow surface.

It was a challenging project. Since it required no acting skill whatso-ever, just skiing, I felt quite confident that I could handle it. But as happens so frequently in life, fate can be fickle. From the height of euphoria one can fall to the depths in a blink of the eye.

And fall I did. I was teaching my class how to master a type of snow considered tricky and dangerous called "windblown breakable crust." Presenting a hard surface that covers the freshly fallen snow underneath, such snow requires precision work and concentration. In demonstrating a series of linked turns, for no particular reason I missed my timing. My left ski got caught in the crust, while my body and right ski continued on, propelled by the momentum. In a crunching, twisting fall, I ended up flat on my face, as though my left foot had been caught in a trap. The left knee gave way under the stress.

I knew immediately that I was badly hurt. The pain was considerable, but my pride and humiliation dictated that I make light of it while getting myself to the doctor with dispatch. I skied home on one leg as best as I could manage. Like Larry Dorcy, I ended up in a solid plaster cast that immobilized my knee.

For me, it spelled the sudden end of the ski season, and neither could I expect to heal in time to perform in front of a camera. Suddenly everything looked bleak. It would be months before I could begin to rehabilitate my knee and regain its normal function. I had signed an agreement as director of sports with the Hotel Tre Croci, a summer resort hotel at the foot of the Dolomites above Cortina d'Ampezzo in northern Italy. My fervent hope was that I would mend fast enough to fulfill my contract. Fortunately, the summer season usually came late to those high-altitude resorts, giving me a glimmer of hope.

As luck would have it, and in good time, many of my problems sorted themselves out. Jerome decided to proceed with his film project and asked me to recommend one of my peers to substitute for me. I suggested Edmund Birkl, as fine a skiing stylist as we had in ski school. He did not disappoint Jerome, and the film was shot in a relatively short time. I managed to hobble around with the help of two ski poles and could assist Jerome on many of the more accessible locations. Above all, I profited from my mishap in learning a great deal about the behind-the-camera technical requirements and visual aspects of filmmaking.

It was an unexpected education, since my curiosity about movies had never waned and I had closely followed the various waves of post-World War I films from many countries. The resurgence in Germany of the Universum Film Aktien Gesellschaft (UFA), a government-sponsored film combine, reached a number of high-water marks with such films as Robert Wiene's *The Cabinet of Dr. Caligari* and Fritz Lang's *Metropolis*, *Dr. Mabuse*, and *Die Nibelungen*, his two-part retelling of the mythological Nibelung saga, as well as many other provocative films. (No, we were not related, although our paths would cross much later in my life.)

After the filming ended, Jerome and Louis convinced me that there was no better way for me to recuperate than to spend a few weeks with them aboard a yacht sailing the Aegean Sea. I was thrilled at the prospect but voiced misgivings that I would be an albatross tied around their necks. My doubts were summarily dismissed; furthermore, they said that en route to Athens, where the boat and a full crew would be waiting for us, we would stop over in Vienna to consult about my leg with the eminent sports injury authority, Dr. Boehler. I was overcome with emotion upon hearing this generous offer and accepted it with gratitude.

We left St. Anton via the Arlberg Express, which conveniently stopped within walking distance from the Hotel Post. We were seen off by a multitude of friends, whom we left behind with twinges of sentiment. For me, this was also good-bye to St. Anton, a place I looked upon as my second home. I did not know if would ever return there.

Crippled though I was, the prospect of seeing Vienna again elated me. We registered at the Sacher Hotel, one of Vienna's historic landmarks and, not to forget, the originator of Sachertorte, a delectable chocolate cake. Most of the group going on the cruise were to gather in Vienna. There would be Jerome; Louis, Dorothy, and Lucille; Jack Barrett, an old college friend of Jerome's; and Maud Oaks, a cousin of the Hills. Yanku Varda, a Greek painter, to be our general factotum and interpreter during the cruise, would join us in Athens.

As promised, an appointment was made with Dr. Boehler at his clinic. My first impression of Boehler was that he was intimidating. He was rather tall and heavyset with a large head, bald and shiny as a billiard ball. I sensed immediately that he was a no-nonsense practitioner of the Hippocratic Oath. He cut open my cast and removed it expediently. Then he examined my knee by bending it every possible direction, which hurt, particularly when he moved it sideways.

"Hmmmm," he said. "I can help you, but it will take two months with your leg remaining solidly encased in a plaster cast from your crotch down to above your ankle joint." I pleaded with the doctor, saying that I was headed on a cruise to the Greek Islands, and that such a cast would be a terrible handicap for me. I asked timidly if there was any alternative. He gave me a steely-eyed, penetrating stare and said, "Young man, do you wish to remain crippled for the rest of your life? It's up to you, but don't waste my time if you have any hesitation." When I left Boehler's office it was with a full-length leg cast, cumbersome beyond anything I had expected.

Despite my renewed doubts about the sagacity of going along on the trip, I was again overruled by the Hills, who said that there would be no turning back now. "We started out together and we are going together," they assured me.

So be it.

GREEK ODYSSEY

The seedy Orient Express, still not fully recovered from the abuse it suffered during World War I, took us to Athens by crossing the entire length of Yugoslavia, traveling through the night. Arriving in Athens, we were met by Yanku Varda at the train station and went straight to Piraeus, the colorful and bustling harbor on the outskirts of that sprawling city. Varda took us to the *Flisvos*, our yacht, which was ready to depart at a moment's notice. It was a sizable ship with two masts as well as an auxiliary engine, so we would not be entirely at the mercy of the wind. There were four spacious staterooms with showers, and a cozy dining room adjoined the smallish galley. Aside from the captain, the crew consisted of a cook, a steward, and one utility sailor doubling as ship's mechanic. These men had separate quarters near the bow.

We were all in high spirits and anxious to cast off, celebrating the occasion with a few bottles of iced champagne. Dinner would be served as soon as we cleared the harbor and headed for the open sea, our destination charted for the island Aegina with its spectacular temple ruins perched on a high promontory.

Alas, it never came to dinner. As the boat glided into the open sea, the gentle rhythm of the waves gradually turned into an up-and-down, swaying, roller coaster ride. One by one, we succumbed to *mal de mer*, with all its unpleasant effects. Seasoned sailors we were not, with the exception of Varda and the crew. It was baptism by wind and sea, initiated by Neptune, ruler of the oceans. Never was a landfall and sheltered harbor greeted with more relief than by our bedraggled and jaundiced-looking group of seafarers. After a good night's sleep in a becalmed cove, we were greeted upon awakening the next morning by a bright sun. An incredibly blue sea and a sky to match made our spirits soar again.

The problem foremost in my mind was how I would be able to see the historic sites we were going to visit. With my heavy cast, walking was out of the question. Someone came up with the idea that perhaps I could be strapped to a donkey, with my cast propped up and belayed straight ahead. To my surprise, the stratagem worked, and I could participate in quite a few excursions. While others walked, I rode in style, but not necessarily great comfort, on my docile beast of burden—much to the amusement of the island populace at every stop we made.

Our daily routine was a simple one. We rose early with the sunrise, ate breakfast, and then got under way for either a land excursion or a sail to the next island. Jerome took time out to photograph and frequently sketched or painted some of the picturesque vistas. Maud was also a painter, as well as a keen student of Greek history and mythology. So was Yanku Varda. A recognized artist, he was an innovative practitioner of collage, an abstract form of picture on canvas made with bits and pieces of materials of different textures and colors. His pictures had a unique and naive charm and became sought after in America. Aside from his artistic talent, Yanku was a delightful, always cheerful companion, full of wisdom, and a raconteur par excellence. He could keep an audience spellbound with his tales, some of which undoubtedly were embellished by his vivid imagination.

All in all, we were a surprisingly congenial group. If for no other reason than just to be part of the activities, I took up painting in water-colors. I had not touched a brush or piece of paper to paint on since my schooldays in Salzburg, but I remembered that, apart from physical education, my only outstanding grades had been in artistic endeavors, which included painting. The professor who taught us art was an exceptionally fine gentleman and an artist in his own right.

Some residue of his inspirational efforts must have left a seed in me to sprout in later years. I became quite engrossed as I struggled gallantly to capture on paper what I saw with my eyes. Some of the resulting sketches seemed to please Jerome and his companions. They urged me to keep going and do some more work. To paint was surprisingly therapeutic and rewarding, though I felt frustrated and inadequate when comparing my efforts in this medium to those of the others.

One of my favorite watercolors, a view of the island of Ios, I gave to Maud Dorcy, since she had wanted so much to join us on this Greek trip but could not. It is a delicate sketch that pleases me every time I see it. Jerome painted my entire cast in the authentic style of an ancient Greek amphora. I wondered how Dr. Boehler would react when the time came to remove the cast.

The distances between islands—some short and others requiring a full day of sailing or motoring—never seemed long. Chios, Andros, Mykonos, Naxos, and Paros were among the many islands we visited. We went as far south as Santorin, with its harbor cradled in the huge crater of an extinct undersea volcano. On one side of the sheer crater wall, a town with a myriad of white-painted houses rose skyward. It was a spectacular tableau, indeed, and yet none of us was tempted to climb the steep path zigzagging up to the village high above. The noon sun was simply too hot.

As we sailed homeward toward Athens, the feeling was unanimous that it had been too good a trip to consider ended. Why not prolong it for another few weeks and circumnavigate the Peloponnese, cutting through the manmade channel at Corinth? Everyone was delighted with the plan. Extending the lease on the boat would be no problem, the captain assured us. However, he would require a day to restock the larder and make minor repairs on the engine. We could use the day to visit the Acropolis, that all-time architectural masterpiece, and some of the other outstanding historical sites. After a hectic day spent dodging traffic and tourists in Athens, we were glad to board the *Flisvos* again.

We had become attached to our crew as well. It seemed as though they had been trained to remain inconspicuous and never to intrude upon the privacy of the guests. The captain knew precisely the capabilities of his boat and the possible pitfalls of navigating the Aegean. Our cook was more than the word implied. He was a chef who had mastered his profession well. Our menus were sumptuous and diverse. We particularly enjoyed the fresh fish caught every day and prepared in many savory ways.

Circumnavigating the Peloponnese was a lengthy journey, much longer than our island-hopping cruise. But it was a mass of land so saturated with history that it would take time to study it. We dropped anchor in many harbors close to shore or tied up along the waterfront where the hub of activity attracted us. Often we mingled with the townspeople in one of the taverns, imbibing ouzo, the potent, anise-flavored national drink. Customarily after dinner, the local orchestra launched into one of those infectiously happy folk tunes, whereupon almost everybody got up and, holding each other by the hand, danced in a circle in a simple but graceful pattern of rhythmical steps.

Unfortunately, weighed down by my cast, I was unable to join these group dances. The cast had turned out to be a problem in another respect. Originally it had been fitted tightly around my leg but without a protective stocking to separate the skin from the plaster. For some valid reason, undoubtedly, the good Dr. Boehler did not believe in such accommodations toward his patients. As my leg shrank more and more, every single plaster-embedded hair (of which I had a profusion) became stretched taut like a violin string. It was a constantly itching, painful, and irritating sensation. Ingenuity solved my predicament. I took a wire clothes hanger and straightened it. At one end I made a loop to eliminate any sharp points. I forced this end of the wire down my leg and gradually severed every single hair from its follicle. It was momentarily painful, but oh, what a relief after it was all done! By now my cast was quite floppy and chewed up, but it still fulfilled its purpose of keeping me from bending my knee.

Three places on this second voyage stand out in my memory. One was Delphi, located idyllically in a deep valley filled with trees and flowering shrubs. Some remnants of the ancient temple ruins were still impressive. The second one was Olympia, where the Olympic games originated. Every fourth year the Olympic torch is relit here by the concentrated rays of the sun and sent on its way to wherever the games are to be held. (How could I have guessed or anticipated then that I would be an "envoy at large" during the summer Olympics of 1984 in Los Angeles?)

I also remember vividly the open-air theater in Epidaurus. Built entirely of stone in a semicircle, it was one of the best-preserved amphitheaters of its kind. The most astonishing thing to me about the theater was its acoustics. Standing high on the uppermost tier, one could hear words spoken in a whisper at center stage as clearly as if sitting in the tenth row. We gave it an extensive test with our own cast of eight, reciting poetry and staging improvised scenes from one of the better-known Greek tragedies. Yanku Varda excelled in this, emoting in the original language.

As must happen to all good things, our trip to Greece came to a harmonious close. Jerome glorified our journey in a large book of photographs called *Trip to Greece*. A limited edition of one thousand copies was privately printed. The book, if one can be found, has become a collector's item. I treasure mine, with its full-page image of my Hellenic plaster cast.

DEPARTURE

Since the time had not yet come for me to return to Vienna and see Dr. Boehler, it was decided that we would all travel to Paris and disperse from there. Some members of our group were returning to America, while others planned to remain in Europe a bit longer. Jerome invited me to stay at his Paris apartment, which was a combined artist's studio and living quarters. His bedroom was in a loft upstairs. The couch in the living room below would double as my bed.

Jerome had a cook-housekeeper by the name of Constance, who came every morning. She made breakfast, cleaned up the place, provided lunch if we stayed in, and also prepared dinner. With her slight lisp and foreshortened peasant physique, she was quite a character. But she was an excellent cook in the homestyle tradition—nothing terribly fancy but always very tasty. I have yet to find a restaurant whose *gigot d'agneau* could top hers.

Jerome and I spent most of the time at home, since it was difficult for me to get around. Occasionally we went to concerts at La Salle Pleyel, where Pierre Monteux was conducting the Paris Symphony Orchestra. He was not what I would call a charismatic or showy conductor who made wild gyrations of arms and body, jumping up and down on the minuscule conductor's podium. Instead, he made hypnotic eye contact with the members of his orchestra and achieved superb results. For the first time I heard the complete cycle of Beethoven's eighteen quartets in a series of four evening performances. It was a moving, soul-satisfying experience. Never to be forgotten was an evening of chamber music in which A. Cortot (piano) and J. Thibaud (violin) teamed with Pablo Casals on the cello to play a selection of the finest trio music ever written. Among these was one of my favorites—Beethoven's "Archduke" trio.

One day Jerome announced that he was going to paint a portrait of me—a head pose in three-quarter profile. He worked diligently at it for days. I was pleased with the progress and thought that not only was it an excellent likeness but also that he had captured a trace of that occasional somber and moody look in my eyes that indicated Slavic genes on my mother's side. When the portrait was finished, he had it handsomely framed and gave it to me. It was certainly among Jerome's finest efforts as a painter and also a stunning and most revealing portrait.

On clear days I liked to sit at an open window facing the Rue St. Simon. With my shirt off, I basked in the warmth of the sun and daydreamed, while Jerome pursued any one of his many avocations, be it painting, playing the piano, writing letters, or reading a book. We had a most easygoing relationship—until one day. While I was dozing off, sitting in the sunlight with my back turned toward Jerome, I could sense him approaching and then standing behind me quietly. Then he bent down and kissed me gently on my bare shoulder and said, "Otto, I love you."

I was stunned for a moment, as I couldn't possibly think of anything to say that would make sense. It had never occurred to me that Jerome might have homosexual tendencies. It is not that I was shocked. I just suddenly realized that in no way could I reciprocate his sentiments and enter into any kind of physical relationship with him. I treasured his friendship and generosity and the unselfish way in which he had taken care of me, and I loved him, too, with the kind of deep devotion sometimes shared between two brothers. I recognized how difficult it would be to talk out this problem that had suddenly arisen between us. If Jerome felt rejected and wounded, it could conceivably jeopardize our friendship and quite possibly bring it to an abrupt end. I would have considered this a personal disaster and traumatic denouement. I felt quite lost and saddened by this turn of events.

For a while our being together was strained, tense, and somewhat clouded. It was a most difficult situation for both of us to cope with. For Jerome to have bared his soul and for me to have rejected his feelings made our situation awkward. It would be to the credit of both of us if we could weather this emotional crisis and find a way to coexist in an amicable friendship. We did, and in time our friendship grew into a solid and lasting bond without ever again touching upon the subject that could have irretrievably ruined our relationship. Romie was immensely popular with ladies. They flocked around him and adored him. He never married, nor did he seem to have any desire for progeny. Nevertheless, he lived the fullest of lives one could possibly imagine, immersed in his world of diverse endeavors.

At last the time came for me to see Dr. Boehler in Vienna. It was anticlimactic. Not a smile crossed his face, not a comment on my artfully painted cast. He simply took a heavy pair of shears, cut down the length of the cast, pried it open, and threw it unceremoniously into a trash bin. He ran his fingers over my knee, manipulating it in various directions until he was satisfied. Then he said, "Your knee is as good as new. Start by exercising lightly at first. Walk, swim, ride a bicycle. Don't play tennis for a while and don't overdo it until you have confidence in your leg. By the time winter comes, you can ski again. Good-bye, and good luck."

That was it. When I glanced at my emaciated leg, with the muscles shriveled to the bone, I couldn't share Dr. Boehler's confidence, but I had to be thankful to him for having restored my knee. As he predicted, I never had a problem with it after it was rehabilitated and normal again.

The first thing I wanted to do was to see my parents in Salzburg. It had been quite a while since my last visit. My father had finally reached the point where he could retire on a partial pension plan. He felt young enough to enter into the private sector and thereby hoped to augment his monthly income. It wasn't easy for him to make the adjustment after having served so many years as a government employee. He became involved in various business ventures, and at that particular time he represented a firm, Graf A. G., whose products were comparable to those of Maggi, the well-established producer of soup cubes and a bottled condiment similar to soy sauce. The competition between these rivals was fierce. There were many disappointments and humiliating experiences for my father to contend with, since any salesman calling upon a store or household was treated as a second-rate citizen. But he stuck with it, and things began to look better financially. He was an admirable model as a family provider.

My sisters, Nelly and Elsa, were self-sufficient. They had flown from the parental nest long before, while Erna still lived at home. Erna was immensely helpful in lightening my mother's burdens of never-ending household chores—even though she turned out to be a martinet. Everything had to be in its proper assigned place, and woe to those who walked on her clean and polished floors without taking their shoes off! This often tested my father's patience, but he mellowed and admitted that she meant well. I made an effort to fit myself into Erna's regimen, keeping my things tidily in place, my clothes folded and put away or hung in a closet. And of course I always took my shoes off upon entering the apartment.

My mother was an inveterate walker and her daily *Spaziergang* was indispensable to her. Occasionally I accompanied her, since she liked company. We chatted about family matters and gossiped about friends and their manifold problems, of which everyone had a surfeit.

I left my family to assume my summer duties at the Hotel Tre Croci. It was just what Dr. Boehler would have prescribed for my rehabilitation program. The hotel was spectacularly situated at the foot of the Dolomites, a range of craggy mountain peaks and perpendicular rock walls, dominated at this section by the massive Monte Cristallo. Offering a variety of difficult routes from which to choose, the place was a haven for walkers and more ambitious rock climbers.

The hotel belonged to the Menardi family, who had upgraded it as it passed from generation to generation and given it a certain cachet. There was a large heated swimming pool of the latest design. Adjoining it was one red clay tennis court. I brought along my golf bag with a complete set of clubs and an ample supply of golf balls, and there was enough of a stretch of terrain to set up a practice range for me. Otone Menardi, the next in line to take over the hotel, happened to be a dedicated skier, which immediately established a cordial rapport between us. Menardi eventually became an official of the Federation Internationale du Ski (FIS), which controlled all facets of worldwide alpine skiing competitions. He was intrigued by my activity of hitting golf balls for practice and asked me to let him try his hand at it. After hitting a few balls, he was hooked. I suggested that we lay out a nine-hole golf course with marked tees and tin cans for cups to drop the ball into, after the flag was pulled out. We surveyed the terrain, and I concluded that we could design a course that, I imagined, would resemble very much the first one ever initiated by an enterprising Scotsman.

We marked the starting point for each hole, known as the tee, stenciling on a wooden box the distance and par, the number of strokes required to sink the ball into the cup on the "green." Of course, we had no greens in the sense of today's manicured, groomed, pampered, and rolled-to-the-perfection-of-a-carpet greens; ours were rough as the surrounding fairways. Unfortunately, due to altitude and sere soil, the grassy cover was spotty and anemic looking. No matter, we had our course. The guests responded immediately, since it was something new to try and it was fun. I found myself struggling at the game yet teaching others the intricacies of a fluid golf swing. It reminded me of somebody halt teaching someone lame to walk, but it certainly did take my summer experience beyond anything I had anticipated. Playing golf ,with all its walking and chasing of errant golf balls ricocheting from rocks, and teaching swimming and feeding balls to eager tennis players strengthened my weakened knee quite rapidly.

It was a pleasant surprise when, toward the end of the season with the days getting shorter and the nights noticeably colder, Jerome came for a visit, bringing Dorothy and Lucille with him. We had a happy reunion, making use of Jerome's racy Bugatti convertible to tour the area and see some of the rewarding scenery and hidden villages. My three companions were about to return to America, and I would not see them again until I arrived in New York sometime in December.

With autumn coming on and before embarking on my longest journey thus far, I wanted to spend more time in Salzburg. My mother had written that she was quite concerned she would never see me again once I crossed the Atlantic Ocean. My father, on the other hand, was thrilled and proud that his only son would accomplish something he had longed to do all his life. He, therefore, would follow my footsteps vicariously, as I had when I trailed him as a young boy on our fantasy adventures to faraway places.

Despite my efforts to keep a low profile, the local newspaper found out that I was on my way to America. To them it was indeed news worthy of reporting. There were less than a handful of Austrian ski instructors in America, and I would be the first one to represent the legendary Hannes Schneider. Once the word was out, I was beleaguered by callers, all wishing they could come along. To them, America was a glory land where self-made millionaires sprouted like weeds in a cow pasture. But I was not in a position to help anyone at that time.

The political and economic situation was in such turmoil not only in Austria but also in Germany, which shared a common border and bond with Austria, that people were receptive to any change that would pull them out of the doldrums of their stagnating existence. Austria at that time was still a free country, but the Nazi movement had infiltrated its six autonomous provinces with alarming speed, like the beginnings of a brush fire soon to burn out of control. The swastika emblem, a visible symbol of Nazism's encroaching presence, was painted on walls everywhere. Young and old joined the ranks of the party with a vengeance. Many of my former schoolmates became staunch Nazis and supporters of Hitler, who appeared like a savior, holding out his hand to lead Austrians to the promised land and fuse their country solidly with the German Third Reich. In fact, Siegfried Überreiter, our *Burschenschaft* leader, became the governor of Styria under the Nazi regime, bailing out at just the right time and fleeing to South America, never to be heard from again. I found the atmosphere depressing. It was also rife with conflict caused by those who did not wish to follow Hitler's pied-piper temptations. The political debate split families into opposing factions, brother against brother, and pitted old friends against each other. It augured a monumental upheaval. I couldn't wait to extricate myself from such political chaos.

I withdrew to an isolated inn high up in the nearby mountains to bide the time until departure and also to finish a piece I had started to write about skiing. My hope was to have it published in an American magazine. The progress was laborious, and my German-English dictionary had a constant workout as I transposed the words I knew in German to acceptable English. My spelling, which left much to be desired, needed to be double-checked in a time-consuming process. I welcomed the quiet environment in which I could concentrate and get the job done.

In the meantime, all the formalities of my American journey had been attended to, as promised by Katherine Peckett. My passport was in order, with all the required entry and working permits in my hands. I was booked in cabin class on the SS *Bremen*, one of the premier trans-atlantic ocean liners built with enough postwar ingenuity to overcome the restrictions imposed upon Germany to prevent a gradual build-up of its once-powerful fleet. My ticket showed a departure date of November 30 from Cherbourg, France, which would bring me to New York on about December 5, 1935. I considered myself one lucky fellow.

A M E R I C A
T H E
B E A U T I F U L

It is strange how some incidents of one's life are indelibly etched into memory, while others, seemingly of major consequence, are forgotten. I have wracked my brain to conjure up my departure for America on the SS *Bremen*, in vain. I know I boarded the ship at Cherbourg, France, since I saved the official ship record that indicated the date and miles logged every day. I can't give a description of the boat or of accommodations or with whom I might have shared the cabin. I do not remember whom I met aboard the ship or what the food and amenities were like. I can only surmise that I was in an ecstatic state of euphoria and bewilderment. In a vague way I can visualize myself leaning against the guardrail, regarding the immensity and loneliness of the Atlantic Ocean, watching the ever-changing play of light and shadow on its surface, observing sun bursts and rain squalls. The voyage was certainly a turning point in my life, an opportunity to start a new life in the New World, THE UNITED STATES OF AMERICA. It sounded so impressive; the words alone sent a tingle down my spine.

I do remember clearly my first sight of America: Ambrose Light. Then I recall a tender pulling up alongside, and immigrations officials, health authorities, and customs personnel boarding the ship. The Statue of Liberty shone like a majestic beacon leading the way to fulfillment.

The skyline of Manhattan appeared, overwhelming and unreal, a *fata morgana*, a city rising out of the sea.

Having heard so many heartbreak stories of immigrants being turned back at Ellis Island, I was grateful to be spared that tortuous procedure. Cabin-class passengers were processed through customs directly in a salon aboard ship, where long tables had been set up to accommodate various departmental officials. With all my papers in order, it was a breeze to pass. Soon I found myself descending the gangplank leading into a turmoil of relatives greeting relatives in emotional embraces, friends meeting friends, porters hauling tons of luggage, and policemen (some on horseback) directing the flow of traffic away from the ship.

I espied Katherine Peckett and Jerome Hill waving to me. It was all so good to set foot on American soil under such fortuitous circumstances. After a barrage of the questions customary on such occasions—How did I feel? How was the trip? What about the weather? Any rough seas? How were the accommodations, the food, etc.?—I was whisked to a waiting car and off to Mayfair House on Park Avenue, where Jerome had a small suite of rooms. One was to be mine during my stay in New York.

NEW YORK, NEW YORK

On the circuitous ride through the streets of New York, I was awed by and gawked at the vertiginous height of the skyscrapers. It felt like riding through a deep gorge with steep canyon walls left and right, almost near enough to touch. As we drove by the open space of Central Park, I was relieved to see the huge, green enclave surrounded by high-rise hotels, office buildings, and apartment complexes. Close by, in short walking distance of the park, was Mayfair House, a hotel of distinction and a home away from home for cognoscenti of comfortable living.

Katherine brought me up to date on the plans for the two weeks before we moved on to New Hampshire for Christmas. I sensed something was bothering her. Eventually, when we had settled in Jerome's suite, she came out with it. "Otto, I have bad news for you. I know I promised it wouldn't happen, but B. Altman sprung it on me by surprise and I can do nothing about it. The store insists on having a demonstration ski slide, contrary to our understanding. In fact, I was told that the slide was already built and waiting for you to find some suitable chemical substance to simulate snow. I'm sorry," she said.

What could I say at that stage? Everything had gone so well up to that point, and I was certainly not going to upset the apple cart. So what if I lowered my self-imposed standards in guarding the purity of the sport I was about to propagate in this country? Katherine told me there would be full page ads in the major daily papers announcing the event, with all the prominent sportswriters invited to cover the opening show. What show? I wondered. I had not the faintest notion how to put a program together on such short notice, one that would hold the interest of an audience and capture the imagination of hard-boiled big-city sportswriters. It was a rather frightening prospect, and to top it all, I had no idea on what kind of imitation snow I would be performing.

It was December 5, and I had to be ready for my one-man show by the evening of December 11—not much time. I realized I would have my hands full for the next few days. I could do none of the sightseeing, museums, theaters, or other diversions to which I had looked forward with eager anticipation. The first order of business the next morning was to see the slide and meet the head of B. Altman, then scour the Yellow Pages of the telephone directory to locate a chemical factory that might have a product that looked like snow, felt like snow, and was slippery like snow. It was a tall order under any circumstances. Crushed ice, which I considered momentarily, would not work for logistical reasons. The amount necessary to cover the slide and then to replenish constantly as it melted was impractical. Katherine and I got into a car with a list of factories, which we had already contacted by phone and presented with our problem. As we approached the end of our list, there was nary a glimmer of hope. Finally, almost as a last resort, we found a crystalline substance, shiny and sleek, in pea-size pellets, which I felt would fill our needs. We ordered a large quantity in sacks with instructions to deliver it without delay to the sixth floor of B. Altman and Company.

I could hardly wait to have the slide covered and give it a try with my skis. Lo and behold, it worked, surprisingly well. But only then did I become aware of the restrictive dimensions of my operative base. The slide was minuscule in length and width. It was also too flat, and my skis were too long. This made it almost impossible for me to make two linked turns at any kind of speed. All this added to my problems in putting a show together.

Slowly a pattern evolved in my mind. I would begin with a demonstration of the basic elements, such as the correct straight running position, snowplow and snowplow turn, followed by the stem turn and sideslipping. Then, I hoped, I could somehow squeeze in one single stem christie before I reached the level floor. What I could not demonstrate I would explain in a chalk talk with a large blackboard. For a grand finale I would run a 16 mm film that I had brought with me, showing Hannes Schneider skiing through knee-deep powder, backed by the majestic Austrian and Swiss Alps, in a dazzling display of the technique he had pioneered. I calculated that the show would last about one hour; afterward, I would answer questions. Now that I had a firm plan I felt somewhat better and more confident.

Prior to the opening, Mr. Woods, the president of B. Altman, invited me to his office with a few of his associates and, of course, Katherine. He was not a man of many words, generally quite reserved and unapproachable, with his pockmarked face, swarthy complexion, and deep-set dark brown eyes. He made a short speech pointing out the novelty of this promotional scheme and wished me luck and success. Then he said, "Otto, in the history of B. Altman, or at least as long as I have been associated with this establishment, there has never been any alcoholic beverage served on the premises. Today, on this occasion, I have broken the tradition by ordering a pitcher of dry martinis. Let's have a toast to this young man, to his courage and poise." Obviously, he was concerned and thought I needed spirituous reinforcement. I had never before imbibed or even tasted a dry martini, but under these pleasant circumstances, I could not very well refuse to share a small glass with the assembled group. A reader may well think, Oh no, he got thwacked and down the drain went the whole show. Not quite, although I did feel a little bit lightheaded and stimulated, which helped to carry me through the evening.

It went well. In fact, it went very well. As predicted, the *New York Times, Herald Tribune, Journal,* and other papers sent their sportswriters, among them Harry Cross, who was looked upon as the dean of sportswriting by his peers. This is a part of his piece for the *New York Times:*

> The exhilaration of downhill skiing was graphically described last evening in the ski shop at B. Altman and Co. by Otto Lang, from the Hannes Schneider Ski School in Austria. Explaining the fundamentals in simple terms, Mr. Lang aims, while here, to broaden the educational features of a sport which is rapidly growing in interest . . . .
>
> Lang carefully explained the different stages in the development of the Arlberg Method of skiing, giving a fine demonstration of the snowplow on the short slide. He also demonstrated the stem turn and christiania.
>
> One look at Lang on skis gives an immediate impression of correct

form, ease, and relaxation.

Although the white mineral covering the slide did not encourage speed, Lang managed to generate enough pace to exhibit several clever jump turns. His explanation of skiing and its principles was aided by blackboard diagrams. He explained the three best known types of skis, for downhill, cross-country, and jumping. There is but one groove on the surface of the downhill and cross-country ski, while there are three deeper-set grooves in the running surface of a jumping ski. The topper to end the presentation was a 16 mm film showing Hannes Schneider in a stunning demonstration of skiing artistry and poetry in motion.

Thank you, Harry Cross. The other sportswriters filed equally commendable reports. One of them, representing the *Daily Mirror*, gave it a humorous touch:

New Yorkers think of snow as white stuff that piles up in streets to keep them from getting to work on time. A deep, dark plot has been uncovered, revealing that certain foreign agents are conspiring to undermine the conviction of New Yorkers that snow is a nuisance, to be disposed of by Mayor La Guardia when it gets too deep.

This propaganda would have us believe that snow falls especially for skiing (people will try to impress you with their knowledge by pronouncing it "sheeing"). The propaganda has made such progress that you can buy a complete ski outfit in most New York stores: drug stores will sell skis wrapped in cellophane next. Under cover of darkness, a group of sportswriters were lured into one of New York's department stores (B. Altman) where one of the "foreign agents" (named Otto Lang) explained the intricacies of skiing.

What B. Altman had set out to do was accomplished. The ski slide became a conversation piece and skiers and nonskiers alike flocked to the sixth floor. What I enjoyed most was the direct contact with people, answering their questions and helping them with the selection of their equipment and clothing. My tenure there was a valuable learning experience. I enjoyed it and everything went smoothly, except for one thing: the climate of the store's emporium did not agree with the chemical substance covering the slide. The originally vibrant, glistening crystals became dull and lusterless. This made them more and more difficult to ski on. The snow might as well have been popcorn, which I was tempted to try as a substitute.

I remember it as the age of innocence in skiing, the wild and woolly days of near self-destructive impulses of skiers, carried away by their enthusiasm and let loose on the slopes without proper schooling and often inadequately equipped. It was also the age of weekend "snow trains" chugging out of Grand Central Station, loaded with ski enthusiasts willing to risk their limbs for the exhilaration of schussing down a ski slope, often at breakneck speed beyond their control. There was a rich field to be mined in teaching those hordes of skiers how to do it right. It was only the beginning of a sport that would envelop America like a tidal wave, from the mountains of New England to the Rockies to the volcanic peaks of the Pacific Northwest to the Sierra Nevada, the Southwest, and beyond. I considered myself privileged to lay the groundwork for skiing's future developments.

In New York, I occasionally managed to sneak away from B. Altman for a dinner with friends. One highlight was a visit to Radio City Music Hall at Rockefeller Center, with its Art-Deco interior. It was the premier showcase for first-run films and offered a stage show without equal, featuring among other outstanding acts the precision dancing, tapping, and high-kicking Rockettes.

At last the time came for my departure for Pecketts on Sugar Hill. After exchanging warmhearted adieus with Mr. Woods, who broke into a rare smile, and the staff of B. Altman, which could not have been more congenial, I boarded the train to Franconia, New Hampshire.

PECKETTS ON SUGAR HILL

On first sight, Pecketts on Sugar Hill reminded me of an Austrian country hotel. It stood on a high bluff overlooking the valley below and Cannon Mountain directly across. Architecturally it conformed to traditional New England style, most pleasing to the eye. The interior decor and ambiance could not have been more attractive, with many family heirlooms integrated into the furnishings. It was like a large home converted into a country inn. The moment I walked in, I knew I would enjoy spending the winter in this environment.

I first met Katherine's parents, who could have easily been the couple who posed for Grant Wood's famous *American Gothic*, with or without the pitchfork. Like most New Englanders, it took them a while to thaw out, and only then did they show the sterling qualities of which they had an abundance. To them it would be a wholly new experience to deal with a bunch of boisterous skiers, overcharged with energy and looking for an outlet.

Two other instructors were already in residence. As Katherine had told me upon hiring me, she had contracted them prior to my entering the picture. I knew them well, since both came from Salzburg, and we had skied and competed against each other in our junior years. One was Siegfried Buchmayr. Short in height, he was tall in spirit and had a great capacity to mix with people and keep them entertained, on and off the ski slopes. He was a colorful character and the epitome of a showman. To show off his physique he often skied in sunny but freezing weather with his shirt off, flaunting his well-proportioned torso to a bevy of New York debutantes. Kurt Thalhammer was also popular with the guests, but more subdued in temperament. He knew there was no point in trying to compete with the irrepressible Sigi Buchmayr. There was no organized ski school since we did not attempt to teach in a coordinated and uniformly agreed-upon method, nor was there a titular head of the school, and everything was quite free and loose. We got along very well and exchanged students to fit in groups with others of equal proficiency.

But we had two major problems at Pecketts. First, incredibly fickle snow conditions. We could never anticipate what it would be like from day to day, or even from a given morning to the same afternoon. We might wake up, look out the window, and see a foot of glorious new powder snow that by noon might be a soggy mess of mush, drenched by rain. By the next morning it might have a surface as hard as concrete, more fit for skating than skiing. The second problem was that the terrain resembled a hilly golf course (which it was during the summer months), lacking any challenge for downhill skiers. It was adequate for beginners, but that was about it. Making it interesting for more advanced skiers was difficult. We had to resort to all sorts of diversions, such as setting up slalom courses or improvising obstacle races. Cannon Mountain bulked in plain sight, but it was more of a summer attraction, for hikers, than a winter one, for skiers. The only trail cut through the mountain's dense forest was narrow and steep with sharp corners, too hazardous for the average skier and even for those few looked upon as advanced. I could not recommend it to my students. Of course there were no groomed trails or slopes at that time; one took it as it was, skiing through cut-up snow with deep, irregular ruts and potholes like small craters left by fellow skiers when they bombed out. It was not yet required etiquette to fill in the holes after a fall, like a conscientious golfer replacing an uprooted divot.

There were compensations for those of us who worked at Pecketts however; gatherings for afternoon tea following an invigorating workout on the ski slopes, rain or shine, created a warm feeling of togetherness. And I had friends close by. Jerome Hill had rented a chalet for the winter near the inn to accommodate his skiing family members and the occasional overflow of friends. As I had seen before, the Hills drew people like a magnet. There was constant coming and going of visitors.

Jerome had brought along the film he had shot at St. Anton for his ski movie and spent a good deal of time editing it into a final cut. Looking over his shoulder, I was fascinated by how he juggled entire scenes and snippets to mold them into a finished entity. I realized that editing was one of the most important components in fashioning the final product. I also became acutely aware of how many steps there were in making a film, each one of equal importance, from shooting raw material to putting it together to adding narration, sound effects, musical score, and a final dubbing. All these facets were combined into a smoothly flowing film, ready to be projected onto the screen. To me it was an absorbing process.

With so much work done, Jerome was not satisfied with the results. He decided to shelve the 16 mm film, start from scratch, and shoot a new version in 35 mm with a professional crew and with me performing in front of the camera. I was now offered a second chance to star in a ski movie, which was indeed an unexpected and appreciated opportunity. Knowing the ski season in New England was short-lived, we decided we would soon strike out for whiter and higher pastures somewhere in the western United States, if necessary winding up in the Pacific Northwest at Mount Rainier or Mount Baker, where snow was guaranteed until late spring. The scenic background of either of these two volcanos, both dormant but showing signs of life, would be spectacular. It was an exciting prospect to look forward to.

In the meantime, the days passed quickly at Pecketts. I used the many rainy days to pursue my objective, which was to write a book on skiing. Specifically, it would describe the progressive structure of the Arlberg technique. I visualized it as a simple, straightforward manual that a skier could easily understand and carry in the outside pocket of a ski jacket. The title I had chosen was *Downhill Skiing*. To my great surprise, in February 1936 I received a letter from Henry Holt and Company, a New

York publishing house founded in 1866 and highly regarded in literary circles.

Dear Sir,

We have it in mind to publish a small manual of ski-ing, perhaps 96 pages of which 32 would be photographs, which would contain in briefest form instructions for beginners. It might contain the idea behind the chief turns and stops, and show the possibilities of skis when expertly handled, without getting into controversial waters. And it might outline what to look for in skis, bindings, clothing, etc., and include a glossary of ski-ing terms.

Such a book could not be a substitute for the longer and more thorough works, but, if priced at about $1.25, it might sell more freely, and help convert novices into amateurs. Your name on such a manual would, of course, assure it of a sale. If you have ever thought of planning a book of the sort, we believe we could publish it successfully, and profitably to you.

We would like to hear from you, and would appreciate it if you would suggest any changes in the above outline, that would seem to you to improve it.

(Signed) Daniel Melcher
Henry Holt and Company

I replied immediately that I was already at work on such a book that was very close in contents and format to what Henry Holt and Company had in mind. I assured them that I would be delighted to proceed with their proposed plan.

Only ten days after the initial contact, we had a deal practically confirmed:

...We are glad to have your letter of Febr. 18th, and learn that you already have a book on skiing in preparation. We are in accord with your ideas for such a book.

It is, of course, too late now to think of publishing the book this spring. We feel that it should be ready for sale by December first, at the beginning of the next skiing season. Then we would have ample time to announce it in advance.

If possible, we should like to see a chapter or so before making a final agreement. If the plan seems satisfacotry, as no doubt it will be, we should be glad to publish it on a royalty basis, beginning at 10% on the retail price, and might be arranged, this to be paid on receipt of the manuscript.

The price of the book should not exceed $1.50, if we are to sell it in any quantity.

Perhaps when you are next in New York I can talk the matter over with you personally.

Sincerely yours,

(Signed) Richard H. Thornton, President
Henry Holt and Company

From then on, every idle moment of my time was occupied with the prospective book, either writing or thinking about it. I wrote every word in longhand, and it wasn't easy, since my vocabulary was still limited and my syntax equally shaky.

One day I was teaching an advanced class when I heard a loud voice exclaim, "Hi, everybody! You mind if I join you? My name is Nelson. I've been watching you guys in action and I think that's just about my speed."

I was a bit startled by this direct approach, expecting the gentleman to address me personally. "Be my guest," I said, and so he joined the class. From that day a warm friendship developed between us, even though our paths went in different directions. Nelson Rockefeller was a grandson of the founder of the Rockefeller dynasty, its fame and wealth of astronomic proportions. Nelson was a lively, outgoing young man, stockily built and well muscled. He obviously loved life. There was no aura or any pretense of the enormous wealth that surrounded him.

Nelson had graduated from Dartmouth College, which specialized in educating and forming a hardy breed of men by having them stay in close contact with nature and learning to cope with its diverse elements. Dartmouth was one of the first colleges with an organized competitive ski program, encompassing downhill skiing, cross-country, and ski jumping on their own home hill, under the guidance of their redoubtable coach Otto Schniebs. Nelson was of that sturdy caliber, and history would prove later his leadership qualities, rising through the political ranks and eventually serving as vice president of the United States.

As the snow dwindled away all over New England, we prepared for our journey west. I knew this would be the end of my tenure at Pecketts. As much as I appreciated the kindness and generosity of the Peckett family, I knew there was no future there for me. I wanted my own ski school in an area where there were high mountains and reliable snow conditions, a place I had yet to find. In any case, the experiment of opening the inn to skiers and winter guests was an unexpected success, and Pecketts' continued to enjoy profitable subsequent winter seasons.

Jerome and I made our travel plans. First we would go to St. Paul, Minnesota, the home of the Hill family, and from there we would travel west, scouting along our route for appropriate terrain and snow cover to shoot our ski film. Mount Rainier, near Seattle, seemed to be our best bet. We marked this area as our primary destination.

To The
Pacific
Northwest

Jerome and I traveled west by train to St. Paul, Minnesota, and during the few days we spent there, I was introduced to the paterfamilias of the Hill clan. A mustachioed, heavily bearded, conservatively dressed man who wore pince-nez, L. W. Hill was extremely private. I felt strangely inhibited in his presence, and he showed an immediate dislike of me. I assume he resented my intrusion into the inner circle of his family without his prior consent and benediction. This of course was very uncomfortable for me.

The house Hill had built for his family on Summit Avenue, not far away from his father J. J. Hill's palatial home, was an imposing brick structure with a multitude of rooms serving as family and servants' quarters. One end of an exceptionally large salon, designated as music room and entertainment center, was occupied by a full-size church organ, its mighty tone enhanced by the superb acoustics of the room's wood-paneled walls and ceiling. The interior decor of the rest of the home was also impressive; it was lavishly furnished, embellished with oriental carpets, and enhanced by a fine collection of paintings of the Barbizon school. J. J. Hill had been an avid collector of European art treasures and furnishings, which upon his death were passed on to his son.

The Hill habitat Jerome and the younger generation liked best was a country cottage on the outskirts of St. Paul near a lake and surrounded by dense forest. The house, called Izboushka ("little house" in Russian), was built entirely of wood and looked much like a dacha in the countryside near St. Petersburg. It was an ideal place for weekend and holiday gatherings, and a trunk full of assorted Russian garments was available to dress up in for parties. The Hills had great empathy for Russian people and the former dynasty of the Romanovs under Czar Nicholas II. I met many of their friends among Russian nobility, painters, sculptors, ballet dancers, and musicians, in the course of the years.

Our stay at St. Paul was of short duration, since we were anxious to reach the snowy regions of the Pacific Northwest. Instead of driving, as originally planned, we decided to go to Seattle by train, over the Great Northern Railway. Quite appropriately, the train, which still runs the same route, was named "The Empire Builder," in J. J. Hill's honor.

DESTINATION MOUNT RAINIER

The journey by train from St. Paul to Seattle was an eye-opener. I was impressed by the luxurious comfort of the train with its corps of well-trained stewards. As I looked out the window, day after day, I was awed by the immense spread of undeveloped land in America. The terrain had every conceivable variety of landscape—ever-changing panoramas of prairies, untouched forests, and high mountains. Occasional farmhouses were surrounded by cultivated fields and corrals for cattle and horses. Finally, after crossing the Cascades, we emerged at Seattle, the portal to the Pacific Ocean. Surrounded by the waterways of Puget Sound and inland lakes, Seattle claims one of the most appealing natural settings for an American city. On a clear day, Mount Rainier, a dormant volcano of spectacular dimensions, looms on its horizon, 14,410 feet high in solitary splendor. I fell in love with this giant mountain before I even set foot on it—which couldn't be soon enough, as far as I was concerned.

We arrived at Mount Rainier on the weekend of the annual Silver Skis Downhill Race, initiated in 1934 by Royal Brougham, the eminent sports editor of the *Seattle Post-Intelligencer*, considered at that time one of the premier dailies in the Northwest. He saw an opportunity to create an interest in the budding sport of skiing and to develop a potential source of advertising revenue by promoting it. Sponsoring a race would be a coup for his paper and provide reams of copy for his sports section.

The race, which attracted skiers from the East and Midwest as well as local talent and even a few European racing stars, started at Camp Muir, a primitive hut built of stone at an elevation of 10,000 feet. The terrain was varied and undulating, interspersed with long, moderately pitched, straight runs. A punishing, steep schuss led to the finish line above the main lodge, Paradise Inn, at 5,200 feet. With a vertical drop of 4,800 feet and a total length of 3.25 miles, it was not technically demanding but a leg killer nevertheless because of the sheer distance covered and the terrain, where one either had to go straight at high speed or make a lot of tiring, time-consuming turns.

The course was left in its natural condition, whether there was a heavy layer of freshly fallen snow, an icy crust, windblown moguls, or treacherous gullies. Race organizers did no packing with skis or smoothing out some of the rougher spots of the *piste*—there wouldn't have been enough manpower to undertake such a chore. For racers, the climb to the starting point, a matter of two to three hours, was laborious and exhausting. The weather could also be a factor, with a sudden bank of dense fog rolling in and obliterating the course.

The inaugural race held in April 1934 was won by Donald Fraser, then a student at the University of Washington. Subsequently he became a member of the U.S. Olympic ski team. Much later he married Gretchen Kunigk, from Tacoma, Washington, the girl who, at the 1948 Winter Olympics at St. Moritz, astounded the world and the European racing fraternity by being the first American skier ever to win a gold medal. In my book Gretchen Fraser is the all-time *grande dame* of skiing and Don has been one fine gentleman and unfaltering friend for all seasons.

The oddest part of the first Silver Skis race was that the competitors lined up straight across the wide open slope at the start, and at the signal all sixty-five of them pushed off simultaneously. This mass start was an invitation to mayhem, with racers building up speed rapidly, crisscrossing each other's lines of descent at random, crashing into each other, or desperately trying to avoid disaster. It must have been frightening for all the participants. Based upon that year's fiasco, the mass start was abandoned and the procedure adopted of sending competitors on their way at one-minute intervals, which made a lot of sense. Still, it resulted in some hair-raising collisions on the course, due to skiers' disparate technical abilities.

The race in the spring of 1936 was a triumph for Hannes Schroll, an Austrian hailing from Bischofshofen, near Salzburg. Hannes and I were old chums from way back and had competed against each other in many junior races. He had been invited to participate in this race with all expenses paid—singled out to be the drawing card, if you will, even though as a professional skier he could not compete against amateurs, according to the rules of the competition. Hannes had come over from Austria to start a ski school at Yosemite Valley. He was a colorful young man, outspoken, candid, and talkative, providing wonderful copy for Royal Brougham's sports pages. One of Hannes's trademarks—other than his jaunty Tyrolean hat securely affixed to his head with a green cord under his chin—was to regale the spectators along the course, whenever he passed a cluster of them, with a lusty yodel. Yodeling was a talent that he used to good advantage on and off skis. Hannes won the race in five minutes and thirty seconds, cutting in half Don Fraser's time of ten minutes and fifty seconds in that memorable first race.

I was merely an interested bystander and observer on the sidelines of the race, resisting any temptation to participate in such a demanding competition. First, I was not in the required physical condition. Second, I could not risk an injury so close to the start of our filming schedule. Instead I sized up the terrain and knew right away it would be perfect for our purpose of making a ski film.

In all the excitement, my presence did not remain entirely unnoticed, as this squib in Royal Brougham's "day after" column notes:

> The most stylish skier on the mountain wasn't Schroll, Hvam, Morbaaten, or any of the other competitors, but Otto Lang, who is at Mt. Rainier making a documentary film on skiing technique. . . . He came down the steep slope with a cadenced dancing swing . . . christianias so birdlike, he seemed to be flying.

After the mob of weekend skiers had disappeared, Mount Rainier took on an entirely different aspect. The majesty of the mountain, sheathed in ice, with the deeply serrated glaciers cascading down its steep flanks from the very summit to the vast rolling snowfields below Camp Muir, was an inspiring sight. The American Indians who lived in the lowlands surrounding the mountain called it Mount Tacoma. To them it was the sacred abode of their deities and kindred spirits. They looked upon it with awe, reverence, and respect—sentiments I could readily share.

Paradise Inn, the lodge where we stayed, was built by the National Park Service in the traditional rustic style, using indigenous rock and timber. Some of the logs were of imposing proportions, in both height and circumference. One could not see much of the exterior of the building since two-thirds of it was covered by snow and only the mansard windows on the top floor peeked out timidly over the vast, white expanse. At times the snow piled up twenty feet high, and one entered the lodge through a tunnel dug through the windblown snowbank. Facing the large lobby with its cathedral ceiling supported by parallel rows of thirty-foot-high columns of shaved tree trunks, one had the feeling of having walked into a house of worship. It was somewhat gloomy since no daylight penetrated the solidly blocked windows during the long winter months. The accommodations were Spartan, as was the heating of the place, which was built primarily for summer occupancy. Two oversize, walk-in fireplaces at each end of the lobby, with huge logs aflame, were a welcome surprise. Wood was in abundance, neatly piled up within easy reach.

Any of the inn's shortcomings were richly compensated by the warmth of the people connected with running the place, from the manager down to the waitresses, maids, bellhops, and sundry personnel. Many of them were college students on "sabbatical," hoping to improve their skiing prowess. They made one feel like a member of a large, congenial family.

In any hotel, the *chef de cuisine* is an important factor in the success of the establishment. Paradise Inn was no exception, with Papajohn as resident cook. Papajohn was definitely not of the Escoffier school of culinary arts, but in whipping up a meal of juicy steaks and potatoes he could hold his own. Short, stocky, and of Greek parentage, with a face as round as the full moon, he lit up the place with his good-natured smile. He loved to mix with people—guests and employees both—and sit around the fireplace to chew the fat, even though he had never put on a pair of skis and abhorred the idea of snowshoeing. He didn't mind at all being followed into the kitchen when the time came to cook dinner. And he permitted one to snoop around and suggest what might suit one's palate for the evening's meal, although, invariably, he ended up serving the ubiquitous steak-and-potato entrée that was the *spècialité de la maison.*

SKI FLIGHT

Mount Rainier's stage was set for our filming venture. Jerome had signed up Hollywood cinematographer Roy Klaffki and his assistant. Roy came highly recommended, but he was not a skier. This had no bearing, however, since at that time reputable cinematographers on skis were virtually unknown. He had worked on locations in the deep of the winter before but never in the same kind of terrain as Rainier. He had learned how to move around on snowshoes and did so with ease. Above all, he had the patience and kindness to bear with our whims—Jerome's, as the director-producer with his artistic penchant for the best results, and mine, as the performing skier in front of the camera; both insisting on having everything technically correct and perfectly executed.

The 16 mm film Jerome had shot at St. Anton served as our blueprint. We started out with the basic, rudimentary steps, as one would teach an infant to walk, and progressed gradually into the mechanics of the stem turn, stem christiania, and high-speed parallel turn, considered the *ne plus ultra* of an advanced skier's repertory. In order to show each maneuver so it was visually clean, we prepared the slope beforehand by packing it with skis to a smooth, flat surface. We were assisted by a group of volunteers drawn from the lodge staff. They enjoyed being part of it and watching the progress of the work, while at the same time benefiting from the free ski lessons.

Fortunately, the weather stayed favorable throughout our shoot, with the sun shining every day, resulting in ideal spring snow conditions that made skiing like gliding on melting butter. In fact, the weather was quite deceptive, leading one to take for granted that it would be like this all winter long. I would experience the opposite, bitter truth of this fallacy in the near future. But then the sun was completely with us, and we had exhausted Mount Rainier in two weeks. We needed a change of scenery, a different backdrop, and new terrain. Mount Baker, north of Seattle near the Canadian border, was our next goal. We had made many wonderful friends during our stay at Paradise Inn, so the parting was both sweet and sorrowful. But somehow I had a feeling I would be back at Mount Rainier. The thought crossed my mind that this might be a promising place in which to open my own ski school.

The drive from Mount Rainier to Mount Baker was a full day's journey, and the closer we approached the final destination, the worse the road became. Narrow and full of potholes, it wound steeply up the mountain. The backdrop of Mount Baker, with wisps of smoke emanating from its perfectly shaped conical peak, reminded us that it was indeed a live volcano, just biding its time until spewing out its molten innards. The scenery was startlingly beautiful, and the terrain compared favorably with many a choice spot in the Austrian Alps. We had been assured of finding powder snow here, and we did: that light and fluffy stuff that leaves glistening rooster tails behind a skier carving high-speed turns. This kind of footage would certainly embellish our film and give it distinction.

If the accommodations at Paradise Inn were modest, the lodge at Mount Baker, with sleeping quarters in a separate building close by, was monastic. But no one really cared that much, as long as there was a place to eat, somewhere to keep warm, and a bed in which to sleep. Again, the people around us were most accommodating and made us feel welcome, extending helping hands in every way they could.

Shuttling camera equipment around in knee-deep snow required additional volunteers. Luckily, there were some steep slopes nearby, untracked and from all reports never skied on before, due to the ruggedness of the terrain.

One such run that I had chosen as part of the climactic run to end the film, had me worried. I had not had the opportunity to reconnoiter beforehand, since this would have left highly visible ski tracks, which we wanted to avoid. I had some apprehensions about unleashing an avalanche as I came down this slope, which would have endangered not only me but also the camera crew and Jerome, placed strategically on an elevated knoll at the bottom, and directly in line with the path an avalanche would follow. It was a troublesome thought and a chance I truly hated to take. I proceeded with great caution, carefully picking my route and the most favorable spots to make my turns. This slowed me down considerably and impaired my rhythm more than I wished. Under normal circumstances and in familiar terrain, I would have just let go and flown down in sweeping, high-speed turns. Also, I could not risk taking a fall, since that would have ruined the whole shot. Suffice it to say that all went well, and what a relief it was! The entire sequence remained intact in the final version of the film.

After we finished shooting film at Mount Baker, Jerome was anxious to start editing the material. I was equally anxious to find a quiet place to work on my book and begin selecting photographs to illustrate the text. I had a fair collection already in my possession, and I had a wealth of material from the surplus scenes of Jerome's film. Some of these were filmed in slow motion and provided me with an invaluable teaching device. I pleaded with Jerome to help me by reading some of what I had written and correcting the most flagrant mutilations in spelling and grammar, but he declined to do so, saying, "This should be expressed in your choice of words and the way you talk, without any meddling by another person. Never mind the spelling and grammatical errors; they'll all be taken care of by your editor." Jerome was right, and circumstances rather than choice dictated that I had to express myself in a succinct and economical style, which was all the better.

The Hill family had a place in Pebble Beach near Carmel, California, which they used frequently to get away from the oppressive heat of the Minnesota summer and the numbing cold of winter. We headed there, since the "big house" was vacant at that time. Maud lived in her own smaller house nearby and would be there when we arrived. The main house, built of wood in the impressive architectural style of the hotels of Glacier National Park (whose design L. W. Hill had also overseen), stood on a high bluff overlooking the Pacific Ocean, with a panoramic view of 180 degrees. It was truly spectacular, with rolling waves crashing against the rocky shore and the spray of water visible for miles. Maud's house, in the style of an Alpine chalet, was tucked away in the woods, yet afforded an enchanting view of the ocean through the boughs of its surrounding pine trees. Her impeccable taste in interior decor, mixing various styles of furniture and using fabrics, made her house a joy to live in.

It could not have worked out better. I settled down to my writing chores, and Jerome worked on editing his film. Both of us made good progress in this beneficial environment. I had sent off a chapter of my book to Henry Holt, as per their request, which happened to be captioned "Teaching and Its Psychology." They liked it, and a contract was in my hands by return mail. I affixed my signature to the standard form, and that was that. I had no agent to negotiate for better terms nor lawyer to double-check the agreement. In this instance there were no surprises or disappointments. I happened to be dealing with a group of honorable people.

Downhill Skiing was fittingly dedicated to Hannes Schneider, who wrote a most gracious and touching foreword to the book. I was pleased that in even so small a measure I could express my gratitude to the man I admired and who had steered my career and life in a most fortuitous direction. I owed him much.

A RETURN TO EUROPE

While the intensive work of book and filmmaking was progressing, Jerome and I discussed plans for the future. We decided that, after we had finished our projects, a group of us would take off for Europe. Maud made arrangements to rent a villa in the Austrian countryside near Salzburg in August, within easy reach of the city and its annual Salzburg Festival. She and Larry would bring along their darling boy, age three, whose nickname was "Charkie" for reasons unknown to me. When we arrived at the villa, a nanny would be engaged to look after him.

"Lady Maud," as I called the elder Mrs. Hill, and her best friend, Mrs. Tina Ward from St. Paul, were also to be part of the group. They would dispatch a brand new Packard convertible across the Atlantic for their use. My responsibility would be to shepherd the two ladies on forays from Salzburg. Knowing and liking the mother of the Hill clan as much as I did, I had no qualms about living up to the trust put in me as both driver and cicerone. The thought of touring Austria in an automobile of the latest design with horsepower to spare titillated me. Furthermore, the prospect of seeing my parents and sisters filled me with joy.

The journey to New York and crossing the Atlantic went smoothly. We all assembled at the spacious Villa Funder in an idyllic country setting on the outskirts of Salzburg. There were enough bedrooms and ample space for everybody. I decided to stay with my parents, however. It meant a great deal to them to have me under their roof.

SALZBURG REVISITED

The weeks in Salzburg flew by with dinner parties, excursions and picnics, concerts, operas, theater performances, and—not to forget— shopping sprees. Much of my time was spent escorting Lady Maud and Tina on various short trips through Austria and Bavaria. They were so dear, laughing and giggling while enjoying the scenery and attractions "off the beaten track," chosen at my discretion. I saw parts of my own country that I had wanted to see, but I had never had the opportunity. We stopped at small country inns for delicious lunches and occasional overnight stays. We had our fill of pastries and *Kaffee mit Schlag*, coffee served with the thickest and smoothest whipped cream imaginable.

At the end of August everybody in our original group dispersed in different directions. Lady Maud and Tina went to Paris under Jerome's guiding hand. Others went to London, and a few headed straight for home. I was sorry to see everyone leave, but I had decided to stay in Salzburg, which everybody understood and supported, since I had seen precious little of my own family, although I did have a chance to take them on a few outings in the resplendent "green beetle," as the Packard came to be known around town. I looked forward to some quiet days of solitude after the excitement of the past weeks and also had work to do. I had been commissioned by *Vogue* magazine to write a piece comparing skiing in Europe to what America had to offer. They wanted it for the December issue, which put considerable pressure on me. *Esquire* also was interested in a piece on the comparative merits of Hannes Schneider's Arlberg method versus the "Parallel Technique" propagated by Fritz Loosli, a Canadian ski instructor. I knew I would have my hands full with these assignments.

I decided to spend as much time as possible with my parents, since I felt I had been neglecting them. My mother cooked some of my favorite dishes, and with every meal we uncorked a bottle of vintage Austrian wine, or I fetched a large mug of beer from the Stieglbrau, a beer garden restaurant across the street. It reminded me of my youth, when I would be dispatched on such an errand and on returning would take a breather climbing the stairs to the fourth floor and sneak a swig of the frothy brew, hoping that it would not be noticed. It was good to see my sisters as well. Nelly was firmly established in the banking business by this time.

A Lang family picnic near Zenica, Bosnia, in 1917.

My father on horseback, 1914.

Nelly, Elsa, and me in Sarajevo, around 1913.

First photo taken when I was a freshman instructor in Hannes Schneider's ski school at St. Anton am Arlberg, 1930. Photo by Schubert.

Hannes Schneider in 1930. Photo by Luggi Föger.

Jerome Hill sculpting at St. Anton, 1930. Photo by Otto Lang.

Returning from an alpine ski tour at St. Anton, 1932. *L. to R.:* Willie Bogner (of Bogner ski fashions), Marius and Bitten Ericksen (parents of Stein Ericksen—I taught them in my class), me, Mary Bird, Hannes Schneider, and Lothar Rübelt (ace photographer). Photo by Lothar Rübelt.

Swimming teacher at Zell am See, 1929.

A student harnessed to the end of the "lifeline" —and not too happy about it.

"Walking on water" using two foldboats at Zell am See, Austria, on my way to see Stefan Zweig, 1929.

The golf links at the Hotel Tre Croci in the Italian Dolomites, 1935.

SALLE PLEYEL
STUDIO N° 1

ENTREE
FAUBOURG ST-HONORÉ
OU RUE DARU

DAMES...... : LUNDI : DE 11 H. A 12 H.
             : JEUDI :

MESSIEURS : LUNDI : DE 19 H. A 20 H.
          : JEUDI :

OTTO LANG

PROFESSEUR DE L'ÉCOLE HANNES SCHNEIDER DE ST-ANTON SUR ARLBERG

COURS DE CULTURE PHYSIQUE
POUR LA PRÉPARATION A LA SAISON DE SKI
(MÉTHODE DE L'ARLBERG)

LEÇONS PARTICULIÉRES SUR DEMANDE
11, RUE BALZAC   ---   TÉL : ÉLYSÉES 87-10

Advertisement in *Neige et Glace* for my physical conditioning classes in Paris, 1932.

Marina and Feodor Chaliapin in Paris, 1936.

With Jerome Hill and Katherine Peckett, 1935.

Riding on a donkey in Greece with my Hellenic cast.

Demonstrating the art of skiing on a slide with chemical snow at B. Altman in New York City. As seen in the *New York Tribune*, December 11, 1935.

The artificial ski slope at the Winter Sports show, New York, 1936.

With Hannes Schneider and Benno Rybizcka at Madison Square Garden's Winter Sports Exhibition, 1936.

Arriving at Mount Rainier in December 1935 to open the ski school.

Brochure for the first ski school at Mount Rainier, 1937.

America's First
Official
Hannes Schneider Ski School
Under Direction of

OTTO LANG
1937
Rainier National Park

36-242 Otto Lang Going Down, Rainier Nat. P.

Going down Mount Rainier in 1936.

The entrance to Paradise Inn at the base of Mount Rainier.

Introducing waterskiing at Glorietta Bay, Coronado, California, in the summer of 1938.

Instructor and student, the first time we met. One picture tells more than a thousand words.

Sinnie (Sinclair Gannon) "subbing" for Errol Flynn in her first attempt at the sport.

Our wedding reception line. *L. to R.:* Dell Gannon (with white hat), Admiral Gannon, Sinnie (the bride), me, Nancy.

Sinnie and I posing for *Fortnighter* magazine on a return visit to Coronado, 1939.

Elsa kept busy as a nanny, and Erna was a trusted but domineering "mother's helper." She also was employed frequently as a baby sitter, a role in which she was reliable. Every shilling she earned she put diligently into a savings account.

My father had worked hard to improve the family's financial condition to the point that they could afford to take a yearly two-week summer vacation in one of the resorts strewn like jewels along the Adriatic coast of Yugoslavia. For them it was like a homecoming, knowing the people and speaking their language fluently. They enjoyed the sunshine and lukewarm sea. Though not an expert swimmer, my mother loved to float around, making sure of a firm foothold beneath her.

Falling back into an old habit, I went to a coffee house almost every afternoon, usually the Cafe Bazar, one of the oldest and most popular in Salzburg. Situated next to the Osterreichischer Hof, the town's flagship hotel, it overlooked the Salzach River. One could be sure that sooner or later a familiar face would enter its hallowed confines, looking for a table, assisted by the practiced eye of the maitre d', who had been with the establishment as long as I could remember. He had the dignity and aplomb acquired through many years of service and a knack of spotting people who deserved to be pampered, be that an old habitué, a well-known actor, or an opera star. For them a table seemed always available, as if by some sleight of hand.

One day I was sitting at a table by myself (often one had to share a table with a total stranger) when I felt instinctively that someone was looking at me and approaching my table. When I raised my eyes from the magazine I was perusing, I recognized the lady immediately, even before she said, "Hello, Otto, do you remember me?" Of course I did. Toddy, as she was called, had been in one of my classes during the winter I spent at the Südbahn Hotel. I remembered her as likable and attractive but without any special physical attributes except for a mischievous sparkle in her dark brown eyes that enlivened her face. There hadn't been a thought of romantic involvement in either of our minds, which led to a pleasant and friendly relationship. Her family was Jewish and her father ran a successful dental clinic in Vienna, where she worked as a receptionist and assistant technician.

I invited Toddy to share my table and as though no time at all had elapsed, we caught each other up with the events in our lives. Since we had never exchanged letters, there was much to tell. Toddy had read in the papers that I had gone to America. She was on sabbatical from her job because the pressures of managing her father's clinic had become too much of a "grind". She badly needed a complete rest and had teamed up with a young lady companion to travel about Europe with frequent random stopovers. Her friend was to meet her presently in this cafe.

Eventually the young lady did appear and join us at our table, apologizing for being late. Her car had had a flat tire, and it had taken a while for her to get help. Judging by her entrance and the turning of heads as she crossed the length of the cafe, she shouldn't have had any problems finding a volunteer to help her change the punctured tire. After having been properly introduced, we fell into easy conversation, as it is wont to happen among people who share common interests and have traveled the world.

"By the way," Toddy's friend said, "do call me Lilo and not Lieselotte." Born and raised in Berlin, Lilo obviously came from a family with an intellectual background. Her father, Gunther Wilhelmi, was a member of the Berlin Philharmonic, playing violin in the string section of that orchestra, which was highly regarded even before Herbert von Karajan, a native of Salzburg, took over and guided it to unheard-of artistic and commercial heights.

Talking with Lilo about music and Berlin intrigued me. Berlin in those days was known for its many avant-garde facets but also known for its decadence, typified by popular cabarets that offered political satire and parodies of sexual aberrations in words, songs, and visual presentations. The city was also the wellspring of some of the finest films made in the prewar era. There was an incredible reservoir of talented directors, writers, stage-set designers, producers, and highly trained actors. Some of these eventually found their way to world fame and material success in Hollywood films. I mention one name that comes to mind, simply because there was a certain physical resemblance between her and Lilo—the inimitable Marlene Dietrich. Both of them had high cheekbones and modeled facial contours, blond hair, blue eyes, seductive curves, and an aura that never fails to attract men.

As a full-blooded male, I couldn't help but be fascinated by Lilo. She was indeed a dish. However, I was well aware that this was no time for me to fall in love and was determined not to start any kind of liaison, tempting though it seemed. All my thoughts were concentrated on America and on getting back there as soon as possible. Besides, it did occur to me that Lilo surely must have a man in her life. Still, it was a pleasant diversion to share time with Toddy and Lilo, inasmuch as they had invited me to take a drive into the countryside with them and later to have dinner at the Schloss Fuschl, an establishment noted for its fine cuisine and beautiful rural setting. The former residence of a noble Salzburg family, the place had the appearance of a square, medieval tower with brightly painted shutters overlooking an emerald lake. It had been converted into an exclusive hotel with a restaurant that was open to the public. I accepted, of course, having nothing of importance on my schedule for that evening.

Lilo's car was a flashy Opel convertible sports car of an opaque, aquamarine color with white leather upholstery and a cramped back seat for two. Once the canvas top was rolled down, Toddy sat in the back and Lilo asked me if I wouldn't mind driving. I had told them about my recent stint as a chauffeur for two elderly ladies, which amused them highly and gave them full confidence in my qualifications. As we cleared the city limits and reached the open road, I felt Lilo slowly nudging closer to me; within a few minutes she was fast asleep with her head nestled against my shoulder. I must admit that it felt cozy and intimate, especially after knowing each other for barely two hours. I enjoyed the fragrance of her body and her perfume. It may have augured the beginning of something I really did not want to happen, but from that time on during the many lengthy drives we made together the ritual repeated itself. Invariably Lilo would fall asleep, snuggled against my shoulder, feeling comfortable and protected.

The dinner at Schloss Fuschl, accompanied by a good bottle of wine and animated conversation, was delicious. Over the meal, Lilo's picture gradually became clearer to me. There was indeed a man in her life, and he played a prominent role in providing her with the means for her carefree, luxurious style of living and traveling about. As owner and president of one of the largest banks in Bucharest, Rumania, Aristide Blanc was an entrepreneur used to playing at high stakes in the global financial markets. This made it necessary for him to travel, and on one of his trips to Berlin he met Lieselotte Wilhelmi at a Berlin Philharmonic concert, when they happened to be seated next to each other. Although Aristide was some forty years older than Lilo (still in her early twenties), they formed a close attachment. Aristide was married and had children, so for the sake of convenience he set Lilo up in an elegant apartment in Vienna, a city easier for him to reach from Bucharest than Berlin. He gave Lilo all the freedom she wanted, except when he wished to see her. He also had bought her the automobile and encouraged her to pursue her interest in arts and languages by enrolling in the University of Vienna. The price for all these luxuries did not seem too exorbitant for Lilo to pay.

At the end of a meal at the Hotel Sacher during one of Aristide's visits to Vienna, Lilo was enjoying an Austrian specialty desert of *Zwetschgen Knödl* (a ripe plum enveloped in fluffy dough and bread crumbs, liberally sprinkled with powdered sugar). She bit hard into a piece of the pit, inadvertently left in the plum, and chipped one of her teeth. The all-knowing concierge gave them the name of Dr. Werner, whose clinic was nearby. It was there that Lilo met Toddy at the reception desk. The dental problem turned out to be of minor consequence and was easily repaired. It also started an enduring friendship between the two girls. The Domnula, or "master of the house," as Aristide was accustomed to be called by his family and close friends, encouraged this association. To some extent Toddy would fill the role of a quasi-chaperon and companion for Lilo when staying at hotels. Such was the case in Salzburg: they occupied two adjoining suites, which made it proper and cozy for all parties concerned.

These little details came to light in bits and pieces during our almost daily encounters for lunch or afternoon coffee. Lilo had told her benefactor about me, and he didn't object to our seeing each other, as long as she kept her evenings—and nights—free for him. In fact, he expressed his wish to meet me, and set up a luncheon date. I found him to be an impressive man, world-wise and sophisticated. He was older looking than I expected him to be, but impeccably dressed and groomed down to his manicured fingernails. It was easy to carry on a conversation with him, touching on diverse topics. He said that he had been in America a few times and expected to return there soon to conclude a major business transaction, which I sensed had something to do with weaponry or war-related items.

Aristide had to know that Lilo would come into contact with other, younger men than he was. But he also knew that few could provide for her as he could. Therefore, he felt quite confident in her loyalty, though not necessarily her fidelity. But he did want to know what kind of a man had entered his territory. By all appearances I had passed muster, and we parted in a congenial manner. He had no reason to be concerned about me—not for the moment, at least.

ITALIAN INTERMEZZO

A few days later, Aristide told Lilo that he had to return to Bucharest on urgent business matters. Since Lilo and Toddy already had planned to tour Italy for two weeks or so, he suggested that they start out even before he left, saying he had a very busy schedule ahead of him. Aristide's sudden decision aroused Lilo's suspicion, and, by intuition, she felt that something was awry. With a little guile and cunning she tracked down through an accommodating travel agent the information that Aristide Blanc had booked reservations for two on the Orient Express—destination Venice. To Lilo it could mean only one thing: there was another woman.

A diabolical plot sprang into her mind, which she confided to Toddy and me. The plan was that we would drive to Venice and meet the train upon its arrival at the railroad station at Mestre, the terminal for Venice. By then Lilo would have purchased widow's mourning attire, shrouding herself in black silk and crepe. She would be unrecognizable until she lifted the dark veil covering her face. This she proposed to do when the Domnula alighted from the train with his paramour. Without uttering a word she would confront her benefactor with a searing expression on her face, as though she had been jilted and wounded to the core of her soul with a silent outcry of "*Ah, perfido.*" Then she would lower the veil, turn around, and walk away haughtily.

When they asked me to join them, I said that I would, providing that I paid for my own room and that all other expenses—food, gasoline, and other incidentals—would be divided by three and that I would pay my share in full. I did not want in any way to participate in the largesse of Aristide Blanc. My proposal was accepted. I also stated that I did not like the idea of Lilo's charade and stated firmly that I wanted no part of it. If they wanted to do it, it was their business. Reluctantly I consented to drive them to the station and remain in the car until they returned. Frankly, I didn't see any point in going through with this demeaning scenario and failed to see what it would prove. Lilo, however, was obsessed by her stratagem and looked forward with childlike anticipation to the moment of her lover's humiliation. Whether for her it was a game of one-upmanship or to create some sort of moral leverage—if there could be a question of morals—or simply to prove to Aristide that she wasn't as naive as he thought, I don't know.

When the day came the plot was executed as conceived. It was choreographed like a well-planned bank heist, with Toddy hiding in the wings and watching the comedy as a vital witness and me standing by with the getaway car outside the station. According to their description, all went as anticipated, and the Domnula was flabbergasted.

As soon as they took their places in the car, we were off to Florence. With its artistic heritage and splendid museums, it would be one of the highlights of our Italian odyssey. We made a side trip to Pisa to check out the leaning tower and verify that it really listed as far to starboard as advertised. It did, even more so. Rome was our next destination, with brief stopovers en route in Siena and Orvieto. After Rome it was Naples and the crown jewel of southern Italy—the isle of Capri. Thinking back on this journey so many years after its occurrence, I find that it is, in my memory, a wash of kaleidoscopic images. We stayed in grand hotels, spent nights in primitive country inns, and ate wonderful food in small taverns. We made hurried visits to museums, paid homage to the best-known edifices along our route, and pondered the decadence and brutality of Roman times.

Somewhere along the way Lilo and I yielded to our sexual desires for each other. We were not in love, nor did we love each other. It was simply the need of two young, naked bodies wanting to be entwined in carnal satisfaction and then to fall into a deep, dreamless slumber. We enjoyed each other's company enormously, without giving any thought to the future. It would last as long as it lasted—and then, who knew what? It was truly a matter of living for pleasures of the moment, and in these Lilo was insatiable, often beyond my capacity to fulfill her. Since Lilo and Toddy always shared a room, Toddy knew what was going on, as for many nights Lilo's bed remained untouched. There was no resentment on her part; all she wanted was for Lilo to be happy. Theirs was a bond of true friendship.

I had been looking forward to visiting Capri. In the minds of people growing up in an alpine environment, Capri represented a sunny paradise with a deep, blue sea in which to swim. After reading a book called *The Story of San Michele* by Axel Munthe, in which the Swedish doctor and author described the building of his dream house in Capri, I longed to see it with my own eyes. We planned to stay for a week, hopefully enveloped in a state of nirvana. Capri lived up fully to its reputation as a romantic Shangri-la.

Our next destination was the Italian Riviera. Through personal connections, undoubtedly initiated by Aristide Blanc, Lilo had rented the vacant villa of Henri Barbusse for one month. Barbusse was a well-known French author of that era, though his stature was diminished due to his open affiliation with Russia and its communist ideology. His villa was located close to the border between Italy and France, adjacent to the French Riviera. We scooted northward following a winding, shoreline route, skirting the Tyrrhenian Sea. For no particular reason, we seemed to be in too much of a hurry to fully enjoy the scenery and picturesque fishing villages along our way.

Upon arriving at the villa, my companions surprised me with a man-servant they had "imported" from Vienna. His name was Leopold Moser, and he was a stocky little fellow with a beaming smile, a smooth-shaven face, and a few solitary strands of hair adorning his otherwise bare scalp. He came highly recommended and looked dapper in his traditional grey suit with the customary green felt collar and lapels. The buttons, fashioned from stag horn, gave it the final authentic touch. Leopold could cook, serve a meal with panache, go to the market and shop for supplies, work around the house, pinch-hit as a uniformed chauffeur, and fix any mechanical failures of the automobile. He was a rare specimen who could run a household single-handedly, going back to the heyday of the Austrian monarchy. The three of us would be seated at an impeccably set table with blinding-white linen, shining cutlery, crystal goblets, and lighted candles; Leopold, having put on a neat-fitting white jacket, served us a five-course dinner, which he had prepared while wearing his tall chef's toque. His offerings never failed to be delicious. I could not help but feel a bit sheepish about the inequities of life, with this single man doing so much work to make the lives of us hedonistic sybarites more pleasurable. But, apparently, that is exactly what gave him satisfaction—and all this taking place in the house of Comrade Barbusse.

Much of our time at the villa was spent swimming and basking in the late autumn sun. A set of steep, winding stairs led from the house down to the sea and a fair-sized rocky cove with a few narrow recesses affording total privacy. We could swim au naturel, without anyone ever taking notice. Occasionally I begged off to stay in the house for a couple of hours and catch up on my correspondence and attempt to do some writing. One such time when I went to join the ladies at the cove, I looked but couldn't find them, nor did I see two heads bobbing out at sea. Knowing that they must be somewhere around, I began to wander haphazardly, puzzled by their mysterious disappearance, when I chanced upon a hidden inlet with a narrow strip of sand. There they were, completely absorbed and unmistakably coupled in an erotic configuration, as graphic as could be. I was stunned and retreated quietly, without having been noticed. I felt I should spare them the embarrassment of being caught in flagrante delicto.

Faced with such a dilemma one might be angered or at least irritated at having been duped. I wasn't. It did illuminate, to some extent, my curiosity about Toddy's sex life. She liked the company of men in a social way but never seemed to be drawn to one of them close enough to enter an intimate relationship. Never had it occurred to me that she might be a lesbian, not interested in any kind of physical contact with a man. Maybe I was simply too naive to have realized what was going on. As for Lilo, I concluded that she was an addict and that sex was her opiate. She couldn't get enough of it, and if it wasn't one way, she was quite willing to get it any other way. Basically she was heterosexual, and I knew that there had been many men before me in her life and that there would be many more after.

From the moment I entered the villa, it had little appeal for me. It was surrounded by a grove of pine trees and, therefore, was somewhat dark and gloomy inside. The decor was a hodgepodge of Art Deco and odd pieces of furniture dating from various past epochs. It was utterly lacking in homelike ambiance. I didn't feel comfortable, and I was getting restless and anxious to get on with my life. I had fallen far behind with my writing on the piece for *Vogue*, and the deadline for delivery was creeping ever closer. Under the circumstances I did not want to spend another two or three weeks in this environment. I felt very strongly that the time had come for me to part company amicably with Lilo. We knew where we stood from the very beginning, and we knew that life would go on quite nicely, if and when we dropped out of each other's sight.

To my great surprise, when I broke my intentions of leaving to Lilo, she was quite upset and unprepared to accept my departure on such short notice. Having arranged for my railroad ticket, with my bags packed and accounts settled, I double-checked my travel documents and noticed with dismay that my passport was missing—without that crucial document I could not cross any frontiers in Europe. After a frantic and futile search, Lilo finally admitted that she had confiscated my passport and hoped that she could force me to stay a while longer. It took much pleading, cajoling, and explaining to convince her how important it was for me to get on my way and prepare for my imminent departure to America, on which all my future depended. Finally, she handed over the precious document and a small leather case containing a beautiful Omega wristwatch made of gold. I felt like a functionary, who having reached retirement age was rewarded with a gold watch for services rendered. No tears were shed, nor any promises made for future reunions when I was dropped off at the railroad depot at San Remo, headed for Salzburg via Milan.

Altogether it had not been an unpleasant experience, but more and more I felt myself sinking into a murky pit, which might well have ended in the realm of the Marquis de Sade, as had been furtively suggested to me on more than one occasion. I was not interested at all in following that route. In fact, I felt the need to cleanse my body and soul through a period of celibacy and solitary meditation. I wanted to just be alone, all to myself.

THE START
OF A NEW SKI
CAREER

Before I left for Italy, I had asked my father to forward any of my mail that seemed important to San Remo, addressed "*Post Restante.*" A batch of letters was waiting for me there, including one from Hannes Schneider. He wrote to advise me that he had been invited to participate in a mammoth winter sports show to be held at the Boston Garden and then to move on to New York's Madison Square Garden. He hoped very much that I would be able to join him and Benno Rybizka, so that we could perform as a trio presenting the progressive steps of the Arlberg technique. We would meet at St. Anton at the end of November, travel by train to Paris, and from there go to Cherbourg and embark on a steamship to America. He also mentioned that we would be skiing on a giant simulation of an Alpine slope covered with crushed ice particles, with a ski jump in the center of the hill.

It sounded exciting to me and had all the earmarks of an extravaganza, such as only American showmen could conceive and put on successfully. Naturally I accepted Hannes's invitation and wrote that I would follow his instructions as far as travel arrangements were concerned. I also warned him that I had to be at Mount Rainier no later than December 15. The winter sports show was an unexpected turn of events and I looked forward to sharing the limelight with Hannes—and in America, no less.

My skiing exhibition on chemical snow at B. Altman seemed like a small carnival act in the provinces compared to the shows in Boston and Madison Square Garden. On arrival from Europe, we three docked in New York, and without even spending a night in the city, transferred to an express train that took us to Boston. Our hotel was conveniently located close to the sports arena. Rooms, food, and incidentals would all be taken care of by the show's promoters.

The ski slope in the Boston Garden was an impressive sight. The foundation, 35,000 feet of crisscrossed steel tubing, rose to a dizzying height to support the contour of the hill, built of wooden planks. Horizontal riders were laid across the width of the slope to keep the snow in place and clinging to the surface. It was quite steep with a sharp transition at the bottom of the slope. The in-run to the fair-sized jumping hill went right into the open sky, through a hole cut in the roof.

The promoters had gathered quite an assemblage of talent: Alpine and Nordic skiers, ski jumpers, figure skaters, snowshoe-runners, alpenhorn tooters, dog sleds with full complements of mushing malamutes, horse-drawn sleds, tumblers, and clowns on skates and skis. Not being used to show biz, Benno and I found this whole scene somewhat disconcerting. It was amazing and reassuring to both of us to see how collected, calm, and good-humored Hannes Schneider was about this whole spectacle. We needed his moral support. "We were hired to do a job and are being paid well for our services," he said. "So let's give the public their money's worth." Hannes was fully aware of the invaluable publicity to be derived from these shows.

The hill was covered with tons of finely crushed ice particles. Elaborate machinery functioned flawlessly in replenishing the melting ice crystals by devouring rectangular blocks of ice and spewing the particles through high-pressure hoses onto the hill. An ingenious drainage system disposed of meltwater. While there was no problem in building up speed on this stuff, skiing on it was not exactly easy and required some adjustments. One would sink ankle-deep into the surface, making it comparable to skiing in soft spring snow on a hot day.

CONQUERING MOUNT MADISON SQUARE GARDEN

We showed well in Boston and even better in New York's Madison Square Garden, which had a considerably larger seating capacity and a more spacious and better-proportioned "ski hill." Once again, I'll let Harry Cross of the *New York Times* relate his impressions:

Skiing hysteria has seized New York with a tremendous grip. Madison Square Garden was again jammed to capacity last night to see leading professional and amateur skiers in the world zip down the man-made mountain covered with snow, which has sprung up on Eighth Avenue's diversified sports forum.

Both downhill runners and jumpers found the going a bit difficult but they didn't mind that. The skier is a species which nothing can stop.

The two distinct schools of skiing, the Central European and Norwegian, were definitively exemplified in the show last night.

The Austrians led the parade with Hannes Schneider the Grand Master of them all, 46 years old and "Ski Meister" who has exerted a tremendous worldwide influence in popularizing "controlled skiing." Accompanied by his two handpicked disciples, Otto Lang and Benno Rybizka, teachers at his prestigious Arlberg Ski School at St. Anton, the trio performed and delighted the audience with their graceful swings and turns on downhill skis, while Sverre Kolterud, one of Norway's leading skiers, displayed marvelous form in the jump and Norwegian style of downhill skiing.

One of the most talented of the skiing stylists in the show is Otto Lang. He has that grace and ease of motion that come only to the performer who has reached the peak of his athletic endeavor. Watching Lang in his slow motion authentic turns down the steep slope in total control, reveals a ski lesson of technical perfection. In turn he does the snowplow, snowplow turn, stem turn, and stem christiania. There is no break in the flow of action. His skiing is effortless and has the grace of a ski gull's flight.

It was certainly a novel experience for the three of us to find ourselves performing before a crowd of thirteen thousand people at each show, with powerful klieg lights following our every movement. There was no doubt that the show created an enormous impact. Eighty thousand people saw the show in New York alone, with the "standing room only" sign often posted at the box office.

Coincidentally, my book, *Downhill Skiing*, appeared in the bookstores at just about the same time. On the whole I was pleased with the results. It was a neatly presented, compact little book, easily understood even by a rank beginner. But as most authors can attest, there is always something to gripe about when faced with the finished product of one's efforts. My main complaint was the less-than-satisfactory reproduction of the illustrations. For economic reasons, the offset printing process was used instead of the more costly but superior gravure process.

Also, the publisher missed a golden publicity opportunity by not combining the promotion of the book with the shows in New York and Boston. Both Hannes and I would have been more than willing to autograph any number of copies bought by the public. Apparently Henry Holt and Company felt that this type of book had limited sales possibilities, as so many of the technical and teaching manuals had established a precedent. I myself was much too naive and inexperienced to know how to market, promote, and sell a book.

When the show ended, we were dined, wined, and feted by friends and representatives of the Austrian and Norwegian diplomatic corps. Realizing that time was running short, Hannes was anxious to return to St. Anton before Christmas. Benno was equally desirous to get to Jackson, New Hampshire, where he was to inaugurate his ski school. I hightailed it to the Pacific Northwest, where I was to open America's first official Hannes Schneider Ski School at Mount Rainier.

THE SCHOOL AT MOUNT RAINIER

My reception at Paradise Inn was as warm-hearted as I could have possibly hoped for. A bus with company executives and me brought us right to the entrance of the inn. The heavy snowfalls that would close the road from time to time during the winter months were yet to come. Alighting from the bus, I was greeted by reporters and photographers representing the Seattle and Tacoma papers and the staff of Paradise Inn. Ken Syverson, who had been in charge of skiing activities at Mount Rainier before I was hired, was also there. Ken had written to me to express his desire to join my ski school, and his credentials and references were reassuring. I would soon learn to appreciate him not only as a good skier and teacher but also as a likable young man. After spending a few days on the ski slopes with him, I knew he would be invaluable to me and designated him my right-hand man.

After settling into my quarters—the best the inn had to offer—the task at hand was to get the ski school launched. While I was in Tacoma, where the Mount Rainier operational headquarters were located, I had ordered the printing of tickets for ski school attendance, the distribution of pamphlets, and the installing of a large sign in front of the inn. Before my arrival, there had been an unexpected amount of free publicity in the newspapers, followed by more of the same as the school's opening weekend approached. I was amazed at the turnout for the first weekend, which augured well, I thought, for the future.

It became immediately apparent that Ken Syverson and I could not handle the number of people wishing to enroll in the ski school and that an apprentice teachers' program had to be initiated at once. This was not too difficult, since there were some hopeful young skiers around eager to become instructors. We took advantage of the weekday lull in ski school activities to push the instructors' program and select the most promising candidates for advanced training. Many of these would eventually form the nucleus of the Pacific Northwest's professional ski instructors corps and carve careers for themselves in the fast-developing sport of skiing, whether as teachers, ski school directors, sports shop owners, area operators, or hotel managers.

Gradually Paradise Inn attracted skiers for extended stays, as people developed the habit of prolonging their customary weekend visits to take advantage of a continuous series of lessons. The guests were mostly long-time residents of Seattle, Tacoma, and other surrounding cities. Many had families with children, which pleased me very much since I had always taken a special interest in teaching youngsters, often holding classes free of charge. The dividends I received from this gesture went far beyond the monetary gains I could have derived.

A case in point was the appearance of young Gretchen Kunigk, then about sixteen years old. In appearance and physique, Gretchen was a Mary Lou Retton type, or like Sonja Henie. She was petite and muscular, well proportioned, and blond, and she radiated charm. She enrolled in the school, and in only a short time I could tell that this young lady had the determination to go far in the skiing world. She grasped important technical points quickly and improved rapidly. At the time I had not even the slightest inkling of what the future might hold for her. Her well-balanced personality and poise, for one so young, impressed me. Furthermore, her infectious sense of humor made her a delightful companion. Though never romantically involved, we found our lives entwined for decades to follow.

I quickly found myself followed about Paradise Inn by a group of young skiers and employees who made me feel like some sort of guru surrounded by his disciples. They couldn't do enough for me, and if circumstances had made it necessary, they would surely have given me the shirts off their backs. Ski school attendance and the occupancy rate of the inn showed all the earmarks of a successful operation.

There was, however, one exception: the weather. There was plenty of snow all the time—too much, in fact. That meant successive days of heavy storms of blizzard proportions piling up snow at a prodigious rate. Periodically, we were cut off from the world until the storm cleared, and the sun came out, and the road was opened again. This situation naturally cut down on the ski school's revenue, especially when a storm hit over a weekend, which unerringly seemed to happen. However, other things kept me busy indoors. I had committed myself to write a biweekly ski column for the *Seattle-Post Intelligencer*, and this absorbed much of my free time.

Unexpectedly, I received a letter from Nelson Rockefeller one day, asking whether I could join him and a group of his friends to ski with them at Sun Valley, Idaho. Averell Harriman, president of the Union Pacific Railroad and founder of Sun Valley, was an old friend of the Rockefeller family. Sun Valley had catapulted onto the American skiing scene within an incredibly short time. It was touted as the *ne plus ultra* of ski resorts, if one believed all the hoopla. This invitation, tempting as it was, put me in a quandary. How could I justify leaving my school, even for a short while?

After weighing the pros and cons and discussing my dilemma with Paul Sceva, the director of Mount Rainier's operations, a decision was reached: by all means I should accept the invitation. Ken Syverson would be perfectly capable of carrying on in my absence. Besides, it would give me an opportunity to see what Sun Valley had to offer—and I should not overlook the publicity value of having been summoned there by Nelson Rockefeller. I accepted Nelson's invitation with pleasure.

SUN VALLEY INTERLUDE

Sun Valley! The name had singular ring to it. When Sun Valley opened its doors to skiers in December 1936, the event created a sensation. The press coverage was extensive, thanks to the astute and imaginative Steve Hannagan, a top man in the field of public relations. *Life* magazine gave it a front cover and featured a lengthy story, extolling its offerings in luxury, ideal terrain, snow, and sunshine in abundance. Overnight, Sun Valley had joined the ranks of the world-class ski resorts. There were a dozen or so comparable resorts in Europe, but none in the United States could match its scope and vision at that time. Sun Valley was a magnet for the "beautiful people," a meeting place for movie stars and moguls, chairmen and captains of industry, Greek shipping tycoons, and peripatetic playboys—and playgirls—of the international social set. All flocked to this wintry Shangri-la.

I found the story of its genesis fascinating. As president of the Union Pacific Railroad and also an avid sportsman, Averell Harriman faced the problem of extricating his railroad empire from the Great Depression. Foresight was always among Harriman's strongest characteristics, as he would prove time and again during a distinguished career as a politician, diplomat, and troubleshooter, serving under five presidents of the United States. What seemed quite logical to Harriman was, first, that the depression could not last forever, and second, that the Union Pacific, with its vast network of tracks and ultramodern rolling stock, needed more passenger traffic and wider use of its freight-carrying capabilities. Hence, the objective was to create a destination point—some outstanding attraction—that could only be reached by the Union Pacific.

Since Harriman had witnessed the rapid growth of skiing in Europe, he commissioned an Austrian skier, Count Felix von Schaffgotsch, to set forth in search of a suitable place in which to build America's premier ski resort. The directives given him were simple: find a place accessible only via Union Pacific; it should not be too close to any large city in order to avoid hordes of weekend skiers coming from a dense population center, and it should have a terrain suitable for every type of skier and plenty of snow and sunshine.

I had met Felix von Schaffgotsch at St. Anton before I came to this country. His brother Friedl had also been a teacher in the Schneider school during my tenure. Felix happened to be a handsome, well-liked young man who belonged to a lesser branch of Austrian nobility. Wherever he went, doors opened easily for him. The task of finding an ideal ski resort, however, turned out to be far more difficult than Felix had ever anticipated. He toured the snowy peaks of Colorado, Wyoming, Utah, and California. Although he found some places close to what he was looking for, there was always one of the vital factors missing.

Finally, he found by word of mouth exactly what he was looking for. Ketchum, Idaho, was a small town situated in an isolated valley in the Sawtooth Mountains. It also happened to be the end of a short spur line of the Union Pacific. A few ramshackle saloons, half a dozen dilapidated storefronts, and the Warm Springs Hot Baths were the main attractions of what had once been a flourishing, wide-open western town when silver mining was at its peak. With mine productivity dwindling and the price of sliver dropping alarmingly, Ketchum had gradually drifted toward oblivion. For the few miners still remaining, pickings were slim.

Sheep raising had developed into a source of income for some, and one of the most prosperous of these was Jack Lane, owner of the general store as well as town oracle and general factotum. With the arrival of the illustrious Austrian count, Lane sensed that something good might be in the offing. Inherently distrustful of city slickers and foreigners, he shrewdly advised the townsfolk to be nice to Felix, show him around, and give him a helping hand—but not to cash any of his checks! (Jack would do very well in later years with a well-stocked sporting goods store.)

After exploring the hills and mountains surrounding Ketchum, with Bald Mountain (9,150 feet) within walking distance and dominating the scenic tableau, Schaffgotsch's spirits soared. Here was the terrain, the snow in quantity and quality, and the sun shining day after day with salubrious warmth. Jubilantly he sent a telegram to Averell Harriman: "Eureka, I have found it! Come and see with your own eyes." Harriman came, and Sun Valley was born.

Purchasing the land posed no problems, and construction of the lodge began as soon as the frozen ground thawed enough to permit pouring of concrete foundations. Equally rapidly rose the poured concrete walls. The texture of the wood forms imprinted in the concrete was retained, giving the building an unexpected appeal. Plans for interior decor also moved along expeditiously. Marjorie Oelrichs, a personal friend of the Harrimans (she would later marry Eddy Duchin), was put in charge of the design and embellishment of the guest rooms, dining facilities, lounges, and kitchen. She supervised the selection of the best fabrics, furniture, accessories, carpeting, and more.

The next most important business at hand was to devise some way to haul skiers up the mountainside. Rope tows had just become popular, but they were ghastly—as if designed to pull one's arms out of their shoulder sockets. There were other Rube Goldberg-type contraptions in various experimental stages, but none was satisfactory as far as comfort, safety, and capacity were concerned. Still, anything was preferable to climbing back to the top of the hill after every run, which was time-consuming and exhausting. Credit must be given to the engineering department of the Union Pacific, with its headquarters and workshops in Omaha, Nebraska, for coming up with a solution. Thanks to the ingenuity of one staff engineer, James Curran, the problem was solved. Skiers around the world should be eternally grateful to him for his invention of the chairlift—perhaps the most popular, efficient, and universally accepted mode of uphill transportation for skiers and summer sightseers.

Sweltering in the heat of a Nebraska summer and an improvised workshop tucked away in a corner of the huge Union Pacific railroad yards in Omaha, Curran based his engineering design on the model of a continuous steel cable with attached hooks that was used to load heavy bunches of bananas onto a freighter. His chairlift prototype hung chairs from the cable instead. To simulate a skier standing on his boards on a slick snow surface, Curran had his first experimental human guinea pigs wear roller skates to coordinate with the forward speed of chair sliding under one's rump. The first chairlifts Curran designed soon went into construction at Sun Valley. They were a bit bumpy at first; the clamp holding the vertical bar to which the chair was attached rolled over the wheel guiding the cable with a thump and jarring jolt. In time, this shortcoming would be ironed out. No longer does one feel a bump when riding a modern chairlift.

On December 21, 1936, less than a year after the site was chosen, the much-heralded opening of Sun Valley took place. With a hand-picked staff, everything was ready. The hotel was packed with important guests and celebrities. The larders were filled with choice victuals and the finest cuts of meat. The wine cellar bulged with selected vintages from the best vineyards in Europe. The ski lifts on Dollar and Proctor Mountains were a marvel to behold.

The only thing missing was the most crucial element—SNOW! Opening day passed in a whirl of social festivities and outdoor activities feasible sans snow. So did Christmas, and still no snow. This posed an awkward dilemma for the management, considering the colossal advance publicity. By New Year's Eve snow finally arrived, but the memory of bare ground lingered, and as one might expect, other winters had similar close calls.

When I arrived at Sun Valley in February 1937, I could not have been more impressed. It was the peak of the season. Wherever one looked, there was a movie star: Gary Cooper, Clark Gable, Claudette Colbert, Ann Sothern, Ingrid Bergman, Jimmy Stewart, and many others. The who's who of the eastern social register were also well represented in the glamorous resort. Nelson Rockefeller arrived at Sun Valley with his entourage in great style in a private railroad car ("The Mayflower"), which undoubtedly had been arranged by Averell Harriman. And there I was, with a delightful and enthusiastic group of skiers under my tutelage. I felt as though I ought to be paying them for letting me come and see this mecca for skiers.

The gathering of the Rockefeller clan was a great success. We had a ball, so much so that I was asked to join them again next winter, same time, same place. This invitation puzzled Averell Harriman. "Why import an instructor all the way from the Pacific Northwest when there is a perfectly respectable ski school available to Sun Valley guests?" And indeed there was. Hans Hauser, my old friend from Salzburg with whom I had skied before my first season at St. Anton, had brought with him a group of his Salzburg buddies as instructors. Hans was a lovable man. He was also an outstanding and stylish skier. Over six feet tall, he cut a fine figure and always dressed according to the latest sartorial trend. The ladies fell for him, head over heels. He could have made a financially expedient marriage, such that he would never have to work again in his lifetime, but he preferred his freewheeling lifestyle.

Before we parted company, Nelson asked about the status of Jerome's film. I explained that the film was finished and ready for distribution but that because it was independently financed and produced, it was not easy to find a distributor. Most of the theater chains across the country were owned or controlled by major film studios in Hollywood, and it was in their interest to release their own films rather than buy independent films, whether they be features, documentaries, or short subjects. Warner Brothers, one of the leading majors at that time, had shown an interest in our ski film but the deal was far from final. The man in charge of the documentary and short-subject division at Warner Brothers was Norman Moray, a fine gentleman and an astute businessman. He had to be, in that cutthroat business.

Documentaries and short subjects were an integral part of a typical movie program at that time, which also typically included a star-studded feature and a newsreel. Generally, a feature film ran one and a half to one and three-quarters of an hour. What was added in order to make a two-hour program was simply considered filler and not regarded as potentially profitable. Since the value of filler was marginal, the rental fee paid by an exhibitor was correspondingly nominal. Some moviegoers anticipated seeing well-made documentaries, newsreels, and short subjects, and considered them an important part of a well-balanced, two-hour program.

Ski Flight seemed to fit well into this category—first because of the novelty of its subject matter and second because it was professionally crafted with loving care and no expense spared to make it an outstanding film. At best, Jerome could hope to break even and recoup his out-of-pocket expenses without any remuneration for his travail and artistic contributions. Nor would I be compensated for my appearance in front of the camera. No matter. At this point, the most important thing was to expose the fruit of our toil to the public. Once the film was completed, however, Jerome went on to other projects and showed no incentive in pushing to have the film booked into theaters. So I had taken it upon myself, with his consent, to act as a middleman.

I told all this to Nelson Rockefeller, who suggested that on my next visit to New York, already planned for the coming spring, I should contact Gus Eysell, general manager of Radio City Music Hall. It just so happened that Nelson Rockefeller was the president of this establishment. He said that Eysell could look at the film and weigh the possibilities of including it in a future program. This direct entrée to a major decision-maker of course was a coup. If Eysell's reaction proved favorable, it would be a cinch negotiating a deal with Warner Brothers. Jerome would be thrilled with the prospect of having his first film shown at Radio City Music Hall. It was a stroke of good fortune. I set all in motion when I returned to Mount Rainier, shipping a print to Eysell and waiting for his reaction.

THIN ICE: SONJA HENIE AND TYRONE POWER

No sooner had I returned to Paradise Inn when another surprise was sprung on me. The film studio Twentieth Century Fox was sending a full complement of technicians and two stars, Sonja Henie and Tyrone Power, to Mount Rainier to shoot a feature film entitled *Thin Ice*. The area would be used to simulate a location in the Alps. I was asked to help them, which of course I was willing to do. A shooting script was delivered to me so that I could size up required locations for the ski action sequences to be shot at Mount Rainier. The movie's plot was a simple one, a love story, naturally, with mistaken identities between two people enamored with each other.

Tyrone Power's star was in rapid ascendancy. After having played a few minor parts in Twentieth Century Fox films, he had caught the eye of Darryl F. Zanuck, respected head of the studio. Tyrone was indeed a handsome young man but was not the conventional "pretty boy" type like some of the other established stars. He had great poise, character, and a winning personality that showed through on and off the screen, especially when he broke into a captivating smile. Tyrone was well aware that he was just at the threshold of a promising career. Even though he had that indefinable "star quality" coming from a theatrical family—his father, Tyrone Guthrie Power, was considered one of the most accomplished thespians of his generation—there was a certain modesty about him. He was eager to learn and improve his acting style.

Conversely, Sonja Henie was what is commonly known as "a natural." She was already a star on ice, with multiple gold medals garnered in Olympic figure-skating competition. Acting came easily to her, from her constant exposure to the public. All that was asked of her was to portray herself. She was "all dimples and twinkles," and she knew how to display them effectively.

The film company arrived at Paradise Inn with tons of camera equipment, wardrobe trunks, skis, snowshoes, personal luggage, and assorted paraphernalia. The crew and cast were all bundled up, with their faces hardly showing, in an array of clothing and styles that must have emptied Twentieth Century Fox's wardrobe department and depleted Western Costume's extensive collection of garments. There was a sense of excitement and anticipation about them, such as an Arctic explorer might have felt when approaching the North Pole.

The success of such an expedition was in the hands of a few key people. Number one was the director, David Butler, captain of the ship, so to speak. He called the shots and ultimately made the decisions, often ones concerning minute details that one would never imagine posing a problem. David was one of the finest directors and a true gentleman who had steered many a Shirley Temple picture to success. A former football player, he was stocky and somewhat overweight but still remarkably agile.

The next man of importance was the unit manager, Ben Silvey. As second in command and in control of the purse strings, he was absorbed in all the cost factors. His job was to keep these under control and bring in the picture at the prescribed budget. Ben moved around with the ponderous gait of an adult hippopotamus and must have tipped the scales at close to three hundred pounds. He was not meant to be a "mountain man" and was ill-equipped for the demands of a severe winter climate. He was far better suited to the flat terrain of a Hollywood studio. On the job, he had the air of a steely-minded executive; nevertheless, he was a kindhearted man with a shrewd sense of humor.

The cameraman with his crew and the assistant director filled out the roster of key people making the feature film. I would learn soon that no one man by himself can make a film of any magnitude; it boils down to teamwork, and every member of the crew contributes in some way. While some contribute more noticeably than others, in the end they are of equal importance. They all have prescribed responsibilities and are depended upon to deliver what is expected from them.

Once the gear was stowed away and the crew installed in their assigned quarters, everyone settled down to wait. It was snowing, but everyone knew that eventually the storm would abate and the sun would come out and shine. Shooting could then begin at full speed. In the meantime, a few days' rest and time to acclimatize to the altitude was welcome.

But it kept on snowing, relentlessly, for a whole week. No matter. There was food and booze aplenty, with roaring fires ablaze at both ends of the lobby. There were games of all kinds to while away the time. During the second week, with no letup in the weather, tempers began to get a bit strained with symptoms of cabin fever showing. I could sense tension and impatience growing among the crew, and it concerned me greatly. Tyrone Power and Sonja Henie had no such problems, however. They had fallen in love with each other, madly and conveniently. Their appearances, as befitted the stars of a feature film, were rare. They kept mostly to their suite of rooms, with meals served in privacy. Luckily, there were no complications in this respect, since both these young and physically strong lovers knew how to spend their time well and wisely. What better pastime could there be?

At last one morning came the long-awaited break in the weather. A few spots of blue sky peeped through the swiftly moving clouds, and there were a few stray bursts of sunlight. The sight instantly buoyed the spirits of the company. It didn't look promising enough, though, to break out the camera gear and set up the first scene. I had a foreboding that this was only a temporary lull in the storm, but I realized it was the psychological moment for activity, as a morale-booster if nothing else. I suggested to David Butler that we put on snowshoes and climb up the mountain to reconnoiter some promising camera setups. Also we could look for a spot to display the Austrian shrine, which was the typical small wooden cross with a roof over it and an epitaph usually commemorating a disaster in which one or more lives were lost. David had never stood on a pair of skis or snowshoes, and for safety reasons I preferred to put him on snowshoes. To my surprise and consternation, Ben Silvey insisted on coming along with us. I knew this would never work; a man of his bulk, nonathletic and physically out of shape, simply could not make it at this altitude. But I did not protest, knowing full well that a few steps and a subsequent fall would spell the end of Ben's alpine conquest. I was proven right and felt greatly relieved, since I did not want responsibility for Ben's having a cardiac arrest.

Walking on snowshoes may look simple and quite natural. It is not. In fact, one feels rather clumsy until one develops the knack of moving forward without stepping on one or the other snowshoe. David did quite well, however. Having been an athlete at one time, he quickly fell into the rhythmical motion of snowshoeing, moving ahead quite readily as we worked our way up the hill. Alas, the sky began to close in again, and a dense fog enveloped us just as we arrived at a flat plateau I had visualized as the perfect spot to plant the portable shrine.

"Here's the place, David," I said. "The scenic panorama is out of this world."

Said David, "How can I tell? I don't see a goddamned thing. I'll just have to trust you."

"Trust me," I replied. "It's all here the way you have it in the script."

That was the end of that somewhat futile expedition, but at least it provided a break in the tedium.

Another time when the sun broke through timidly for a few minutes, Sonja and Tyrone also made an appearance, saying that they wanted to brush up on their skiing technique. Sonja had claimed all along that she was an experienced skier from way back, while Ty admitted modestly that he was just a beginner. One look at Sonja convinced me that no doubt she was one hell of a world-class skater, but as a skier . . . *nyet*, as the Russians would say. Certainly in her younger years she must have done a lot of cross-country skiing in Norway, but as for her skiing in Alpine terrain, I knew that virtually all the action sequences would have to be filmed with doubles. This would have been a wise decision in any case in order to avoid the possibility of an accident that could hold up production and cause a critical and costly delay in the schedule.

After three weeks of waiting and not one foot of film exposed, word came from the studio: "Pack up and head for home." Only the camera crew and a skeleton contingent of helpers would be left at Paradise Inn. On David Butler's recommendation, I was to take over direction of the scenes required. Very carefully he explained all the details to me, and together we dissected the script, scene by scene. It was a good indoctrination for my first assignment as a Hollywood director. Having worked with Jerome on his two ski films gave me a measure of confidence.

Ironically—and as always seems to happen—no sooner had the

homebound group left than the sun came out, to stay with us long enough to complete the assignment. There were delays and frustrations, however, mainly caused by the cumbersome method of moving equipment and crew members when changing camera setups. With the exception of a few skiers, everybody was on snowshoes. All the equipment had to be hauled on toboggans, carried by hand, or strapped to the backs of a handful of local Sherpas.

Finding a skier to double for Tyrone was relatively easy; to cast one for Sonja was more difficult. Gretchen Kunigk was the obvious choice, although she had not yet acquired the skill and ease of an expert skier. She was the exact same size as Sonja, and Sonja's wardrobe fit her to perfection. I could not say the same thing for myself. When an emergency arose, I donned Sonja's outfit to double for Gretchen. Seen from the front and at a great distance, with a blond wig and cute woolen ski cap propped on my head, I could get away with this masquerade while streaking down the mountainside. The rear view was considerably less photogenic, especially at close range. To accommodate my larger chest and waist measurements, all the seams had to be cut open with a razor blade and held together with safety pins. I had volunteered to do this stunt only with the strict understanding that no still photographs were to be taken of me "in drag." So none were taken—to my subsequent, lasting regret for having been such an old-fashioned prude. Today, I would treasure having even one photograph of this brief intermezzo.

OF SKIS AND SKI POLES

We struggled through the remainder of the winter season until the middle of April. In terms of snow conditions, we could have stretched the season into June, but by the end of March, "ski fever" had subsided with the first warm days of spring. People were anxious to start summertime activities. By that time, I, too, was longing to get off the mountain and into a sunnier climate.

David Butler had urged me to visit him in Hollywood, and his tempting invitation was most timely. But before I headed for southern climes, I had business to attend to in Seattle. First, I was working on a design for skis that would have my signature affixed to them. They would be made of hickory and have sectional strips of steel screwed to the running edges in order to carve smoother turns on hard-packed or icy snow. The measurements of tip, waist, and tail would conform to the dimensions of the best European models I had tested through the years. The local firm of Anderson & Thompson would be the manufacturer, and they hoped with this signature model to gain access to the national market.

I also had an innovation in ski pole construction in mind, a design that would replace the clumsy and poorly balanced wooden poles then in use. During my tenure at B. Altman in New York, I was browsing around the sporting goods department when I caught sight of a set of golf clubs with shafts made of gleaming metal. This immediately sparked my imagination, and I was determined to apply the same principle to a ski pole. It would be strong, flexible to a certain degree, and lightweight. The trademark stamped on the golf clubs was "True Temper," and I made a mental note to track down the manufacturers.

I found out that the shafts were made by American Fork and Hoe Corporation, a firm located near Cleveland, Ohio, which specialized in the manufacture of agricultural implements. I decided to present them with a schematic drawing, including an experimental triangular and slightly curved metal tip. It never occurred to me to think of applying for a patent before showing my idea to anyone. Shortly thereafter I contacted them by letter with my proposal and their answer was, "Come and see us. We are interested and will take care of all your expenses."

I met with them successfully en route to New York after I had seen David Butler in Hollywood. The True Temper division liked my proposal and accepted the basic design, suggesting a few minor modifications. They would proceed with production and have the poles ready for shipment by late summer. There was only one hitch: they did not want to become involved with final assembly of the pole, which required attaching the basket above the tip and the leather handle with a strap around the wrist for a firm grip. As long as I was tied up with Anderson & Thompson in producing my signature ski, it seemed logical that they would take on this final assembly of the pole and market it with the ski. I placed the call to Seattle. The company was not only willing but, in fact, eager to take on the poles, thereby adding an additional prestige item, with my name on it, to their line of ski equipment. My remuneration would be on a modest royalty basis. I was such a greenhorn in business dealings! I was in a position to corner the ski-pole market and assure myself of a lifelong annuity. I should have never entered into any negotiations without the advice of a lawyer, but for some reason I felt it was up to me to handle my affairs. How wrong I was.

In any case, I was proud to have pulled off this deal and to have a ski pole to complement my ski. The finished poles looked stunning and lived up to my expectations of performance. But alas, Anderson & Thompson did not have the marketing expertise nor the money to promote this product as it should have been. It sort of just fizzled out, and when World War II came along, all unnecessary steel items had to be eliminated for armament purposes. Ski poles fell into this category. To my regret I never pursued this brainchild of mine any further. Other metal ski poles came along after the war, Anderson & Thompson went out of business, and the upshot of it all is that I don't even have a pair of the original ski poles in my possession. I wish I had, just as a curio.

From New York I intended to embark on another trip to Europe. Though not planned originally for this summer, the trip was inspired by Bob Littler of Seattle. As owner of an exclusive store and local arbiter of fashion trends in men's apparel and a sharp dresser himself, Littler asked me to go shopping for him in Austria. He commissioned me to buy a collection of ski clothing and handmade boots for his select clientele or for anyone wishing to place an advance order for garments to be tailored according to individual measurements. He placed an impressive ad in the local papers announcing that I would be present at Littler & Company's stylish haberdashery for three days only to take orders personally.

I have always taken pride in the selection of my own ski apparel and equipment, and this habit was now paying big dividends with an all-expenses-paid trip to Europe and a chance to pleasurably earn some pocket money as a buyer for a store, without any risk on my part. The results of Littler's merchandising stratagem surpassed all expectations. I had a stack of orders in my hands when I left Seattle, and more were forwarded to my parents' address in Salzburg. After my return to Seattle in the fall, the whole collection sold out within two weeks, and that included a large number of items I had bought "on spec." Bob Littler was happy, and although not a skier himself, he sported some of the more colorful après-ski jackets and sweaters during social gatherings at Paradise Inn. One could not help but like the man. He was bright, gregarious, fair, and a very astute business man with imagination.

After my Hollywood visit and the American Fork and Hoe meeting, next on my agenda was heading to New York and seeing Gus Eysell at Radio City Music Hall. Eysell happened to be of Austrian ancestry and, although not a skier himself, was quite taken by what he saw in *Ski Flight*. He was willing to show the film with one of his coming attractions, but it would have to be shortened in order to fit into his programming. I foresaw no problem in re-editing the film to this length, since in some ways it was redundant. An audience of dedicated skiers could sit mesmerized and watch skiers in action for hours, but not so an average movie audience. They came to be entertained. Eysell, with his inherent instinct for showmanship, was quite right. Shortening the film would improve its impact. Better to leave an audience wishing for more than to lose their interest. When I told Norman Moray of Warner Brothers that he could count on a first showing of the film at Radio City Music Hall before its nationwide release to theaters, Moray worked out a deal with Jerome. Financially, it would just about cover his expenses, but the exposure and recognition would be artistically rewarding for him as well as putting a proud feather in my hat.

I spent a few days in New York as Nelson Rockefeller's house guest and marveled at his impressive art collection. Then I was on my way to Europe for a summer of leisurely travel and, of course, shopping. I planned to spend some time in Paris with Jerome and then we would drive his Bugatti to Cassis sur Mer, a small seaside village in the south of France, close to Marseilles. Jerome had bought a house in Cassis and had put a lot of work and money into converting the simple abode into a livable home with a studio in which he could paint in the luminous light of southern France.

It was good to be back in Paris, next to London, one of my favorite cities. Jerome had told me that Marina was also in Paris and counting on seeing me. Looking forward to this reunion, I contacted her as soon as I arrived. She invited me to come to dinner at her family's home in Rue d'Eylau.

To sit at a table with Feodor Ivanovich Chaliapin, surrounded by members of his family, mostly female, was indeed a memorable experience. Not only because he was a world-renowned operatic star, but more than that, he was an imposing man, larger than life in every respect. He had performed in every capital on the European continent, in Great Britain, America, Australia, South America, and other venues. His repertoire was astounding, and he had elevated opera to a new stature, fusing music, voice, and acting into a powerful new entity. His concept of the character he portrayed was considered at times revolutionary and controversial, since he broke away from the customary style of declamatory singing, in which a performer stood virtually still and used little facial expressions to convey the meaning of words and music. In this respect Chaliapin was undoubtedly an operatic genius.

When I saw him in Paris that evening in 1937, he was no longer performing on a regular basis. Occasionally he appeared at charitable fund-raising affairs, and I was invited to one such gala at the Paris Opera, where he sang excerpts from Modest Mussorgsky's *Boris Godunov.* What's more, he asked me to come with Marina to his dressing room and watch him put on his makeup to portray the ill-fated czar of all Russians. That in itself was a performance and ritual well worth seeing. With meticulous care, he proceeded like a master painter with deft brush strokes, applying layer upon layer of makeup until he had captured the haunted mien of the mentally tortured Czar. He would be singing the demanding hallucination scene that night, as he had innumerable times before, interpreting its meaning more fully than had any performer before him. It was a triumphant, riveting performance. He stood ramrod straight in his floor-length, heavily embroidered imperial robe and crown, well over six feet tall. He WAS the czar and ruler of all Russians. It is no wonder that he owned this role and had performed it all over the world to the total satisfaction of audiences everywhere. Alas, only a year after this memorable evening, Feodor Chaliapin died at sixty-five years of age, leaving behind him an extraordinary legacy. It was far too soon to have his brilliant career ended so abruptly.

Jerome and I left Paris, and when we arrived at Cassis sur Mer after an unhurried journey, I could see why Jerome fell for the spot. It was a small fishing village, unspoiled and as yet undiscovered. There was a well-protected, minuscule harbor with a lighthouse on a nearby promontory, and the idyllic view from Jerome's house overlooked this maritime panorama backed by pine-forested hills and rocky cliffs. No painter could resist transposing its constantly changing moods onto canvas. As always in a Hill house, there was the coming and going of friends, musicians, poets, painters, and just plain travelers, who, in passing through, called on Jerome. Conveniently, the Hotel des Roches Blanches was just across the street and could feed and house the overflow. One of its culinary specialties was "*Loup de Mer,*" a tasty fish caught by local fishermen. Music, poetry readings, discussions, games, and charades, spontaneously improvised by Jerome, were the entertainment. Much of the time was spent on the beach below the house in the spectacular setting of a rocky cove. Often Jerome would bring along his 16 mm camera and shoot scenes that he would eventually incorporate in a film of his. For me it was a summer of relaxation and total freedom.

Once my shopping chores were completed, the time came for me to embark again for my return trip to America. One of the first things I did when I arrived in New York was to check with Norman Moray on how the shortened version of *Ski Flight* looked. "I like it," he said. "Come and see for yourself." I was pleasantly surprised by what I saw on the screen. The film editors at Warner Brothers had done a thoroughly professional job. There wasn't really anything I missed and the film moved along with pace, leading to the final climactic run down the mountainside at Mount Baker. I was quite confident that Jerome would accept the changes in this shortened version, since he had retained a print of the original version for his personal archives and for posterity.

After seeing the edited version, Gus Eysell said he was ready to schedule the film for a January 1938 showing with Walt Disney's premiere of *Snow White and the Seven Dwarfs*. How much luckier could two fellows be than to have their first joint cinematic effort shown at the world's most renowned entertainment emporium in the illustrious company of the lovely Snow White and her seven droll companions?

There was also an invitation awaiting me in New York to participate in another winter sports show. I declined for a number of reasons. First, I felt once was enough, and second, I had another scheme in mind. It struck me that having an automobile was of the utmost importance in order to move expeditiously between places, as I was required to do. Financially, I was not in a position to purchase such a luxury. So, I figured, why not try and earn it by endorsing the product of an automobile manufacturer that was willing to enter into a trade-off?

I had my eyes set on a small Dodge convertible with a rumble seat. Through a bit of research, I got the name of the advertising company that handled the Dodge Division account of the Chrysler Corporation. I arranged a meeting in which I would present my idea of tying skiing, my name, and a Dodge automobile into an eye-catching ad, which would be a refreshing novelty. They went for it. All that remained was to work out the details of setting up the shoot, and they wanted it done in a hurry to take advantage of the approaching winter season. To find a place with real snow in a convenient location at this time of the year seemed unrealistic and impractical. "We'll set it up on a stage, cover the trees with snow, put a Dodge car on a piece of simulated road against a mountain backdrop—and we're in business," said the art director. As simple as that, and I sensed that the man knew his business and spoke based upon his past experiences of a shoot in snow country.

"And where would I fit in?" I asked, somewhat perplexed.

"Oh, that's no problem," I was told. "We'll have a couple of good looking broads in ski togs, each holding a pair of skis and you'll be standing nearby in your best Tyrolean ski outfit and presumably giving them some pointers about skiing."

And that is exactly the way the ad appeared full page in the *Saturday Evening Post* and other national magazines, except that one of the girls was sitting in the driver's seat of a Dodge sedan, leaning out the window. I stood next to her in a jaunty, nonchalant posture, skis slung over my left shoulder, Tyrolean hat and jacket on, giving my most fetching smile. The other girl was at my feet, sitting on top of her skis—doing what, I couldn't possibly fathom. Oh yes, there was a huge backdrop of Mount Rainier, a few scraggly pine trees here and there covered with ersatz snow-flakes, and enough of a piece of road covered with snow to accommodate the car. As phony as this Alpine tableau appeared to me on the set, it looked quite realistic in print with an elliptical insert showing me in an action shot in deep powder snow leaving a rooster tail behind me. Then of course came the plug, which was the sole and primary purpose of this whole effort:

> Otto Lang, champion skiing stylist and instructor, pictured above with his new 1938 Dodge, and also at left, says: "You'd think there would be few thrills left for me. I thought so, too, until I started driving my new Dodge to and from my ski schools at Mount Rainier and Mount Baker— 300 miles each weekend. That car is not only the finest performing Dodge ever built, but the most thrilling car to drive I've ever owned."

How true, how true—considering that this was indeed the first car I would own. A few weeks later I received a message at Paradise Inn from the Dodge dealer in Tacoma: "Come and get it! Your Dodge convertible is waiting for you." What a day it was when I took delivery of this vehicle. It had a robin's egg blue exterior (my favorite color) with beige leather upholstery and a rumble seat, much in style then, for extra passengers and luggage space. To me it was a small miracle and a deal accomplished by a straight swap without any money exchanged. I signed a release form and with a handshake the entire transaction was sealed.

A Second Year In The Northwest

While looking forward to my second winter at Mount Rainier, I felt a nagging apprehension, not knowing what to expect from the weather. Tons of snow falling for days on end, keeping skiers away from the mountain, could be ruinous for a ski school operation. I had opened another ski school at Mount Baker, where the terrain was actually better suited for skiers, with a great variety in open slopes, vertical drop, and pitch. It had all the basic ingredients, except for good weather. Mount Baker's existing accommodations were spare with only a limited of number of beds for overnight guests. But what the facility lacked in ambiance was made up by the people who ran the place. They were pioneers of a sort and true lovers of the sport, since there was little financial reward for their efforts. If they made it through the season without going deep into debt, it was considered a triumph.

Of course, there were no lifts to take skiers up the hill, not even jerry-built rope tows, such as the one that came into being at Mount Rainier that winter. There, two local gentlemen, Webb Moffett and Chancey Griggs, pooled their savings and installed a rope tow, consisting of a used automobile engine with a pulley attached to it that advanced a one-inch-thick rope over a series of automobile wheel rims. The rims were fastened to high poles set in a straight line, leading to a flat spot on top of the hill. A skier had to grab the often icy or, at other times, wet and slippery rope, which raced through a gloved hand until friction tightened the hold, similar to the clutch in an automobile. Then the skier either began to move slowly or, if he grabbed the rope too firmly, shot forward, as if launched from a cannon, to fall flat on his face. This would obstruct the next skier's progress, who fell on top of the one already prostrate, entangling his skis and struggling to get out of the way. There was an infinite variety of prat- and pitfalls, like devious traps, along this journey, and it was always a relief to arrive at the top. At the terminus a skier would let go of the rope, his fingers cramped and shoulders stiffened from the long haul up the hill. As primitive as this conveyance was it was still preferable to laboriously climbing up the hill. The fare: $.25 a ride or $1.50 for the day.

Besides weather and facilities, another problem facing me was not only to provide additional ski instructors for Mount Baker but also to commute between the two places on alternating Mondays, usually the slowest day as far as the ski schools were concerned. This meant leaving one place late Sunday afternoon, spending the night in Seattle, and arriving at my destination on Monday at noon. Considering roads and weather, the trip was an adventure at times. One of my pleasures was driving my own automobile, which I had baptized the "Blue Beetle." It was a reliable workhorse, albeit not the best vehicle for winter driving with its canvas roof top. It never failed me.

Occasionally, I would make an appearance as a guest jumper at a competition, usually laying the track for the opening jump. Seattle was a stronghold of nationally acclaimed Norwegian jumping competitors, and many became good friends of mine—Olav Ulland, Hjalmar Hvam, and Olav Rodegard, to name just a few. Olav Rodegard, in fact, developed into one of my prize instructors. He was a picture-book stylist and a superb teacher, and he stayed with me for many years. These clannish Norwegians chided me about being one of those sissy Austrian downhillers, afraid to take a man-size jump. I proved otherwise and gained their respect when I went over the giant hill at Leavenworth. I was nervous and scared, having been out of practice for some time, but it changed the whole picture. Some even came to me to brush up on downhill technique. They were all splendid athletes and gifted skiers, as I assured them, but few knew anything about the mechanics of a turn. I told them so frankly, and they reluctantly became acquainted with the basic snowplow turn, which they soon realized was the foundation of a successful

Alpine technique.

Carting along a pair of jumping skis added to my load as I drove back and forth between places. Much longer and heavier than my regular downhill skis, the jumping skis jutted out from the rumble seat. Equally cumbersome, the one luxury I hated to be without was my portable, electrically operated Victrola, one of the first on the market, plus a stack of heavy 78 rpm records, mostly of a classical nature, which were my favorites. Inconvenient as it was, hauling the Victrola was well worth the effort, providing me with quiet moments of repose after a long day's workout on the slopes.

Staying overnight in Seattle was a pleasure and a treat. Johnny Graham, co-owner and manager of the Camlin Hotel, often put me up in the presidential suite on the top floor of the hotel or, if it happened to be occupied, its equivalent. These accommodations were luxurious and far beyond my means if I had had to pay for them. Luckily they were complimentary.

Aside from my duties as director of two ski schools, there were other projects, such as writing for newspapers and magazines, demanding my full attention. I was even talked into appearing on stage and giving a dissertation on skiing, highlighted by two ski films I had on loan from the Austrian government. I had never done that kind of an appearance before and couldn't help but be nervous. Fortunately, I committed myself to only two of these shows, one at the Metropolitan Theater in Seattle and the other in Bellingham, close to Mount Baker. In both instances, the houses were packed, and if I had wished to do so, I could have taken the show on the road as an innovator in this type of entertainment and as a predecessor to the inimitable John Jay, Warren Miller, "Doc" Frank Howard (a dentist by profession), and others who succeeded in making a respectable living out of this art form.

In fact, Warren Miller started out as one of my instructors at Sun Valley. After an adventurous interlude as the first bona fide "ski bum," he rose to become recognized as the master among his cinematic peers and was known as "king of the ski flicks." As it happened, two of his students were executives of Bell & Howell Corporation, makers of a popular 16 mm camera by the same name. Warren talked them into loaning him a camera, and therein lies the start of a fabulous career. After producing more than forty-five crowd-pleasing films, he is still going strong. The inventiveness of his camera crews is outstanding, as is his commentary and the rhythmically pounding original musical scores and his acerbic one-liners. The late autumn screenings of his films are the ski world's annual kickoff for the coming winter.

Sadly, I was unable to attend the premiere of *Ski Flight* at Radio City Music Hall. Traveling to New York by train in those days was time-consuming, and I simply had too many commitments. Gus Eysell was thoughtful enough to send me the official program, and in looking through it, I could conjure up the spectacle, remembering the tingle down my spine when the house lights at Radio City dimmed to the sounds of invisible musicians tuning their instruments, and then the one-hundred-man orchestra, elevated by a hydraulic lift, appeared in full view. In the hushed silence, Maestro Erno Rappé raised his baton to conduct a selection from Gounod's opera *Faust*. Then followed the elaborate stage show, featuring, of course, the fabulous Rockettes. The main attraction in the program Eysell sent me was the world premiere of Walt Disney's *Snow White and the Seven Dwarfs*. I could not have wished for a more fitting vehicle to accompany *Ski Flight*. The show ran for a house record of six weeks, and *Ski Flight* received its share of accolades for the novelty of its subject matter and lyrical photography, backed up by the splendor of Mounts Rainier and Baker. And there I was, bigger than life, gliding down pristine snowfields on the biggest screen in existence in front of an audience of five thousand.

I couldn't help but think of myself as a young boy, watching the Norwegian mining engineer carving telemark turns on the snow-covered hills near Sarajevo. I also thought of the film snippets I collected in the projection booth of the theater in Zenica and of the scolding I received from the mother superior as a result of my activities. I was at the threshold of a dream partially fulfilled, with a career in filmmaking still in the nebulous future. But it was an auspicious beginning, even though I couldn't enjoy the full impact of the thrill until a month or so later, when a special premiere of *Ski Flight* was arranged in a Seattle movie theater.

COACHING THE HUSKIES

On the shortest possible notice, I was asked by the athletic department of the University of Washington to coach its ski team, which was scheduled to compete against Dartmouth College, a powerhouse among eastern collegiate skiing teams, at Sun Valley during the last week of December 1937. The contest would comprise downhill, slalom, and cross-country racing, with ski jumping not counting for points but included as an exhibition event. That would give me about eight days to prepare the Huskies for this first encounter, billed and publicized widely as a crucial test between two colleges representing East against West.

When I met the squad at Mount Rainier for our first workout on snow, I was pleasantly surprised to find them in excellent physical condition and in high spirits. I was also aware that with barely a week's time to train them, my role would be primarily that of a supportive morale booster and team manager. The university's ski program was still in its infancy, and the team was woefully lacking in technical skill and competitive experience.

Dartmouth, on the other hand, had already established a winning tradition, well supported and subsidized by their athletic department. For years their team had been coached by Otto Schniebs, a renowned teacher and a stickler for mastering the fundamentals. He was succeeded by Walter Prager, a stellar Swiss racer and experienced mentor. His was a seasoned and battle-tested squad that dominated interscholastic meets in the East. The star of their team was Dick Durrance, a versatile athlete still in his formative years, who shortly thereafter would become a world-class racer and an American legend.

Here is an excerpt from my column in the *Seattle Post-Intelligencer.*

The Husky team had an intensive series of workouts with downhill, slalom, and cross-country on their daily schedule. My endeavor was to keep the squad in good condition and instill into its members a modicum of confidence, without any radical changes in their inherent style of skiing. The time was much too short to experiment and try to force upon them a risky transformation. It would have only confused the boys.

We managed to get in a few high-speed runs under fine weather and snow conditions from the top of Pinnacle Peak, across the valley from Paradise Inn. The objective was "to let the skis go" and keep them flat on the snow, while lowering the body posture into an aerodynamic configuration to reduce the wind resistance factor.

The following days I laid out various combinations of slalom gates at nearby Alta Vista, a terrain ideally suited for such a purpose. Most of the time was spent in working on technical details to "smooth out" the turns and eliminate the harsh jerkiness. Jerking the skis around results in a loss of time, which may be only a matter of split seconds, but multiplied in repetition these can add up to precious full seconds. It takes but a few ticks of the clock to win or lose a race.

After timing by stopwatch each of the aspirants during practice sessions in the three events, the final selection of the six members to form the team was decided upon. Five would participate in each event, of which the first four finishers would count for points. The sixth man would be held in reserve in case of injuries or illness. The team shaped up as follows in alphabetical order: Bob Barto, Bob Higman (Captain), Otis Lamson, Walt Page, Ragnar Quale, Lonnie Robinson.

The squad left their training quarters on Friday to spend Christmas at home and, except for a light workout on the U. W. Stadium running track on Sunday morning, they won't be standing on skis until they arrive on Tuesday at Idaho's highly touted winter oasis.

Arriving at Sun Valley on a sunny morning with a fresh layer of much-needed snow covering the slopes, the Husky team had its first startling glimpse of that glamorous resort. They had never seen anything like it before. Averell Harriman, keenly interested in the successful organization of this event, had arranged to roll out the red carpet for both teams and give their members VIP treatment.

At first glance, the nattily dressed Dartmouth contingent, in their uniforms and up-to-date equipment, was impressive and a bit intimidating compared to our haphazard "come as you are" dress code and antiquated ski equipment. The impression was borne out during a joint practice session on the cross-country course since most of the Dartmouth team seemed over six feet tall and devoured the terrain with long rhythmical strides.

Dick Durrance, the shortest of this group at five feet, five inches, unfortunately was out of action. The day before on a downhill practice run, he was following his patented formula—that the fastest and shortest route between two points is to take it straight—and took a spectacular double somersault fall, which resulted in a wrenched knee and twisted ankle. To have him out of the competition would be an advantage for our team, even though we genuinely regretted being deprived of seeing him compete. Throughout his career and late into his life, Dick had proven himself to be an exemplary sportsman and most likable companion. His style of skiing, quite individual and tailored to suit his physique, hardly changed at all and served him well.

On Friday morning the Dartmouth Five, consisting of Dave Bradley (Captain); Steve Bradley, John Litchfield, and Warren and Howard Chivers, sauntered confidently up to the starting line of the cross-country course, poised and ready. These Dartmouth runners literally galloped away with the four best times. Not quite as devastating were the results of the slalom race on a masterly course laid out by Hans Hauser, the Sun Valley ski school director. I had hoped after this somewhat encouraging showing that the Huskies would do even better in the downhill, but it was not to be. Again the Dartmouth boys showed their superiority by grabbing the first four places. The University of Washington suffered a resounding defeat, but nevertheless it was an invaluable learning experience for the team. There were no excuses or regrets expressed, and the camaraderie between the two competing squads augured well for repeat encounters. Mine was not an auspicious debut as a coach, but it did give me much hope for the University of Washington ski team, with plenty of talent on hand and an ample backup pool of promising young competitors to draw from.

Personally, I had one of the nicest experiences during my short stay at Sun Valley. A bunch of us fellows were having a great time practicing on the jumping hill at Ruud Mountain. I took my turn in the constant flow of jumpers sailing down the hill, which was impeccably engineered and groomed, allowing a maximum distance of 160 feet. It was virtually "fall proof." With a chairlift running right alongside, it was the neatest layout I had ever seen. While I was waiting for my next turn to jump, a solidly built, stocky gentleman turned around toward me and said in an unmistakable Norwegian accent, "Yee'd make a gead yumper. Are yee one of those college hot shots?"

"No," I said, "I'm only the coach of the University of Washington ski team." I gave him my name and he just looked at me for a while and said, "Yomping Jimminy, I'll be darned. I've heard a lot about yee. My name is Alf—Alf Engen, that is." It so happened that I had also heard a lot about Alf Engen, a premier ski jumper who, with his two brothers, Kare and Sverre, had cleaned up in jumping competitions across the country. All three of them also excelled as soccer players. "Why are we wasting our time here?" Alf asked, "Would yee mind letting me follow yee down Dollar Mountain for a few runs?" So we did, by taking the next shuttle bus to Dollar Mountain, just a few miles away.

From the first turns I saw him make, looking back over my shoulder, I realized that he was an extraordinary talent who had a natural affinity with snow—not so surprising, since he had grown up in Norway and most likely had been put on skis when he was a mere toddler. His turns were fluid and smooth, caressing the snow, a pure joy to watch. From that day on, Alf and I became friends and our paths crossed often through the years. I followed his meteoric career as a racer, competing in both Nordic and Alpine events. His crowning achievement, aside from his sizable collection of jumping trophies and hill records, was winning the U.S. combined four-way championship, the ultimate hallmark of a great athlete. After phasing out his competitive ambitions, he became a first-rate instructor and director of the ski school at Alta, Utah, holding that post until he was past eighty. Even at that age, he still skied with vigor and style. He was looked upon as the guru of deep-powder-snow skiing, for which Alta was famous.

During this visit to Sun Valley I also met Averell Harriman. With his lean aristocratic stature and handsome face, he played the majordomo to perfection. He had a modest private cottage built for himself and his family. Kathy, his youngest daughter, was an avid skier, and between the two of them, they kept a close watch on the management, always striving to improve things with innovative touches. Averell invited and appreciated constructive suggestions but had a raw nerve when anyone mentioned the perennial scarcity of snow during the Christmas holidays. I made the mistake of casually referring to this shortcoming in one of my newspaper columns, commenting that a little more of it would be beneficial in covering up the snarling rocks sticking out on some of the runs. Even though I gave the highest praise to Sun Valley as a superior destination resort, my remark did not sit well with Averell, and he expressed his pique in a letter referring to our opposite dilemma in the Pacific Northwest, whose surfeit of snowstorms left little room for benevolent sunshine such as Sun Valley offered. *Touché!*

I told Averell before I left that I would be back again in February to ski with Nelson Rockefeller and his party. This obviously pleased him, but I also sensed a fleeting moment of displeasure in his mien as he wondered why Nelson, his good friend, found it necessary to send for me all the way from Mount Rainier. Fortunately, gentleman that he was, Averell Harriman never permitted such picayune matters to be carried on as a grudge, as our subsequent relationship in future years would prove.

MOUNT HOOD

From Sun Valley I took an overnight train to Portland, Oregon, where I was met at the station by one of my instructors to be driven up to Timberline Lodge at Mount Hood for my week in residence there, where I had opened a third ski school. Mount Hood had become an outstanding year-round tourist attraction. Its scenic grandeur was equally as impressive as that of Mount Rainier and Mount Baker, although not quite as dramatic and massive in appearance. But Mount Hood had one superior asset—the recently opened Timberline Lodge. One of the few structures in the mountains of the Pacific Northwest built for winter use, it had the looks of a veritable castle, able to withstand the fiercest winter storms.

Credit President Franklin D. Roosevelt (who attended the grand opening of the lodge the previous summer) to have included this imposing structure in the Works Progress Administration program. What is so attractive about this mountain lodge is, first of all, its architecture, echoing the symmetrical purity of the volcanic peak rising behind it to 11,245 feet. Wherever possible, indigenous material was used in the exterior structure and in the interior decor of the hotel. The huge beams supporting the roof were hand hewn with ancient tools. Rough blocks of stone were artfully fashioned into walk-in fireplaces and dividing walls. Wrought iron fixtures and metal accessories, from chandeliers to copper ashtrays, as well as fabrics for drapes, bedspreads, wall hangings, furniture, and upholstery coverings were all handmade following traditional designs of the ancestral Indian cultures of the area. And so it went down the line in every detail, giving the interior amenities such as bedrooms, lounges, dining facilities, and the famous Blue Ox Bar, with its huge stained-glass mural, a cachet all their own. To stay at the lodge with its luxurious appointments was a special treat. I looked forward to enjoying the comforts of one of the spacious suites made available to me.

When I opened my ski school at Mount Hood, I was faced with the same weather conditions as at Mount Rainier and Mount Baker. Luckily, however, the mountain had a few wind-protected glades that made it possible to conduct classes even in inclement weather. I gave my full attention to the daily classes. There were also plans afoot to hold the U.S. Nationals in downhill and slalom at Mount Hood in late March 1938—an event that would attract the cream of American racers and also elite European racers, many of whom had come to this country as ski instructors. I was asked to lay out the courses for both races. In scouting the terrain around and below Timberline Lodge, I skied a huge bowl, down the road but easily accessible, which I felt would lend itself perfectly for a challenging slalom course, as good as any in Europe. The downhill course was a problem since it would have to run straight down the wide-open slopes, starting halfway up to the pointed peak of Mount Hood, which would result in speed but would not be much of a test of skiing ability, due to the lack of variety in the terrain. We compensated for this with a number of strategically placed control gates that forced the racers to make some high-speed turns.

I was fortunate in having young Ariel Edmiston as my deputy at Mount Hood. I could always rely on his good judgment and cheerful personality in dealing with people. At Mount Rainier I still had Ken Syverson with me, who was technically the best instructor to come out of the Pacific Northwest. At Mount Baker I had Millet O'Connell from St. Paul, Minnesota, highly recommended to me by Louis Hill, Jerome's older brother, who knew about skiing and teaching from our days at St. Anton. Milt, though not an eye-catching skier, had a solid knowledge of the fundamentals and the ability to pass it on to his students. He was a college graduate who did not aspire to make teaching skiing his life's vocation; his ultimate objective was, after a winter sabbatical or two of skiing, to continue with his studies and eventually become a lawyer. This he did, with great success. Each of these men had a number of assistant instructors working for them in order to divide the students into groups according to their individual proficiency. This was a tried and proven system for speedier progress.

More and more I realized that mine was not an ideal situation. I felt all along that I was trying to be in too many places at the same time and committing myself to too many extracurricular activities. After all, my primary objective was to teach skiing and run my ski schools. I longed to stay in one place for a while. I had very little time for personal pleasures, such as reading a good book or listening to music. And I had no intimacy. Young and in the public eye, I was surrounded by attractive women, but for various reasons I avoided becoming involved with any of them.

A REUNION WITH FRIEDL PFEIFER

As planned, I made another quick trip to Sun Valley to meet with Nelson Rockefeller and his party. This time there was no shortage of snow such as I had encountered on my two previous visits. And, as I had heard even before I arrived, a dramatic and sudden change had taken place. Hans Hauser and his instructors from Salzburg were no longer in charge of the ski school.

Friedl Pfeifer, hailing from St. Anton and a former member of Hannes Schneider's staff, had been designated by Averell Harriman himself to take over. Friedl had chosen as his assistant Peter Radacher, a boyhood friend of mine from Salzburg. Though small in size, Peter was a determined and successful racer. He also had a happy disposition and at the same time was a serious instructor. Friedl had made his reputation as a stellar world-class competitor in downhill and slalom racing, and he had a trunk full of trophies and medals to prove it.

I wrote about Friedl for my column in the *Seattle Post-Intelligencer.*

> The ski school under Friedl Pfeifer, the newly appointed director who replaced Hans Hauser, is working efficiently with classes filled to capacity.
>
> The teaching has immeasurably improved in concept, style, and a unified plan of progression since Friedl Pfeifer took over.
>
> Since Friedl came to Sun Valley with and, specifically, as the coach of the American Ladies Olympic Ski Team, he will now have to find some free time in his busy schedule to devote to his wards, a most attractive group of young ladies, attired in their becoming official uniform of provocative long red stockings and short, dark blue skirts. He is so proud of his team and so are they of their coach.

Although I was not aware of it at the time, this unexpected reunion with Friedl would lay the foundation for another important turning point in my life.

Friedl was born and raised on a farm in St. Anton. Of the fourteen children born into the Pfeifer family, only twelve survived. Friedl went through grade school fitfully, not being able to establish a rapport with his teacher, a vindictive and narrow-minded priest. Part of the problem was that Friedl, rather than going to mass, went skiing, which, as he grew older, became an all-consuming obsession. Very soon it was apparent that he was the fastest and technically most advanced skier among his peers. He began to win races and people began to notice his exceptional talent. One of these was Hannes Schneider, who offered the youngster a job as an apprentice instructor, the lowest position in the ski school pecking order. As Friedl said later, "My job was mainly to pick up the stragglers after classes ended in the afternoon."

Friedl was not an easy mixer, and it took awhile for him to make friends among the clan of somewhat haughty ski instructors at Hannes's school. But with his racing career blossoming, he was soon awarded the recognition he deserved. Because Friedl was frequently away at races, rather than have him teach classes, Hannes assigned him as a private instructor and skiing companion for those individuals who requested such a service. This inevitably brought him into contact with the well-to-do. He learned the manners of a gentleman and broadened his experience far beyond his modest background.

Although Friedl and I worked together in St. Anton for a number of winters, we were not close friends. He was gone most of the time, covering the racing circuit all over Europe, and came home only sporadically, laden with honors and trophies. Then in 1935 I left for America, partly due to the specter of Adolf Hitler's political ambitions and inexorable climb to power. All was not well at St. Anton, where a small core of avowed Nazi followers was spreading discontent in the ski school and among the people of the village. Friedl was one of the few among Hannes's loyal instructors who would have nothing to do with Nazism. He, too, decided to leave Austria. He did so reluctantly, but wisely.

Ernst Skardarassy, a friend of Friedl's who taught skiing in the Zürs area, across the mountains from St. Anton, had been to Australia during its winter to teach skiing. He was about to depart again for another stint and invited Friedl to join him, assuring him of a job and good money to be made. By this time Nazi authorities were in control of Austria. Through Skardarassy's connections he managed to get an exit visa, and although there were some anxious moments at the border, they got out of the country and were soon on their way to Australia via the Suez Canal. This was farewell to Austria for Friedl. He had made up his mind that as long as Hitler was in power, there was no point in his returning home, only to be forced to join the Nazi military ranks.

After a successful winter in Australia, Friedl and Ernst disembarked at San Francisco, California, on their return journey. Ernst was on his way home to Zürs, Austria, where he had a small hotel to run. Friedl decided to look for a position in the burgeoning ski world of the eastern United States. He had friends and valuable connections in New York. Enterprising and curious as both men were, they decided to buy a second-hand automobile and drive across the country. One of the obilgatory stops on their itinerary was Sun Valley. Once they arrived there, Friedl looked around to see what all the shouting was about and what Sun Valley really had to offer. He did not think much of the skiing terrain. The lodge, although architecturally pleasing and luxuriously appointed, stood isolated from the ski slopes at Dollar, Ruud, and Proctor Mountains and could only be reached by a shuttle bus circulating between places. Sun Valley was not perfect.

Nevertheless, Friedl saw some possibilities in regard to Sun Valley's future development, even though he was perplexed that Count Felix von Schaffgotsch had chosen this location. He also wondered why Felix, a man not qualified in any way as a skier nor as an alpinist, should have been given the responsibility of finding a suitable location for a major ski resort. From his casual observations, Friedl Pfeifer calculated that it would take an awful lot of money and much work to develop Sun Valley into a world-class destination. His eyes were magnetically drawn time and again toward Bald Mountain, another few miles away. It was massive, 9,150 feet high, heavily forested but with a series of wide, treeless glades and huge open bowls above timberline. Baldy, in Friedl's opinion, would be the salvation of Sun Valley. As it turned out, he was right.

Arriving at New York after an enlightening and adventurous journey, with the car sold at a profit, Ernst took off for Austria and Friedl was on his own. He contacted Alice Kiaer, a seasonal habitué of St. Anton and close friend of Hannes Schneider. The daughter of Walter Damrosch, eminent musicologist, social lion, and conductor of the New York Philharmonic Orchestra, Alice knew everybody in *Who's Who*. She was also the godmother and self-appointed patroness of the U.S. Ladies' Olympic Ski Team. With Europe cut off due to the incendiary political situation, Alice had to find an alternate facility suitable as a training ground for her team. It was quite natural that her friend and fellow ski aficionado Averell Harriman was willing to help out by offering the amenities of Sun Valley to the ski team, with much of the cost to be absorbed by Sun Valley management and the Union Pacific Railway. Averell, with Steve Hannagan, the New York-based public relations man in charge of the Sun Valley account and an astute flack in promoting high-class resorts (Miami was his crown jewel), sensed that this would be a golden opportunity to add to the luster of Sun Valley.

With Friedl's timely appearance, the matter of finding a coach for the team was solved. There wasn't a more qualified person within reach, and Friedl was glad, willing, and ready to accept the position. Alice introduced Friedl to Averell Harriman, and they took an immediate liking to each other. Averell listened attentively as Friedl told him his impressions of Sun Valley; Friedl gave a forthright and honest appraisal of what in his opinion needed to be done without delay. Averell was well aware that he was talking to a man with extensive knowledge of a number of well-established ski resorts in Europe, acquired during his racing career, and he hoped to take advantage of his expertise.

A good deal of publicity was triggered by Friedl's arrival at Sun Valley with the Ladies' Olympic Team. And, of course, Averell was also there with his daughter, Kathy, to greet them. Now Friedl had the opportunity to present to both of them two ideas of what he visualized should be done to the resort. First, he said, develop Mount Baldy into a skiing mountain by cutting a number of ski trails through the dense forest. Second, build a chairlift in three separate but adjoining sections to the top of the mountain. Harriman and his daughter were convinced and determined to begin these improvements as soon as the snow melted in late spring.

A problem arose in pinpointing the location for a day lodge on the mountain, an absolute necessity for providing shelter, nourishment, and rest room facilities. The Union Pacific wanted it—if it had to be built—at the very top of Baldy, exposed to the whims of the elements. Friedl and Averell opted for a spot on an elevated knoll above the terminal of the second lift, within easy reach of the third loading station. They argued that if the third section of the lift had to be shut down during a storm, a day lodge on the mountaintop would be unreachable and its purpose nullified. Grudgingly, the powers ensconced in Omaha acquiesced and approved a structure to be built in the octagonal shape of a roundhouse, similar to the type used in railroad yards to turn around locomotives. The Roundhouse it would be called thereafter, and it became a popular and strategic meeting place on the mountain.

When Averell Harriman asked Friedl for a his candid evaluation of the Sun Valley Ski School, his opinion, though presented in diplomatic terms, was negative. Friedl liked Hauser well enough as a man and respected him as a former ski-racing opponent, but he did not think that he was cut out to be, nor that he particularly liked, being director of the ski school. Of Hauser's instructors Friedl had a considerably lower appraisal. They were certainly far below the caliber of instructors he had worked with at St. Anton, who were dedicated first to their profession and who were careful to be discreet in their personal lives. Not so Hauser's group, some of whom were chronically late for classes, often appearing unkempt and unshaven after a night's debauchery. As teachers, Friedl rated them as inadequate, lacking experience and the traditionally self-imposed discipline of the profession.

Averell's solution was a simple one: he asked Friedl to take over the ski school then and there. With some reluctance Friedl accepted, knowing full well that he would have to make some drastic changes. Hans Hauser could stay on as an instructor if he cared to do so, but as far as the rest of his staff was concerned, those who wished to continue teaching would have to conform to a new regimen of stringently enforced rules, including a nightly 11 P.M. curfew and strict observance of punctuality and personal grooming.

Of course, my reunion with Friedl could not have been more amicable. We had much to talk about, and he assured me how happy he was with the turn of events in his life. I was glad he found a niche in an environment he liked and a secure position with enormous prestige. He was in complete charge of all activities concerning skiing and was intimately connected with the future of Sun Valley. Friedl showed no displeasure in my appearance as a guest instructor for the Rockefellers. He knew from his own experience that certain clients, who liked to have their own private instructor, counted on and made arrangements far in advance to have him available. Albeit brief, ours was a most joyous reunion, and we parted closer friends than ever before.

CALIFORNIA, HERE I COME!

When the time came to close up shop in the Pacific Northwest with the termination of the 1938 ski season, I made plans to move south, longing for California sunshine. My long-range plans for settling down permanently were uncertain. I was still trying to find myself and consolidate my ultimate goals in life. A primary objective and driving motivation was to escape the poverty and privations my parents had endured for so much of their lives. I dreamed of having a home of my own, if ever so small, in an idyllic spot. I hoped to get married eventually and have a family. I had always been drawn toward children with genuine affection.

These things were in the future. For the moment, I intended to make a leisurely drive south to San Francisco along the spectacular route skirting the Pacific Ocean. I would spend a few days with Maud Hill at Pebble Beach (her marriage to Larry Dorcy, alas, was disintegrating and headed for divorce) and continue as far south as the Mexican border. I thought that after a few weeks of thawing out in a salubrious climate, I might return to Europe for the summer. Jerome and Maud had already booked passage on the *Ile de France* and planned to spend most of the summer in France and Austria; they urged me to join them. It was certainly tempting. I had saved practically all of my winter's earnings and had a bank account with $1,500 in it, which to me, in 1938, was a small fortune. I knew that my job in the Pacific Northwest was awaiting my return in December, so for the first time in my life I felt financially secure.

I learned that on the island of Coronado, across the bay from San Diego and reachable by ferry boat, was a splendid hotel named after the island. On the west side it faced the Pacific Ocean, and on the east Glorietta Bay, which separated the island from the mainland, with San Diego as a picturesque backdrop. There were tennis courts, a golf course, and an outdoor heated swimming pool of Olympic proportions. That was all I needed to know.

THE HOTEL CORONADO

When I pulled up in front of the Hotel Coronado, I was favorably impressed. It was much larger than I had anticipated, built entirely of wood, with turrets, mansard windows, and balconies encircling its structure, all embellished with imaginative curlicued scrollwork so characteristic of Victorian architecture. The exterior was painted a gleaming white and accented by a red-tiled roof. Enhanced by grassy slopes, tropical vegetation, high palm trees gently swaying in the ocean breeze, and a profusion of varicolored bougainvillea climbing up the walls, it was a sight to gladden one's aesthetic senses, and had the cachet of a European hotel somewhere along the Mediterranean. As I found out later, it was a mecca for sun-starved pleasure seekers from the frozen Midwest, who booked reservations a year in advance and returned time and time again.

Entering the large reception hall leading to the front desk, I marveled at the sumptuous decor, in sharp contrast with the Spartan appointments of Paradise Inn. A wide staircase leading from the upper floor provided the proper showcase for ladies in evening dresses to glide down to the dining room or to some gala in the adjoining ballroom. Next to the staircase was an old-fashioned elevator with touches of gold-plated wrought-iron grillwork. Without reservations, I was fortunate to be booked into a small room overlooking the huge, green quadrangle courtyard with colorful flower beds. Mine might have been a temporarily vacant maid's room, neat and cozy. I could not have picked a more suitable place in which to restore my winter-weary spirits.

Dining and evening affairs at the Hotel Coronado were dressy with a salon orchestra playing appropriate music for the occasion. The dining room was a remarkable structure that could seat hundreds of people at elegantly appointed tables for smaller and larger groups. The vaulted ceiling, made entirely out of wood without any visible structural support, was considered a masterpiece of woodcraft artistry. It gave the room a cathedral-like feeling. The cuisine was outstanding and the staff trained to render the type of service expected at Claridge's in London, the Danieli in Venice, or the Ritz in Paris.

In the course of such a hedonistic life, I found out that the managing director's name was Alberto Campione, an Italian, as his name implied, trained in the European tradition. He was a part of Hotel Coronado legend. Like a movie star, he had that indefinable quality making him a star in his own right. Dressed in fine hand-tailored Italian suits, silk shirts, and Cartier cufflinks, with a dapper mustache, slickly parted black hair combed back à la Rudolf Valentino, and vivacious dark brown eyes, he had a winning way with his guests, especially elderly ladies. They doted upon his chivalrous manners, which he accentuated with hand kissing and flattering comments. I met him, since it was his wont to greet every one of his guests in person, and we established an easy rapport.

Having arrived alone after a winter spent on the snow-covered volcanic peaks of the Northwest, I had a certain mystique that Alberto cultivated by introducing me to the flowers of female society gathered in his pleasure emporium. In no time at all, thanks to him, I found myself not lacking in company, if I wished to pursue the social activities connected with hotel life. I was not too keen on becoming involved with this sort of hectic lifestyle, having traveled all this distance to escape from it.

Alberto had various helpers to enliven his little empire. One of them was a lady in her fifties, regally gowned and crowned with an assortment of wide-brimmed, fancy hats. As the paid "social hostess," her job was to get people to mingle with each other, to get the right people to meet their proper counterparts, according to her own chosen standards of protocol. Another lady, perhaps a bit older, not nearly as imposing, was the bridge teacher and indoor games impresario. Her job, other than teaching, was to match the playing partners compatibly. Not being a bridge player made it easier for me to back out legitimately from this sedentary pastime. I spent most of my idle hours on the tennis courts, in the pool (the ocean was still too cold), and on the golf course. Also I enjoyed sailing about Glorietta Bay in one of those neat little boats of the "Rainbow" class.

Before I had left San Francisco I had bought a pair of water skis, which I carried south sticking out of the rumble seat of my car. I hoped I would have the opportunity to try them out at Coronado. They were ungainly-looking things, almost eight feet long and a foot wide, and they weighed a ton—monstrous. At that time, the sport of waterskiing was in its infancy in California, and when I made my first tentative practice runs on Glorietta Bay, it caused quite a flurry of curiosity among the onlookers. Before I knew it, there was a big picture of me in action on the front page of the sports section of the *San Diego Union.*

Immediately, I was swamped with requests from guests wanting to be initiated into this novel sport. One among these was Tony Gaines, a young man approximately my age, who was Campione's assistant manager and all-around factotum. Small of stature and quite good looking, Tony was also of Italian ancestry. Fluent in many languages and a social butterfly, he was in his element. His main function for the hotel was to keep the younger people happy and physically exhausted, if such a thing were possible, by having them participate in all sorts of sport activities and contests. Waterskiing immediately caught his imagination as an added attraction for the young.

As I was ready to pack my bags and head back to San Francisco and possibly Europe with the Hills. Tony asked me whether I was willing to dispose of my water skis at a fair price. "Why not?" I said, "They are yours. Just take it off my hotel bill, whatever you think is fair."

"Oh, on second thought," interjected Tony, "why don't you stay here with us for the whole summer season. Alberto and I have talked it over and would love for you to join our team. We would work out a financial arrangement that would make it worthwhile for you." I was stunned. Though my plans were vague, I was not prepared to spend the whole summer at Coronado.

"What would I do here?" I asked.

"No problem," Tony said. "Just having you around would be a great help to us, the way you get along with people. Also, you could start a school for waterskiing, which would be the first in California, if not the U.S.A. You could take charge of our Rainbow Fleet, arranging for weekly regattas and instructing neophytes in the art of sailing. All that would keep you nicely busy and working in an environment you would like. We would provide you with a room and free run of all the eating facilities plus a commensurate salary. Fair enough?"

"Fair enough, indeed," was my tentative reply, "but give me time to think it over. I'll head for Los Angeles to see some friends and let you know within a few days about my decision. Is that okay with you? Tell Alberto I am complimented and that his offer is very tempting."

With my car packed and ready to leave, I stopped at the front desk to pay my bill and saw to my great surprise that my room had been given to me complimentarily in return for my skis. Not a bad deal as trade-in for a pair of cumbersome implements I was glad to unload. As Tony escorted me to my car, he urged me again to consider their offer. As I turned on the key to get my engine started he waved to me and shouted, "*Arrivederci, caro amigo. Buon viaggio. Ritorna presto!*" The moment I boarded the ferry to San Diego, I knew I would be coming back.

I spent the night at La Jolla, up the coast a little way from San Diego. I had heard so much about the place and found it to be a charming and unspoiled seaside town with a Spanish colonial ambiance. From my room at the Valencia Hotel, the view was unobstructed and inspiring, with foaming waves rolling in all the way from Hawaii in rhythmical cadence. La Jolla seemed like an idyllic spot to keep in mind for the future, with its unmatched climate a mean average of seventy degrees year-round and abundant natural assets.

The next morning I called Tony Gaines at Coronado and said, "I'm coming back!" And so I did, challenging destiny for whatever it held in store for me. Stepping into my new job was easy, given my teaching experience and the jobs I'd held in other resort hotels in Europe. I scheduled the waterskiing activities for the early morning hours before the wind came up and made the water too choppy to teach beginners. Waterskiing, on first try, was not quite as easy as snow skiing. The trick was to get started and stand up with the knees slightly pushed forward to act like shock absorbers in an automobile. After a few faulty attempts, most beginners caught on. Much depended also on the dexterity of the boat driver, who had to have a gentle touch in getting the skier launched from a sitting position, and then had to accelerate gradually so that the skier would stay afloat on top of the water. A sudden jerk at the start or hitting the throttle too suddenly would inevitably unseat the skier and land him flat on his face and belly, dragging him under with a mouth full of brine.

Not surprisingly, those who succeeded in standing up and making a full circle around Glorietta Bay were ecstatic when they returned to the dock. Word spread quickly that this was IT for a novel thrill—and a sport with a future. This prediction turned out to be correct, but with a difference. Today's skis are sleek, streamlined, lightweight, and maneuverable, unlike the unwieldy models we had to contend with. It is gratifying to know that I had a hand in pioneering this sport.

When the breeze came up later in the day, Glorietta Bay was made for sailing. The Hotel Coronado boathouse was another Victorian gem, sitting right above the water and surrounded by a colorful fleet of sailing vessels. For a soul-satisfying sport, sailing a boat with a steady flow of wind billowing the sails is a unique sensation and can become addictive. Adding to the excitement was the social life of the hotel, in high gear around the clock, whether hosting a tennis tournament for guests mixed with a sprinkling of Hollywood celebrities, a regatta followed by a victory celebration, or a poolside luncheon with a fashion show. And, of course, there were a gamut of evening entertainments. I had no regrets about deciding to stay at Coronado for the summer, although I was busier than I had ever anticipated.

A MEETING WITH DESTINY

Life magazine planned to shoot a pictorial layout on waterskiing at Coronado that would feature a sequence of Errol Flynn and Patrick Knowles taking a lesson from me. Flynn, a handsome and eccentric movie star, was also well known as a versatile sportsman and even better known as a notorious womanizer. Waterskiing would be new to him as it was to the equally handsome and versatile movie star Patrick Knowles, at the peak of his career. The day and time was arranged, and the stage was set with ten young women attired in play- and swimsuits to flesh out the tableau. They were the daughters of high-ranking naval officers and the recently married wives of younger officers. They were indeed a pretty bouquet of pulchritude, which any casting director would have been proud to present.

The day and hour came. Time passed. We waited . . . and waited . . . and waited some more, but no stars showed up. The situation became a bit awkward, and we attempted to kill time by joking and getting acquainted among ourselves. Eventually, Patrick Knowles made his entrance, not at all in heroic style. In fact, he looked awful: weary, hungover with bloodshot eyes, and in no condition at all to participate in a waterskiing session. He apologized profusely and said, "If you think I'm in bad shape, you should see my pal, Errol. He couldn't even get out of bed." As I heard later, there had been a party the evening before with much drinking, ending up in some sort of a bacchanal with Errol Flynn, the center of attraction, swigging champagne out of a lady's slipper.

It was up to the director of this shoot to salvage something out of the day. After a few moments, he said to his assistant, "Let's just go ahead and pick the prettiest one among these ten dames, and we'll shoot a sequence with her taking a lesson from Otto Lang. Those two Holly-wood bums! Good riddance to them!"

Sinclair Gannon, considered the prettiest, was chosen to substitute for Errol Flynn. Sinclair was the daughter of Rear Admiral Gannon, commandant of the Eleventh Naval District, with headquarters in San Diego, and Mrs. Gannon, of the Tripplet family of Austin, Texas. Sinclair's sister, Nancy, ten years older, was also married to a naval officer, Captain H. Gearing, and lived in Coronado. According to the story told to me, the admiral had fervently hoped for their second born to be a boy but instead was blessed with another girl. To console him, the baby was given the name Sinclair, which was also his first name, and called Sinnie by family and close friends. And a strikingly lovely girl she was at age twenty.

Sinnie disclosed to me that she was totally nonathletic and that the only sport she excelled in was swimming, which we both felt might come in handy in this particular part she was to perform. In any case, she was willing and game enough to serve as a guinea pig. Soon we had her seated on the dock with skis on her feet and the boat poised to take off. After my preliminary instructions on how to anticipate and react to the gradual start of the boat, I gave the driver the signal to go. When the coiled rope, released by a helper in the stern of the boat, was stretched to its full length, Sinclair, from her sitting position on the dock, took off in a perfect swan dive over the tips of her skis, letting go of the handle and submerging with barely a splash. She surfaced doubled up with laughter and said, "Let me try it again. I think I know now how to do it." The second attempt was a breeze. She stood up and sashayed off behind the boat, as though she had been doing it all her life. It was an impressive performance. There were many more runs and many pictures taken, but none ever appeared in *Life* magazine. Sinclair, apparently, was no substitute for Errol Flynn as far as *Life* was concerned. Nor was I. Fortunately, I managed to get hold of some of these photos for my collection.

That was the beginning of the romantic association between Sinclair Gannon and me. It was not love at first sight, but a gradually growing deep attachment, until one day we became aware that we had fallen sublimely in love with each other. It was an unmistakable, mutual feeling of exaltation, which left no doubt about it.

Sinnie was a few inches shorter than I, her eyes grey-green, her complexion flawless, her face, classic, framed by a mane of dark brown hair that lent itself to all manner of imaginative coiffures. With her long and shapely legs and proud posture, she could have made a living as a fashion model. Fortunately for me, she had no such ambition.

Not only beautiful, Sinnie was also bright and witty with an uncommon command of the English language. She used her large vocabulary to formulate sentences of singular distinction that reflected her personality. Where and from whom she picked it up I could not fathom, since her academic career was not distinguished. Being the daughter of a rising naval officer meant changing posts and domiciles frequently. It also meant a variety of schools for the Gannon girls. Sinnie spent some years in a school in Honolulu run by Catholic nuns, which must have had some beneficial influence, although it never converted her from her Episcopalian faith. The triumph of her spotty education was her graduation from a San Diego high school, not cum laude, I was assured. But above all, she had always been an avid reader of books, which undoubtedly was the main source of her verbal acumen. Other than a smattering of Spanish, she spoke no foreign language.

It was apparent that people enjoyed seeing us paired as much as we liked being together. Two people who didn't appreciate our togetherness, however, were Admiral and Mrs. Gannon. The time came when I was invited to a small, family dinner given at their home. Their living quarters at the naval air station, not far from the hotel, were impressive in a functional, yet elegant way. I could sense immediately that Sinclair's parents were not too happy about their daughter's fast-developing attachment to an itinerant *sportsmeister*, such as I was.

Our relationship had become the talk of the town, especially among navy wives and their daughters. After all, Sinnie had many eligible suitors among the officers from junior grades up to captains, who vied for her attention . . . not only to love her and be loved in return but also to further their career by marrying the admiral's daughter. The admiral doted on her and quite naturally dreaded the day when he would have to let go of her. The very thought that this infatuation could develop into something quite serious and of a lasting nature was unthinkable to the admiral and his wife, who always deferred to her husband's judgment. Sinnie's sister Nancy was the only one of the family on our side. She thought, and said so spontaneously, that she felt it utterly delicious and *soooo* romantic the way the two of us had found each other. She was convinced we were meant for each other.

In any case, the dinner conversation did not flow as one might have wished for the occasion. In fact, it was a strain for all of us. Admiral and Mrs. Gannon probed discreetly, hoping to uncover details about the background, breeding, and family history of the mysterious stranger who had so suddenly intruded into their orderly lives. This was understandable, but what could I tell them to alleviate their concern? There was not much to brag about in my background. That I thought the world of my parents and loved them dearly? That we never had enough money and just struggled through as best we could? I could talk about my sisters (one of whom was retarded) and how they managed to earn a livelihood, thereby reducing the financial burden of our parents. And to top it all, I wasn't even an American citizen yet. I was certainly not a very promising prospect. I am sure they speculated as to how they could terminate this amorous interlude, and I couldn't blame them a bit.

In the old days, such a dilemma was often solved by sending the well-chaperoned daughter on the proverbial Grand Tour of Europe. This the Gannons could not afford. Despite the admiral's status, his salary would not have permitted such an extravagance. The family's quarters were large and spacious with meticulously maintained grounds. The interior was, to use the naval expression, shipshape, at virtually no cost to them. There was a retinue of Philippine sailors of low rank at their beck and call, including a cook and steward to serve the meals. Sinclair once told me that she was so rottenly spoiled that she never bothered to pick up a dress once she dropped it to the floor and stepped out of it, since there would always be someone to tidy up her room afterward.

It was a relief to all of us when the evening was over. Nancy and Sinnie saw me to the door. They both gave me a hug, a cheerful smile, and a peck on the cheek, with Nancy saying, "Don't worry, Otto. It will all come out all right. We know our pop. His bark is fiercer than his bite." The encounter had been disconcerting, and had I been a midshipman or officer under his command, I would have been scared stiff. But since he was not my boss, I merely felt somewhat chastened by his stern attitude and the steely look in his grey-blue eyes. There was no doubt in my mind that Sinnie was the girl I wanted to marry, but I was also aware of the obstacles ahead of me, comparable to a frontal assault on Mount Everest. At that point I hadn't even asked her whether she entertained any matrimonial thoughts. I had to be patient and bide my time for the right moment to propose to her.

Despite the devastating first encounter with Sinnie's parents, our love for each other grew stronger every day. I considered giving up my job at the hotel, since my interest in fulfilling my contractual obligations had obviously slackened. I discussed this matter with Alberto Campione, and fully aware of the situation and romantically inclined himself, he assured me that I was doing just fine and persuaded me to stick with the job until the summer came to an end, which was not too far off. The days flew by with all the activities surrounding us. Sinclair hinted that she wished to learn how to play tennis so that we might have a sport to share together. In my free time at the end of the day I took her to an isolated private court, away from the busy and highly visible tennis center adjacent to the hotel. I began feeding her balls by hand and introducing her to the basic strokes. Fairly soon we managed to hit some balls across the net facing each other. As much as she tried, with her right hand blistered and her arm sore, I felt that her heart was really not in this sport. Often we had a chuckle when she chased a soft lob, which I had purposely lofted high over her head, and I told her that she reminded me of a butterfly collector fumbling to catch a rare lepidopterous specimen with her net. Our tennis activities gradually petered out with no regrets on either part.

We both loved to ride side by side on horseback along the long sandy beach before the sun went down. This appealed to Sinclair as she had learned to ride in Honolulu. Our rented horses from a nearby stable were quite docile and easy to handle. One evening as we were streaking along in a spirited gallop, with the sun sinking below the horizon in a fiery display, I burst out in a spontaneous display of courage and yelled to her over the sound of the surf, "I love you! Will you marry me?"

There was a stunned look on her face and a long silence, which seemed like an eternity to me, as she reined in her horse to slow down. Both of us came to a standstill. She looked at me quizzically and said, "I wondered why you waited so long to ask me. Of course I will. I love you too, and it would make me very happy." Filled with emotion, all I could say was, "Thank you, thank you, for wanting me."

Shortly thereafter, Jerome and Maud showed up unexpectedly at the Coronado. They were about to leave for Europe and had come either to take me with them or to say good-bye. I was delighted to see them and, of course, couldn't wait to introduce them to Sinnie. They were the closest to what I considered my family in America. As I expected, they took to each other with gusto, and an immediate rapport was established among the three of them. Jerome was quite taken by Sinclair's personality and verbal élan. Maud unstintingly admired her beauty and natural poise. Of course, we told them of our plans to get married and the problems facing us.

Sinnie and Nancy had the brilliant idea of giving a dinner party at their parents' home in honor of Maud and Jerome. It would give me some credence to show that I was the close friend, and almost adopted son, of the Hill family. The dinner party was a great success. Maud and Jerome were delightful storytellers, with me frequently the butt of their comical tales. I didn't mind at all, since it resulted in much laughter and a more congenial atmosphere than that fiasco of our first ill-fated dinner. The dinner conspiracy was helpful to some extent in improving the admiral's negative attitude toward our relationship, but there was still much work to be done before we dropped the bombshell on Sinclair's parents.

Every summer season at the hotel was climaxed by a supergala charity evening, with dinner, entertainment, and dancing, to raise money for institutions such as hospitals or organizations dedicated to the care of the physically or mentally impaired. A number of visiting artists would perform and the most talented members of the staff would be requested to display their theatrical forte, whatever it may be. Tony Gaines was in charge of the affair. He asked Sinclair and me to perform in a lip-synched rendition of the famous love duet from the opera *La Bohème* by Puccini. Sinclair and I consented and thought it would be quite appropriate to make our first official public appearance as the opera's two star-crossed lovers. We rehearsed diligently for days on end. Our costumes, rented from a Hollywood establishment, were quite authentic, and Sinclair, when all fitted and made up, looked ravishing, though not as emaciated as the consumptive Mimi would have looked. I stuffed a small cushion into my shirt so that I would have a protruding belly like so many famous tenors. When the curtain rose with a full moon dimly lighting the scene, there we were, Sinnie and I, with our lips moving appropriately, projecting much feeling into the famous duet of lovers to be. Judging by the ensuing applause, our performance was a success.

By that time, the month of August was about gone, and we thought it was high time we informed Admiral and Mrs. Gannon of our plans. Sinnie did not want a lengthy engagement and wanted to get married within a few weeks once the date was set. Should her parents try to stall for time and hope thereby to thwart the marriage, she assured me that she was prepared to elope by crossing the border and having the ceremony performed in Tijuana. This was not my idea of starting out on this most important and hopefully long-lasting voyage of our lives. Furthermore, there was really no pressing hurry, no "emergency," as some

gossipy rumormongers might have liked to assume. Her virginal innocence was totally intact, as she told me, and I had no reason to doubt it.

My idea was for both of us to formally inform her parents of our
decision to get married and, as was customary in the old country, for the
prospective groom to ask for the hand of the daughter. I sensed that her
parents' attitude toward me had improved somewhat, especially Mrs.
Gannon's, quite possibly due to Nancy's influence. The admiral remained
an enigma to me, but at least there was some hope.

Another family dinner was set up and everyone knew that this would
be *the* climactic encounter. Surprisingly, there was a minimum of tension among us during dinner, which deceptively made me feel as though
I were already part of the family. After dessert was served, the admiral
suggested that the two of us adjourn to a small sitting room for our
coffee and after-dinner liqueur. "I know you wish to talk to me, Otto,
and so would I to you," the admiral said quite congenially.

He explained that he and his wife were entitled to know about my
future prospects as a wage earner and where Sinclair and I planned to
settle down when the time came to start a family. He pointed out that his
daughter had been pampered, and that in addition to their love, they
had given her everything they could afford—in other words, it would be
a tough act to follow. I was well aware of all this, and of his doubts as a
father, and wished to give him a reassuring answer. But how could I, not
knowing myself what the future had in store for me?

The admiral was a proud man, with an outstanding service record as a
naval officer. Born in 1877 in Texas, he was appointed to the United
States Naval Academy at Annapolis, Maryland, in 1896. He graduated
with academic honors and had excelled in football, wrestling, swimming,
and boat racing. Subsequently, he worked his way through the ranks on
various ships and tours of duty. He served as the aide to the commander
in chief of the Atlantic Fleet and, later on, to the commander in chief of
the Asiatic Fleet on the USS *Saratoga*. In 1912 he assumed command of
the USS *Elcano*, which operated on the Yangtze River in China during
the turbulent overthrow of the Manchu Dynasty. He went through World
War I in command of the USS *Saranac* and emerged with a distinguished
service medal, cited for "exceptional meritorious service in a duty of great
responsibility engaged in laying mines in the North Sea." After the war,
he had a turn as commandant of midshipmen at the naval academy. In
1936 he became the head honcho of the Eleventh Naval District at San
Diego, which included the large installation at North Island, Coronado.

To his way of thinking, I was a nobody, an immigrant without a college degree, with an anemic bank account, and with no visible means of support, living hand-to-mouth. He deeply resented my intrusion into his regulated life and my efforts to wrest his daughter away from him. The more we talked, the more I felt I was losing ground. He threw one final question at me. "Tell me, Otto, what happens if you break one of your legs and can't teach or perform your duties in the pursuit of your livelihood?"

After a few moments of deliberation, I pulled out my trump card. "Admiral, sir," I said, "broken legs heal and, fortunately, my brains are not in my legs. I can write, as I have proven, for newspapers and magazines. I have had a book published by Henry Holt and Company in New York. I have lectured to audiences filling every seat in movie theaters. My intention is to take the best possible care of your daughter. I love her and will provide and share with her everything I have."

The conversation ended on this far-from-reassuring note. The admiral had not said yes or no. He had left me dangling in anguish. He returned to the dining room to join the ladies, and I wandered out into the garden to collect my thoughts. I loathed the idea of eloping with Sinnie, as it would have been so hurtful and humiliating to her parents. But I did not want to capitulate and lose her just to appease her father.

THE NUPTIALS, NAVY STYLE

What transpired in the dining room in my absence was relayed to me later. Apparently, the admiral had won the verbal skirmish with me but had lost the final battle. After our conversation, Nancy jumped to her feet like an angry tigress, and facing her father eyeball-to-eyeball, kicked him in the shin, making him wince in pain, and said, "How can you be so cruel. I hate the way you treated Otto and put him through an inquisition. It was like someone pulling a butterfly apart, wing by wing. Shame on you, even though you are my father. We are all in favor of Sinnie and Otto getting married and you'd better realize and accept it. Now you go back to him out there in the garden and tell him so and apologize."

The wedding was set for October 2, 1938, at 4 P.M. at the residence of Admiral and Mrs. Gannon at the naval base at Coronado. Contrary to our desire for a simple and intimate family ceremony, the Admiral and Mrs. Gannon wanted our wedding to be a big social event with all the pomp and flourishes of naval tradition. Choosing a cleric to perform the ceremony was a simple matter. Since I was a nonpracticing Catholic and

Sinnie's family was Episcopalian, we opted unanimously for an Episcopalian minister. I didn't care, so long as it was legal.

Nancy would be the matron of honor, and her husband, Captain Gearing, my best man. The admiral would give the bride away, and there would be a bevy of Sinnie's former schoolmates and navy juniors as bridesmaids. That left me absolutely alone, as far as family representation was concerned. For my parents or one of my sisters to come to America would have been an enormous financial hardship, if not impossible. The Hills were either traveling abroad or scattered elsewhere. I had made some friends in the Pacific Northwest, but none close enough to invite to my wedding. Also, for them the travel distance would have been considerable. Of course, there would be Alberto Campione, who thrived and shined on such occasions, and Tony Gaines, his indispensable sidekick. Had it not been for these two asking me to return to Coronado for the summer, the festive celebration would never have taken place.

A few weeks of concentrated preparations preceded the day of the wedding. The bridal gown had to be designed and hand sewn by a seamstress chosen by Mrs. Gannon, who was herself an accomplished practitioner of this art. The dresses to be worn by the bridesmaids had to be selected and fitted. I owned a nicely tailored tuxedo, but since the attire was to be ultraformal, I would have to rent a coat with tails. The thought of going to my own wedding in a rented outfit bothered me very much, but it would have been silly to buy tails for just this one wearing. Furthermore, I was assured that this was customary practice in America.

Some four hundred engraved invitations had to be mailed out. The Gannons were very popular in the San Diego area, and by even modest calculations, the newlyweds could expect to collect a sizable amount of loot. Sinnie's choice for china was an elegant design from the reputable English manufacturer Spode, and the cutlery, fashioned by the Messrs. Kirk, renowned silversmiths of Philadelphia, was one of my favorites.

Much on my mind was the choice of an appropriate engagement ring and wedding band. It occurred to me to ask Dell (Mrs. Gannon), whose taste I considered impeccable, to assist me in the choice of these items. Gladly she offered to do so, and we slipped out one afternoon and went to Jessop's, the most fashionable jeweler in San Diego. I had no inkling what such ornaments might cost and was a bit taken aback, though trying not to show it, when the bill was handed to me. But at least I was reassured that my offering would be worthy of my wife to be.

One assignment given to me specifically was to confer with the leader of the marine band of some forty-five musicians to select musical accompaniment for the ceremony. For some reason (whether it was sheer stupidity, flaunting tradition, or inadvertent snobbery I can't remember) I skipped the traditional "Here Comes the Bride," thinking it was commonplace and trite. I selected a composition by Brahms, a haunting adagio from one of Rachmaninoff's symphonies, and a soulful melody by Schubert. The problem was that this elite marine brass band had never been asked to play that type of music. The conductor told me that he would have to hunt up the score from a library or the local symphony's archives and have it transposed to fit a military brass band. He said he would be happy to do so, accepting this challenge and welcome change of pace from the traditional repertory.

As daylight broke on the morning of Saturday, October 2, I was already wide-awake and tense with anticipation, with a number of last-minute details on my mind. I had moved from the hotel to spend my last night as a bachelor in a guest room at the home of Nancy and her husband, my best man. My personal belongings were stowed away in the rumble seat of my car, as was a large suitcase containing Sinnie's travel necessities. The car was to be ferried across the bay to San Diego and driven to the admiral's reserved landing dock so that after the wedding, having crossed the channel in his official navy barge, we would find the car waiting for us, ready to start off on our honeymoon. Realizing that it might be too late in the evening for a lengthy drive, I booked reservations at a small country inn, highly touted for its ambiance, at Rancho Santa Fe, less than an hour's drive from San Diego.

I was told by Nancy there was a phone call for me. I picked up the instrument and said hello. An agitated voice blasted into my ear, "This is Sigi. Sigi Engl from Kitzbühel, in Austria. I am here in San Diego. Remember me?" Of course I did. Sigi and I had raced together as youngsters. He became a top instructor at the local ski school and also made a name for himself as a world-class downhill and slalom competitor. "I'm in San Diego visiting with friends who were in my class in Kitzbühel. I have a job teaching at Yosemite National Park next winter. My friends told me that they read in the paper you are getting married this afternoon. Can I come?"

"Of course you can," I answered. "I would be delighted to see you. Let your friends explain to you how to get here. If there was more time I would pick you up."

"Don't worry," he said, "I'll make it. I always carry my compass."

"That will be a great help," I said. "Oh, before I forget, get out of your lederhosen and put on a dark suit."

"I've got one!" he replied, laughing heartily. "Looking forward to seeing you and meeting your bride. I bet she is something else! Yodely, hoo, hoo!"

So by a strange coincidence, Sigi Engl turned out to be the only other Austrian representative at our wedding, and he wasn't even what I would call a close friend of mine at the time. Nevertheless, I was pleased to have a fellow countryman there.

When, at the stroke of four, Sinnie appeared at the far end of the garden in her resplendent white bridal gown on the arm of her father in his bemedaled, gold-trimmed, full-dress uniform, I was overwhelmed. They approached us in a slowly measured walk, Sinnie with a radiant smile on her face, the admiral with dignity.

To me it was like a dream: the beautiful garden setting with a red carpet rolled over the green lawn to create a path; the marine band with their highly polished instruments glistening in the afternoon sun, playing the music I had selected; the hundreds of people, ladies in their finest frocks, men in formal dark suits or showy dress uniforms. It was all too much for me to absorb. I felt like a disembodied persona watching the spectacle from a distant observation point. Not in my wildest imagination had I ever expected to be a vital participant in such an elaborate scenario. How I managed to get through the ceremony, reciting the vows and putting the ring on Sinnie's finger with hands shaking, remains only a hazy memory. Finally the minister intoned, "I hereby declare you man and wife." And looking at me he said, "You may kiss the bride now," which I did with enormous joy in my heart and great relief, whispering into her ear, "You never looked more beautiful. I love you."

The reception took place in the Gannon's home with a huge buffet table set up and champagne flowing freely. Nearby, on another large table, the wedding gifts were displayed. To me it was unbelievable. It was as though someone with a magic key had opened the door to Aladdin's secret treasure chamber. The wedding cake, looking like a huge replica of the Tower of Babel, was cut with the admiral's ceremonial sword, and the bridal bouquet tossed in the direction of the fluttering bridesmaids and other marital candidates, all vying to catch it for a good omen. I briefly introduced Sigi to Sinnie and her family. When last seen in the mass of people, he was happily working the crowd, holding a glass of champagne in one hand and juggling a small plate of finger sandwiches in the other.

Among the throng of guests there was much speculation as to how this wedding had all come about—and so fast. It was not easy to explain, and even harder to comprehend, considering the circumstances. But, there we were, Sinnie and I, husband and wife, for better or worse, in sickness or health.

At last the time came for us to make our exit as unobtrusively as possible, change into civvies, and walk down to the admiral's barge anchored a short distance from the house. This we did quickly, and shortly thereafter we were piped aboard and at sea, with a large tricornered pennant fluttering in the breeze from the fantail and proclaiming in large letters "JUST MARRIED," for all the world to see. What an exit. What a day. And what a beginning to our conjugal odyssey.

As we approached San Diego, Sinnie suddenly gasped and whispered in my ear, "Oh, dear, oh, dear. How dumb of me! I forgot to bring my overnight case with my toiletries and nighty in it." So I asked the captain of the barge if he would be kind enough to make a smart U-turn and have a sailor dispatched to go to the admiral's quarters to fetch the delinquent overnight case. One could hardly expect a respectable bride to go off on her honeymoon without a nighty, I explained to the captain. He agreed with a nod and a knowing smile and turned the barge around.

With all these delays, we arrived late—and exhausted—at our honeymoon cottage at Rancho Santa Fe. We stayed there for the next five days, enjoying to the hilt our being left alone. We slept late in the morning, ate as though each meal was our last, lounged at the pool, went for long walks, made love, and talked and talked about our dreams for the future.

On October 7, we celebrated Sinclair's twenty-first birthday, just the two of us. The next morning, we took off for a journey, without a set schedule and no advance hotel reservations anywhere. We had toyed with the idea of a quick trip to Europe, since Sinnie longed to meet my parents and sisters and get a glimpse of Salzburg and the Austrian countryside. We discussed the pros and cons and decided to wait until the following summer. Hitler had marched into Austria with his Nazi storm troopers and taken over the country in March, and I was leery of taking her there and hoped that by next summer the political situation would have stabilized. Also, being frank with her, I explained that our budget was a bit stretched at the moment and that we had to wait for the coming winter season to replenish our treasury. We had our car and our wardrobes. We could expect no financial windfall from any other source.

That is why we decided to make ours an American honeymoon, to see together some of the states we had yet to discover. Our adventure would take us through Arizona, New Mexico, Colorado, and Wyoming, where we planned to spend a week or so on a bona fide working cattle ranch owned by friends I had made while teaching them to ski at Mount Rainier. The sights we saw, the people we met, the relics of native Indian heritage we encountered, the small towns and larger cities through which we passed, the motels and fancier hotels in which we stayed formed never-to-be-forgotten images in both our memories.

At my friends' ranch in Sheridan, Wyoming, the waning Indian summer days, warm and sunny and crystalline clear, and the nippy nights, often leaving a touch of frost in the morning, were invigorating. We took lengthy rides on cowboy ponies and helped herd cattle. We could see high mountains in the distance already dusted with a layer of snow. There was only one serious drawback: an invasion of pesky flies, which were hard to keep off our faces, out of the house, and away from our plates as our meals were served. They were a bloody nuisance.

Continuing our journey, we wound up eventually at Louis and Dorothy Hill's home in St. Paul. They had invited us for a lengthy stay in their attractive home in a posh residential section of the city. Dorothy and Louis were gracious hosts and urged us to stay even longer. But time was running short and we had to think seriously about getting to Mount Rainier.

We arrived at Paradise Inn the first week in December after a memorable journey covering thousands of miles. Everything taken into consideration, Sinnie had been a delightful, undemanding, entertaining, and loving traveling companion, interested in every facet of our progress across these vast stretches of land. How she would adjust to spending the winter in this totally alien environment, an isolated mountain refuge at five thousand feet above sea level, perched against the west flank of Mount Rainier, with limited creature comforts and few diversions, was of utmost concern to me. Only the passage of time would answer this question.

MY THIRD WINTER
IN THE
NORTHWEST

In early December 1938 Sinnie and I arrived at Paradise Inn in a blizzard. The lodge was already half-buried and soon would be accessible only by a tunnel dug through layers of accumulated snow. Mount Rainier was enveloped in a frenzied dance of wind-whipped snow flakes rendering it invisible. We would see it eventually in its overwhelming splendor between storms, when the sky suddenly cleared and the sun came out to lend an incandescent and mystical appearance to this giant of a mountain. It would be my third winter running ski schools in the Pacific Northwest, but for Sinnie, who had grown up mostly at sea level in the salubrious climates of southern California and Hawaii, it was a new, strange environment. Such a winter could turn out to be the ultimate test of marital devotion, and I was fully aware that it would be up to me to find ways to ease her into the often hostile surroundings.

Nobody was in sight to greet us when the bus pulled up in front of the entrance. Then, surprise!—when we entered the lobby we were faced by a double row of people holding high crossed ski poles for us to walk under with much cheering and hoopla. I introduced Sinnie to all my old friends as we gathered around a table set up with snacks and hot coffee. There was Ken Burke, the handsome young manager of the lodge, and Jean, his comely wife; Papajohn, the rotund resident chef; Ken Syverson, my right-hand man; and some of my other ski instructors, plus old and new employees preparing for the opening of the lodge before Christmas. I was glad to see Hank Nelson again, an indispensable jack-of-all-trades whom I could count on to do anything I asked of him. Sinnie and I were shown to our quarters, a smallish suite of two connecting rooms, as good as the inn had to offer, as these friends shouted, "Pick her up and carry her over the threshold!" So I did.

When we were alone Sinnie told me, "I know I am going to like it here. These people are so genuinely friendly and real—nothing phony, nothing pretentious about them."

"That's the way I feel about them, too," I told her. "It must be the hardy pioneer spirit they inherited from their forebears."

We talked until late into the night. As we bedded down, tired, drowsy, and already half asleep, Sinnie mumbled, "I want so much to learn how to ski. Will you teach me?"

"Of course I will, with pleasure," I replied. "Sweet dreams, my love."

"Yeah, but I'll take lessons only from you and no one else."

"It's a deal," I assured her. And with this last exchange sleep overcame us.

Sinnie learned to ski quite well in a relatively short time. It was not surprising to me, based on her first experience on water skis. She progressed to the point that I thought it might be beneficial to her to join a regular class, but she rebelled and said, "Oh no, no way! Remember we had a deal that you would be my sole instructor." So we had, and so it stayed.

Sinnie also adjusted well to living in the lodge in its wintery isolation. Our travels between the three lodges, with overnight stays in Seattle or Portland, provided welcome diversions. Of the three, she preferred Timberline Lodge, which was was more like a traditional luxury hotel and had the singular cachet of a true mountain hotel, such as one might find in Austria and Switzerland. As winter went along, all three ski schools functioned well, and weather cooperating, I projected a fairly rewarding season financially.

Money would be helpful since we were planning on a lengthy summer trip to Europe so that Sinnie could meet my parents and sisters. We could not meet them in Salzburg, the logical choice, because Austria as it used to be no longer was; as of March 12, 1938, it had become a part of Hitler's Third Reich. We thought of possibly going to Yugoslavia, a safe and neutral country, where my parents usually spent their summer vacations, enjoying the salubrious climate of the Adriatic. Also, we could visit some of the small towns in Bosnia and Herzegovina. But because of the political situation, we would have to weigh carefully whether we should proceed with our plans.

My Austrian passport was no longer valid, and I would have to be issued a new one by the German consulate. I was now considered a citizen of Germany and therefore subject to its military laws, including the one that required every able-bodied man up to a certain age to serve a tour of duty and to be available, whenever called upon, should Germany become involved in any kind of military conflict. In a letter from my father, I was surprised to learn that I might actually be recruited for military service under the new regime, even though I was well on the way to becoming a naturalized American citizen. Of course, I had no intention of ever serving under the Nazi flag.

To my great chagrin I sensed that my father had been carried away by the initial euphoria of Austria's reunion with Germany. While he never joined the Nazi ranks as a registered member, he was clearly mesmerized by Hitler's charisma, as so many were. My father's pro-Hitler sentiments divided the Lang family, splintering its unity of many decades through good times and bad. It was five against one. I tried to rationalize how and why my father could be so misguided. I concluded that perhaps he thought this was a way to end his business career with dignity and pride of accomplishment, after so many years of humiliating experiences as a sales representative of various, often ill-chosen, products. I could fathom but not condone his feelings. It was a wrongly conceived illusion on his part that a few years later he would rue bitterly.

I was dismayed when word reached me that Hannes Schneider was caught up in the political maelstrom. Apparently, Hitler's triumph was a jubilant fulfillment for a cell of hardcore Nazi followers in St. Anton that included some of Hannes's ski instructors. They had kept low profiles in order not to jeopardize their jobs. Hannes had been an outspoken critic of Hitler and his cohorts; after the takeover, he was arrested and led away to prison at four in the morning. The ski school was taken over by one of the renegade instructors, Hannes's two children were away in boarding school, and Ludwina, his wife, was left alone as a political pariah. There remained, however, a cadre of loyal townspeople, other ski instructors, and legions of influential former ski-school students in Europe and abroad whose faith in Hannes was unshaken. They tried everything in their power to set him free, to no avail, until Dr. Karl Rosen, a devoted friend and longstanding skiing companion of Hannes's, appeared on the scene. He sprang into action as soon as he heard of his friend's incarceration.

It happened that Rosen had some leverage, reaching up to the highest authority of the government, the Führer himself. His association with Hitler went back to when Hitler was at the very beginning of his meteoric rise to power as the head of the National Socialist German Workers Party. After Hitler's precipitous *putsch* of November 9 and 10, 1924, went awry, he and his coconspirators were incarcerated and required to stand trial on charges of high treason and attempting to overthrow the government by force. The punishment, if not death by hanging, could be a lengthy imprisonment. Without financial resources to retain a top lawyer, they were assigned a defense attorney by the Bavarian High Court. Hitler insisted that he, personally, would undertake his own defense and that of his coconspirators, but Dr. Rosen, a lawyer of considerable reputation, who lived in Garmisch-Partenkirchen, untainted by any political affiliation, was the court's choice.

How much and to what extent Rosen contributed in developing Hitler's defense stratagem was never revealed publicly. Somehow he must have ingratiated himself to Hitler, since he continued to have access to him when he rose again to power after a short time spent in prison and reached the highest pinnacle as president, chancellor of Germany, and commander-in-chief of all its military forces. Rosen held a personal IOU to cash in at an appropriate moment, and that moment had come. He asked to have Hannes Schneider put into his custody and permitted to live in his home at Garmisch-Partenkirchen. He would personally vouchsafe Schneider's presence, when and if his case came up for trial. He also offered to serve as Schneider's defense attorney.

Dr. Rosen's proposal was accepted since Hannes's month-long incarceration, on flimsy charges and with his trial not yet scheduled, had become a source of embarrassment to Germany. Hannes moved into Rosen's comfortable home as his honored guest. His family could visit him, and together they planned for their uncertain future. As far as Hannes was concerned, if he could not have his ski school at St. Anton, he wanted out and regretfully would leave what was formerly Austria to settle in a foreign country where he had friends to help him get started anew.

Like a deus ex machina, unexpected help appeared in the form of Harvey Gibson, a heavyweight financier. President of the powerful Manufacturers Trust Company in New York, Gibson had frequent dealings with another financial wizard, Hjalmar Schacht, the redoubtable exchequer of Hitler's Third Reich. The Germans desperately needed to restructure their existing loans, far in arrears, and to obtain additional long-term loans to prop up their economy and subsidize military buildup. A shrewd Yankee trader in the New England tradition, Gibson insinuated to Schacht that quite possibly things could be worked out one way or the other, but only under the proviso that Schneider be exonerated and allowed to leave Germany with his family. It was a clever, calculated ploy.

Gibson, also a skiing enthusiast, had a solid plan for Hannes's future. He owned a hotel and substantial acreage in hilly North Conway, New Hampshire, and it was his dream to develop the area into one of the East's most attractive winter and summer resorts. He was well aware that Schneider, with his reputation and expertise, would be invaluable in bringing this dream to fruition. Coincidentally, Benno Rybizka had stayed on in America after the winter sports shows in Boston and New York to open ski schools at Jackson and North Conway, also thereby paving the way for Hannes.

Hannes accepted Gibson's proposal with gratitude, knowing that at last he and his family would have a new home and a future. It was now a matter of waiting for Hjalmar Schacht to perform his role as middleman in consummating the deal.

Hannes wrote to me:

> I hope that I shall succeed to land at North Conway, New Hampshire. Mr. Gibson is undoubtedly the only man who could accomplish this for me. Ludwina, unfortunately, is not well physically and her nerves are also run down. We want to leave under any acceptable circumstances. All four of us want to do so.
>
> The contract offered to me by Mr. Gibson is generous and sufficient for us to live comfortably.

The agreement was a five-year guarantee encompassing free room and board for the four of them in a spacious, fully furnished house, with a cook, plus a salary of $3,000 for each winter season of four months. During the summer months, Hannes could pursue other interests, as long as they did not conflict with the master plan of developing North Conway. After having served three winters, he could bow out of his contract, if he wished, or have it extended.

Once permission was granted by the "highest authority" for Hannes and his family to leave Germany, everything happened at breakneck speed, as though the Germans couldn't wait to get rid of Hannes and sweep the whole affair under the rug. Passports, travel permits, and tickets were secured expeditiously, thanks to Gibson's far-reaching connections. Hannes met his family in Munich and they went on to Paris to collect their United States entry visas. Before they knew it, they were aboard the *Queen Mary* headed for New York.

HANNES SCHNEIDER RETURNS TO AMERICA

On February 12, 1939, a bitterly cold morning, the local train pulled into the North Conway station in a cloud of billowing white smoke. A large crowd of townspeople was gathered there to celebrate the historic arrival of Hannes Schneider and his family. Of course, Mr. and Mrs. Gibson with Benno Rybizka were there to welcome them, as was the parish priest, who would become Hannes's English tutor and golf partner.

I cannot resist quoting excerpts from Ludwina and Hannes's joint letter dated February 19, 1939. Ludwina wrote (in German):

Many thanks for your dear letter. Thank God we arrived here safely and, above all, were received most hospitably. Leaving home came almost too precipitously, to comprehend what was happening. Within three hours we had to be packed and leaving by train for Munich, where we were to meet Hannes. From there passing through Strasbourg on to Paris and, after a night's rest, on to Cherbourg to board the *Queen Mary*, which brought us across the vast Atlantic Ocean. We had a few very stormy days at sea, which prevented Herta from enjoying any of the good things to eat and kept her feeling miserably in bed until the day before our arrival in New York. Herbert also had his share of seasickness and I was quite frightened, but managed to put on a good facade, and so did Hannes, of course.

We spent one day in New York and it is now a week since our arrival here. We have a comfortable house to ourselves, central heating, radio, telephone, an excellent cook, who looks after our nourishment needs in a touching way. After having been separated for such a long time, we are so happy to be together again as a family, for which we have to thank Mr. Gibson. He has really gone all out for us.

It's a pity that we are separated by such a great distance. On Tuesday we are planning a " *Tiroler Abend mit Knödel und Sauerkraut.*"

No doubt the time will come when we can verbally communicate, to which I look forward. Hearty greetings to your bride, whom we hope to meet soon.

To this Hannes added:

Thanks very much for your last letter. As it stands now the four of us
have a visitors visa for six months. Without Mr. Gibson's help we could
not have gotten the necessary passports and U.S. entry papers. For this I
shall be eternally grateful to him. Now we still need his help to extend
these temporary visas, as we have every intention of becoming American
citizens.

Otto, when one has gone through what I had to endure, one cannot
help but to be grateful and happy to be a human being (*mensch*) again and
to be offered the opportunity to earn a living. I know you would appreciate this. Believe me, I have learned to know the people of St. Anton and
still cannot believe that so many would turn against me overnight.

Now I shall take my time to look things over and see what needs to be
done and where to start.

I hope that we shall see each other in the spring so that I can fill you in
on all the details of the past year.

At the present I am happy and content to be privileged to be here. We
are very, very well taken care of and have everything we need.

I shall keep in touch with you and let you know how things progress
here.

To know that Hannes and his family were safe and happy was truly an
emotional relief. It seemed quite unbelievable the way it all happened. I
looked forward to a possible reunion late in spring.

SKI SEASON FINALE, 1939

The remainder of the 1939 winter season went by like a breeze. I had
two major events to oversee. One was the U.S. National Slalom Championship for men and women at Mount Hood on April 1 and 2, for
which I had already done a considerable amount of groundwork. It
promised to attract an outstanding field of competitors, many of international caliber. The other was the climactic annual Silver Skis Downhill
Race at Mount Rainier two weeks later.

As predicted, the national slalom championships attracted a star-studded field of racers with a distinct international flavor. I covered the event
for the *Seattle Post-Intelligencer:*

Enjoying most favorable weather and snow conditions . . . a balmy
spring day and bright skies . . . about 100 men and 35 ladies raced through

45 slalom gates at the Ski Bowl here today, competing in the National Slalom Championship.

That was for the first run only. After the race committee had sifted the chaff from the wheat, 28 men and 15 ladies made the "cut" to participate in the second run, which with the combined time of both runs would produce the ultimate champion.

The hero of the day was Friedl Pfeifer. Friedl is the newly appointed director of the Sun Valley Ski School, the latest instructor coming from St. Anton am Arlberg to make good in America. He is a product of Hannes Schneider's teaching staff.

Pfeifer's first run in the slalom was of such superiority, elegance and ease that he can rightly be called the "Nijinski on skis," whereas his second run was a masterpiece of cool-headed judgment. Although again he made the best time, I sensed that he was holding back. The reason for it was that in the very first gate he crossed his skis on account of a crust having formed on the somewhat rutted course, and due to the late afternoon hour and fading light with the sun going down. Alertly he managed to pass through the gate without falling and from then, playing it safe was foremost on his mind. His technique is most polished and quite unusual. Not that he uses a different technique, but he manages to initiate and set his turns considerably earlier than any other competitor, while pushing his knees a few inches farther ahead, resulting in a fluid succession of seemingly effortless turns. Thus he just seems to float ahead of his skis. It is this perfect combination of great talent and serious training which makes him the world-class skier he is.

Pfeifer's time for two runs was 2:38.1. Closest to him was the irrepressible Dick Durrance, Dartmouth prodigy, running in his own aggressive style. His time: 2:44.6.

Toni Matt (also hailing from St. Anton with a distinguished racing record in Europe and now teaching in New England) posted the third best time with 2:49.1.

Peter Radacher (assistant to Friedl Pfeifer at Sun Valley) came in fourth and Walter Prager (coach of the daunted Dartmouth Ski Team), who eclipsed a shaky first run with a brilliant second effort, wound up sixth (2:54.9).

The first Northwest skier to place was Olav Rodegard, who tied for ninth place with Pete Garret skiing for Yale, his alma mater. Bob Barto, of the University of Washington ski team, was tenth.

Two Swiss girls, Erna Steuri and Nina von Arx-Zogg, dominated in the women's division, finishing first and second. They are superb skiers, these

Swiss lassies.

Were it not for an unfortunate accident, the results of the women's slalom might have been different. Marian McKean, at present arguably America's best woman skier and stylist, hit a pole so hard in the upper portion of the course that she dislocated her shoulder and was forced to withdraw due to acute pain and immobility of her shoulder. What a pity.

Personally, I was impressed by the showings of Gretchen Kunigk and Grace Lindley. I did not expect either of them to fare as well as they did. Little Gretchen did especially well (10th) considering the fact that she had not entered any competition all winter long.

Since I was in charge of picking the terrain and setting the gates for the slalom course, I was most gratified that the event went over so flawlessly and for the compliments paid to me by all competitors, for giving them such a fluid course following the formation of the natural terrain.

Two weeks later, on April 15, we had another glorious sunny day for the Silver Skis Downhill at Mount Rainier. Weather was the key to the success of this race, as I wrote in the *Seattle Post-Intelligencer*:

HEAR YE, HEAR YE NOW:
So diminutive Peter Radacher of Salzburg, Austria, wins the "Silver Skis Downhill." He raced away with the first prize in the most thrilling competition of this winter.

It was a perfect day, partly sunny and the snow lightning fast. What is more important, it was not tricky. The racers could give it all they had and could trust the snow cover. Starting at Camp Muir 10,000 feet up (4,000 feet below the summit) the course dropped 4,800 vertical feet to the finish line near "Paradise Inn."

The only part of the course which buried many a hope, virtually a hundred feet before crossing the marked finish, was the last big "schuss" down (straight run) from the top of Edith Creek Basin to the flat outrun fully exposed to the sun. It had softened considerably and acted like a trap, snaring some racers at full speed. Other than this small patch of slushy snow, the course was in exceptionally good condition.

Radacher's victory was not unexpected, but the way he accomplished it reminded me of a finely trained thoroughbred horse, running a perfectly paced derby…

A roar and shrieks of disappointment rose from female voices among the crowd of spectators when Don Fraser took a head-over-heels rolling spill and bit the snow at that treacherous transition before crossing the finish line.

We were about to close shop at all three places shortly after the race at Mount Rainier. It was the appropriate climax to what I considered a hectic but successful winter season, notwithstanding the occasional and inevitable pitfalls. Although I had no binding agreement in writing, I knew I was welcome to return the following season, and, in fact, expected to be back. None of the three resorts was in a financial position to give me a firm contract. I was not seriously considering making a change, but in the back of my mind I longed to find, and felt that surely there must be, a place somewhere in the United States with a more stable climate, ample snow, and sunshine.

Our tentative departure date was somewhat delayed because Hannes Schneider called to ask whether it would be all right for him and his children, Herbert and Herta, to come and see us. They were ready to start out by automobile on a journey across America from North Conway to Seattle. Ludwina, not in the best of health, preferred to enjoy the comforts of her cozy home and not make such a lengthy and, for her, overstrenuous journey. After visiting with us they planned to link up with Friedl Pfeifer at Sun Valley, where Friedl had arranged for Hannes to go on a hunt for elk and mountain sheep. This was a tradition Hannes had followed religiously every summer in Austria. At my enthusiastic response, he said, "We will be leaving tomorrow bright and early and should be in Seattle in a week or less. *Auf Wiedersehen!*"

I wanted him to see Mounts Rainier, Baker, and Hood, which I was sure would be among the highlights of his family's trip. To welcome Hannes in the Pacific Northwest so soon after his arrival in America would be certainly the chocolate topping on the cake of my winter season. After a joyous reunion and a few restful days at the Olympic Hotel in Seattle for the weary cross-continental travelers, Sinnie, the Schneiders, and I drove up to Mount Baker and later to Mount Rainier. Hannes was in seventh heaven surrounded by spectacular ice-sheathed volcanic peaks and astounded by the wide-open terrain above the heavily forested land below. He saw great potential in both areas, as had I on first sight, until I explained to him that the difficulties in running a ski school here were similar to the ones he encountered in the East: fickle weather conditions. Many a time he had complained mournfully about this in his letters to me, which I fully understood from the winter I had spent in New Hampshire. But I was glad that he saw these mountains in their full glory and on their best behavior during the sunny days we shared there together.

In the evenings, sitting close to a log-burning fireplace, we talked heart-to-heart for many hours. So much had happened in the years since I had left St. Anton. The details of some of the dramatic incidents in Hannes's life even his children had never heard before. Sinclair was totally absorbed and fascinated by his tales and had struck up an instant rapport with him, as though they had known each other for years. Although I found him to be in good health and surprisingly fit, the sorrow and anguish he had endured had left telltale marks on his rugged face. His once dark hair had taken on a silvery hue above his temples, which only added to the wood-sculpted character of his mien. But his spirit and optimism remained undaunted.

Ready to get on the road after a brief sojourn at Mount Rainier, the group of us decided to travel south in tandem for a stretch, with a stop-over at Timberline Lodge. This, of course, was very much to Hannes's liking. He was immensely impressed by the architectural concept of the structure and interior design of the lodge, acclaimed nationwide by now.

I had to stay on a few more days in Portland to attend to the launching of a line of ski clothing under my name. It was manufactured and distributed by White Stag, with a stylish horned stag as its logo. The owners were a Mr. Hirsch and his son, Harold, a Dartmouth graduate steeped in the development of this sport. This business association would blossom into a long-lasting family friendship of many decades.

As much as I regretted it, we had to part company with Hannes at that point, since he was trying to follow a schedule before going to Sun Valley to meet with Luggi Föger, who had settled at Yosemite National Park in California and was running the ski school there. As we bid farewell to each other, I realized what a heart-warming experience it had been for all of us who had come into contact with Hannes Schneider during his short visit—a great man, bigger than life itself.

DOMESTICITY

With our "blue beetle" packed to the gills, Sinnie and I set our bearings for San Francisco. Coming by automobile from the north and crossing the Golden Gate Bridge, we saw the city spreading out before us like an oversized Japanese folding screen. The tableau was engraved in our memories. We checked into a small hotel on Post Street near Union Square and saw all the prescribed sights, riding up and down the steep hills on clanging cable cars. It was a great satisfaction to me to share these experiences with Sinnie, especially since she had never before been to this city. To see her face light up in wonderment and appreciation at some of these sights gave me much pleasure.

Leaving San Francisco, our plan was to find a cottage to rent in Carmel-by-the-Sea, which was not far from the Hill family compound at Pebble Beach. At that time, in the 1940s, Carmel was a small town with a singular charm, attracting artists from many fields—unlike the bustling tourist center it would become years later. The scenery was unsurpassed: the ocean pounding against the picturesque coastline, crowned with wind-bent, gnarled trees. There, also, were two splendid championship golf courses: one the fabled Pebble Beach course, and the other at Cypress Point, both championship courses of the highest difficulty yet enjoyable—though trying to less proficient golfers, which included me.

CHEZ NOUS

After scouting around Carmel for a few days, we located the little house of our dreams in a shady forest glade within easy reach of a market and other shops. Very aptly, a small carved rustic shingle above the entrance said "Chez Nous." This is exactly what we wanted it to be. Though only rented for two months, it would be our first home all to ourselves, where we could play at keeping house in its rudimentary forms. It would also give me a peaceful environment in which to pursue my writing assignments. From there we could branch out for short day trips or overnight excursions in various directions.

Staying at Chez Nous was a delightful interlude. We had more fun puttering around the kitchen together, trying to concoct savory meals. The results were not always the finest examples of the culinary arts, but we learned as we went along. I remembered well that when we decided to get married, Sinnie had very forthrightly warned me, saying, "Otto, my dear, I must confess to you I don't know a lick's worth how to cook. I don't even know how to poach an egg properly. And, as you know, I smoke a lot."

"Never mind," I said. "Honey, anyone can learn to cook, but no one can learn how to be as beautiful and bright as you are. About smoking, we'll see what can be done. It shouldn't be such a big deal to quit." I was wrong in this assumption, of course, and I did not realize at that point how much harm smoking would cause her in years to come.

By the time our lease was about to expire, the weather pattern also began to change at Carmel. By some meteorological quirk, a dense fog descended upon this coastline during the hot summer months, while only a few miles inland, the sun shone brightly with a clear, blue sky.

We had ample time to mull over our plans for the remainder of the summer and our projected trip to Europe. We decided to go ahead with it, in spite of the threatening political clouds hovering over most of Europe. We reasoned it might be our only chance in the foreseeable future to see my family and have them meet Sinnie. In corresponding with my father, we scheduled our trip to avoid the peak summer tourist season and wait until early autumn to gather *en famille* in Selce, Yugoslavia, a small town on the shore of the Adriatic Sea.

Sinnie and I had to get our passports and visas in order, which we planned to do in Los Angeles. I hated the thought of traveling with a German passport, but there was no alternative. Another minor problem was that my parents and sisters were limited in the amount of money they could take out of Austria and change into foreign currency, in this case dinars. We remedied the problem by transferring dollars to a bank in Yugoslavia, collectable upon their arrival.

Until our departure to Europe, we accepted the invitation to stay with Sinnie's parents at Coronado. They were looking forward to seeing us and at last showing us all our accumulated loot, carefully catalogued and stored with them. Of course, we had a fair idea of what was there because Sinnie had been busy for weeks on our honeymoon writing thank-you notes. Frankly, I was pleased to spend some time at Coronado. It would bring back poignant memories and erase some of those not entirely happy. The admiral's negative attitude toward me had improved, and we seemed to be on the way to becoming good friends, judging by his congenial letters. Sinnie's mother and I had never had any problems, and we felt pleasantly comfortable in each other's company. And of course Nancy was a jewel in her own way; our friendship never faltered to the very last day of her life.

Staying at the admiral's living quarters on North Island was a treat. Also, on our frequent visits to the Coronado Hotel, we were still regarded as the glamour couple of the previous summer season.

A TRIP TO EUROPE

Sinnie and I had discussed alternatives for our trip abroad and I asked her how she would feel about crossing America in an air-conditioned sleeper bus and then boarding an ocean liner in New York and sailing to Naples. I thought we could spend a week or two in Italy and travel leisurely north by train, with stopovers in Rome and Florence, to Yugoslavia.

The idea of traveling by sleeper bus amused Sinnie. "How did you ever come up with this idea?" she asked, a faint smile on her face. I explained that I had seen an ad in the paper and thought it would be worth investigating. We would be traveling in something similar to a train sleeper car, stopping for breakfast, lunch, and dinner at prescheduled places and making obligatory pit stops for refueling. Every evening after having dinner at a hotel restaurant with shower facilities available, we would return to the bus, which would be spruced up and converted into private lower- and upper-berth compartments during our absence, ready to go to bed. Next morning, while we were having breakfast, the process would be reversed. With the bus traveling day and night with drivers changing at regular relay stations, we would be in New York in less than a week. "Also," I added, "it's the most economical way by far to make such a trip. We could schedule our departure to give ourselves two or three days in New York before boarding the SS *Napoli.*"

Sinnie agreed, and said it sounded exciting. When we divulged the plan to Admiral and Mrs. Gannon, they were at first nonplussed by this quixotic idea, but with some explanation, they warmed to it, admitting it was a novel approach to seeing America. We proceeded with the arrangements and firmed up our reservations with a deposit. I informed my family of our itinerary and suggested when and where we could meet. They would be even more surprised than Sinnie's parents were, hearing about our crossing America by sleeper bus.

Only a few days before our scheduled departure for Europe, I received a letter from Friedl Pfeifer. Translated from German, the gist of it was:

> Even though I have little hope that you might still be available, I shall not pass up the opportunity to ask you to join me here at Sun Valley as my assistant and codirector of the ski school.
>
> Otto, if you have not committed yourself and signed a contract, I am now in a position to offer you a financial deal, which I feel would be attractive to you.
>
> Also, I have been assured by the management that there would be a suitable and pleasant job for Sinclair, since Union Pacific Company regulations require that both husband and wife have to be on the company payroll in order to be provided with adequate living quarters on the premises.
>
> Please answer my letter immediately, or even better, contact me by phone, so that I know where I stand regarding this matter. This would be a golden opportunity for us to work together.

During my last visit at Sun Valley, Friedl and I had toyed with the idea of our working together. Nothing came of it since the timing was not right. Friedl mentioned to me that he and Averell Harriman had touched upon this possibility, but Friedl doubted that I would consider such a proposal. What with my own ski schools and having recently married, he feared that I might find it demeaning to accept a secondary position. When Friedl contacted me, I didn't feel that way at all.

It had been a good and productive three winters for me in the Pacific Northwest, but upon soul-searching analysis, the prospects were discouraging. Mount Rainier, with its Paradise Inn battered by time and the elements, was never meant to become a destination winter resort. Its location in a national park limited possibilities for expansion. And while the inn was quite acceptable for the relatively short summer season, it was inadequate for the winter months. After a trial period of a few seasons, it was shut down during winter and remains closed in winter to this day. The same shortcomings applied to Mount Baker, only more so, since it was harder to reach and had insufficient living accommodations at the ski area. Mount Hood with its Timberline Lodge was in a better position, due to its proximity to Portland. I knew that the future of these three places as destination resorts was dubious and that only Mount Hood had a chance in succeeding as a year-round attraction.

These thoughts tormented me as I weighed Friedl's offer. After all, Sun Valley was America's glamour ski resort. It had a magical allure for skiers, and they flocked to it to mingle with celebrities, business tycoons, and movie stars. It had become a winter mecca. I thought of Sinclair and our future together, undoubtedly with some additions to our family soon to be expected. Sun Valley offered the kind of environment I had long hoped to find, and it was being presented to me on a silver platter. I had absolutely no qualms about Friedl's and my getting along with each other, as we both had shared Hannes Schneider's philosophy of how to organize and run a ski school. It would be a matter of teamwork by two like-thinking leaders. With an ache in my heart, remembering all the effort I had put into building up my ski schools and the many genuine friends I would miss, I decided to accept Friedl's offer. I told him that we planned to travel in Europe for about six weeks but that by the first of November I would be at his disposal.

Thus, my tenure in the Pacific Northwest came to an end, but I was amply rewarded by becoming recognized as the father of skiing in that part of the country. Also, I knew that the corps of local instructors I had trained would carry on the legacy I left in their trust.

With this weighty decision off my chest, Sinnie and I embarked on our cross-country trek by sleeper bus. It was a pleasant journey, surprisingly comfortable as far as our creature needs were concerned. Everything was well thought out and organized. We knew from the beginning that it would not be a deluxe tour and it wasn't. After leaving California and heading eastward through Arizona, New Mexico, Texas, Oklahoma, Missouri, Indiana, Ohio, and Pennsylvania to New York City, our final destination, we felt awed at having crossed the width of the continent in five days and four nights of continuous traveling, close to 3,500 miles.

There was also a noticeable physical and mental reaction best described as "bus lag."

The few days we allocated ourselves to see New York were not nearly enough. To my great disappointment, Nelson Rockefeller had sailed for France a few days before our arrival. I did take Sinnie to Radio City Music Hall, and she found it as striking as I had. Another highlight was an evening at the Savoy Club in Harlem, where Jerome Hill had taken me on my first visit to New York. It was at the peak of its popularity, and for the cognoscenti, it offered jazz music at its best with an ebullient floor show put on by an all-black cast, from which many a famous tap dancer, composer, and singing star emerged.

In a way it was a relief to be shown to our stateroom on the SS *Napoli*. The ship was far from a luxury liner; however, our compact cabin with a porthole looking out at sea suited us just fine. The ship sailed under the Italian flag, had only one class of accommodations, and was almost one-third less expensive than the more fashionable flagships.

One image from the voyage sticks out in my mind as though it happened yesterday. Close to us on deck was an elderly couple sitting side-by-side in their deck chairs at the fantail of the ship, its sparkling wake receding toward the horizon in a straight line. The husband was obviously in a state of harmless semisenility, whistling over and over an aria from Verdi's opera *Nabucco*, while conducting with his right hand an imaginary orchestra, in his mind undoubtedly Milan's illustrious La Scala. Every so often his wife, with a touchingly loving look in her eyes, would reach over to pull his arm down and then put her index finger across her lips, signalling him to be still. Like a child, he stopped, a bewildered expression on his face, but not for long; soon he would start whistling again with renewed vigor. This went on day after day, whenever the sun was shining, which bathed him in a glow of serene happiness, while his wife sat at his side, her posture hinting at sadness and resignation, probably reliving some of the happier times in their lives. I could not help but wonder what kind of life theirs had been, and now in the fading years of their marriage, what lay ahead for them.

Distant at first, Naples gradually came into view, backed by Mount Vesuvius with a silvery column of smoke rising skyward from its perfectly shaped volcanic cone. Naples has been acclaimed as one of the twelve most beautiful cities of the world, and so it seemed to us, at least when approached by sea. It turned out to be a typically busy harbor town with narrow streets and steep staircases badly in need of cleanup, overcrowded with beggars and peddlers hawking their wares. As in most harbor cities, there was much poverty in evidence.

We had not planned to spend any time in Naples and transferred from the boat directly to a bus that would take us to Amalfi, farther south. We had made reservations to stay at a small, highly recommended hotel perched on a cliff overlooking the tiny harbor. The accommodations were all they were promised to be. Stepping out from our bedroom onto a wrought-iron balcony overflowing with a profusion of potted red geraniums, white begonias, and other flowers, we could see the tiny harbor below and the isle of Capri across the sweeping bay of Naples. Sinnie was quite taken by this enchanting tableau, commenting that it must be surely one of the loveliest panoramic views she had ever beheld.

We sat down for dinner by candlelight in the intimate, elegant dining room and perused the menu. After giving our selections to the waiter, Sinnie looked at me with a pained expression and mumbled, "I fear I'm going to be sick. Please excuse me." With one hand cupped over her mouth, she rushed out. I knew she would not return and notified the waiter to cancel our orders. Then I hurried to our room to find her lying on the bed doubled up in pain and bathed with perspiration. I guessed it was a case of ptomaine poisoning. To make sure and to get her some immediate relief, I asked the hotel manager to send for a doctor. With only little delay, he arrived at our door, introduced himself courteously, asked a few questions, and took her temperature. Upon his inquiry when, where, and what she had eaten last, I answered that both of us had eaten the same meal on disembarking from the ship: a cup of chicken bouillon and a small portion of seafood salad with a glass of wine.

"Ah, *insalata marinera, ecco,* that's it," he said. "The seafood salad did it. You are the lucky one, but your *signora* has a bad case of intestinal dysfunction. It may not be too serious. With some medication and a good rest for a few days, she will be all right. Not to worry. It happens all the time, and this is why I carry a supply of this special medication in my black bag. Follow the instructions on the label and let me know tomorrow morning how things went through the night. She will not want to eat much for a few days, but make sure that she has a lot of fruit juices to drink, coffee, or tea, but no liquor. *Ciao.*"

Sinnie recovered quickly. Two days later, she was sitting comfortably in the sun on our balcony, while I put my miniature watercolor box to good use, toiling diligently on a small painting of the view from our balcony. Today it hangs in my study for me to look at frequently with nostalgia.

Originally, we had hoped to include a few side trips from Amalfi, such as to Sorrento, Pompeii, and Herculaneum. Our schedule having gone somewhat askew due to Sinnie's illness, we had time to see only Pompeii on our way back to Naples. From there we would board a train to Rome for a brief stay and then continue on to Fiume on the Italian-Yugoslav border. A coastal steamer would then take us to our rendezvous spot with my family at Selce. Our visit to Pompeii absorbed the better part of a day and was well worth the time we spent there. Buildings, private homes, shops, public plazas, mummified bodies of people and domestic animals, priceless artifacts, pottery, mosaics, frescoes, and fountains, representing the whole spectrum of human activity in that long past era, had been unearthed from the debris of Mount Vesuvius's catastrophic eruption in A.D. 79. One of the showpieces featured by the mercenary (and obligatory) guides was the remains of the local bordello, obviously well frequented as proven by a few clients caught in flagrante delicto, oblivious to the cataclysmic events taking place outside. For a few extra liras, the guide, with a salacious smirk, would draw open a curtain to unveil a pictorial rendition of priapic deformity in abominable taste— only to demonstrate that in all cultures, pornography was and still is part of people's lifestyle. One day of peeking into the distant past was enough for us. Herculaneum, which, from what I had heard, was far more esoteric than Pompeii, would have to wait for a return visit.

In Rome one incident stands out in my memory. We happened to stroll into a huge open plaza—the Piazza Venezia—filled with thousands of people to hear Mussolini, "Il Duce," standing on a balcony, exhorting a mesmerized audience in the manner of Hitler, whose leadership he followed. In front of us stood a group of ranking Nazi officers. In their immaculate white dress uniforms, short haircuts, ramrod straight posture, and soulless cold staring eyes, they gave me an unexpected jolt and reminder of what was happening between Italy and Germany, which had formed a military entente. I said to Sinnie, "Let's get out of here. It makes me sick to my stomach."

And on that discordant note, we left Rome by express train headed for Fiume.

WAR BREAKS OUT IN EUROPE

After a lengthy train ride and a pleasant two-hour journey from Fiume on a miniature Adriatic coastal steamer, we tied up at the dock in Selce, a fishing village near Crikvenica. To our great surprise we saw my sister Elsa waiting for us.

It had been a while since I had seen her last, and she looked healthier and lovelier than ever before, radiant with pleasure. The three of us threw our arms around each other. Of course, to meet Sinnie was primarily what Elsa had come for, but also there had always been a close bond between us. She bubbled over with the latest news from our family and explained that as she had already used up three days of her week's vacation, every remaining day was precious. Our parents and older sister, Nelly, were to arrive within the next three days, just before she had to leave. Elsa said there were some letters for me at the post office.

We adjourned to our hotel, more like a pension or private home converted into a guest facility, with a view from our window of the picturesque harbor. I left Sinnie and Elsa, seeing how quickly they had taken to each other, and walked to the post office. Two letters were handed to me. I recognized my father's calligraphic handwriting immediately. Looking at the posting dates on the stamps, I opened the earlier one first. It was filled with anticipatory excitement, giving the exact date and time of their arrival. Also included was a minutely laid-out itinerary for our long-planned trip through Bosnia and Herzegovina, with visits to Zenica and Tesanj. Typical of my father, he had studied the railroad and bus schedules, calculated the distances between places, and looked into hotel accommodations within our means. Like a professional tour guide, he would make this journey an undiluted pleasure.

Then I opened the second letter, written only a few days later. What I read hit me like a punch into the solar plexus. "Get out of Europe as fast as you can and head back to America! We are at the brink of war, with Hitler's army poised to invade Poland and his air force prepared to unleash an aerial assault on this country, which will assuredly force it into submission. What will follow," my father wrote, "no one can predict, but it will certainly have serious consequences internationally and could well be the prelude to World War II. Our travel permits have been rescinded and we are not permitted to leave Austria. You cannot possibly imagine how distraught we are that our plans have evaporated. Had we only planned to meet a few weeks earlier, it might have all worked out. We know that at least you will see Elsa. You must let us know when and how you are going to proceed with your plans to return to America."

A few minutes, after I left the post office in a daze, one of the clerks came running after me, yelling, "*Gospodin* Lang, wait! A telegram for you has just arrived."

I signed the receipt and opened the telegram. The message was worded diplomatically: "In view of your precarious health problem urge you to follow instructions in my last letter without delay. Love to all, Papa."

Now I had to relay this distressing news to Sinnie and Elsa. My sister was perturbed but not surprised by these political developments. We made arrangements to leave for Zagreb, which was the closest direct rail link. While in Zagreb I wanted to call on the American consul to solicit his advice and assistance if necessary. With sadness in our hearts and tears in our eyes, we parted company with Elsa in Fiume. She boarded her train to Austria, while we headed for Zagreb.

There, the American consul told us that there was really nothing he could do for us except to suggest emphatically that we grab the next train to Paris. We rushed to the nearest travel agency to book a compartment, and luckily were given the last one available, first class on the Orient Express, coming from Istanbul and going to Paris. It was indeed a stroke of good fortune, since it would be the last Orient Express for many years to cross Yugoslavia. According to my travel documents, I was an expatriate of Austria traveling with a German passport and heading for France. Given the current political climate, this was not a pretty picture, but Sinnie, composed and calm, never doubted for one moment that we would find a way to get home to America.

By the time we finished a late lunch at the station restaurant, the fabled Orient Express had glided into the depot and come to a smooth halt. We boarded the train, reveling in the luxury of first class. Soon we were on our way, silently and barely perceptibly in motion. I excused myself from Sinnie, explaining that I had some business to transact with the wagon-lit attendant. I found the gentleman sorting papers in his compartment at the end of the car, with his door open. He bade me to enter. I explained to him my predicament and furtively slipped a munificent sum of folded bank notes into his pocket, saying, "Could you please see to it, when we cross the border into France, that we are not disturbed in the middle of the night by a border patrol officer yanking our door open, shining a flashlight into our faces and saying, '*Passeports, s'il vous plaît.*'"

He nodded his head and said, "I understand perfectly. A young couple on their honeymoon on the way home to America, not wishing to be disturbed. You leave your passports with me. I can handle this. For you, it is not a pleasant situation to find yourself in."

I shook his hand and said, "That will be much appreciated. *Merci beaucoup*, Monsieur."

Our attendant kept his word. Very tired, we slept late into the morning, and no one opened our door until we heard a knock and his voice saying, "*Madame et Monsieur, nous sommes ici, une demi-heure jusqu'à Paris. Bienvenue!*" As I opened the door and was greeted by his smiling face, he handed me a breakfast tray with coffee, hot milk, and croissants on it—and our passports—and said, "*Bon voyage à vous pour Amerique!*" I discreetly slipped an additional bonus into his coat pocket.

Arriving in Paris and passing a newspaper kiosk at the station, I glanced at the headlines, screaming, "HITLER INVADES POLAND. GERMANY AT WAR." France and England would declare war on Germany within a day or two, confirming my father's prognostication of the chain reaction to follow. There was no time to waste. We hailed a taxi at the station's exit and asked the driver to take us to the American Embassy.

The embassy was housed in a stately mansion, formerly the palatial city residence of an aristocratic family, near the Place de la Concorde. Around the front entrance and inside the office section, a fair-sized crowd was milling about or standing in line, obviously people stranded and seeking advice or foreigners trying to obtain permits to enter the United States. Although I did not expect that much could be done for us, I felt it would be wise to register with the embassy and hopefully consult with one of the officials in regard to our situation. When I mentioned to one of the marine guards on duty that Sinclair was the daughter of Admiral Gannon, the commander of the Eleventh Naval District at San Diego, his face lit up and he said, "I served under Admiral Gannon's command. I think you ought to see the ambassador's naval attaché, Captain Ellis Stone. Follow me."

We were ushered into Captain Stone's office with hardly a delay, and after we explained our predicament, he thought about it for a while and said, "My suggestion is for you to leave Paris today. Go to Le Havre, where we have a consulate and where it would be your best chance to get on a boat sailing to America. I'll give you a letter to present to any French official in case you run into complications." He asked us to wait in the reception room while his secretary typed the letter. We thanked him sincerely for his courtesy, shook hands, and departed.

The letter read as follows:

AMERICAN EMBASSY
OFFICE OF THE NAVAL ATTACHÉ
2. AVENUE GABRIEL
PARIS

1er septembre 1939

Je, soussigné, Ellis S. STONE, Attaché Naval près l'Ambassade des Etats-Unis à Paris, certifie que je connais personnellement Monsieur Otto LANG marié a la fille de l'Amiral Sinclair Gannon, de la Marine Américaine. Monsieur et Madame Lang sont arrivés à Paris ce matin, venant de l'Europe Orientale; ils ont leur passage retenu à bord du S/S *De Grasse* de la Compagnie Générale Transatlantique.

Monsieur Lang est citoyen autrichien et par conséquent voyage avec un passeport allemand. Toutefois, il a déjà obtenu ses premiers papiers en vue de sa naturalisation américaine, et, conformément aux lois des Etats-Unis, deviendra citoyen américain en Novembre, cette année. Il possède le permis No. 1256919 pour rentrer aux Etats-Unis.

Au cas où Monsieur Lang se trouverait en difficulté vis-à-vis des Autorités Françaises du fait de son passeport allemand, je serais tout particulièrement reconnaissant à celles-ci de bien vouloir communiquer avec le bureau de l'Attaché Naval à l'Ambassade des Etats-Unis d'Amérique. Pour moi, en effet, les sentiments et l'intégrité de Monsieur Lang ne font aucun doute.

Ellis S. STONE,
Capitaine de Vaisseau,
Attaché Naval près l'Ambassade
des Etats-Unis d'Amérique.

It was certainly some token of reassurance to hold in my hand and see us through the next phase of our odyssey. We got into a cab heading back to the railroad station, but not before instructing the driver to take us on a roundabout detour to give Sinnie at least a few glimpses of Paris.

Trains to Le Havre ran frequently around the clock, but due to the political crisis were overcrowded. We managed to squeeze into an already occupied compartment with two spare seats, aided by a savy porter. Finding a place to stay at Le Havre wasn't easy either, being even normally a very busy harbor town. It was too late to go to the consulate that evening, but we planned to do so first thing the next morning.

Sam R. Wiley, the resident consul, was beleaguered by people when we arrived there, all beset with problems similar to ours. Eventually we were able to explain to him that we actually had confirmed reservations on the French liner SS *De Grasse* but that it was not scheduled to sail until September 20. He said that was not realistic and urged us to book passage on the earliest departing boat for America. He told us it would take some doing and a bit of luck, as at this moment all boats were overbooked and jammed with waiting lists of passengers anxious to get aboard.

"What I would recommend," he said, "is for you to get out of Le Havre and go to a smaller town, such as Honfleur or Étretat, for example, and sit it out there until you secure passage to America. It is a almost certain that France will declare war on Germany and so will England. There will be real bedlam here, with everyone trying to get out of France at the same time. For now this is, unfortunately, all I can do for you. Keep in close touch with my office, and should you run into any kind of trouble on account of your German passport, contact me immediately in person."

We made the rounds of the shipping agencies, leaving our names, without any promise of a booking in the immediate future, and were informed that the SS *De Grasse* had been withdrawn from public service and was reserved for military use. The next morning we turned on the radio and heard that as of that day, September 3, 1939, France and England were at war with Germany. All German nationals were to report to the nearest police prefecture and prepare to be interned for the duration of the war.

From Le Havre to Étretat was only a short bus ride, which made it convenient to keep abreast of shipping activities. It was a small summer resort and fishing village, renowned for its scenic appeal. We found an unpretentious pension where we could hibernate. As is customary in Europe, when one registers at a hotel or pension, one is obligated to turn over one's passport at the reception desk, and it is then taken to the police prefecture or local mayor's office to be registered. I had avoided this procedure at the hotel in Le Havre during our overnight stay there by explaining that we were in transit and leaving town early in the morning. In a small village such as Étretat, this requirement was much more lax and not of any real urgency. However, after two nights and days, I was asked to turn in our passports. I told the desk clerk that I had accidentally left my passport at the embassy in Paris and that it would be mailed to me *post restante* at Étretat, would they please bear with me for a few days. They kept asking, "No passport yet, Monsieur? *Non?*"

"No," I would say. "Very inconvenient this delay, isn't it?" I could sense that by our reclusive behavior we had become somewhat suspect to the owners of the pension, increasing the tenseness of the situation.

Finally I was told, "Look, Monsieur, passport or no passport, the mayor wants to see you both immediately at his office." Sinnie and I agreed to tell the mayor, forthrightly, the cause of our dilemma. The mayor would understand that I was not a Nazi spy with an American wife.

Not at ease at all, we walked the few short blocks through cobblestoned streets to the picture-book *Mairie* and presented ourselves to his honor, the mayor. Officious as any seasoned government functionary would be, he simply said, "Madame et Monsieur, vos passeports, s'il vous plaît." I'll never forget the look on his face when first I put Sinnie's passport, adorned with the American eagle, on his desk and then plunked mine down on top of it, emblazoned with the detested swastika. He recoiled as though I had placed a poisonous viper on the desk. Without waiting for an explanation, he said to me sternly in French, "You were supposed to have turned yourself in to the French authorities three days ago in Le Havre. I command you to do so without any further delay. Take along a toilette kit and a change of clothing. That is all you are allowed to bring with you. This is an order and I shall report your attempt to hide out as a German citizen. *C'est tous. Allez-y!*"

It was a distressing moment for me, realizing the mess I had dragged Sinnie into. After the shock subsided, we settled down to discuss our options. I said that, if it had to be, I would report to the French authorities and go to an internment camp and hope to be released soon through the intervention of American authorities. After all, France and America were allies. I insisted that rather than wait for me, Sinnie should return to America by grabbing the first available space on a boat.

"Absolutely and unequivocally no!" she said. "I'm not going to be separated from you. Wherever you go, I go, even if I have to be interned with you."

"Honey," I said, "they couldn't take you in, even if they wanted to, because you are a bona fide American citizen. Besides, you could do us both much more good by being free and helping me to be freed."

Then I remembered Capt. Ellis Stone. He had said, "Should you find yourself in real trouble, don't hesitate to get in touch with me immediately through the consul in Le Havre." As I was in real trouble, that is what we decided to do. I would pack my internment bundle separately, ready to report, in case there was no alternative. But first we would consult by phone with Captain Stone to see if he knew of a way out. When we arrived at the consulate we explained the urgent necessity of getting in touch with Captain Stone. Shortly thereafter we were admitted into Sam Wiley's office.

"Sir," I said, "we are in trouble, plenty of it, and we hope that Captain Stone and you might help us."

After presenting the events that had brought us to him, and the fact of my being actually on the way to an internment camp, he said without a moment's hesitation and without even placing a call to Captain Stone in Paris, "Now I can help you legitimately. Bring your bags up here. Both of you are staying with me at the consulate. I have a spare room left, and you are not going anyplace until I put you safely aboard a ship sailing to the U.S.A. One of our own ocean liners is on the way to evacuate American citizens, and I'll find a way to get you aboard. Make yourself at home and be of good cheer!"

Were we ever! What a relief to us both.

About twelve of us refugees were housed temporarily in the consulate. It was an interesting and congenial group. Among them was a stunningly beautiful young lady, dark haired, blue eyed, with a complexion of porcelain and svelte physique, chaperoned by her ever-present mother. She had just finished a lengthy, highly successful engagement at the famous Lido de Paris supper cabaret as a fan dancer, tantalizingly exposing her naked body with only a minuscule G-string covering her most private part. No, we could not induce the young Lido de Paris star to put on a show for us. She said it would be totally inappropriate in such intimate surroundings. It was designed for a sensuously lit stage with an audience of hundreds glued to every movement of her cleverly manipulated billowing fan. It was, therefore, genuinely artistic and not objectionable on a stage, in public.

Ours was a gathering of oddly mixed characters like in a mystery movie, but we all got along well, sharing room and board, courtesy of the U.S. government, with our gracious consul as host. We were permitted to take short walks and often went to watch the activities in the harbor. I happened to talk to one chap, Peter MacCann, an Irish schoolteacher, who was on vacation and also stranded, but for a different reason. He had a chance to get on a boat but didn't have enough money to pay the inflated ticket price. "If that is your problem," I told him, "consider it solved. How much is your fare?" He told me the amount required, a few hundred francs, which I handed to him.

"Oh, thank you!" he said. "Thank you ever so much. You are so kind, and I'll pay you back as soon as school starts and I have some money coming in."

"Mr. MacCann," I said, "this is not meant as a loan. I don't want you to pay me back. The very thought that I could find myself in your situation makes it more than worthwhile to me." He gave me his address and I gave him ours. It pleases me to remember how such a small gesture could mean so much under certain circumstances.

As a reminder that we were at war, every evening before sundown an RAF squadron of Spitfire warplanes arrived practically at rooftop level over the city, whooshing, swooping, whirling, and diving about like a flock of swallows on their crepuscular hunt for insects. It was a cleverly patriotic, spirit-rousing, spectacular evocation of England's brotherhood with France and determination to conquer *Les Boches.*

One foggy morning, almost as though appearing from nowhere and accompanied by the mournful sounds of a foghorn, the SS *Washington* arrived in the harbor. Approaching the landing pier at a snail's pace, she loomed higher and higher, like a mighty fortress built of steel, proudly flying the Stars and Stripes. It was a wonderous and uplifting sight. At eight o'clock the next morning, we assembled in the entrance hall of the consulate, all packed and ready to be taken aboard ship. There was a festive mood among us evacuees, knowing that at last we were on our way home.

We had been forewarned that all married couples would be assigned separate sleeping quarters by gender in order to double or even quadruple the occupancy of each cabin. Temporary field cots would be set up along the corridors and in every suitable space to accommodate passengers for the duration of the five-to-six-day voyage. The ship would be loaded like a military troop transport in war time. Even the large swimming pool, emptied of water, would be converted into a vast dormitory. Thus many passengers, normally accustomed to traveling in the luxury of cabin class, would find themselves relegated to a cot in the swimming pool. A few luxury suites were, however, reserved for high-ranking State Department officials. Meals were to be served military style in shifts. Considering the circumstances, nobody seemed to mind, and only a few complained of the regimen. Fortunately Neptune was in a benevolent frame of mind. The crossing was one of the smoothest imaginable, and the ship performed flawlessly. To all of us crowding the deck, the Statue of Liberty never looked more beautiful as we steamed into New York harbor.

After we passed through all the disembarkation formalities, Sinnie and I hugged and kissed each other, laughing and saying, "Welcome home to America." I tore my passport into shreds and dropped it into the nearest garbage can. I did not wish to have another one until I was an American citizen.

We spent a few days in New York at the Algonquin Hotel before heading west. The first order of business was to stop at the Western Union office to cable my parents in Salzburg and Sinnie's in Coronado that we had safely arrived in New York. The next thing on my agenda was to get in touch with Friedl Pfeifer. There were many details to discuss in firming up the joint operation of the ski school for the coming winter season, and I was eagerly looking forward to this sudden turn in my career. Friedl wired that he would meet me in California, either at Los Angeles or San Diego, whichever was more convenient for me. That would work out well for us since we had planned to return to Coronado before moving to Sun Valley for the winter.

Before we left New York, I wanted Sinnie to see a Broadway show. Though 1939 was not a vintage year for Broadway, we settled on the musical *Dubary Was a Lady*, with Ethel Merman as a rising star. We enjoyed the show immensely. While in New York I also picked up an assignment to write a piece for *Esquire* magazine, which would keep me busy for a while since I was not a fast writer and toiled over my prose.

Taking the Twentieth Century express train from New York to Chicago and from there the Santa Fe Chief to Los Angeles, we got to California in the fastest time possible in those days. Sinnie's parents welcomed us and we settled down comfortably in our quarters. Within a week, a letter arrived for Admiral and Mrs. Gannon that verified our tales of adventures. It was from Peter MacCann, the Irish schoolteacher, who upon reaching Dublin, had immediately cabled the Gannons that he had seen us both well in Le Havre. He followed it up with a touching letter of gratitude for our having helped him get home. The admiral replied with a letter that was equally heartfelt, since both he and Mrs. Gannon had been so grateful for news of their wayward children's whereabouts. Admiral Gannon also wrote warm thank-you notes to Captain Ellis Stone and Sam Wiley. Captain Stone's reply threw a discerning light on the political embroglio in Europe. To paraphrase his letter, to him the world on the whole seemed to be in an awful mess, with the worst of it yet to come.

L I F E

A T

S U N   V A L L E Y

Arriving at Sun Valley with Sinnie for the 1939-1940 winter season seemed to establish a new home base for us. Pat Rogers, the manager of the lodge, put us up in a spacious corner room overlooking the ice rink and the new Harriman cottage. Teaming up with Friedl Pfeifer turned out to be a happy combination—of two characters of almost opposite temperament. Still, we managed to get along with a minimum of friction for several reasons. First, I admired Friedl as a superior athlete. Second, he was scrupulously honest and fair-minded. Third, he had a delightful sense of humor, which did not readily spring to the surface but when it did, exploded into a cascade of uninhibited laughter. At heart he was an unabashed sentimentalist and, therefore, vulnerable; he had trained himself not to display his innermost emotions in public. In short, he was a gentleman.

Friedl had hand-picked a staff of instructors, balanced in experience. Although we had the framework of a successful ski school, patterned after the Hannes Schneider School at St. Anton, he and I recognized that certain changes in teaching methods would have to be made, without violating the basic principles we had learned in Austria. For one thing, skiing was growing in popularity, and as the sport evolved, continuous improvements were made in ski equipment. Manufacturers of skis, bindings, and boots had come up with new ideas, especially the innovation and perfection of steel edges, which made a great difference in controlling the skis in motion. For another, American skiers were much different from European skiers, more impatient. Our students were more interested in reaching a semblance of proficiency than in perfecting certain basic maneuvers. It was all well and good to practice snowplow turns ad infinitum on a gentle slope at the bottom of a hill, but what our students really aspired to was getting to the top of the mountain to ski safely down an appropriate run. That's what the sport of skiing was all about, the freedom and speed felt while soaring down a mountainside.

Friedl and I felt strongly that we needed to adapt the ski school's curriculum to this American temperament. We knew the teaching process had to be expedited and shortened, and believed that Dollar Mountain was the ideal training ground to put a streamlined version of the Arlberg technique to a test. With the mountain's variety in pitches and undulating slopes, beginners and intermediate skiers could make remarkably rapid progress. By the end of fewer than a week's lessons, with practice on Dollar Mountain, a majority of fledgling skiers were up on Baldy, considered the ultimate yardstick to gage one's progress. This would not have been possible in the old days.

In many people's minds the profession of ski instructor was glamorized. They visualized it as a life of luxury with free room and board, lift tickets, and unlimited opportunity for carnal fulfillment. Certainly an instructor's life could be fascinating, since it brought him in touch with multiple layers of society, from everyday working people who had saved up their money for a week's vacation at Sun Valley to potentates of industry and Hollywood celebrities. But the intensity of putting a class of twelve to fifteen people through a day's workout on skis was mentally and physically tiring. Patience is an instructor's prime requisite, mixed with a dose of well-timed humor and the capacity to make learning fun. He has to have the knack of instilling in his pupils a desire to come back the next day to learn more. And since each individual demanded and expected a certain amount of personal attention, it was the instructor's greatest gift to make each student feel that he or she was to him the most important member of his class.

In those early years at Sun Valley after a heavy storm with tons of fresh snow piled up on the practice slopes, we instructors often would have to get up at daybreak and, joined by the full complement of ski patrolmen and mountain maintenance personnel, head out to the slopes to flatten the snow. Lined up across the width of the slope or trail, we would step-by-step pack down the deep layer to a solid surface that would keep skis on top. This could take hours and had to be finished in time for the morning class at ten o'clock. Frequently, during lunch hours (noon through two o'clock) instructors were booked for private lessons, leaving barely enough time to gulp down a bowl of soup or grab a sandwich before afternoon classes started at two. When the day's share of outdoor work was finished, there was the obligatory daily meeting to turn in collected tickets, discuss the day's events, share information about students to be either advanced or fitted into a lower class, and attend to other matters pertaining to the next day's schedule. Occasionally a constructive critique of someone's performance concluded the session.

By 5:30 P.M., the instructor was free to socialize, if he was so inclined. While the corps of instructors at Sun Valley were not subjected to a monastic regimen, their nocturnal outings were a matter of private choice and discretion. As long as their activities did not give rise to gossip and as long as they appeared clean shaven with eyes wide-open, neatly dressed, and bushy-tailed on time for work the next morning, no one could fault them.

No matter what the weather was—snowstorms, bitter cold, biting polar winds—there were always a few gung ho aficionados who could not be deterred from going out and taking lessons. Bad weather, of course, could dwindle a class down to two or three participants. It was a guest's prerogative to choose as he felt, to go out or stay indoors in a warm place; not so for an instructor.

In my book *Downhill Skiing*, I had written about a teacher's spiritual rewards:

> Skiing is not exercise only, not merely a sport—it is a revelation of body and soul. We should look at it as an art akin to ballet, like dancing to imaginary music. . . . On the teacher's side, there is the rich satisfaction of seeing his pupils' progress, to note the gleam in their eyes after a thrilling run, down a smooth trail or a series of christianias in deep powder snow, with white rooster tails flying behind. This joy, which comes from the depth of their souls, is the teacher's joy too, and his most precious recompense.

A well-functioning ski school was a major asset to Sun Valley, but a well-run hotel was of paramount importance. The responsibility of managing the lodge was placed by the Union Pacific Railroad Company in the hands of Pat Rogers, and a felicitous choice it was. Pat Rogers was among the very best hotel managers I have known. He was the epitome of an "innkeeper" in the finest tradition. He considered every one of his guests his personal ward and couldn't do enough to make them feel comfortable. He was tireless and irrepressible, although he could be ornery on rare occasions, when the performance of an employee did not measure up to his expectations, as many who worked for him can attest. No matter where a trouble spot surfaced, Pat would show up to have it fixed in a jiffy.

During the summer season, Pat organized a baseball league for employees. He acted as a star player, captain, and coach for one of the teams. Woe to the teammate who should have the misfortune to drop an easy fly ball with men on base or commit some other inexcusable boo-boo. In a high-pitched, agitated voice Pat would shout at the crestfallen player, "Get off the field! You're fired!" Baseball was sacred to him, to the extent that he frequently he lost his normal composure. However, at the end of a game, the heat of battle tempered, Pat returned to his more docile and rational self, reinstating the temporarily jobless player with apologies for having lost his cool and the advice, "Now, son, you go out there and practice some more, so it don't happen again. You hear now, boy?"

I admired Pat Rogers through our lengthy association and, next to Friedl Pfeifer, regarded him as my boss but also as one of my best and most supportive friends. All in all, he was both beloved and respected by guests and employees, a high tribute for one in such a delicate position.

HANS AND VIRGINIA

The history of Sun Valley is rich in romance. Some local love stories were sweet, such as that between Marty Arrouge and his pupil Norma Shearer, who was a stunningly beautiful lady and an all-time great star of the silver screen as well. Theirs was a fairy-tale love match. I was best man at their wedding, which was held at the Church of the Good Shepherd in Beverly Hills. Their marriage was durable and their devotion to each other shone brightly throughout Norma's all too brief life span.

Another instructor who found his true love at Sun Valley was Wayne Poulsen, later a driving force behind the development of Squaw Valley. He was assigned as private instructor to a Greek shipping magnate, Stavros Niarchos. Stavros proved to be a night owl, addicted to high-stakes gambling, and spent much of his time at the Christiania Club in Ketchum, which was the *ne plus ultra* casino among the many local gambling parlors. Customarily, Stavros would show up sometime after lunch, or maybe not at all, after a heavy night of action at the gambling tables. That gave Wayne a lot of time to kill, which he used to teach a plucky young debutante from New York how to ski—for free, on Stavros's time.

Sandy, the debutante, came from a respected family that was well established in business. They occupied the large penthouse suite of the Sherry Netherland Hotel as their permanent home. After seeing the film *Sun Valley Serenade,* Sandy was so enthralled by the valley's romantic ambiance that she made reservations for a lengthy stay—unescorted. Need I say more? By the end of the winter, Wayne and Sandy's daily association had become permanent, resulting in wedlock. Many children followed, all of them first-rate skiers of Olympic caliber. After fifty years of a very colorful life together, and fourteen grandchildren, they continue to live happily ever after.

Friedl Pfeifer also found the girl he dreamed of. He was passionately smitten by Hoyt Smith, a lithesome ingenue from Salt Lake City. Her father was a prominent banker, who, along with Mrs. Smith, was unfortunately not in favor of and, in fact, highly antagonistic toward his daughter's romantic entanglement, which threatened to become binding. In a situation similar to mine and Sinnie's, her parents had expected their cherished offspring to come up with a better match than an obscure ski instructor from Austria's hinterlands. But love prevailed. After an attempt to elope, the determined lovers were wedded in a festive ceremony that turned out to be the highlight of the Salt Lake City social season.

Hans Hauser was another ski instructor who found romance at Sun Valley. Hans was a lovable man. He was also an outstandingly stylish skier and a racer of renown. Over six feet tall, he cut a fine figure. Reportedly—and from sources who ought to know—he was exceptionally well endowed in the male department and had uncommon staying power. No wonder the ladies fell for him, head over heels. He could have had his pick among numerous heiresses, but his destiny lay elsewhere.

I was out on Dollar Mountain when I was told I had an urgent call from Pat Rogers. When I contacted him he told me that a lady had checked in that morning without reservations and had asked for the best suite of rooms in the lodge. (Since it was the middle of January, a slack period, the house count was low, and this unexpected revenue was a windfall.) The woman requested that I call her right away to make arrangements for a private instructor. During my lunch hour I went to see the lady in

How to earn a new Dodge the easy way. This
ad appeared in the *Saturday Evening Post* and
other national magazines, 1938.

Averell Harriman, founder of Sun Valley, in 1936. Photo courtesy of the Sun Valley Historical Society, Ketchum, Idaho.

Kathleen Harriman, in 1948. Courtesy of Sun Valley Resort.

Herding a flock of future champion skiers at the ski school at Sun Valley, 1948. Courtesy of Sun Valley Resort.

Arriving at Sun Valley with Sinnie and baby
Peter in the winter of 1939–1940.

Teaching Peter to ski—for the camera,
only. Photo by E. L. Chapin for Steve
Hannagan Associates.

Mark with Sinnie at Sun Valley, after having won
first prize in a race, 1948.

Peter ski-jumping at Sun Valley,
stopped in mid-air, 1950. Photo
by Otto Lang.

The Sun Valley Ski School, 1949. Emile Allais stands in the center to the right of me; Warren Miller is on the top right end of the back row.

Action shot of Otto Lang at Sun Valley.

With Darryl F. Zanuck at the lift up Mount Baldy, 1940.

Sometimes it's fun to be the director. Filming *Snow Eagles* for RKO-Pathé at Alta, Utah. From left: Audrey Roth, me, Dodie Post-Gann, Gretchen Fraser, Billie Deeke (cameraman), 1944.

With Virginia, Darryl, and Dick Zanuck on Baldy, 1941.

Sun Valley Serenade poster. The movie starred Sonja Henie and John Payne.

Skiing with the Shah of Iran, Mohammed Reza Pahlavi, at Sun Valley in 1954. There was no snow early that December, so we drove up to higher country at Galena every morning, just the two of us.

Awarding one of his many racing trophies to Toni Matt. Matt directed the Sun Valley Ski School for one winter, 1948.

At Marty Arrouge's wedding to Norma Shearer, Beverly Hills, California. I was best man; Sylvia Fairbanks was the maid of honor.

The director's chair—a Max Barsis sketch.

My first movie camera.

A scene from *Basic Principles of Skiing*, a training film I shot for the Tenth Mountain Division prior to World War II, at Sun Valley, 1941. Photo by Watson Webb, Jr.

A rare action photo of the master and disciple. Hannes Schneider and me during the filming of *Ski Meister* for RKO-Pathé, 1944.

Peter, Sinnie, Mark, me on our last family outing at Sun Valley, 1952.

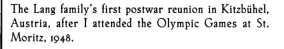

The Lang family's first postwar reunion in Kitzbühel, Austria, after I attended the Olympic Games at St. Moritz, 1948.

Hannes Schneider and family arriving safely in North Conway, New Hampshire, after having left Austria under duress from the Nazis.

her suite. She showed me her large assortment of skiing apparel, all first-rate, brand-new, and very expensive, bought at Abercrombie & Fitch in Chicago. "I don't like any of this junk," she said. "It's crummy. Take me to Piccard's and let's get me some good-looking duds."

Fred Piccard, an astute Swiss businessman with impeccable taste, was regarded as the ultimate arbiter in skiing fashion at that time. We adjourned to his elegant store, which adjoined the lobby of the lodge. Here the lady proceeded to duplicate everything she already owned in ski apparel. Rarely have I witnessed such a buying frenzy. Exchanging looks of amazement, Piccard and I just shrugged our shoulders. While the lady was trying on a new pair of ski boots, I noticed a gold bracelet dangling from her wrist. The letters attached spelled out V-I-R-G-I-N-I-A. When all the purchases had been added up, Virginia pulled a fat roll of hundred-dollar bills from her bag. She removed the rubber band holding them together and peeled off a number to pay for her purchases. These were to be sent to her suite, pronto!

Suddenly it struck me: Virginia . . . Chicago . . . money. . . Beverly Hills . . . Bugsy Siegel . . . Virginia HILL! That was indeed who she was, as I found out later when checking with the front desk. The woman was well-known for consorting with a mobster with notorious Mafia connections. We had a tiger by the tail. I could tell this "tough dame" would need special handling. Who would be the best man for the job? Who could assert himself with authority yet at the same time make her stay pleasurable? Hans Hauser was the obvious choice. With his vast experience in the ladies' department, he could surely handle the task of being her private ski instructor.

Hans took the assignment readily. He and Virginia got along right from the start. Virginia was not a bad sort. Far from pretty, she was a bit dumpy and of considerable mammary amplitude. A disconcerting habit of hers was to pull out her eyelashes, hair by hair. In spite of her gangster's moll demeanor, she made friends easily. She was especially popular with the help and the bellboys, of course, since the hundred-dollar tip was her trademark—what the hell, it was just as easy to peel off a century note than to fish around in her bag for a measly buck. But Virginia could also be tough, as I found out during one of Sun Valley's seasonal warm spells. The snow turned to molasses while rain pelted down like a tropical downpour. Not a soul, not even the hardiest skiers, were tempted to go out. Except Virginia, that is. My phone rang. An irate voice said, "Where the hell is Hans? I want my lesson! I'm waiting for him."

"Virginia," I said, trying to placate her, "it's raining cats and dogs. You wouldn't want to go out in this sort of weather."

"Never mind that. I'm paying for the instructor, come rain or shine. I want the son of a bitch to report to me immediately!"

Hans obliged, and their relationship grew cozier by the day. Pretty soon, I noticed Hans carrying a wad of hundred-dollar bills, too. He had become Virginia's confidant, lover, and exchequer, a dispenser of cash and tips, though he operated on a scale far less lavish than Virginia's.

Gradually, an influx of shady and ominous characters, all in city clothing, arrived in Sun Valley to call on Virginia, afterward leaving furtively without ever putting on a pair of skis. Virginia knew a lot, having been Bugsy Siegel's paramour for years, before he was mowed down gangland-style at his lavish Beverly Hills residence. To this day it remains a mystery where the money came from, and why it came floating into her hands, supposedly delivered by personal messengers, all neatly piled in old shoe boxes. Her presence made the Sun Valley management more and more uncomfortable, and the FBI also moved in to conduct their own investigation. We reached the point of wanting to get rid of Virginia, "and the sooner the better," as Pat Rogers said.

Late one evening there was a knock on my door. It was Hans. He had come to tell me that he intended to marry Virginia Hill. They had both agreed to it. Hans's news did not come as a total surprise to me, but it was a shock, nevertheless. As if I were his big brother, I tried to dissuade him from taking this rash step. It would cut him off from all his friends, I warned, and—to be very blunt—it might ruin his life. Gradually Hans seemed to grasp the magnitude of his decision and his resolve began to falter. By then it must have been three o'clock in the morning. I was dead tired, but I was determined to change his mind. As Hans shook my hand before leaving, he reassured me, saying, "You're right, Otto. It would be a foolish thing to do. I'm not going through with it. Thank you for talking to me." Feeling immensely relieved, I went to bed convinced that I had done a good deed for an old and dear friend.

The next morning the news was flashed to me: Hans and Virginia had eloped, clearing out at the crack of dawn. They were going to get married by the nearest justice of the peace somewhere en route, wherever they were headed on their honeymoon.

While this was the end of the Sun Valley chapter, it was by no means the end of the story. The tale unfolded like a Greek tragedy, inexorably leading to the destruction of the two principal players. Hans ran into trouble with the immigration authorities because his visiting permit had expired. Rather than be deported, he skipped out of the country without Virginia and went to South America and eventually back to Salzburg. Meanwhile, Virginia had her own troubles. In a government investigation of organized crime, the Kefauver Committee asked her to testify at its hearings. Looking demure in a Greta Garbo-type flop hat, she appeared on national television and created a sensation. Her presence made the stodgy members of the Senate committee sit on the edge of their seats, as if expecting her to burst any moment into a tirade of choice four-letter expletives, as she had done in the privacy of chambers.

For once, though, Virginia behaved like a lady. Because the committee could not pin anything on her, only by the time-proven stratagem of putting the Internal Revenue Service on her trail was justified punishment ultimately meted out to her for income tax evasion and fraud. She was stripped of all cash on hand. Her house and personal possessions, including jewelry and furs, were confiscated. Somehow she managed to escape the country to rejoin Hans in Salzburg.

But neither of them was welcome there. Virginia's notoriety had been widely publicized in the world press following her television appearances during the Kefauver hearings. As often happens under stressful circumstances, their marriage began to deteriorate, even though Virginia had given birth to a boy, whom Hans treasured and looked after in a touching way. Also, Virginia's supply of money was cut off as mysteriously as it had been provided to her in previous years.

She finally couldn't take it any longer. Virginia died of an overdose of drugs and alcohol. Whether premeditated or accidental remained unexplained. But all signs pointed to suicide. Two years later, despondent and weary, Hans ended his own life by hanging himself with a rope from a wooden beam in the ceiling of the small restaurant-*boîte* he owned. When I heard the tragic news, I was shaken to the core. After all, to a certain extent—though innocently—I had initiated this harrowing chain of events by selecting Hans to be Virginia Hill's ski instructor.

DFZ

Early one morning, during the winter of 1941, the phone rang in my room in the main lodge at Sun Valley. I was barely awake. On came the voice of Averell Harriman. "Otto," he said, "could you come over to our cottage for breakfast? There's something I want to discuss with you."

The Harriman cottage, close to the lodge, had a splendid view of the valley and surrounding mountains. It was a modest but most comfortable structure, built in a pseudo-Alpine style. Shortly after I knocked at the door, Averell opened it and invited me to enter. He was an impressive-looking gentleman—tall, lean, handsome, sun-tanned, and elegant—and patrician in manner and speech. We sat down. He poured me a cup of coffee and came quickly to the point. "I have a problem, Otto, and I hope you can help me solve it. A close friend of mine has been here for a week with his wife and three children. We're fierce adversaries in the game of croquet. He's also a passionate polo player. But he can't seem to make any progress in learning to ski. This is very discouraging to someone with considerable pride in his physical abilities. So he's ready to pack up and leave.

"I don't want to lose them," Averell went on. "Aside from my personal attachment to them, they're too important for Sun Valley and its future. If they go away with a good experience, many Hollywood stars, producers, directors, and socialites will follow in their footsteps and come here, too. So it's really imperative to keep them here with us." My mind was racing ahead to guess who this crucially important personage might be. "I would like to ask you to take personal charge of this situation," he said. "I have already discussed it with Friedl, and he's totally in accord with this plan. We both feel that if anyone can turn this situation around, you are the man to do it."

I assured him I would do my very best to help out.

"Good!" he said. "Then meet me in the lodge lobby at eleven, and I'll introduce you to Mr. and Mrs. Zanuck."

"Darryl Zanuck?" I gaped.

Averell looked at me quizzically. "Do you know him?"

"Not really," I said. "But I worked for his movie company on location once, a few years ago." Working on *Thin Ice* with Tyrone Power and Sonja Henie at Mount Rainier had whetted my appetite for filmmaking. My encounter with Darryl Zanuck at Sun Valley would mark a turning point in my life and career, to a degree I would never have imagined. In time it also developed into a close family relationship with him, his wife, Virginia, and their three children, Darrylin, Susan, and Richard.

As a skier, Darryl had trouble finding that perfect balance point for his body, the "sweet spot" that makes skiing easier and almost effortless. He perched precariously on his boards, and the slightest change in terrain or speed would make him topple face forward into the snow, his ubiquitous Havana cigar quashed by his face. He would fall sideways or backwards at the slightest provocation. No wonder Darryl thought skiing was the pits. The worst part of it was that Virginia, an accomplished dancer, caught on quickly and waltzed ahead of him, as did the Zanuck youngsters. As is usually the case with children on skis, they surpassed their parents in no time at all, and this oedipal challenge also threatened his paternal pride.

Actually, there was something peculiar in Darryl's attitude toward skiing. He seemed to fight his skis rather than coddle them into changing direction. I had to teach him how to go with the flow of the terrain and to be loose, relaxed, and free with all his movements, shifting his weight from one ski onto the other yet having both skis under complete control. With skiing as with other endeavors, Darryl refused to give up. It took much work, patience, and even some mental therapy to overcome all of his hang-ups, but in the end, he persevered, proving once again that he had the mettle to overcome any physical adversity. After that the Zanuck family came regularly to Sun Valley, and brought a long stream of camp followers in their wake. Averell Harriman's bid to retain Zanuck's good will paid off.

In time Darryl's son, Dick, inspired by his father's movie accomplishments, also became a distinguished producer of many outstanding films. With Lili, his wife, he built for his family an attractive Alpine-style mansion, an architectural showcase, on a piece of land I had once pointed out to him as highly desirable. Thus, the family tradition that combines filmmaking and skiing lives on and will undoubtedly continue to do so. Dick's sons already show the makings of champion skiers.

DFZ spent the last years of his life as a near-recluse in Palm Springs, under the care of Virginia, to whom he had returned after a separation lasting seventeen years, mostly spent abroad. She was a loving wife to the very end, in spite of his extramarital peccadilloes, of which there were a considerable number.

During Darryl's final years, I spent many a weekend with him at his Spanish-style hacienda at Palm Springs. We watched television by the hour, a medium Zanuck had detested and denigrated, until he realized that it was here to stay. He then proceeded to blend it artfully and successfully with his filmmaking endeavors. We sat around the shady patio, overlooking the large swimming pool and his beloved croquet court, on which many a tense match had been fought. We talked about old times, the halcyon days of movie making, when the major studios stood like mighty fortresses against changing economic tides. Darryl's mind was beginning to fade, and his memory suffered, to his great annoyance. He slept a lot but physically appeared to be in good shape. In his lucid moments, his comments on present-day state-of-the-art filmmaking were revealing and perceptive, as always.

Later, Virginia sent me a photograph of their fiftieth wedding anniversary celebration. He was cutting the cake, nattily dressed in a white military dress jacket, his chest bemedaled. Behind him was a credenza filled with trophies, mementos, and photographs. Among them were a half dozen Oscars, the prestigious Irving Thalberg Award, and the Lifetime Achievement Award from the Academy of Motion Picture Arts and Sciences, which was about as high as one could rise in this business. Fittingly, his last picture and biggest box office success was *The Longest Day* (1962), depicting the invasion of Normandy, a crucial step in ending World War II.

When Darryl died in December 1979, I was one of the six honorary pallbearers at his funeral. A few years later, when Virginia followed him, I was again among the six asked to escort her on this last journey, to be laid to rest next to her husband. Virginia was one of the strongest and bravest ladies I was privileged to know and have as a friend. It wasn't exactly easy for her, being the wife of Darryl F. Zanuck. Sometimes it wasn't easy being his friend, either. But, for me, our close association was always stimulating, challenging, and professionally fulfilling. And never for a moment was it dull!

SUN VALLEY SERENADE

Averell Harriman's efforts to keep Darryl F. Zanuck and family at Sun Valley were well rewarded. It would have taken a lot of money to pay for the kind of publicity that was generated simply by his presence. When vacationing at Sun Valley, DFZ initiated a studio operation on a small scale, and a steady flow of writers, producers, directors, and film editors came to confer with him about ongoing and future film projects. He had made arrangements to have access to the local movie theater, the Sun Valley Opera House, when it was not scheduled for public performances.

His regular studio projectionist, well versed in the routine of running the "dailies," was summoned to Sun Valley. The dailies represented the day-to-day progress of every film in production, which could be half a dozen at a time, all awaiting Zanuck's comments and approval. I was fortunately invited to attend many of these screenings, usually scheduled after his skiing outings from noon to four o'clock on Baldy. Often a film in its first rough-cut assembly would be included, needing to be trimmed to the required length for theatrical release. To a certain extent this was flexible, depending upon how well the film held up. Darryl Zanuck's comments and suggestions regarding the deletion of entire scenes, portions of dialogue, lack of or excessive use of close-ups, camera angles, and so forth, anything that affected the smooth flow of continuity and the overall impact of the film, were jotted down in shorthand by Molly Mandaville, his trusted production assistant and confidante of many years. Sorted out, condensed, typed, and mimeographed, these notes were then dispatched to all persons at the studio connected with the particular film in work.

Darryl had an uncanny instinct, following his own tenet that "motion pictures had to move and never should stand still," in order to keep an audience's attention riveted. He was highly respected as a top-notch editor by his peers. Even though his was the final word, when he encountered opposing opinions from his associates, it was a matter of give-and-take in regard to making proposed changes. He listened, respected, and considered their points of view, but the ultimate burden of responsibility, right or wrong, rested on his shoulders. However, and to his credit, he never shied away from admitting that he may have made an error in judgment.

These sessions, except for a short break for dinner, often lasted past midnight into the wee hours of the morning. I found it incredibly stimulating and exciting to watch the sequential progression of creating a film. I was fascinated by the process and amazed by the myriad intricate details required to come up with a burnished final product, ready to be shown in theaters worldwide. For me it was an extraordinary learning experience under the tutelage of a man recognized as one of the brightest minds and creative filmmakers in the Hollywood pantheon.

Sinnie and I also became part of the Zanucks' social life, alternating between quiet family dinners and large parties, of which there was an abundance at Sun Valley. Virginia Zanuck, the mother of three strapping youngsters, took a great liking to Sinnie's inherent vivaciousness. When she found out that Sinnie was expecting a child, she took it upon herself to become her guardian angel and couldn't do enough to make her feel comfortable, dispensing sage advice as a seasoned mother would to one awaiting her firstborn.

The culmination of Darryl Zanuck's contribution to the fame of Sun Valley was his production of the film *Sun Valley Serenade*, which put Sun

Valley on the map as a world-class ski resort and, in fact, made it a legend. The actual shooting of *Sun Valley Serenade* was preceded by many story conferences in Zanuck's office at the studio with the producer Milton Sperling and the writers Robert Ellis and Helen Logan. A last session to finalize the shooting script was scheduled to take place at Sun Valley. Since I had been assigned by Darryl as technical advisor on all matters concerning skiing and also to direct the ski action sequences for the film, I was asked to participate in this story conference held in the Redwood Room at the lodge.

There was one unresolved problem in the story line, which required the two principles, Sonja Henie and John Payne, to be thrown together in some manner to progress their love affair. Ideas were presented, kicked around, dissected, and discarded. I listened attentively but kept quiet, since I felt it did not behoove me to interfere with the pros in this skull session. In my mind I had worked out a scenario that would force the two principles, stranded through certain circumstances on a little-used ski trail, to seek refuge in a nearby unoccupied but fully furnished mountain cabin. What better place to kindle the flames in an idyllic love tryst? Timidly, while the others were still groping for ideas, I raised my hand and asked whether I could present my idea. I was given a nod by Darryl to proceed. After I finished explaining my scenario, there was an ominous silence that made me feel that surely I had bombed and should have kept my mouth shut.

Everybody waited for Darryl to express his reaction first. At last he spoke. "That's it," he said. "It's a perfect setup to progress our love entanglement in the right direction. Let's do it Otto's way." The scene played in the finished film exactly the way I had originally presented it. If nothing else, it may have left a spark of recognition in Darryl's mind that there was more to his ski instructor's enthusiasm for films than met the eye.

Bruce Humberstone, under contract to Fox, had been assigned to direct the film. The plan was to shoot backgrounds and establishing shots of the locale with doubles for all the principal characters, to avoid the expense of bringing them to Sun Valley. The script of *Sun Valley Serenade* was not of that distinction. It was a pleasant love story designed to feature the skating talent of Sonja Henie, a multiple Olympic gold medal winner, playing the part of a Norwegian adoptee in youthful pursuit of John Payne, as a member of Glenn Miller's famous band. Miss Henie was a naturally gifted actress, when cast in the right role, and her skating numbers were to be elaborately staged and choreographed at the studio on an ice rink taking up the floor of an entire stage.

Sun Valley with its scenic offerings was to be a major player in this wintry romance, whereas the remainder of the cast, all under contract to Fox, such as John Payne, Milton Berle, Lynn Bari, and Joan Davis would contribute valiantly to the somewhat simplistic story line with songs and comedic shenanigans. What really was expected to lift this picture above the average musical was the Glen Miller Orchestra performing some newly composed melodies with appropriate lyrics, such as the theme song "It Happened at Sun Valley."

After the Humberstone unit finished shooting and returned to the studio, as had Darryl Zanuck, I was to do my job as a second unit director, staging with doubles a playful but exciting chase on skis down Baldy Mountain with Sonja Henie in hot pursuit of John Payne and vice versa. Darryl had told me before he left that he wanted me to come to Hollywood as soon as the season ended at Sun Valley, to be on hand when the interiors were shot at the studio. Also, I would help in piecing together the footage I had shot at Sun Valley, which would need a number of close-ups of Henie and Payne on skis, shot against a moving background, to be integrated with the live action shots. This was an assignment I looked forward to, and I was told it could last anywhere from four to six weeks. With a princely weekly salary and per diem, more than I collected in one month of my salary at Sun Valley, it was an unexpected bonanza. I hoped that this might open the door for me to switch over some day from ski teaching to filmmaking on a permanent basis.

Working at the studio was a fairy-tale fulfillment—so much to see and learn. The weeks went by and within a short time my lucrative financial windfall would be coming to an end. But before it did, I asked Darryl's secretary for an appointment to see him just for a few minutes. At the set time I was shown into his office, which I was seeing for the first time and about which I had heard much. It was huge, the size of a fairly large swimming pool, and psychologically intimidating as one approached him sitting at his desk after a lengthy walk on a deep soft carpet. His oversize antique desk made of a rare wood was at the opposite end from the entrance door. As one might have expected, the room was beautifully furnished by one of the top interior designers of the studio with fine period pieces and artifacts intermixed with mounted trophies of his and Virginia's safaris in East Africa. There was an assortment of large upholstered chairs and tables in various groupings to accommodate story conferences and production meetings with department heads. Though stylish and sumptuous, it was still a functional office.

Graciously he pointed at a chair for me to sit down. Facing him across the expanse of his desk piled up with stacks of scripts and shooting schedules, I noticed a credenza against the wall with a galaxy of silver-framed family photographs. "What's on your mind, Otto?" he asked me without any light-hearted preamble. This was strictly on business time, not to be used for banal chitchat.

"Darryl," I said, "this has been an absolutely wonderful experience working on *Sun Valley Serenade*. I cannot thank you enough for having given me this opportunity."

"You have done a fine job for us," he replied, "and we at the studio appreciate it."

"Well, now, ah . . . I'm making an awful lot of money on my weekly paycheck, but before my cup runneth over, I would like to ask you to cut my salary way down so that hopefully I could stay on and learn the business from the bottom up."

He gave me a startled, quizzical look with his blue eyes, and after a thoughtful pause, he said, "I want to tell you something, Otto. You are the first guy that ever walked into my office and asked to have his salary cut, contrary to many other SOBs who come into my office to ask for more." I blinked with surprise and hoped that my stratagem would work.

"Okay, you're on," he said. "We'll cut your salary to one third of what you are making now, to start with. I'll assign you as a third assistant director to my friend William Wellman, who is directing *Oxbow Incident*. Report to Joe Boehm, his first assistant director, and he'll put you to work. Good luck, and keep in touch."

That was the way I began my career in films, fully employed by Twentieth Century Fox, with the understanding that by the first week in December, I would return to Sun Valley for the winter season in my former capacity.

W A R   Y E A R S

With my immediate future determined, Sinnie and I looked around for a small furnished house to rent for the summer months. We found just what we wanted in Benedict Canyon, one of the less-traveled arteries connecting Beverly Hills with the San Fernando Valley. The house was one of the ubiquitous miniature villas built in a pseudo-Spanish style of architecture. It would serve for the time being, but in the back of my mind, I was determined to look for a house of our own to buy outright. We had saved enough for a sizable down payment, and with real estate prices depressed and favorable loan terms available, our monthly payments would be far less than the rent we paid. Of course, we did not have a stick of furniture, but from our wedding gifts we did have a surfeit of fine china, silver cutlery, and all sorts of decorative bric-a-brac.

Until we found our own house, however, we had a comfortable place to live, an automobile I could drive to work, a solvent bank account, and a suitable home for Sinnie to await her accouchement sometime in June. We were as happy as two people could be.

THE OXBOW INCIDENT
When I reported to Joe Boehm for my first day's work on the set of *The Oxbow Incident*, I knew that I would be lowest on the totem pole.

The word had spread that I was Darryl Zanuck's favorite ski instructor, which in a way helped me get established but in another way had the odor of nepotism. I resolved to rise above it and prove that I could deliver what was expected from me, regardless of how I got the break.

Luckily Joe Boehm was a likable man and slightly bemused to see me starting out in such a humble position, which actually was nothing more than a gofer. He must have remembered starting his own career in a similar situation. Thoughtfully he found ways to give me more authority and responsibilities to bolster my ego. Eventually he put me in charge of a whole bunch of horses, which were part of the on screen posse in pursuit of three suspected rustlers and purported killers. For editing purposes, I had to make sure that the number of horses, color, and position matched in every scene. When someone asked what my function was on this picture, I explained I was counting horses' asses.

Eventually I was introduced to William Wellman, director of the film. One of the best in his craft, he also happened to be a colorful character with an extraordinary personal history. Having been a combat pilot in World War I with the Lafayette Escadrille, he told harrowing tales of dogfights and airplane crashes, one of which left him with a permanent limp. He was full of life and energy and great in directing men in his films. They trusted him and his judgment implicitly.

The Oxbow Incident had an exceptional screenplay by Lamar Trotti. Based on Walter Van Tilburg Clark's novel, acclaimed as one of the truest westerns, it also had a stellar cast with Henry Fonda in one of his most moving performances. Dana Andrews, Anthony Quinn, and others rounded out the players in the grim drama of three innocent men being hung by a posse of lawless rednecks without a legal trial presided over by a judge. Henry Fonda played one of the dissident characters in the crazed lynch mob who could not avert the tragedy. The picture became an enduring classic due to Wellman's sensitive direction and outstanding performances by every single member of the large cast.

As the shooting of the film went along, I got to know Bill Wellman a little better and admired his integrity as a filmmaker. He used to kid me a lot and called me "dat Austrian somesing . . . ," imitating my pronounced accent, all in good fun and without malice. I felt proud to have been part of the filming of *The Oxbow Incident,* in even a minor capacity.

Sinnie gave birth to our first child, a boy, on June 7, 1941. We named him Peter Anton, for no one in particular. Sinnie had endured bravely and without complaining the prolonged process of labor. When I was told by the attending obstetrician, after a tortuous wait of many hours, that both mother and infant were well, it was an enormous relief. I could hardly wait to be admitted to see Sinnie and share with her the joy of the arrival of this precious addition, which made us a family.

After another half hour or so, the nurse beckoned me to follow her to Sinnie's room. I found her sitting up in bed leaning against the pillows at her back, wanly smiling. I was fully expecting to see her much more spent and weary. Though the strain of her ordeal had left its mark on her face, it only made her look even more beautiful. I told her I loved her, and sat gingerly at the edge of her bed so that I could hold her hand when the door opened and the nurse brought in the baby for us to see together for the first time.

He was all spruced up, healthy in color with a pink glow and a full head of dark hair. Loosely wrapped in a lightweight blanket, he was fast asleep with a cherubic smile on his face. The nurse passed him to Sinnie to hold, and after a while she handed him to me, ever so gently. When I held that tiny bundle of humanity cradled in my arms, leaning his head against my chest, I felt indescribable elation and overflowing tenderness coming from my heart. I vowed that I would do all in my power to make his life a happy one, to be a protector, provider, and teacher for all seasons. We were fortunate to have a perfect little fellow, as pronounced by the pediatrician after a first examination. I was convinced that ours was the most beautiful, most perfectly formed baby I had ever seen, bar none. Isn't that the opinion of every father and mother? I think it is.

Sinnie stayed in the Good Samaritan Hospital for only a few days after her childbirth. I was as nervous as can be, and trying to cover up my state of anxiety, when I picked up mother and child and bundled them carefully into my car to start the long drive home. I felt that I carried something fragile, comparable to the delicacy of two priceless Fabergé Easter eggs. Only when I got them home did I relax and feel safe, protected by the solid walls of our Spanish abode.

When Virginia Zanuck heard that Sinnie had given birth, she sent her driver to deliver the bassinet in which all three of her children had spent the first months of their infancy. It was an elaborately appointed, large, white wicker basket on a high stand, with flounces, flourishes, and a baldachin of the finest linens plus a kitten-soft blanket, fit for a princeling to start out in life. Also, there was a beautiful bouquet of roses from the Zanucks awaiting Sinnie upon our arrival at home.

For a time, every day of our lives was a succession of moments of amazement, observing the progress of a growing infant. Even at that early stage, certain characteristics of Peter's behavior came to the fore, and one kept wondering whether he would be like his father or more like his mother. I was besotted with love for our little boy and looked upon his arrival as one of the best things that ever happened in my life.

To add to our marital bliss, we also found the house we wanted to buy on Coldwater Canyon, another of the thoroughfares connecting Beverly Hills with the valley. What attracted us was the house's short distance from Beverly Hills and the rural aspects of its surroundings with orange groves on both sides of the street. The house itself offered nothing outstanding architecturally; it was an L-shaped structure in the simplest California bungalow style. The backyard abutted the steep hillside and was rather small. It would have barely accommodated a swimming pool of modest proportions, had we wanted to build one. Still, for us it was a prayer answered. We moved in as soon as all the legal formalities were resolved and the deed signed. It occurred to us that it would be easily rentable for the winter months while we were at Sun Valley. We furnished it with pieces mostly bought at weekend auctions, managing to find an assortment of furniture with antique character.

Everything was going well for us. Then on Sunday, December 7, 1941, news of the Japanese attack on the U. S. base at Pearl Harbor hit with the impact of an exploding bombshell, as it did in millions of homes all over the United States and the world at large.

War with Japan was inevitable, which was shortly verified by President Roosevelt's electrifying announcement over the radio that "a state of war existed between the two nations." America had already fully committed its vast resources to stand by the side of England and France in their war against Hitler. Now it was expected to enter the conflict full-scale with its mighty fleet of ships, air force, and ground troops.

I wondered how all the turmoil would affect Sun Valley, a luxury resort. I contacted Pat Rogers and Friedl Pfeifer, and they said that as far as they knew, Sun Valley would open for the winter season a week before Christmas. That being the case, Sinnie and I made preparations to leave for Sun Valley. The house rented out quickly, and we signed an open-ended lease agreement for four months, subject to a mutually agreed upon extension clause.

In Sun Valley, we were pleased and surprised that Pat Rogers, in view of our family addition, had assigned us new quarters with two bedrooms, a living room, and a small kitchen in a wing of the Challenger Inn, overlooking the steaming, circular swimming pool with a panoramic vista featuring Mount Baldy. Friedl had meticulously assembled a first-rate ski school staff, mostly returnees from the previous winter and a few new additions. To my amazement, bookings for the winter season were coming in fast and furious, which augured to be one of the most successful seasons ever, as though people wished to have one last fling before the whole world became immersed in a political cauldron.

We had barely settled down when the FBI swarmed in. A rumor was circulating that there were spies among the Austrian ski instructors and hotel personnel, secretly collecting and disseminating information by short-wave radio. Employees of even remote German ancestry were suspected to be undercover agents for Hitler. It is quite possible that a few among these might have been sympathetic toward Hitler and Germany's desire to rid itself of the burdens imposed by the Treaty of Versailles. Others may have sided with the majority of Austrians, who welcomed Hitler's annexation of their homeland. But to be marked as spies and potential saboteurs was ludicrous. It paralleled the situation whereby all Japanese people, including those naturalized as American citizens, were herded en masse and interned in detention camps scattered around the country.

Of course, as most of us felt then and as history has proven, the internments of Japanese and Sun Valley Germans were nonsense, part of the pervasive war hysteria based on the ill-conceived suspicions of a few fanatics who had been carried away by misguided patriotism. Still, off to jail went Friedl Pfeifer, Sepp Froehlich, and Hans Hauser. Hans was implicated because his brother, Max, no longer on the ski school staff, was a ringleader of the Nazi youth movement in Salzburg. Hans Hauser—the bon vivant of Sun Valley—a "schpy?" I might as well have been the pope in Rome, if that kind of logic persisted.

I am positive that I was thoroughly investigated by the FBI about my background and political affiliations and activities, which amounted to next to none. Furthermore, on November 21, 1941, I had become a bona fide American citizen, sworn in at Los Angeles. Last but not least, I was married to the daughter of Admiral Gannon. I was declared clean and thereby escaped the FBI dragnet.

As second in command of the ski school, I took over its direction in Friedl's absence. With testimonials and letters of recommendation in regard to his innocence pouring in, including one from Averell Harriman, who was then in a high position in President Roosevelt's war cabinet,

Friedl was released by the middle of February. Still taunted by some of the local firebrands, he was morally and spiritually depressed by this un-called-for vendetta that he took a voluntary leave of absence and moved to Salt Lake City with his wife, Hoyt. Later on, to prove his devotion to this country, he signed up voluntarily for military duty and went into training with the mountain troops, still in embryonic stages. Many other Austrian instructors followed in his footsteps.

As a family man with a wife and child completely dependent on my support, I registered for the draft as required by law and was classified II-A, thus legitimately allowed to bide my time until I was called for duty. I would be lying if I pretended I was gung ho to go to war. At heart I was a dedicated pacifist and abhorred war, convinced that war rarely offered a solution to conflicts. I did feel strongly, though, that to quash Hitler's ruthless aggression and killing of innocent people was imperative. When my time came, I knew I would join the forces in helping to do so.

In spite of these political shadows, Sun Valley did indeed have one of its best seasons ever, and snow was plentiful. All the old guard showed up—the Hollywood movie stars, producers, and directors. Darryl Zanuck came with his family, but only for a short stay. He had been asked to take over a top position in the film division of the Signal Corps, a branch of military service that attracted a great many creative talents of the film industry. Frequently they were recompensed with an officer's commission. Before Darryl left he asked me to make a training film for soldiers to learn how to ski so that they could operate as combat units in Alpine terrain. It made sense to me, and I asked Darryl whether I would have a script to work with and if he had any specific directives. "What do you need a script for" he asked. "You know what to do. Just make a film to teach some city wimps how to get around on skis in snow."

"Okay," I said. "I can do that." In my mind I formulated a picture that would be so visually enticing that any young man would say, "Man, that's for me. That's a lot of fun. Just imagine a vacation on army time gliding around on skis!" So when the ski school season ended, I mustered a platoon of twelve skiers to put through their training paces. Most of them were resident ski instructors supplemented with some skiers already enlisted in the mountain regiment in its formative existence.

The filming went well but we still had to shoot some interiors in an army barracks at the studio showing how to mount bindings, fit boots, and care for the equipment in general. In one sequence pertaining to waxing skis, I chose a young actor who was very short, good looking, and delivered his few lines like a polished performer. His name was Alan Ladd, and he rose quickly to stardom—but not, I can assure you, because of the bit part he played in a training film entitled *The Basic Principles of Skiing*.

A personal reward that resulted from my association with this film was becoming friends with Watson Webb, Jr. I had met Watson briefly when he came to Sun Valley to hand deliver a finished film to be run for DFZ's final approval. The film, *I Was an Adventuress* (1940), was directed by the irrepressible Gregory Ratoff, a far better actor than he was a director, and starred the beautiful Russian ballerina Vera Zorina, Erich von Stroheim, and Peter Lorre. It turned out to be a cinematic disappointment, mainly because von Stroheim and Lorre hammed up their parts so badly that it became a farce. Zorina, also, when not delicately poised on the tips of her toes, floated around like a rudderless ship. Gathered at a hurriedly arranged dinner with Gregory Ratoff, Molly, me, and other members of the staff who were connected with this film, Darryl said, "Boys, we've got a lot of fixing up to do."

Crestfallen, Ratoff, sitting next to Darryl and beating his chest, with large crocodile tears pouring down his puffed-up cheeks, exclaimed in his heavily accented Russo-American idiom, "Daarrreel, it is all my fault. I am going to kill myself. I'm so sorry."

"That is not necessary and wouldn't do any good, Greg," Darryl said. "And it's not all your fault, only some; so calm down and we'll see what we can do." Ratoff was one of the favorite clown princes in Darryl's entourage, and DFZ genuinely liked him as a person. He also knew a consummate faker when he saw one. Ratoff's tears dried quickly and he gulped down the huge steak on his plate like a hungry wolf. Yet despite his reputed wizardry, Darryl couldn't salvage this picture. The returns at the box office were minimal, with negative reviews to match.

Watson Webb was the assistant cutter on that film, and since he was coming to Sun Valley and had skied in the East, he brought along his boards. That's when we met for the first time. Then he was assigned as film editor on *The Basic Principles of Skiing*. We not only worked well together but became lifelong friends.

If ever someone was born with a silver spoon in his mouth, it was Watson Webb, Jr., an eastern blue-blooded aristocrat who graduated from Groton and Yale. I asked Watson whatever induced him to enter into the film business. He told me that, as long as he could remember, he had been a film buff. The right opportunity came along when one of his many uncles, Sonny Whitney, who fortuitously had connections with the film and theatrical world, told Watson that an important filmmaker and studio head was coming to spend the weekend at their Long Island estate. Knowing Watson's absorption with films, his uncle suggested that he drop by and take advantage of the opportunity to meet Darryl Zanuck in person.

Watson met DFZ as planned and hinted at how much he wanted to become part of the film business; he said he would be willing to start at the very bottom doing anything—carrying film cans from one place to another, working in the mail room, or even taking a job as a janitor. Zanuck was duly impressed by the willingness of a Yale graduate to humble himself to such a degree in order to get a foot in the door. Watson was offered a job and started as a third assistant in the film cutting department of Twentieth Century Fox. His first assignment was indeed hustling those heavy film cans from one place to another. This was better than a janitorial job by far in Watson's mind, because at least he could smell, look at, touch, and feel the texture of the film. Much later, on one of my visits to his home, he showed me with great pride his first weekly paycheck, framed under glass and hanging on the wall in his study. It amounted to $24.50.

Watson didn't have to work to earn a living and pay his rent. But he chose to pursue his goal, and rose to the rank of full-fledged feature film editor and director. He made a host of friends, whom he entertained elegantly, much different from the ostentatious style of the Hollywood nouveau riche, in his home in a quiet neighborhood in Brentwood close to Gary Cooper's house. When Watson's mother, Electra Webb, passed away, he decided to give up his motion picture career and took over the directorship of the rapidly expanding Shelburne Museum she had founded near Burlington, Vermont. He served most successfully in that capacity for decades, putting into effect his own innovative ideas. The museum became a state of Vermont landmark and a national treasure under his guidance. On the thirtieth anniversary of the museum's opening to the public, he invited a flock of his close friends to attend the celebration, flying them in as his guests from all over the United States and Europe. I happened to be among them, and it was truly a memorable party. Nor will I forget the many idyllic weekends the Lang family spent at Watson's summer retreat, a spacious house at Lake Arrowhead.

Watson was a perfect and generous host. He beautified whatever he touched and by doing so gave pleasure and inspiration to his friends.

After *The Basic Principles of Skiing* was delivered to and applauded by the military brass, I stayed on for the summer (1942) working at Twentieth Century Fox. I had graduated from third assistant director to an untitled position that kept me busy with a variety of chores, such as scouting for suitable location sites. Another of my assignments was to direct a series of vignettes for theatrical release about the behind-the-scenes work of various craftspeople involved in making a film, with Darryl making a brief introductory speech on camera to introduce each segment. For example, what does a cameraman's job (now "Director of Photography") entail? How does an art director function, or a set decorator choose the furniture for a specific period, including draperies, paintings, artifacts, and accessories down to a lady's thimble, called for in the script, with all these items stored and catalogued in a studio repository the size of a Bekins warehouse? It was mind-boggling to walk through such a warehouse floor by floor and see everything from a Louis XIV canopied bed to a primitive ax of a cannibalistic New Guinea Stone Age man or an authentic Egyptian sarcophagus with the original shrouded mummy still in it. I enjoyed making these "shorts" very much, since it gave me the opportunity to become acquainted with many of the men and women in key positions essential to film production.

Occasionally Darryl invited me to ride one of his spirited polo ponies stabled at his ranch in the Malibu Hills. When I say "spirited," I mean exactly that. Darryl was an excellent equestrian, as were his select riding companions. I was a greenhorn compared to them and had to fight not to be unseated, galloping over often rugged terrain with low tree branches whisking by my face and making sudden sharp turns at full speed around menacing rock formations. I never gave Darryl the satisfaction of seeing me hit the dirt, which I am sure would have been a vindication to him for the occasional rough times I gave him on skis. I was told that some of guest *caballeros* emerged bruised and bloodied after such a ride, and one ended up with a broken leg. Luck just happened to be on my side.

With the approach of autumn I was amazed to see Sun Valley still in operation after a busy summer and getting ready for another banner winter season. I carried out the preparatory arrangements of firming up contracts with the corps of ski instructors. For those who had been drafted or had voluntarily signed up, replacements had to be found. On the whole it appeared to be business as usual, but I had some doubt in my mind whether it would remain that way. Reluctantly, I put up our house for rent.

We arrived in Sun Valley early in December finding everything normal with concerted preparations in progress to make the Christmas holiday a festive one. With *Sun Valley Serenade* a surprisingly big box office hit, a whole new strata of ski aficionados booked reservations to fill the lodge and Challenger Inn with not a room to spare.

WARTIME OCCUPATION

Suddenly, before it had even opened officially for the 1943 winter season, the ax fell on Sun Valley. W. M. "Bill" Jeffers, president of the Union Pacific Railroad Company, was appointed the nation's "rubber czar" and transportation coordinator by President Roosevelt. To his patriotic way of thinking, there was no justification for Sun Valley to remain open, and the order came to close the resort for the duration, effective immediately. It was a logical and long-overdue decision. There was, of course, pandemonium in the valley, with cancellations and demands for refunds and displacement of personnel—including me—now without jobs just before Christmas.

Within a few days I had a phone call from the owners of Snow Valley, a small ski resort in Vermont close to the village of Dorset. "Now that Sun Valley is closed, would you consider coming East with some of your instructors to open a ski school here?"

"I would have to think about it," I told them, "and I'll get back to you." Returning to Beverly Hills with our house just rented out had no appeal to me. Also, I knew that the studio would be drastically cutting back its production schedule, and with Darryl Zanuck gone to war, it would not be the same. I talked it over with Sinnie and we decided that I should accept the offer. We would weather the winter somehow. Fred Iselin and Elli Stiller, two top instructors at Sun Valley, expressed an interest in joining me, which I welcomed, since we would be servicing two areas, Snow Valley and Bromley Mountain, separated by only a short distance.

With some trepidation, I called back to inform the Snow Valley people that I accepted their proposal and that we should settle all the financial details before we left Sun Valley. Not until we had settled at Snow Valley did I realize what a mistake I had made and how much I would rue my decision. The competitive jealousy between the owner of Bromley—Fred Pabst, the American brewery scion of Germanic ancestry—and the Jewish owners of Snow Valley reminded me of a fight of attrition between two Mafia factions. It was an unpleasant climate to work in, even though we did meet some solid New Englanders, such as Bill Parrish and Mary, his wife, who ran a small country inn near Peru, Vermont.

As much as I hated to do so, I suggested to Sinnie that she and Peter should accept her sister Nancy's invitation to stay with them. Captain Gearing had been transferred to Annapolis for a short tour of duty at the United States Naval Academy before taking command of a destroyer headed for the Pacific theater of war. They lived in a big, comfortable house with lots of room, while in Vermont we were squeezed into a small apartment and quite isolated from everything, which was uncomfortable for Sinnie. She agreed that it would be a temporary solution; we would reunite at Annapolis after the ski season ended. It would be the first time we were separated for any length of time, and the parting was not easy.

Fred and Elli were a great comfort to me. They had brought along their Saint Bernard dog from Sun Valley, and he was a real character. He had a tendency to wander off and explore the neighborhood when life became too boring where he was. One day while I was having lunch with Fred at the ski area, he was paged to pick up the phone and was told that his dog had dropped in at a homestead some miles away. He asked the caller to please put the culprit on the horn. With a stern and commanding voice, Fred said to the Saint Bernard, "Now you son of a dog, you get your ass home, and I mean right now without any delay. You hear me?" and he hung up. Within a short time, the oversized pooch, out of breath, waddled into the day lodge with his tail flapping around happily and went straight up to Fred as though to say, "Here I am. You see what an obedient dog I am?" Fred burst into gales of laughter and said to me, "This isn't the first time this has happened, but he never fails to come home when I tell him to."

Never were three people happier than Elli, Fred, and I when the ski season in Vermont came to an end. I couldn't wait to get to Annapolis. When I arrived I found Sinnie looking radiant after an almost three months' separation. Peter was even more robust and seemed to have grown an inch for every month we were apart. Living with Nancy and her two youngsters, Hilyer, a girl, and Sinclair, a boy, both lovable and bright, had been beneficial for Peter, and had enriched his vocabulary, notwithstanding a few words of questionable meaning.

With Captain Gearing's departure on his refurbished destroyer imminent, we decided to stay put. I wanted to look for a job more compatible with the war effort, short of enlisting, since my patriotic conscience had begun to needle me. In scouting around for suitable employment, I chanced upon a shipyard in Annapolis with a "Help Wanted" sign on display. I walked in and asked them what kind of manpower they were looking for, and I was informed that someone with experience in carpentry and shipwrighting was wanted. "Well," I said, "I'm your man. I've used a saw and hammer for many years and have put things together. Also I have fiddled around with sailboats." I got the job.

What was being built there at an accelerated pace were patrol torpedo boats, or PT boats. Very maneuverable at top speed, they could fly like a dart over the ocean and sting like a hornet, unloading deadly torpedoes against an enemy warship. Mission accomplished, they could vanish expeditiously or go under heroically, riddled by a hail of bullets. That stirred my imagination, and I was looking forward to working hard with my hands and not so much with my brain.

My pressing problem was to find a place to stay overnight, since commuting between the house in the countryside and the shipyard was out of the question due to gas rationing and no bus line servicing this particular area. I was fortunate to run into a stranger who had a sailboat, with adequate sleeping facilities and a small galley, berthed at a dock nearby. I talked him into renting it to me for a nominal fee during weekdays; on weekends it would be at his disposal. I promised to do some maintenance work to keep his boat shipshape.

Living on the boat, though restricted by space, was actually quite comfortable, and under different circumstances could have been cozy and romantic, disregarding the fact that the first thing I found awry was the hand-pumped toilet. To fix it tested my mettle and required many hours of tedious and filthy work, taking it all apart and putting it back together again. I did it, and from then on it was clear sailing, securely belayed to the stationary dock. Luckily I was hooked up to a power line and had an electric heater to keep me warm and plenty of light in my cabin with a surprisingly well-stocked library. Except for being separated from my family, it was not a bad arrangement and very convenient for me to go to and from work on foot. I was always able to find a ride or was picked up by Nancy to stay for the weekend with the family.

The work at the shipyard was as monotonous as I had expected it to be, comparable to working on an automobile assembly line. After only a few weeks I became disenchanted by the sloppiness and negligence of the work crews. In fact, I was appalled at times and concerned about the safety of the sailors and officers who would have to man these fighting units. As a single individual there was nothing I could do to improve the situation. My discreet hints to the foreman about quality control fell on deaf ears. "What do you expect me to do?" he said, "With the type of people I have to work with and depend upon?" There seemed to be a definite shortage of more qualified and responsible laborers in that part of the country.

The following winter proved to be as severe as it could be at Annapolis, and only because of weekly family reunions, culminated by a touching Christmas celebration, was I able to persist in my personal contribution to the war effort. The best Christmas present came from Sinnie when she said, "Honey, I have a surprise gift for you. Guess what? We are expecting—and by the end of August, we should have an additional bundle of joy."

"There seems to be always something good following some unexpected setback," I said as I hugged and kissed her. "I've wanted so much to have a companion for Peter, be it a brother or a sister," I told her. "This is truly the finest gift I could have hoped for." A merry Christmas it was indeed for all of us, in spite of Captain Gearing's being at war in the Pacific and my being somewhat isolated on a boat, but at least never in danger of being shot at.

At last spring burst forth, and having stuck with my job even though I objected to the inferior quality of work I saw being done, I felt the time had come to make a change. Surely there had to be a more satisfactory outlet for my capabilities.

RKO-PATHÉ, NEW YORK

I had followed regularly the film presentations of RKO-Pathé with its weekly newsreels, short subjects, and documentary films. Some of these, such as a series entitled *This Is America,* were highly patriotic in order to bolster the morale of American citizens both at home and at war. It occurred to me that perhaps I could better serve my country—and myself—by making these kinds of films. I asked for an appointment with Fred Ullman, the head of the documentary division of RKO, with offices in New York. When I met him, I was instantly impressed by his casual demeanor and the sophisticated manner in which he conducted our lengthy interview. When I left New York, I was hopeful but not at all certain that I would be joining this organization, which impressed me as thoroughly professional.

No sooner had I arrived back home than a telegram from Jay Bonafield, the head of production and Fred Ullman's close associate, was delivered to me. It read, "Would you like to start Monday or as soon as possible?" I was elated by this unexpected break, even though it meant moving to New York. I quit my job at the shipyard and wired back that I would report to work as they requested. After discussing our options with Sinnie, we decided that she and Peter would stay with Nancy at least until September, when our second child would be born, and then we would decide on our next move.

My gut feeling was that this RKO-Pathé connection would work out well for me. After my first week of indoctrination in the office and meeting most of my peers, I was positive it would be so. These were a group of dedicated no-nonsense professionals. The amount of product they put out weekly was prodigious, and it could have been accomplished only by the close teamwork of producers, writers, camera crews, and directors.

My job was primarily to direct segments of a popular series called *Sportscopes*, which were ten-minute one-reelers featuring outstanding sports figures. My first assignment was a short subject on horseshoe pitching. Thinking of it as a test of my abilities, I went to work on it as though I were directing *The Grapes of Wrath*, bringing every bit of my ingenuity and inventiveness to the job. I knew little about horseshoe pitching and, from what I did know, was reluctant to even classify it as a sport. Well, I found out that it isn't as simple as it appears the first time one tries it and that as an inexpensive pastime it had attained surprising popularity not only in rural areas but also among city dwellers. Even in New York there were a surprising number of practitioners to be found in many city parks.

To start with I titled the segment "Barnyard Golf," of which there was no similarity at all between the two. I then discovered that the reigning U.S. champion was a Basque with an unpronounceable name and that the runner-up and future star was a young Midwestern farm hand who had enlisted as a private in the army and was stationed in Washington, D.C. If I could get these two together in a *mano a mano* contest staged with the Lincoln Memorial or the White House as a background, it would give me something to shoot for a climactic ending. The private in his uniform and the Basque shepherd in his everyday work clothes would make a patriotic tableau. I also was tipped off that there were two portly housewives in St. Louis, Missouri, the Schmitz twins, who were wizards at the game. Supposedly they had all sorts of tricks up their sleeves and even toured the rural hinterlands, showing off their quasicomedy act. I even managed to have the Honorable Thomas E. Dewey, Governor of New York, make a cameo appearance. He was supposed to toss out the first horseshoe in a championship tournament in Central Park. Never one to miss a photo opportunity and a chance to mix with the populace, he did show up, posed for a few pictures, but declined to throw a horseshoe, concerned that it might tarnish his neat image that resembled a groom on top of a wedding cake.

My stock rose appreciably with RKO after this filmmaking tour de force. The conclusion must have been that anyone who could make something out of such subject matter must have something to recommend him. From then on things became easier for me as I trod more familiar ground in the subjects assigned to me and others that I suggested, prompted by my own desire to film them. One that gave me special satisfaction and I had no problem in selling to the company was a segment about Hannes Schneider. Hannes also agreed to it enthusiastically knowing that it would be good publicity for his ski school and North Conway.

I realized that North Conway did not have the necessary terrain to make an exciting film about skiing per se. My solution was to include scenes filmed in the summer, showing the village ambiance, the house where Hannes lived with his family, and scenes of Hannes coming out the front door, headed for the "mountain." Here he would be seen swinging a heavy ax and chopping down trees to widen a ski trail, cutting high grass with an authentic Austrian scythe, blasting rocks, and strewing about handfuls of grass seed to smoothen the ski slopes. Then I would segue into the winter activities and the ski school operation, ending with a chase down the mountain, such as it was. When all done, it made for a nostalgic little film with some historical connotations. I named it *Skimeister*, and an original print reposes in the archives of the National Ski Hall of Fame in Ishpeming, Michigan.

I made other ski films, including one shot at Alta, Utah, starring that indomitable all-round champion, Alf Engen. He was surrounded by a group of the finest skiers at that time, such as Gretchen Fraser, Dodie Post, Audrey Roth, Jack Reddish, and Dick Movitz, to mention a few, swooping down a real mountain in deep powder snow. Another film mainly depicted ski jumping and featured Alf Engen teaching youngsters how to build a ski jump and supervising their first attempts at age six to fly on skis. This segment was climaxed by a jumping exhibition on the big Howelson Hill at Steamboat Springs, Colorado. It so happened that the last and longest jump of the day was nailed down by the legendary and most likable Torger Tokle, on military leave. Shortly thereafter he returned to the front in Europe and was killed in action. His passing was a vast loss to the skiing fraternity, but the memory of his record jumps is indelibly etched in the annals of U.S. skiing.

One project that still haunts me was the two sportscopes I was assigned to direct in the Texas panhandle. They were to be two separate pictures, on duck hunting and quail hunting, both featuring Eltinge Warner, the editor of *Field and Stream* magazine, and Gene Howe, owner and publisher of the *Amarillo Globe and News*.

Gene Howe's Big Bull Ranch was our headquarters for a shoot of about two weeks. The main house built of logs was well protected by a cluster of shady cottonwood trees. It was a large, comfortable place with the definite feel of a lived-in family home. I was looking forward to working there with my crew of two, cameraman Billy Deeke and his assistant, two of the best. One may think of the Texas panhandle as an arid and dreary spread of flatlands, especially for photographic purposes. I did not find it that way at all, knowing that beauty in nature can be discovered in almost any kind of landscape with the right juxtaposition of light and shadows, blue sky and clouds.

Shooting the duck-hunting film, which I named *Mallard Flight*, required that we select spots at a nearby lake to build blinds for our hunters to hide behind and to place the decoys in the water at nightfall. The next morning just before sunrise, we set up our camera on a tripod. As the sun rose slowly to give us enough daylight, we would be ready and waiting. I hadn't even said "Action!" when ducks by the hundreds, lined up like separate squadrons of fighter planes in perfect formation, rose over the horizon, headed for the lake glistening in the morning sun. Even to me, a nonhunter, it was a stirring sight.

While the ducks were still in the air, the hunters rose and started shooting. It was actually like an ambush, with ducks dropping into the water as fast as the hunters could reload their shotguns with fresh shells until they reached their legal limit. To me the most marvelous part of this shoot was filming the work of Gene Howe's trained two-year-old Chesapeake retriever. He burst into the water on command when the shooting ended and with unerring accuracy picked up each duck, one at a time, and gingerly, without bruising it, held it between his teeth, swam to shore, and laid it at the hunter's feet. Then off again he went to bring back another one. Within two or three mornings, filming at different locations, we had all the material we needed.

Then it was time for the quail-hunting film. I had never seen a quail shoot, so I figured the best way to find out was to ask that they show me. We set out with a special wagon for dogs, holding two highly trained pointers. Their job was to locate and corner coveys of quail but not to flush them until the hunters on foot had caught up with them. They stood like marble statues, muscles taut and tails high, until on command they stormed the thicket and flushed the birds into the air to give the hunters a shot at them in flight. After seeing this demonstration, I said, "Gentlemen, with our heavy camera equipment, we could never coordinate it in time, to get set up with the camera on a tripod, with all this action taking place simultaneously." Our cameraman agreed with me.

The solution I proposed was to build a wooden box with a loose chicken-wire lid. The box, with four to five quail in it, would be held by a man in his lap, hidden behind a thicket of heavy brush. This way we would control where the dogs were coming from, and once they were *On Point* (the title of the subject), the hunters would join the tableau. On command, the dogs would jump the thicket, while the man hidden behind it would lift the lid on the box to free the birds, thus giving the hunters a clear shot. We would need about seventy-five quail to work with.

On paper it sounded feasible. We all agreed that it would be worth a try—except Eltinge Warner. He blew his top exclaiming that under no circumstances would he be part of this fakery nor condone it, speaking as the editor of *Field and Stream*. "If this is what you seriously plan to do, count me out," Eltinge said.

"Too bad," I countered. "Then we might just as well abandon this film."

In his quiet and resourceful way, Gene Howe went to work on Eltinge and finally convinced him that there was nothing wrong with my proposed scheme and that it would be only fair to give me a chance to try it. "After all," he told him, "Otto is an experienced director and ought to know what he is talking about."

Actually, I didn't and was just groping in the dark.

"So from where are we going to get these seventy-five captive quail?" Warner asked somewhat sarcastically. That would be no problem, Gene assured him. He had already talked to the game warden, who was working closely with us. He could trap for us, within twenty-four hours, all the quail we needed, he said, and he had already gone to do so. Promptly a day later, the game warden drove up in his sedan with a beaming smile on his face.

"Where are the birds?" I asked. "All back in my trunk," he replied. "They're in a big bird cage, at least one hundred of them."

"That's great!" I complimented him. "Could I take a peek at them?"

"Sure enough," he said as he proceeded to lift the lid of his trunk. At that moment, with a loud whir and frantic fluttering of wings, a whole bunch of birds flew away before he could slam the lid shut again. The fragile wooden cage had broken apart, and the remaining quail were now loose in the trunk.

"Don't worry," the warden said, "I'll back the car into the garage, drop the door closed, open the trunk, and catch all these suckers one-by-one with my own hands." And so he did.

We set up the scenario as I had planned. A man held the box in his lap, and the dogs were let loose to scent the quail. But nothing happened. They never came near the hidden box. My whole scheme was an embarrassing failure. Eltinge Warner stood by my side quietly triumphant as he watched this fiasco of mine.

Now, I really had to go out on a limb. I analyzed the situation and concluded that of course the dogs hadn't picked up the scent of the birds because they were locked in the box unable to move or flutter their wings. My tortured but still fertile mind came up with a revised scheme: Dig two holes in the ground behind a cluster of shrubs, deep enough to hold two men squatting with their heads above ground level, each holding two birds in each hand, letting them wiggle with some freedom. We went out, dug the foxholes, and put two ranch hands in them, holding the birds as planned. If this worked and the dogs came to a point properly, we would have complete control of the situation.

On signal the game warden let the two pointers loose, and after a few tentative preliminary snuffles with their noses to the ground, they headed for the thicket as though on a wire and came to a sudden stop in the classic "on point" stance. It worked to perfection. We moved from place to place, setting up our scenario and repeating the action until we had used up our supply of quail. Even Eltinge Warner mellowed reluctantly and joined the group of hunters, which included Sybil Harrington, looking very chic in hunting attire, who later became one of the great patronesses of the Metropolitan Opera in New York.

Was it worth all the trouble and time spent on these two sportscopes? I'll let the critics speak. One wrote:

Mallard Flight coupled with *On Point*, this pair of sportscopes from

RKO-Pathé, under the direction of Otto Lang, cannot possibly miss an Academy Award for this type of short subject.

Gene Howe, Jim Haggard, and Eltinge Warner, Editor of *Field & Stream*, make up the hunting cast while a super Chesapeake retriever displays some prowess seldom seen on the screen, if ever. Opening scenes offer a close-up of mallards in flight that is one of the handsomest shots ever gracing anybody's short subject.

. . . *On Point*, the other Academy contender for our money, features Jack and Jake, a pair of bird dogs, the likes of which you never saw before on the screen. The work of these two "pointers" is unerring. All of which adds up to an outdoors sports subject which is definitely tops.

No, these two films were not among the four nominated for an Academy Award later in my film career.

While working on these sportscope films, I had moved into furnished bachelor's quarters in a brownstone near a direct bus line to the RKO offices on Madison Avenue. But this small apartment would be inadequate for us as a family. Although millions of families lived quite happily in Manhattan, I leaned toward the suburbs or a nearby smaller town. On one of my rare free days during the week and without any tangible leads, I headed for Grand Central Station, bought a ticket, and alighted at Larchmont. It appealed to me on first sight—not too long a train ride, not too small nor too large a town. There were tree-shaded streets, parks with splashing fountains, attractive houses with flowers abounding and often even white picket fences. I stopped by a realtor's office and told them what I was looking for. The agent said I might be in luck. There was a doctor, married with children, who was planning to take a sabbatical in Europe for one year starting October first. "It's a lovely home," I was told, "and in easy walking distance to the railroad station in case you need to commute."

"Could I have a look at it?" I asked.

"Generally, only by previous appointment, but let me make a call and find out if we can arrange it on such short notice."

The answer was yes, but not until one o'clock. I grabbed a bite to eat and then went to meet the doctor and his wife at their home. Still young, both of them happened to be ardent skiers (one of their reasons for going to Europe) and when they heard who I was and where I came from, the good doctor went to a large bookcase filling an entire wall and pulled out a skinny little volume and handed it to me. It was *Downhill Skiing*, a bit frayed around the edges and showing distinct wear.

"Is that you?" he asked. "It has been our bible, accompanying us on many trips to the ski country. Also, we remember seeing your film *Ski Flight* at Radio City Music Hall. Beautiful show."

I reciprocated that gracious introduction by telling them how much I liked their place and that I was convinced we could be very happy living there. They showed me around the house, which was furnished in an upscale but livable style and had plenty of space. I really could not think of anything better and instinctively knew that Sinnie would agree with me. From then on I would be joining the hordes of daily commuters, leaving the house early in the morning to catch the 7:33 A.M. train and pushing my way through the rush-hour traffic in New York to connect with the 5:27 P.M. leaving Grand Central. But I felt it would be well worth it to escape the nerve-jangling way of life in a big city and to have wonderful weekends to ourselves in such verdant surroundings. All there was left for me to do now was to organize the grand exodus, "*mit Kind und Kegel,*" as my mother, who was great on homilies, would have said. After Sinnie gave birth to our second child, we would travel by train from Annapolis, Maryland, to Larchmont, New York, and all our excess paraphernalia would follow us by UPS.

To Sinnie's and my surprise, our second child arrived prematurely. Sinnie called me as soon as she could and told me the news, "It's a boy! What shall we name him?" I was surprised and overcome with relief, having planned to be with her but finding myself stranded on location for a film. I told her how grateful I was that all went so well and that she was in such good spirits. "As to the name, I leave it up to you. Surprise me." It turned out to be Mark Stuart. My first encounter with baby Mark was as exciting and an equally emotional high as when Peter was born. I held him lovingly cuddled in my arms, while Peter repeated, "My broder, my broder." It was a blessing to have two healthy little fellows, unblemished in every respect. I hoped they would be lifelong buddies.

We enjoyed living in Larchmont, but we did not like the daily commute and the frequent short-term separations dictated by my chosen profession. We found autumn and spring delightful in the East, but the arctic winters and Calcutta-like hot, humid summers to be draining. Both Sinnie and I longed to get back to California and to settle down in our own cozy bungalow. But that would have to wait for a while.

I was involved in directing a segment in the *This Is America* series entitled "They Fight Again." It was to be narrated by Quentin Reynolds, one of the most sought-after commentators for his quiet yet sonorous voice and the honesty of his trademark narrative style. The story line was a simple one about the rehabilitation of an aviator shot down in combat and severely wounded after a crash landing. Along with many others physically disabled or mentally disturbed by the war, he was guided back to health through a carefully developed program of rehabilitation. The purpose of it was to enable the injured fighters to return to their former civilian professions or to resume their military careers, if they so wished.

Making the film was a novel experience, since all the participants were actual patients who had no acting experience at all, with the exception of the aviator character, who was played by a young New York stage actor. Working with these troubled patients was fascinating, especially those who had serious mental problems and had to relearn their manual skills and develop their faculties like young children. Most of the film was shot on location at Pawling, New York, at a boys' prep school taken over by the government and turned into a complete medical and rehabilitation facility, staffed by the best specialists available. The cooperation extended to us was exemplary, and therefore, the shooting went smoothly and the results were gratifying. As one critic reported:

> "They Fight Again," newest of the *This Is America* series, is the most significant and most memorable of all the subjects yet issued in this series.
>
> Here is something for anxious America to see. An inspiring first pictorial account of what our government is doing to rehabilitate our war wounded.
>
> All America will take heart from it, for it shows visually what a grateful nation is trying to do for its heroes, not only to save their lives, but to restore their productive potential.
>
> Quentin Reynolds delivers the commentary, and if you heard him on "London Can Take It" two years ago, you'll know what to expect.
>
> To see "They Fight Again" is a "must" for every American.

While we were filming in Pawling, Lowell Thomas, who had a home nearby, dropped in to say hello. I had never met him before, but had had previous contact with him was when he wrote me a letter thanking me for sending him a copy of *Downhill Skiing*.

R.C.A. Building N.Y.
December 3, 1936

Dear Mr. Otto Lang:

Many thanks for the book. I received it before your letter arrived, took it to my office, and found it so fascinating that I couldn't get any work done until I finished reading it. I believe every skier in the country will want a copy.

I am more anxious than ever to master the Arlberg Technique.

I hope you enjoy your work in the Puget Sound region (Mount Rainier and Mount Baker). Many years ago I spent considerable time out there and regard it as one of the most delightful sections of this planet.

Cordially yours,

Lowell Thomas

Of course I forwarded a copy of this letter to Henry Holt and Company, and they jumped on it and wanted to use it for a quote—a request to which Lowell Thomas most graciously consented, and which undoubtedly helped to sell out the first edition. In 1992, when I wished to purchase a copy for my own library, only with the help of a professional out-of-print book finder did I manage to buy one for $16. The original cover price was $1.25.

Meeting Lowell Thomas in person was most fortunate. I do not know of any other man who has had such an adventurous life and career. When I first met him he was fifty-two and wound up like a human perpetual motion machine, always on the move to somewhere. Standing five feet seven inches, give or take an inch, there was not an ounce of surplus fat on his slender but well-muscled body, and he had the intrepid gaze of an explorer. He cut a dashing figure with his thick growth of dark hair neatly parted and a pencil-thin mustache, which became part of his cachet, enhanced by the ever-present pearl-grey Stetson.

One word of advice Lowell never forgot, which was given to him by his father, was to always speak clearly, to pronounce each word correctly with proper attention given to the grammatical structure of every sentence, and to cultivate a distinct and resonant tone of voice. By the time he reached the apex of his career, he was a master of elocution, and his voice flowed as smooth and clear as honey poured out of a jar. It became a voice known all over the world.

After brief meetings between setups at Pawling, Lowell extended an open invitation to me to visit him any time at his baronial estate. Henceforward, our paths would cross frequently, socially and professionally. I never expected that we would share so many adventures together. Over the years, I received hundreds of personal letters from him, now collected in three thick folders.

With our rental agreement on the house in Larchmont about to expire, Sinnie and I decided not to look for another one. We did not want to spend another winter in the East. Since our own house in Beverly Hills was becoming available again, we opted to pack up and head for California. In many ways I regretted leaving RKO-Pathé. Ours was more than just a pleasant and productive working association. Fred Ullman's family and the Lang family had become good friends, and we frequently shared weekends together.

Although the war was winding down and victory was in sight, we still had to attend to the formality of getting permission from the draft board in Ketchum, Idaho, where I was registered, to make this change in domicile. I explained in a letter that better job opportunities were offered to me in Hollywood. Permission was granted for me to leave.

We found a second-hand La Salle sedan whose stylish, sleek design appealed to me, with a set of retreaded tires. If we kept our fingers crossed, they might get us all the way to California. Our plan was to apply for the necessary gas coupons that such a lengthy journey would require, then load up the car to its capacity with all our personal belongings. I would drive with Peter in stages cross-country, while Sinnie and Mark would follow by train, arriving after we had settled down in our house.

I looked forward to this journey with young Peter, going on four. It would be an adventure that both of us would remember as a rare time of closeness between father and son. It seems to me that we made a rather leisurely journey of about nine days. We avoided staying overnight in big cities and chose small towns close to the road with convenient motels. The daily routine was a simple one: getting up at daybreak, eating a substantial breakfast, making a brief stop for lunch, and timing our driving day so that it ended no later than four o'clock. By that time, Peter was a soggy, sticky mess, having indulged in chocolate bars, soft drinks, chewing gum, and candy, crawling back and forth between the front seat and the back window, using a pair of skis as a gangway and sharing the view of the receding road with three duck decoys I had brought along. The first thing to do when we settled in our room for the night was to strip Peter of all his clothing and dump it into a sudsy wash basin. Both of us would step under a hot shower where I struggled to soap him down from head to toe until he fairly sparkled. After that we shared a little playtime and diversion by whatever means was available, then early dinner and early to bed, with me reading him some of his favorite stories or, better yet, concocting one of my own improbable fables, which absorbed his full attention before we dozed off to sleep.

I treasured every minute of this experience and wouldn't have missed it for anything. Peter proved himself to be a delightful traveling companion, full of curiosity about the passing scenic cavalcade, questions and more questions—where we would stop next, about his mother and "broder," Nancy and her children, playmates in Annapolis and wondering whether he would find some in California, a place he barely remembered. Also he wanted to know all about my mom and pop and sisters, where and how they lived and when we would ever see them. I assured him we would as soon as the war was over. It pained me very much that communication with my family had virtually ceased. With postal service cut off, I had been without a word from them for over two years.

Despite an unseasonable snowstorm in California, which blocked our progress temporarily and forced us into an unscheduled overnight stay, we dropped into the Los Angeles basin in buoyant spirits. The La Salle performed beyond my expectations, and only about ten miles from our final destination did it almost give out on us. We limped to a halt in front of 1861 Coldwater Canyon with a leaky water-pump hose, the engine steaming and hissing as though ready to blow up momentarily. After I turned off the ignition key, Peter and I gave each other a big hug and kiss on the cheek. We were home and glad to have arrived safely. Sinnie and Mark joined us as planned. At last we were where we wanted to be and together as a family, looking forward with high hopes for peace on Earth for all to come in the following years.

POSTWAR
YEARS

My first assignment back at the Twentieth Century Fox studio was on *13 Rue Madeleine*, a film to be directed by Henry Hathaway, a passionately dedicated filmmaker and seasoned hand under contract to Twentieth Century Fox. Hathaway also had worked his way up through the ranks. He did not have a formal education, but he gave himself one as an omnivorous reader of daily newspapers, magazines, classics, historical novels, westerns, and science fiction. He started out as a propman and set dresser but was determined to become a film director some day, which he did step-by-step and by being in the right place at the right time, such as when he jumped into the breach and took over on a Gary Cooper film for a director who had fallen ill on location.

I had met Henry at Sun Valley with the Zanuck entourage. With no interest whatsoever in skiing, he had spent most of his time observing—and reading. He couldn't have been a nicer and kinder man socially, but on the set he could become a tyrant, obsessed by his directorial ambition and always striving for the best results, without any compromises. Many of his coworkers and actors, male and female, found it difficult to perform with him at the helm, until they realized that all he really wanted was one hundred percent of each individual's effort, no less than he was willing to give himself.

13 RUE MADELEINE

I looked forward with some reservations to working on *13 Rue Madeleine,* not knowing exactly what my function would be but also realizing that it would be rewarding to watch Henry at work. The semi-documentary film starred James Cagney and Annabella, the charming French actress. The story took place in England and France, and featured a highly specialized secret commando unit that was to parachute into France to join a group of French resistance fighters. It was the kind of film that cried for realistic scenic backgrounds away from the studio. Since it was impossible to go to England and France to shoot the film during wartime, the studio decided to use Quebec for the French segments and Boston and its environs for the English portions of the film. My job was to scout for suitable locations in both places; for example, I had to find a building that would simulate the headquarters of the German high command and gestapo in Le Havre, a place quite familiar to me. We also would need some typical French village streets.

With the addition of a few appropriately placed signs and some cosmetic touches, the existing narrow streets in the older part of Quebec could be easily converted to suit our needs. The countryside, only a short distance away from the city, was ideal to represent France as seen in picture postcards. We were looking for an isolated peasant farmhouse built of indigenous stone to serve as a hideout for the Maquis. The one found was perfect in character, with a realistic patina of age. The only problem was its owner's reluctance to let us use his stone house and trample the ground around it, planted with sprouting onions. He kept groaning, "*Mes poireaux, mes poireaux. Qu'est-ce qu'on va faire de mes poireaux?*" I assured him that whatever damage might be done to his onion field, he would be reimbursed generously in cash. He simply couldn't fathom such wanton destruction, even though we would pay him more than double the price his harvest would bring at the local market. Finally, we made a deal.

My choice for the gestapo headquarters happened to be the imposing residence of the archbishop of Quebec. "You think you can get permission for us to use it?" Henry asked me. I said that I could certainly try. When I entered the archbishop's palatial home I did not have much hope that I would succeed in my mission. My stratagem was to be absolutely forthright, telling him that ours was a film to glorify the courageous and covert activities of the French resistance fighters, helped by an American commando unit. Knowing that Quebec and its citizens had great empathy for the plight of the French people, I thought we might have a chance.

"And what would that entail as far as we are concerned?" his eminence asked in a soft voice.

"Well," I said, "we would only want to use the exterior of the building and the impressive iron-gated entrance into the courtyard and not come inside the building at all. It would represent the headquarters of the Nazi military occupation forces in Le Havre."

There was a lengthy pause before he said, "This is not an impossibility, but let me think about it."

At least I had a foot in the door, and when I told him that James Cagney, the popular American actor, and Annabella, a well-liked French actress, were the stars in this picture, I sensed that we might be in luck. It would be such an asset to the picture.

The next day I was summoned to see the archbishop again. "Now, tell me what exactly would be required from our diocese to assist you in shooting these scenes?" he asked me.

"First of all," I said, "we would need to fly a large swastika banner from your flagpole above the entrance. Second, we would want to place two sentry boxes to the left and right of the wrought iron gate with two Nazi soldiers guarding it. A black Mercedes-Benz sedan flying swastika pennants on the front fenders would arrive and the gate would be opened to let it pass. And that's about it."

I could tell by his expression that he had not quite expected such a display of Nazi presence, but to my pleasant surprise he said, "You have my permission to do it. Go ahead." With my thanks and discreet suggestion of permitting us to make a commensurate donation to the diocese, I bade him adieu with a respectful bow. We shot the scene as planned; to see the archbishop's palace bedecked as a Nazi stronghold must have been an unexpected sight for the Quebecois.

I felt that Henry Hathaway appreciated my contributions and dedication to the job and my choice in locations. What helped me very much on this particular assignment was that I had been able to bring Sinnie with me for two weeks before the full complement of the crew from the studio arrived. We stayed at the beautiful Chateau Frontenac Hotel, and she accompanied me on my scouting trips. We had been fortunate in finding a highly recommended nanny for Peter and Mark through Virginia Zanuck, but we were never at ease leaving our boys in the care of others. Sinnie was such a good mother with a delightful sense of humor and playfulness, so stimulating for growing little boys. When the time came for her to go home, I hated to see her leave. We had been separated far too often, but there was no alternative unless I had remained a director of ski schools, which would have permitted us to be together. I missed my family very much, and I realized it was not the best situation for us. Also, I could foresee that as long as I was working in films, there would be prolonged separations. But such was the challenge and magic of filmmaking that once ensnared by it, breaking away was hard, comparable to breaking an addiction.

While the film crew was still shooting in Quebec, Henry asked me to find him a B-24 airplane, which was used for parachute drops at this time in the war. Quite possibly he could have used another type of aircraft, but being a stickler for authenticity, Henry wanted a B-24. There were not too many of these around, and they were not easy to locate. I made a number of phone calls exploring possible leads when I struck gold virtually next door. There was a B-24 in Montreal. I hopped on a plane to Montreal, and while circling the airport prior to landing, I saw the B-24 parked in an isolated area with some other supposedly obsolete aircraft. It looked to be in very good condition from my bird's-eye view.

On the ground I was told that yes, indeed, the B-24 was for sale and that it was in such good condition it could be flown to Quebec. That would not be necessary, I told the man handling the sales of surplus war matériel. The plane never needed to leave the ground for our scenes, and we would come to Montreal to film them. All our action would take place in the cockpit and cargo hold, while preparations were being made in the cargo space to drop a load of paratroopers into occupied France. I was taken to inspect the plane and couldn't believe what I saw. Here was a B-24 in near perfect condition, with four powerful Pratt-Whitney engines and oversized metal propellers reflecting the sun. "It might be of interest to you to know," the man said, "that Winston Churchill used this plane when he came from England to meet with President Roosevelt at the historic Quebec Conference. The tanks are still filled with fuel, and the plane is safely flyable with some checking and tuning-up done on it. You'll also notice," he continued, "the wood-paneled interior, which is considerably more luxurious than the run-of-the-assembly-line type of this plane."

So it was, and I was quite stunned. It seemed preposterous that this beautiful and classic airplane was languishing on the tarmac. Somewhat apprehensively, I asked, "How much would you want for this baby?"

"Seventeen hundred dollars."

"Come again?" I asked incredulously, certain that I hadn't heard him correctly.

"Seventeen hundred U.S. dollars, firm, that is the price," he said again. "But don't forget, you can sell the high octane fuel, also the four engines, propellers, and all sorts of paraphernalia separately and turn over the rest to a junk dealer, once you are done with your shooting."

"It's a deal. We want it," I told him. To prove that such a deal had been made, I saved the bill of sale and still have it as a priceless memento. By the time we filmed our required shots, we not only recovered what the plane had cost us but actually made money by selling the fuel and the various components. Today a B-24 in the same condition would be a museum showpiece worth a small fortune.

When we moved onto Boston we were lucky to find a school with the appearance of an English manor house to serve as a training facility for our commando units. After a lengthy search I also found the perfect location to serve for a night-crossing exercise by a group of fully equipped commandos: a grassy meadow bisected by a meandering stream and bordered by leafy trees. The scene would be shot in the daytime with appropriate filters to make it appear like a moonlit night. I walked through the meadow to the crossing spot only to discover that the whole area was infested with black snakes. Knowing that many people have an instinctive aversion to snakes, even harmless ones such as those were, I wondered whether I should make it known to the cast and crew or just shut up and hope that the snakes would make a timely retreat, as they were likely to do when warned by approaching footsteps. I chose the latter course, and not a single snake made an appearance. It made a gem of a scene.

Due to Henry's superior direction and first-rate performances by the cast, led by the dynamic James Cagney, *13 Rue Madeleine* was a critical and box office success. As *Time* magazine said, it was "Far and away the roughest and toughest spy chase yet gleaned from the bulging files of the OSS," a sentiment which was echoed by a majority of other critics.

On May 8, 1945, World War II was officially over in Europe, soon to be followed in August by the collapse and surrender of the imperial Japanese war machine. It was not a time to rejoice, but a time to reflect and be grateful that one of the greatest tragedies ever to befall mankind had come to an end. It was a time to gather the shards of what was left in the aftermath of this carnage and get on with the immense job of putting the shattered world economy back on its feet. The first news to reach me about my family in Salzburg came unexpectedly at war's end from a Lieutenant Colonel R. V. D. Janson. His letter was so welcome and thoughtful. I was elated to find out that my parents and sisters had survived and coped relatively well with the vicissitudes of war.

July 27, 1945

Dear Mr. and Mrs. Lang:

I saw your family the other day. They were most happy to get all the news about you. They had heard about you from several other officers but nothing definite, so it was quite a relief. The whole family is still in Salzburg and everything is okay with them. Even their apartments have been spared from air-raid damage by lucky chance. Your father, in spite of his age, is still vigorous and very lively. He is in love with his daughters and works at a tobacco storehouse, which enables him to indulge in his favorite vice, smoking.

Your mother is said not to have changed her good looks very much although her nerves, owing to her predisposition, have been shattered by all the excitement of war and other troubles, etc., so she very rarely gets enough sleep, but generally feels quite all right and enjoys her walks without air-raid alarms. She is terribly anxious to see your two little boys. So you must come here without delay whenever the opportunity should occur.

Your sister, Eleonore (Nelly), has temporarily left Schider's firm to work for the U.S.A. military government of the city. She has not married yet and not on account of lacking offers (the last one being from a GI 23 years old), but owing to a general feeling of disinclination to do so.

Elsa, due to circumstances, has lost her previous position but does a wonderful job now (fully appreciated by the people concerned) in keeping house and interpreting for a CIC unit. Unfortunately, she seems to have inherited your mother's disposition concerning nerves and sleeplessness, but she is looking young and attractive so that nobody would believe it.

Erna, as you know, "a difficult case," has been engaged to a certain Seppl or Franzl, who unfortunately seems to have been killed or imprisoned in Italy during the last weeks of war. Anyway, he is missing and your family is very sorry about it.

Later on, when you will be able to send parcels, sugar would be the stuff most appreciated besides fatty food supplements and, of course, chocolate for the girls. They would love to have photos of the little boys and send heaps of love to both of you, with kindest regards to Maud and Jerome.

Russ Janson

As it turned out, Janson lived in the military guest house in a villa on the outskirts of town, which Elsa managed, and she enlisted his help to open channels of communication. Now it became possible for us to send letters back and forth and for me to send frequent packages of nutritional goodies and a variety of items according to a wish list. For example, my father urgently needed a repair kit to fix the inner tubes of his bicycle tires. My mother pined for (of all things) a garter belt, and my sisters wanted a modest supply of cosmetics, hand lotion, lipsticks, hair combs, needles and thread, stockings, bras, and a cigarette lighter for my father.

Three of my good-sized packages, containing an assortment of goods as though I had robbed a country store, arrived just in time for Christmas, and what a celebration it was according to a letter from Elsa. She wrote, "You cannot possibly imagine how happy we were to get all these things from you which we needed so badly. Especially all the little added surprises by you we missed so much." My father followed up with a letter composed of a lengthy poem written in the inimitable style of one of the all-time great humorists and poets of German literature. Unfortunately, I cannot provide a translation to do justice to my father's attempt to imitate the illustrious Wilhem Busch, but all things considered, he did very well, enumerating every item contained in the three packages and extolling their merits and expressing the appreciation of each recipient for these, in their minds, priceless treasures.

For the four of us here in America, looking forward to our imminent departure for Sun Valley, which would be officially reopened for the coming winter season, it was also one of the happiest of Christmas holidays.

CALL NORTHSIDE 777

It took a while for Sun Valley to reorganize its operation from military rest center to popular ski resort. But as skiers expected, Sun Valley reopened to the public for Christmas 1946. I had been corresponding

regularly with Pat Rogers during the interim years and would be returning to my former position as codirector of the ski school. I had taken a
mutually agreed upon leave of absence from Twentieth Century Fox for
the winter season in order to resume my duties.

Friedl Pfeifer was still the titular head of the ski school, but having
returned from the war with only one lung, due to a near fatal shrapnel
wound, he had taken a great interest in developing his own ski resort at
Aspen, Colorado. Like me, Friedl was not quite ready to cut the umbili-
cal cord with Sun Valley, which was a prestigious and enjoyable association, and he planned to commute between Sun Valley and Aspen. Both
of us felt a sentimental loyalty toward Sun Valley and wanted to make
sure, if and when either of us did decide to make the break, that the
school would be left in the hands of someone who could carry on the
tradition we had established. It was important to us to preserve the
image of Hannes Schneider and his brainchild, the Arlberg method.

A solid core of Tenth Mountain Division veterans, formerly affiliated
with Sun Valley as instructors, rejoined the ski school. Some others had
not survived the war; they would be missed by all of us. But by the time
Sun Valley opened for the season, we had assembled a ski school staff of
superior caliber, quite possibly the best in the United States. With Christmas at the threshold and snow falling, former habitués and hordes of
newcomers flocked to the resort. It was comparable to the memorable
grand opening of 1936, except that this time there was snow in
abundance, transforming Sun Valley into a winter wonderland. Sinnie,
too, was glad to be back. She had made a lot of friends and enjoyed the
carefree lifestyle of Sun Valley, as did Peter and Mark, who thrived on
the diet of fresh air, healthful sunshine, and frolicking in the snow.

When the Zanuck clan and their entourage returned, Darryl and I
reestablished our daily routine of skiing together for a few hours in the
afternoon and then walking over to the Sun Valley Opera House to run
the studio dailies and films in various stages of completion. One aspect
of skiing with DFZ that appealed to me very much was riding with him
on the ski lift up to the top of Mount Baldy. In stormy or cold weather
the lift attendant provided us with a weatherproof poncho to wrap around
our shoulders and sit on to keep us warm for the lengthy ride. When the
sun was shining, the conversation flowed freely. But often we enjoyed
the repose of complete silence, letting our thoughts wander or watching
the skiers below us, carving graceful turns, while we glided smoothly up
the mountain past snow-laden, ice-encrusted fir trees resembling

surrealist sculptures. This was part of the beauty of skiing—to enjoy the splendors of the winter landscape.

On one beautiful sunny day with the world aglow, riding up the mountain with Darryl I mentioned to him a story I had read in *Reader's Digest* that morning, preceded by a short piece in *Time* magazine a few months earlier on the same subject. I thought the story might make a fine feature film in the semidocumentary vein, based on the success of some other films of this genre released by Twentieth Century Fox.

"Give me a brief synopsis," Darryl said. I compacted my account into as brief a continuity as I could. An ad had appeared in the *Chicago Times* offering $5,000 to anyone who could provide evidence that a young man convicted of shooting a policeman was innocent of committing the crime. The editor of the paper, in checking the general layout, caught the ad and thought there might be a human interest story behind it. He summoned one of his ace reporters, James "Mickey" McGuire, showed him the ad, and asked him to follow up on it. Reluctantly the reporter agreed. He believed the man was guilty as hell and that whoever had placed the ad was naive enough to be conned out of $5,000.

It turned out that the person who had placed the ad was the mother of the accused man. McGuire located her at her work, on her knees scrubbing the marble floor of a cavernous office building. She told him she had saved up $5,000 through many years of back-breaking janitorial work and that it represented her life's savings. She was willing to put it up as a reward, knowing that her son was innocent. After a lengthy interview, and somewhat moved by her indomitable faith but still skeptical and unconvinced, the reporter went back to his editor and suggested they drop the story. But the editor was adamant that he give it one more shot and investigate a promising lead. If nothing came of it, he could go ahead and close out the story.

With the image of the old lady scrubbing away on a seemingly endless corridor in his mind, he did follow up on that lead and, overcoming his initial resistance, interviewed some of the people connected with the trial. To his great surprise, he ended up in a crusade to prove that the mother could be right. Her boy and a friend of his seemed to have been railroaded by the Chicago police into a ninety-nine-year sentence. The victim, Officer Lundy, had been the sixth policeman gunned down in recent weeks, and somebody had to be convicted. McGuire located and interviewed the prisoner's divorced wife, now remarried, and she too had nothing but the best to say about her former husband and father of their son. Then he made an appointment with the warden to visit the prisoner at the Joliet penitentiary. McGuire asked him whether he was willing to submit himself to a lie detector test, to be administered by Leonarde Keeler, then the foremost authority and practitioner in this new field of criminology. The prisoner agreed to the test, and it proved negative.

Now full bore, the reporter went ahead with his investigation, with conspicuous headlines in the *Chicago Times*. A new hearing was granted because evidence was found to have been suppressed and withheld and because the defendant's half-drunk court-provided attorney was shown to be incompetent. The man was found innocent and released from prison. The mother's faith was vindicated. The editor's hunch was right. Mickey McGuire enjoyed temporary celebrity. And the *Chicago Times* increased its circulation.

Glancing at Darryl occasionally taking deep puffs from his ever-present cigar, I sensed that I had touched his creative imagination during my lengthy discourse. I had seen this expression on his face before. After a lengthy silence he said, "That's quite a story. Let me see those pieces in *Reader's Digest* and *Time* when we get off the mountain." He then said, "What I think we should do is for you to fly to Chicago as soon as you can. Make arrangements to see McGuire, the reporter, and meet the editor. Dig deeper into the story and find out about their willingness to cooperate with us in case we should want to make a film based on this material. Also talk to the mother and her son, see what kind of a deal we could make with them." He later issued a memo:

TWENTIETH CENTURY-FOX FILM
CORPORATION STUDIOS
BEVERLY HILLS, CALIFORNIA

INTER-OFFICE CORRESPONDENCE ONLY

DATE	January 15, 1947
TO:	LEW SCHREIBER
FROM:	DARRYL ZANUCK
	LYMAN MUNSON
cc:	JASON JOY
SUBJECT:	"TILLIE MAJCZEK STORY"
	JULIAN JOHNSON
	OTTO LANG
	RAY KLUNE

We are preparing to obtain the rights to a true story which was written up in the December issue of *Reader's Digest,* 1946, and also in *Time* magazine August 27, 1945. The title of the *Reader's Digest* article was "Tillie Scrubbed On."

We will have to buy permission from the mother, the son, and other members of Mrs. Majczek's family in Chicago. We will also in all probability have to buy clearances from the reporter on the *Chicago Daily Times* named James McGuire. All of these people will be portrayed in the picture.

It also may be necessary for us to negotiate through *Reader's Digest* to obtain the rights to their story by William F. McDermott and Karl Detzer. It may not be necessary to buy their story insomuch as the facts contained in it are the same facts contained in the *Time* article. Our lawyers will have to determine this.

It is the intention now to send a lawyer from our New York office to Chicago to meet with the people concerned. Make arrangements for Otto Lang who will produce the film to go to Chicago to meet with our lawyer so that Lang can be present when these people are originally produced, as Lang has a clear definition of why we want to make the film and how we are to go about it. Perhaps he will even want to screen for them in Chicago a print of *Boomerang* as we intend to follow this same technique of production.

I would like a junior writer, someone who is good on research, to also accompany Lang so he may make notes and get as much of the human interest material as they can find. I suggest Leonard Hoffman.

You should talk to Moskowitz on the telephone and set a date for them to meet in Chicago so they can have a conference previous to approaching the principals in the case.

If we obtain all the necessary clearances and rights, Otto Lang and Leonard Hoffman will prepare a rough draft sequence by sequence treatment and then I am going to try to get Quentin Reynolds to do the screenplay. He is not a construction man but all the construction will be finished and he will be the ideal man to step in on this material.

DFZ

With Pat Roger's and Friedl's consent to a foreshortened winter season for me, I left Sinnie and the boys at Sun Valley and went to Chicago as Darryl instructed, fortified by the presence of a Twentieth Century Fox legal advisor from the New York office. The response from all parties involved in this story in Chicago was not only favorable but actually enthusiastic, as I cabled to Darryl Zanuck. He promptly answered:

> Delighted you have made good progress. Have our attorneys decided whether or not it is necessary for us to buy article from *Reader's Digest?* Personally, I do not think we have to purchase same as we do not want to use the same title they used. How long will you and Hoffman stay in Chicago, as I would like to get started on first draft treatment as soon as possible. Is it okay for Harry Brand to break story from here?

Out of these preliminaries emerged *Call Northside 777*, a feature film, which Darryl Zanuck assigned me to produce. While I was still in Chicago, the wheels of production were already starting to turn, as per this interoffice communication from DFZ:

> Quentin Reynolds is back in town and available. I think he would be perfect to do the Chicago story which I am temporarily naming *Call Northside 777*.
>
> He would work in collaboration with Leonard Hoffman and of course under the supervision of Otto Lang. Call him and find out what he wants for the deal. I imagine Lang and Hoffman will be back by the end of this week from Chicago with all their research material. Let me know the kind of deal he wants before any commitments.

Upon my return to the studio, a deal had been made, which pleased me very much. I wrote to Reynolds:

> I have just returned from Chicago, where I had many talks with all the principals involved in this human drama.
>
> I couldn't be more pleased to know that you might take part in the making of this picture. I think it is one of the finest stories to have happened in a long time, and it should make a most worthwhile film; even better than "They Fight Again"—the picture we made together at RKO-Pathé.
>
> I am sending you the blow by blow account according to the *Chicago Times*. Also a very leisurely account of the happenings as told to me by James McGuire, *Chicago Times* reporter, while a steno-typist took down his words.
>
> I feel that with these two features at your disposal you will get quite a clear picture of the case. Please feel free to call me if you desire any further

information. In fact, I am looking forward to seeing you again very soon.

Things really began to hum at the studio now that the primary requisite of putting a writer on the screenplay had been achieved. Thoughts were next directed to the question of who would portray the mother, Tillie Majczek, a key role in this film. As was customary, names by the dozen were tossed back and forth, with everyone searching their memories for fine performances given by character actresses. Darryl suggested Ethel Barrymore. I could see the merits of having someone of Ethel Barrymore's star quality in the film, but I couldn't quite see her in this role. I visualized Tillie as a downtrodden, smallish woman with a face creased by hardship and sorrow almost from her childhood on. Miss Barrymore, no matter what part she played, always came through to me as overpowering, simply by her physical appearance and almost regal presence. After a search lasting almost until the start of actual filming, Kasia Orzazewski, a Polish actress from of a branch of the Polish National Theater in New York, was cast in the part. She was unknown in Hollywood film circles and had had only minimal, if any, film exposure at all. But she *was* Tillie Majczek. We never regretted our choice.

To write the saga of how a film progresses from its inception to a finished product could fill the pages of quite an interesting book, with all the ups and downs, reversals of fortune, changes in decisions already made, casting selections, and a multitude of other problems. This is exactly what makes the art form of creating a film so fascinating and challenging. It is a finely spun spider web in which many minds and hands are closely involved at every phase. One often has to wonder: How on earth will it all fall into place?

To my great regret, we soon faced the first reversal of fortune. Quentin Reynolds happened to be a superb journalist, but he could not adapt his craft to fit the demands of a dramatic screenplay. We had to make a change in writers, which is always a painful decision, especially when it concerns a man of great talent and reputation in a related field. It fell to me to be the bearer of these bad tidings, as I wrote in a memo of March 18, 1947, to DFZ:

> I took Quentin Reynolds to lunch and broke the bad news to him. He was, as could be expected, distressed and felt that he had "flopped." I explained to him that the blame is not entirely his and that the decision was necessary in the best interest of the picture.

He bears no grudge but would like to complete the second draft on which he is working presently. He figures it would take him approximately three more days and it would ease his conscience to have the job completed as best as he knew how to do it.

I felt that would be fair enough and told him to go ahead.

Darryl and I subsequently wrote warm, personal letters to Quentin, thanking him for his contributions and assuring him that he need not feel that the blame was equally ours and he had failed.

His replacement was Jerry Cady, a proven journeyman writer of screenplays, who could always be counted on to come through with an acceptable script. He took over the assignment at the end of March with instructions to leave the continuity of the Reynolds draft intact and to concentrate mainly on character development and dialogue.

While Jerry Cady was busy with his rewrite, I made a quick trip to Sun Valley to fetch my family. Luckily, through the kindness of our renters, we could move back into our house ahead of time. When I returned to my office, Cady handed me eighty-five pages with more to follow shortly. But, alas, a hitch developed, as per my memo to DFZ:

Memo to DFZ from OL, April 21, 1947:

Jerry Cady complained of a severe migraine headache, which hit him over the weekend. He felt that a change of atmosphere would be very beneficial for him to expedite his work.

He would like to go to Phoenix, Arizona, for a while and finish the script there. We have about 120 pages thus far. Two big scenes remain to be written—the one when the reporter goes to the mother to tell her that he is backing out and the final scene at the parole board hearing.

Personally, I would prefer that he finish his draft of the screenplay here at the studio and then go away for a rest.

I promised Jerry Cady that I would consult with you before giving him a final answer. I do not want to antagonize Cady at this juncture and arouse his belligerency, but in view of the pressing time element, I feel that this would be a rather inappropriate moment to go away.

Jerry Cady got over his migraine headache and turned in his draft of the finished script for my and Darryl's approval. This resulted in another lengthy story conference in his office, which was recapitulated in a thirteen-page memo, not containing any major changes but a great many helpful and constructive suggestions to improve the script. Cady did his polish job as per Zanuck's notes and finished his version of the script, but still not entirely to our satisfaction. It lacked that indefinable something that raises a good script to a loftier plateau. We needed to find yet another writer.

> Memo from DFZ to OL, May 28, 1947:
> I want Jay Dratler to do the final dialogue polish and pinpointing of characterizations on C.N. 777. But I do not want him to disturb the existing continuity nor do I want him to delve into any further research. Have him read the script dated May 23 and then let him read my notes which I dictated in your presence.
> If you run into any minor continuity adjustments, please call them to my attention before you make any changes.
> I do not want to disturb the construction of our story line unless we are positive it is an improvement.
> Dratler should study the script over the weekend so that he is ready to go to work on Monday.

Jay Dratler had the reputation of being an excellent "dialogue doctor." He could catch the subtle idiomatic speech inflections of a diversified cast of characters in a story. He was also well known for his eccentric work habits and the hours he kept. In his mid-thirties, sinewy and physically fit, with a crew cut, he would arrive in his office and strip down to his minuscule bikini-type underwear before he was ready to go to work. High strung and taut, he would pace up and down his office, mumbling to himself, and then sit down at his typewriter to put the words on paper.

At this stage a director for *Call Northside 777* had to be assigned. After a number of suggestions were discarded for one reason or another, we zeroed in on Henry Hathaway. Darryl expressed doubts that Hathaway, who had just finished shooting a demanding film (*Kiss of Death*), would be ready to dive into another one so soon.

"Why don't you try it anyway," Darryl said to me. "Show him the script and get his reaction."

Henry Hathaway liked the screenplay very much, with some reservations, which I assured him would be given the fullest consideration. In principle he committed himself to direct the picture, a decision I immediately communicated by phone to Darryl. We were so pleased to have Henry aboard as captain of the ship. By another fortuitous coincidence, Jay Dratler had worked with Henry before and they got along well in spite of occasional professional differences. I knew that Henry respected Dratler and vice versa, and it would be immeasurably helpful to have Henry involved with the final revisions of the shooting script.

With Henry at the helm, we could also attract actors in the star category. They trusted his judgment, even though he could be tough to work with at times. We still had not cast the part of the reporter, which called for a star performer. At one point, Henry Fonda expressed interest in playing this role, and he would have been not only very good but also an asset at the box office. Conflicting time schedules eliminated this prospect. We tried to interest Jimmy Stewart in the role, and DFZ was very high on the possibility of having him in the film. But Stewart, after reading the script, had some objections regarding the manner in which the reporter's character was presented.

> Memo to DFZ from OL, July 11, 1947:
> Henry and I have carefully weighed the best strategy of approach in regard to reaching a final agreement with Jimmy Stewart.
> Jimmy is opening in a limited run of the stage play *Harvey* in New York next week, and most likely his mind is totally preoccupied and not exactly in a receptive mood to talk about another project until his theatrical commitment is finished.
> Inasmuch as we are making better progress with the revised script than we expected and plan to leave in two weeks for a preliminary reconnoitering trip to Chicago, it might be best if we went straight to New York first and have us go over the script with Stewart.
> If anybody can sell the story to Jimmy, it is Henry.
> I am inclined to believe that we would be in a much stronger position if we were able to present a completed shooting script and discuss it verbally with Stewart, rather than to read to him over the phone the changes we have made.

Zanuck agreed and the good news was that Jimmy Stewart accepted the part of the reporter and would be available as soon as his commitment for *Harvey* had been fulfilled. We selected a few more New York stage actors, whose names and faces were relatively little known in films, a status we aimed for whenever possible, to round out the cast.

Richard Conte, under contract to Twentieth Century Fox, balked when he was assigned to play Joe Majczek, to an extent that he was prepared to forfeit his weekly salary and go on suspension. After some heart-to-heart talks with Henry Hathaway, he changed his mind, and I am sure he never regretted it, since the role turned out to be an actor's plum.

We were also fortunate in casting Bette Garde, a veteran of the New York stage, to play Wanda Skutnik, the owner of the small grocery store fronting for the speakeasy in which Officer Lundy was killed. She was the only witness who had a good look at the man who fired the gun. Coerced and pressured by the Chicago police, who were pushing for a conviction, she fingered Joe Majczek in a lineup, just to satisfy them. Incidentally, she was the only one of the participants in this drama who refused to sign a release to be portrayed in the movie, and we had to change her name. The actress who played her had to be tough, mean, and devious. Bette Garde turned out to be perfect for the part. Another New York stage actor was chosen to play the second husband of Joe's wife, a role which demanded much sensitivity. The actor was E. G. Marshall, a fine actor who accomplished it with consummate conviction.

With our job finished in New York, Henry and I headed for Chicago and the next phase of our production, scouting locations. We nailed down all the original sites to be used as authentic backgrounds in our film, and we also met with most of the surviving participants who had been involved in this drama many years ago. We met Tillie Majczek for the first time in person and were impressed by her modest demeanor, faith, and dignity. We knew immediately that our choice of the actress to portray her was perfect.

We also traveled to the penitentiary at Joliet to meet with the prison warden, who assured us of his full cooperation, offering us the run of the place and giving us permission to use his private office as a set. Not only would it save us an enormous amount of money not to have to duplicate many of these interiors at the studio, but also it would give us that much sought-after documentary feeling. It was my first visit to such an institution, and it was a sobering and emotionally draining experience to see men so regimented in every move they made and deprived of any shred of freedom and privacy. The physical layout alone, in its immensity, was awesome. I couldn't help but to wonder whether this was the best possible solution for the punishment of criminals and where it would lead in years to come.

Henry and I also attended a lie detector test given by Leonarde Keeler to an alleged murderer. We watched the session through a one-way window in a hidden room the size of a closet, with the sound of the dialogue piped in. It was a fairly complex procedure with a multitude of electronic connections linking the man's body to a sensitive recording apparatus, somewhat resembling a seismograph. We both concluded that it would be difficult for an actor to handle all the mechanical details of monitoring this apparatus while speaking his lines in a realistic manner. The best solution, we felt, was to try and convince Leonarde Keeler to portray himself in the film.

Keeler was opposed to the idea because of his total lack of acting experience. He also felt that it would be unprofessional, as a practicing physician, for him to act in a film with the suspicion of self-aggrandizement. We assured him first that there would be no need for him to act at all. From what we had seen, his performance in giving the test was beyond reproach. Then we reminded him that since there was still some reluctance in the legal acceptance of such tests, would he not prefer to demonstrate it in an authentic way? After all, it would be the first time that a lie detector test would be seen by worldwide audiences in a feature film. Keeler was impressive and good-looking, tall and reserved, with a controlled intensity that would enhance immensely the importance of the procedure in the prosecution of criminal cases. Eventually his opposition wilted under our barrage, and he consented, reluctantly, to do the scene. I might add that this scene was one of the suspenseful highlights of the film, and his performance could not have been topped by any actor, even Spencer Tracy.

With this phase completed, we headed back to Hollywood to set up a shooting schedule and arrive at an overall budget for the film. To calculate the budget, every department had to submit its projected share of the cost, down to the penny, which, when all added up, would represent the final figure. Should this figure be too high, it would have to be gone over with a fine-toothed comb and pared in areas not absolutely necessary to the film. As a rule, once the budget was set, both the producer and director were obligated to see that the film stayed within its designated boundaries.

The allocated budget for *Call Northside 777* was $1,579,813.94, which was somewhere in the middle range of the thirty-four pictures scheduled to be released by Twentieth Century Fox in 1947. These were the projected costs of some of the main items: story rights: $5,500; screenwriters:

$90,046.81; musical score: $24,600; director (under contract): $91,000; producer (me): $24,500; cast: $297,500 (of which Jimmy Stewart received $200,000); production department services: $352,825.12; obligatory administrative overhead charge: $173,779.53. Additional items amounted to $520,062.48. Our starting date to begin shooting in Chicago was set for September 22, eight months almost to the day from when the project was put on the active list, with a projected finishing date of November 26, 1947. After a lengthy session on some final script changes with DFZ, and the customary skirmishes with the official censorship of the Breen Office, we were on our way back to Chicago with a compact crew of about thirty studio employees, which would be supplemented by members of the local labor pool in Chicago, as required by union regulations.

Normally, once a picture starts shooting, it is the director's prerogative to be left alone and not have a producer on the set looking over his shoulder. For some reason, however, Henry accepted my being around and close to him on the set during the entire shoot, which I appreciated very much. I had learned when, and knew instinctively how, to keep myself in the background and, at the same time, be readily available should he need me. Everything went very smoothly with hardly any temperamental outbursts or altercations among the crew or actors. The cooperation of all city and county officials, the police, and the press was exemplary. So were the first rushes, as memos and letters showed:

To Otto and Henry from DFZ, September 27, 1947:
I have been thrilled with the rushes. I think it is the best material of its kind I have ever seen and I say this frankly and sincerely. Jimmy Stewart looks great, Conte is excellent in his scenes and so was the actor from New York who plays Tomak. The girl looks wonderful in the brief scene that I have seen her in.

Memo to Henry and Otto from DFZ, October 13, 1947:
I want to congratulate you for the manner in which you have handled the Chicago location on C.N. 777—both from the standpoint of quality and quantity.
Not only did you come in under schedule, but I have never seen more effective scenes made anywhere by anyone. This should be a lesson to us in future location pictures and I am asking Ray Klune to hold it up as an example for our future location pictures.

Memo to Henry and Otto from DFZ, October 25, 1947:
The rushes last night were excellent. I am excited by the wonderful relationship between Jimmy Stewart and Lee Cobb. This is just the thing we were looking for but never were really able to put into work.

We had finished shooting in fewer than the allocated days and also came in under budget, thanks to Henry's astute direction and a superb crew. We were fortunate in having Watson Webb, my good friend and also Henry's, assigned to us as film editor. Watson was fast, meticulous, imaginative, and savvy in condensing the raw material on hand to show to its best advantage in the finished film. After a few screening sessions that went late into the night, as was customary with him, DFZ suggested a few last editorial touches and gave his final blessings to the film. Then it was turned over to Alfred Newman, composer, conductor emeritus, and head of the music department, to add his musical score. Meanwhile, the sound effects technicians went to work to prepare it for the dubbing process, in which all the composite elements would be fused together. Suddenly, *Call Northside 777* had to be rushed to completion to meet an earlier release date than was previously planned, as a replacement for a film that had fallen behind schedule. The film was done.

It was time for me to return again to Sun Valley for my three months as director of the ski school. I looked forward to it but regretted the interruption of my film career, which had gotten off to a good start. Before I left, I wrote one last memo to DFZ:

To DFZ from OL, December 11, 1947:
I would like to take this opportunity to thank you from the bottom of my heart for having given me this opportunity to take part in the production of *Call Northside 777*.
It was a great privilege and something I had hoped for, but hardly expected to materialize. I know that without your help and constant supervision, it would have been well-nigh impossible for me to see this picture on the screen in its present form.
I am planning to leave tomorrow night and it will be wonderful to greet you and your family at Sun Valley.

One point of curiosity, that remained unresolved in many viewers' minds was whatever happened to Ted Marcinkewicz, who was convicted of the same crime as his friend Joe Majczek. They had served their sentences in different penitentiaries and had been represented by separate lawyers.

Had Ted Marcinkewicz not spent the night at Majczek's home after Officer Lundy was gunned down, Joe would never have been connected with the crime. I had received a rather poignant letter from Ted on prison stationery shortly after our first exploratory visit to Chicago:

> Dear Mr. Lang:
>
> A recent issue of the Chicago Daily Times revealed that you were in Chicago obtaining information concerning the Joe Majczek case with the intention of producing a movie based on his conviction.
>
> Being his co-defendant, I take this opportunity to appeal to you for a little careful consideration when you portray me in the sotry. I, too, am innocent, so I ask you in my kindest manner to please deal kindly with me in the story of Tillie Majczek and her son Joe because my case is at present under consideration for a pardon before the Pardon Board and any misrepresentation or falsification can irreparably ruin any possibility of a pardon....
>
> I am as innocent of the crime as Joe Majczek was, Mr. Lang, and with my case before the Pardon Board now--and they may keep it pigeon-holed for another six months or more--please do not destroy the only chance I have for my exoneration and freedom. You may characterize me in any way you desire once my innocence is established officially but, until then, I ask you as a gentleman to give me a chance until the Pardon Board and the Governor of Illinois render a decision....
>
> My subconscious persists in making me think you are of Lithuanian descent. I must have read it somewhere, perhaps, in the Luella Parson's column. I am of Lithuanian descent also. So, if for no other reason, please give a brother Lithuanian a break, will you?
>
> Very truly yours,
> Theodore Marcinkewicz #13995
> Illinois State Penitentiary

Of course, I answered his letter immediately:

> Dear Ted Marcinkewicz:
> Thank you for your letter and let me put your mind at ease in regard to the picture which we are going to produce about the case in which you

and Joe Majczek were involved. I have given a good deal of thought to your particular situation, and have emphasized on various occasions to exercise consideration in the portrayal of your character so as not to spoil any possible chance of your receiving a pardon in the near future, if the Parole Board deems a pardon is justified. Our intentions are to follow the factual story as closely as possible with a minimum of dramatic license.

As a matter of fact, the way the script is shaping up at the present time, I feel that this picture, if anything, will do you a great deal of good, since we are definitely portraying your character in a favorable light—rather than to point an ominous finger towards you.

Wishing you success in your appeal to the Pardon Board.

Very sincerely yours,

Otto Lang, Producer

In February 1948, after the picture was released nationally, I received a number of congratulatory letters from people all over the country. One of these was from Ted Marcinkewicz.

February 24, 1948

Dear Mr. Lang:

With unbounded happiness I am writing to express my deepest gratitude for the pains and care you had taken to portray me without injury in "Northside 777." Thanks a million, for being so considerate.

The recent numerous opinions and comments regarding the picture since it has been shown in the Chicago Theatre has confirmed the many glowing terms James McGuire used when speaking or writing about you, and I now agree with him whole-heartedly. You must be a kind, thoughtful, and an extraordinary sort of a fellow who should be considered a rarity in this selfish world of ours. It is strange indeed to find a person of such good character, morals, and ethics as you possess, in the highly unethical group in which you work. My faith is somewhat restored in humanity after knowing you.

With the highest esteem and a fervent prayer that I can someday repay you, I remain.

Gratefully yours,

Ted Marcinkewicz #13995
Menard Penitentiary

I did not deserve all the accolades showered upon me by a hapless prison inmate as there were many others involved in fashioning the screenplay who were concerned about protecting his interests and not showing him in a negative light that could compromise his chances for being granted a pardon. Shortly thereafter, Ted Marcinkewicz was pardoned and set free.

Steve Hannagan, the renowned flack, sent me this note:

> Here are the New York reviews on *Call Northside 777* that will make you feel young and spry again. I have seldom seen the New York press agree with such unanimity, that this picture is completely splendid.

The picture did very well at the box office and recouped its original investment in multiple figures.

SUN VALLEY REDUX

During the previous summer, while I had been fully occupied with *Call Northside 777*, Friedl Pfeifer tendered his resignation from Sun Valley, realizing that in order to accomplish what he set out to achieve at Aspen, he had to give the project his undivided attention. It was an unexpected blow to all of us. I was given the title of executive director of the ski school, and it was up to me to find a replacement to head the school's daily operation. I wanted a man with an extensive teaching background, preferably one who had made a name for himself as an international Alpine racing competitor.

Naturally I veered toward someone from St. Anton and turned to Hannes Schneider for suggestions. Hannes had one teacher on his staff at North Conway who seemed to offer the qualifications I was looking for. The question was whether Hannes could spare Toni Matt, his ace instructor. Also, would Toni be willing to assume the responsibility of running a ski school on his own?

After many phone conversations and letters exchanged with Hannes and Toni, who was delighted to have been offered this position, I cabled Hannes, who had left on a visit to St. Anton am Arlberg:

IF AGREEABLE WITH YOU, TONI MATT CAN HAVE THE SUN VALLEY SKI SCHOOL STOP

His affirmative cable came the next day:

AGREEABLE WITH ME ABOUT TONI MATT STOP MANY THANKS

I knew that Hannes was always willing to have one of his instructors advance to a more promising future, and I knew Toni from the days when I taught at St. Anton. He had been trained as an instructor under Hannes's strict supervision. A powerful young man over six feet tall, he had also acquired a certain charisma as a world-class racer. At war's end, after serving his tour of duty as a ski trooper with the Tenth Mountain Division, he rejoined Hannes's school at North Conway and had become one of his most popular instructors and an asset to the ski school. He added to his stature and gained everlasting fame when in a race he schussed the notorious and close-to-perpendicular head wall at Tuckerman's Ravine on Mount Washington in New Hampshire. No one would have believed it was possible to do so and live to tell about it. Toni himself told me that he never intended to do this, but on his first turn at the very top of the head wall, his skis got away from him and there was no way for him to check his speed. As he was hurtling down the mountain, he realized that it was a matter of either continuing his straight descent or sitting down and taking an ungodly head-over-heels fall, skirting sharp rock outcroppings and risking bodily injury. He decided to tough it out, keeping his skis lined up straight, with a prayer on his lips, until he reached the gentler run out at the bottom of the ravine, leading into a narrow trail to the finish line, setting a course record, minutes ahead of his closest competitor. It was a landmark performance that he vowed he would never repeat—nor would anyone else ever want to challenge it.

I had invited Toni and his wife, Stella, to come west and visit me in Beverly Hills for a few days to go over the many details of his new job. Toni appeared to me to have matured enormously since I had last seen him. In a quiet way, he justified my confidence in having selected him for this job. Upon my arrival at Sun Valley, I found that Toni had the ski school operation well in hand and had gained the respect of his peers. It was, therefore, with a modicum of confidence that I pursued my long cherished dream to attend the Winter Olympic Games 1948 at St. Moritz in Switzerland. It would be my first Olympics.

I was no longer writing my regular column for the *Seattle Post-Intelligencer* and its associated wire service, but they welcomed my occasional contributions. In fact, Royal Brougham, sports editor and my mentor, suggested that I cover the Olympics for his paper as a special correspondent. Of course, this idea appealed to me enormously. Pat Rogers also thought it would be a terrific opportunity to garner some international publicity for Sun Valley, with me acting as the resort's official goodwill ambassador. Another advantage of writing for the *Seattle Post-Intelligencer* would be my accreditation as an official member of the press corps with access to the select observation posts reserved for the press and to the Olympic Village, where the athletes were housed. Pat Rogers also volunteered to book a room for me at the venerable Palace Hotel in St. Moritz. Owned and managed by the Badrutt family for generations, the Palace offered glamour and exclusivity, luxurious accommodations, superb cuisine, and a fine wine cellar, enhanced by excellent service.

I had discussed with Sinnie, long before entering into these arrangements, how she would feel about my leaving her alone again with the two boys. She assured me that she would be quite comfortable and well cared for in the company of a few very dear friends. One of these was Mary Ellen Moritz, the wife of the extraordinary Dr. John Moritz, who would contribute so enormously to the knowledge and treatment of ski injuries. They became our closest friends over the course of the years. It is only fitting that the hospital at Sun Valley is named in honor of John Moritz. With the road cleared and my conscience appeased, I booked a seat on a TWA Constellation, and in a remarkably short time I found myself in Paris. Cross-continental and overseas flying were standard modes of travel by then.

The United States had entered a very competitive squad of athletes. Foremost among these was Gretchen Fraser, née Kunigk, who had learned to ski in my school at Mount Rainier. Now a resident of Sun Valley, along with her husband, Don, also a renowned racer, Gretchen was touted by the American press as a dark horse and potential threat to the elite European women skiers in downhill and slalom, as was the up-and-coming Andrea Mead, the youngest member of the U.S. squad. Art Devlin from Lake Placid, New York, a stylish internationally acclaimed ski jumper, with courageous Gordon Wren from Steamboat Springs, Colorado, headed the U.S. jumping team.

I knew I would miss the opening ceremony, but my objective was to concentrate on the Alpine events and ski jumping. After scanning half a dozen European papers to catch up on the latest reports from St. Moritz,

I filed my first piece with a Paris dateline:

Glancing through the pages of European and, especially, sport sections of Swiss papers, one can easily detect that the American Olympic Ski Team is regarded as the "Glamour Squad" of the Winter Olympics 1948, but nobody seems to think that we have any potential winners, except for perhaps an isolated "dark horse" breaking out from the pack. . . . The unanimous opinion is that technically the Americans are on a par with the best in Europe. Whether they'll have the speed, stamina and racing expertise remains the question to be answered in the very near future.

The U.S. Team has impressed everybody by its physical fitness and dignified conduct. To add to this the specially designed Olympic uniforms with their variety of changes has caused a good deal of favorable comment.

Except for the loss of Art Devlin, our premier ski jumper, due to an unfortunate re-injury of his knee in practice, and "Dodie" Post's broken leg, which eliminates both from competition, all team members have survived the preliminary training period and tests in good condition, disregarding minor cuts and bruises.

There was a great fuss made by the French team in regard to the choice of the Men's Downhill course. They claimed it was too easy and would favor the "waxers" and technically inferior racers. Reports from other sources passed onto me describe the course as tough and demanding on the legs of the racers. There is a succession of devilish bumps toward the finish line, which will undoubtedly take its toll unmercifully with legs tired and thighs numb.

The Swiss don't believe in levelling out bumps as we are inclined to do on our courses, such as the Harriman Cup Course down the Warm Springs Trail at Sun Valley.

Our Ladies Team also has a tough assignment and formidable obstacle to overcome facing such proven competitors as Celina Seghi (Italy), who seems to equal the prowess and finesse of France's Georgette Thioliere and Sweden's ace, May Nilsson.

Our hopes rest upon an inspired performance by reliable and cool-headed Gretchen Fraser and Andrea Mead's aggressive and uncommon aptitude in the Slalom.

Going by express train from Paris to St. Moritz was like old times. I had always enjoyed traveling by train and watching the scenery pass by, but especially so on this trip after crossing the border into Switzerland.

The constantly changing vistas of small villages, lakes, and snow-covered peaks left me with a feeling of joyous anticipation for the rest of this journey. St. Moritz itself was a fairy-tale village, clinging to the steep flank of a mountain and overlooking a frozen lake below. The surrounding mountains with their wide-open terrain above timberline seemed tailor-made for skiers.

Someone must have done an awfully good public relations job in advance of my arrival; I was received by the Badrutt brothers at the Palace Hotel as though I were a celebrity. The narrow streets of St. Moritz were enlivened by crowds of people and horse-drawn sleds. The buoyant atmosphere and spirit of camaraderie augured well for the smooth flow of all competitive events.

St. Moritz, Switzerland, February 2, 1948
(Special *Post-Intelligencer* Correspondent, via cable)

Well, I was wrong. American ski racers will have to wait another few years to catch up with the Europeans. Our best entries in the Men's Downhill didn't do so well in the Winter Olympics 1948.

They ran into trouble on the upper section of the course. I put some of the blame on the wrong selection of the wax applied to running surface of the skis to make them slide faster. Much time was lost due to this shortcoming.

Also, the series of bumps approaching the finish line at high speed took a toll among the U.S. foursome. . . .Technically, American racers are virtually equal to their opponents, but they lack in experience and cunning of frequent big-time racing competitions and also need to master the art of "waxing."

Alas, the American women downhillers did not fare much better. They either fell or were too cautious in their attack of the course.

Gretchen Fraser, our Northwest girl, was steady as a rock, but rather conservative, which nevertheless placed her 13th, far behind the three favorites and winners . . . However, there was still a glimmer of hope that Gretchen might score in the combination of slalom and downhill, with slalom being her forte.

Andrea Mead, of the U.S.A. Team, could have been a strong contender and was ahead of the field by three seconds at a mid-course interval timing spot. Shortly thereafter she took a bad fall, ending up in the deep snow off the course, which ruined a daring effort on her part.

The weather, course and snow conditions were perfect....

St. Moritz, Switzerland, February 3, 1948
(Special Post-Intelligencer Correspondent, via cable)

... Gordon Wren of Steamboat Springs, Colorado, gave an impressive display of his undaunted and courageous excellence on [the] beautiful jumping hill. While he could keep up with Ruud's length of jumps he could not match his impeccable style in the air, floating like a bird on wings to a perfect landing. Gordon Wren's fifth place, breaking through the phalanx of world-class Nordic ski jumpers, was a remarkable achievement, which throughout the practice sessions and final competition, impressed the judges and enthusiastic spectators most favorably. Hip, hip hurray for our Gordon Wren!

It was a day to rejoice when I sat down to file my last report from St. Moritz.

GRETCHEN FRASER IS TOAST OF AMERICAN SKIERS
St. Moritz, February 4, 1948 (via cable)

American skiers can cheer up. Today's Olympic slalom for women proved that our racers deserve to be considered as serious contenders after all.

Gretchen Fraser convincingly vindicated her 13th place showing in the downhill by placing first in the slalom and thereby winning the first Gold Medal ever accorded to an American skier in an alpine event. To add to this, her personal best, she was also awarded a Silver Medal based on her sum total of points in the combination of downhill and slalom, barely edged out of first place by Trude Beiser of Austria, with a minuscule margin of a few hundredths of one point.

Little Gretchen is the toast of American skiers and cheered by them wherever they gather in St. Moritz tonight.

It was a proud moment when she stood on top of the three-tiered Olympic victory stand to receive her well-earned Gold and Silver Medals.

She has fittingly climaxed her colorful racing career by these victories. It was a turning point in American skiing—an historic achievement, considering the field of international competitors.... Gretchen's victory proved immensely popular here in St. Moritz. She has been flooded with congratulatory cablegrams and her room resembles nothing less than a florist's showroom—simply a mass of flowers. How proud my good friend Don Fraser, back home in Sun Valley, must be of his petite, plucky spouse.

She plans to leave for Norway after the games' closing ceremony to visit relatives she has never met, but who by now surely must be well aware of her Olympic triumph.

From Norway she will fly home to the Pacific Northwest to be honored as the Queen of American skiers.

The time had come for me to leave also. But I was obsessed by one wish, which was to take a ride down the famous Olympic bobsled *piste.* Somehow, with the help of Andreas Badrutt, I managed to get myself invited on a practice run by the captain of an alternate squad of the Olympic Swiss team. As a deadweight passenger in the middle of the bobsled, I was told to take my assigned place and sit still, keep my head down, and go with the flow of the serpentine course. What impressed me most was the feeling of sudden onrushing speed, emphasized by the thumping impact of the steel skids pounding against the rippled surface of the ice and the steeply banked concrete-hard walls of the embankments. It felt like being catapulted from a cannon and hurtled relentlessly toward the finish line. It was a ride to be remembered— totally different from traveling at high speed on skis.

I knew that I could not possibly come to Europe and not see my parents and sisters. It had been over ten years since our last reunion, and they would have never forgiven me if I had failed to visit them. Traveling by express trains through the night in a sleeping car berth, I could gain time to spend a few days with them. Deliberately, I waited to advise them of my arrival until I was in a position to give them an exact date. For expediency and to save my mother from the pressure of buying provisions and cooking meals for all of us, which she would have insisted on doing, I suggested that we meet at Kitzbühel, only a short train ride from Salzburg. I told them that I would arrange for room and board for all of us in a small *gasthof,* which would take care of all our needs and give us lots of time to visit with each other. Overjoyed and completely surprised, they accepted my invitation without protest.

It turned out to be a perfect solution, and our family reunion could not have been more rewarding, after our long separation and the hardships they had endured during the war. I was pleased to see that physically they appeared to be healthy, though still slender after a limited diet. The food packages we sent regularly via CARE had helped immensely, they told me, but they preferred by far the packages Sinnie and I had put together. Psychologically, I could tell that both my parents had aged

beyond their years. Especially my father, who had always borne the responsibility of being the provider against difficult and often insurmountable odds. Nelly and Elsa seemed to have weathered the privations of war
somewhat better. That they were younger had a lot to do with it.

Nelly had a good job with Americans in Salzburg, and Elsa also worked
with the American military as a house mother and tour guide. Both attractive and fluent in English, they had an advantage in procuring these
types of jobs. Erna couldn't come, but I was told she was our mother's
mainstay in keeping house, going to the market, and helping with daily
chores. Lovingly and respectfully my father referred to her as the house
"dragon," since she insisted he take his shoes off whenever he came in
the house to keep her highly polished floors spic-and-span. There were
other regimens to which he had to submit, often unwillingly, to keep
peace in the household. He told me some of these comic episodes with a
sense of gallows humor and a small dose of resentment, but never with
acrimony. That was one of my father's lovable character traits, to keep
peace and spread good will, with a smile on his face.

Of course, the recurring topics of conversation were Sinnie and our
two youngsters. The burning question was: "When are they coming to
Salzburg?" I had to dig up all sorts of anecdotes and funny happenings to
make the family laugh and vicariously visualize our way of life. To own
one's house and have an automobile in California was to them like paradise on this Earth. In many ways it was, I assured them, and I considered
myself very fortunate. All too soon the time came to end this whirlwind
family visit and fly back to America. The joy of such a reunion is always
somewhat dampened by the inevitable parting, which, in a family such
as ours, was always quite emotional. I reassured them that this was just
the first of many more such visits and that soon they would see Sinnie,
Peter, and Mark. I meant to keep my promise.

Filled with an overflowing cornucopia of impressions and memories,
I boarded my train back to Paris as they stood at the station platform
waving to me until we were out of each other's sight. It was a wonderful
finale to my first Olympic experience.

I WAS A MALE WAR BRIDE

I felt an overpowering longing to get back to Sun Valley and be
reunited with Sinnie and our two boys. I looked forward to staying put
for a while, skiing with them during my free time, and making ours
more of a family life. Peter was going on seven and Mark would be four

in August. I had taught them the rudiments of skiing, to which they had adapted quite nicely.

Peter liked ski jumping from a small hill I had built for him and his classmates on Dollar Mountain. By some misunderstanding during a practice session one day, he took off thinking that my signal indicated that the track was clear. In fact, some of the youngsters were diligently ski-packing the landing strip. When Peter reached the lip of the takeoff and found his landing spot blocked by packers, now in hasty retreat, he instinctively recoiled and stepped on imaginary brakes in midair, desperately trying to halt his progress. I was looking through the finder of my camera and caught him in action with his skis braced and askew, arms flailing, and a corresponding expression of surprise on his face. He never forgave me for immortalizing this particular embarrassing moment in his life. I, on the other hand, enjoy looking at this photograph, smiling every time I rummage through my collection of family memorabilia, knowing that there was really no danger to him and no harm done other than a dent to young Peter's pride.

Mark was the more studious and cautious skier, always trying to stay well in control. Sinnie on skis was graceful and composed, rarely taking a fall. She considered the prostrate position on snow and the struggle to get back on her feet unladylike and humiliating, best avoided. As Max Barsis, the charming and talented cartoonist in residence at Sun Valley, said in his Austrian accent of Sinnie, "She skis like a 'swain' gliding along a placid pond." At heart she never was what I would call a driven skier and could take or leave it as the occasion came her way. This suited me just fine. The last thing I wished was to have her pursue skiing only to please me.

In order to fulfill the Union Pacific Railroad Company's requirement that both spouses be employed by Sun Valley in order to qualify for company housing, Sinnie had a part-time job at the sports desk in the lodge, which was sort of a glorified concierge's all-purpose information center. It was attended in shifts by her and two male employees, who had formed a congenial and effective trio.

Darryl Zanuck and I resumed our habit of skiing together and then going over to the Opera House to look at the daily rushes and films in progress. A constantly changing coterie of creative talent floated in and out to take part in the convoluted process of filmmaking. With *Call Northside 777* a box office and critical success, my stock had risen considerably with DFZ, and he assured me that I had a position waiting for me at the studio by the end of the skiing season. What it would be I couldn't guess.

At Sun Valley, I tried to cut down on my social obligations as much as possible, to spend more time with my family. This was also what Sinnie preferred, having dinner at home in our comfortable apartment rather than following the nightly ritual of cocktail parties and dinners at the lodge, Ram, or Trail Creek Cabin, or any one of Ketchum's many restaurants as an alternate choice. It could be exhausting, attempting to keep up with all the après-ski activities. In no time at all spring was around the corner, bringing increasingly warmer and sunnier days.

The ski school under the leadership of Toni Matt had functioned well, and on the whole it had been a successful season. There was one exception: Toni Matt had become involved in a love affair, not uncommon among ski instructors, but his became public. His wife, Stella, with true Sicilian ardor, entered into her husband's amorous entanglement and put an end to it. Their marriage was salvaged, but the management was soured by this tumultuous love triangle, and Toni's chance of returning next winter was forfeited. When Hannes Schneider heard about this denouement, he was truly disappointed and quite put out, as I was, again faced with the unenviable task of finding someone of Friedl Pfeifer's stature to fill this important position.

I knew that my arrangement of taking a leave of absence from Twentieth Century Fox every winter would not work for any length of time. I had to decide either to make Sun Valley my full-time career or to cross all the way over the line into the film world. In my heart I knew that my choice would be Hollywood, despite its labyrinthine complexities, intense competition, and Byzantine intrigues. Thus far, I had experienced only a very small dose of it, but it was enough to realize that it would be far different from the relatively carefree life offered to me at Sun Valley. I decided to give my split career one more year and then let destiny take its course.

No sooner had we settled down in our home in Beverly Hills than I was told I would be heading for Germany as part of the crew working for Howard Hawks on a film entitled *I Was a Male War Bride*, starring Cary Grant and Ann Sheridan. Hawks was a highly respected and successful filmmaker, with a string of box office hits to his credit. Working with him would be a step in the right direction. But it also augured the beginning of a pattern of prolonged separations from my family. I did not look forward to this, nor did they. I realized that being left alone with and taking care of our two growing boys, and overseeing the important beginnings of their primary schooling, would put an additional burden on Sinnie. I had fully expected to share parental responsibilities with her, not only as the provider of the means but also as a father by my presence and companionship. Under the circumstances my choices were limited, inasmuch as I was hooked on filmmaking and hoped to become a full-fledged director of feature films eventually.

One recompense to look forward to on this latest assignment was that surely there would be opportunities to visit my parents in Salzburg on free weekends. So I left for Germany with somewhat mixed feelings. My function, while not precisely delineated, would be that of a standby second unit director for extraneous shots with doubles and scenic backgrounds. For expediency and economic reasons, these could be handled by a second unit requiring a minimal crew. Our headquarters were in Heidelberg, as romantic and beautiful a town as there was in Germany and, surprisingly, one of the few cities that had been spared Allied bombing attacks. It was a terrible shock to me to see towns I had known for their singular beauty and historical heritage and had visited many times now devastated and virtually flattened into gigantic heaps of bricks and rubble. One could not possibly imagine that these cities would ever rise again. But rise they did, as the passage of decades would prove.

The shooting of *I Was a Male War Bride* could best be described as a cinematic breach birth. The schtick was Cary Grant's playing a French officer who falls in love with an American Wac (Ann Sheridan). In order to get him legally into the United States, he had to impersonate a female American officer in full military drag as a war bride, to be granted an entry visa. Among the many problems was that Cary Grant did not feel very comfortable in this charade of a sex change. We were hampered by inclement weather and the difficult working conditions in post-war Germany, and our progress was slowed down alarmingly.

With Charles Lederer on hand, the screenplay writer and a close friend of Hawks's, scenes were frequently rewritten and dialogue improvised while shooting. This innovative approach to making films was not unusual with Howard Hawks and often contributed to making his films look fresh and spontaneous. It didn't work in this particular case. Many scenes had to be reshot and others added when the company moved to England. Eventually, the film was completed with more shooting at the Fox studio in Hollywood.

What I personally learned from this experience was that Howard Hawks was an imposing and dominating figure who was difficult to get close to. Consequently, there was a noticeable lack of communication between him and the members of his crew, who waited for directives and specific instructions in regard to the day-by-day shooting schedule. Often we found ourselves sitting around, anxiously waiting for decisions on locations, military personnel, and material requirements. Yet, when the film was finally finished, way over the estimated shooting schedule and the allocated budget, it was not a total flop. But it was far from being memorable, and mainly dependent on Cary Grant's and Ann Sheridan's star power at the box office and some of Howard Hawks's ingenious comedy touches, of which he was an acknowledged master.

I did see my parents twice for brief visits at Salzburg and became aware that the city had sustained heavier damage than I had previously thought from Allied bombings, mostly in the newer part of the city and in the area around the sprawling railroad station, main post office, and communications center. One stray bomb had come close to hitting their apartment building, causing considerable damage in the neighborhood. At the sound of each ear-piercing alarm, indicating the approach of enemy aircraft, they dashed from the fourth floor down into an underground shelter, to sit out time and time again the nerve-wracking interlude, waiting for the all-clear signal. With her composure already stressed to the edge, this was particularly hard on my mother.

I was relieved to find them both in much better spirits and healthier looking than when I had seen them in Kitzbühel. A steady flow of food packages and other necessities from us in America had given them new hope and fortitude to cope with the aftereffects of war. With a firm promise that on my next visit to Europe some of my family would be coming with me, I headed back to what I considered my home, the good old U.S.A.

In retrospect I have often wondered why I was sent to Germany on the film. I felt that my contributions were insignificant. But then, who was I to question my boss's decision to send me where he saw fit? This I would find out later on in my film career.

EMILE ALLAIS AND THE FRENCH TECHNIQUE

In thinking about the Toni Matt debacle and the future of the Sun Valley Ski School, I felt intuitively that the school, as well as the resort, needed a shot in the arm to revitalize it, to renew its former preeminence and glamour. We needed an attraction—a celebrity with the charisma of a superior ski racer who could also teach. The name Emile Allais came to my mind, a world-class racer whom I had met during the Winter Olympics at St. Moritz.

Emile Allais was the toast of that era in international slalom and downhill competitions. He also spearheaded a movement to introduce a new technique and teaching method based upon his personal racing style, which began to be promulgated as the "French technique." The main objective was to liberate ski schools from the dogma of the Arlberg technique and to shrink Hannes Schneider's stature as the guru of Alpine skiing. Spirited confrontations, often with ugly and out-of-order personal attacks directed toward Hannes Schneider, sometimes developed between the two factions.

To Emile Allais's credit, he never stooped to such lowly tactics. He respected Schneider for what he had done for skiing, even though he felt that his idea of rejuvenating and improving the basic structure of the Arlberg technique was justified. In return for the gentlemanly way in which Allais propagated his aims and goal, Schneider respected him as a worthy opponent and not as an enemy. After all, Hannes philosophized, there was always a possibility that another man could come up with a better mousetrap. He was willing to listen but not ready to concede.

It would be a daring step to invite Allais to join the Sun Valley Ski School, not as director but as a guest instructor. I saw him becoming involved with the top class of skiers, while we would continue teaching the established curriculum to beginning and intermediate skiers. I had no idea whether Allais would be interested in such a proposal. Before I approached him, I solicited some opinions. As I might have expected, my loyal and well-established instructors were dead set against it, saying, "Otto, are you out of your mind? Allais is an ambitious young Frenchman and a skiing ace, riding the crest of a popularity wave. He'd be after your head and trying his best to get your job. Don't do it!"

I wrote a letter to Kathleen Harriman, who was her father's alter ego concerning Sun Valley, since he was immersed in the political problems of the Democrats. Kathleen cabled promptly:

YOUR PLAN FOR ALLAIS SOUNDS ABSOLUTELY TOPS STOP AM SURE AVERELL WOULD APPROVE, PARTICULARLY IF YOU CAN GET ALLAIS ON THE CONDITION THAT THE SKI SCHOOL WOULD RETAIN ITS INDIVIDUALITY AND NOT BE COMPLETELY DOMINATED BY HIS TECHNIQUE STOP BEST OF LUCK TO YOU IN

SECURING HIM STOP AM WRITING MORE STOP LOVE TO YOU AND SINNIE

I also contacted Hannes to get his reaction. He was completely in accord with my brainstorm as a great stimulant for the resort and for American skiing in general. It would create attention, and he was confident the two techniques could coexist, and to let the results of such a worthwhile experiment dictate the future. He reassured me that I had nothing to fear in regard to my position, nor did he, as father of the Arlberg technique. Only time would tell which of the techniques deserved to last.

I wrote to Emile Allais, laying out the details of my proposal in a letter. His reply came promptly on May 15, 1948, from New York, where he was waiting to board a ship for Chile. He had spent the winter teaching at a Canadian ski resort, and from what I had heard through grapevine gossip, it was not quite to his satisfaction. He wrote:

> . . . Now, for myself, I do not intend to go back to Canada next winter. I have always had in mind coming to the States and as I have received two or three very interesting offers, I shall accept one of them. Needless to tell you that I would prefer to come to Sun Valley as I have always considered it THE place in the States.
>
> During the short time you and I spent together at St. Moritz, I had the conviction that between the two of us, we might achieve pretty good things for skiing.
>
> I, too, am very broad-minded in regard to technique and would suggest keeping your Sun Valley technique and just add a few improvements and perhaps some slight changes.
>
> I am sailing on May 16, so I shall ask you to write to me in Portillo, Chile, with perhaps a copy to Cristobal (Panama), where I shall stop around May 20. We can make arrangements by correspondence, but it would have to be soon, as there is one place to which I must give an answer on June 15.

I responded:

> . . . I was delighted to hear from you so promptly and it must have been intuition on my part to have reached you just before you sailed. . . . I am even more enthusiastic now to have you with us at Sun Valley. You have reassured me completely that we can find a mutually rewarding base of cooperation.

I shall be absolutely frank with you, so that you know exactly where you stand before you make a final decision. As you probably know, my official title is "Executive Director of the Sun Valley Ski School," and I have been asked by Mr. Harriman to continue in this capacity for at least one more winter, as I am splitting my time working for Twentieth Century Fox during the summer months and Sun Valley during the winter season.

Last winter I engaged Toni Matt as the head instructor, with great hopes, which unfortunately did not materialize and I shall spare you the details. To be brief, Toni is out.

In the meantime (and before I even thought of contacting you), I had promised Johnny Litchfield, an American born and raised skier, the job Toni held. His title is head instructor, while I remain the overall director. Naturally, I intend to live up to my promise and I am sure that you will understand when you meet Johnny. He is a Dartmouth College graduate and has been a valued instructor of the Sun Valley Ski School for many years. Inasmuch as all the "executive positions" have been filled, I would like to create a position for you, which would carry importance and dignity and be in keeping with your reputation. I thought that perhaps you would like to be in charge of all racing activities and top classes among the guests who wish to improve their technical skill.

We would, of course, work closely together, and any suggestions you care to make would be most welcome and always given utmost consideration. Perhaps this is not exactly what you visualized, but it is better to be truthful now, than to lure you to Sun Valley merely to capitalize on your name. We would like you to become one of us and for many years to come. There will be changes undoubtedly, as I may want to step aside soon to pursue my film career and let others have a crack at my job. In my opinion, there is a definite future for you at Sun Valley.

I then verified the financial and housing arrangements for him and Georgette, his wife, wishing them a good summer, or rather winter, as they happened to be in the southern hemisphere. Emile accepted the offer in principle, with one request, that I increase his guaranteed salary for one season by $1,000. This was easily arranged and the contract signed in triplicate by all parties concerned.

In his next letter, Emile wrote that no sooner had he mailed the signed contract than he received an offer to head the ski school and development of the White Face Mountain area near Lake Placid, at a guaranteed minimum salary of $6,000—twice the amount he had signed for with

Sun Valley. I resolved that somehow, someway, we would see to it that Emile did not regret his decision to sign with us.

Emile Allais arrived at Sun Valley much heralded by the press. It was looked upon as a coup on my part to have brought the two feuding factions together under one roof. As it turned out, there was no feuding worth mentioning. To the contrary, we all enjoyed Emile's presence and graciousness. He was a gentleman in every respect and comported himself accordingly. All of us ski instructors, including me, were most anxious to participate in one of his skiing seminars, and all of us tried to master the "ruade," which was the signature of his technique. It was a christiania with the skis held parallel, and in order to initiate the change of direction, one lifted the tailends of both skis off the snow and started the turn in midair to head the skis in the opposite direction. I found it to be a physically taxing maneuver, but very useful under certain conditions, such as a crusted or deeply rutted snow surface. The sight of a bunch of skiers doing the ruade reminded me of a flock of bunny rabbits hopping around and frolicking in the snow.

Emile was very popular with the guests enrolled in the ski school, and to be in his class of top skiers was a much sought-after privilege. I offered him any class he wished, to take over on an experimental basis, be it rank beginners or intermediate skiers struggling with their stem turns. He declined with a sly smile and said, "*Merçi beaucoup, mon cher copain,* you are all doing just fine and I don't think I could do any better." Of course, by that time our concept of the original Arlberg technique had been perceptibly streamlined, with less emphasis on the basic stem position. It made a lot of difference in progressing students more quickly.

I was truly sorry when the season came to an end and we would part company, since Emile had been offered a lucrative deal to take over the ski school at Squaw Valley and further the development of this up-and-coming winter resort. I wished him good luck. He deserved to be the director of his own ski school. Alas, after only two years, Emile left Squaw Valley because of "conceptual and artistic differences" between him and Alex Cushing, the owner, who had acquired the reputation of being not easy to get along with.

Emile returned to France to take over as technical director for the country's development of ski resorts. Our friendship endured through the years, and the last time I saw him he lived semiretired in Flaine, an ultramodern ski resort in whose creation he had been involved. He supervised his own large sport shop and still skied with vigor and the infectious enthusiasm for the sport that had brought us together. We took a run together and, as I followed his tracks down the mountain, I shouted at him, "Hey, Emile, what about the ruade?"

Looking over his shoulder he yelled back at me, with a wicked grin, "Extinct as the dodo bird."

HOLLYWOOD
POTPOURRI

In the early summer of 1949 I was asked by Twentieth Century Fox to go again to Europe, this time to shoot action sequences and scenic vistas of Paris for a film based on the short story "My Old Man" by Ernest Hemingway. It was a story with a horse-racing background, to be shot at the famous racetracks around Paris and one in Italy. The screenplay adaptation was written by Casey Robinson, who would also produce the film. No director had been chosen as yet, which was not exactly in the best interest of the project. John Garfield would portray a crooked jockey who was idolized by his young son and whose wife had left him. In the story, complications arise when the son finds out that his father threw a race to pay off a debt to a Mafioso. Interwoven into this plot was a love story between the jockey and a young Frenchwoman, played by Micheline Prelle, who assumed the role of surrogate mother to the boy.

The opportunity to go back to Paris was tempting, but it would mean again being separated from my family. I said that I would go if I could take my wife with me and if the studio would pay for her transportation. It would be exciting to revisit Paris under more serendipitous circumstances, compared with our brief stop at the outbreak of World War II. My proposal was accepted, somewhat to my surprise, since the arrangement was not a precedent the studio wished to establish. Sinnie and I decided to enroll Peter and Mark in a highly touted summer camp for boys at Lake Arrowhead. They wouldn't mind spending a summer away from parental badgering to tidy up their room, take a bath, brush their teeth, put on clean clothes, eat with a fork, "Don't slobber your food," and so on, and so on.

I knew that it would be no second honeymoon for us, since the demands on my time were compelling and unpredictable. The film took priority over personal lives and desires. But I knew Sinnie would adjust to almost any situation, and the diversions offered by Paris—its sights, shopping emporiums, and boutiques—would keep her amply entertained. We would still eat many meals together and stay in the same suite at the Georges V Hotel, one of the choicest in Paris, off the Champs Elysées near the Arc de Triomphe. The trip was one of the nicer perks of working on films in foreign countries and made up for many of the shortcomings.

UNDER MY SKIN

Working on "My Old Man" was fascinating, with a camera crew, grips, various assistants, helpers, and doubles—all French, with little knowledge of the English language. I had no experience of the intricacies, protocol, and finer points of thoroughbred horse racing in Paris, a citadel of the sport, but I learned fast and managed to get what needed to be put on film.

Sometimes this was difficult. For example, it nearly took an act of God to obtain permission at Auteuil, one of the prime racetracks, to set up two of our mobile cameras in the shrubbery of one of the hurdles during an actual steeplechase. We had planned it so one camera would film the approaching field of bunched-up horses, lifting over the camera, and the other would catch the landing and falls, if any. A third camera would cover the actual jump from a three-quarter side angle. This would provide us with an exciting cutting continuity, using pieces of each camera's point of view. I explained to the racing stewards that our two camouflaged cameras could not possibly distract the approaching horses, since they would be activated by a hidden wire along the hedge leading to a switch in the hands of a standby cameraman. After much deliberation, they granted their permission, and it worked like a charm. From then on I had relative run of the place with my camera crew. Always double-checking that we were not interfering, the stewards began to rely on my good judgment.

We worked at the beautifully landscaped racecourses of Auteuil, St. Cloud and Longchamps. On a sunny afternoon an explosion of color— flower beds, well-dressed people, jockeys in their silks slowly riding their lithe and prancing horses to the starting gate—was a sight to gladden one's imagination. We had hired the Dutch trainer of a prominent stable as our technical advisor. Monsieur Mynher D'Okhuisen, a savvy and seasoned connoisseur of horse flesh, was immensely helpful in providing racehorses and jockeys and selecting locations for action sequences. At his invitation and to my greatest pleasure, I joined him and his grooms for the early morning workouts. We met in the Bois de Boulogne before sunrise to ride racehorses on mile-long practice tracks cut through tall trees and on the softest sandy surfaces. It was a smooth and exhilarating ride, such as traveling on a cloud might be.

I worked my tail off and the hours were long, but having Sinnie with me made all the difference. We did manage a visit to the Louvre, saw a few other historical sights, and enjoyed an occasional escape to one of Paris's famous nightclubs. There was only one unpleasant incident, which occurred when I had an exchange of heated telegrams with Casey Robinson, when he berated me for some shortcomings.

To OL from Casey Robinson, August 12, 1949:

WHEN CAN WRITE WILL BUT THIS A SPIN STOP WHY DID YOU NOT ANSWER MY CABLES ABOUT YOUR NOTES THAT YOU HAD PROMISED ME AND ABOUT FLOOR PLANS, JOCKEYS' ROOMS AUTEUIL AND CHANTILLY STOP ALSO DID YOU EVER COVER WITH STILLS INTERIOR TRACK HOSPITAL AS YOU TOLD ME YOU HAD STOP WITH PHOTOGRAPHY BEGINNING AT STUDIO IN FOUR WEEKS THIS CEASES TO BE INCONSEQUENTIAL MATTER STOP WHERE ARE THE SHOTS YOU TOLD ME YOU HAD TAKEN FROM TURNS SHOWING GREAT DISTANCE TO GRANDSTANDS IN BACKGROUND CANNOT FIND THEM AND NOW BEGINNING RUN UNDEVELOPED NEGATIVE IN SEARCH STOP ALSO AM DESPERATELY MISSING ANY GEOGRAPHY SHOTS OF HORSES GOING AWAY FROM CAMERAS WHICH LACK I BELIEVE IS DIRECTLY TRACEABLE TO AN INCIDENT WHICH HAPPENED RIVER EIGHT JUMP ON OUR FIRST DAY OF SHOOTING WHEN I

ASKED CAMERAMAN TO PAN AT THE HORSES AND YOU ASKED
ME NOT TO CREATE CONFUSION SO THEREAFTER I LET YOU
DIRECT CAMERAS AND AS A CONSEQUENCE AM HAVING TO
GROW AN ACRE OF GRASS ON BACK LOT TO GET SOME FUNDA-
MENTAL SHOTS STOP IF I SOUND ANGRY AM ONLY TALKING TO
YOU LIKE BROTHER STOP KINDLY ANSWER MY CABLES, BEST,
CASEY

I could understand his frustration sitting in an office at the studio far
removed from the action, but I was irritated enough to lash back, at the
risk of being relieved of this assignment, which was in his power to do. I
replied:

FRANKLY, AM NEITHER ACCUSTOMED RECEIVING NOR ANSWER-
ING CABLES SUCH AS YOUR LAST STOP FLOOR PLANS JOCKEY
ROOMS AIRMAILED STOP WILL PROVIDE STILL OF HOSPITAL
ROOM CONSISTING OF TWO BEDS WASHSTAND AND WHITE
WALLS AS YOU SAW WITH YOUR OWN EYES BEFORE YOU START
PLANTING ACRE OF GRASS SUGGEST BEING PRACTICAL AND
CONSIDERING JACK MUTH MAKING EXACTLY SPECIFIED
ADDITIONAL SHOTS IF NECESSARY STOP

The hatchet was buried shortly thereafter, with his reply:

MANY THANKS YOUR CABLE AND PHOTOS STOP STILL IN TAIL-
SPIN BUT THINGS STRAIGHTENING AROUND STOP SINCERELY
MISS YOU STOP

After we had finished our quota of designated shots in France and
were preparing to move the unit to Italy for a few days of work, I was
informed by the studio that they wanted me instead to move to London
to work on a film about to be put into production. They would assign a
second unit director to handle the remaining sequence in Italy.

When the film was released Ernest Hemingway's terse dialogue and
consummate writing skill had lost its punch in the process of being transposed into a screenplay for a mawkish film without much distinction
entitled *Under My Skin.*

NIGHT AND THE CITY

After we arrived in London, Sinnie decided to stay with me only a week longer. She felt she should be home in time for our Peter and Mark's return from summer camp. I agreed with her reluctantly and looked forward to sharing a few more days with her in England. Our digs in London were again superlative, in the classy Dorchester Hotel. At the registration desk, a cable and a fat, large envelope were handed to me. Both were from Sam Engel, a veteran producer at Twentieth Century Fox and a close associate and personal friend of Darryl Zanuck's and his family. I knew Sam from the studio, and Sinnie and I had also had some social contacts with him and Ruth, his endearing and statuesquely beautiful wife. Sam was a dedicated, hardworking, and very serious filmmaker. But in private, he was a gregarious, fun-loving storyteller and usually the life of the party. Sam would be in London for only a short time to launch the picture and then return to studio. I would be staying on to represent him during the entire shoot in London. I opened the cable, which read:

EAGER TO HEAR CONFIDENTIAL FRANK OPINION OF SCRIPT STOP PLEASE PHONE OR CABLE THANKS REGARDS, SE

We had barely unpacked and settled down in our suite, when I sat down to read the screenplay of *Night and the City*, which was in the fat envelope handed to me at the front desk.

I cabled back to Sam shortly thereafter:

ON FIRST READING FIND SCRIPT ARRESTING AND EXCEEDINGLY WELL WRITTEN STOP TIGHTENING IN SOME SECTIONS AND SHORTENING IN GENERAL ADVISABLE STOP SHOOTING WITH ACTUAL LONDON ATMOSPHERE AS BACKGROUND SHOULD MAKE IT A FINE PICTURE REGARDS, OL

The story centered around the sleazy manipulations of a ruthless crook and entrepreneur in the milieu of Greco-Roman wrestling. It was the fading era of classic wrestling, unlike today's farce of grotesquely overweight, out-of-shape, ridiculously attired behemoths, strutting and clowning and playacting. Jules Dassin was to be the director, which was an excellent choice for this type of a film. He had very recently brought in a picture entitled *Naked City*, shot entirely in New York. A box-office bonanza, it was well received by film critics and followed the popular concept of "cinema verité," which was to make exteriors and interiors look as realistic as possible, without any cosmetic corrections. This was effective in black-and-white films, with the contrast of often dark and moody shots against an occasional overly bright pool of light for certain effects. It tried to capture life at its most raw; that attempt also applied to the dialogue and acting style. It signaled a breakthrough and would become standard procedure in future films. It also influenced the development of television's hard-hitting docudramas.

I did not know Jules Dassin personally, but I knew of him and his work. He was a daring and imaginative director, always looking for interesting and unconventional camera angles, shooting off a crane from high up or using a dolly to move the camera, keeping in step with the action and actors. This gave the audience a feeling of "verité," of being right in the epicenter of the scene. I had used this technique to a limited degree in my documentary films, handicapped by the cost of renting the appropriate equipment and the extra time such shots took.

Sam Engel had lined up a well-balanced cast of American and British players, namely Richard Widmark and Gene Tierney, supported by Googie Withers, Herbert Lom, and Francis Sullivan. One of our actors, also serving as a technical advisor, by the Polish name of Stanislaus Zbisko, was at one time a popular hero and bona fide world champion. Even at his advanced age, with his arthritic knees, gnarled fingers, and flabby physique, his inherent dignity and honesty still carried him through the scenes with some spirited wrestling action in the ring. He remembered well some of the cunning moves in his repertory going back to his long-past glory days.

There were a multitude of problems and constant delays on the picture, including the fickle English climate. Our cameraman, who had done beautiful work in many films, attempted to light every setup to look like a painting by Rembrandt. It was far too slow and time-consuming and, therefore, costly, until we finally convinced him to settle for inferior Rembrandts, with fewer lights and without the customary refinements of studio photography. Also, Jules was a perfectionist and consequently slow. He insisted on extensive rehearsals and many takes to obtain what he expected from his actors. This, in turn, unleashed a barrage of cables from Sam Engel, criticizing our slow progress, berating us, and cajoling us to make headway, hopeful of regaining some lost days on our schedule. I found myself caught in the middle, as the anvil being pounded on relentlessly. The cost of cables alone must have been staggering. Just for fun, I counted the number of words in one lengthy message. It added up to 594 words, and that may not have been the longest among the many I received.

Fortunately, Dassin and I got along well. I believe I managed to influence him to reevaluate his "artistic integrity" and to accept the fact that sixteen takes of one scene was far too many when we were already eight days behind schedule. As has been shown in reviewing the high number of takes of a particular scene, often the first, third, or fifth take are equal to or even better than the last one. Psychologically, a director finds himself trapped, once he gets into the higher numbers of takes, to print the last one so as not to make a fool of himself. Jules certainly bent to my suggestions and so did Mutz Green, our Rembrandt protégé and cameraman.

It was some consolation that General Lyman Munson (retired), who was then in charge of the Twentieth Century Fox London office, wrote some complimentary words about me in a letter to DFZ:

> Otto has been invaluable. He is constantly on the floor or in the cutting room with Jules Dassin, and also is handling all the second unit work. This has meant many stretches of 20 to 24 hours without sleep and I think he has been a major factor in keeping the picture from going more over schedule than it is. As you remember, the picture was 8 days over schedule at one time and that a yeoman's job has been done in keeping Julie from slipping further behind than the 13 days, which are now on the score card.

Within a few days, DFZ came from Paris to London for a short stay, and after he viewed the first rough assembly of the film and current rushes, I cabled the following report to Sam Engel, which I was sure would be a great relief to him.

DARRYL RAN 6800 FEET OF ASSEMBLED FOOTAGE STOP HIS REACTION DOWNRIGHT ENTHUSIASTIC IN PRACTICALLY EVERY RESPECT SUCH AS DIRECTION, PERFORMANCES AND PHOTOGRAPHY STOP HE THINKS WIDMARK'S CHARACTERIZATION OF FABIAN SHAPING UP SENSATIONALLY AND IN ACADEMY AWARD CONTENTION STOP THERE ARE A FEW

MINOR ADJUSTMENTS TO BE MADE IN NOSSEROS OFFICE BUT NO SUGGESTIONS WHATSOEVER TO CHANGE ANYTHING SHOT WITH WIDMARK STOP COMPANY REHEARSED ALL THURSDAY ENTIRE SEQUENCE AT BARGE AND FINALE AT HAMMERSMITH BRIDGE TO HAVE EVERY MOVE AND LIGHTS IN POSITION STOP AM CONVINCED THIS WILL PAY OFF ALTHOUGH AT FIRST THOUGHT IT MAY APPEAR EXTRAVAGANT STOP RETURNING NEXT FRIDAY MORNING STOP WILL AIRMAIL WRITTEN REPORT, REGARDS, OL

Finally, Sam Engel broke down and wrote a most conciliatory letter to Jules Dassin, of which I quote a short excerpt:

> In my book, you go down as one of the freshest breezes that has hit our business in a long time. You have worked diligently, creatively and with sincerity of purpose that merits full marks for you, no matter whether we get a hit or not, no matter whether it is within its budget range or not.

So it was done. The shooting in London was finished. My job was accomplished. All the remaining work would be done in Hollywood.

Jules Dassin had lost eighteen pounds during this ordeal, and Richard Widmark, slender as he was, lost thirteen pounds, which he could ill afford. Also, he was mentally so exhausted that he needed a rest period of indefinite length, and the start of his next scheduled film had to be postponed. I overlooked weighing myself in all the rush and commotion of my last days in London, but I knew that I was also physically and mentally bushed.

"Julie" Dassin, and I had become close friends, surviving together the bad days and enjoying the few good ones, and we remained so. I was thrilled when later on in his career he left the mark of his special talent on such classic films as *Topkapi* (1964), a suspense thriller that takes place in Istanbul and *Never on Sunday* (1960), starring Melina Mercouri in a delightful portrayal of a Greek "lady of pleasure," plying her trade in Piraeus, near Athens. But NEVER on Sunday! Julie wrote the screenplay, acted in the film (not his forte), and produced and directed it as well. Melina and he married eventually and settled down in Greece, her homeland, to live happily ever after. She died in spring 1994.

FIVE FINGERS

It was my habit to browse around in a bookstore whenever I had some time to spare and wherever I might be. In a favorite store of mine in Salzburg I had picked up a book called *Der Fall Cicero*, translated from German into English and published in London as *Operation Cicero*. Eventually, it wound up as a feature film, which I produced under the Twentieth Century Fox banner, entitled *Five Fingers*. The book related a true and suspenseful spy story that took place in Ankara, the capital of neutral Turkey during World War II. The author, L. C. Moyzisch, an Austrian Nazi, played an important part in the story, even though he was only a lesser functionary in the German embassy, which was headed by Franz von Papen, a.k.a. "the Old Fox," who was Hitler's designated ambassador to Turkey.

I was absorbed by the book and thought it could provide the basis for an excellent suspense film, filled with skullduggery and double crosses in the sordid milieu of international espionage. I knew by this time that the seed of an idea for a film first had to be planted, then nurtured through its many stages of growth, until, finally, it emerged ripened to fruition. So, in the middle of February, riding on the chairlift up to the top of Mount Baldy seated next to Darryl Zanuck, I found an opportune moment to present an idea for a film based on *Operation Cicero*.

At the top of the lift in preparation for our run down to the Round-house, Darryl lit a fresh cigar and said to me, "Let me tell you, Otto, I'm intrigued by what you told me and interested in this property, but our release schedule is all set through the end of this year. Nevertheless, I am going to instruct our literary purchase department at the studio to check on the availability of this property and, if it is available, to make a deal for the film rights. Also, I would want our legal department to look into the ramifications of obtaining clearances, as there would be some very prominent political heavyweights involved in this story. Once we have all this settled, which could take some time, we would schedule it for a next year's production slot. You can then take over as the producer. In the meantime, I have some other plans to keep you busy when you report to the studio. Let's go! You first, I'll follow." Needless to say, I felt and skied like a bird on wings and Darryl didn't lag much behind me either on this beautiful sunny day in the perfect snow conditions that Sun Valley frequently offered.

Darryl was right about the political heavyweights, of course. There were some prominent personalities exposed in this bizarre story. One of these was the British ambassador to Turkey, Sir Knatchbull-Hughesson, whose fortresslike safe was rifled regularly by his trusted valet of Albanian origin. He, in turn, photographed and sold to the German embassy the contents of these classified communications at an exorbitant fee. He used the bumbling and nervous L. C. Moyzisch as a middleman for these transactions and was given the code name of "Cicero" by von Papen to be used in interoffice communications between the Nazi hierarchy in Berlin and the embassy in Ankara. The information obtained by the Germans, had it been properly interpreted, could have had a serious effect on the outcome of the war. They had the actual date, place, and hour of the planned Allied invasion of Normandy in their hands, thanks to Cicero, but never followed up on it because they believed they were being purposely duped by the British.

When Sun Valley closed for the winter season, I had made up my mind. It was with considerable emotion that I bade farewell to many friends, loyal and hardworking instructors, and especially Pat Rogers, who had been a tower of strength in his support of the ski school and a steadfast friend through all the years. But the time had come for me to concentrate on my career in filmmaking. Certainly I would want to return to Sun Valley as often as I could to ski or to visit during the summer months with my family. For now, it was good-bye.

A pleasant surprise awaited me upon checking in at the studio. Darryl had sent word for me to come to his office, where he informed me that the studio had acquired the film rights to *Operation Cicero* and that the project was a definite go. Certain technicalities still had to be sorted out by the legal department before the picture could be put on the active schedule. He asked me to be patient and to keep myself occupied with the preparatory research.

The lawyers concluded that the only person who could possibly have reason to sue Twentieth Century Fox for invasion of privacy was Sir Knatchbull-Hughesson. That wasn't likely, however, since he would be portrayed as a distinguished diplomat and gentleman, acting in the best interest of his country but embarrassingly unaware that he was being flimflammed by his wily valet. The other key figures were public personalities in the political limelight and, therefore, without recourse when subjected to scrutiny and portrayed in a film. At last the road ahead was clear for us to move ahead.

I was most fortunate in having Michael Wilson assigned as the writer on this project. I liked the man and his quiet, self-assured demeanor very much. There was nothing flamboyant about Michael in his inherent modesty, which made me feel instinctively that we would get along well. Our first story conference in DFZ's office was revealing and, as always, fascinating. Darryl's enthusiasm for a new film project was infectious and supported by his accumulated knowledge. In addition to the three of us, Molly Mandaville was present to take copious notes of the proceedings. Darryl started off by expressing his philosophy of documentary feature films:

> ... The great value of any semidocumentary picture, such as *The House on 92nd Street, Street with No Name*, and *Call Northside 777*, lies in the fact that while the story need not be true in every case, it must be presented in such a way that the audience *thinks* the whole story is true. This is the greatest value in these pictures and it's something you simply must have. If you can't make the audience believe your story is an actual happening or based on an actual happening, you're in trouble. You can dramatize and take certain liberties and licenses, as we did in the pictures mentioned previously, provided you start out with a convincing opening. If you start out with a feeling of authenticity, you immediately have the audience on your side and they tell themselves that while this seems an incredible story, it must be true. ...

> I see this film as a *Raffles* type of a story. Raffles was a thief and robber, yet he always had the audience pulling for him, because of his daring exploits, his willingness to take risks. Also, Raffles committed his crimes purely for gain. He was not out to save the world or get revenge on anyone, he simply wanted to make a bunch of bucks.

> We must look at this as a *Raffles* story. We must get into it as much mystery and suspense as possible. It has to be intriguing and daring. It has to have elements of risk and danger.

> We should not have the man who tells this story be on the side of the Allies nor the Germans.

> The "hero" of our picture should be Cicero, the spy. At the end, we want the Allies to be chasing him and the Nazis chasing him and, if it is possible, to devise it so that the audience will be rooting for him to escape.

> Cicero must be the perfect servant—not overdone, of course. He can talk on any subject. During his years in service in various embassies he has picked up astounding knowledge. While he has a nice relationship with the British Ambassador, it never slips from a master-servant basis, and Cicero, himself, is the one who maintains this. He never forgets that he

is a servant. He keeps his place.

After giving us this most helpful dissertation on his personal vision of the film, Darryl sent us away with his best wishes. We could not have asked for better guidelines, and we looked forward happily to our joint creative effort.

After a few days of intensive discussions between the two of us, Michael sequestered himself in his office in the studio's writers row, saying, "You'll see me in a few weeks from today." Three weeks later he came to my office and handed me his treatment, which was a short version of the story outline and continuity from beginning to end, with only a few scenes with actual dialogue between the principal characters included. After reading and evaluating his treatment very carefully, I was impressed by his professional job. Yet I felt there was an element lacking that would lift the story above the plateau of a good spy movie dominated by an all-male cast. When I told Michael my misgivings, he said, "To tell you the truth, Otto, I had the same apprehension, but felt obligated to follow DFZ's guidelines. Maybe that was my mistake, and I take the responsibility for it."

"No, not at all," I reassured him. "You've done a first rate job, but let's take a chance and see whether we can come up with an idea to give this story the trump card it needs. I'll take the blame if it misfires."

So we began to kick around a number of ideas. During one of these brainstorming sessions, I began to improvise, saying to Michael, "Picture this." I painted the scenario that Diello [his Albanian birth name long before he became Cicero the spy] was in the service of a highly respected Polish diplomat, who had also been an ambassador to many countries and at present was serving a tour of duty in Warsaw. His wife, the Countess Staviski, was a well-known beauty and social hostess in diplomatic circles. As can happen and often does, Diello, the ambassador's perfect valet, finds himself smitten and physically attracted to the countess in an infatuation which, though unrequited, was subliminally tempting to the countess. This could have led only to unpleasant complications and, at her request, Diello was dismissed, to her husband's disappointment. Without much delay, given highest recommendations through the diplomatic grapevine, he found an equally attractive position with the visiting British ambassador to Turkey, residing in Ankara.

I said that since in 1939 Poland was overrun by Hitler's Luftwaffe and

Panzer divisions, Count Staviski might have been killed and Anna, his wife, could have escaped by the skin of her teeth and only a minimal amount of zloty (Polish currency) in her handbag. She could find asylum as a political refugee in neutral Turkey, and settle down in Ankara to live the life of a beautiful but impoverished aristocratic grande dame, who was still part of the international diplomatic social set and frequently invited to receptions and dinners for foreign dignitaries, statesmen, and industrial captains. Here then, I suggested, we have a situation with Diello, once her servant and now in the chips, still yearning for her affection and in the enviable position of being able to support her in a life somewhat resembling the style she was accustomed to. He made it possible for her to settle in an elegant villa on the outskirts of Ankara and provided her with commensurate financial support, all earned from his lucrative spy activities.

From there, I said, we could develop the story in any direction we chose and concoct a situation that will create a valid motivation and make it imperative for Diello to take ever-increasing risks in order to horde more and more British pounds, with the ultimate objective of both of them leaving Turkey for a country in South America and living there together in connubial bliss, far from the war that has engulfed all Europe and England.

Michael listened intently and was, in fact, spellbound by the time I finished. He told me that he thought it was a promising angle to pursue. In a surprisingly short time, he came back with a revised treatment, springing to life the Countess Staviski, who never existed in real life but could have quite believably. I was buoyed by the results.

It was up to me to present this radical departure to DFZ. I realized it could easily cost me my job, with a succinct note from the boss saying, "You're fired. Pack up and vacate your office as of this moment." I gave him the revised treatment with this note attached:

Michael Wilson has finished the preliminary treatment on *Operation Cicero*. I am very pleased with the results.

At the risk of arousing your ire, we have introduced a totally new character, triggered by your advice "that one can take dramatic licenses and liberties, as long as it is believable to an audience."

This is believable and helps us immensely in dramatizing the story to an exciting fade-out in the end.

With a sense of foreboding I awaited the phone call that I knew would come from Esther Roberts, Darryl's all-knowing, diplomatic secretary, who said only, "Story conference tomorrow at 2 P. M., Mr. Zanuck's office. You and Michael Wilson."

Michael and I had lunch together before this meeting to steady our nerves for the possible verbal explosion that might come and be culminated by DFZ's saying, "How dare you make such a change without consulting me first? You're both fired!" We made the long march the length of Darryl's office, which at that point seemed the full length of a football field, and when we arrived at his desk, he said to us in an amiable tone of voice, "Sit down, boys. We've got some work to do." Then he took off marching up and down his office, swinging his foreshortened polo mallet with gusto, expounding on the great potential of this story. Not a word regarding the addition of the countess, not a pat on the butt like a football coach might give his quarterback and wide receiver after a successful touchdown pass. But at least our jobs appeared to be safe. We ended up having a productive session that resulted in a green light for the screenplay.

This flexibility was one of DFZ's redeeming traits. When he was faced with something unexpected but constructive in the development stage, he would accept and, in fact, welcome it, as though he almost expected it, even though it did not originate from his own, unfailingly creative imagination.

It always gave me such pleasure to get home after a day's work and my regular nine-to-five office hours, knowing that my two little fellas were anxiously waiting for me in the late afternoon. It was our habit, whenever possible, to take a long walk before dinner. There were a lot of rugged hills and rocks to climb in our neighborhood, reachable by a short automobile drive. I made it a point to make our prospective destination a surprise by asking Peter and Mark, "How would you like to go on a safari to Kenya, Africa?"

"Oh, yes!" they chimed. "That's our favorite and just what we hoped for." We let our imaginations roam freely and visualized some of the magnificent creatures populating the vast stretches of sun-baked land surrounding Kilimanjaro. There would be sightings of a mother lioness with her cubs. We always liked to check up on them and noticed how much they had grown. There were rhinos, antelopes, giraffes, and zebras. Not much luck with elephants on a given day, but we knew they were around, probably feeding farther south, where the tree branches and leaves were succulent. Occasionally we happened upon an overweight hippopotamus, blissfully wallowing in a pool of muddy water, opening the huge cavity of its mouth to intimidate us.

In past expeditions, we had journeyed to the rain forests of South America and hacked a path through the dense jungle, encountering the extraordinary fauna and flora of that continent. We had also been to the Australian outback to visit its game preserves, with the highlight of watching a colony of platypuses, surely one of the most anomalous of nature's creatures, playfully chasing each other with remarkable speed and dexterity under water. All this reminded me so much of the imaginary voyages my father took me along on as a youngster. But never ever could I have foreseen that Peter would actually own and run a private animal preserve ("Safari West") with close to two hundred exotic species from Africa and other places at his ranch in California's Napa Valley.

Returning home, after one of these expeditions, hungry and dusty, the three of us together jumped into the shower with much merriment before our dinner was served by a housekeeper, who also cooked. This gave Sinnie a breather and some time of her own, when she didn't have to shop and haul groceries or chauffeur the boys around to school, playgrounds, and parties. Television in those days was still in the distant future, and, therefore, evenings were spent mostly with homework, reading, and games, playing music on the Victrola, and just "family togetherness." Those were the best of times.

While Michael Wilson toiled away on the final draft of the screenplay, I left him alone. My confidence in his ability was enormous, and I had a hunch that what he wrote would be right on the button. Meanwhile, there were other pressing matters to be considered in regard to *Operation Cicero*. To my surprise and regret, DFZ changed its title in a moment of inspiration to *Five Fingers*. I was puzzled by this new title and expressed my feelings in a memo to DFZ. He sent back a reply, explaining in detail how he came up with the title, with an almost childlike drawing of a hand with five outstretched fingers and accompanying annotations, "Greed. Power. Freedom."

"So be it," I said to myself, knowing that titles were subject to change until the last moment before a film goes into its final stages. Darryl, I noticed, had a penchant for numbers in the titles of this type of documentary feature film.

In preparing for our planned shooting of *Five Fingers*, we needed to be certain we had the full cooperation of the Turkish government. Without it we could never expect to film important exteriors, such as the British and German embassies in Ankara. From our research we knew that the British embassy was functioning normally, whereas the German one had been shut down tight since the collapse of the Nazi regime. In 1950 it was under the Turkish government's jurisdiction and in its trusteeship. There would be many other locations as well in Ankara and Istanbul to which we would want to have access.

A Turkish gentleman had been recommended to me by the William Morris Agency in Hollywood for consideration as a technical advisor and middleman in smoothing our paths with local government officials in Turkey, wherever we planned to set up our cameras. His name was Adil Özkaptan. Born and raised in Istanbul, with a respected old family name and Moslem background, he would have a built-in entrée to many officials and places we wished to use in our film. Also, he spoke English fluently and was a fervent patriot, very much interested in bringing film-makers to his home country to show the world at large what Turkey had to offer in scenic beauty, historical cities, and other film-related advantages. Naturally, I hired him. He was a soft-spoken, always well-dressed gentleman with impeccable manners but persistent in obtaining what he was after, as I learned soon. Adil Bey, as he wished to be called, according to Turkish custom, became invaluable to me personally and to our filming unit in general for a very nominal salary. Soon he addressed me as "Otto Bey," and our friendship lasted through decades thereafter.

What we needed next was to have a director assigned to the picture in order to make some definite decisions regarding cast, sets to be built at the studio, and where and how much of the film to shoot on location in Turkey. Since Twentieth Century Fox had a fully staffed production office at Sheperton Film Studio near London, serious consideration was given to the possibility of producing this film out of England, which offered certain financial advantages. Darryl asked the London office to submit an estimated budget of how much the film would cost to make there to compare with the studio budget here. When the comparative budget estimates were examined, London lost out—and I was immensely relieved. As I wrote to Fred Fox, Virginia Zanuck's brother, who was in charge of the London office:

> In the event the picture is made out of London, my personal problems are difficult. I have been so much away from my family during the past years and I cannot leave them here for another lengthy stretch. I would

have to bring them with me or else my wife and children would surely leave me.

By this time, Joseph Mankiewicz had been assigned to direct *Five Fingers*. This pleased me very much. Joe was a highly regarded screenplay writer and director, whose last film, *All About Eve*, had brought him two Academy Awards for best screenplay and direction. Through the ever-so-active studio grapevine, Joe had heard that there was an exceptionally good story and script written by Michael Wilson about to go into production. He obtained permission to read an advance copy of the mimeographed script, and after having done so, he asked Darryl to let him direct the film. DFZ agreed with some trepidation and with the proviso that Mankiewicz could not change the structure and continuity of the scenario, nor could he rewrite any of the major dialogue scenes, as he was likely to do. Of course, this would not prevent Joe from changing a word here and there and adding some of the acerbic barbs for which he was rightly famous.

Darryl told me in private the reason for his wariness, was based on his previous experiences of working with Joe Mankiewicz. Concerning his talent, there was no question and only high praise. However, many of his coworkers resented his egotistical credit grabbing and pushing his name into the limelight, as though he were the sole creator of a film. This did not sit well with the film's writer, producer, cameraman, editor, and composer of the musical score, among others. I cannot help but admit that I was concerned about how he would react to my being the producer of this film—whether he would just ignore me and treat me as an inferior pawn. I was determined not to let this happen and prepared to stand my ground with much encouragement from DFZ.

Joe Mankiewicz was sensible enough to realize that it would be too costly and impractical to send a fully staffed Hollywood unit with stars, yet to be cast, to Turkey, which was somewhat unknown territory for filmmakers. He proposed, therefore, to go to Turkey himself with a small second unit to select and shoot the backgrounds and establishing shots with doubles and, thereby, capture on film the flavor of Turkey. Also, this would help him immensely in acquainting himself with the mores and exotic ambiance of this country. This made a whole lot of sense. DFZ, Ray Klune of the production department, and I were wholly in accord that this was the best way to proceed. And we were fully aware that few directors of Joe's stature would have been willing to do this.

As far as the casting of the principals was concerned, it seemed to me to be one of the easiest tasks in which I was ever involved. Right from the beginning, when I visualized the looks and aristocratic demeanor of the Countess Staviski, I thought of Danielle Darrieux, the French actress, and I could not see anyone quite as well suited for this part, with her piquant face, elegant figure, and delicious French accent. There was hardly any opposition to casting her for this part, and she got it. Joe's preference for Diello, the suave and wily Albanian valet, was James Mason, and what inspired casting it turned out to be. Joe's Austrian wife, Rose Stradner, was also an actress, and they had some of the best Austrian and German stage and screen actors among their wide circle of personal friends, which made it easy for him to cast the important supporting actors. He selected John Wengraf to portray Franz von Papen, who not only happened to have a startling physical likeness to von Papen, but also captured the insouciant verbal repartee and "cool" of the seasoned diplomat he portrayed. A most fortuitous choice to play the fussy L. C. Moyzisch was the popular Viennese actor, Oscar Karlweiss. He added a wonderful touch to the bumbling secondary attaché, who suddenly and inadvertently found himself drawn into this bizarre drama as a key player. Also, it was a blessing for us to have cast Walter Hampden as Sir Knatchbull-Hughesson, the dignified and compassionate British ambassador to Turkey. He was such a man, every inch of his height.

On June 13, 1951, our compact unit of seven people, led by Joe Mankiewicz, arrived at Istanbul's Yesilköy Airport. Joe requested that I accompany the group, which was somewhat of a surprise to me, knowing of his antipathy toward the stereotypical Hollywood producer. Gerd Oswald was to be his first assistant and also the unit's business manager to handle all financial transactions. Norbert Brodine, a dear, very quiet, middle-aged gentleman who was a talented cinematographer, with his regular assistant cameraman, David McEwen, was with us, as was Jack Dimmack, a versatile technician, electrician, carpenter, and you name it. George Davis represented the studio's art department, and his contributions regarding the selection of various exteriors and interiors turned out to be invaluable, apart from being a jovial companion.

Ours was a congenial group, intrigued and challenged by the assignment that had brought us all to Turkey for the first time. From the moment we set foot on Turkish soil and entered the main hall of the airport, we experienced a culture shock of sights, sounds, people, and general confusion. We were greeted by Adil Özkaptan and Hilmi Bey, a handsome young man who was assigned to us by the Turkish police to be with us at all times. Had he been Greek, he could have posed for a classic sculpture of a Hellenic Adonis. We were steered expeditiously through customs and whisked by automobile to the venerable Pera Palace Hotel, which at one time long past might have been a five-star hotel but through neglect and economic straits had lost its sheen. Still, it was centrally located, with a panoramic view overlooking the Bosporus.

The multitude of graceful, needle-pointed spires of ancient mosques with their gilded domes made me think that Istanbul must surely be one of the most photogenic cities in the world. Toward evening, we were escorted by our Turkish guardian in mufti to take a closer look at the harbor by crossing the Galata Bridge, which links the Occident with the Orient. We passed close by a freighter being unloaded by a gang of porters, when Hilmi Bey nailed one of the porters with a stern look and said something to him in Turkish, which caused him to drop his load with a thud. With lightning speed, he picked up a fist-size stone, hurled it at Hilmi Bey's head, and ran off. To pursue him would have been futile as he melted into the mass of people.

A crowd gathered immediately around the wounded officer, some shouting to grab the fugitive and others jabbering and jeering because one of the none-too-friendly onlookers identified Hilmi as an agent of Istanbul's secret police. Blood was streaming down Hilmi's face from a gash above his temple. Slightly dazed and bewildered, he tried to stanch the flow with a handkerchief. This sudden eruption of violence was a startling introduction to Istanbul for all of us. We rushed the officer to a nearby hospital where his wound was cleansed, sutured with a dozen stitches, and dressed with a bandage around his head. The damage turned out to be not as serious as it looked. After he regained his composure, I could not refrain from asking him what he had said to the porter to cause such a violent eruption of temper. He replied, "All I said to him was 'So you're back again, Ibrahim. I'll catch up with you later.'" He explained to us that the man was wanted for questioning in a recent homicide case.

Although we tried to dissuade him, he insisted on continuing with our preplanned tour of the famous *souk* (bazaar) of Istanbul, which would provide an important background for the climactic chase in our scenario, when Diello is pursued by both Nazi and British counteragents. Once past its entrance portal, one finds oneself transported to a different world, something like a scene from the Arabian *Tales from the Thousand*

and One Nights. It was a maze of narrow, dimly lit streets with shops of every conceivable kind squeezed in tightly next to each other, with shouting street hawkers moving through the dense crowd and shopkeepers beckoning to customers. Others could be seen gesticulating and haggling with prospective buyers. We were surrounded by the unmistakable smell of mutton being roasted on a spit over a bed of charcoal and the pervasive aroma of freshly brewed coffee.

We expected foul-ups and delays once we started shooting, and there were many of these, mostly caused by small-time bureaucrats who wished to flaunt their importance. Controlling curious crowds that closed in on us the moment we set up our camera was another major problem and a source of exasperation to Joe, who was used to having complete control over a set at the studio.

Overall, shooting in Istanbul was rewarding because it had so much to offer photographically and lent itself admirably to a dramatic spy story, such as *Five Fingers*. Ankara, on the other hand, was a modern city built to serve as Turkey's new capital with just enough of the old Turkish quarter left to suit our needs. Its British and German embassies, which were two of our main reasons for coming, were where we ran into real trouble. The Brits would have nothing to do with us and wouldn't even permit us to take an exterior establishing shot of the embassy and its grounds. We were *personae non grata*, and quite understandably so, since the Cicero affair was one of the more embarrassing chapters in the annals of England's foreign affairs. We fared not much better with the unoccupied German Embassy. The key to its solid wrought-iron, double-gated entrance, and also to the building itself, was in the hands of a Turkish government official, who wouldn't budge an inch in his resolve to keep us out. It took all the perseverance, diplomatic pressure, and veiled threats we could think of to convince the Turks that no possible harm would come to the building since we had no intention of entering it. All we wanted to do was film the entrance gate with the guardhouse and the long driveway leading up to the front door of the embassy. It was quite a unique setup for us and important to the picture.

Finally, after we had almost given up, word reached us from a high government official that the gate would be opened and we could proceed with our planned shots. The premises needed a bit of sprucing up, like someone with a long overdue haircut. Fortunately, most of our scenes were night shots and, therefore, most of the obvious defects blended into the darkness of the background. One important item to be attended to was to raise a large Nazi banner over the embassy, flying it from a tall flag pole, some twenty feet above the roof. Our jack-of-all-trades became a stunt man, as Jack Dimmack volunteered to climb the wobbly steel pole to thread a lanyard through a loophole near the top. It was a tense few minutes for all of us, watching him climb hand over hand up the rusty pole, as there was no telling whether it might topple after having been exposed to the elements for so many years. It worked, and the ignominious Nazi flag flew once again over Ankara.

We had a similar problem in Istanbul, where we needed a Nazi banner to replace the large Turkish flag flying from the imposing mayor's office building, high up on a hill overlooking the city. This was to represent Gestapo headquarters in Istanbul. It would have been a simple matter to change flags for a few minutes to get our establishing shot, but the mayor wouldn't permit it under any circumstances. Little did he know that the wizards in our special effects department at the studio could perform this exchange in a jiffy and at a relatively minor cost. With the British Embassy unavailable to us in Ankara, George Davis found us a perfect substitute in the Kirkeby mansion in Belair close to the home studio. It would later be featured as the mansion of television's "Beverly Hillbillies." Attach a replica of the British monarchy's heraldic shield to the iron gate, and *voilà*, the British Embassy in Ankara. Such are the devious ways of Hollywood make-believe.

The harvest reaped from our "Turkey shoot" was rewarding and would certainly enhance the film. To our astonishment, near the end of our stay, the real Diello (Cicero) made contact with us, followed by a covert appearance in Ankara. He spoke only to Joe for about fifteen minutes in a dingy coffeehouse. A few of us caught a glimpse of him walking by. He looked far from what one might have expected—short, pudgy, and bald with an almost grotesquely large head—altogether unattractive. He had not come to ask for money but to ask whether Joe could help him emigrate to America. He insinuated that he was not welcome in Turkey and that the government would rather have him gone. Joe explained to him that this was out of his orbit and could only be handled by the American consulate. I never followed up to find out what happened to Diello in the end.

There was one unfortunate aftermath to this location shoot, when Joe Mankiewicz made some derogatory remarks about Turkey, its government officials, and police in an interview with Art Buchwald, which appeared in the *Herald Tribune* and also in the Paris *Samedi Soir*:

I don't remember ever in my life that I worked under such difficult terms. As if it were not enough that the Turkish secret police were following us everywhere, they were monitoring our phone conversations and censoring telegraphic messages. From the moment we arrived in Turkey, every one of us were followed. Our trip was a true-to-life police story.

I was surprised to hear this, since I had thought that Mankiewicz was quite satisfied with the all-around support we received. If he thought of our officially assigned police guard as putting us under constant surveillance, it was certainly not to spy on us and primarily to protect and help us.

This was substantiated by a note from Anthony Muto, our resident Twentieth Century Fox representative in Washington, D.C. He was summoned to the Turkish ambassador's office and severely reprimanded for this diplomatic faux pas committed by our director, in view of the help the Turkish government had given us. He denied categorically any of the allegations published in Buchwald's column. This is what Muto wrote to me:

> I don't think that you will ever have a problem returning to Turkey, but I do know of one chap connected with this film who would be given a very exceptional reception in the subterranean dining hall of the Pera Prison in Istanbul.

It took quite a bit of diplomatic fence-mending on my part to assuage the ruffled egos of Turkish officials by a set of apologetic letters.

As brilliant a writer, dramatist, and director as Joe Mankiewicz was, he also had a dark side. To work with him and watch him ply his craft was a privilege. He was a perfectionist and expected others to give him their very best. He was exceptionally good in guiding his actors. He chose them well to fit their parts and then succeeded in getting the best performances from them. I was titillated by some of his directorial touches. Both verbal and physical, minuscule and almost unnoticeable at first sight, they integrated themselves smoothly into a seamless whole. For example, there was a scene in which Colonel Richter, a Gestapo envoy sent from Berlin to Ankara to shed some light on Cicero's murky past, found himself tapping his foot, waiting for him impatiently at a secluded mosque. As custom demanded, he had to take his shoes off, revealing a big toe popping through a gaping hole in his sock. It was so incongruous to see this man in his civilian clothes, dressed to the hilt, with a hole in his sock. Many people in an audience might not have even noticed it, but those who did got a spontaneous chuckle.

Back at the studio, the picture sailed through right on schedule. DFZ was excited about the rushes and so was I. We ran into one serious road-block after shooting the last crucial scene of the film, showing Cicero in splendid solitude in an elegant villa, overlooking Rio de Janeiro. His paramour, the Countess Staviski, had betrayed him and fled to Switzer-land with a sizable sum of his amassed fortune in British five-pound notes in her baggage. Visibly brooding in the middle of his dinner, im-peccably served by a butler, he was interrupted by another servant who announced the arrival of two gentlemen for whom it was imperative to see the master of the house. They introduced themselves as representa-tives of one of the largest and most reputable banks in Brazil. The pur-pose of their urgent visit was to inform him that all the British bank notes he had deposited in their bank were counterfeit, perfect in master-ful craftsmanship by German engravers but worthless nonetheless, after a thorough scrutiny by the Bank of England in London. Whereupon, they handed over to him a stack of the counterfeit five-pound notes, paid to him by the Nazis. Taking a long look at his visitors with an in-scrutable expression on his face, Diello got up, walked to the edge of the terrace high above the glittering lights of the city below, and with a burst of laughter tossed the bank notes into the wind while crying out, "Anna, poor Anna!"—aware that all the money she had absconded with was also worthless.

When I first saw the rushes of this scene with Jim Clark, our editor, I was disturbed. Somehow the quality of this all-important scene struck me as lacking. It just didn't come off right. It was difficult to pinpoint, whether it should have been more of an evocation of self-pity at finding himself financially ruined or pity for Anna whom he still loved. What I missed in his laugh was an undercurrent of *schadenfreude*, a most fitting German word to describe one's enjoyment of another person's misfor-tune—in this case, the Countess Staviski, to whom fate had dealt a much deserved comeuppance.

I wanted to make sure that I was not prejudiced in my impression, and I asked Darryl to please have a look at the scene. If a retake was necessary, we should plan on doing it immediately since we were virtu-ally at the end of our shooting schedule and it should be done before the elaborate set was dismantled. After seeing the scene, DFZ concurred with me and suggested that I talk to Joe about the necessity of a retake.

Going to Joe and ask him to do that was not a task to which I looked forward. It could have easily led to an alienation of our, thus far, very pleasant working relationship. Joe took it very calmly and said to me, "Well, let's look at it. I'll ask Jimmy (Mason) to come with us." After they saw it, they both agreed it needed to be reshot. They knew that there was an indefinable something missing and perhaps a slight over-dose of hysteria in the scene. The scene was redone and was perfect on the first take. I admired Joe and James Mason for their professionalism, as they could have destroyed me by saying, "That scene is fine. Who is that *nudnik* of a producer to tell us that there is something wrong with the concept of this scene?"

With the film finished and in Zanuck's hands for the last editorial changes and touches, Joe was despondent and had little faith in its success. He left for New York with the intention of fulfilling a long-cherished wish to find a place in the countryside near this metropolis as his permanent residence. Upon arriving in New York, Joe was asked by the home office to make himself available for the customary press interviews prior to an opening and to be present for private showings of the film to select audiences. He refused to do so, thinking that the film would be a flop, and wrote a scathing personal letter to DFZ complaining that he (Zanuck) had ruined his film, which to his way of thinking had been "cut with a lawn mower."

This letter was mailed three days before the gala premier at the Roxy Theater in New York. The morning after the premier, there were nothing but rave reviews in the papers. The New York critics were unanimous in their praise. Frantically, Joe got on the phone and called Esther Roberts, Zanuck's secretary, imploring her to intercept the letter he had written and destroy it. It was too late. The damage was done. As it turned out, Joe deservedly garnered the lion's share of kudos. One prominent critic raved at length about the masterful editing job done on this film. *Five Fingers* was a box office success when it was released in 1952, surpassing Twentieth Century Fox's fondest expectations.

On a personal level, I can say that Joe paid me the highest accolade a man can accord a fellow man when he asked me, before he moved to New York, "Otto, could you do me a big favor? Would you be willing to take in my beloved dog, which to my chagrin I have to leave behind? You are the only man I would trust with this."

How could I possibly refuse this eloquent plea? As it happened, we did not have a dog at that time, and our house and grounds were perfectly suited to this addition to our family. The boys were elated, while Sinnie and I had some reservations, even though she loved dogs and cats. The dog, named Timber, was a magnificent purebred German shepherd with registration papers to prove it. It was a big dog, powerful and loving, which by its sheer weight and impulsive joy of being alive, simply overpowered one without any malice. It was too much to handle for us, and many of our visiting friends were frightened by its stormy but harmless way of greeting them. With much reluctance I had to find an appropriate new home for the dog. I never had the heart to tell Joe about it.

Much later in life (1993) when I had settled in Seattle, I talked to the impresarios of the month-long International Seattle Film Festival, suggesting they invite Joe Mankiewicz as their honored guest and include a retrospective showing of a few of his best films. They were extremely responsive to the idea and asked me to contact Joe. This I did in a letter, presenting the details of his proposed visit with expenses fully paid and underlining the prominent stature of this festival. After a lengthy wait, I eventually got an answer:

Dear Otto:

I'm sorry to have kept you waiting for my reply to your kind invitation. Seattle has always been atop the list of "some day I must see it" ambitions.

I am, however, a pretty creaky old guy who can't just go "schussing" around the country at will. Which is a very clumsy way of thanking you very, very much for your invitation, but I simply cannot commit myself so far in advance. Actually, I am working very hard at what I hope will be an informative autobiography, which consumes most of my brain all of the time.

Could the kind invitation be postponed to a later date and could there be some indication of what the occasion will be?

As ever,

Joe

A few weeks later, Joe Mankiewicz died of a massive cardiac infarction at his home in Bedford, New York. If not a giant, he was a near giant and a lasting credit to his profession. A review of "our" movie in the *New York Times* "Guide to Movies on TV" calls it an "ace" and makes the point:

> Five Fingers: A spy thriller, as trenchantly sophisticated, clever, tingling and colorful as anyone could hope, based on a true World War II story.
> This highly literate affair is superbly paced by Director Joseph L. Mankiewicz and superbly played by a grand cast headed by James Mason as the suave conniver and Danielle Darrieux as a smooth, Polish ex-countess, and others add to the high stylishness and itching suspense, straight through to a neat, ironic pay-off.

WHITE WITCH DOCTOR

Occasionally, I have a recurring nightmare in which I am stranded with a camera crew in a remote spot in the jungles of the Belgian Congo (now Zaire), toiling away for months on end, without ever being informed by the studio of the results of our labor. Nor are we ordered to return home, though the cost of our prolonged stay mounts considerably with every week that passes. In this vivid dream, the crew members, working in the sweltering heat and exhausted by the insect-infested, sultry climate of equatorial Africa, are close to the breaking point. We are in a state of bewilderment and acute anxiety. We feel as if we are forgotten men, condemned to spend the remainder of our lives in exile. Waking up, bathed in perspiration and tormented by frustration, I realize with a sense of great relief that it was just a bad dream, far removed from—yet inspired by—reality.

I had read a book called *White Witch Doctor* and brought it to Darryl's attention. He liked the synopsized version he read and bought the film rights to it. The book, written by Louise Stinetorf, an autobiographical first novel, attracted me for a number of reasons. It was the story of an elderly, somewhat frail Christian missionary in Africa who was joined by a young novice missionary who had decided to follow in the older woman's footsteps, dedicating her life to the cause of healing and converting the natives to a better way of life. A close relationship develops between the two women, but the older missionary dies, leaving the still untrained young novice to carry on with the legacy now left in her hands.

I liked the whole premise of her subsequent struggle because it was so offbeat and unlike the conventional Hollywood concept of films taking place in Africa. A key element in making the movie would be to find a tribe that would be attractive to portray in a film and visually arresting. The title, *White Witch Doctor*, was intriguing and, for once, not in need of changing. It was a catchy theater marquis and billboard title, certain to interest the movie-going audience.

I had already spent a considerable amount of time researching tribes in the Belgian Congo and even in East Africa. The Belgian Congo, as presented in the book, appealed to me much more, even though it lacked the number of animal species prevalent in East Africa. But, after all, this was not an African adventure story, dependent on encounters with wild animals. Before we even started the preliminary development of a screenplay, I knew I would have to make a short reconnoitering trip to Africa.

I assumed that DFZ and I were on the same wavelength, thinking similarly about transposing this book into a screenplay of uncommon values. Not so, I found out during our preliminary story conference, over which DFZ presided. Also present were Sy Bartlett, a writer under contract to the studio, and the indispensable Molly Mandaville. The shock hit me like a ton of bricks when DFZ laid out his concept of the story and the guidelines to be followed in writing the screenplay:

> We do not want a picture based on the "exploits of a woman missionary" struggling for courage in the African jungle. We want a picture about two interesting people, a woman missionary and a white hunter, a story full of physical excitement, physical violence and SEX. We do not want a picture about a woman struggling to cope with sickness, locust, and other depressing things.

I was devastated after hearing of this radical departure from the original book. It was diametrically opposed to what I had in my mind. I kept asking myself: Why did we buy this book? Was it just because of its catchy title?

Faced with this dilemma, I felt the most honest decision would have been for me to withdraw from the project. But having brought in this property and instigated its purchase, I could not very well do that. Besides, I had enormous respect for DFZ's expertise, sense of drama, and box office projections. I also admired his enthusiasm and the decisive manner in which he approached the creative first steps of a new film. So, even though I was personally disappointed by the course he had charted, I decided to stick with it, hoping that with the development of the continuity, some of the esoteric elements in the book could be salvaged and incorporated in the screenplay.

I had a lengthy meeting with Sy Bartlett and turned over all my research notes and pertinent visual material to him. My reaction after this session was rather negative, as I could not detect even a smidgen of enthusiasm on Bartlett's part about this project. He looked upon it merely as an assignment that would require an enormous amount of time and research in order to come up with an acceptable preliminary treatment. After Bartlett turned in his first lengthy treatment, and after it had been read by DFZ and me, a change in writers was decided upon. The assignment was given to Edmund North, an esteemed practitioner of his craft.

Edmund North would need at least four weeks of research and writing, and I felt that I could use this interim period to go to Africa. In addition to looking for a suitable tribe to portray, I would also size up the physical problems and logistics of location shooting in Africa. I laid out an itinerary for my proposed journey, which was approved by the studio. First I planned to go to New York to consult with the head office of missionary groups in the Belgian Congo, on whose assistance and cooperation we would depend to a great extent. Next, I would fly to Brussels to open channels of communication and obtain the approval of the Belgian government to take a sizable film crew into their colonial territory. Without their assured cooperation and endorsement of such a project, it would be a hopeless undertaking. After concluding these introductions, I would board a plane for the long flight to Léopoldville (now Kinshasa), the official seat of the colonial government of the Belgian Congo.

In spite of my research, this part of the globe remained unknown territory to me, evoking a feeling of tremendous emotional uplift and producing a tingling sensation down my spine when I set foot on the tarmac at steamy Léopoldville. From that first day in this colorful and mysterious country, Africa cast a lifelong spell on me.

I was met at the terminal by a representative of the colonial government by the name of Jean Labrique. He was assigned to guide me through the pitfalls of bureaucratic procedures and to acquaint me with the mores of the country. He took me to the Régina Hotel, purportedly the best in the city. The hotel was a sprawling compound with many airy corridors to let the breeze, what little there was, waft through open doors and windows. My room was sparsely furnished and comfortable enough. The bed was shrouded by a tight-fitting net, forming a baldachin over one's prone body at night as protection against mosquitoes, those bloodthirsty foragers. I had been forewarned of this and had provided myself with an ample supply of quinine tablets to be taken daily as a safeguard against malaria.

I was anxious to locate a tribe that we could use in our film. From my research, I was particularly intrigued by the Bakuba tribe, ruled by a hereditary king in the province of Kasai. Luluaburg, the provincial capital, could be reached by plane in a few hours' flight from Léopoldville. I knew the Bakubas were a people of uncommon artistic heritage, as weavers of cloth and builders of homes with walls and partitions ornamented with intricate geometric patterns woven of palm fronds. They excelled as carvers of wood and ivory. They forged raw metal into an array of weapons and decorative objects using a primitive but effective blast furnace, which was activated by a series of interconnected airtight animal bladders.

The court ceremonial life centered on the king's large enclosure with his 376 wives (fewer than the customary 500) and a dozen courtiers. They held frequent celebrations connected with births and deaths, harvest festivals, and religious rituals, such as spectacular dances in which masks were used to impersonate good and evil spirits. I was truly excited to make contact with this particular tribe and be introduced to their reigning monarch, Nyemi Bope Mabinji.

Conveniently, there was a large mission station and government field office located near Mushenge, the hub of the Bakubas' realm. The local Belgian official, who also spoke the native language, volunteered to be my guide and interpreter. Only through him would I be able to communicate with the king and his subjects.

I met the king, who was informally dressed in a dark blue loincloth, in a secluded courtyard close to his thatch-roofed "palace." On his head he wore a small conical hat of delicately woven raffia fibers, such as most of the men around him sported. After the customary introduction, he invited me to sit down with him on a round log in the shade of a banyan tree. Slowly I presented to the king the purpose of my visit through the interpreter at my side. It must have sounded very strange to him, since he had never seen a film.

Nyemi Bope Mabinji was a man of hefty proportions with his belly spilling over the loincloth tied below his naval. My guess was that he weighed over three hundred pounds and was six feet tall. His face was puffy and unhealthy looking, and his eyes held the sadness of a sick man. However, when he put on his official regalia, which added another fifty-five pounds to his weight, he appeared completely different, waddling along slowly with his feet apart for better balance. The ceremonial outfit consisted of an unbelievable number of cowrie shells sewn onto a multi-colored knee-length pleated skirt, with heavy sets of brass rings on both ankles and both arms. His crown consisted of a beaded band around his forehead with a veritable bouquet of exotic bird feathers sprouting and spreading from the top of his head. This gave the illusion of additional height to impress his duly obedient populace. He was an all-powerful but also benevolent monarch, and his word was the law.

I was well prepared to document what I saw with my still cameras and brought back with me a wealth of pictorial research material, touching on many facets of Bakuba culture. To witness the fascinating pomp and panoply of this tribal lifestyle would be a feast for the eyes of movie audiences. Logistically, I felt it would be feasible, but not without sacrifices by the crew as far as their own creature comforts were concerned. I was well aware that it would not be practical to bring our principal characters to this part of the world and that we would have to work with doubles.

As long as I was in Africa, I wanted to observe some other tribes in this territory, such as the Wagenias near Stanleyville (now renamed Kisangani), who had bridged a side channel of the turbulent Congo River in this section of its long journey. I saw a maze of rickety walkways consisting of haphazardly crisscrossed bamboo poles tied together with vines, to which the Wagenias fastened large conical fish traps. They lived well and thrived commercially from their abundant year-round catch. Seeing this structure, with fishermen young and old precariously perched over the rushing water, convinced me that the trip had been very worthwhile. It had taken me a few days of travel on a Congo River paddle wheel steamer, with many stops at isolated landings, to reach this destination. The ship was overcrowded with people, naked children running around, goats, pigs, monkeys, chickens, and even a crocodile with its jaws bound together, stoves to cook on, mats spread out for sleeping in every nook and cranny—all squeezed tightly into corridors and below deck in steerage like sardines. I will never forget the singular beauty of the passing scenery, totally pristine for hundreds of miles.

Another tribe, which I felt compelled to investigate, was the Mangbetus near Paulis. They were known as the "Longheads," as it was their custom to bind the heads of infants and children through a progression of years into an oblong shape, which was considered a mark of distinction for men and beauty for the women. Upon my inquiry, I was assured that this reshaping of the cranium had no ill effects on the normal development of the brain.

A delightful interlude during my cross-country journey to the east was my encounter with the "littlest people" on Earth, the Pygmy tribe. These nomads inhabited the seemingly impenetrable jungle of the Ituri Forest, bisected by a red dirt road mixed with clay. This road proved to be hazardous when wet from rainfall, as an automobile would slither and slide haphazardly on the gooey surface. Nevertheless, it was an important link connecting the West with East Africa.

I drove on through Uganda, with its magnificent fauna-saturated national park, and stopped in Rwanda Burundi to see the royal Watusi dancers perform. The dancers were a highlight of the film, *King Solomon's Mines*. My cross-continent journey ended in Nairobi, a cosmopolitan city compared to others in Africa. Kenya was also the Africa of white hunters, carnivores, and gentle grazing species, engaging in the daily drama of the stronger eating the weaker. I had the satisfying experience of visiting the Nairobi National Park Animal Preserve, with the gamut of African fauna roaming around freely and pursuing their lifestyles as though they were in the farthest corner of the African veldt, miles away from civilization. Nairobi, with its up-to-date hotels, teeming commercial center, and international airport, was the departure point of my journey home, with a connecting flight from London to New York.

Laden with presents, I arrived home after a long flight with many refueling stops. For Peter and Mark I had native bows, finely tooled arrows, and other African memorabilia. For Sinnie I found some eye-appealing artifacts and trinkets. A number of these had been given to me by the king of the Bakubas as personal gifts to take home and were from his large collection of tribal treasures, safely housed in a special hut in his compound. Bringing these gifts to my family assuaged my feelings of guilt at having left them alone so long at a time when our two youngsters were so much in need of their father's presence and companionship— not to overlook Sinnie's needs. No presents in the world could compensate for these lengthy separations imposed by the demands of my profession.

When I checked into my office at the studio after only a weekend's respite to readjust my out-of-order body clock, having crossed so many time zones, I found some bad news awaiting me. Edmund North had not succeeded in developing a satisfactory treatment for *White Witch Doctor*. He admitted that it was not up to his usual standards and suggested that possibly it wasn't the type of material best suited to him. Regretfully, we decided to withdraw him from this assignment, without hard feelings on anyone's part. I disliked intensely making these changes, especially when it involved a writer of Edmund North's reputation. It meant starting over from scratch.

I was summoned to DFZ's office to give a report on my African journey. He was pleased to hear that we were assured the cooperation of the government and of missionaries in the Belgian Congo. He was as tickled as I was that the Bakuba tribe would participate in our film, thereby adding immensely to the authenticity of the story. He also voiced his displeasure regarding the lack of progress on *White Witch Doctor*. I suggested that he assign Michael Wilson to *White Witch Doctor*. After hesitating, Darryl said to me, "That would be okay with me. But I want to bring something to your attention which troubles me very much. I have received a warning from the highest security sources of the USA that Michael Wilson is suspected of belonging to a communist cell of dissident Americans. He is under investigation and surveillance now and we'll just have to see what happens."

I was flabbergasted and well aware of the House Un-American Activities Committee, known as HUAC, headed by Senator Joseph McCarthy and his cohorts, causing havoc in the Hollywood film community. I told DFZ that I could not conceive of Michael Wilson being a dedicated communist, having worked with him closely over a long period of time and gotten to know him as a personal friend. Yes, I said, he was a champion of the underprivileged and impoverished and rebelled against the unequal distribution of wealth among the peoples of the world. But did that make him a communist? If so, then I, too, was a communist, for I shared his concern for these people.

"Trust me, Otto," he said, by now somewhat irritated and impatient. "I know what I'm talking about, as my information comes straight from the top man of the FBI in Washington."

That could only be J. Edgar Hoover (not so lily-white himself, as it turned out later.)

I told Michael Wilson about my conversation with DFZ and asked him point-blank, "Michael, are you in any way involved with the Communist Party in this country?"

He looked me straight in the eye and replied, "No, I'm not, but it's nobody's business if I were, since the Communist Party is not outlawed in the U. S. A."

I believe Michael Wilson told me the truth.

Michael went to work on *White Witch Doctor* with zeal. It was a subject matter much to his liking. In a remarkably short time, he presented me with a very promising and workable treatment pulling the story together. It touched upon all the important elements contained in the book and, at the same time, made an exciting adventure story.

Very soon thereafter the bombshell burst, when Michael walked into my office, his face white as a sheet, fire in his eyes, and anger in his voice as he told me that he had been subpoenaed by HUAC. He realized that the consequences could be very serious for his career and family as he was determined not to bow to the dictates of this committee. Wilson was dismissed by Twentieth Century Fox with a minimum of civility, and as far as the Hollywood studios were concerned, he was considered "unemployable" from that day on. He chose to go into exile in Paris, where he was warmly welcomed and accepted in French filmmaking and literary circles. He kept busy writing under a pseudonym and was paid handsomely under the table without his name appearing on the screen. In 1978, Wilson died embittered and dissillusioned, and seven years later, the Academy of Motion Picture Arts and Sciences exonerated him. Posthumously, he was given credit and an Oscar as the cowriter with Carl Foreman of the classic film *The Bridge on the River Kwai*, to add to the Oscar he received prior to his departure from the United States for the screenplay *A Place in the Sun*. It was a proud moment for his wife and daughters, but it would not bring back to life a man who had stood by his conviction and paid the price for it.

Ivan Goff and Ben Roberts took over where Wilson left off on *White Witch Doctor*. They had the reputation of being fast and inventive, blending their individual talents successfully. I found them pleasant to work with, as they concocted a shootable screenplay from the material on hand. They even succeeded in keeping Dr. Mary, the frail, elderly missionary, alive long enough to leave her mark, which was balm to my heart, since I considered her the wellspring of this whole story. She had been a character that Darryl had vehemently opposed.

In casting the picture, we ran into a problem. Susan Hayward, who was under contract to Twentieth Century Fox, was our first choice, not only because she was a contract player, but more so because she was the actress best suited to portray the young missionary. When so informed by the casting office, and without even having read the script, she declined, saying that she was in the final stages of another film and was too spent to jump right away into another assignment. We already had a commitment from Robert Mitchum to play the macho and adventurous white hunter. The combination of the two would have been perfect, but Miss Hayward was adamant in her resolve. DFZ asked me to meet with Miss Hayward personally in an effort to sway her. I saw her between setups in her private bungalow. I could sense immediately that she was indeed physically fatigued and also emotionally distraught by the impending dissolution of her marriage, which brought tears to her eyes as she spoke of it in my presence. No wonder she was not willing to commit herself for another picture—and one to be filmed in the Belgian Congo, of all places.

There was no point in applying any kind of pressure nor in doling out devious morsels of promises. Very quietly I gave her an abbreviated account of the story line, emphasizing that this was not solely an adventure film and love story between two disparate human beings, but that it also dealt with the human condition among the native people and therefore was of some moral value in appreciating the contributions of unselfish missionaries. I assured her that she would not be required to go to Africa. That put her mind somewhat at ease. I left, asking her to take more time to think about it, adding that I would have a script delivered to her to read at her convenience. Not very long after the meeting, Susan accepted the assignment.

There was an up-and-coming young English director on the lot, who had most recently steered Marilyn Monroe, then a relatively unknown starlet, through the shoals of her first feature film, *Don't Bother to Knock*. He had also been successful with some documentary film work in his home country. We felt he was the kind of director to entrust with this film. Roy Baker was a slightly built, rather frail-looking gentleman with impeccable British manners. The crucial test would be to see how he handled the preliminary shooting with a small second unit, using doubles and working with the native Bakubas in the torrid climate of the Belgian Congo.

As I anticipated, this was a "hardship shoot," if ever there was one. I was part of it from beginning to end. Despite the cooperation of all parties involved, filming the episodes with the Bakubas was more demanding than anyone expected. The constant heat, day and night, was debilitating. Providing adequate nourishment and keeping the food fresh was a continuing problem. The requests for cold liquid refreshments were endless. Housing was makeshift and as good as could be had under the circumstances. We even arranged to have some railway sleeper cars put at our disposal. Rinky-dink though they were, and without air conditioning, they provided a modicum of privacy but little respite from the heat.

Pale-skinned Roy Baker was ultrasensitive to the sun and found it difficult to function normally. Africa was anathema to him. He detested all those buzzing insects and the creatures that crawled up and down walls and the others that slithered along the ground. One evening when I came to call on him, I noticed that all the windows were shut tight and that the room was suffused with a haze of insecticide. I was worried he might asphyxiate himself. When he fell victim to a severe intestinal disorder, which forced him to withdraw from this assignment and return to England to regain his health, I took over direction of the second unit and saw it through to its completion.

After we finished our work with the Bakubas, who turned out to be willing and surprisingly natural actors, we flew to Stanleyville to film the Wagenia fishermen. We also made arrangements to include the "Longheads" in our film. When we arrived at the Longhead village, we had an unwanted surprise waiting for us. I had told the chief during my reconnoitering trip that we might possibly be back to film them. On his own impulse, in the meantime, he gave orders to spruce up the village. What I had seen originally was a number of thatch-roofed huts with earth-colored mud walls, decorated with an array of African animals painted in a primitive style. I was very much taken by the sight of this native art form. Now, all the walls were painted a gleaming white, with all the animals eradicated. Also, I noticed that many of the men, including the chief, had scrounged together all manner of dilapidated European clothing, such as T-shirts with holes in them, frayed short pants, and pointed worn-out shoes with socks. One of them even had garters to hold up his socks as the ultimate in European chic.

We were not amused, even by the hilarious incongruity, and I let the chief know this through our interpreter. The shoot was off, I told him. We couldn't use their village in its present state, and the remnants of European clothing were totally out of place. He was very disappointed and said they would restore their *shambas* to their original appearance and promised they would revert to wearing their native attire. "How long would this take?" I asked. The chief's brow furrowed and his eyes squinted in deep thought. Then he held up eight fingers.

"All right then," I said. "We will take a gamble on this promise and be back in a week." As it happened, I had some shooting to do with the Pygmies in the Ituri Forest that would occupy us while we waited for the Longheads. When we returned, the village was restored to its original appearance. We shot some beautiful footage and enjoyed the experience enormously, quite possibly because it was our last stop prior to our journey home. We had also collected a prodigious amount of authentic native costumes, spears, shields, drums, masks, and other artifacts, all to be shipped back with our camera equipment. They would supplement what we already had in our studio collection.

Back at the studio, Henry Hathaway took over the direction of the film with his accustomed expertise, adding a number of his own directorial touches to improve the picture. Yet, even a superb musical score contributed by Bernard Herrmann, an extraordinarily gifted composer who had elevated the caliber of music written for films to the highest level, did not give the picture the sheen and distinction I had hoped for.

This was succinctly expressed in a review in *Newsweek* magazine that was echoed by other national critics when the film was released in 1953:

> Africa is such a photogenic land that almost any handsome camera job done on it will have appeal. This Technicolor film, a sentimental adventure story largely taken in Hollywood, is interlaced with striking sequences obtained in the Belgian Congo area occupied by the Bakuba tribe 1,200 miles inland from Africa's West Coast. With Leon Shamroy, three times an Oscar winner, as chief cameraman, the luxuriant Congo is richly suggested, the Bakubas are caught in their fantastic dances, and there are African specialties, such as the Wagenia tribe fishing with great conical wooden traps in a dramatic river rapids.
>
> The script by Ivan Goff and Ben Roberts, after a novel by Louise A. Stinetorf, is a rather schmaltzy and familiar matter. . . . In the course of the action, Director Henry Hathaway supervises a good deal of animal business and some romantic moonlight business. Miss Hayward is a piquant missionary, Mitchum sidles through the clearings with wholly masculine aplomb, but it is the genuine Bakubas, in mask and paint, who have the best of things here.

The picture did surprisingly well at the box office. A large number of missionaries who saw the film and whom I expected to be most discerning and critical liked it on the whole. And so did Louise Stinetorf, who expressed her delight in a most gracious letter to me:

My husband and I went to see *White Witch Doctor* last evening, and we both want you to know that we enjoyed the film immensely. The story wasn't as I wrote it, of course, but I well know that it couldn't have fitted into the pattern of our present-day movies as I wrote it.

You and your writers whipped it into a tight, fast-moving plot that was true to the characters of many white men in Africa and did not discredit the missionaries.

The native "shots" were wonderful—the mat walls, the ocher pictures on the mud huts, the Congo sternwheeler, the fishing traps, the costuming and dancing, and the devil masks.

There are so many other things I could say, but I am not going to make this a long letter. I just want you to know that I am not piqued as you seemed to think I might be by your changes in my story. On the contrary, I think you did a wonderful job and turned out a delightful picture. Thank you for being so kind to my "Little Mama" [played by Susan Hayward].

A gracious lady indeed. Now that I have cleansed my memory of shooting in Africa, I hope this will also be the end of my recurring African nightmare.

H O L L Y W O O D
E N C O R E

I knew that producing films was not my ultimate career objective. A successful producer required certain intellectual qualities that I felt I did not possess; I lacked the educational background and had no theatrical experience to speak of. Yet by instinct, guts, and perseverance—and thanks to Darryl Zanuck's indefatigable support—I had succeeded in producing three prestigious feature films, all three moneymakers. The only one among these that progressed smoothly was *Five Fingers*. The other two, *Call Northside 777* and *White Witch Doctor*, were heart- and back-breakers from beginning to end, draining me and straining my marriage and family life. I did not want to put myself through that sort of wringer on a continuous schedule. I made up my mind to have a hiatus from producing films. I wanted to direct films instead, to be handed a finished script and transpose it into a motion picture.

I decided I would concentrate on getting directorial assignments, even if they were only of a second-unit nature. Being a second-unit director was not always rewarding, since second units were used primarily to save money, shooting scenic backgrounds and action sequences with doubles. But the work was essential. With a competent second unit director and the sleight of hand of camera technicians at the studio, remarkable results could be achieved at nominal cost.

I did not have to wait long for a project. Twentieth Century Fox assigned me to direct the second unit of *Lord Vanity*, a film based on the best-seller by Samuel Shellabarger. It was a massive undertaking, and I'm not sure if I was given this assignment as a show of faith or as a punishment.

LORD VANITY

Lord Vanity was a swashbuckling eighteenth-century historical drama abounding in daredevil action sequences. It reminded me of Dumas's classic *The Count of Monte-Cristo*, with its political intrigue, multitude of characters, costume pageantry, horse-drawn coaches, chases, duels, and perilous escapes from prisons, the hero doggedly pursued by a sneering villain. I had the first draft of a shootable script for preparations that would lead us to England, France, and Morocco. Once abroad, we would have a crew of at least fifty-five technicians to transport, house, and feed, supplemented by local help, in addition to actors doubling for the principals. For me it was a job on a scale and scope I had never handled before.

In England we had two main locations: one was the estate of the Earl of Pembroke at Wilton, near Salisbury, and the other was the city of Bath. The earl's palatial manor was designed and built by Inigo Jones, one of England's most prized architects. We had the fullest cooperation of the earl, a tall, gangly gentleman with a high brow due to a receding hairline. Always dressed casually and slightly rumpled in his well-worn tweeds, he also seemed to like to imbibe spirits.

Wilton was an exceptionally beautiful palace. I had only one problem there, which was that the main entrance was so inconspicuous as to resemble the back entrance to the servants' quarters. With ladies dressed in their finest silks and furs and bedecked with jewelry and their elaborately costumed escorts alighting from highly decorated coaches with caparisoned horses to enter the manor for a festive ball, this entrance seemed incongruous. I conferred with our English art director, asking whether we could build a small mobile portico with four Grecian columns and a roof to be butted onto the entrance to make it more impressive. "No sweat," he said, "providing the earl agrees to it."

The earl consented without blinking an eye, when reassured that this would be a lean-to, an easily removable "prop" that would not damage the manor's façade. So, with my apologies to Sir Inigo and hoping that he may not have found cause to turn about in his grave, I made the change. Upon our departure from Wilton, the earl handed me an art-fully framed rendering of the original architectural ground plan of the manor with its vast gardens. It is one of my prized possessions, passed on to my son Peter, who accompanied me on the trip.

Peter participated in some scenes in *Lord Vanity* as an extra—once as a gardener raking the lawn and another time as a blackamoor, dressed in silk knee breeches and silver turban with a white ostrich feather, who was the front carrier of one of the ladies' sedan chairs. He did not particularly enjoy that part of the trip, but he did enjoy seeing London and living with me at the five-star Savoy Hotel and flying on his own to Austria to meet my parents for the first time.

On his return to London before leaving for home, he made the acquaintance of a well-known English character actor in our group, who was also an authority on and breeder of kestrels, the smallest and pretti-est of the falcon species. A collector of animals, Peter somehow managed to talk the actor into selling him a matched pair. Hence, I found myself stuck with two birds, which had to be smuggled into our room at the staid Savoy Hotel. We fed them choice morsels of filet mignon (broiled bloody-rare) left over from our dinner, wrapped in newspaper, and spirited into our room. Somehow the word got around, resulting in a newspaper story and a picture of Peter and his two birds at the airport about to board the plane for home.

When Peter arrived safely at home with his two precious wards, he put them in a cage with two other birds of a related species. Next morn-ing, he rushed to his aviary, anxious to greet his newly acquired birds. To his amazement, both were gone—eaten alive by two beastly caracaras, Mexican hawks that were voracious carnivores. The caracaras were now sitting happily on their perches with their bellies bloated. Peter's tears flowed freely.

The city of Bath was our next location in England. I found its architecture classic and remarkably well preserved from the time Romans occupied the city. We took full advantage of the atmosphere and enjoyed our stay of a few days immensely. Wherever one looked, there was a perfect movie set, suitable for many situations.

Next we went to France, where major segments were to be shot in and around Paris. We worked much of the time in the countryside, using some of the lovely châteaux and forest lanes. We took over the gardens of Versailles for a few days, with hundreds of costumed extras promenading around the manicured grounds, backed up by the magnificent palace with its elegant statuary and splashing fountains. The script called for a theater, which we concocted by attaching "Theatre Royal" in large bronze letters above the entrance doors of a suitable building on palace grounds. This scene, shot at night, resulted in a spectacular tableau, with faux nobility flowing toward the theater's main entrance.

Another big setup with hundreds of costumed extras was a bucolic fair, staged in the vast expanse outside the iron gates to the palace, with a traditional Punch-and-Judy show set up on a rickety stage, vendors hawking their wares, lots of children and dogs running around, jugglers, fortune-tellers, fire-eaters, contortionists, and freaks on display. From this scene, the camera panned to a horse-drawn cart, packed tightly with prisoners in tattered garb and escorted by a complement of guards on horseback. The cart turned into an open gate leading to the military barracks with an adjoining prison compound. Among the cutthroats, thieves, and murderers was also our hero, Lord Vanity.

One problem in shooting this scene was the look of the smooth, paved main street, totally out of character for the era we hoped to portray. This our versatile art director corrected ingeniously. He had an oversized piece of plywood cut in the pattern of cobblestone paving. Using this template, he repainted the entire street, with shadings, rocks, and chipped-off corners, to look like a well-used thoroughfare. With the added sound effects of the horses' clattering hooves and the noise of the rolling and creaking wheels of the primitive cart, the illusion would be perfect.

Our final destination was Morocco, a country I was visiting for the first time. The three Moroccan cities of Marrakesh, Rabat, and Fez, with their scenery, architecture, Arabic mores, and diverse populations, offered sights reminiscent of archaic times. Our locations there required a fair amount of set dressing to reflect the period of our story. For example, we had to recreate a quarry with hundreds of convicts, Lord Vanity among them, laboring under abysmal conditions. The rim high above them was ringed by fierce-looking Arab horsemen with rifles ready to fire at the slightest sign of insurrection. Workers toiled with rudimentary hand tools and makeshift machinery on improvised wooden trestles like something from the Middle Ages. Others pulled large, square blocks of marble on wooden sleds, a vicious guard driving them with a long-tailed leather whip.

It took a concerted effort to convince the local Arab extras to be lashed. I explained that it was painless, since the simulated leather thongs were made of lightweight cotton. But it was against the edicts of the Koran to be mistreated in such a demeaning way. "All right," I said. "Then one of you beat me first. No bodily harm nor spiritual shame will come to me." This one of the men volunteered to do, and with their fears assuaged, we shot the scene as planned.

We recreated another scene as well. From the stone fortress at the seaside town of Agadir, a long rampart faced the sea with slits in the parapet for cannons to be fired at approaching invaders. Unfortunately, only a few of the original cannon barrels remained. Again, our art director solved the problem. He commissioned a local artisan to create thirty more cannons with a plaster mold and the clever use of paint. Soldiers stood by, manning each battery, looking down the full length of the rampart. It provided a spectacular background for the suspenseful escape of Lord Vanity by sea from his fortress prison. Since we worked on an unspecified budget, a very rare happenstance, and had an imaginative crew, we could afford these rather extravagant embellishments.

While in Marrakesh, absorbed in our preliminary preparations, I received a letter from DFZ with a copy of the enclosed interoffice memo:

TCF TELEVISION PRODUCTIONS, INC.
INTER-OFFICE CORRESPONDENCE

DATE   September 18, 1954

TO: Charles Brackett
                  Sid Rogell
FROM   Darryl Zanuck
cc: Lyle Wheeler
            Charles LeMaine

SUBJECT: *LORD VANITY*

I ran all of the material on LORD VANITY last night, and I was enormously impressed by Otto Lang's work.

I will go so far as to say that I think he handled the doubles, the atmosphere and the camera setups with amazing imagination and skill.

I was tremendously impressed with all of the sequences at Bath, particularly the Normandy Inn. This sequence had more flavor, action and genuine period atmosphere than anything I can remember from a second unit company in a long while.

The same was true of the stagecoach relay station. Every setup has atmosphere and really unusual and intelligent conceptions. I hope that the director of the picture can capture this same authentic atmosphere. There is not a dull setup in any of his material.

The only bad photography is in Lord Marny's estate in the night sequences where they carry the torches but these two angles which shoot away from the house can easily be eliminated or remade here as there is nothing in the background except lawn and trees.

The long shots of Lord Marny's estate are magnificent—even the night ones. The enlistment scene was excellent. This is a case of a director using real imagination. He saved us money by eliminating all of the other scenes that were in the script and by boiling it down to this one scene with the poster. What is effective about Otto's work is that he manages to crowd all of his atmosphere into the exact section of film that we will eventually use.

I was also very impressed by the king's house and by the way Otto worked out what may prove to be a very effective tag ending to the picture. It has dignity and importance.

The gate shot leading to the king's estate is ordinary but it is only ordinary because for some reason in this setup he used entirely too few extras. The set looks skimpy. However, we need to use very little of it and as a matter of fact, we could eliminate it entirely and come on the coach as it approaches the magnificent shot of the king's house.

I personally feel very bad about having sent the first wire to Otto and I have sent him another one as I was actually given new hope for the whole picture by the wonderful values I saw on the screen last night.

If any of the carriages are out of date there is nobody in the world who will know the difference. But I cannot believe that they are actually out of date or out of period because Otto is very careful about these items and I know that he had reliable research. From the standpoint of anyone's complaint about the costumes on the extras, Freddy Fox has told me that this might be an error, but there was no opportunity to make wardrobe for the extras and they had to rely upon the wardrobe rental companies.

I certainly am no expert on carts, carriages or period costumes, but I'll be damned if there is anything that jarred me or seemed out of key.

Otto managed to re-create, for me at least, the spirit of England at this period. I would trust him with any second unit job anywhere in the world after seeing this material and, furthermore, I would be very inclined to trust him with a full-fledged directorial assignment on a picture that called for pictorial values.

DFZ

Alas, nobody ever saw this film in theaters or on late-night television. The picture was shelved before being born. Because of script problems, and realizing that to make it would have been exorbitantly expensive, the powers that be decided to cut their losses, reputed to be already over a million dollars, and *Lord Vanity* disappeared like a sinking ship into the briny deep.

LOVE IS A MANY-SPLENDORED THING

I was next assigned to be second-unit director for *Love Is a Many-Splendored Thing*, which was released in 1955. The film was to be directed by Henry King, one of the most revered directors under contract to Twentieth Century Fox. Darryl Zanuck entrusted him with some of his major films without a moment's hesitation, knowing that he would get a quality product from Henry—as good, bad, or indifferent as the screenplay might be. Though frequently nominated, Henry never took home an Oscar. A hardworking, dedicated, and honest filmmaker, he shunned the limelight as a fashionable Hollywood director. He was a quiet-spoken, highly intelligent gentleman, and I looked forward to working with him and for him.

Most of the action for *Love Is a Many-Splendored Thing* would be filmed in and around Hong Kong, as photogenic a location as one could wish for. The beautiful screenplay faithfully captured the sentiments and tragic love story contained in Han Suyin's much-acclaimed book. Jennifer Jones and William Holden, cast as the two doomed lovers, both insisted on going with me on location rather than being doubled. They would dispense with the customary attention of wardrobe people, makeup personnel, and other such studio frills. All Jennifer Jones wanted (she was then Mrs. David Selznick) was her regular hairdresser. Holden would take care of his simple makeup and be his own valet. Fair enough, the studio said, and Henry King agreed. This opportunity to work with two stars was a wonderful break for me. Not only were they stars in their profession, but they were also two exceptionally warm-hearted and likable human beings.

Jennifer was considered by some who had worked with her to be aloof and difficult to reach. I did not find her so at all. She was thoroughly cooperative, always on time, friendly, and receptive to suggestions, which she executed with aplomb. That she, as a happily married lady, chose not to socialize, was quite understandable. I am sure that the long distance phone conversations between David Selznick and her must have run into a tidy sum of money—he being well known for his loquacity.

Bill Holden, as I had anticipated, was a joy to work with. A special bonus was the developing friendship between us. Bill was the personification of the romantic lover in films. He was also a connoisseur of Chinese food and was a welcome guest at the best eating places in Hong Kong and on barges afloat in Aberdeen Harbor. Through him, I received an education in the art and appreciation of Chinese cuisine. Also, he had the best tailor in town hand stitching his suits, and he insisted that I, too, refurbish my sartorial appearance—for a ridiculously low price.

When we returned to the studio, Henry King had high praise for the work we had done. There was one scene, however, that Henry wanted to reshoot at the studio. It was the important and crucial scene when Jennifer Jones found out that her lover had been killed in Korea. She stormed out of her schoolroom and ran through the crowded, narrow streets of Hong Kong, heading for "their hill" overlooking the city, where she hoped to find solace in this favorite spot of theirs in happier days.

I had set up the scene very carefully, to be shot in one of the busiest streets in the native shopping district, with real people going about their business and not a single paid extra among them. This would force Jennifer to push her way through the crowd, distraught and haunted by her sorrow. The camera was to be hidden behind a curtain in back of a utility truck with Chinese lettering, ready to record Jennifer's run through this busy street. No one should be aware that she was an actress, playing a part in a film. I made a dry run with Jennifer sitting next to me in the driver's cab and showed her the approximate line she should follow in relation to the camera car, moving slightly ahead of her. It worked like a charm when Jennifer slipped furtively out of the truck. No one, other than a normal casual reaction by shoppers and bystanders, paid any attention to Jennifer, who, of course, played her part masterfully.

It couldn't have worked any better, but as long as we were prepared for it, I suggested we make another run following the same route to get some additional cuts, with a different lens, for the director to have a choice to enhance this sequence. It didn't work nearly as well as our first run-through. It was amazing to see how people had caught on when the same truck and the same lady came running by a second time in tandem. Their reaction was totally different and typical of people realizing that this was for a movie, pointing at her and some running after her.

When Henry King looked at this scene, back at the studio, he felt entitled to give it his own interpretation, since it was a climactic moment in the film. Whereupon the entire length of a narrow street on the studio's back lot was dressed at considerable expense to simulate a street in Hong Kong, populated with a hundred extras, appropriately costumed, with rickshaws and such, to reshoot Jennifer's run. Not a single foot of this reenaction was used in the final cut. The realism and intimacy of the real Hong Kong street and Jennifer's reactions to it could not be duplicated on a set. Everything was a bit too perfect and premeditated in the re-shoot. Jennifer was perfectly lit, with not a strand of hair out of place, and her makeup impeccable. It looked like the studio-set scene that it was.

Not that I was gloating with satisfaction that the footage I had shot in Hong Kong was used. Henry's was simply a genuine effort to improve the scene, which somehow didn't pay off. There was no harm done, and no hurt feelings; it was just part of professional filmmaking. What counted with me was that I learned a lot. I felt I was ready for a directorial assignment for a full-length feature film in the big leagues.

At the time, in the early 1950s, a crisis arose in the film industry when box office returns hit rock bottom and threatened the survival of movie studios and theater owners. What caused these alarming setbacks, which recurred from time to time, was not always easy to pinpoint. Studio heads believed that something new, a fresh approach, something out of the ordinary had to be offered as bait to lure people back into the theaters.

CINEMASCOPE

A French inventor and cinema devotee had developed a new "anamor-phic" lens. It acted like a wide-angle lens by squeezing a given image onto a standard 35 mm film frame, so that its width was almost doubled when projected on the screen, while its height remained the same. To do so, a corresponding lens had to be inserted into the projector to "unsqueeze" the image to its original appearance. Looking through a frame of film shot with an anamorphic lens, one sees that human figures and objects appear elongated, and they remain so if projected with a regular lens. Twentieth Century Fox, through its chairman, Spyros Skouras, and one of his camera experts, had shown great interest in this process, which was called CinemaScope. When it was brought to Darryl Zanuck's attention and demonstrated to him, he immediately jumped at it, convinced that this new gimmick might be the bait to bring people back into the theaters.

For his first film in this new medium, Zanuck chose a subject matter as old as the Bible itself. The film was entitled *The Robe* (1953), based on the best-selling novel by Lloyd C. Douglas. It depicted the fate of Christ's robe, which had been handed to a Roman centurion standing near the cross, before Christ was nailed to it. The screenplay was written by Philip Dunne and directed by Henry Koster. Richard Burton, at that time almost unknown, starred in the epic, with Jean Simmons. Leon Shamroy, Fox's ace cameraman, exploited the new CinemaScope process to its fullest. The entire production was a typically daring gambit by Darryl Zanuck that paid off handsomely. It was a huge success and put Fox back on its feet financially.

The next film done by Fox in CinemaScope was *How to Marry a Millionaire* (1953). It was written and produced by Nunnally Johnson with a star-studded cast. The subject, a trio of female gold diggers on a marital hunt for a millionaire in Manhattan, was ideally suited for the new medium and done with panache and Hollywood glitz. In movie jargon, it was a smash hit. Nunnally Johnson, a soft-spoken Southern gentleman with a delightful sense of humor, which was reflected in his writing, stood tall in the hierarchy of creative talent at the studio and was one of Darryl Zanuck's most appreciated associates. He was exceptionally versatile and could write screenplays for comedy, westerns, and dramatic stories.

Night People, filmed in 1953 in postwar Germany and released in 1954, did not fare nearly as well. It was shot in color and in CinemaScope format. Written, produced, and directed by Nunnally Johnson, it was an attempt at a triple play that misfired. The somber cold-war suspense story set against the dreary background of war-torn Germany would have probably been better suited for the standard 35 mm black-and-white treatment. Even sterling performances by Gregory Peck and Broderick Crawford could not induce the public to see the film.

I had a peripheral involvement with *Night People*. My job on the film, as so many times before, was ambiguous. I simply did what I was asked to do and helped out wherever I could. One assignment was to occasionally accompany Mrs. Nunnally Johnson as her German-speaking interpreter on shopping expeditions in Munich and Berlin, searching for antique china, heirloom silverware, and sundry artifacts. Dorris Bowdon had made her feature screen debut as Rosesharn in *The Grapes of Wrath*, John Ford's finest and most memorable achievement, honored by an Academy Award. The film was written and produced by Nunnally, based on John Steinbeck's classic book. A romance between screenwriter and actress ensued, and Nunnally married Dorris, who sacrificed her promising acting career to become a loving wife and devoted mother of three children.

Close to the end of shooting *Night People*, I had a phone call from DFZ asking me to meet him in Paris to talk about a project he had in mind for me. I joined him at the exclusive Lancaster Hotel off the Champs Elysées to learn the details of the project. He explained that in order to round out the showing of a CinemaScope feature film in a theater to a full-length two-hour program, he needed fillers, shot in CinemaScope, of ten to twenty minutes in length. He wanted me to direct these. Spyros Skouras had suggested a documentary on Greece, but I felt it should be something with more movement and excitement. DFZ concurred, and suggested filming the "Flying Scotsman," one of the most publicized high-speed trains in England. I countered with a proposal to use the Italian ETR300, which started its journey in Milan and ended it in Naples. It was the latest in design and fastest, bar none, and we would have the marvelous scenic background of Italy and its historic cities. Darryl agreed. Immediately the production wheels were set in motion; the release date was set before the Christmas holidays.

The challenge of working in this new dimension excited me. I was also pleased that Charles Clarke, a veteran and most knowledgeable cinematographer, revered by his peers, would be my cameraman. In very little time we had gathered a polyglot crew and were off to Milan to get clearances for filming the train. While waiting for these formalities, we filmed some of Milan's historic sites and monuments as an introduction to the documentary.

Our first planned shot of the ETR 300 was a camera angle from the control tower, which directed departures and arrivals of trains. Milan was one of the busiest rail hubs in Italy. We knew the exact departure time of our train, and as we waited expectantly, a most extraordinary thing happened. Out of the dark, cavernous terminal emerged a sooty old locomotive, belching clouds of smoke and pulling a dozen vintage passenger cars behind it, slowly gathering speed. On an impulse and knowing that at any moment our train was going to appear on the adjacent parallel track, I gave the signal to roll the camera. As the old steam engine, huffing and puffing, pushed ahead, our train emerged from the terminal, slithering into the bright sunlight like a streamlined silver snake, rapidly accelerating until it caught up and passed the antiquated train.

The timing was perfect as we could keep both trains in the frame of the picture to follow the silver train as it disappeared into the distance.

I knew we had a knockout introduction that would have been hard if not impossible to stage. From there on we followed our train as it progressed down the length of Italy. This required many days of catching it at different spots on its daily run. We also followed its speedy progress from an airplane, with the camera mounted below one wing and activated by a switch inside the cockpit, where the cameraman looked through a matching frame of vision outlined in black pencil on the window in front of him. Unfortunately, our Italian contact man had not obtained the proper military clearances to film this type of footage from a private plane, so when we landed at the Rome airport, we were accosted by some militiamen who demanded that we turn over our exposed film. We gave them what was in the magazine attached to the camera, and with a wink of complicity between Charles Clarke and me, we solicitously handed over a roll of unexposed film sealed in a can in lieu of a roll of exposed film in another can. This subterfuge worked, but it would still leave me short some of the best aerial views we filmed.

Another problem was that back at the studio the film editor told me that we could not have any dissolves due to technical problems and the high cost of each dissolve. We could have a fade-in at the beginning and fade-out at the end of the film. As it so often happens in life, this worked to our advantage rather than detriment. These straight cuts, instead of being jarring to an audience, carried the viewers along as though they were sitting in the train. Alfred Newman added a superb musical score to the film, using sections of classic compositions in the Roman genre.

I changed the name of ETR300 to *Vesuvius Express* for the film's title. It caused much excitement at the studio and was nominated for an Academy Award in the documentary category. That it did not get an Oscar was partially due to our inexcusable slip-up of omitting Charles Clarke's screen credit as cinematographer, which cost us a number of votes from the cinematographer's union. I was most chagrined to find out about this, but with a release date set, we could do nothing to correct it until much later—too late to rectify the damage.

Another one of these short subjects, *Jet Carrier*, was also nominated for an Academy Award. It showed a day of activity on the venerable USS *Yorktown*, with some hairy, near-crash landings on the carrier's postage-stamp-size deck, as seen from the pilot's point of view. I also enjoyed immensely doing a film on Paul Mantz, the legendary stunt flyer of the era. He was extremely camera wise and had the knack of reducing the danger quotient of each daring stunt to a minimum. Later, in spite of precautionary measures, he crashed and died in the experimental jury-rigged plane during the shooting of a dangerous takeoff for the film *The Flight of the Phoenix* (1965), after an already successful first take registered on film.

An interesting change of pace for me was the filming of *The First American Piano Quartet*, a popular ensemble that had toured the world over. Johnny DeCuir, one of the most inventive art directors in the business, had designed a set of a series of twelve-foot-high mirrors linked together at an angle. With the four pianos set in front of it, it appeared as though there were a multitude of them. This was a spectacular setup, but hellish for the cameraman and his lighting gaffer to illuminate without showing pieces of electrical equipment or reflecting the camera in one of the dozen mirrors. It took the better part of a day to solve this problem, but we did.

My idea was to open the shot with the pianos and players in semi-darkness and with the first note of Claude Debussy's "Claire de Lune," a beam of light would touch the first of the four players, and then the other three would become visible as though lit by the rising moon, to have the whole set bathed in a silvery, bluish mood. It was a nice idea and it worked well until the first full rehearsal when a hitch developed. Adam, the lead player and the first to be caressed by the touch of the moon-beam, was as bald as a billiard ball. I realized that this would provoke a big laugh from the audience. So I said to him, "Sorry, Adam, we simply have to plop a wig on your head." Adam protested, saying that being bald had no bearing on his artistic integrity and that he had performed successfully in hundreds of concerts as a bald piano player. Only after I explained to him the scheme of our lighting treatment did he consent to wear a stylish and becoming wig.

The second piece was Enrique Granados's fine composition "Malagueña," one of my personal favorites. This shot, thank God, was without mirrors and had only the backing of a heavy, blood-red curtain. Johnny DeCuir gave us one of the largest and most ornate crystal chandeliers from the studio repository to hang over the set. My thought was to begin the sequence from a high angle on a moving crane, shooting through the chandelier, and as the music progressed, to lower the camera to eye level, focusing on Adam (still wearing his wig) and then traveling slowly along the row of pianos and holding all four of them in the frame.

Then the camera would gradually rise again and pull back to the original high-angle starting position, shooting through the chandelier. It was a complex move for the crane operator and cameraman to time and coordinate with the length of the piece. I wanted to do it in one single continuous move without an intercut, but in the end, I had to insert a few close-ups. Once spliced together, these cuts blended smoothly into the floating camera movement.

The last number, John Philip Sousa's "Stars and Stripes Forever," was backed by a phantasmagoria of flags, colored streamers, and balloons, and the camera treatment was done in a kind of jazzy manner with many cuts and angles of the piano players. Altogether, this musical program represented a fine piece of teamwork by all hands involved. It also was nominated for an Academy Award.

FAMILY UPS AND DOWNS

After having lived for a number of years at 1861 Coldwater Canyon, Sinnie and I came to realize that times were changing. Traffic on this throughway to the San Fernando Valley had increased markedly as automobiles raced by in both directions, which also increased the noise. Also distressing was that many hundreds of acres of the beautiful orange groves surrounding us had disappeared to make room for stately mansions and subdivisions. Suddenly, Coldwater Canyon had become fashionable, and many affluent people in the movie industry were choosing to build there, tempted by its rural proximity to Beverly Hills. With our two growing boys in need of a little more breathing space away from the steady flow of traffic, we decided to sell the house. As it turned out, we disposed of it at a sizable profit.

The next house we bought was in Brentwood, not too far from Santa Monica and the Pacific Ocean. Located in a quiet residential area with a network of pleasant side streets, ideal for walking and bicycling, the house was a traditional Spanish-style edifice with shady trees and ample lawn front and back and an adjoining two-car garage, which would serve as much-needed storage space and a workshop for the boys. Both of them had become avid animal lovers and collectors of any species they could lay their hands on, be it cat, puppy dog, raven, peregrine falcon, long-tailed pheasant, rabbit, homing pigeon, frog, or snake. Of course, this luxury of space and privacy was reflected in the corresponding increase in our monthly overhead, what with mortgage payments, higher taxes, the services of a gardener, and the maintenance of this type of older home.

Much larger than our previous house, the new home also needed more furniture, new carpets, and drapes, almost too much for Sinnie and me to handle on our own. Luckily, I was making good money, more than I had ever had. Fully expecting that it would continue in this vein, I suggested to Sinnie that we seek the help of a professional interior designer. I had seen and liked the work of Paul Frankl, who was of Austrian ancestry, and his American wife, Mary. Sinnie thought the Frankls would be far beyond our price range and that it would be useless even to contact them. Although I agreed with her, I reasoned that no possible harm could come of inviting Paul to come to our house, look it over, and give us an idea of what it would entail, without entering into any kind of commitment.

Paul and Mary graciously accepted our invitation, and from the very first moments of our encounter, we seemed to feel a mutual empathy toward each other. Paul, short and somewhat frail looking, with brown eyes, a bald head, and the expression of a wise owl, was the creative brain, while Mary, good looking with solid American genes, represented the management arm of the business. Paul had also made himself a niche as a furniture designer for a major manufacturing company in the Midwest. His designs, somewhat avant-garde compared to the prevailing trend, were highly aesthetic and elegant. He used a variety of fine woods, beautifully detailed and finished, with an innovative polished surface of glazed off-white cork for tabletops and smaller side tables. His furniture was distinctive and sold well.

During my stay in Japan in 1951, when I was the second-unit director for the pleasant but quite forgettable musical *Call Me Mister*, starring Betty Grable and Dan Dailey, I had collected some odd pieces of furniture and artifacts, such as a large antique cocktail table, exquisitely finished in emerald green lacquer, and other smaller pieces of quality, which I had bought in Kyoto. I also brought back two high, six-panel folding screens, entitled "A Thousand Flowers," depicting the whole range of flora found in Japan. The two screens, one hanging in our living room above the fireplace and the other filling a side wall in the dining room, immediately attracted Paul's attention since they were obviously of museum quality. I had picked them up in Tokyo from a private collector, who still had a limited selection on hand, some of a beauty I had rarely seen before. I should have bought all of them as an investment. Sinnie and I had also bought a few antique pieces at various auctions, and among these, of great appeal to me, was an authentic captain's stand-up writing desk of satin-smooth walnut from a New England sailing ship. Altogether, ours was a hodgepodge of odds and ends, attractive by themselves but in need of coordination to make a harmonious decor. Neither Sinnie nor I wished to live in a "decorator's home," but we surely could use some help and advice.

I explained to Paul and Mary that our financial resources were limited, unlike the clientele with unlimited funds with whom they were accustomed to doing business. As we strolled through the house looking at various usable pieces, I pointed out an old-fashioned lighting fixture in the dining room ceiling, left by the previous owner, and casually remarked to Paul, "Of course, this unsightly piece will have to go."

"Now, wait a minute. Don't be so hasty," Paul said. "We can fix it up by painting all its leafy metal branches black with some touches of gold. Then, by adding a few more crystals and replacing the lightbulbs, you'll have a charming chandelier at a minimum cost." The same thing happened when I pointed out the old-fashioned paneled door of a hallway closet, thinking it would have to be replaced. Again he came up with a simple solution to bring it up to date and give it a contemporary look. The upshot of all of this was that not only did we "do" the house with the Frankls' help, but we also became the closest of friends, visiting each other frequently and dining at their home in Palos Verdes and vice versa. When all was finished, the house was comfortable to live in and elegant in an unostentatious way, with a mix of new and old pieces.

One day, in moving a heavy piece of furniture around in the living room, I felt a sharp pain in my lower back, as though someone had sunk a stiletto into my lumbar column. I dropped to the carpet flat on my stomach in great pain, unable to move, as though my legs were paralyzed. I could do nothing but wait until Sinnie and the boys returned home from the grocery store. Despite their trying to help, I could not get up, and the pain was excruciating. Between tears and laughter about this awkward situation, I asked them to call Dr. Edward Le Mancheck, who had taken care of some lesser ailments of my self-abused body.

Dr. Le Mancheck arrived promptly and, after a preliminary examination, diagnosed that undoubtedly I had severely bruised a nerve when a lumbar disk slipped its mooring. He pulled out of his black leather satchel a syringe, large enough to tranquilize a horse, inserted a long, sharp needle into a vial filled it with morphine and then injected it into my back. With the pain relieved, and everyone helping, I managed to get upstairs to our bedroom. Le Manchek ordered me to remain in bed, flat on my back, for at least eight days. Prolonged rest and caution in all activities was his prescription. When I got back on my feet again, the back of my left leg was numb and insensitive to pinpricks from the buttock to the heel, including all of my toes. While a bruised nerve does regenerate, it takes years and years to do so. My back never healed completely and bothers me still, temporarily incapacitating me from time to time. I have learned to live with it, and with appropriate caution and exercises to keep the back muscles in tone, I adjusted to this common impairment.

Next was Sinnie's turn. A small nodule appeared on her throat, which needed to be examined by a doctor. She went to one recommended by a friend. His suggestion was to surgically excise the nodule. A date was set, and Sinnie went to St. John's Hospital in Santa Monica. The nodule was removed and as a routine procedure sent to the lab while she was still on the operating table. The report came back that it was malignant. This, of course, was a horrendous shock to us. The surgeon decided to close the incision and reschedule the operation, which now had taken on a much more serious dimension. I was heartbroken when she was wheeled back into her room. I dreaded telling her, when she came out of anesthesia, what we were faced with. I knew how courageous she was and able to face any crisis, but this one was out of her control and beyond her willpower.

At that point, a nun who acted as a trained medical assistant to the surgeon came into the room and said, "Mr. Lang, quite confidentially, I would like to tell you that Dr. F. is not qualified nor experienced enough to perform this complex operation. He is a certified ear, nose, and throat man, but not allowed to go beyond that, into the chest cavity. I would strongly recommend that you select another surgeon with the proper credentials. Please keep this information between us. I did it because of my sympathy for your wife and to make sure she has the best care in this critical situation." I was most grateful to her for her forthrightness and thanked her profoundly. I had the operation postponed until I could find another doctor. The surgeon who had performed the initial surgery was furious and threatened to sue me because I had besmirched his reputation and also because by delaying the surgery, I endangered the life of my wife. I stuck by my decision and found a Dr. Weber, who was highly recommended as a specialist in this field. It was a fortuitous choice, and Dr. Weber came through as a hero in all of our hearts. The cancer had spread in its beginning stages, but as Dr. Weber told me after the operation, "I think, hope, and pray that I cleaned it all out and she should have no problems from here on."

Sinnie recovered rapidly, and Dr. Weber made only one mistake: when she asked him about her smoking habit, he told her he saw no reason why she shouldn't smoke, as he himself enjoyed his daily ration of cigarettes. At that time smoking was considered an innocuous and harmless addiction, with both doctors and smokers unaware of its dangers. Nevertheless, I was grateful to Dr. Weber as, undoubtedly, had he not entered the picture, Sinnie would have been doomed to an early demise.

As has been said before, all good things come in threes—so, too, I found out, did bad things. Next was young Peter's turn. As I was told by an eyewitness, Peter was riding his bicycle and had come around a corner at high speed to find himself headed at an angle into a slowly approaching automobile. He lost control of the bicycle and crashed into the front fender of the car. The results were devastating.

Fortunately, I was at home when a neighbor rang the bell and pounded at the door to say that Peter had been in an accident. I rushed to the scene, where a small group of people had already gathered and had moved him off the street into a bed of red geraniums. The sight of him made me want to burst into tears of despair. Here was our firstborn, a handsome young boy, with his left leg almost sheared off by the sharp metal edge of the car's front fender, with jagged pieces of white bone sticking out of an open gash above his ankle, and blood all over, pouring from his wound. He was pale, frightened, and speechless, in a sort of traumatic shock. The pain had not set in yet.

There have been few times in my life when I have been utterly dismayed, and this was one of them. But it was not a time to lose my head. I was told that an ambulance had already been called. My next thought was to stanch the flow of blood with a tourniquet by using my belt and tightening it around the leg below the knee. Then I just held his hand, put my head next to his, and whispered to him, controlling my emotions, "It'll be all right. Dr. Le Mancheck will put your leg in a cast and it will heal and be as good as new. We all love you and will stand by you, no matter what. So don't worry, it's just bad luck that it happened to you."

By that time the ambulance had arrived, and as he was carefully lifted onto a stretcher, I realized that the damage to his leg was much worse than I had thought. It was a mean-looking compound fracture of the tibia and fibula with the leg just hanging on by stretched ligaments and

Jimmy Stewart in *Call Northside 777*. Courtesy Twentieth Century Fox.

A scene from *Call Northside 777*. Courtesy Twentieth Century Fox.

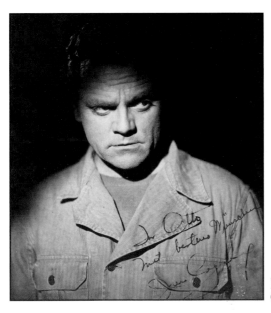

James Cagney in *13 Rue Madeleine*. Courtesy Twentieth Century Fox.

With director Joseph Mankiewicz during the shooting of *Five Fingers* in Ankara, Turkey. Courtesy Twentieth Century Fox.

James Mason and Danielle Darrieux in *Five Fingers*. Courtesy Twentieth Century Fox.

My informal first meeting with Nyemi Bope Mabinshi, king of the Bakuba tribe in the former Belgian Congo, prior to shooting *White Witch Doctor*.

Nyemi Bope Mabinshi in his ceremonial robe and ornaments, acting in front of the camera. He is seated on the back of one of his prostrate underlings.

Masked dancers, Bakuba
tribe.

With Lowell Thomas at Alta, Utah,
1948.

With Bill Holden during the filming of *Love is a Many-Splendored Thing* in Hong Kong.

A scene from the ill-fated film *Lord Vanity*, showing the portico I added to Inigo Jones's masterpiece, the Earl of Pembroke's manor.

Sinnie in Istanbul, during one of our travels together. Photo by Otto Lang.

My father, Mark, and my mother in Salzburg, meeting for the first time. Photo by Otto Lang.

My sister Elsa with her daughter Anne, visiting us in Beverly Hills, California. Photo by Otto Lang.

The *Globemaster* plane, being loaded with Cinerama gear to shoot *Search for Paradise.*

The Cinerama crew "camped out" inside.

"Captain" Chris Young and "Sergeant" Jim Parker arriving at Gulmarg, Kashmir, with skis in tow in *Search for Paradise.*

The Cinerama raft anchored on the turbulent Indus River, with the mountain Nanga Parbat in the background.

Lowell Thomas and Charles Mayo (wearing top hats) in Nepal during King Mahendra's coronation procession, 1958.

The Mir of Hunza and the crown prince, holding court.

For a Cinerama coronation sequence, the Royal couple's elephant in our parade.

The King and I. Contrary to his "godlike" image that he presented in public, Mahendra wore a smile and went without his customary dark glasses when I met him.

Saturday Review

JANUARY 11, 1958 / 25¢

Grand Prize in Color—"Blind Beggar," Ceylon, Otto Lang, Leica, Kodachrome.

U.S. PASSPORT POLICY—TWO VIEWS
Joseph N. Welch & The U.S. State Department

AMERICA AT THE BRUSSELS FAIR:
ARE WE LOSING THE CULTURAL RACE, TOO?

1958 WORLD TRAVEL CALENDAR— ANNUAL PHOTO CONTEST WINNERS

My award-winning photo, "Blind Beggar," taken in
Ceylon, as it appeared on the *Saturday Review*, 1958.

With flier Paul Mantz during
the filming of *Movie Stunt
Pilot*, a documentary about
his work. He also flew his
B-25 for all the aerial
sequences in *Search for
Paradise*.

shreds of sinew. It would be a major orthopedic achievement to make his leg right again. The thought that he might lose it frightened me.

Dr. Le Mancheck was shocked when he saw the damage, as I could see by the concerned expression on his face during his examination. He told me in private that it was very serious and that it would take all his expertise—and a huge dose of luck—to save Peter's leg. It would be a protracted healing process with infection almost inevitable and difficult to control. He was not overly optimistic, but he assured me he would do everything in his power. This all happened while Sinnie and Mark were away on errands. I knew how they would feel when I told them what happened. The three of us were in a state of shock for days.

Dr. Le Mancheck kept his promise, although it was nip and tuck for quite a while. As he had predicted, a massive and tenacious infection hindered the knitting process of the bones. Two more operations were required to combat the insidious effects of osteomyelitis, which was finally brought under control by Le Mancheck's medical skill and perseverance. Peter was in a cast and wheelchair for months, and after that he hobbled on crutches for a long time. On top of it, he had to have a mastoid operation, unrelated to his accident. All through this ordeal, Peter's high spirits and sense of humor never faltered, endearing him more than ever to his parents. His leg eventually healed but was left with a deep indentation in his shin bone, covered by a thin layer of scar tissue. It would always be a cause of worry, with the ever-present danger of a reinjury and subsequent reinfection of the bone.

TV VERSUS FLICKS

It took awhile for Twentieth Century Fox to join the mainstream and make films for television, that burgeoning new medium, mainly because Darryl Zanuck had little faith in its future. He called TV "that idiot box," and while he grudgingly admitted that there was some merit in its broadcasts of sports events and topical newsreel-type subjects, he could not see it as a purveyor of dramatic shows and big-time musicals. This surprised me since he had always been a pathfinder and innovator.

Spyros Skouras, on the contrary, feeling thwarted in his creative ambitions, grabbed the television opportunity to establish himself as a creative talent. He entered into an agreement with General Electric to provide them with a weekly one-hour TV show. Skouras, with the assistance of another frustrated filmmaker, Sid Rogell, who succeeded the very able Ray Klune as overall production manager at Fox, took the bull by the horns and produced the first segment, a truncated version of *The Oxbow Incident*, with a revised script and new cast.

At that point, Darryl Zanuck stepped forward and brought the whole scheme to a crashing halt. He took over the project with the statement that as long as he was the head of the studio, no piece of film released by Fox would be shown to the public without his approval. This was only one of many explosions between the feuding Skouras and Zanuck factions. With Skouras on the East Coast, running the business affairs, and Zanuck on the West Coast, functioning as the creative partner, the future of Fox did not look promising. With General Electric in accord and obviously feeling much safer with DFZ at the helm, the opening segment of the series was postponed for six weeks. It was to be known as the *Twentieth Century Fox Hour*, with a new schedule of films planned. The already completed version of *The Oxbow Incident* was put aside temporarily.

I was summoned to DFZ's office and told that he wanted me to take over and be in charge of this series under his supervision. I was unprepared for this turn of events and, frankly, not very pleased by the offer. My primary objective was to become a director of feature films, and this assignment would obviously steer me in a different direction. I tried to explain to Darryl that I was a total neophyte in television techniques and its demands. "Nonsense," he said. "It's all the same. As simple as making films."

"Not quite," I said, trying to justify my reluctance. "It's like painting a picture, one in watercolors and the other in oil." Still, one did not turn down a job offered by DFZ, and so I accepted, knowing from the beginning that I had entered into something I might regret.

After a series of meetings with executives from General Electric and Young and Rubicam, their New York advertising agency, the decision was made to schedule "Cavalcade" as the kickoff show on October 5, 1955, of *The Twentieth Century Fox Hour* on CBS, sponsored by General Electric. That would give us approximately six weeks in which to prepare a shooting script, cast the picture, build and dress the sets, shoot the film, and edit, score, and dub it. *Cavalcade*, an original stage play written by Noel Coward, in which he also starred, had had a successful run on Broadway. In 1932 it was made into a film by the old Fox studio, prior to its becoming Twentieth Century Fox, which garnered Oscars for best picture, for its director, Frank Lloyd, and art director, William Darling. The story depicted a sprawling chunk of British history by following the

341 HOLLYWOOD ENCORE 341

lives and fates of an upper-class English family and their household staff during the final phases of the Boer War around the turn of the century.

What we needed desperately was a screenplay writer, preferably an Englishman, who could deliver a television movie shooting script in the shortest possible time. I suggested Alistair Cooke, who was not only a distinguished writer, but also one who had left his mark on this new medium through his association with *Omnibus*, a critically acclaimed and popular weekly TV show. My choice was unanimously seconded as the solution to our problem. David Brown, then the story editor at Fox, having a personal entrée to Mr. Cooke, contacted him immediately. Cooke was available and enthusiastic about doing the job, for which he asked a fee of $5,000 plus travel and hotel expenses.

In the meantime, we were also trying to assemble a cast. We were most fortunate in finding Merle Oberon and Michael Wilding available and excited about playing the two lead roles. They would make a handsomely matched couple, very believably upholding the English tradition of loving devotion and dignity. A sizable number of servants and other characters had to be cast, and these roles were filled by experienced English actors. Everyone had to be fitted for period wardrobe. There were ladies' hairdos to be tested and wigs and beards selected for the men. As director we chose Lewis Allen, also of English ancestry. With the preliminaries settled, all departments at Fox worked hand in hand to pull the production through in a time span to which studio filmmakers were totally unaccustomed.

On Friday, August 26, 1955, a letter arrived from Alistair Cooke:

Dear Mr. Lang:

Mr. Klinger's office will be picking up the finished script this afternoon and air-mailing it, special delivery to you at the studio.

It was a lot of fun to do, especially to visualize on a television screen, instead of one of those vast panoramic Twentieth Century Fox inventions whose name escapes me.

I hope and believe the script will speak for itself and require no gloss of "principles" or "approach" plucked at by hindsight to justify incompetence. The only thing I would say is, after three years of watching immaculate scripts turn into blurred and spotty features on the screen, that I have kept in mind always the painful fact that over sixty percent of the home television sets of this country are 17-inch jobs. Consequently, in avoiding all the pomp and spaciousness of vast montages, and cumulus clouds marching in step with Crusaders, I have tried to reduce the story to small images, even about great events. I would personally rather avoid all the marching regiments, and Apocalyptic horsemen, and "War is mud" space-shooting which so impressed us all around 1930.

We shall doubtless talk after you've seen it, so there's no point in going into details. You will see that I have kept the same newspaper vendor throughout. Thirty years is not such a long time for an Englishman to stay in one job.

My schedule has been boiling since I began this last weekend. I have to go up to Maine on Monday and Tuesday to make a film for *Omnibus*. And then the U. N. Disarmament Commission will require my scribbling presence. It doesn't look too hopeful for my getting out your way; and therefore I have composed the script with the more care and loving polish. But it should not be hard to touch up this and that according to your judgment. I am taking a copy away to the country now and will do a more thorough timing. If I find it too long, I will pencil in suggested cuts.

I do wish I'd heard about this a month ago. I'd have been out to you by the first California Zephyr—my favorite type of transportation. However, the script would probably have taken a longer, if more pleasurable, time to finish.

Good luck to you in your new and fearsome project.

When, by the way, is this one scheduled to appear? My greetings to Mr. Zanuck.

Very sincerely,

AC

My impression after reading the script was that it was indeed written for television, a format very familiar to Alistair Cooke, but unfamiliar to us die-hard filmmakers. Consequently, everyone panicked. We did not have the courage, nor were we ready for such a radical departure. We chose to stay on safe ground and follow our habitual path of making a movie instead of a drama adapted specifically for television. I admired Cooke's concept and dialogue, which leaned faithfully toward Noel Coward's original stage play rather than the movie script. I have read and reread it many times since and always wondered what would have happened if we had followed through and shot it with only minor rewrites.

At that time it was obvious to me that the script needed some work—a compromise between film and television approaches that, unfortunately, would not be the best resolution and something of a cop-out. But the lack of time dictated an immediate decision. Also, I had had a note from Merle Oberon and Michael Wilding, who were totally confounded and alarmed by what they had read. Alistair Cooke could not come west due to his minor surgery scheduled to be performed in New York, nor could I go there at this critical time. The only alternative was to engage a local writer, Peter Packer, an Englishman and friend of director Allen Lewis. They had worked together on another project and were attuned to each other.

The three of us virtually closeted ourselves in my office and worked nonstop with Alistair Cooke's script as the basis, for two days and late into the nights. I wrote conciliatory notes to Merle Oberon and Michael Wilding, telling them not to fret as everything would be set to rights in the revised shooting script. I also wrote a letter to Alistair Cooke, which I was sure would not please him and only aggravate his antipathy toward Hollywood filmmakers, including me:

> First of all, I hope that the surgery performed on you did not prove to be of too serious a nature and that by now you are resting comfortably.
>
> It is indeed a pity that we both had to work under such adverse circumstances on this first collaboration—due to the pressure of time and your pending operation. We started shooting on Tuesday, September 6, and it was really a battle to get the script ready, the many parts cast, and the wardrobe selected and fitted in this incredibly short time.
>
> Rather than to explain in great detail what caused me to be concerned after studying your first draft, I am sending you a copy of the shooting script. You will notice that a good deal of your material has been retained. In going over your latest notes that arrived this morning, alas—late again due to the miserable postal service, I find that most of your suggestions have already been incorporated in the present shooting script. I thought that your opening narration was by far superior to what we had and we shall make use of it. This, however, can wait until the last moment as it only involves a narrator's voice.
>
> In view of the fact that in this emergency, we had to put another writer on this assignment, when it became evident that you couldn't possibly make the trip, I would like to check with you on the credits. Peter Packer, the man who jumped into the breach and worked with me and the director virtually through two days and part of the nights—deserves recognition and I hope you will agree with me that he came through with a commendable job.

We are planning to use the following credit announcement:

Noel Coward's
"CAVALCADE"
Teleplay by
Alistair Cooke
and
Peter Packer

I trust that this will be agreeable with you as we are very anxious to have your name in first place.

Please let me know how you are coming along, and I hope that you will look us up on your next visit to California.

As a footnote to our story of frenzied preparations, I received a communication from the CBS censorship office after they read our script, advising me to delete certain objectionable parts:

Page 56, Fanny's second speech: Don't say "damn" . . . Change to something milder.

Bottom of same page, Joe's speech: "You don't regret it—any of it?" Fanny's answer: "Not a moment."

CBS prefers that these two lines be deleted entirely, since they could be interpreted as referring to illicit sex which, in the network world, can only bring regret and remorse. If you feel that similar speeches are needed here, they must leave no doubt that these two are chaste.

Ah, for those bygone days of innocence.

As per our schedule, the picture was shot in a week including one Saturday and sometimes working into the night. Considering the length of the script and the many moves required, it was a tour de force. Lewis Allen had come through with an outstanding directorial job, and the acting was uniformly good, with all actors speaking British English, without any discrepancies in the dialogue. The show premiered in prime time on October 5, 1955. I received this telegram from Frank Fagan, a top executive at General Electric:

DEAR OTTO WHEN PETE LEVATHES AND I TALKED TO YOU ABOUT THE PHILOSOPHY BEHIND THE ENTIRE 20TH CENTURY FOX

GENERAL ELECTRIC PROGRAMS, YOU HAD A VISION OF THE LEVEL TO WHICH EACH PROGRAM SHOULD REACH. TONIGHT " CAVALCADE" REACHED THE FULFILLMENT OF THIS VISION.

I AM SENDING THIS WIRE TO YOU BEFORE THE CRITICS HAVE A CHANCE TO TELL THE PUBLIC BECAUSE I WANT YOU TO KNOW THAT I PERSONALLY THINK THIS IS A LANDMARK IN TELEVISION. MY KIND REGARDS AND BEST WISHES TO YOU.

New York's media response to our inaugural television show was better than that given to any of the other film companies' competing programs. The *New York Times* and the *New York Daily News* reviews were good. The *New York Post* and *Journal* were satisfactory. *Motion Picture Daily* was good. A "breakthrough" it was not, and I did not expect it to be. Said one reviewer:

> On the whole, though, I'd say all hands did about as well with "Cavalcade" as was possible in the time limit they had. There was no evidence of the sloppy, back-of-my-hand-to-you attitude which characterized some recent major movie companies' output for TV.
> It was done with dignity and care. Wilding and Miss Oberon behaved with what I imagine is about the right degree of gentility and of the others in the cast, Noel Drayton and Nora O'Mahoney were notable as their servants.

We skipped a week after the premiere of "Cavalcade," gaining a most welcome breathing spell to put the final touches on "Laura," which would be our second segment in the series. The theatrical version of this film had been a resounding box office success. Directed by Otto Preminger, it became an enduring classic, seen time and time again on television and in movie theaters specializing in revival programs. It translated very well into TV format and, with its intimate story, was much more suited to a television audience than was our kickoff show. With John Brahms as the director and Dana Wynter, Robert Stack, and George Sanders in the leading roles, "Laura" was arguably one of our best if not the best show in this entire series.

For our third show, the already finished and unwarrantedly maligned "The Oxbow Incident" was a welcome gift. It was very well directed by

Gerd Oswald, a friend of mine who had also come up through the ranks, and I could find nothing to criticize. Nevertheless, I could understand why Darryl Zanuck did not want it to represent the opening salvo for *The Twentieth Century Fox Hour.* The grim, downbeat subject matter was not likely to start the series off on a high note.

In a letter to DFZ, vacationing in Paris, I wrote:

> As far as the overall operation of TCF-TV is concerned, there is still much to be discussed and straightened out. I realize that nothing can be done in this respect until you return.
>
> I have been so preoccupied with our two first segments and thinking ahead in terms of what next after "Oxbow Incident." Consequently, I have not had much time really to look into many details pertaining to reorganization or personnel changes, of which undoubtedly some will have to be made.
>
> From my personal point of view, I can see the potential of my job. But I must also admit and tell you in all honesty that under the existing setup and jousting in management, it would be quite a hardship for me to stay with the position I hold at present, unless it becomes more clearly defined.
>
> The pressure and struggle to sort out stories and put them in work continues unrelentingly—since up to date, none of the 11 properties, selected originally by the Skouras-Rogell regime, has provided us with a shootable screenplay.

When DFZ returned from his vacation, he dove into cleaning out this Augean stable. He wrote a memo to Sid Rogell, who was an experienced production manager but, in my opinion, not gifted as a creative mind in selecting and developing stories into screenplays, with copies to me, Lew Schreiber, Buddy Adler, and David Brown:

> I received the copy of the progress report which Michael Kraike sent you. This shows a lot of activity, but who has read or approved these projects that are now apparently being written and ready to be cast? I refer particularly to "One Life" and "Yacht on the High Seas." I want everyone mentioned to study these properties, and this includes "Parnassus on Wheels," "The Age of Reason," "Philemon Complex," "The Thieving Magpie," and "Small Back Room."
>
> When you say, "The following assignments are to be handled by David Hempstead," I assume that you refer to the situation before Otto Lang

was brought into the picture. Are you certain that Michael Kraike has been clearly advised of his new duties and especially of the fact that nobody except you is above Otto Lang?

I assume that Otto and you will want to continue to use him as your production executive.

The thing that really disturbs me is that we have gone ahead and signed people for various casts and we have put a number of original stories into work and apparently we have been relying entirely on the judgment and taste of Michael Kraike and one of his associates, Jules Bricken.

It now becomes more than ever essential that we organize ourselves properly and carefully analyze and evaluate these properties.

To obtain quality and to protect ourselves it is going to be essential that Otto, David Brown, Julian Johnson and others qualified to do so must read and evaluate these projects and give us their opinions before we go any further with any of them.

Quite understandably neither Sid Rogell nor Michael Kraike was pleased with this turn of events. Personally, I valued Michael Kraike as a filmmaker and a veteran of studio infighting and did not want him to feel that he was demoted. I showed my respect by consulting with him regularly and freely on many problems. It was a continuously draining and mind-numbing process. I did not like my ambiguous position and responsibilities, nor did I look forward with joy and excitement every morning to going to work at the studio. I could not suppress the feeling that I was the wrong choice for this job. Basically, I was a one-project, one-film-at-a-time type of person and was convinced that I would function much better as a director, given the chance.

Darryl Zanuck eventually brought in another executive producer to relieve Sid Rogell of his television responsibilities, claiming that he could not fill two full-time jobs simultaneously. I also came to the decision that the time had come for me to resign. After much soul-searching, realizing that it could be one of the most important decisions of my career and possibly the biggest mistake I ever made, I submitted a letter of resignation to Darryl. He most graciously accepted my withdrawl, expressing his regrets but understanding the reasons for my wanting to pursue a different course. He also thanked me profusely for stepping in when needed to get *The Twentieth Century Fox Hour* off to a good start. My personal relationship with Darryl Zanuck and his family was not affected by this decision, and we would remain close friends.

I was free and prepared to enter the highly competitive field as a freelance director. First of all, I would have to get myself an agent who made the regular rounds of the studios. At home we would have to make some adjustments in our family modus vivendi and tighten our purse strings. In the interim I looked forward to having some time off and to rethinking my priorities.

CINERAMA

Soon after I left Fox, and at a time I needed it most, Lowell Thomas asked me to direct his next Cinerama spectacular, which would be the third he had produced in this medium. His two previous Cinerama films, *This Is Cinerama* and *Seven Wonders of the World*, were long-running box-office mega-successes. Lowell and I had seen each other frequently, though our visits were brief and impromptu, due to our peripatetic lifestyles. We kept in touch through letters, bulletins regarding our ongoing projects, and occasional phone conversations. We even managed to ski together a few times.

The more I got to know Lowell, the more I realized what an extraordinary person he was. He was the splendid narrator of his own adventure films and spokesman of *Movietone News*, a newsreel shown weekly in theaters around the world. As a journalist he was the voice of the longest-running daily newscast, on CBS, every program beginning with his distinctive "Good evening, everybody," and signing off with "So long until tomorrow." He published a hardcover book every year on diverse subjects, more than fifty titles in his lifetime. He was happily married to Fran, his college sweetheart.

I had the pleasure of staying with Lowell and Fran as their house guest on many occasions. Their authentic Georgian-style mansion in Dutchess

County, New York, was surrounded by green meadows, woods, a private lake, and its own golf course, featuring both the longest and the shortest holes in golfing annals—one of Lowell's quirks was to always reach for the out of the ordinary. A red barn had been converted into a working office and broadcast studio. Theirs was an idyllic and peaceful place, embellished by Fran's spacious rose garden; tending it with her own hands was one of her fondest avocations—it brought forth a registered hybrid yellow rose known as the "Lowell Thomas." Its floral beauty was equalled by its fragrance, as I can attest after growing some in our own garden at a later time in my life.

Some time around the spring of 1950, Lowell had haphazardly dropped in on Hazard Reeves, an old friend of his, just to say hello and find out what was new in New York's cinema circles. Reeves was a recognized electronics genius and authority on sound reproduction. He told Thomas that he had developed a stereophonic sound system way ahead of its time; it engulfed an audience seated in a theater with sound coming from every direction. Reeves then took Lowell on a surprise visit to Fred Waller, who was considered a wizard in the field of cinematography and film projection. Waller had been working for years on a three-eyed movie camera whose images, when projected on a specially designed screen, would envelop an audience and create the sensation of being right in the center of the action. Reeves's and Waller's advances in film technology were combined into one package spelled Cinerama.

With his instinct for showmanship, Lowell was so impressed by a demonstration reel of this process that he locked into it instantly and formed a partnership and corporation with the two gentlemen to produce a feature-length film to be shown in select theaters. A considerable investment was needed to convert theaters to Cinerama specifications. First, it required an intricately designed wall-to-wall curved screen with a series of vertical louvered strips of fabric to eliminate reflections. A concrete base at floor level was necessary to anchor the three projectors, whose light beams crossed each other to project three separate filmstrips and filled the screen with a 160-degree image. In addition, a stereophonic sound system had to be installed, with four speakers mounted behind the screen, two on each opposite wall, and one in the rear of the theater.

An audience of political dignitaries, socialites, press critics, and glitterati filled the Broadway Theater in New York, to capacity on September 30, 1952. Unostentatiously, the first Cinerama show opened with Lowell Thomas's casual remarks in a short prologue shown on the conventional screen. Then the curtains slowly drew back to reveal the huge wall-to-wall curved screen, nearly reaching the ceiling, and with a whomp and a shriek, the audience found itself hurtled into a vertiginous roller-coaster ride while sitting in their theater seats. To some, the illusion was so frightening that they were nauseated. It was what one could rightly call a smash opening, followed by lyrical images of the world's scenic attractions, a stunning operatic sequence shot at La Scala in Milan, showing on a grand scale the triumphant victory march in Giuseppe Verdi's *Aida*. The final topper was a flight across America by stunt pilot Paul Mantz in his converted B-25 plane, especially equipped to accommodate the 850-pound Cinerama camera. Skimming rooftops over cities, vast stretches of farm land, across the Rocky Mountains, and dipping down into the Grand Canyon, it was a flight never experienced before by an audience. With a musical score that included "America the Beautiful" and "God Bless America," the film soared to a stirring finale. The critics of all major newspapers and magazines were unanimously impressed and effusive in their accolades. Cinerama was a hit.

This Is Cinerama was followed by *Cinerama Holiday*, with Louis De Rochemont, a former *March of Time* producer, at the helm. This second film did well, though not as strikingly well as Thomas's initial presentation. Next came *Seven Wonders of the World*, produced by Lowell, which, as the title implies, covered the world with panache and great showmanship, although it did not have the surprising box office impact of the first Cinerama offering.

With the financial success of Cinerama, the original group of Thomas, Reeves, and Waller parted company amicably and sold out, everyone having made a bundle. Cinerama, Inc., changed hands a few times and wound up with Stanley Warner as its sole owner. The Warner company had added to its lucrative business of ladies' brassiere manufacturing two businesses it hoped would be even more lucrative: theater ownership and film exhibition. Cinerama was its prize possession. As an independent producer, Lowell Thomas made a deal with Stanley Warner to finance and exhibit his next show; he had not for one moment lost faith in Cinerama's potential. It was at this juncture that he invited me to come aboard as director of his next film. I was honored to have been singled out for the assignment.

SEARCH FOR SHRANGRI-LA

At Lowell's invitation, I flew to New York to meet him and then to drive together to his home near Pawling. As we drove, we talked about preliminary requirements for the film and, in particular, the necessity of having a story line to follow—hopefully before we began shooting in some distant land. One event and date was definite: the coronation of King Mahendra was to take place in May 1956 at Katmandu, the capital of Nepal. Lowell thought it quite possibly could be the last of such spectacles, considering the deterioration of political relations among nations in that part of the world. The event would compare favorably with India's fabulous durbars during the period of the British Raj, promising a surfeit of pomp and pageantry. There would be a parade of painted elephants carrying brocaded howdahs filled with dignitaries from many countries, Croesus-rich maharajahs, and nobles from neighboring feudal states, all resplendent in uniforms or colorful native garb. Lowell expected the extravaganza to be a high point of our film.

Fran and Lowell's beautifully appointed home was the perfect environment in which to develop further ideas for our film. We both agreed that a personal story should be woven into the film, rather than making it an outright travelogue that, beautiful and spectacular as it might be, could limit the size of the audience.

Lowell told me that President Eisenhower had appointed him and Dr. Charles "Chuck" Mayo, head of the famous Mayo Clinic, to represent him at King Mahendra's coronation. This would give us a valuable entrée to many places and festive events. Lowell also informed me that through his personal connections with the air force brass in Washington, D. C., he had been granted the use of a Globemaster, the largest transport plane at the time, engineered to fly long distances without refueling. The plane would be capable of accommodating our crew of some thirty technicians and staff and the tons of equipment required for a Cinerama shoot.

Officially, the plane and its flight crew of twelve were undertaking a routine long-range training flight. Just by chance, since we were headed in the same direction, they offered to give us a ride in their airplane, what with all the empty space to spare. It would take us across the Atlantic, southern Europe, the Middle East, and on to India, where we would switch over to a commercial airline to Katmandu. After we finished shooting, the Globemaster would pick us up again in New Delhi. This lucky windfall saved us a sizable amount of money in plane fares and cargo charges, but troubled Lowell. He felt obliged to include the Air Force in the film in some way to appease his conscience and to justify the complimentary use of the Globemaster. I assured him that one of us would come up with an idea to solve this problem.

After a few days of walking through the woods by myself and ruminating, I was struck by a possible story line. I told Lowell my idea for a possible scenario. Let's assume, I began, that when he embarks on the Globemaster for the journey to Nepal, he meets two or three Air Force pilots not belonging to the crew. They are on a month's furlough and have hitched a ride to India. One of them is a captain, an iconoclastic introvert, seeking the secret of a fulfilled spiritual life. Another one, a sergeant, is his regular crew chief, who decided to come along on his captain's odyssey, having nothing better to do. Both are single, with the captain just having come through a painful dissolution of his marriage. The sergeant is all for variety in his pursuit of female company and Lucullan pleasures. A third one could be an avid white-water kayaker, anxious to fulfill his dream of running some of the turbulent rivers in this part of the world—a sequence which, if we wished to shoot it, would be reminiscent of the roller-coaster ride in the first Cinerama show. But, I added, our main story line should concern itself with our captain and his sidekick sergeant in a sort of Don Quixote and Sancho Panza relationship.

I continued by saying Lowell could invite all three to join the Cinerama crew for the coronation at Katmandu. From then on, we could follow them in their adventures through various countries and situations they encounter. One is looking for spiritual solace and enlightenment and the other for the cushiest and most comfortable lifestyle possible at a minimal expense. That would give us the opportunity to play them against each other. I could already visualize some very funny scenes and conversations between the two. It would be, in fact, a "search movie," perfectly suited for Cinerama. Why not call it *Search for Shangri-la*, that out-of-this-world mythical place in Hilton's book, *Lost Horizon*?

I then proposed a stirring finale. At the termination of their furlough, both men would decide to go back to their Air Force jobs, maybe as part of the Thunderbirds air force demonstration team. They realize that, after all, this is their Shangri-la, high up in the sky, zooming, diving, and pirouetting in their jets at top speed. I could see the mind-bending aerial acrobatics of these fly-boys in precision formations, shot from Paul Mantz's B-25.

Lowell thought it was an excellent springboard for a film and at the same time a gesture of thanks and appreciation to the Air Force. With this seed planted in Lowell's mind, I left for home, looking forward to spending the Christmas holidays with my family. I thought it would be a wonderful surprise to take them all to Sun Valley, which we did and enjoyed immensely. I had hoped that in the interim, Lowell would arrange to have a writer assigned to the project, to develop the story's continuity. But when I returned to Pawling in February, nothing had been done in this respect, and I became alarmed. Lowell was quite cheerful, as was his nature, and full of enthusiasm. "Don't fret, Otto," he said. "We'll find a writer for you, but first let's get this coronation at Katmandu out of the way."

While in New York, I also was indoctrinated into the Cinerama process, its capabilities and drawbacks. Lack of mobility, on account of the camera's weight, was one thing, and moving it around required a four-wheeled metal cart, almost as heavy as the camera itself, used to shift torpedoes around aboard navy vessels. Keeping everything clean and in line with three separate films running through three synchronized cameras was another factor. Harry Squire, the head cameraman, a grizzled grey-haired veteran in good physical shape, had the look of a weathered, blue-eyed New England sailing ship's captain. He was kind, composed, and patient, never using a swear word and reading his obligatory Bible chapter every evening. As a cinematographer, he was superb. He knew everything there was to know about the process and had meticulously trained his own assistants. All of us got along well, with rarely an argument. As I would find out later, Harry's and my eyes were similarly attuned to the best composition of a given tableau, be it with people or scenic shots.

Casting the three characters for the film was easily done. Lowell preferred nonprofessional actors, especially since the rigors of shooting on location would be considerable and every crew member might have to help out physically. For the role of the captain, we chose Chris Young, a dedicated skier with no acting experience but some background in documentary filmmaking. He fit my concept of the character remarkably well; he was gaunt of face and relaxed in attitude. For the sergeant, we felt that Jim Parker would be the perfect choice. Jim was a dear and droll fellow, a natural mimic with a delightful sense of humor. I knew Jim well and liked him very much. He had been an instructor in my ski school at Mount Rainier, and a good one. Steve Bradley, a friend of Lowell's, whom I didn't know, was to take the part of the kayaker and be our white-water river expert. All three were good skiers, so naturally I speculated that somehow, somewhere we might be able to include a skiing sequence in a faraway land. I asked them to bring their skis along, just in case.

NEPAL

Arriving at Katmandu, we found it to be a beehive of activity, with only a few days left before the coronation ceremony. We were shown to our quarters in a building that normally served as a school but had been converted temporarily into makeshift bedrooms, a living room, and office space. Our meals were prepared by a professional caterer, imported from India and hired through our local intermediary, and were of surprisingly good quality. The compound, known as "Cinerama City," was the hub and central staging area for our activities.

Katmandu, with its narrow streets, barely wide enough to let an elephant pass through, was a sight to behold . A profusion of peoples of fascinating ethnic origins had traveled for hundreds of miles on foot from villages in the foothills of the Himalayas, Bhutan, Sikkim, Pakistan, and India to attend these rare ceremonies. King Mahendra was revered as a divine being. The timing of the coronation would be calculated to the second by the official court astrologers and high priests, who had studied the signs and observed the configuration of heavenly stars.

The first day of our filming at Katmandu began with the king, accompanied by his consort, riding on top of the largest elephant I had ever seen. It was lavishly decorated and both its heavy tusks had been shortened to half their original length. The procession came to a halt at the gate of a temple, one of the most sacred shrines, dedicated to Hanuman, the monkey god. Traditionally, the coronation ceremonies were performed in its courtyard, and we had set up our camera close to the entrance. As the king's elephant stopped and ponderously lowered its bulk into a kneeling position, we watched the royal couple descend a short ladder propped up by a mahout against the howdah and enter the courtyard. They were followed by a parade of elephants depositing the monarch's courtiers and high-ranking military and foreign dignitaries, all dazzlingly attired. It reminded me of a Hollywood gala affair with stars stepping out of their luxury limousines. This arrival scene set the tone for the whole sequence to be shot in Nepal, conjuring up a make-believe fairy-tale land. It was an impressive tableau, exotic and ready-made for the three-eyed Cinerama camera, which would fill the curved screen with crowds of spectators squeezed together like sheep in a corral.

Inside the courtyard we had fought for and secured the most favorable camera position to capture the lengthy religious rites. While waiting for the action to start, we stole a few cutaway shots and close-ups of dignitaries and invited guests seated in galleries surrounding the courtyard. These short glimpses of different faces would enable the film editor to compact and shorten the religious formalities. At precisely the exact moment, the astrologers and high priests peering at the celestial constellations gave the signal to commence. The king was crowned. We had a ringside seat to the whole show.

With the jubilant assemblage milling around and lingering in the courtyard, we hustled to a parked jeep we had rented. With our camera mounted on the jeep, we would precede the coronation procession through the narrow streets of the town out into open country and eventually ending at the royal palace. This triumphal march would give the populace the spectacle they had been waiting for. All went well as the royal cavalcade moved along, with us keeping a proper distance in front of the king's elephant. Then suddenly, without warning and in one of the narrowest streets in town, with only a few inches to spare on either side, our jeep conked out. It would not budge in spite of the frantic efforts of the driver to restart the engine. In the meantime, the royal elephant was inexorably closing in on us. I shouted to the driver to keep the jeep in neutral gear and to the assistant cameraman, I said, "Mike, let's you and me jump out and push the sucker until we hit a spot to pull out and let the parade pass." Like trained commandos, we bolted over the side and began to push, while Harry kept the camera rolling until, out of breath and drenched in sweat, we found a place to pull aside, in a perfect position for our camera, to let the whole parade pass by in front of us. And then who should come along but Lowell Thomas and Dr. Mayo in their diplomatic cutaways and top hats, standing high atop an elephant, waving to the populace.

I restaged a vintage automobile being transported on a wooden platform borne on the shoulders of hundreds of men from the low plain of India over rocky mountain trails to the plateau of Katmandu. Not so long ago, with no drivable access roads, this was the only way to bring an automobile into Nepal. We also shot a scene in the royal palace garden where the British ambassador was to receive a decoration of the highest order and to give an honorary sword to King Mahendra. A detachment of immaculate Gurkha soldiers stood by as a guard of honor, with their captain in command, sword in hand. We had rehearsed the scene carefully before the ceremony began. The camera would roll on the smooth lawn from a longer shot, passing the Gurkha complement with the captain standing in front, closing in on a tighter shot of the principals. Plain and simple to execute, it seemed, but when we started to roll our camera, the captain inadvertently moved half a step closer to our path. There was no way of stopping the moving camera once we started, since we would lose the shot, nor could I motion to him to move back, since he was facing away from us toward the ceremony in progress. I just hoped that we could pass by him without a collision.

We almost made it. The cart with the heavy camera and operator standing on it rolled over the toes of his left foot. As I turned around to apologize, I noticed he winced in pain and shot me an angry look, spitting out some words in Nepalese between his clenched teeth. When I asked one of our Nepalese cart pushers what he had said, it was translated verbatim: "As soon as this ceremony is over, I'll catch up with this bastard . . . and kill him!" Meaning me! Luckily, as I was informed subsequently, only the captain's left big toe was bruised. The velvet soft lawn had cushioned his toes as the cart rolled over them.

In keeping with the traditional Nepalese belief that their king descended from a god, King Mahendra always wore dark glasses and never smiled when he could be seen by the populace. It so happened that during a reception at the royal palace, I found myself amiably conversing with him—he smiling, and without his dark shades.

During his stay at Katmandu, Lowell hoped to convince the Chinese delegation to give him permission to take the Cinerama camera and crew to Lhasa in Tibet. It would have been a major coup, since in 1950 Tibet had been overrun and brutally annexed by Mao Tse-tung. With the Dalai Lama's perilous flight to exile in India, Tibet had been cut off completely from the outside world. As was to be expected, Lowell never even got to first base with the Chinese delegation. So he decided to fly ahead of us to New Delhi to meet with Prime Minister Jawaharlal Nehru and to inveigle him to let us go to Leh in Ladakh, another hard-to-reach Buddhist outpost, thinking that, in a way, perhaps the isolated location was even better suited for our captain's search for "the light of spiritual transcendence." Here, again, a very critical political standoff between Pakistan and India torpedoed this attempt, as Prime Minister Nehru would not assume responsibility for our safety. That left us with two other alternatives: Burma, or the island of Ceylon, now better known as Sri Lanka. Because of transportation difficulties into Burma and supply logistics, we opted for Ceylon, since it posed the fewest problems at the time.

While Lowell was pursuing his diplomatic mission, the rest of us stayed on at Katmandu for another ten days to film in the photogenic rural countryside and smaller towns. Also, still without a writer, I had to fabricate some comedy situations involving our roaming sergeant to be fitted somehow into our nebulous story line. Comedy, though never easy, was relatively easy to do with Jim, due to his natural talent as a comic. Some of the gags, as he cabled after seeing our first shipment of rushes upon his return to New York, Lowell found very funny. He urged me to come up with more of this kind of footage.

KASHMIR

We caught up with Lowell in Kashmir, the fabled vale, with its Shalimar Gardens, romanticized in poetry and songs. It was a place pretty close to paradise on earth, in many people's minds. Since Lowell would be with us for only a few more days, with pressing business and broadcasting duties requiring his return to New York, we had to work him into as many sequences as possible before he left.

All of us in the crew enjoyed immensely working in Srinagar, the capital of Kashmir. We lived in a fine hotel where the food was good and the people were friendly, cooperative, and artistic. It was the kind of place our fictional sergeant would have relished. He could live happily in luxury on an ornate, fully furnished wooden houseboat with a flock of servants, including a cook. Merchants in their floating dugout canoes would bring victuals, vegetables, fruit, flowers, and sundries right to his floating doorstep on Dal Lake. Every boat had its name painted on a wooden shield, and the sergeant's was aptly named *Buckingham Palace*. Without doubt it was the largest and most luxurious of the fleet. In such a setting, Jimmy really acted it up in style and loved it, with rent and living expenses prepaid, courtesy of Cinerama, Inc.

I had plans to shoot a skiing sequence high up in the mountains at Gulmarg, an established mountain station for summer tourists conveniently reached from Srinagar. The information given to me regarding snow conditions was encouraging, even though it was already late spring. After Lowell had gone, we organized our expedition, loading up a dozen or so sturdy packhorses. Small as they were, their resilience and endurance were remarkable in such rugged terrain and high altitude, which had a distinctly deleterious effect on us.

My intention was to include the trek as part of our much anticipated skiing episode. We made a number of brief stops to show the progress of our caravan climbing the rocky and winding footpath, filmed against the backdrop of snow-covered mountains. During one of our halts, I noticed another, smaller, film unit following us. Wherever we stopped, they also stopped to set up their camera in the exact spot and take the identical shot. After we reached the wide-open plateau at Gulmarg, where we planned to spend the night in individual pup tents, the other unit also took time out for a rest a respectable distance from us. We handed out the lunch boxes and munched on our sandwiches, occasionally looking at what was going on in the other camp and wondering who they were. My curiosity drove me to wander over casually and introduce myself. There was a considerable language problem since they were a Russian documentary film unit from Moscow, as their leader and director told me after introducing himself. His name, Roman Karman, rang a distant bell as one of his country's top documentary filmmakers.

Seeing that their lunches were rather skimpy compared to ours, I invited them to come over and share our bounty of sandwiches, of which we had a surplus. In no time at all, and in spite of communication difficulties, we established a friendly rapport. Politics and the strained diplomatic relations between our two governments did not enter into our conversation. Of course, what intrigued them most was our monster Cinerama camera. I saw no reason to hide it from them, assuming that they already had detailed drawings and specifications for this camera—if they didn't, they wouldn't be Russians with their widespread network of spies in the United States. However, for them to be able to touch it and look through the viewfinder was an unexpected treat. After lunch and much shoulder slapping, handshaking, and calling-card exchanging, the Russians went their way and we began to set up our tents for the night.

Months later, back in Hollywood, I was interviewed by Hedda Hopper, the powerful movie and gossip maven. She wanted to interview me about our adventures while filming *Search for Shangri-la*. I thought our Russian encounter high up in the mountains of Central Asia might be of interest to her. Not so at all, and did it ever backfire! To her way of thinking, I must be a pinko Russian sympathizer and card-carrying communist to have enjoyed a friendly rapport with the "enemy." The interview came to an abrupt ice-cold ending, with Hedda Hopper excusing herself as being late for another appointment, leaving me with egg splattered on my face and the lunch tab to pick up. Neither Cinerama nor my name made it into her column.

Back at Gulmarg, early the next morning at daybreak, before anyone was even awake, I was on my way with my skis slung over my shoulder to explore a long, wide couloir filled with snow, which looked good to me and accessible enough to take our camera partway up. To my surprise, a young boy appeared seemingly out of nowhere, dressed in the native garb of a flimsy cotton shirt down to his ankles, a knitted skullcap, and no footwear. He insisted on carrying my skis, guessing where I was headed. Of course, it was utterly ridiculous to me to have this skinny lad carry my skis. But he followed me doggedly, nagging me and hoping to earn some money by rendering me this service. I gave in as I began to breathe harder and let him carry one of my skis. Whereupon, he sprinted ahead of me and led the way skipping from rock to rock, picking the best route along a ridge not covered with snow. Even after we reached some frozen patches of snow, he just kept on walking, sure-footed as a mountain goat. When I shook my head in disbelief pointing at his bare feet, he just gave me a beguiling smile, as though saying "not to worry," it was nothing and he did it all the time.

After a few hours of steady climbing, the sun came out full force and began to transform the hard snow surface into the thin buttery layer of crystals prized by skiing connoisseurs as ideal spring snow. As I began my descent, crossing the couloir from side to side, with turns linking into each other almost automatically, without any physical effort, I felt as though I were floating down the mountainside in weightless liberation. This was it, a perfect slope for our skiing sequence. By the time I had arrived at the end of the snow line, taken off my skis, and walked the rest of the way down to our camp, I realized that an audience had gathered.

Among them was a gentleman in military uniform. He stepped forward and introduced himself in fluent English as the commandant of the troops billeted at Gulmarg to guard the border between Pakistan and India. He had been apprised by one of his soldiers that a man with skis, accompanied by a native boy, was climbing up this mountain couloir, which was considered a restricted zone of strategic importance and off-limits. As he told me, he had observed every one of my moves through his high-powered binoculars and, since I carried no camera nor seemed to make any notes about the terrain, he would not make an issue of it. But, he said in a stern voice, "Sir, if you entertain any thoughts to film skiers coming down this couloir, I cannot give you permission to do so." Naturally, I was downcast at seeing my plans shattered. "But let me tell you," he continued, "I so much admired your skiing performance that I wish you could stay and give me and the troops a few lessons in skiing your way. As a small token of my admiration, permit me to give to you this souvenir from one skier to another." He handed me his swagger stick with a round silver knob and his regimental insignia engraved on it. I was touched and thanked him for his kind gesture.

A piece of still-unfinished business remained to be attended to, which was to take care of my ski bearer. I handed him enough baksheesh to buy himself a pair of shoes and some warm clothing. I shall always remember his radiant smile of gratitude.

We broke camp that same day and returned to Srinagar to map out our next move.

SHOOTING THE INDUS RIVER RAPIDS

From the beginning I was apprehensive about the white-water segment of our movie. Before leaving the States I had spent considerable time looking at 16 mm films of well-known practitioners of this sport running the Colorado River through the Grand Canyon in Arizona and other rivers of similar ferocity in Utah, Idaho, and Wyoming. As I became fully aware of the dangers, I was convinced we should not attempt this feat except under the guidance of experienced river runners. Neither I nor anyone in our crew had this kind of experience.

Steve Bradley and Colonel Ata Ullah, who was retired from the Pakistani army and whom we had hired to be our liaison in Pakistan, had completed their scouting trip of the Indus River and were waiting for us at Rawalpindi, Pakistan, which would be our base of operation. They had drawn up a map of the section they felt would lend itself best to our purpose. Of course, they had seen it only from the banks of the river, not from a boat. No one else had rafted the Indus before, which cuts through a narrow valley between the Himalayan and Karakoram mountain ranges. Ours would be the maiden voyage, starting at some point upriver from the hamlet of Skardu and ending some miles below it.

The first thing I wanted to see was the type and size of rubber raft that had been sent to us from New York. Since a large outdoor swimming pool adjoined our hotel, I suggested we inflate the raft. It is hard to describe the shock I felt when I saw what had been sent to us. The camera alone took up most of the space. When fully loaded, the raft was so wobbly that I would not permit anyone to even try to row it across the pool. To take this kind of toy raft on the Indus would be suicidal. I decided to scrub the mission until we were adequately equipped and in the hands of skilled white-water men.

I shot off a cable and letter to Lowell in New York:

AFTER THOROUGH DISCUSSION WITH BRADLEY, COL. ATA
ULLAH AND KEY PERSONNEL, PLUS PRACTICAL EXPERIMENT-
ING WITH OUR RAFT IN LARGE SWIMMING POOL, OPINION
UNANIMOUS STOP IT WOULD BE POSITIVELY RECKLESS
ATTEMPTING INDUS RAPIDS SEQUENCE WITHOUT EXPERI-
ENCED RIVER MEN AND ADEQUATE RAFT SENT TO US STOP THE
RAFT HERE CANNOT SUPPORT CINERAMA EQUIPMENT AND
MANPOWER REQUIRED TO HANDLE BOAT STOP THEREFORE
HAVE DECIDED TO POSTPONE SHOOTING INDUS SEGMENT
AND ORGANIZE HUNZA EXPEDITION FIRST STOP SUGGEST
DISPATCHING IMMEDIATELY TWO TOPNOTCH EXPERTS SUCH
AS BUS AND DON HATCH WITH TWO OF THEIR LARGEST AND
MOST RUGGED ASSAULT TYPE RAFTS STOP THIS OUR ONLY
CHANCE OF SUCCEEDING WITH A REASONABLE MARGIN OF
SAFETY FOR CREW AND EQUIPMENT STOP SINCE BRADLEY
PREFERS TO BOW OUT AND RETURN HOME SEE NO POINT IN
INTRODUCING HIM AS THE THIRD CHARACTER STOP LETTER
FOLLOWS STOP

Gilgit, Pakistan
June 12, 1956

Dear Lowell:

We arrived yesterday morning in Gilgit, the starting point for our
Hunza expedition.

Mr. Mohammed Kiani, the political agent (governor) of the Hunza
District, received us in a most congenial and hospitable way. He is an
intelligent, handsome, and tall man, with great charm and worldliness.

Considering the fast change in our plans we had to make on account
of the "raft fiasco," we were most fortunate in getting reorganized so
quickly for our Hunza trek and to have moved from Rawalpindi to Gilgit
our entire crew and all of our equipment (now at last pared down to a
manageable amount) in two flights, within one day.

Planes have waited often from one to eight days and even two weeks
to get in and out of this isolated place on account of weather conditions
and flying so close between towering mountain ranges and a makeshift
airfield with a short runway to land on. The flight route was spectacular

and I doubt whether it can be equaled in any other part of the world, except perhaps the Andes and the Himalayas, of course.

One of our planes had to return to Pindi, with only one engine running. Apparently, an alarm signal indicated that the other engine might possibly be on fire. Fortunately, this proved not to be so. The plane took off again an hour later and everybody arrived safely in Gilgit.

Great concern regarding military security hereabouts, in photographing restricted areas (airports, bridges, and approaches to river crossings). In spite of it, everybody is extremely cooperative and rather broad-minded in understanding our problems.

Of course, Col. Ata Ullah is tops as you predicted. Knowledgeable, experienced, aggressive, respected, and enthusiastic about the job at hand. It would be certainly a different story and struggle to get things moving without him.

We are starting our journey to Baltit (the residence of the "Mir" of Hunza) on foot, followed by a caravan of horses, some to be ridden by crew members and others packed to the limit with all our paraphernalia. I am figuring on three days of walking and two nights camping out, with a number of photographic stops en route to capture the precarious narrowness of the footpath, often clinging to vertical rock walls, with the Hunza River rushing by some 400 feet below. The trek alone will be a thriller on the screen, rest assured.

I shan't go into the details of the Indus River sequence, as I assume that Bradley will have briefed you on all the problems facing us in this respect.

I have rarely seen a man more relieved, when I called the whole thing off. It was obvious to me that he did not have a particular affinity nor desire to negotiate the formidable Indus River gorges in a foldboat.

Steve seemed to be skeptical and believed that even with the type of equipment and manpower I requested, it would be extremely hazardous, if not impossible, to do this sequence.

I do not share his opinion and am willing to try this stunt, given at least a 50/50 chance as far as the safety of the crew and equipment is concerned.

We have a good deal of work to be done here and it is the kind of work that is slow and requires much patience, but we will push ahead as rapidly as possible, since I have no interest in procrastinating this assignment any longer than necessary, in the best interest of the finished product, by which you and I will be judged.

Everyone is in good health and fairly good spirits. As you well know from your own experiences as an expedition leader, there are times of stress and strain among any group of people thrown together at random for such an extensive and strenuous trip, living in close quarters.

Albeit there is no reason to be worried or to complain.

You stay well!

Best wishes,

OL

Perhaps Hunza was the kind of the place James Hilton imagined when he created Shangri-la in his book. On first sight, I wondered what we were going to photograph, other than its extraordinary remoteness on the border with China's Sinkiang province and scenic beauty, to make it look like an inviting retreat. Then I began to dig deeper and discover what made this mountain-locked territory such a legend. The population is relatively small, and ethnologists, doctors, and nutritionists have been puzzled as to why so many of them exceed the hundred-year mark in longevity, with a few even claiming to be 120 years old. I met some of these centenarians, and they looked remarkably fit for their age.

From what I observed during our short visit, I thought there might be a simple explanation. High altitude and climate have a lot to do with it. They are Moslems of the Ismaili sect, and the Koran itself dictates certain restrictions that are very conducive to a prolonged life. Their diet is frugal to the point of monotony. They rarely eat meat of any kind, and when they do, it would be an occasional chicken or lamb, prepared in a curry stew with rice or barley as a side dish. No beef or pork. Their bread (*chapati*), which is made of unleavened wheat flour and resembles pita bread, is healthy, tasty, and full of natural vitamins. They eat a lot of home-grown vegetables and fruits, especially apricots, which seem to thrive in this climate. These are sun-dried on the flat roofs of their houses to be consumed year-round. Even the apricot pits when shelled are considered a healthy byproduct, providing supplementary vitamins.

Smoking is marginal, and I remember seeing only pipes. Alcohol is nonexistent. There are no roads, footpaths connect the houses, and often there are many steps to climb. Virtually all traffic moves on foot with the exception of the more affluent landlords, who own horses. These ponies are mostly used for their wild polo games, which are played in a rather small rectangle, enclosed by a shoulder-high stone wall, with the spectators seated on embankments and the local band wailing, shrieking, and booming tom-tom drumming, inciting the polo players to give their best. Other than an occasional ceremonial sword dance for special celebrations, this is quite possibly the only form of entertainment offered to the public, and the rivalry between teams is fierce.

The *mir*, or ruler, of this small autonomous state under the jurisdiction of Pakistan lived with his wife, the rani, and family in an attractive but relatively small house, very much in the style of a modest villa in the Austrian or Swiss Alps. He and his family were part of the people and cared for each other. He was looked upon as the paterfamilias and benevolent autocrat. He was their judge and dispenser of justice, with homicide and major crimes virtually unknown. Most of the complaints, presented at weekly sessions in an open courtyard adjoining the *mir's* residence, would deal with infringement of water rights, grazing privileges, property disputes, and other mundane matters. Occasionally, a case of petty theft might be on the docket. His verdict was final, never questioned, and always adhered to.

Since the courtyard looked so bleak and unphotogenic, I had to dress it up with a few artistic touches. I attached huge horns of ibex and Marco Polo mountain sheep to the wooden posts encircling the *mir's* podium. I placed his ornately carved chair on finely woven Pakistani carpets. I also covered the hard-beaten clay surface of the courtyard with carpets. The spectators, in their best native attire, were seated in the round. With the judicial proceedings followed by a choreographed sword dance, the scene was quite picturesque after all, with some panoply and less pomp. I requisitioned a red flyer wagon belonging to the young son of the English teacher hired by the *mir* to teach his son and daughters how to speak and write English. With his permission I mounted our camera on it and used it for a traveling shot. Slightly wobbly and bumpy as it was, it still gave us a Hollywood production touch.

I truly enjoyed my visit with the *mir* of Hunza, his family, and all the Hunza people I came in contact with. Altogether, it was a grand, memorable, and thoroughly worthwhile journey, which I knew would enhance our film immensely. Upon our return to Rawalpindi, I decided this would be a good opportunity to give our entire crew a few days of rest and relaxation. We had been working steadily and traveling for weeks without any rest days.

Lowell had engaged Bus and Don Hatch, a father-and-son team from Vernal, Utah, and they were waiting for us in Rawalpindi. The Hatches were two of the best, most experienced river guides, who knew every gaping hole and jagged rock formation along the white-water rivers in America. Bus was fifty-six years old with an athletic build and sun-burnished face that belied his years. Don, lean and wiry, in his twenties, was a schoolteacher, family man, and passionate saxophone player. In his free time, he assisted his father in guiding tours down various rivers. His father had taught him everything he knew, and together they made a formidable team.

Our plan was to get on the next flight to Skardu and make an exploratory run down the stretch of the Indus suggested to us by Steve Bradley and Colonel Ullah. We would use one of the rafts flown in with the Hatches from America. We had no intention of using a camera on the trial run; the primary objective was to size up the problems awaiting us. For three days we made early morning pilgrimages to the airport only to have the once-a-day flight canceled at the last minute, due to dense fog in the mountain passes. On the fourth day, before we had even recovered from the surprise of being airborne at last, we passed seemingly within arm's reach of the utterly forbidding and awesome-looking mountain giants. Soon to our right appeared Nanga Parbat, 26,660 feet high and unbelievably beautiful, sheathed in a thick armor of ice. It deserved its sobriquet "Killer Mountain," based on the toll of lives it had claimed of many intrepid high-mountain climbers.

The political agent at Skardu met us at the airstrip and put his jeep, the only one in town, and his driver at our disposal. He was to take us and our gear as far as the trail was drivable, following the steep bank of the Indus. We stopped the jeep a number of times en route to give Bus and Don an opportunity to survey the rapids. Judging by their remarks and the meaningful looks they exchanged, I knew we were in for quite an adventure. When the jeep trail gave out, Bus selected a spot on the riverbank for our starting point. The tedious process of inflating the raft with a hand pump kept us busy for the better part of the day. Bus also had to build a wooden support structure at the stern, to which the outboard motor would be attached. From another board he made a bench across the raft to which the two oars would be fastened. The bench would also serve as the captain's bridge. When evening came, we were well along with our preparations and weather permitting, planned an early morning start.

The rubber raft to take us down river dated back to World War II. Linked together with others like it, it had served as an anchor boat for pontoon bridges or ship-to-shore landing assaults. Ours was a ten-year-old model, built for rugged service. It was twenty-seven feet long, with a slightly turned-up snout to ride smoothly over waves. In width, it measured seven feet, with an inflated rubber roll of about thirty inches in diameter encircling the entire boat. This made it virtually unsinkable, although there was the distinct possibility of its turning upside down in very rough water. It was designed to carry huge loads and, in fact, proved itself capable of doing so. The skin was made of a strong canvas lining covered on both sides with a heavy layer of neoprene, resulting in one of the most durable and indestructible fabrics ever devised. The raft glided smoothly over jagged rocks. It bent and twisted, following the contours of the water. It could be hauled ashore and dragged over the roughest terrain without showing any signs of damage. It expanded to the size of a small whale when fully inflated and with the air let out and neatly folded, could be stowed in the luggage compartment of any standard automobile.

The next morning, after a hurried breakfast, we checked out the outboard motor and raft, packed our remaining gear into a supposedly watertight compartment and fastened our life jackets. Last minute instructions were given to me as to what to do and what not to do. Above all, I was told to keep a firm grip on my safety line and when the going became rough, to hang onto it. We cast off at 6:45 A.M., and were carried with astonishing rapidity toward the middle of the river. Bus was seated on the captain's bridge facing downstream, manning the oars, while Don was at the controls of the outboard motor. Gliding over the rippling waves was pleasant and exhilarating. In no time at all, we could hear a loud roar as we approached the first rapid. Bus and Don did some quick maneuvering to get the raft lined up into the proper approach, and the boat headed straight toward the tip of the deceptively smooth-flowing tongue of water that led into the heart of the rapid below.

A few tense commands and split second adjustments and then Bus yelled at the top of his voice, "Hang on, Otto!" The raft dropped as though headed into a bottomless chasm and then doubled up and twisted like a pretzel. Torrents of water alternately buffeted and buried the raft with relentless fury. The outboard motor was shrieking and spinning away, trying to get a purchase in the foaming white water. The thought flashed through my mind that this could easily be the end of this short trip! If we capsized, would I be able to fight my way out of this watery inferno before being crushed against the rocks and carried away in the incredibly swift current? But with the same suddenness, the raft shot out from the boiling cauldron into quiet waters. I was in one piece! That was my baptism to river running.

Bus and Don just laughed and ordered me to start bailing water with a bucket attached to the bridge with a rope. This was a welcome diversion since it kept me busy and didn't allow me much time to analyze the situation. What good would it have done anyway? We were in it up to our necks. Besides, watching the way Bus and Don worked our raft inspired utmost confidence. They were real professionals.

I thought the rapid we had just passed through was a whopper, and that surely there couldn't be any worse ahead of us. But there were—not just one, but a succession of them. As my confidence increased, I began to actually enjoy the upheaval of elements, although the pervasive feeling of apprehension at getting through the next rapid safely never ceased.

Bus gave orders to prepare for a landing. The raft had taken on much water and needed our combined efforts in bailing. Also, he wanted to look over the next set of rapids, which he had observed from the jeep trail and marked in his memory. Landing was a matter of precision timing. Bus picked a likely spot ahead of us and maneuvered the raft close to shore, then Don and I jumped simultaneously out of the boat with a line in our hands to pull the boat around and secure it to a nearby rock. What a relief it was to be standing on terra firma again!

Bus and Don studied the configuration of the rapids ahead of us and discussed their plan of attack. This next assault was going to be one of the toughest, they told me, for here was one raging rapid immediately joining forces with another of equal ferocity—and then one more after that. They gave some thought to lining the unmanned raft through the rapids, while walking along the shore, but ultimately decided against it. Their pride simply wouldn't permit it, although it was a fairly frequent procedure on guided tours, when it was a question of safety for inexperienced passengers. Back in the raft we felt the maximum impact of the water unleashed against us. Suddenly I felt myself lifted into the air with such irresistible force that I could barely hold onto my safety line. I was floating in space with the raft pulling away underneath me. The backwash of a wave caught me and tossed me right back into the raft.

We landed again to bail water and to scout the next series of rapids, which turned out to be relatively cooperative. Eventually the river calmed down, broadened, and smoothed out as we came around a bend and saw the ancient fort of Skardu on a high promontory ahead of us. As we walked ashore, a stream of natives came running down the slope. They were clothed in ragged outfits with long strands of matted hair spilling from under woolen pancake-shaped hats. They must have thought we had arrived from another planet and looked at us askance, as creatures with obviously little sense, having chosen this route. They knew their river well, as did their forebears. It was a mean one. It returned nothing. No human body nor animal carcass had ever been retrieved from the Indus in that section of its descent.

We had been underway for about six hours, but it seemed like a span of time that could not be measured in hours and minutes. We opened a tin of sardines and dug out some soggy crackers and cheese to snack on. Eventually, I asked the Hatches what they thought of the Indus. Their response was, "It's as rough and wild as they come." The volume of water carried by the Indus was enormous, reaching depths from thirteen to thirty-two feet, depending upon the season of the year and runoff from glaciers. The speed was constant and relentless, with little chance to get straightened out between rapids, unlike the Colorado River, whose rapids were separated by stretches of calm water. Don said that the deepest hole he had ever fallen into on a river and the biggest wave that had ever hit him were right here on the Indus.

Although I was confident after this exploratory run that our plan was feasible, I concluded that Skardu was not the place for our operational headquarters. It was too inaccessible; furthermore, I felt that this section of the Indus was far too hazardous. Bus and Don concurred. I decided to concentrate our efforts in the Gilgit area, which I had hurriedly scouted after our Hunza trip and had kept in mind as an alternate possibility. Pictorially, it had the further advantage of Nanga Parbat looming in the background.

The question still to be answered was, how would our raft respond when loaded down with our heavy camera equipment and the added weight of six men? I can report that it responded magnificently. In fact, the added load turned out to be an advantage as it settled the raft deeper into the water and made it more stable. In regard to the crew, scaled down to a minimum, I can say that I have never before encountered a more heroic and willing group of coworkers. Their attitude and courage went far beyond the call of duty. We had some hair-raising experiences, and my belief that this stretch of the Indus would be less hazardous than the one at Skardu was erroneous. It was every bit as challenging but easier to reach and to cope with logistically.

On the last day, on our final run before dismantling the raft, tragedy struck us. What promised to be an easy passage turned into a nightmare and disaster. Here is a portion of my report to Lowell Thomas:

On July 20, we prepared to launch the raft early in the morning for our last run on the Indus and then pack up and return to Gilgit.

As usual, there was much activity with last-minute preparations and many people clambering all over the boat prior to our departure. The raft had to be repumped with air to full capacity, motors started and warmed up, the magazines loaded with film, attached to the camera, lenses cleaned, and all of it tightly wrapped under a waterproof light cover for protection against the onrushing water and spray. Also, drinking water and some provisions were taken aboard.

This would be our last sortie on the Indus and everybody was in a happy frame of mind. The selected crew for this ride consisted of:

> Mike Zingale—on camera
> Peter Passas—on camera
> Bus Hatch—captain and oarsman
> Dusty Wallace—motorman
> Otto Lang—motorman
> Jim Parker—utility man

Don Hatch, in his small boat, would precede us, so that we could take a follow shot of him going through the rapids with Nanga Parbat in the frame ahead of him.

Harry Squire, our elderly ace cameraman, who had insisted on being with us in the raft on every previous trip, had come down ill with high fever and was forced to stay in bed, much to his chagrin.

Jack Priestley, his regular camera operator, who had developed an acute phobia toward wild water rafting and was mentally and physically incapable of adjusting himself to it, also begged off from going on this last trip.

Jim Parker, who had been frustrated and so eager to get aboard, finally was given a chance to have his wish fulfilled. Jim had worked so hard all along wherever his help was needed, only to see the raft float away without him aboard. Now, at last, he was to be part of the crew on board.

I had my hands full and mind concentrated on giving instructions to the Hatches on how to coordinate all our moves. As was my habit, I always asked: "Is this OK with you?" and "Is there any question in regard to the crew's safety?"

In this case, we were assured of smooth sailing by the looks of the rapids seen from a distance. So, off we went from a shallow channel formed by a large gravel bank between the shoreline and the middle of the river.

We were moving slowly at first, until we picked up full speed when we hit the main current.

Bus gave the order for me to run my motor in reverse while Dusty Wallace would run his in forward speed. This would give Bus the reserve power to either slow down or speed up at a given command, in guiding the raft with his oar strokes into the desired camera position, while keeping Don in sight going through the rapids.

No sooner had we hit the main current and were approaching the first rapid, when things began to go awry. One of the motors conked out, which had never happened before. Bus's attention was concentrated on watching Don ahead of us, while trying to keep at a desired shooting angle and holding the proper distance between the two boats. There was nothing to be alarmed about, except that I noticed with a certain uneasiness that we were rapidly drifting in sideways toward the center section of the rapid, which suddenly looked much more portentous and threatening than any of us had anticipated. We hadn't been underway for more than a few minutes, when all of a sudden the raft dropped into a deep hole and within split seconds on the rebound was tossed high up in the air like a child's toy by one of the angriest waves I had seen on this river.

All I can remember was seeing the camera high above my head in a torrent of foaming water, before I was pitched out from the raft and sucked under by a swirling spiral of water.

While I was thrashing and fighting to get back above water for a breath of air, I was dizzily spun around and became disoriented as to which way was up. It seemed like an eternity. There was only one thought in my mind—that unless I got to the top and my head above water, it would surely be the end of me.

Suddenly, I burst into the open, retching, gasping for air, and heaving to get rid of the water I had swallowed, when about 15 feet away from me loomed the raft turned upside down with Mike Zingale and Dusty Wallace holding onto a rope. To reach them was the longest 15 feet I ever swam, to hold onto the same piece of rope, as we were still constantly buried by water in this boiling caldron. Gradually, the three of us by swimming with one free arm, maneuvered the overturned raft toward shore, fortunately helped by a back eddy of quieter water.

There was no one else in sight, and we thought that surely we must be the only three survivors.

Suddenly, Jack Priestley appeared from behind the stern of the boat, groggy and half-conscious, as we helped him stagger to shore. Then Bus stumbled forward with blood running down his face from a deep gash on his head. That made five of us safe! What a relief to see at least that many alive, but where were the others? Jim, Don, and Pete Passas?

Next to appear was Don Hatch. He had ridden out the rapids in his small boat without difficulty. As soon as he could, he landed and was on the lookout to help anyone he spotted. Then Pete Passas showed up. He was the one who told us that he caught a last glimpse of Jim before he was carried away by the rushing current. They were tossed out simultaneously off the raft to portside, according to Pete. Both popped up together, with Jim clinging to him, when another wave buried them again and separated them.

Pete, a strong swimmer, had been carried away down river, made it to shore, and walked up to us.

Only now was the tragic and full impact of this catastrophe revealed to me, when I found out that Jim was aboard without a life jacket. What happened was that at the last moment before our departure and without informing me of his change of mind, Jack Priestley had come aboard. He felt compelled, in view of Harry Squire's illness, to overcome his inherent phobia to take Harry's place on this final ride. Neither Pete Passas nor Mike Zingale were asked to go ashore, to conform with our past practice to carry only two men of the camera crew aboard. Furthermore, Priestley had asked Jim to relinquish his life jacket for him to wear, which left Jim unprotected.

Why Jim did not request to be let off the boat and why nobody else in front of the boat (twenty-seven feet long) shouted out that there was a man without a life jacket aboard remains an unfathomable mystery to me, as we had been so cautious and conscientious in this respect up to this last ride.

After we realized that Jim had been swept away by the current, we walked along the river shouting out his name, trying to find some trace of him, to the point where the next rapid started. No human being caught in this one would have survived.

It was all in vain. Jim was surely dead. Shortly thereafter, Col. Ata Ullah drove up in his jeep with Chris Young, and after hearing the tragic news, he immediately organized a search party of some local inhabitants, who knew the terrain well, to continue looking further down the river. Their conjecture was that the only hope of finding Jim alive or his dead body, would be in a large swirling back eddy some miles down river. They stood watch there for a long time with neither a trace nor a clue to follow-up.

Chris Young, on his own, also searched the riverbanks with his field glasses and found some boards and pieces of our equipment floating around in an eddy, with our camera a total loss and no trace of Jim.

Whether a life jacket would have saved him was certainly a matter of serious afterthought, but too late to rectify. Even though Jim was physically extremely fit and an excellent swimmer and athlete, a life jacket would have been immensely helpful to him in fighting his way to shore.

The fact that he vanished so quickly led me to believe that he must have been stunned and incapacitated by being struck on the head with a heavy piece of equipment when it was torn loose from its moorings.

The six of us who emerged alive were mentally badly shaken and distraught but physically unharmed, except for some bruises and minor cuts. Poor old Bus had one hell of a time extricating himself, as he found himself trapped under the raft, entangled in a coil of rope. With a super-human effort, he worked his tangled left leg free from the rope while fighting to catch a breath occasionally from the air trapped between the bottom of the rubber raft and the churning water. He was hurt more than any of us, patched up with bandages, and limping about painfully for days afterward. For a man fifty-six years old, his was an extraordinary feat of strength and willpower to have come out of it alive.

Ironically, Jim was not meant to be part of this river expedition from the very beginning. In order to be extremely mobile, we had whittled the crew to a minimum number. Jim was not to appear in his role in this particular segment and, therefore, I had asked him to stay behind in Rawalpindi with the three members of the sound crew and other dispensable personnel. In the last moment and after Jim begged me to do so, I included him in the river expedition, knowing how willing and helpful he could be, but also telling him in advance that his chances to ride the raft were marginal.

While we were encamped near the river, I asked him to return a jeep to Gilgit and then to take a plane to Rawalpindi and transact some important business matters for me. He left us with a sad look in his eyes. To my great surprise, Jim reappeared the next day at our encampment at Thelechi and informed me that he was able through phone calls and wires to accomplish what I had asked him to do. It seemed as though destiny was inexorably leading him back to the chosen spot of his demise, like a moth attracted by a bright flame and fluttering around it, which could only lead to ultimate destruction.

Jim told me how much he loved this part of the world. He loved the mountains, the Indus River, and the native people. Nanga Parbat became his idol and he couldn't take his eyes off it. He referred to it as "my mountain."

Once at night, when the full moon was out, he asked me to take a look at Nanga Parbat with its silver saddle mysteriously shimmering in the starlit sky.

Only a day before he was struck down so cruelly, we were sitting on a rock and he was talking to me in a reflective mood. He said, "You know, Otto, I love this mountain and countryside so much. I wouldn't mind at all if I spent the rest of my life here."

We were about ready to board the raft. I was changing from my heavy walking boots into a pair of tennis shoes. Jim was all set in pair of shorts without wearing a shirt and excited to be finally going on a ride in the raft.

Casually I asked him upon noticing a nodule on his back, whether he had ever paid any attention to it. "No, I never thought of it," he said.

I suggested that such a swelling could possibly be the cause of potential trouble, thinking of the possibility of a malignant tumor.

"Thanks anyway," he said. "I'll have a doctor look at it when I get back home. Come to think of it, my mother had a similar growth removed from her back and just in the nick of time."

These were the last words I heard Jim say. And the last glimpse of him I caught was fastening his life jacket on the raft.

Jim's body was never recovered. At the Rakhiot Bridge crossing the Indus River at the approach to Nanga Parbat, there is a stone column inscribed with the names of all the mountain climbers who have lost their lives trying to conquer this magnificent "Killer Mountain." The traveler there will also find a bronze plaque with Jim's name on it, which reads:

In Memory of
James Parker
Who lost his life exploring the
rapids of the Indus, within sight
of Nanga Parbat, Jim's favorite
mountain, during the filming of
"Search for Paradise."
July 20, 1956

Reunited again with the members of our crew waiting for us in Rawalpindi, we gathered for a wake in memory of Jim. We reminisced about his jolly disposition, things he had done, words of wisdom he had spoken, and anecdotes of funny situations he was involved in. It helped us to assuage our grief over this tragedy and kept us wondering why it had to be he, plucked from life in this untimely way.

Also, the torturous questions kept nagging me: What went wrong? Why had it happened? Could it have been avoided? And if so, how? Was it a case of gross negligence or a case of multiple human errors in judgment? There is no clear-cut answer to any of these questions, and very often the contributing factors overlap and touch ever so closely to an indefinable borderline, that a verdict as to where the guilt lies is impossible to determine.

A cable from Lowell awaited me at the Flashman Hotel:

DEEPLY SADDENED AND SHOCKED BY JIM'S TRAGIC DEATH AND FULLY SHARE YOUR GRIEF STOP WILL GET IN TOUCH WITH HIS MOTHER AND BROTHER STOP SUGGEST ALL OF YOU RETURN HOME EARLIEST POSSIBLE WITH GLOBEMASTER STOP IF ANY MEMBER OF CREW IN DISTRESS SEND HOME BY COMMERCIAL AIRLINER STOP UPON YOUR RETURN ALL OF US TOGETHER CAN FORMULATE PLANS TO COMPLETE PICTURE STOP

We had a lengthy meeting to decide whether all or any one among us wished to go back. To my great satisfaction, the unanimous decision was to stay and get on with the job at hand, using our backup camera and equipment to complete the filming. Don Hatch, who had contracted a mild case of typhoid, was under medical care. He and his father would leave for home as soon as Don was well enough to travel, with their mission accomplished. Our plan was to fly to Ceylon with a short stopover in New Delhi, as I wanted to include a short sequence of India in our film, especially the Taj Mahal at Agra. I informed Lowell of our decision, which I was sure would please him. Ceylon lived up to all our expectations of a lush and beautiful island. With its many Buddhist shrines, it was ready-made for the captain's search for his mythical paradise.

The routine, after we arrived in a place that not one of us had ever seen before, was for the crew to get settled in their quarters, check out our equipment, and recharge their batteries during a day off. I would hire an automobile with a local driver and qualified guide to cruise around the countryside looking for likely sites to fit our requirements. I enjoyed these solitary location hunts as I could let my imagination roam freely.

The Buddhist monastery at Kandy, a small town in the highlands of the island, was a perfect setup for us. As I circled the premises looking for the best camera angles, I chanced upon a beggar, seated on a straw mat, holding a bowl outstretched to collect alms, completely motionless. He was a striking-looking old man with a flowing white beard and dark brown skin. Since I wore thick rubber-soled boots, he did not actually hear me, but sensed my presence without turning his head. I realized then that he was totally blind. Even though the sky was overcast with only diffused sunlight, not strong enough to cast a shadow, I still felt compelled to take half a dozen exposures with my 35 mm camera on Kodachrome film. I was struck by the composition of this man sitting there as though absorbed in deep meditation. I did not think that this picture would be of any particular importance—except my own personal satisfaction—until some months later that year. I entered one of the slides in *The Saturday Review* World Photography Contest. It was the first time I had ever submitted one of my photographs to such a competition. To my great surprise, it won the grand prize out of close to nine thousand entries from all over the world and also made the cover of the magazine.

I had named the picture *Blind Beggar*, and this is what one of the judges wrote about it:

> . . . We admired the photograph of the "Blind Beggar" . . . for its beautiful flow of composition, its carefully related moving masses, and its grace and extreme naturalness.
>
> The picture held up so remarkably well throughout the judging process mainly because of its thought-provoking quality. It is the sort of picture that needs no text to successfully convey a whole series of ideas.

The prize was an all-expenses paid trip for two to Japan. Having had my fill of traveling for the time being, I suggested they send me the equivalent in cash, which they did. Through the years, I have presented many one-man shows of my photography in museums and galleries in various cities across the United States. My *Blind Beggar* still remains the much-acclaimed pièce de résistance of my collection.

Homeward bound at last, after three hectic months of shooting on widely dispersed locations in central Asia, we were grateful to see the Globemaster parked on the tarmac and waiting for us to board.

SEARCH FOR PARADISE

Arriving home after such a lengthy separation and being reunited with my family was almost like a joyful rebirth for me. We landed at Los Angeles at two o'clock in the morning, and I was met by Sinnie, fortunately with a station wagon large enough to accommodate all the loot I had brought back on the plane. Peter and Mark had given instructions to wake them up, no matter what time it was, the moment we stepped into our house. So we did.

Of course, every present had to be unpacked immediately, and by the time we went through the whole lot, it was six o'clock in the morning. It was as though Santa Claus had arrived in the middle of August. Peter went immediately to work, helped by Mark, to clean up the two sets of horns given to me by the mir of Hunza as a parting gesture. One set was from a Himalayan ibex and the other from a Marco Polo mountain sheep, both of trophy dimensions. It was well worth lugging these huge impediments halfway around the world to see how much they were appreciated.

While we were filming in Hunza, a caravan of a dozen camels and a few yaks had come through from the Sinkiang region in China on their way to Karachi, following the ancient Silk Road. Supposedly Alexander the Great's soldiers followed the same path and halted at Baltit long enough to father some blue-eyed, light-skinned offspring, whose genes are still noticeable in Hunza today. The line of camels arriving at the venerable caravanserai was truly a poetic sight. The traders, in their tattered, grimy, gamy clothes and rakish headgears unpacked and displayed for us some of their wares gathered across China and let us have first pick, at prices so low they were hard to believe. It ended in a veritable buying frenzy by our crew and the *mir's* family.

Most of Sinnie's gifts came from this source, which I supplemented with some of the delicately painted lacquer boxes for which Kashmir was famous, precious unmounted gemstones, and an assortment of elegant saris. To me, that was always the most fun, to look for and bring home specially selected gifts, not always of a practical nature.

By the time the sun rose above the hills, we were a droopy-eyed foursome ready to get some sleep. There was so much to tell each other of what had happened in these past months that there was not a dull moment. The boys looked so healthy and buoyant and Sinnie as pretty as the image of her I always carried with me. Alas, after only two weeks at home, I had to leave again for New York, as we still had a film to finish with no definitive ending set. Lowell was anxiously awaiting me so we could solve this problem together. He still had not come up with a writer, even though he had gallantly tried. He kept reassuring me that between the two of us and Prosper Buranelli, his writer of long standing under a personal contract, we could lick this problem by ourselves. I was not so sure.

"How long will it be this time?" Sinnie asked me with a sigh.

"Oh, no more than three weeks," I tried to comfort her.

"Isn't it fortunate that having grown up as a 'navy brat' I learned to brace myself and accept long separations, but one never gets used to it. Without you being with us, life around here just isn't the way it ought to be. We miss you so much." I could only reassure her by telling her how much I loved her and our two boys and that someday soon there might be a change for the better in this respect in our lives.

The first order of business upon my arrival in New York was to go to Oyster Bay with Lowell and screen hours and hours of the film we had shot. There was an incredible amount of footage, some of it quite beautiful, exotic, and spectacular. The big job now was to blend it all together into a cohesive continuity. We still needed a rousing climax to end the film, with the captain deciding to rejoin his Air Force unit and look upon it as his paradise found. We decided not to include and exploit Jim Parker's tragic demise.

This was now the time to take full advantage of what the Air Force had to offer. For example, we planned to photograph a mass parachute drop at Fort Bragg of eight hundred soldiers with their combat equipment in a scheduled training maneuver. Eight hundred parachutes blossoming like giant white flowers against the blue sky should be quite a spectacle never seen before in a movie.

Next I wanted to recreate visually the impact of the mysterious sonic boom effect, caused when combat planes broke the sound barrier traveling a speeds of Mach 1 or higher, resulting in shattered windows. This was a frequent topic of conversation in those early days of supersonic aircraft. How to present it visually was a challenge that fascinated me. I approached the powers that be at the Eglin Air Force Command in Florida with my scheme. I wanted to set up a large framed pane of glass on an open runway and have a plane break the sound barrier upon approaching it. The impact would surely shatter the glass into hundreds of shards.

The reaction to this idea by the officers in charge was exasperation: "Here we go again! Another one of those dreamers. The people from *Life* magazine just left here, after trying to do this trick. They drove us nuts. We wasted more time with planes breaking the sound barrier just to suit them, but their glass wall never showed a crack, while at every pass a whole bunch of windows in nearby office buildings, residences, and hangars exploded like firecrackers. We had to stop it, as it simply became too dangerous for personnel working around the base."

After thinking about it, I came up with a proposal. Would they allow us to build a small shack on the runway with a solid roof and a large panoramic front window facing the oncoming plane? Our gambit, as I discussed with Harry Squire, was to place one camera inside the shack, activated by a remote switch. A second camera would film the plane as it flew directly over the shack at low altitude, breaking the sound barrier, so that we could hold both the plane and the shack in the film frame. The assembled military brass listened to my naive and unscholarly exposition with a somewhat jaded ear, but as long as it wouldn't cost them anything, they were willing to go along. For them it might provide a comic diversion.

The day came when our neat-looking little hut was ready, with one camera inside and the other at a three-quarter angle outside. The pilot in the air was primed and waiting for the command to begin his run at higher altitude, swoop down, and level off to break the sound barrier. Then came the tense moment with the plane coming at us and I signaled both cameras at the top of my voice, "Roll it!" Just as I had hoped, after the resounding boom came the explosion of splintered glass from the window of the shack. My hunch had worked. The onrushing blast of air against the window, combined with the recoil of the compressed air inside the shack, shattered the window. Cut together, it was quite a startling piece of film. The audience felt as though they were sitting inside the shack, seeing the plane approaching, and then—WHAM!—an explosion of such force as to scatter the shards of glass away from the shack, rather than into the laps of the onlookers. The camera crew and I were proud of this shot, which left its mark not only with stunned audiences in the theater, but also with the doubting military, who had gathered to watch this show concocted by a bunch of amateurs in the highly sophisticated field of supersonics.

All that was left to complete the film was to shoot the very last sequence, featuring the Thunderbird Demonstration Team. As I had visualized from the very beginning, our best chance to get some exciting and unusual footage was to be right up in the air with them, high enough above ground to give them freedom for action and also safety, as they performed their precision aerobatics. That was when my old friend Paul Mantz came into the picture with his converted B-25. Though not the fastest plane and unable to keep up with the Thunderbirds, it was rigged to serve as a camera plane like no other in existence at that time.

After talking it over with Paul and the captain of the flying squadron, we concluded that we in the B-25 would stay on a straight course, conforming to the best direction of sunlight for us, and at a set altitude, while they would swoop by us at top speed and perform their maneuvers before the camera mounted in the nose of the B-25. Then we would reverse the procedure and place the camera at the tail-end mount of the plane to capture the flight formation of four planes coming straight at us and flaring out into one of their patented configurations, passing us as close as safety dictated.

All this footage with its changing angles would be intercut by Harvey Manger, who with his corps of assistants had edited every previous Cinerama film, into a fluid sequence for a skyrocketing grand finale for *Search for Paradise* (the film's title after copyright problems arose with the title *Search for Shangri-la* from the estate of James Hilton). Lowell Thomas, Prosper Buranelli, and I began the all-consuming process of laying out the narration for the sequential continuity of this film. Eventually, it would have to be meticulously timed to the length of each segment and every foot of film.

For Cinerama, with its elaborate sound system, the choice of a composer for the musical score was paramount. My first choice was Bernard Herrmann, with whom I had had a congenial and productive relationship on previous films. Unfortunately, being much in demand despite his reputation as a tempestuous, talented curmudgeon, Herrmann was booked far ahead and not available to us. We decided on Dimitri Tiomkin, "Dimi," as he was addressed collegially, and what a character he was. Aside from his inherent talent and extensive background as a concert pianist and composer, he was also funny and often unreasonably demanding. He had elevated many a film above its mediocrity, and in so doing had collected four Oscars for his invaluable contributions. At one Academy Award ceremony, I was present when he was handed another

Oscar. In his acceptance speech, he humbly admitted that above all, he had to thank for much of his success Messrs. Brahms, Beethoven, Mozart, Tchaikovsky, Rimsky-Korsakov, Borodin, and Berlioz, among others. It brought the house down and endeared him even more to the audience.

I got to know Dimi and his wife very well. Albertina, called "Bettina," was a former Austrian ballet star who had brought her own company to the United States to perform with great success as the "Albertina Rasch Dancers." They were quite a pair, Dimitri and Bettina. He, with his fractured Russo-American accent, temperamental and domineering, and she with her lilting Austrian diction, equally capricious and strong-minded. I spent a lot of time at their home and enjoyed listening to Dimi's composing at his piano, while Bettina was in the kitchen preparing a Viennese dinner. As Dimi told me himself, he was working on a film score, doodling on the piano, searching for a melody, when the kitchen door opened and Bettina stuck out her head and said, "That tune you just played, let me hear it again. I think it is catchy and perfect for this film." The film was *High Noon* and the tune he wrote for its title song was "Don't Forsake Me, Oh My Darling." *High Noon* was the surprise hit of 1952, nominated for a parcel of Oscars right down the line: best picture, best producer (Carl Foreman), best actor (Gary Cooper), best director (Fred Zinnemann), and best song (Tiomkin and Ned Washington, who wrote the lyrics). Gary Cooper and the team of Tiomkin-Washington walked away with an Oscar each, while, as is so often puzzling, Fred Zinnemann was left empty-handed.

So it was that the team of Tiomkin and Washington was commissioned to write the score and lyrics for *Search for Paradise*. By the time winter came along, I was back at Sun Valley. The phone rang, and Sinnie picked it up, listened, and handed it to me, saying, "It's Dimi, for you." Dimi and Ned were on a connected line, excitedly telling me that they wanted to play a song for me they had just finished for our film. It was all about the beauty of Kashmir. They rendered it over the phone with Dimi playing the piano and Ned singing the lyrics he had written. "How do you like it? Isn't it terrific!" they exclaimed in unison after they had finished. What could I say other than to agree with them that it was indeed a great song and my congratulations. I was moved that they would spontaneously phone in a song they had just completed.

By the time I returned to New York at the beginning of summer, all the components were assembled: the film was edited, the narration written and timed to fit, and Dimi's score with a number of calypso-type songs ready to record. Robert Merrill, the renowned baritone of the New York Metropolitan Opera, was to sing the songs, enhanced by a large chorus conducted by Dimi. We ran into a major problem when Dimi suddenly refused to record his score at Oyster Bay because the improvised studio had inferior acoustics. He insisted on recording at Carnegie Hall. I sympathized with Dimi's wanting the best quality possible, and so did Lowell, though the added expense of renting this hall and installing the necessary sound equipment was not included in the budget, which at that point was considerably overextended.

Dimi persisted and won. Late the night before the scheduled recording session, I was awakened out of a deep sleep. Dimi was on the phone, upset, frustrated, and close to tears, saying, "I'm so mad I'm ready to quit. I need to have one more violinist for the orchestra to play an important solo passage and Nat Lapkin categorically refused to pay for it." Lapkin was our exasperated exchequer trying to keep the ship afloat.

"Now, now, Dimi," I said. "Calm down and don't let this anger you. Let me see what I can do. Go to bed and get some sleep. We need you rested and happy for tomorrow's recording session. Good night and sweet dreams." Dimi got his additional violinist and couldn't have been happier. For me to have been a part of this recording session at Carnegie Hall for a film I had directed was a singular emotional thrill and a career high.

Search for Paradise opened on September 24, 1957, at the Cinerama Theater on Broadway in New York, with the customary fanfare, klieg lights, celebrity ado, and Lowell's and my name in bold letters on the marquis. I wasn't present, since I was working on another film abroad. The reviews sent to me were less than mixed and did not bode well for the financial returns. What I had feared all along came through in critical reports: Cinerama missed a great opportunity to come up with a different kind of Cinerama film. The germ of a good story idea was neglected as an insignificant side issue. Most of the brickbats were aimed at Lowell Thomas. *Variety* carried a lengthy review, which I quote in part:

> Producer Lowell Thomas has over-starred himself, being in on script, narration, the song lyrics (with Ned Washington), and also credited for the basic idea. He is the principle principal, the major and sergeant remaining mostly just part of the scenery.
>   . . . Dimitry Tiomkin's music on the whole is a strong score, if

occasionally too prominent and loud and now and again deliberately coy.

. . . Overall, the toil and sweat of the technical crew's crawling Asiatic terrain must be respected. Some of the color photography by Harry Squire is superb.

. . . Otto Lang has captured many a beguiling native type and custom. His direction and the editing of Harvey Manger and Lovel E. Ellis are top credits.

These excerpts echoed the general consensus by other reviewers in the United States and abroad. This did not come as a surprise to me. It was a film prematurely rushed into production, without a script and only the skeletal bits of a storyline never fully developed into a screenplay. I felt bad about the reviews and did not agree with the scathing criticisms of Lowell. Cinerama, after all, did not fit the conventional pattern of films shown in theaters and was a specialty and an extravaganza promoted with great success by Lowell Thomas. The important thing to me was that our friendship and his desire for us to work together again actually emerged fortified. I could not have asked for a finer tribute than he paid me in a letter to Stanley Warner:

> For all that I know, and as a result of the time I spent with Otto in the field, I think he has done an extraordinary job as a director and executive. I know of nothing tougher than running an expedition, especially if those involved are not there on the same basis.
>
> When I think of the troubles we had with the whole flock of directors on *Seven Wonders of the World*, well, I believe my judgment was right in saying to myself that Otto, for this type of an enterprise, may be the best man in Hollywood or anywhere.

I looked forward to working on another film with Lowell under more felicitous circumstances, and we did team up a few years later on a 16 mm project that ended up as a one-hour TV special, "The Land That Time Forgot," shown in prime time.

I was in the final stages of shooting a documentary film in New Zealand when Lowell phoned me at Rotorua, suggesting that I meet him in New Guinea. He had been invited by the Australian government to attend the annual gathering of aboriginal tribes, with some tribes in isolated pockets still living in the Stone Age. He asked me to bring along my New Zealand camera crew so that we could film a short segment to be shown to prospective investors as a lure to finance his next Cinerama production. The timing was perfect, and travel arrangements were made to fly from Auckland, New Zealand, to Sydney, Australia, and on to Port Moresby in New Guinea. Mark was with me, since Peter had already been with me on a previous assignment in New Zealand. For Mark to accompany me was an unexpected windfall. I intended to send him around the world on his own, and I would do so once we were finished with our job in New Guinea.

We met Lowell at Mount Hagen, the hub of this highland territory. At that time, Mount Hagen was primitive, unspoiled, and touched only peripherally by a veneer of civilization. There was one rinky-dink hotel of limited capacity and a Jesuit missionary station, with a church built of corrugated sheet metal, hot as Hades. We had to bunk in native huts built of palm fronds with thatched roofs. The outdoor shower consisted of a large bucket with holes punched through the bottom. A native boy climbed a ladder to fill it with hot water.

The gathering of the tribes was to take place in a few days' time. Sixty thousand natives, bare-breasted women and men in skimpy loincloths, with arrays of bird of paradise plumage atop their heads, were to parade into an open field. To welcome Lowell, we were sitting around a rough-hewn table under a shady tree in front of the hotel with a few government officials and pioneer settlers, laying out a shooting schedule. The thought occurred to me that as long as we were here with a camera crew and sufficient raw stock on hand, why not make a full-length documentary instead of a short segment. From what little I had seen, I was confident that I could deliver a worthwhile portrait of this little-known spot in New Guinea and its people.

My "cast" was conveniently sitting right around the table with me: Lowell, the district commissioner (a handsome, tall, and rugged military type) the Aussie schoolteacher (who taught classes and also trained local graduates to be teachers) Father Ross (a bundle of energy in the form of a five-foot-two-inch Jesuit priest from Kansas, with a flowing white beard, and pale cornflower blue eyes with an intense steely look) Michael Leahy (a farmer, coffee grower, and cattle rancher) and the young district patrol officer with his bride on a short visit to headquarters, soon to return to his distant outpost, reachable only by small aircraft. He and his wife would certainly offer a unique segment of life among the most primitive people living on this island, where cannibalism was rumored to be still rampant.

After getting to know Father Ross a little better, I found him to be one of the most impressive men I had ever met. He had come to New Guinea years ago with a pistol under his black cassock and the courage of a lion to establish the first Christian outpost in this part of the island. He spoke pidgin English to perfection, salted with a few choice swear words of his own. Just to follow these people around on their daily routines would provide a wealth of material for a documentary film, for which I did not need a script and could do by instinct. The gathering of the clans to pay their respects to the governor general, in his bemedaled white uniform and ostrich-plumed topi and escorting his beautifully dressed wife, a diamond coronet above her forehead, would add a British colonial touch to the ceremony. Lowell was enthusiastic about my idea, so we made the film in record time, flying around in a small Cessna to various native settlements and covering the activities around Mount Hagen, where a low "long hut," the length of a football field, with smoke pouring out the thatched roof from open-hearth cook stoves placed on the hard-beaten soil, housed thousands of natives.

After we finished this fascinating interlude of filming in New Guinea, Mark went on his way with an around-the-world ticket in his bag and sufficient funds to carry him through a month of travel on his own, with stops in various countries at his discretion. When he returned from his odyssey, having seen the wonders of ancient Greek ruins, Egypt, and Europe, I asked him, "Mark, if you were given the chance for a return visit to the country you liked best, which would it be?" Without a moment's hesitation, he answered, "New Guinea."

Lowell and I headed for home, convinced that he had what he needed to promote his next Cinerama production. Sadly, it was never to happen. As hard as Lowell tried to promote Cinerama, the money simply didn't come forth; Cinerama was on the downswing. After *Search for Paradise*, there was one more Cinerama picture, *South Seas Adventure*, produced by Carl Dudley. I was asked to direct it but declined, having had my fill of Cinerama. With only a limited number of theaters scattered around the world and the expense of installing projection equipment that cut down the seating capacity, it simply couldn't survive. It was one of the greatest disappointments to Lowell that the baby he had nurtured with such enthusiasm and success was destined to be so short-lived.

WAR ZONES

Home again after my return from New Guinea, I became aware of the growing popularity of television and its enormous potential. I knew that television had a bright future as a mass medium. As a freelance director, I felt it was imperative I get a firm foothold in this new medium. I wanted to learn all there was to know about writing for television, camera techniques, shooting schedules, and budgeting for series segments and specials. My first contact with Ziv Studio, one of the pioneer television production companies, paid off. Based upon my track record and credits, I was a welcome addition to their ranks. Ziv was, at that time, perhaps the most active independent purveyor of TV fodder for home consumption. The name "Ziv" sounded puzzling, like an acronym for an industrial conglomerate, but it was named for Frederic W. Ziv, founder of the company. He ran his own advertising agency out of Cincinnati, Ohio, and veered into television with weekly series, such as *The Cisco Kid* and *Boston Blackie*, among others. One of his most successful and popular series was the hard-hitting police drama *Highway Patrol*, starring Broderick Crawford, well remembered for his Oscar-winning performance in *All the King's Men* (1949). I was hired on a no-contract basis to direct segments of *Highway Patrol* and eventually direct segments of other series produced by Ziv at its small Hollywood studio. The director's pay for each segment was moderate, but the opportunities for learning were wide-open and exactly what attracted me to Ziv. I never regretted it.

I looked forward to working with Broderick Crawford, whom I had met when I worked in Germany on *Night People*. Broderick was a powerfully built man with an imposing presence off screen and on. With his growling voice and staccato delivery, he always left an impression on audiences. I considered him a consummate actor, if cast in the right part, as he was in *Highway Patrol*. However, I found out soon that there was a problem with Broderick, namely his dependency on alcohol.

All went well on the first day of shooting until after the customary one-hour lunch break. Having had a more-than-liberal quota of vodka tonics with his lunch, Broderick had difficulty moving around the set and remembering his lines. This put me in a serious bind, since I had over thirty pages of screenplay to shoot and a tight schedule of two and one-half days for each segment. Every lost minute was costly, and the pressure, even under the most favorable conditions, was relentless. There was no provision in the budget for overtime. In fact, promptly at the stroke of six o'clock, the plug was pulled, leaving the set in darkness.

To keep on schedule with Broderick Crawford became a definite problem. My strategy was to shoot all the scenes with extensive movements and "business" before lunch and to concentrate on stationary shots and close-ups after lunch. When all the bits and pieces of film were edited and spliced together into a coherent scene, I doubt anyone could have detected Broderick's condition. Whether or not he was under the influence, he remained his amiable self—although I could sense his frustration and embarrassment. However, in his defense, I must also say that the job always got done in the end, with Broderick standing tall in his role.

My next assignment for Ziv was to direct an episode of *Target*, a new series just put on the air. I was satisfied with the results of this segment, entitled "Turn of the Tide," and my stock with Ziv rose noticeably based on a favorable review in *Variety*.

After being off target the first couple of weeks it has been on the air, the Ziv series of the same name came through with an exciting action-filled episode, "Turn of the Tide," on Monday night.

Director Otto Lang's excellent work on characterization and his fine pacing kept it moving all the time.

As a reward, I was entrusted with directing the pilot for a new series entitled *World of Giants*, starring Marshall Thompson. Thompson played a perfectly formed and highly intelligent human being, except for one drawback: he was minuscule. In physical appearance, he came closest to the fairy-tale character Tom Thumb. Each segment dealt with his efforts to survive in a "world of giants," meaning all those surrounding him. In order to make Thompson appear diminutive, all the sets, furniture pieces, and accessories had to be built on a larger scale. A pencil, for example, would be the size of a long broom handle; a telephone, with all its details perfectly reproduced, would tower like a fortress above him, and dialing it required herculean effort. The climax of the pilot segment was for him to extricate himself from a wire wastebasket, where he had taken refuge from a cat as ferocious as a saber-toothed tiger. The series had a short run, due to the exorbitant production costs.

I stayed with Ziv for about three productive years and went through their entire repertory of shows, including many westerns such as *Bat Masterson*, *Rough Riders*, *Tombstone Territory*, *McKenzie's Raiders*, and others. At Ziv there was a certain camaraderie and frontier spirit. Our motto was to get the best possible product with the least money spent at the shortest possible shooting schedule. Naturally, quality had to suffer.

As a freelance director, I also accepted assignments from other studios. There was Metro-Goldwyn-Mayer (MGM) with *Man from U.N.C.L.E.*, Four Star Studio's *Rifleman*, *The Zane Grey Theater*, and *The Deputy*, for which I had the rare opportunity to direct Henry Fonda in a television appearance. I enjoyed working with Ann Sothern in her own series filmed at Desilu Studio. She was such an accomplished actress in any kind of a show, be it a dramatic story, light comedy (her forte), or a musical where she could sing and kick up her heels. Ann had also learned to ski well at Sun Valley and moved there permanently.

The two of us, after being invited by Mark, went to see *Oklahoma*, presented by the students of Hollywood High, from which he was about to graduate. Mark was involved in the scenic design of the show, having shown artistic talent. It was an enjoyable, surprisingly high-caliber performance. As is customary, Ann and I went backstage after the show to meet some of the participants. Ann told me that the boy who had played "Curly" had enormous appeal and showed talent. I thought the young lady playing the second lead, Taffy Paul, had great potential. She was pretty and quite at ease in her part, singing, dancing, and emoting with natural charm. Some weeks later, when we were about to start shooting a new segment of her series, Ann said, "I have a surprise for you, Otto. Remember the young girl you liked in *Oklahoma* at Hollywood High? I have signed her for a part in my next show, which you are going to direct." Not that it was the two of us who catapulted Taffy into stardom; her talent alone eventually did so. With her name changed to Stefanie Powers, she became an enduring star of TV and films. Our friendship has remained equally steadfast.

One of the most endearing and fascinating series of which I directed a number of segments was *Daktari*. Marshall Thompson (at full size) had the leading role as a field veterinarian in Africa. Yale Summers portrayed his assistant, and a daughter was included to add some feminine interest in this saga of the African veldt. But all of us were fully aware that the real stars of this show were Judy the chimpanzee and Clarence the cross-eyed lion. The series was the brainchild of Ivan Tors, who enjoyed success with other popular series such as *Sea Hunt,* starring Lloyd Bridges as a scuba-diving explorer and scientist, and *Flipper,* starring the captivating dolphin by the same name. Of all the memories I have of working with Ivan Tors, the one I treasure most is of Judy, the brightest, funniest, most directable creature. One of her favorite pastimes, when I was sitting in my folding director's chair, immersed in my script, was to take a running start at me and topple me over, chair, script, and all. Of course, in response, I dramatized my surprise by rolling over a couple of times on the ground. It made her laugh with joy.

Two contacts who always seemed to come up with an assignment for me at the right time were Carl Dudley and David Jacobson. Carl was an amazing businessman who promoted documentary and travel films. Through him I got to know the world even better; assignments for his two TV series, entitled *It's a Wonderful World* and *This World of Ours,* took me to faraway and fascinating countries. We worked well together. He knew that once he gave me an assignment, he could count on me to bring back interesting footage that would cut well into a cohesive half-hour TV show. Most of his films were made with the cooperation of foreign governments, which often footed most of the bill since they were anxious to have the exposure on television to attract tourists. They provided not only air transportation but also automobiles and hotel accommodations. Traveling under government sponsorship and being accompanied by an official representative opened many doors to locations not always accessible by the average traveler. Through Carl, I made films in Indonesia, featuring the island of Bali and the lesser-known island of Sumatra. I traveled extensively throughout the Philippines. I saw Thailand, Australia, New Zealand, Fiji, and many more countries. I shall always be thankful that our paths crossed.

The other contact, David Jacobson, I met through his wife, Jean. She had been Jerome Hill's secretary for many years and, more than that, his girl Friday, handling any kind of situation. David worked as a producer for Bransby Studio, a small film company in New York City. As Bransby, the owner of the company, got older, he handed over more and more responsibilities to David, until eventually Bransby retired and left the studio and all its facilities to David under a mutually favorable financial arrangement. David ran the company successfully and with great enthusiasm. Most of the income was generated from promotional films for various commercial enterprises. But a major portion of the company's revenue came from training films ordered by the U.S. military. To my surprise, these films often were quite sophisticated in their approach. I became involved with a number of David's films during some of the dry spells in my career and always enjoyed working with him. He was bright, knowledgeable, and realistic in making out a schedule and budget.

One film I directed was part of the chaplain's training program for soldiers. The story was an allegorical drama about a conflict of conscience between the sheriff in a small western town and his young deputy. There was a vicious killer on the loose, and the sheriff had to face him in a possible shootout. The question was whether the deputy, who was against using a gun to kill, would back him up if need be. When it came to the dramatic moment when the sheriff walked out into the deserted street, would the deputy stay put or follow him against the dictates of his conscience? After the lights came on, the objective was to open a discussion among the viewers and to hear what they, as individuals, would have done in such a dilemma. It was an interesting and challenging premise for me as a director, and certainly a departure from the norm in training films.

We needed to cast a good actor for the part of the sheriff, reminiscent of the character played by Gary Cooper in *High Noon*. The man that came to my mind immediately was Clint Walker. I had directed many segments of *Cheyenne*, a weekly TV series in which he starred as sheriff. Clint was a tall, impressive-looking man with a chiseled face, and a good actor. If he could be enticed to take this role for a film with limited public exposure and a nominal salary, it would be truly an asset.

I was quite friendly with Clint beyond our working association. When he became interested in learning to ski, I helped him get started at Holiday Hill in the nearby San Bernardino Mountains. He was a fast learner and very soon was skiing on his own at Mammoth Mountain. To his misfortune he took a bad spill and, by a most unusual happenstance, fell onto the sharp metal tip of one of his poles, embedding it in his heart. He was rushed by ambulance to the nearest hospital at Bishop, some forty miles away. He arrived there blue in color and near death. Miraculously, undoubtedly due to his superb physical condition, he survived the ordeal. He was still mending after weeks of convalescence at home when I called offering the part of the sheriff to him. At first he was reluctant and apprehensive, but after discussing the details of the role, the length of the film, and the schedule, he said he would do it and felt confident that he was up to it physically.

The plan was to shoot the film in Tucson, Arizona, where there was a studio with an extensive western town set. Clint was very particular about the authenticity of the period clothing he wore, the way his horse was saddled and bridled, and the make and caliber of the gun he carried in his holster. The gun provided by the studio prop man didn't satisfy him at all, and replacing it on such short notice posed a problem. Fortunately, John Huston was directing a western there with Paul Newman about the life of Judge Roy Bean. When I mentioned my predicament to Paul, he said spontaneously, "Tell Clint to pick any one of my guns. I have a dozen of them in my dressing room. Whichever suits him best, he's welcome to it." Clint got his gun and the shooting of the film proceeded smoothly. We had the nicest letter from the commander of the Chaplain's Corps thanking us for having brought Clint Walker into the picture and for the way it all worked out to their satisfaction. David and I were also pleased with the results.

A challenging assignment came in 1964, when Walter Strohm, then production honcho at MGM and also a dedicated skier and longtime friend of mine, called to offer me the job of handling the second unit work for *Viva Las Vegas*, a musical featuring Elvis Presley and Ann Margret. George Sidney, a veteran Hollywood director, would be in charge of the proceedings. The character portrayed by Elvis Presley in this film was a Grand Prix automobile racer, and the script called for such an event to be set up in and around Las Vegas. I was to stage this extravaganza, with an allotted budget of $300,000. To begin with, the problem was that never before had there been such a race held at Las Vegas, nor was there any likelihood of there ever being one in the future. It would be counterproductive to the casinos, whose primary aim was to keep as many people as possible indoors and gambling at all times.

My responsibility was to improvise a racecourse and to follow my creative intuition. The course I chose started and finished in Las Vegas's main street, aglow with the garish neon displays of casino names and entrances. It wound through the scenically spectacular Valley of Fire, then went up to Mount Charleston and across Boulder Dam on an out-of-the-way, narrow road, with cameras shooting from a high hill overlooking the imposing concrete structure. The ultimate objective was to make the racecourse action visually exciting, not necessarily logical or according to protocol. This goal was fully achieved.

I had surrounded myself with a group of the best stunt men and race-car drivers, with Carey Lofton, a top man in the field, as their coordinator. We staged spectacular chases over the undulating Valley of Fire roads. There were meticulously staged crashes, one with a car hurtling out of control end over end down a steep embankment. Miraculously, the car came to a halt in front of the camera and crew placed on a high wooden platform. Had it rolled a few feet farther, it could have mowed down the men positioned there. One prays for such things not to happen and breathes a sigh of relief when stunt filming is over. There is always a bit of luck involved, in spite of the most minute calculations and precautions taken.

A tragedy nearly happened to us after we had finished shooting around Las Vegas and returned to the studio. In cutting the footage together, we found that we needed a few more angles in order to effect a smooth bridge between two sequences. To find a matching location at Lancaster, less than a two-hours' drive from the studio for one day's work, was no problem. It would involve the full complement of cars still in the race. In this particular scene, with his car bottled up in the middle of the pack, Elvis decides to outsmart his competitors by taking a shortcut on a stretch of dirt road and reappearing in front of them back on the paved road.

Whenever I worked with stunt men, I invariably explained to their coordinator what sort of an action the script indicated, how I visualized it, and where I suggested placing the camera. In this case, Elvis's double was Carey Lofton, whom I liked very much personally and respected professionally. I told him to work out this stunt with his guys and go through it mentally, calculating every contingency. I told him we were in no hurry and to take their time and let me know when they were ready for a take. My final advice was always, "Look, I don't want anyone to get hurt. It's not worth it to me, nor your men, since it's only for a piece of film of a few minutes' duration. So please make sure to take care of yourselves." Stunt men take pride in their work and are fully aware of the dangers of their chosen profession, but they still do take chances.

As hours went by in preparations, I was becoming a little apprehensive. I could tell by Carey Lofton's intensity and the expression on his face that this was not as simple a stunt as it had first appeared. More physical preparation and working out of the timing were required than anticipated. To ease the tension, I suggested we break for lunch and do the shot later. During lunch, Carey drew a diagram for me on a napkin of the sequential progression he had worked out with his team. I assured him that it was just what I had hoped for.

After lunch, when everything appeared to be in place and I said "Roll it," things went haywire. When Carey Lofton hit the dirt road at full speed, he was not aware how soft it was. This not only threw him off line but also threw up a huge cloud of dust that obliterated the approaching phalanx of other cars. When Carey regained control of his car and hit the middle of the paved road, the other cars, whose drivers were blinded by the dense cloud of dust, caught up with him, and one of them crashed broadside into Carey and tossed his car into a ditch across the road near the camera position. It was a sickening sight. First, the harsh metallic thump of two automobiles in collision, and then the realization that Carey Lofton and the other driver must be hurt. By some good fortune, the other cars passed by unimpeded.

Carey took the brunt of the impact and was seriously injured with broken ribs and internal damage, as we found out at the emergency hospital in Lancaster. He recovered eventually and is still pursuing his hazardous occupation as a stunt man. The other driver, though badly shaken up, got off with only minor injuries. These men are a tough and indomitable breed. To me, watching this debacle was an experience I shall never forget. It would have been horrible if one of these men had lost his life—just for the sake of a piece of film.

The payoff to all this came in a review of the film in *Variety*.

The film is designed to dazzle the eye, assault the ear and ignore the brain. Las Vegas, of course, is the setting of this superficial contrivance about an auto-racing buff trying to raise funds to purchase an engine for his race car with which he hopes to win the Grand Prix. His main obstacle is a swimming instructress (Ann Margret), who doesn't approve of his goal, but ultimately softens.

This hackneyed yarn provides the skeletal excuse for about ten musical interludes, a quick tour of the U.S. gambling capital and that one slam-bang climactic sequence that lifts the film up by its bootstraps just when it is sorely in need of a lift.

This depiction of an auto race is one of the most exciting passages of its type ever put on film. The driver's-eye-view position in which the audience is placed as the cars swoop over the swoops and dips of the desert highway engenders a genuine sensation of giddiness in the spectator—much like that generated by the roller coaster ride in *Cinerama*.

The pickings are lean outside of this show-stopping kicker.

FLIGHT FROM EGYPT

Twentieth Century Fox, with whom I had an ongoing relationship, acquired the motion picture rights to *Justine*, one of the four books comprising Lawrence Durrell's *Alexandria Quartet*. This drama of love, political intrigue, and racial and religious conflict is played out against the spectacular scenery and historic background of Egypt. I was surprised the Egyptian government gave Twentieth Century Fox permission to film it in their country. The author's portrayal of Egypt and its citizens may well have been close to the truth, but it was far from complimentary, depicting the basest instincts of sexual lust, depravity, and drug abuse and contrasting the abysmal poverty of the lower classes with the decadent lifestyle of the rich. I was hired to direct the shooting of establishing shots in Egypt.

The Egyptian government stipulated that Twentieth Century Fox commit itself at the same time to producing a documentary film on Egypt to boost tourism. Although this put a double load on my shoulders, it also assured me of complete government cooperation and an entrée to many historical sites that normally would not be accessible to filmmakers.

To get the most out of this "double shoot," with the least amount of money spent, we would keep the crew down to a minimum and use European technicians, supplemented from the local Egyptian labor pool. The films were to be shot in wide-screen Panavision, with cameras, lenses, lights, and other requisite items to be provided by a rental establishment in London. The camera crew itself would come from Rome, which offered a selection of seasoned veterans to choose from. An accountant attached to the Twentieth Century Fox office in Rome would take care of all financial transactions and payroll on location. I would be the only

American with the unit. Piero Portalupi, a highly respected cinematographer, and his regular assistant and operator, Cesare Leone, were the most vital cogs in this operation. I liked them from the moment I met them in Rome and sized them up as experienced pros.

Arriving at the Cairo airport and passing through customs was facilitated by the presence of a government representative assigned to be our constant companion and intermediary during the shoot. Mohammed, as every third male seems to be named in Islamic countries, turned out to be a gentleman and a dignified functionary. He knew his way around Egyptian bureaucracy and also knew the rules of the game—when, where, how much, and whom to bribe, as circumstances dictated. The main hall of the airport reminded me of an oriental bazaar with all the hustle and bustle. Men wearing skullcaps and loose-fitting cotton robes down to their ankles and women in black shapeless gowns, their eyes peering through a slit cut in the hoods covering their faces, contrasted with international tourist groups in various attires, loaded down with fake artifacts and souvenirs, waiting to check in for their departures with slightly dazed expressions on their faces. We were booked into the Nile Hilton Hotel, the newest in town, but lacking the charm of the venerable Mena House Hotel, close to the Pyramids. The Hilton, overlooking the Nile and conveniently located next to the National Museum, a veritable treasure trove of priceless antiquities, would be our headquarters in Cairo.

I never expected Egypt to have such an impact on me. One may see stunning pictures and read detailed descriptions of the Sphinx and the pyramids, but when I saw them for the first time rising from the desert plain, I was overwhelmed. As I stood diminutively at the foot of these monumental structures, they appeared so much larger than I had ever imagined. They were truly among the "Seven Wonders of the World." Looking up at the massive head of the Sphinx, cruelly mutilated by fanatical Mameluke cannoneers who used it for target practice, I was struck by a possible theme I could develop for the documentary. Wouldn't it be interesting to tell the story of Egypt as seen "through the eyes of the Sphinx," narrated by a voice in the first person? A cavalcade of historical personages had stood in front of it: Greek poets and philosophers, conquering Roman centurions, Caesar and Cleopatra, Napoleon with his vaunted grenadiers, Churchill, Roosevelt, and many others through the ages. They would make a fascinating parade going back to the days of the pharaohs.

Filming locations for such a story, we traveled the length of Egypt, following the Nile with innumerable stops at historic sites from Abu Simbel, close to the Sudan border, to Alexandria, where the Nile joins the Mediterranean Sea. It was at Alexandria, comparable to one of the finest city vistas along the French Riviera, where most of the action for *Justine* took place. The heat was oppressive throughout our stay, but since we were quartered in the best available tourist hotels, we were fairly comfortable.

Aside from being congenial companions and seasoned cinematographers, Piero Portalupi and Cesare Leone proved adaptable to any circumstance. We were somewhat restricted in our ability to photograph interiors because of the limited amount of lighting equipment at our disposal. For example, in order to photograph King Tutankhamen's underground burial chamber in the Valley of the Kings near Thebes, we had to get permission to bring in lights with a generator. Even though King Tut's grave had been plundered to some extent by grave robbers, an enormous number of priceless objects were left untouched and were later retrieved, to be saved for posterity at the Cairo Museum.

When faced at the museum by the dazzling sight of Tutankhamen's sarcophagus and funerary mask, sculpted out of the purest hammered gold and arguably one of the most elegantly executed likenesses of a human face in existence, I was stumped as to how we could photograph it, protected as it was within a glass enclosure, without showing the mirrored reflections of surrounding statuary and other artifacts. I saw no other way in solving this problem than to have the glass case dismantled and removed, so that with an improvised backdrop of fabric or cardboard, we could isolate King Tut's funerary coffin from its surroundings, thereby avoiding any reflections. This was a hitherto unheard of request, and it took some negotiation to convince the director of the museum to cooperate with us. He said no and stood his ground firmly until we impressed upon him that our request would show Tutankhamen's mummy to the world as one of the highlights of the documentary film commissioned by his government. This swayed him, and although apprehensive, he acquiesced and the glass enclosure was lifted gingerly from its base.

We were in awe, eye-to-eye with over three thousand years of history.

While we deployed our lights and positioned the camera appropriately, I dispatched two of our smartest crew members to find us any suitable fabric or cardboard panels to rig up a backdrop for King Tut, and to do so in a hurry before the director might have a sudden change of mind. It turned out to be a beautiful shot, lit by Piero Portalupi, who took pride in being the first cameraman to photograph King Tut unimpeded by a glass partition. Mind you, this was some twenty years before the Egyptian government packed up Tutankhamen's gold mask and other artifacts and dispatched them on a sensational world tour to raise funds for the Cairo Museum, badly run-down and in need of improvements.

We had a similar problem in obtaining permission to light the superb frescoes in the underground necropolis of the Nobles. These wall paintings had retained the freshness of their original color due to the dry climate and lack of moisture in the chambers. They portrayed in great detail every facet of life in Egypt in those bygone days, and were indeed artistic masterpieces.

Since part of the story in *Justine* dealt with the religious conflicts between Copts, Moslems, and Greek Orthodox believers, we visited a Coptic monastery, far removed from civilization and squatting like a small fortress in desert no-man's-land, encircled by a high wall and guarded by a fortified entrance gate. Once inside the confines of this monastery, with its pink buildings, verdant greenery, blooming flowers, and wooden walkways high above, harmony and peace reigned supreme. Absorbed and preoccupied with our daily shooting schedule, we paid little attention to what was going on in the outside world. Nevertheless, one could sense a certain apprehension among the people, fearing that the tense political situation between Israel and Egypt could erupt at any time into war.

My first awareness that something was in the offing came while we were setting up our camera on a high rooftop for a sweeping panoramic shot of Alexandria's fabled Corniche, with its tree-shaded boulevard, government buildings, embassies, private mansions, and pointed spires of mosques. The official military representative who had been added to our crew asked us to limit the scope of our pan shot to what he indicated, designating a point of beginning and ending. I complied with his request, without prying into the reasons for this restriction, which did not matter that much. Later I found out that the city, its harbor, and the surrounding terrain were bristling with camouflaged ground-to-air missile installations, off-limits to photographers.

Also, quite casually, he suggested that the time had come for us to seriously plan our speedy exit from Egypt. I assured him that this was exactly what we had in mind, and there remained only one more scene we had scheduled to film in Cairo. This was a night shot of the Sphinx, lit up for the Son et Lumière spectacle. As planned, we made the shot of the ghostly Sphinx peering out of the darkness. This done, it was a wrap.

We sat down at the adjoining restaurant for dinner and a small celebration. I announced that as a surprise I had booked reservations for our crew members to fly out the next day on a TWA Constellation to Rome, which did indeed surprise them.

My plan was to stay on for two more days to expedite all the shipping formalities for our exposed and unexposed film and to clear our camera equipment through customs, as nothing could be left behind to be sold by someone on the black market. But when I woke up the next morning, June 5, 1967, and turned on the radio, it blared the news: Egypt and Israel were at war. Amid the confusion in the crowded lobby I saw the headlines of the morning paper, screaming in large letters:

FIRST ENCOUNTER IN AERIAL COMBAT BETWEEN ISRAELI AND ARAB PLANES, A DEVASTATING LOSS TO ISRAELI AIR FORCE

I stepped out the front door of the hotel, with air-raid warning sirens shrilly wailing, to take a look at the sky. Some planes were visible high up with black-and-white puffs of smoke exploding around them. I watched this bizarre, almost surreal spectacle for a while, not for a moment considering seeking cover. Returning to the lobby with people milling around aimlessly, I saw my three comrades in arms and we sat down in an empty corner for a war council among ourselves. As it turned out, the TWA noon flight on which I had made reservations for them but which they had asked me to cancel in order to enjoy a shopping day was the last scheduled flight out of Cairo. Together we had to act fast and somehow get ourselves out of this gridlock, cut off from transportation by air or sea.

My first inclination was to call on the American ambassador and ask for his advice on how to get out of Egypt. Arriving at the embassy compound, a short walk from the hotel, I found it ringed by a cordon of police on horseback, quite possibly there to protect it from being set on fire by overzealous Arab radicals. I identified myself to one of the mounted police officers, stated my wish as an American to see the ambassador, was allowed to pass. When the ambassador caught sight of me, he shook his head and said, "I'm surprised you're still here. You'd better get out of Cairo as fast as you can. No one can predict where this is going to lead and how it is going to end."

"But how?" I asked. "What would you suggest?"

"I can't help or assist you in any way. Get yourself a caravan of two cars, load up all your gear and people, and head for Alexandria. You might be lucky and get aboard a ship. That's about your best chance. Bon voyage, and let me know when you arrive home."

I could tell he was awfully glad to get rid of me.

It was up to Mohammed, our official Egyptian "godfather," to get us out of Cairo. He came through in style by hiring two cars with drivers and offering to provide us with an official letter, signed by the chief of security forces, to clear our passage should we run into a military checkpoint en route. When I hinted to him that we would feel more comfortable if he accompanied us, his affirmative response was instantaneous, with only one request, to let him go home to inform his wife where he was headed and to pack a small bag with a change of clothing and his toiletry kit. He also said it would be obligatory to obtain a government clearance to take the large carton containing all of our exposed film out of the country. Unfortunately, the office was closed that particular day, but he could arrange for us to stop by that official's home to have the rubber stamp affixed to the package and pay the nominal service fee. While Mohammed and I did this chore, my three co-musketeers would load up the two cars and we would be out of Cairo within a short time— and none too soon. The euphoria of the citizenry on the streets was swelling rapidly, convinced of a devastating initial blow dealt to the Israelis and victory in sight, *inshallah.*

Our drive to Alexandria turned out to be uneventful, except for dodging through heavy traffic all headed north toward the only viable exit port from Egypt at the time. Arriving in Alexandria, which had taken on the appearance of a beleaguered city, we pulled up at the Grand Hotel, where we had stayed before, only to be told at the front desk that there wasn't a single room available in that or any other hotel. In fact, it was pointed out to us, Roberto Rossellini, the well-known Italian director, and his crew of thirty-five people were camping out in the lobby.

Piero Portalupi and Rossellini were old friends and upon seeing each other started much hugging and backslapping in true Italian tradition. Our crew was introduced and informed that Rossellini had been shooting one of his much-prized full-length documentary films when he was abruptly forced to close down and seek a way to get himself and his crew back home to Italy. We explained that we were in a similar situation, except that at least our work had been completed. Ours was a bit more complicated, with the presence of an American and Englishman in our group, personae non grata in Egypt at the moment, in view of the close political affiliation of the two countries with Israel. "Not to worry," Rossellini assured Piero, "We're in the same profession and bound together, like a family."

The concierge of the Grand Hotel (whom I had tipped generously during our previous stay) slipped me a piece of paper with the address of some sort of a bed-and-breakfast place along the broad esplanade overlooking the bay. We were pleasantly surprised to be offered the last unoccupied suite with enough beds to accommodate all five of us. It wasn't bad at all, airy and clean with a splendid panoramic view. We made arrangements to take our meals at the Grand Hotel, which also gave us the opportunity to observe Rossellini in action. Presiding like a field marshal from his command post in the lobby, he dispatched couriers in all directions to gather information on what was going on in town and, specifically, intelligence of prospective boat movements into and out of Alexandria. It was like watching a scene from one of his movies.

We sat around for two days, waiting, guessing, anticipating, listening to rumors, until at last it was verified that an Italian excursion boat on its weekly run between Naples and Alexandria would arrive in the evening. It would be ready to board the next morning and depart at eleven o'clock. Obviously, Italian citizens would have preferential treatment in being evacuated. Piero and Cesare vowed they would stick with us, whatever happened. They wouldn't think of leaving us non-Italians behind.

Every effort to buy passage legitimately or otherwise failed. The ship was already overbooked far beyond its maximum capacity. When morning dawned the next day at five o'clock, we were loaded up and ready to drive to the embarkation pier, tickets or no tickets, so that we would be among the first ones in line to pass through customs when the gate opened. Mohammed reassured us again and again that he would not leave us until he saw us safely aboard ship and waving to him from the upper deck.

There was a bit of a holdup at the customs counter, due to our number of pieces of personal luggage and camera equipment. With Mohammed's helpful prodding, we were almost done, when in the last moment, one of the customs officials decided to confiscate our box of unexposed raw stock of something like five thousand feet. He claimed it might be useful for his country's cinema division to have this raw stock, even though we explained to him that it could not be threaded into a standard 35 mm camera. But since he insisted, I did not make a fuss about it, figuring we had gotten off cheaply, and before he had the idea of confiscating our high-priced Panavision camera as well.

On a hunch, before we entered the customs hall, I asked Piero to take my own personal twenty-five rolls of exposed film with his luggage through the inspection. It was a lucky hunch, indeed, since the first question asked by one of the officials was whether I carried any personal rolls of exposed film in my luggage. I told him no, I did not, which was the truth, and passed. Our English assistant cameraman happened to have a few canisters of exposed film on him, and they were promptly taken away. Piero and Cesare, showing their Italian passports, weren't even asked and slipped through unaccosted.

We settled down to wait with our pile of luggage next to the entrance gate to the staircase that led up to the boat deck. While we waited, a man whom Mohammed knew vaguely approached us. He knew we were looking to buy space on the boat and said he had just seen a man who had four tickets to sell. Of course, they would be at black market prices. I handed him a fistful of dollars and told him to go and get them, the price was of no consequence. He disappeared, and time passed. Half an hour, then an hour, and more waiting. I had almost given up hope of seeing him again, and berated myself for being such a trusting schmuck. How could I have handed him all that money, not knowing who he was, and what made me believe that he would return?

By this time the gate was opened leading to the dangling stairway alongside the boat for passengers to board. Still no sign of our man, when suddenly he popped out from the crowd, with a long face and obvious look of disappointment. Slightly out of breath, he said, "So sorry, when I arrived there and thought I had a deal, a Lebanese merchant stepped forward and offered double the amount I had negotiated. Naturally I lost out. Here's your money back. Again, so sorry and good luck." And he left me holding in my hands the exact amount of money I had given him, before I could even offer him something for his valiant effort.

"OK," I said, "This is it. The moment of truth. Everyone grab a suitcase in each hand and let's line up our porters with full loads. Up we go, there's no alternative." We said good-bye to Mohammed, with heartfelt thanks for all he had done for us, and began the steep climb up the staircase, with me in the lead. The incredible happened! No one asked for tickets; no one stopped us. We walked through the narrow entrance gate to the upper deck, with two guards just standing and gawking at the parade of porters and us passing through, as though we owned the ship.

We were aboard to stay, with our luggage neatly piled in a corner on the upper deck. I suggested that we casually walk away from each other but keep our eyes open in case something untoward happened. We sidled up to the ship's railing and waved down to Mohammed, who waved back at us before he turned to leave.

Not until late in the afternoon did we begin to move slowly out of the harbor. Then there was another delay with a shrill alarm and warning that Israel underwater commandos and demolition crews had infiltrated the harbor. There was a crackle of shots and much excitement, before it was concluded to be a false alarm, and we continued out to sea leaving Egypt behind us.

It has always amazed me how conveniently the human mind and body adjust to unaccustomed circumstances, which in our case were far from bad. We had ample time to scout around the boat before our departure and discovered a cache of folded deck chairs, the old-fashioned wooden ones, of which we requisitioned four and set them up next to our luggage depot to bed down for the night. Our two Italian benefactors knew their way around, resulting in Cesare showing up with four blankets and bath towels. Piero, in the meantime, had arranged with the maître d' of the dining room to have us seated for the third serving in the first-class section. Instead of the normally 500 people aboard, there were 750 crowding the ship. We were happy and looking forward to sleeping under the stars, not realizing that by morning we would be drenched to the skin with dew. Eventually, long after we left Alexandria, a man came around to check the tickets. He wasn't surprised at all to find stowaways and simply added up what we owed, which I paid, and that was it.

When we arrived at Naples after two days en route and were scheduled to dock at night, the captain of the ship was instructed to kill time for lack of docking facilities and circle until daybreak around the volcanic outcrop of Stromboli, still very much alive. It was then that Roberto Rossellini took over and regaled us with stories about directing the film *Stromboli*, starring Ingrid Bergman. He gave us a glowing account of his torrid and illicit love affair, while the fiery glow of the volcano appropriately lit the scenario. It was the scandal of the decade.

We docked at Naples early the next morning. By that time, the Arab-Israeli war was over. It came to be known in history books as the Six-Day War. During the course of it, Egypt lost the entire Sinai Peninsula bordering on the Suez Canal. Syria lost the strategic Golan Heights, and Jordan was humiliated. Contrary to the headlines in the Cairo papers that morning when the war broke out, the Israeli air force had annihilated the Arab military forces on the ground and in the air. We were met at Naples by representatives from Fox, who had flown from Rome to Naples, on the chance we might be on this boat.

Justine was released in 1969 and didn't cause much of a ripple. Directed by George Cukor, one of the best among his peers, and photographed by ace cameraman Leon Shamroy, it featured Anouk Aimée, Michael York, and Dirk Bogarde, not exactly powerful marquis names. Above all, the screenplay failed to do justice to a fine literary property. It would have taken the consummate skill of a filmmaker such as David Lean to make a success of *Justine*. The documentary on Egypt was scuttled, and all the beautiful footage we shot was relegated to the studio stock library.

When I saw DFZ upon my return to the studio, he told me that he wasn't worried for one moment about our safety. He knew that somehow we would find a way to get out of Egypt with our exposed film and camera equipment. My finest reward was the twenty-five rolls of still film I took, which yielded the material for one of my best one-man photo shows, which was displayed in museums and galleries in many cities in the United States. Its title: "Egypt."

LA JOLLA INTERLUDE

Sinnie, Peter, Mark, and I moved from Brentwood to a smaller, more centrally located home in Beverly Hills on Wetherly Drive, one block above Sunset Boulevard near Doheny Drive. It was a spacious California-style bungalow with a basement converted into living quarters and a playroom. The mortgage and maintenance on our Brentwood house were too costly for us to carry. Also, we all wanted a swimming pool, and there was really no convenient spot to build one there. At our new home, Thomas Church, a friend and preeminent landscape architect, designed a beautiful pool for us overlooking Beverly Hills.

We stayed at this house for some years and eventually moved to La Jolla. The reasons for this move were manifold. The traffic on Sunset, the most direct access route to our house, had become unbearable. From Doheny Drive up to Vine Street in the heart of Hollywood, Sunset had developed into a favorite cruising venue during the late 1960s, with a mix of drug dealers, pot smokers, pimps, and prostitutes crowding the sidewalks. To get to our house at night, we had to take a circuitous detour to avoid all this congestion.

Also, to my utmost dismay, Sinnie had developed an alarming affinity for alcohol, aside from being a chain-smoker. She had had her fill of the Hollywood scene and social life. She longed to go somewhere far away from this lifestyle that was forced upon us by the demands of my profession. She chose La Jolla because of happy memories and roots established there before I entered her life. I did not mind this decision, even though it would disrupt my career and earning capacity since I would not be so readily available for assignments due to the distance between Hollywood and La Jolla. To be truthful, I too looked forward to a more peaceful environment away from the hectic Hollywood merry-go-round.

I was also hoping to salvage our marriage, which had definitely eroded. Our initial togetherness had been damaged by too many unwanted separations for extended periods, and the effects were felt by both of us. Although Sinnie did accompany me on some of my location trips, we realized that being together on location wasn't all that satisfactory. I was on the run and preoccupied with my film work, while she wandered about by herself in a foreign country. It was the best we could do, but it was not enough to nurture and sustain a once-solid marriage. We did manage finally to get to Salzburg for a long overdue reunion with my parents, which was one of the highlights of their lives and also of ours. We spent some happy weeks together in London with a side trip to Edinburgh, Scotland. Istanbul with its exotic ambiance and historic past enchanted her. There were other countries, such as France, Australia, New Zealand, and Indonesia, that we visited together.

Sinnie's happiness was of the utmost importance to me, and her condition distressed me. I was willing to abandon my film career if it would help to rekindle the flame of our crumbling marriage. I felt that the move to La Jolla would be a constructive step in this direction, but somehow I would still have to provide for all of us.

We sold our home in Beverly Hills without much trouble and bought a new home in La Jolla. It belonged to a widow, who could no longer take care of such a large house. It stood high up on Country Club Drive, overlooking the golf course with a distant vista of the Pacific Ocean. Our closest neighbors were James Copley and his wife, Helen, whose property adjoined ours. Jim was publisher of the *San Diego Union*, the *Evening Tribune*, and a chain of other newspapers, including the Copley Wire Service, with eight hundred national outlets. He also had a hand in a number of other business ventures, all of them markedly successful. He was a kind man with consummate taste, civic-minded and philanthropic.

The Copleys' home was a solidly built Spanish colonial mansion, with immaculately groomed grounds and flower beds. Ours, in comparison, was like a sharecropper's shack, much in need of attention.

To have the Copleys as our neighbors was an unexpected and welcome surprise, and we began to visit each other's homes frequently. Sinnie, as Admiral Gannon's daughter, and Jim, having served as a reserve naval officer during World War II, found an instant rapport. One enjoyable aspect of our lives was our joint preoccupation with beautifying our home. Helen and Jim followed our efforts with genuine interest and discreetly offered occasional suggestions, which often proved to be very helpful. Despite the vast gap in material advantages, we felt comfortable with Helen and Jim, and they adopted us, introducing us to their circle of friends and including us in elegant black-tie soirées and casual dinner parties.

Among the most fascinating were Theodor Geisel and his wife, Audrey. He was better known as Dr. Seuss, the author of such popular books as *The Cat in the Hat* and *How the Grinch Stole Christmas*. Sinnie and I shared many an intimate dinner at the Geisels' home perched on a knoll overlooking La Jolla. I also spent some quiet hours with the good doctor, watching him create his fantasy creatures, and felt complimented when he asked me to take photographs of Audrey and him surrounded by some of his creations. Since he was very private, this was a rare privilege.

My main concern was to get Sinnie back on track and our faltering marriage set to rights. We decided to seek help from a psychiatrist and marriage counselor, who had been trained in Vienna. Her husband was an outstanding scholar. They soon became close friends of ours and helped us to reconcile and face some of our problems. But when it came to Sinnie's most urgent personal problem, she categorically refused to join an Alcoholics Anonymous support group, though I offered to accompany her to make it easier for her.

For me, only an occasional imbiber of spirits, a glass of wine, or a beaker of beer, and never having smoked a cigarette, it was difficult to comprehend why it would take so much effort to shed an obviously harmful habit. Couldn't one just make up one's mind and say, "That's enough, I have had it and I'm quitting as of this day?" Easier said than done, as many who have confronted this problem know. As a concerned bystander, I was completely helpless. To be constantly on the prowl for cleverly concealed caches of liquor, to preach and rant were not solutions and, furthermore, only debased both parties concerned. Patience, understanding, and sympathy helped but did not cure Sinnie's addiction. It was a constant, day-to-day battle. I was always hoping that by some miracle we would wake up one morning and everything would be as it was in happier days. It only got worse.

Finally, Sinnie acquiesced and let me accompany her to an Alcoholics Anonymous meeting. I was shocked to hear about the struggle and pain so many had had to endure. They were young, elderly, male and female, affluent, and poor whose meager allotment was spent on liquor. To see these people and hear their stories was heart-wrenching and gave me a new perspective on Sinnie's problem. Sinnie's reaction was negative. She said to me, "I don't belong with these people. I'm not a drunk." And that was the end of our first AA experience until much, much later. One of the recovering consultants said to me, "When she hits rock bottom, she will feel differently and return to us as a last resort."

Since we lived on what I earned, supplemented by frequent withdrawals from our savings account, I had to look for some film assignments. Preferably they would be of short duration and within the United States. When I was required to go abroad, I always stipulated that Sinnie came with me. Many of my jobs were promotional films for resorts or industrial enterprises in the United States.

I was also invited by the University of San Diego to teach a summer seminar. In retrospect, it was one of my most rewarding experiences, even though the honorarium paid to me was minuscule. The university was run by a group of Catholic nuns, and Sister Murphy was the one I dealt with primarily. Remarkably world-wise and open-minded, she had a cheerful personality and winning smile. Before we entered into an agreement, I was invited for dinner, presided over by the mother superior and her entire staff. I was seated as the guest of honor next to her at a long refectory table in the main dining room. The table was covered with snow-white damask and glassware, china, and cutlery of the finest quality. I stole a closer look at these implements and noticed that they showed a variety of different monograms, indicating that they had been donated to the university by deceased benefactors.

Evidently, I passed muster, and when my first class of thirty-five assembled, it consisted of faculty members, nuns, secretaries, college students, "flower children," and long-haired renegades. The curriculum was simple. I began each session with an introductory dissertation on the behind-the-scenes workings of filmmaking. I arranged to have a guest speaker for each session, chosen from among my peers in Hollywood.

After a short break, we ran a film of my choice, about which the class would have to write a critical appraisal. The overall response was gratifying, and each session of the two-month-long seminar flew by. I was asked to repeat the seminar the following summer, and I was approached by a branch of the University of Southern California in La Jolla to initiate a film seminar there. As tempting to me as it was to become a "professor" without a college degree, I declined. The amount of time necessary for preparatory work would be enormous, and the financial rewards would not be commensurate with the required and time-consuming preparations. Also, my curiosity was aroused by a bulletin I had read in the trade papers about Twentieth Century Fox having reactivated their production plans to film the Pearl Harbor story. I had been aware of the project for a long time and wondered if at last it might go forward.

T O R A !
T O R A !
T O R A !

As a freelancer, I was frequently engaged by Twentieth Century Fox, especially when foreign backgrounds were involved. Much of this was due to my continued close relationship with Darryl Zanuck and his son, Dick, who had risen to an important executive position in the company hierarchy. When the studio put the story of Japan's attack on Pearl Harbor on its production schedule for 1968-1969, with high hopes for a potential blockbuster, I was instantly intrigued. Obviously, it would have to be a top-budget picture that would require extensive location shooting in Japan, the United States, and, of course, the site of Pearl Harbor on the island of Oahu.

Over the course of the years, a number of abortive attempts had been made to produce a film about the historical chain of events leading to Pearl Harbor. But every one of these attempts died aborning. The scope of such a film and the exorbitant budget it required forced the project to be relegated to a back burner. The right time to produce it finally came along when Darryl Zanuck, courageously looking for innovative material, decided to tackle this property with his accustomed vigor. This was in 1967, twenty-six years after the actual attack on Pearl Harbor had taken place.

The departments at Twentieth Century Fox involved with the

preliminary preparations for the Pearl Harbor film soon faced difficulties of a monumental and heretofore unimagined scale. For example, there wasn't a single Japanese aircraft carrier in existence; they had all been sunk in the course of battle. The same applied to cruisers, destroyers, and submarines—all resting at the bottom of the Pacific Ocean. There wasn't a single flyable "Zero," the most potent and deadly attack plane used by Japan at Pearl Harbor, left anywhere, nor were there any of the "Vals" and "Kates" used for low-flying torpedo attacks. All of these would have to be faithfully duplicated. The ships would have to float and the planes would have to fly.

As overall producer for the Pearl Harbor film, Darryl Zanuck selected Elmo Williams, a veteran filmmaker, although he himself would hold the reins as executive producer. Elmo also had an extensive background as a film editor (*High Noon*), a knowledge that would come in handy for this type of film. Richard Fleischer, also with his solid track record, was designated director of the American portions of the film. In an extraordinary and imaginative departure, famed Japanese director Akira Kurosawa was engaged to direct the Japanese portions. These sequences would constitute approximately one-third of the entire film, and Kurosawa would be autonomous to a certain extent but still under the jurisdiction of the studio. He was then already a living legend in Japan and recognized worldwide as a superior filmmaker. One might say that he was one of the original *auteurs*, with complete control over every phase of the films he directed, produced, and often coauthored. He was so powerful and revered among his peers in the Japanese film industry that they bestowed upon him the honorary sobriquet of "Emperor."

So the stage was set for all the key participants involved in filming the project. One thing remained: the screenplay had yet to be written. This would be a task of major proportions in view of the delicate and often embarrassing complexities surrounding the attack on Pearl Harbor. Instances of bungled situations and negligence of high-ranking officers in the War Department came to light after the fact and were subsequently covered up. The writers assigned to this project were a trio of acknowledged pros. Larry Forrester, a British journalist and prolific author of books and screenplays was to write the American portion of the screenplay, while two Japanese writers, Hideo Oguni and Ryuzo Kinoshima, long-time friends and coauthors of some of Kurosawa's finest films (*Seven Samurai, Throne of Blood*) were to establish continuity and write dialogue for the sequences to be shot in Japan. Such an arrangement suggested a situation fraught with complications, aside from the mind-boggling logistics a film of such documentary reality would demand.

None of the black-and-white newsreel footage could be used, since *Tora! Tora! Tora!* (a Japanese navy code meaning "Tiger! Tiger! Tiger!," confirming "all systems go, attack at full force") was to be shot in 70 mm, wide-screen Panavision. Every foot of the actual attack would have to be reenacted. This meant that there would be plenty of work for many, and I wanted to get aboard the project, which promised to be one of the most prestigious films ever attempted by Twentieth Century Fox. With my background and expertise in foreign locations I knew I could contribute something of value. I wrote a note to DFZ and Dick expressing my desire to join the *Tora! Tora! Tora!* team. Both seemed favorably inclined to have me associated with the project, although they pointed out that Elmo Williams's voice would carry the weight of the final decision. I had high hopes that it would be in my favor.

Writing the shooting script could take months, and I didn't want to sit around and wait for their decision, so I took a few short-term assignments in the meantime. One of these was to shoot some second-unit sequences for *Gypsy Moth*, a picture directed by John Frankenheimer for MGM, starring Burt Lancaster, Gene Hackman, and Deborah Kerr. The story dealt with two daredevil sky divers and required a great deal of aerial photography. I enjoyed working for Frankenheimer, tough as he was, a stickler for perfection. Watching his imaginative direction and choice of camera angles was stimulating.

As my stint with the Frankenheimer unit was coming to an end, toward the end of July 1968, I received a cable from Dick Zanuck at our location headquarters in Wichita, Kansas:

ELMO WILLIAMS IN TOKYO BUT FROM EVERYTHING I CAN GATHER HE IS DEFINITELY PLANNING ON HAVING YOU ON THE TORA TEAM.

Of course I was elated, but my state of euphoria was quashed by a phone call on September 10 from Elmo Williams. He explained that after much deliberation and soul-searching, he had decided to give the position to Ray Kellogg, a studio colleague of mine for many years. I was truly disheartened and vented my wounded feelings in a letter to Dick Zanuck:

Dear Dick:

Elmo called me last Thursday to tell me the bad news concerning my hopes to become associated with T.T.T. It was kind and considerate of him to phone me personally and explain the reasons for his decision. Of course, I must agree with the choice of Ray Kellogg. He has all the qualifications and then some, aside of being a fine gentleman and human being. There is *none* better qualified when it comes to this type of challenge of a multiplicity of "special effects," which is truly his forte. The choice was a wise one.

Still I am dismayed, to put it mildly. I wanted this job so very much and fought for it fiercely. But, as your father would say, *c'est la vie.* We all have to swallow these bitter pills from time to time, except that I have had too many to swallow of late.

Best always,
OL

Dick answered my letter immediately.

Dear Otto:

I was very moved by your letter, but before anything I want to get things straight on T.T.T. I was in Europe last week when Stan Hough [production head at Fox] wired me that both he and Elmo had decided on Kellogg rather than you. I was as shocked as you were since I had been under the impression for a long time that Elmo had preferred you. I wired back that Elmo should call you personally (or see you) as I knew it would come as a blow to you.

I asked Stan to canvass our entire production program, both films and television, and look for an assignment for you. This he is doing. Both Stan and Elmo are fine and honest men and their selection of Kellogg over you was strictly based upon their judgment, which I must respect and do have faith in.

All I can say is that everyone speaks very highly of you. I believe in your talent, but most of all your friendship is very important to me.

Best to the family.
Love,
Dick

I decided that the best thing for me to do was to put *Tora! Tora! Tora!*

out of my mind and to go on making films wherever and whenever the opportunity came along. This was the price of freedom as a freelance director. Then, around the first week in November, I received a call from Stan Hough asking me to come to the studio to discuss shooting some preliminary scenes for *Tora! Tora! Tora!*

Hype being an important factor in the beginning of shooting of any big-budget picture, the idea was to time the kickoff of this epic on December 7 in Washington, D.C., the anniversary of the attack on Pearl Harbor. The studio would capitalize on a bonanza of nationwide publicity. When I reported to Elmo Williams at his office, he handed me the screenplay with the scenes marked to be shot in Washington, which we discussed in great detail. He said that I would even have the luxury of working with some of the actors cast for certain parts instead of using doubles. The camera crew and other technicians would come from New York, which would reduce the budget considerably for a projected eight-day shoot. Elmo had to leave the next day for Hawaii and on to Japan to coordinate the extensive preparations for the start of shooting there. Ray Kellogg was already in Hawaii preparing the special effects for the battle scenes. Elmo confided to me that he felt much more secure knowing that I would be handling the important Washington segments, with crowds of people and individual actors to be directed.

The New York contingent of the crew in Washington was made up of total strangers who knew each other only by reputation. As it turned out, ours was a felicitous and workmanlike association. Of course, there were a few problems of a technical nature, which is almost inevitable. After a few days of scouting for locations and securing the necessary clearances, we rolled the camera for the first scene to be filmed of *Tora! Tora! Tora!* on Pearl Harbor Day, 1968.

It was clear but bitterly cold in Washington. Fortunately, there was no snow on the ground, which was to our advantage, since most of the scenes to be filmed took place in late autumn. But we had to shoot one scene depicting Washington in the middle of summer, and that was a problem—all the trees on Constitution Avenue were bare. Somehow, some way, we had to cover up this deficiency. Between the cameraman and me, we decided to place the camera on a high platform and shoot down onto the street. By placing a tree branch with green leaves in a corner of the image, we would create the illusion that all the trees along the avenue were still in foliage. Dressing the crowds of extras in summer clothing would enhance the illusion. There were to be ladies in summer dresses, sailors in their whites, and other military personnel in summer khakis. Nannies pushing perambulators and a dozen or so vintage cars, some with their canvas tops down, scooted along the avenue. As a crowning touch I placed an ice-cream vendor with his push cart on wheels below the camera in a visually strategic spot.

We rehearsed the scene a few times, with all the extras bundled up in wool hats, ear muffs, gloves, and heavy overcoats. When the moment came for a take, all these heavy winter accouterments had to be shed and stowed out of sight. On the command "Action!" over a loud hand-held bullhorn, the whole summery tableau came vividly to life, but we were not close enough for the camera to detect the goose pimples of the shivering extras. I felt so sorry for the people involved that it was a relief to yell, "CUT!" whereupon, a veritable stampede ensued to the caches of winter clothing. Rarely does such a scene work out to everyone's satisfaction on the first try, and, if only for protection, a second take is customary. Everyone was relieved when it was done and over with after only a second take. We all got a kick out of the ice-cream vendor. Despite the freezing cold, his business was thriving. No wonder; the ice-cream cones were the real thing—and free.

In another scene, I was with the camera crew, all bundled up like Eskimos, in front of the Capitol and me collecting dead leaves. I released the leaves to let them float by the camera at the appropriate moment to conjure up a visual image that winter was around the corner. Altogether, it was one of the best second-unit shoots I have ever been involved in, thanks to a splendid crew. To all of us it was professionally satisfying that we had launched the shooting of this historical epic. The studio was elated that we accomplished it in four days, and Elmo Williams was pleased and highly complimentary after seeing the results. However, I had no illusions that this would lead to my joining the *Tora! Tora! Tora!* team on an extended assignment. Once the Washington episode was completed, I knew I would be on my own again, looking for a job.

HOLDING THE TIGER BY THE TAIL

A few months later, I was working on a film for my old friend, David Jacobson of Bransby Studio, at McCoy Air Force Base in Orlando, Florida. By that time *Tora! Tora! Tora!* had evaporated from my mind. Occasionally, I heard rumblings that all was not going well with the Kurosawa unit in Japan—in fact, that there were major problems. I had heard that the "Emperor" was irritable, demanding beyond reason and tyrannical with his own Japanese crew and cast. At that point I really couldn't have cared less.

Out of the blue, I received a call from Stanley Hough, asking me if I would be available to go to Japan and take over as associate producer, due to Kurosawa's sudden illness, which might keep him hospitalized for a lengthy stretch. This was an extraordinary and unexpected turn of events. I asked when they would want me to be in Japan; his answer was, "Yesterday." I explained to him that while, of course, I wanted to accept the assignment, I could not just pack up and leave a picture halfway completed. It would take me a few days to find a replacement. "Do so and let us know as soon as possible. Darryl, Dick, and Elmo want you," was his reply.

David Jacobson reluctantly agreed to let me go, if I could spring myself loose from the military and come up with a viable substitute. This being a weekend, it wasn't easy to find the officers to whom I needed to explain my problem. Their initial resistance softened when they heard about *Tora! Tora! Tora!* and the position offered to me, but there was still one captain whose consent would be decisive in letting me go. He might insist that I stay to fulfill my contractual obligations. When I called his home on Sunday morning, his young son answered the phone, telling me that his dad was in the shower and that he would go and get him. "No, no, don't do that," I said. "I'll wait and call him back in fifteen minutes." The last thing I wanted to do was to pull the captain out of the shower and have him in a foul mood. But apparently he had heard the phone ring while drying himself off and came to the phone posthaste. I presented my case, assuring him that I would arrange for a colleague of mine, Gerd Oswald, to take over.

There was a prolonged and pregnant-with-suspense pause. At last he said, "You're sure the guy taking your place is good?"

"Positive," I said.

"Okay, you can go," he said. "Work out the details with David."

I called the studio to inform them when I would be arriving at LAX, and they in turn advised me that they would dispatch a limo to meet me and that the driver would take me straight home to La Jolla to say goodbye to my family and to repack my bag for a lengthy stay in Japan, maybe two months or more. The driver would wait for me and take me back to the airport to board a plane to Tokyo. As simple as that, I was on my way to Japan. Fortunately, Mark was living with us at the time and would look after Sinnie so that she would not be left alone.

Our temporary headquarters in Tokyo were at the fashionable Okura Hotel. Elmo was already there, having rushed over from Hawaii, where the American unit was shooting. Gradually, the details of the Kurosawa debacle were passed on to me by Elmo and Stan Goldsmith, the studio's liaison with Kurosawa Productions, Ltd. The rumors about Kurosawa's bizarre behavior were not only true but became even more alarming after the actual shooting began at the Toei studio in Kyoto. One can only speculate what might have led to the downfall of this creative genius of the Japanese film industry.

One major factor may have been his idea to cast nonprofessionals as some of the key figures in the military hierarchy. Kurosawa thought it would be refreshing to see new faces and to have men of great dignity from the business world, such as the president of a bank or chairman of an industrial cartel, assume the roles of Admiral Isoroku Yamamoto and Admiral Nagumo, the moving forces behind the attack on Pearl Harbor. It simply didn't work. Days were spent rehearsing a single scene, with take after take not yielding the desired result. Gradually, this ground down Kurosawa's composure. He had a hard time controlling his frequent outbursts of temper and refraining from insulting members of his crew whom he blamed for the various delays in shooting. Never known as a fast director to begin with, he was as slow as molasses on this picture. Furthermore, how Japan, as perpetrator of one of the most treacherous yet most brilliantly executed attacks in military history, would be portrayed was of great importance to all Japanese and was undoubtedly of great concern to Kurosawa.

He stooped to every known device to boost the morale of his principal amateur actors. For example, to make the actor playing Yamamoto more aware of his exalted military status, he laid a red carpet from his dressing room to the stage set. There a military band struck up a martial tune, while the whole crew stood at attention and saluted him smartly. All to no avail, and Kurosawa knew it. The business executives, after the first exhilaration of being a part of this epic, soon became disenchanted by the tedious routine of filming. They longed to return to their sumptuous offices. The tension on the set became increasingly explosive, and the results of Kurosawa's efforts increasingly negative. It must have appeared like a dead-end street to Kurosawa, who had never before had to deal with such a fiasco of his own making.

Then a freak accident occurred that threw Kurosawa into a tailspin. A heavy piece of lighting equipment broke loose from its moorings high on a bamboo trestle and crashed to the stage floor, missing Kurosawa by inches. He suspected a diabolical plot to eliminate or at least immobilize him. Henceforth, everyone on the set had to wear a hard hat. Things went rapidly from bad to worse until finally it became quite apparent that Kurosawa had flipped, caused by either a nervous breakdown or acute mental tension. Even his closest coworkers of many years agreed that this was an undeniable fact. Frantic cables between Elmo Williams in Hawaii, Darryl in Paris, and Dick Zanuck in Beverly Hills led to the decision to close down the Kurosawa unit, pay off the actors and crew, strike the stage sets, and return the rented props.

After being examined by a panel of reputable Japanese doctors, Kurosawa was informed of the precarious state of his mental health. He vehemently denied their diagnosis, claiming that he felt perfectly fit to continue directing the film. He protested vociferously the studio's decision to close down their joint venture. The decision stood firm. Kurosawa would have to be institutionalized for a minimum of two months and undergo intensive psychiatric treatment.

How to deal with such a delicate situation, as far as the Japanese press and public opinion were concerned, was indeed a problem. In Japan, one doesn't just *fire* a man of Kurosawa's stature, regarded as a national treasure. Utmost diplomacy would be required by officially announcing that "due to severe fatigue," Akira Kurosawa had resigned as the director of the Japanese portion of *Tora! Tora! Tora!* This did not wash well with the notoriously sensation-hungry Japanese press corps, nor with the loyal movie-going public, of whom there were millions in Japan. It was further exacerbated by Kurosawa's continued statements to the press that he was in fine health and ready to resume his directorial obligations.

When Darryl Zanuck got drawn into this whole mess, well remembering how Kurosawa had let him cool his heels for hours in a dingy little office at Toei studio before permitting him to come on the set and observe him shooting a scene, he was furious to say the least. Aside from the enormous costs in time and money lost, it was a humiliating setback for the studio. Darryl's reaction was to junk the few minutes of usable footage shot in Japan and rewrite the screenplay so that the entire film could be shot in Hawaii and at the home studio.

After a cooling-off period of a couple of weeks and a reevaluation of the situation in Japan, it was decided among Darryl, Dick, and Elmo to make a completely new start—in Japan. After all, there was a sizable investment in standing sets on hand, such as the full-scale upper structure and deck of Yamamoto's flagship *Nagato*, and a replica of the flight deck of the aircraft carrier *Akagi*, which spearheaded the attack on Pearl Harbor. There were a great number of interior sets: realistic ship's quarters and offices and even a ceremonial reception hall in the Imperial Palace, where the emperor was to hold an audience. It would have been an enormous waste to lose all these sets, which had already been paid for. And that is where I came in.

Elmo, Stanley Goldsmith, our unit manager, and I set up a new schedule. In view of the enormous amount of work to be done, we decided to engage two Japanese directors. One would direct all the dialogue sequences in various interiors and exteriors, while the other would concentrate on the pure action shots, such as practice bombing runs and, most importantly, the preparations for takeoff of the Japanese attack planes from the *Akagi*'s flight deck. The *Akagi* set was not built for planes to take off nor land, and since there was no Japanese aircraft carrier extant, this dramatic sequence had to be shot using an American vessel. Normally, with a film of this type, the various branches of the armed forces cooperate in making their equipment available at a nominal fee to cover operating expenses. In this case, the navy balked. They could not see themselves providing an American ship to simulate the *Akagi*.

Eventually permission was granted to use the carrier USS *Yorktown* to double for the *Akagi*, but with certain restrictions. First, the squadron of thirty-two Zero fighters, converted faithfully from American AT-6 trainers, would have to be ferried by barge the night before the shoot and hoisted by crane onto the deck of the *Yorktown*. At daybreak, with the sun just rising over the horizon, they would be permitted to launch the whole squadron one by one, but only once for each plane. No landings would be permitted on the carrier deck. The planes would have to land at the North Island airstrip at the naval air station at Coronado. This whole scheme worked beautifully without a single mishap and would intercut perfectly with the action yet to be shot in Japan on the *Akagi* set, showing all the preparations.

One of the first orders of business was to sign up the two directors. We started with half a dozen of the top directors available, interviewing them at length and screening clips of their films. Some of them seemed reluctant to step into Kurosawa's shoes, as though it would be almost sacrilegious to do so. We could not afford to make a mistake, but we gambled when we decided upon Toshio Masuda for the sequences with dialogue and Kinji Fukasaki for the action footage. Both of them had originally studied to be teachers and had drifted into the film business, accumulating an extensive list of feature film credits. They were highly recommended to us as dedicated workhorses. Of the two, Masuda-san was the more outgoing and relaxed, somewhat familiar with the English language but not sufficiently to communicate without the presence of an interpreter. In contrast, Fukasaki-san was as taut and high-strung as a thoroughbred racehorse. In the end both worked out well, albeit I had to learn to accept their preferred working hours and methods of shooting, so different from ours in the States. I realized very soon that it was more expedient to let them do it their way rather than to try to convert them to our way of doing things.

Recasting the picture took some time, even though a number of the actors originally selected by Kurosawa were re-signed for the same roles. This applied more or less to the camera crew, technicians, and other helpers. Casting the actor to portray Admiral Isoroku Yamamoto was difficult and protracted, until we finally settled on Soh Yamamura, a seasoned professional of stage, screen, television, and Kabuki theater. Although not resembling Yamamoto in physical appearance or facial likeness, he was a felicitous choice. He gave us a solid and believable performance with much dignity.

Another casting problem was finding an actor to play the Japanese ambassador to the United States, Kichisaburo Nomura. By this time Elmo had left for Hawaii, leaving me holding *Tiger! Tiger! Tiger!* by the tail. Facing the end of my fruitless search to cast this important part, I found myself in Osaka in the dressing room of a revered Kabuki actor, who was putting on the traditional makeup of a fierce Samurai warlord. After the proper ceremonial introductions, we began to talk with the help of one of the interpreters who was at my side at all times. Shogo-san (Shimada, his second name) did not speak a word of English nor understand the language. This posed a serious problem. However, he was six feet tall, well built, and his face closely resembled the character to be portrayed. I was impressed by his dignified countenance, and to be honest, I had no second choice. He assuaged my concern about his linguistic shortcomings and assured me that if I made him a tape of his lines, he could learn them phonetically. "No problem," he said through the interpreter, "I have done this many times before."

I told him I would be glad to do so, disregarding that his English learned by rote would come out with the lilting Austrian accent of my speaking voice. In any case I was so impressed by his quiet confidence that we made a verbal agreement then and there a few minutes before he made his stage entrance for an eight-hour-long performance in a demanding role. I had a hunch that it would work out fine, knowing there would be a voice coach on the set at the studio in the Hollywood, where this scene was scheduled to be shot. When I told him this, he was thrilled with the prospect of a journey to America. Suffice it to say that he came through with flying colors and fooled everyone into thinking he was fluent in English.

One last casting problem remained: the part of Mr. Grew, the American ambassador to Japan in Tokyo. He, too, was a man of above-average height with a distinctive face. By sheer coincidence, at a reception at the American embassy, I met a gentleman who was the publisher of fine books on Japanese culture, mores, homes, and gardens. His likeness to Ambassador Grew was startling. Notwithstanding Kurosawa's debacle with nonprofessional actors, I was tempted to tread the same path. After all, his part consisted of only a few short dialogue scenes in the ambassador's office, and he could just pretend they were part of his book-publishing business. I was willing to take the gamble, but when I approached Mr. Weatherwax with my proposition, he turned me down flat. He told me he was not an actor and had never aspired to be one and that he would fall on his face with a resounding thud. "No," I said, "you wouldn't. I can tell. With a little patience and proper coaching and direction you would do well."

Gradually he became a bit intrigued by the whole idea, and when I told him that we would have three business suits made for him by the finest tailor in Tokyo to fit the period, which he could keep after we were through shooting his short scenes, he said, "All right, you talked me into it." He did not disappoint us. Masuda had a fine time working out his moves and staging the scenes he was in, with the great satisfaction of directing his first American actor in his debut. For us, his was truly a fresh face and well worth the minimal trouble encountered once he got over his initial camera fright.

To get away from Tokyo and head for Kyoto and our headquarters at the Toei studio complex was a great relief. Tokyo, a bustling, overcrowded metropolis, reminiscent of ants converging upon a giant anthill, was not among my favorite capital cities. To compound this impression, the majority of people wore surgical white gauze masks over nose and mouth, supposedly as a disease preventative. Kyoto, to the contrary, the ancient imperial city, had managed to retain its soothing beauty in the long-

420 TORA! TORA! TORA!

established tradition of Japanese architecture juxtaposed by a variety of trees, shrubs, flowers, and artfully composed rock formations, often with a cascading waterfall. I remembered Kyoto well from my first visit to Japan, but as I soon found out, many things had changed. There were bigger, more modern hotels, some high-rise office buildings, and other landmarks with glaring neon lights. But as a whole, Kyoto still stood out as having preserved much of its ancient heritage.

Office as well as stage space was claustrophobically cramped at the Toei studio, quite different from our large and spacious facilities in the U.S. Accompanied by Stanley Goldsmith, who had been with Kurosawa from the outset of shooting and had witnessed—and survived—the gradual downfall of the cinematic giant, I looked at the still-standing sets. I was impressed by the quality of the scenic designs and details of the various sets until I took a look behind them. A maze of bamboo poles tied together in an intricate pattern held the walls in place, with a gangway on top to serve as a lighting platform. This alone indicated to me how different this shoot would be.

Our first actual shooting in Japan was scheduled to take place at Kyushu, the southernmost island of Japan. It was there that our two warship sets were built, standing on dry land with bows barely touching the sea. The nearby village in which we were quartered was an isolated place that mostly attracted summer tourists. This being the middle of winter, it was cold with frequent, pelting rain mixed with snow. The expectancy of sunshine, based on past records, was only nominal. However, these unpleasant weather conditions, while not conducive to filming, would match the atmospheric pattern during the actual training exercises that had been held in these waters and that could be expected while en route to Pearl Harbor.

The sight of the two ships was quite overwhelming, especially the *Nagato*, a towering superstructure with a battery of heavy-caliber guns pointing out to sea. The flight deck of the *Akagi*, which was originally designed to represent only the middle portion of the flattop with the bridge in the center, was reinforced and extended fore and aft at the insistence of Kurosawa, with the hope that the Japanese aviation authorities would consider it fit enough for takeoffs and landings. As it turned out, the set was simply not adequate for such a purpose. The risk of a fatal crash was enormous, and the insurance premium would have been prohibitive. Nevertheless, the set served us well.

One of the most impressive scenes shot on this location was the ceremonial change of command on the occasion of Admiral Yamamoto's taking charge of the *Nagato*. I couldn't help but wonder how Masuda would handle this situation logistically: get the extras, dress them properly, train, and feed them. It was then that I grasped for the first time the ingenuity and professionalism of director Masuda and his crew. They came up with five hundred or more sailors dressed in white uniforms, drawn from a nearby university. Some of the students, as was common then, wore their hair long, and for those willing to shear their locks, a special bonus was offered.

For this scene the camera had to be placed in such a way, on the deck of the *Akagi*, shooting toward the *Nagato* for the establishing long shot, that the audience would not be aware of her standing on dry land. The five hundred sailors were lined up in rows all over the ship's deck and superstructure as though it were festooned with a thousand of them. The camera crosscut to the deck of the *Nagato*, shooting down at the admiral's barge, with Yamamoto and his staff approaching the ship, and then cut to the military band on deck, which was striking up a fanfare with everyone snapping to attention. By that time the admiral's barge had supposedly docked alongside the ship, and he was shown climbing up the last steps of the staircase and being piped aboard. This whole scene, when cut together, played perfectly smoothly and set the tone for the Japanese portion of the film. My confidence in Masuda's directorial ability, imagination, and inventiveness was enormously fortified. Also, I was pleased with the appearance of the cast members, with their precision in speech and stern demeanors so characteristic of their military discipline.

By disposition a notorious optimist, I thought that surely after this promising start we would move along at the same pace. I was wrong. Many delays were caused by the fickle winter weather. This caused aggravating delays in our shooting schedule and forced us prematurely to use up our limited number of cover sets. Another problem was the workday's starting time. Our Japanese crew preferred beginning the day's shooting later in the morning than we were accustomed to. They compensated for it by working late, often into the night when daylight was not required. Their concept of using and scheduling time was so different from ours. Also, their method of setting up an interior scene, lighting it, rehearsing the dialogue and moves, and finally shooting it took ever so much longer than we were used to. We saw ourselves falling alarmingly behind schedule, which, of course, was costly and upsetting to the home production office.

With every passing week the pressure on the three of us Americans— Stan Goldsmith, me, and Lloyd Anderson, an experienced production manager we had brought over to stick with the Fukasaki unit—increased. I spent much of my time traveling between the two units wherever they happened to be shooting to try to expedite their progress. I had to use my good judgment and sense of discretion so as not to offend Masuda or Fukasaki. They both took enormous pride in their work and strove for perfection. They were most sensitive to any criticism unless it was presented diplomatically. At times I had to point out to Masuda that it would be preferable as far as American audiences were concerned to tone down the exaggerated style of some of the actors, saying the style expected in their traditional Kabuki drama would not be suitable for a film of this type. He reacted appreciatively to my suggestion, without regarding it as an offense to his ego. After all, he realized that this was an important part of my job.

Fukasaki was overly sensitive in this respect and misconstrued any constructive suggestions as a criticism of his work. At one point I informed him that, in accordance with Elmo Williams, one of the more complicated sequences would be eliminated. It was superfluous and would only retard the flow of action. Fukasaki was incensed and took it as a personal affront, thinking that it was a lack of trust on our part that he was not experienced enough to film this sequence of aerial bombardment. It was simply that we did not need it, and it took me a long time to convince him of this.

When at last we moved our operation from Kyushu back to Kyoto, we had high hopes that the tempo of our daily output would accelerate. To a certain extent it did, but we would never catch up with days already lost. On the whole, the actors were cooperative and patient with a pronounced esprit de corps. In one case, both crew and actors worked until after midnight, on their own time and without any additional compensation, to enable a key player to leave early in the morning for a previous TV commitment in Tokyo. I admired the professionalism of some of the major stars in our cast, such as Soh Yamamura (Admiral Yamamoto) and Eijiro Tono, a lovable, grizzled old veteran with a pockmarked face, who portrayed Admiral Nagumo, commander of the fleet attacking Pearl Harbor. Tatsuya Mihashi, another versatile actor, played Minoru Genda, the technical genius behind the execution of the daring assault. We became good friends and kept up a correspondence for years thereafter. Then there was Koreya Senda as Prince Konoye, a member of the imperial family and a high functionary in the political arena. He was a stylish performer who could have fit with ease into the Shakespeare repertory offered by the Old Vic in London. These were the reasons we had come to Japan, to get a different overall feeling from the scenes shot there with Japanese directors, actors, and technicians. This goal was achieved and was favorably noted by many critics after the film was released.

By the end of March, everyone's composure was stretched taut because of the slow progress of our unit. Our primary objective was to overcome by any means available the unexpected emergencies and hold-ups to get the job done. We were inching ever closer to the day when we could say, "This is a wrap!" The home studio was fully aware of our dilemma and made every effort to bolster our morale, such as this cable from DFZ:

DEAR OTTO HAVE RECEIVED COPY OF YOUR COMPREHENSIVE LETTER TO DICK AND HAVING BEEN TWICE WHERE YOU ARE NOW I KNOW WHAT YOU HAVE BEEN THROUGH BUT I DO NOT SYMPATHIZE WITH YOU IN THE LEAST AS YOU WANTED TO WORK AND I THOUGHT AN ASSIGNMENT IN A NICE SOFT SPOT LIKE KYOTO WOULD PROVIDE YOU WITH THE WORK YOU WANTED STOP JOKING ASIDE YOU MUST STICK IT OUT TO THE BITTER END, WHICH I KNOW YOU WILL STOP AFFECTIONATE REGARDS, DARRYL

We were left with one more major hurdle, and that was mastering a new technical process called "front projection" as opposed to the customary "back projection" system. In back projection, the background of a given scene is projected onto a transparent screen with the projecting apparatus behind it. Then the actors, never having been near the location shown on the screen, are put in front of it to emote and speak their lines while being photographed by a camera in front of them. It was a time-consuming affair, since it required a perfect "plate" (the strip of film projected) both in density of detail and lighting, which then had to be matched exactly with the lighting thrown on the actors standing before the screen. When successfully executed, the effect was startlingly realistic. For example, one could show a medium shot or close-up of a skier racing down a slope at full speed without even having a pair of skis attached to his feet. When done badly, it was jarring and awful.

"Front projection," still in the final stages of development, promised to deliver better quality and a substantial economy in time. This required shipping to Japan all the necessary equipment, plus two top technicians familiar with the system. It also meant that we had to hire a hall to accommodate the installation as there was no stage of that size at Toei studio nor was there a hall large enough in Kyoto. We settled on the convention center of the nearby city of Osaka.

Osaka, a thriving commercial center and harbor town, was too far from Kyoto to commute; therefore, we had to move our temporary headquarters there. Other than the magnificent and well-preserved Osaka Castle, I remember it as a colorless industrial city. It seems to me that once our equipment was in place, I was encapsulated in the huge cold convention center hall during our entire stay. The premises were not equipped to serve as a studio, so everything we needed for camera, lighting, and prop platforms had to be built. Many of the medium shots and close-ups of Japanese pilots in the cockpits of their combat planes were done there with the plane placed on a platform against a blue backing. In the laboratory the real background would be superimposed through optical manipulations.

An assortment of other set pieces was to be photographed against this special blue backing. Although this process had the advantage of eliminating the back-projection setup, front projection became a source of prolonged delay, and the results were discouraging and minimal. Not being as technically versed in the process as I could have wished, I was completely frustrated. Finally, in despair and feeling the pressure of time upon us, we asked the studio to send Bill Abbott, one of the best cameramen in the special effects department, to come bail us out. Even after Bill Abbott took over, our struggle continued, and for some reason the problems were never satisfactorily resolved.

Dick Zanuck sent me this cable:

DEAR OTTO JUST RECEIVED YOUR LETTER AND APPRECIATE IT VERY MUCH STOP I KNOW THAT YOU ARE DOING THE BEST JOB YOU CAN UNDER VERY AWFUL CIRCUMSTANCES AND WE ARE LOOKING TO YOU TO CONTINUE FIGHTING IT OUT SO THAT WE GET THE BEST POSSIBLE FOOTAGE ON THE SCREEN STOP REGRET HAVING SENT THE FRONT PROJECTION SYSTEM UNTIL

WE HAD IT ABSOLUTELY PERFECTED BUT THIS OF COURSE IS
HINDSIGHT STOP I HOPE THAT ABBOTT'S EXPERTISE WILL BE
OF VALUE AS WHAT I HAVE SEEN THUS FAR HAS BEEN TERRI-
BLY DISAPPOINTING BEST REGARDS DICK

At one point we resorted to one of the most primitive ways to shoot
some tight head close-ups of pilots en route to Pearl Harbor and some
quick extremely close reaction shots during the actual attack on Pearl
Harbor. We had two grips hold up a large piece of cardboard painted
with a blue sky and fleecy clouds, which was then moved slightly up and
down and slowly backward. To further simulate the effect of the plane in
flight, we had a wind machine blow a blast of air into the open window
of the cockpit. It was almost embarrassing in its crudeness, but in that
particular situation it worked.

At last the day came when we had to be out of the hall and could write
THE END to our frustrating cinematic saga. We had a lovely wrap-up
party in true Japanese style, sitting on the floor of a fine restaurant with
our legs awkwardly tucked under the low table, and a bevy of heavily
made-up geishas in elaborate kimonos and hairdos serving food and freely
dispensing potent, warm sake. It healed some of the wounds inflicted
during our battle of wits, but like so many experiences in filmmaking,
the unpleasant memories fade, while the more pleasant ones linger.

Akira Kurosawa recovered from his untimely malaise after we left Japan and resumed his successful career with his reputation untarnished,
still revered by his loyal followers. As for *Tora! Tora! Tora!*, the film was
released in 1970 to mixed reviews, even though highly acclaimed for its
extraordinary reenactment of the fiery inferno of December 7, 1941,
from a technical and visual point of view. For this, all kudos must go to
Elmo Williams, Dick Fleischer, and Ray Kellogg with his team of special
effects technicians and corps of fearless stunt men. But the public at
large, while impressed by the documentary fidelity of the film, did not
flock to the box office. The picture never recouped its staggering production costs. Nevertheless, it has become a cult film that appears regularly
on television every December 7.

HOLLYWOOD SILVERBACK

The income from *Tora! Tora! Tora!* provided Sinnie and me with a
much needed infusion into our anemic bank account. As luck would

have it, after I had been home for a few weeks, Jim Copley created a position for me in the Copley Film Unit, headquartered in La Jolla. It operated on a modest scale and dealt primarily with the production of educational and promotional 16 mm films.

As was to be expected, the head of this unit was concerned about the intrusion of an experienced filmmaker into his domain, which consisted of a tightly knit staff of about eight people. With my film and television credits, he might have thought I intended to gradually take over the department. Such a thought never entered my mind. I was more than willing to subjugate myself to his established modus operandi and to work in congenial partnership. I had no ambition to climb the rungs of an executive ladder. Jim Copley knew that, and I knew he was proud to have me on his staff. My thought was that I would stay with the Copley organization until it was time for me to retire. I was so pleased and happy to have found a suitable job so close to our home in La Jolla, with normal business hours and a monthly check to count on. Nevertheless, I felt it would be difficult to overcome the undercurrent of resentment toward me at having been foisted upon the film unit by Jim Copley.

My prediction was not too far off, as time would tell. I found out, and not for the first time, that creeping-up age was a deterrent. To these young men, I was a used-up silverback with a Hollywood stigma, whereas they leaned toward a new trend promulgated by graduates from the University of California at Los Angeles film school. It was a well-established school, staffed with highly competent teachers. But that did not guarantee that every graduate would emerge as a *wunderkind* with revolutionary ideas about filmmaking. I have seen so many of this type fall flat on their faces after an initial success at directing a film. On the other hand, some of these graduates did rise to fame and fortune. The one hired by the head of Copley Productions was a dud, and the first film directed by him was as amateurish and inane as any I had ever seen.

Frequently, Jim Copley and I had lunch together to talk about movies, sports, and current political events. He never asked, nor did I bring up, how things were going in the film unit. I was sure that the company grapevine took care of that. During one of these luncheons in the club room of the Valencia Hotel, we happened to touch upon the upcoming 1972 Winter Olympics to be held in Sapporo, Japan, on the northernmost island of Hokkaido. He knew that I had covered the Winter Olympics at St. Moritz in 1948. He also knew that I had had a hand in the Squaw Valley Winter Olympics in 1960, where I had improvised, with the full approval of Willy Schaefler, chief of Alpine events, an "instant replay" procedure to resolve problems of competitors missing a slalom gate or straddling a pole that would disqualify them.

I had arranged for a large grocery van to be transformed into an on-site film lab, manned by a horse-racetrack camera technician familiar with the quick print process. Six cameramen chosen from among my friends were placed strategically along the racecourse. The cameras and raw stock film were provided to us gratis by Eastman Kodak. Each cameraman had a set of skiing runners assigned to him, and as soon as a one-hundred-foot roll of 16 mm film was exposed and properly identified as to position and number of gates covered, it would be shuttled to the lab and within fifteen minutes developed and dried to run through a projector. It turned out to be an invaluable tool in settling disputes between competitors and officials, almost as soon as the race was finished. Though only a crude forerunner of the sophisticated electronic instant replay system now used for sports events, ours did the job.

Knowing my skiing background, Jim said, "How would you feel about going to Sapporo to cover the 1972 Winter Olympics as a special bylined reporter for the *San Diego Union* and Copley Wire Service? It would be sort of a coup for us to do so."

"I'd love it," I said, "if we could arrange for a leave of absence from the film unit."

"That would be no problem," he assured me, with a twinkle in his eyes. "I want you to meet with Jack Murphy, our sports editor. The two of you would work closely together. You to cover the technical aspects and excitement of the ski events, and he to take care of the color aspects, at which he is tops."

I had been an admirer and avid reader of Murphy's daily column in the sports section of the *Union* and considered him indeed a fine writer with the ability to bring out the human interest angle, whether he was writing about a sports hero or about his close companion, Abe, a smart, coal-black Labrador with a mind of his own. To work with Jack Murphy would be an honor. Shortly thereafter, the three of us met for lunch and all the details were settled. Jack admitted he was relieved to have someone like me along, as he knew next to nothing about skiing. I could not help but take an instant liking to the man.

Official certification procedures through the U.S. Olympic Committee would entitle us to pick up our credentials, press badges, and housing arrangements upon checking in at the Olympic Village in Sapporo. I would catch up with Jack just in time for the opening ceremony since I had to finish work on a film in its last stages of completion. Then off again I was to Japan. I felt like a bird of passage, destined to restlessly migrate between countries and cities, even continents.

My assignment from Kenneth D. Zumwalt, Sunday editor of the *Union*, was to get him a picture that he could feature on the front page of the Sunday paper, showing the American team in the opening ceremony. Fortunately, my plane arrived on schedule at Sapporo. I gave instructions to deliver my luggage and skis to the press center at the Olympic Village and hopped into a taxi. Arriving at the ice arena that was the site of the ceremony after a mad dash through traffic, for which Japanese taxi drivers are famous, I saw a long snake of people lined up to enter the building. Not knowing anything about the layout, I realized that without my press badge, I would have some difficulty getting in on time.

I glanced to my left, searching for a solution to my dilemma, and spotted a large fenced-in snowfield where the teams were forming up in preparation for their entrance into the arena. That's where I ought to be, was my instinctive thought. I straddled the shoulder-high wire fence, dashed across the snowfield, sinking up to my knees, and made it just in time, huffing and puffing, to grab a shot of the U.S. team casually forming up. They were to follow the Russian team already lined up ahead of them. My only chance to get in position to take a picture of the American team making its entrance was to join the Russian team at the tail end and march with them into the arena. I raised my camera to the smiling, laughing Russian athletes and said, "Americanski, me press," while pointing back at the American team following us at some distance. As soon as we cleared the guarded entrance, I waved good-bye to the burly fur-hatted Russians, using three of the five Russian words in my limited vocabulary, "*Bolshoya spasiba, daskorava*," meaning "Thanks a whole bunch, you guys. See you later."

I then veered to one side, having taken a quick look at the position of the sun, and was ready to take the other angle requested by the editor, which was of the American team marching into the arena. This entrance prompted a jubilant outburst of cheering and waving of miniature American flags. Once inside the arena, I was on my own. I got all the shots I wanted of the opening ceremony, including a close-up of the Japanese torchbearer climbing the steep staircase to light the Olympic flame, the signature of all Olympic games. I even got a shot of Emperor Hirohito with his customary unsmiling facial expression, heavily guarded and isolated from the surrounding populace. Altogether, it was a delightful and fitting ceremony, auguring one of the best organized, executed, and most successful Winter Olympics ever.

When I caught up with Jack Murphy at the Olympic Village, the first order of business was to dispatch by airmail the roll of film I had shot, keeping my fingers crossed that there would be something usable in it. Jack would file his first report by telex.

A few days later I received a cable from Kenneth Zumwalt:

THANK YOU FOR THE NICE COLOR PHOTOS FROM SAPPORO. I HOPE YOU ARE AS PLEASED WITH THE FINISHED PRODUCT AS WE ARE. WE HAVE HAD MANY COMPLIMENTS FOR THE PAGE AND YOUR COLOR PHOTOS MADE THE PAGE.

That was the beginning of two most enjoyable weeks. Jack and I were assigned an apartment in a complex of small townhouses that had been built specifically for the Olympics. It consisted of two bedrooms, a living room with fireplace, and a kitchen we never used as the nearby cafeteria offered a variety of tasty meals.

We were working in tandem and virtually inseparable, except for the times I took off to run the Alpine courses, accompanied by an official. To me that was one of the most memorable treats, skiing down the velvety Olympic racecourses. The downhill course itself was a marvel of imagination and ingenuity, virtually hewn from a rocky peak, interspersed with stands of dense forest. All of the terrain was part of a national park; the proviso was that every single tree felled to make room for the steep serpentine downhill course would have to be replaced by a new tree planted in the exact same spot, all evidence of mechanical incursions would have to be erased, and the mountain's original appearance restored. The chairlift and its iron towers were also to be dismantled after the games ended. Another venue, the majestic Okurayama seventy- and ninety-meter hill was an architectural masterpiece, integrated into the surrounding landscape to endure for decades.

What could be more gratifying for Nippon than three Japanese ski jumpers standing proudly on the victory podium to receive gold, silver, and bronze medals for their stylish, birdlike, long-distance flights at the inaugural competition? The American contingent, unfortunately, did not fare well in the Alpine events. Had it not been for our ladies team, with

Barbara Cochran winning a gold medal in the slalom and Susan Corrock's surprising third place in the downhill, there would not have been much to report.

Physically, covering the Sapporo Olympics was somewhat tiring since the scattered venues were separated by substantial distances. The miniature buses servicing these areas were built for people of short stature and did not accommodate our long legs. Also, pushing one's way through the thousands of spectators and frenzied press corps, rushing to get to their observation posts, was wearying. When the games were over, both Jack and I were tired but nevertheless stimulated by having been part of a unique experience.

During my two weeks' absence from the Copley Film Unit, I was able to think more realistically about my future there. By the time I returned to La Jolla, I had made up my mind to resign. There was one last business matter to attend to, and that was to supervise the dubbing in Los Angeles of film I had directed prior to leaving for Japan. After a few days of rest at home, I drove to Los Angeles, finished the dubbing session, and hastened back to La Jolla, having mailed in my resignation letter. It was short and concise, stating "health conditions" as the reason for taking this step. Tooling along the road back to La Jolla, my racing-green Jaguar purring like a contented cat, I felt a sense of relief. Also, I felt some regret as far as Jim Copley was concerned, whom I did not want to lose as a friend and hoped would understand my predicament.

As I approached Encenitas, a small town on the coast north of La Jolla, I felt a sharp and very painful stab in my chest. The pain radiated into my left shoulder, down the arm, and into my leg. I felt as though I was about to vomit. My mind began to get woozy. All I could think of was pulling off the main road at the nearest gas station. I realized I needed help. Stopping at the station, I asked the attendant whether there was an emergency hospital nearby.

"Not that I know of," he said, "except for the Scripps Clinic Hospital, farther south."

Of course, I knew the Scripps Clinic. "Well," I said, "I'll just pull to the side out of your way and rest for a while before I go on."

As I was sitting in my car with the engine turned off, leaning back with my eyes shut, I heard a lady's voice saying, "Excuse me, I couldn't help but overhear your conversation with the attendant, and looking at you, I don't think it would be safe for you to drive on in your condition."

"Oh, thank you so very much," I said. "I think I'll be all right after a little rest. I've been under a lot of pressure lately, and it may also have something to do with the lunch I ate in a hurry at a Mexican taco joint. It has happened to me before and gone away."

"Let me do this," she replied. "My husband is getting something at the drugstore around the corner. I'll go and fetch him. He can drive your car, and I'll follow you. We'll drop you off at Scripps. We are headed in that direction anyway."

Before I could say a word she was gone. Within ten minutes she was back with her husband, a handsome-looking young man, who said to me, "Slide over, I'll drive."

So off we drove. I didn't know his name, nor did he know mine. I was thankful he was driving instead of me. The conversation was halting and monosyllabic until I said, almost to myself, "I wonder if this could be possibly a heart attack," never having given it a thought before.

"Oh, my God," he said. "If that's what you think it is, we'd better get you to the emergency hospital in a hurry." Whereupon, he revved up the Jaguar's r.p.m.s as though he was a race driver heading into the home stretch.

We arrived at the hospital entrance with a screeching halt. He jumped out of the car, ran around to open my door, and helped me out. I told him I would be all right and could make it on my own to the front desk. It happened to be a quiet Saturday with no one waiting ahead of me. The attending nurse came up to me and asked, "Can I help you?"

"Yes, you can," I said. "I think I'm having a heart attack and I need a doctor."

She gave me a scrutinizing look and asked me, "What makes you think so?" as though suspecting I might have had a few drinks too many or overdosed on some potent drug.

"Look," I said, "I'm in great pain and need help, believe me."

"Okay, okay," she said. "I'll get a doctor." Soon a doctor appeared in his white smock. He took one look at me and motioned me to follow him. He led me into a small cubicle with an examining table, directing me to lie down. He checked my pulse, pulled out his stethoscope, and put it to my chest. He listened with a furrowed brow, then turned to a nurse, who had followed him, and gave her a few terse instructions.

Suddenly there was bedlam in the cubicle. My shirt was pulled off; so were my shoes and pants. Instruments were hooked up and connected to my body and an injection was given to me. Indeed, I had had a heart attack and a massive one at that, the doctor told me later, and I was very lucky to be alive. A little more delay and I would have been a goner. I was over the first critical step, but far from being out of danger, I was told. They didn't even want to move me from the cubicle into a hospital bed for the time being.

To my dismay, I could never thank the young couple for having helped me, nor could I identify them. They left the keys to my car at the reception desk. They came into my life in a moment of dire distress and vanished without a trace.

Sinclair came to see me after she had been notified by phone where I was. She was inebriated and frightened, her face ashen with worry, wanting to be helpful. Immediately she asked sternly whether the doctor who was taking care of me was a qualified heart specialist. If not, she demanded that he be replaced by the best available doctor in town. Weak and listless as I was, I tried to pacify her and whispered to her, "Dr. Brown is just fine. I like him. He saved my life. I see no need to make a change. He knows what he is doing." I was classified as being in critical condition and was moved into the intensive care section, where I stayed for ten days until I was moved to a regular-care hospital room. Mark came to see me immediately, and Peter also rushed to my bedside from Los Angeles. I assured them "Pop" was over the hump and would mend.

What amazed me was the number of get-well notes and cards I received and how many friends came to see me. Among these was Jim Copley, who told me how sorry he was that his good intentions had misfired in regard to my joining Copley Films. He reassured me that my resignation would have no effect on our personal friendship. So it remained until he passed away. Jack Murphy came to cheer me up. We had formed such a close bond in Sapporo, as he wrote in his column after having seen me at the hospital:

> In Sapporo, Otto was my colleague, delightful companion and personal expert. He explained what I was seeing and made it comprehensible.
>
> I imagine Otto was the only newspaper correspondent who skied all the Olympic courses except the jumps. He'd go down the alpine runs on Mt. Eniwa or Mt. Teine one day, and then watch the actual race with me on TV, covering the full length of the course. Having skied down the mountain, he knew what to expect and his practiced eye missed none of the details.
>
> We had a fine relationship. Otto interpreted the Olympics to me and I

typed out his essays for transmission by cable, after he had composed them in longhand. That seemed an equitable arrangement and I look forward to seeing Otto to rehash our adventures in Sapporo again, after he recovers from his momentary setback.

Softened by my constant pleading to let me go home, where I could recuperate much faster, Dr. Brown reluctantly permitted me to do so, but only if I promised to abide by his firm instructions. I would have to restrict my physical activities, not lift anything heavy or climb any stairs, and rest a lot with a minimum of mental stress.

This I agreed to, but as it turned out, my domestic environment was not at all a peaceful haven of convalescence. After two days at home, I packed a small valise and left a note that I was checking into a motel, where I would stay for a while undisturbed and unreachable until I felt stronger. I got into my car and drove off to find a place in a quiet neighborhood, where I signed in for a room. I carried my bag, fortunately a light one, up a flight of stairs as though I wanted to challenge fate and against Dr. Brown's orders. I passed this test without any harm coming to me.

Within a few weeks I had a commitment to direct a promotional film for a resort to be shot in and around Lucaya-Freeport on an island in the Bahamas. I had hoped to bring Sinnie with me, but it was not to be. Our marriage was floundering on the brink of a permanent dissolution. I knew I could not fulfill this commitment, since I was physically and mentally in no condition to do so. But I went anyway, turning over the direction of the film to Allan Caillou, who had written the script for it. Resting in the sun, swimming in the opalescent Caribbean waters, and watching the progress of filming from the sidelines helped me a lot in conquering my pervasive lethargy. I would need all my strength to rebuild my life and heal the damage inflicted by my heart attack. Dr. Brown had put me back on my feet, for which I would be grateful to him forever, but I had a long and arduous road ahead of me.

When I returned to La Jolla, Sinnie and I agreed to a temporary separation. She would stay on in our house, and I would move into an apartment. Neither of us wanted an immediate divorce, and we both hoped that we might still straighten out our personal problems. I moved into the Oakwood apartment complex at the outskirts of San Diego, populated mostly by singles of a much younger generation than I was. It was not an uncomfortable place to live, with all sort of amenities, pleasant surroundings, a gym, and a pool, but a home it was not. After a year of living separately, financial requirements dictated that we sell our home and Sinnie also move into an apartment complex in Coronado.

This was certainly the nadir of my life, and it would take a long time for me to pull myself together and even want to go on living after a failed marriage. It was as though I had lost all my incentive and motivation to struggle on.

Sinnie and I remained in communication through letters and phone calls but rarely saw each other. If we did it was emotionally draining to both of us. As the AA counselor had predicted, Sinnie would have to hit rock bottom before she decided of her own will to return and seek help from that organization. This occurred when early one morning I received a phone call from her, desolately telling me that during the night two strange men and a woman had broken into her apartment through the glass patio door on the ground floor. She told me that she had been beaten up and that the place was in disarray. Furniture had been toppled and a tall standing lamp broken in pieces while she fought them off, screaming for help, which forced them to retreat in haste.

I immediately called the manager and told him that I would be over and that I was incensed by his lax security measures that had permitted such a break-in to occur. After a long silence, he said to me, "Mr. Lang, I checked out the situation as soon as I was notified of it, and all I can tell you is that there was no break-in, no sign of a forced entry, and the patio door was securely closed. None of her valuables were missing or even touched. Yes, some of the furniture was toppled over helter-skelter, as though a fight had taken place, but there was no one to fight. It was all in her mind, a vivid hallucination caused by you know what and verified by a row of empty vodka and wine bottles in the kitchen. She must have hit her face against the sharp edge of a table or a fallen chair. I'm really terribly sorry and I don't know whether we can keep her here unless something is done to help her."

I rushed over to the apartment and was shocked by the look of her battered face and bruised body. I called for an ambulance to take her to an emergency hospital and tried to calm her down, telling her that she had reached the low point of her addiction, with her brain playing tricks on her. She agreed. This was the crucial turning point the AA counselor had warned us about. Sinnie realized she had sunk to the bottom of the pit, and she made up her mind to join Alcoholics Anonymous.

After two years or so living in limbo, we decided on a divorce, which

Mark and me enroute to New Guinea.

Peter and his wife Dale (Hagmann) with their two boys, Patrick and P. J. at Wetherly Drive, Beverly Hills, 1965.

Scene from *Tora! Tora! Tora!*,
Admiral Yamamoto's flagship
Nagato as seen from the aircraft
carrier *Akagi*.

With Japanese director Toshio
Masuda during the filming of *Tora!
Tora! Tora!* at the Kyoto studio.

Directing Clint Walker in the television series *Cheyenne*.

Directing Philip Ahn in *The Man From U.N.C.L.E.*

Visiting with my sisters Nelly (left) and Erna (below) in Austria.

My father, Alfred Lang, in a photo taken in 1929 when he was fifty-five years old.

Connie Wiley and her daughters Paige (left) and
Laurie (right) at Belvedere, California.

Peter and Didi at home at the
Rio Vista Ranch in Santa Paula,
California.

A pick-up "trio" for the ABC-TV special, *Beethoven: Ordeal And Triumph*, staged with John Secondary and Helen Jean Rogers. None of us were musicians off camera.

With cameraman Bill Hartigan during the shooting of *Beethoven: Ordeal And Triumph*.

With President and Mrs. Gerald Ford at the Vail/Beaver Creek ski classic, 1985. The Fords signed the photo, "To our friend Otto Lang, with warmest regards." Photo by Pepi Gramshammer.

Earl and Carol Holding, present owners of Sun Valley.

With Emile Allais at Vail in 1985.
Photo by Pepe Alemparte.

Friedl Pfeifer and his inamorata Sharon Crose at our Sun Valley reunion, 1993. Photo by Otto Lang.

June Campbell. Photo by Connie Campbell.

At home in Seattle. Photo by June Campbell.

was handled quite amicably, each of us engaging a lawyer to work out the details. According to California laws, we split our joint checking and savings accounts fifty-fifty and divided the furniture, artifacts, books, and so on, according to each person's wishes and satisfaction. I would support her financially and make it feasible for her to live in relative comfort, which was my intention all along. So ended the story of two once-young lovers, which began like a fairy tale with a festive wedding at Coronado and, sadly, terminated there in a dismal final parting after thirty-four years of matrimony.

I am grateful to have lived to see Sinnie gain control over, but never quite overcome, her addiction to alcohol and to see her make new friends among the old ones she already had in Coronado. She was part of an active AA group that met frequently to socialize, study Spanish, and travel together on short trips. We remained close friends, but it would never be the way it used to be, once upon a time so very long ago.

L I F E   W I T H
P E T E R

Despondent after my heart attack and its aftereffects, and saddened by the dissolution of my marriage, I saw no point in staying on at La Jolla. I felt it would be best for me to return to Los Angeles to earn a living and be close to the center of filmmaking. My son Peter lived there, and I thought it would be nice to be near him. My life was soon connected to his in ways that I would not have imagined.

Prior to his bicycle accident, Peter had been a good student earning commendable grades. After his accident, he was forced to spend months wearing a cast, be confined to a wheelchair, and undergo constant medical treatment. Even though Sinnie and I tried not to coddle him, emotionally we were distraught by the thought that his infected leg might not heal properly and still have to be amputated below the knee. It made it difficult to treat him as though there were nothing to worry about. By the time Peter returned to school, he had fallen behind in his studies. He seemed to have lost interest in the tedious process of getting an education. When his leg was healed, Sinnie and I decided to send him to Chadwick, a private school in Palos Verdes with a strictly regimented scholastic program. As a special favor to us and also because of their fondness for Peter, Mr. Chadwick, the headmaster, and his wife took him in as a boarder in their home—coincidentally adjoining the residence of our dear friends Paul, Mary, and Paulette Frankl. We made it a point to see Peter on weekends and to drop by the Frankls' for a visit or dinner.

What Peter wanted most was to be independent, earning a living as soon as possible. He dropped out of Chadwick before graduating and tried his hand at various jobs, among these automobile salesman and tuna fisherman. He joined a Hispanic-Portuguese crew on a lengthy journey from San Diego down into Mexican waters and farther south to Costa Rica in pursuit of tuna. In those days, tuna were caught on barbless metal hooks on lines attached to stout bamboo poles, rather than by purse seining, as nowadays. A school of fish would attack the hooks, baited with a few white feathers, in a feeding frenzy. Each fisherman tossed a hooked tuna over his shoulder onto the deck with a coordinated sweeping motion. With twenty or more men fishing simultaneously and wielding their poles in a crowded space, it was a hectic and dangerous workout, with hooks and fish flying through the air. Spending eight weeks at sea with a rough and free-wheeling group of men must have been tough going for a young American apprentice fisherman. It was an education of a different kind, and the fact that Peter was paid more than the agreed-upon percentage of the sale of the catch upon returning to San Diego proved that he had held his own.

After this, Peter determined, more than ever, to be his own boss. This was the goal he set for himself, and he followed it from then on. He started his own business of repairing, refinishing, and reupholstering furniture, learning the trade as he went along. He set up his shop in a World War II Quonset hut near the intersection of Sepulveda and Santa Monica Boulevards in Los Angeles. Primitive as it was, it served him well and helped him to build up a clientele.

With the business growing, a felicitous event occurred in Peter's life: he fell in love with and married Dale Hagmann. Dale came from a well-to-do family and was a graduate of Westlake, a distinguished school for girls in Holmby Hills. A pretty girl, vivacious and a charmer, she endeared herself to Sinnie and me instantly. Peter and she appeared to be well-matched, a happily married couple working together, she in the office as a general factotum and gofer, and Peter in the shop and out in the field. Offspring soon came. Peter Justin ("P. J.") was first, in 1962, followed by Patrick Foster in 1963. With their parents' mix of genes, these two couldn't help but be adorable young boys who grew into striking young men, both close to six feet tall. During P. J. and Patrick's early childhood, Sinnie and I were still living at Wetherly Drive; naturally, they came frequently to visit us and frolic in our swimming pool. Peter and Dale appeared to be destined for a happy and congenial family life.

It did not last. What brought on the rift and eventual divorce remains a mystery to me. I know that Peter was in love with Dale and she with him. This unexpected reversal was distressing, and at first I could not believe it. I tried my best by letter to change Dale's mind, but she answered in a tear-stained reply that her mind was made up. Perhaps the constant strain of working together every day of the week while taking care of two growing youngsters, keeping house, shopping, cooking meals, and at the same time wondering how to keep one step ahead of bill collectors were too much for Dale to bear. Peter was heartbroken when the divorce became final. Dale and he remained friends and communicated with each other, bonded by the lives of their two boys.

After the divorce, having outgrown the crowded and awkward layout of the Quonset hut, Peter moved his shop to a much larger building in an industrial area near the Los Angeles Airport. In addition to his restoration and upholstery business, he began to design furniture, featuring reproductions of classic antiques. One of his first creations was a bench inspired by a buggy seat, built of oak with ornamental wrought iron and upholstered in fine leather. In time, his styles branched out into various periods of history up to contemporary designs. The quality of his workmanship was first rate. The business culminated in the presentation of a handsome catalogue, encompassing all of his furniture lines, thereby establishing Peter Lang as a name to contend with among furniture manufacturers.

Peter remarried, as had Dale before him. It took time and perseverance to woo Diane Doheny ("Didi," as she was called by her friends), another California beauty, petite, bright, and glamorous, into marrying him. Hers was the well-known Doheny family, long-time Californians, oil- and land-rich. The wedding ceremony, performed in the garden of Didi's home, was a simple but joyous celebration with parents of both the bride and groom in attendance. Didi had married once before and had two children, Randy and Diane; their father and Didi's former husband, Randy Forbes, had married Dale. The four children befriended each other and got along well.

With Didi at Peter's side as a partner, his company sprouted wings. Together, they opened a showroom in the new, prestigious Pacific Design Center (the "Blue Whale") on Melrose Avenue in West Hollywood.

One day, quite unexpectedly, Peter said to me, "Dad, Didi and I would like to open a showroom at the Ice House in San Francisco, but only if you are interested in managing it. We need someone we can trust, someone who has the personality and presence you have. We could teach you the managerial part of the job in a hurry." The Ice House, a group of old-fashioned brick structures, had served at one time as office buildings and warehouses. Henry Adams and his wife, Claire Ellen, had done a terrific job in converting the buildings into a showcase for interior designers and their clients. I did not deliberate long before accepting Peter's proposal. The thought of living in San Francisco intrigued me and, above all, I would have the security of a well-paid job, although it would be an enormous challenge for me as a relative newcomer to make a success of the showroom. Above all, I did not want to disappoint Peter and Didi.

We flew to San Francisco, looked at the Ice House, and contracted for suitable space. In a month or so we opened for business, adding lamps, pictures, artifacts, and fine accessories to our furniture collection. My work at the Ice House was stimulating. People came through in a constant flow, looking around, asking questions, and placing orders. I made many new friends among the in-house staff and the visiting designers. With so many diverse showrooms on different floors, the place was a veritable treasure trove.

San Francisco is one of the most fascinating and attractive cities in the world. I was fortunate and found a compact bachelor's apartment high up on Taylor Street. From my balcony overlooking the city I could see the ultramodern Transamerica building pointing like a gigantic spire into the sky. Across the street was a miniature park with trees, shrubs, and flower beds designed by Thomas Church, who—once upon a time—had designed our swimming pool at Wetherly Drive. I also had a friend there: Maud Hill, still living in Woodside in her country mansion, whose grounds had also been masterfully landscaped by Church. She came to town frequently, staying in her townhouse, close to where I lived. After divorcing Larry Dorcy, Maud had married the irrepressible Austrian skier, Hannes Schroll, an extroverted character if ever there was one. I also made new friends. Among these, two of my favorites were Jim and Helen Nassikas. Jim was president of the classy Stanford Court hotel and with Edgar Stern the guiding spirit behind the creation of Deer Valley, a Utah ski resort and skier's dream fulfilled.

On a weekend visit at Maud's house in Woodside, I met one of her friends, a lady who happened to be an interior designer and had done work for Maud in both of her homes. The lady's name was Corinne Wiley. After a pleasant lunch, we adjourned to a nearby tennis court to play a game of doubles. I was completely out of practice and realized very quickly that I was not in Connie Wiley's league. Rather than humiliate and embarrass myself, I chose to watch her and her two teenage daughters play. Laurie, the older daughter, and Paige, the younger, were both in the full bloom of their youth and very attractive, with an impish streak of rebellion, so common at that age.

I was drawn to Connie by her athletic good looks and serene composure. When I told her that I ran the Peter Lang Showroom at the Ice House, she promised to drop in and visit me the next time she was there. She did come by and her intended short visit extended into lunch. Gradually came dinners and an invitation to visit her at her Belvedere home. Right from the beginning I felt comfortable with Connie and her daughters. In time she told me about her two failed marriages and struggle to provide a living for the three of them. Her two girls despised her last husband; incapable of establishing a rapport with them, he treated them shabbily and made their lives miserable. Correspondingly, this made Connie's life unbearable and resulted in an unpleasant divorce. Connie was just getting over her depression and obviously was not in any kind of a mood to become attached to another man in any way.

Still, we developed a friendship. We saw more and more of each other until eventually I was accepted as a member of the family, commuting from my apartment in town to Connie's relaxed home, built by her parents on the shore of Belvedere Lagoon, with her sailboat and canoe tied to the dock a few steps away. Over the course of the following years, Connie and I undoubtedly had some of the very best times of our lives. We went to concerts together and became devoted fans of Seiji Ozawa, then resident conductor of the San Francisco Symphony. We went to the opera, saw plays, and attended dinners and parties given by her many friends. In the winter months, we skied together at various resorts and traveled to Europe and Mexico, all while she was pursuing her profession and studying for her final exam to become a certified interior designer.

Sadly, these times did not last. Connie and I parted, even though we remained the best of friends and devoted to each other. There was no high drama, no rift or personal conflict. It is something I find very hard to explain. Whatever happened, I take the blame for our parting.

One of the factors was that Peter was hit by an unexpected, major financial setback. He had purchased a shipment of oak at an advantageous price, based on the large size of the order, but it unfortunately turned out to be insufficiently cured. Consequently, most of Peter's finished and shipped-out pieces of furniture began to develop cracks, especially the tops of tables and smaller pieces that were inlaid in a parquet pattern, meticulously fitted and glued together. They had to be shipped back to the factory and replaced, since Peter guaranteed his workmanship. Financially, this was ruinous and meant retrenching in every possible way, leading to the closing of the San Francisco showroom.

That left me without a job, but I decided to stay on in San Francisco and look for other work. In fact, I was offered a position as a staff salesman with one of the other showrooms at the Ice House, but that was not what I wanted. Working with and for Peter and Didi was fun, but I could not reconcile myself to doing it for anyone else. I tried instead to find a suitable position related to films and photography, and even considered going into the wedding photography business, which I was told could be lucrative. The opportunity to take a crack at it came when Scottie, the resident photographer at the Ice House, begged me to pinch-hit for him since he had inadvertently double-booked himself. When I told him that I had never covered a wedding before, he said, "Don't worry, it's a piece of cake. Just be there on time. With your background in photography, everything will take care of itself."

I was there as directed at the Norwegian Church on Hyde Street, but barely in the nick of time, as I was under the impression that the wedding was scheduled for an hour later. I met the officiating *preste-mann* (priest), who explained to me what was going to happen. I didn't know the name of the bride or groom and had no time for further inquiries since they were about to make their entrance, descending a staircase leading into the chapel. Positioning myself to take the introductory picture, I was startled at my first sight of the pretty bride. Daintily clasping a small bouquet of spring flowers, she rested her hands on her bulging stomach, reminiscent of a weather balloon about to be launched. I figured she was close to nine months pregnant and, therefore, that it would be best if I framed all my shots to exclude her tummy and waist, which I did.

With the ceremony over and the guests milling around, I finally met the bride and groom. She was Danielle Steele, carrying her first child, just under the wire to be born in wedlock. When she and her new husband heard my name, they seemed to know who I was. After we moved to Chez Robert for the wedding banquet, I found myself seated and treated as an honored guest rather than as a hired photographer. Later on, Danielle even invited me for tea to see Nicholas, her son born two weeks after the wedding, and also to meet some members of her family. She commissioned me to take portraits of her, which were far less glamorous than the ones that appear nowadays on the back covers of her umpteen best-selling novels that made her a multiple millionairess.

Nothwithstanding this bizarre initiation, I learned that wedding photography was not for me. I arranged for some one-man photography shows, displayed at I. Magnin and Neiman Marcus, and sold a few pictures, but not enough to convince me that I could make a living out of photography and the occasional travel pieces I wrote for magazines and newspapers. I realized I could not stay any longer in San Francisco and be with Connie. I would have been uncomfortable living with her without a job, and, if we should marry (which we never discussed), unable to support her with my limited resources and alimony obligations to Sinnie. Connie's previous two husbands had been incapable of supporting her, and I didn't want to see her saddled with a similar dilemma again. Reluctantly, I withdrew from the scene.

I returned to Los Angeles to be with Peter and Didi, who always welcomed me. But I also realized that it was not in the best interests of Peter and Didi to entwine my life so closely with theirs, having heard too many stories about the stress imposed upon a young married couple saddled with an elderly parent. Also, I could foresee that Peter's life would become even more peripatetic than mine. He was a mover, shaker, and doer, and about as hard working and ambitious a young man as I have ever known.

Soon after I rejoined them, Peter received a proposal to sell his factory. It was a deal hard to turn down. The fickleness of the furniture business and the cutthroat competition of the Midwestern and Eastern manufacturing giants were major considerations. So Peter sold the company, but kept the showroom in the Pacific Design Center, which had become more or less Didi's domain. Peter then decided to go into residential home building. After obtaining the required licenses, he set out to build himself a house on a lot on Cherokee Lane off Coldwater Canyon, only a few blocks from where Sinnie's and my first house still stood, almost unchanged. In addition to the attractive main house, Peter built me a small chalet adjoining the carport near the entrance gate to the property. He also added a swimming pool with large rock formations placed around it that were reflected in the glassy black surface of the water. I loved my little condo-type pad with its living-room fireplace and compact kitchen downstairs. The bedroom-studio, bathroom, and plenty of closets were upstairs. I felt as snug and cozy as I ever had in my private domicile. Our neighbors were Robin and Jessie French, a delightful and congenial couple. Jessie was an artist and "primitive" painter. Robin, her husband, was involved in the film business. A few houses up the lane lived Yale Summers, who had costarred in the *Daktari* series. Below us, adjoining the property line, lived Hermes Pan, the much honored dance director, whom I knew when we both worked at Twentieth Century Fox.

Next Peter started wheeling and dealing in land development projects, moving from one place to the next. He and his partner, Earl Miller, acquired a choice spread of a hundred acres of land in Franklin Canyon. It was a most desirable location, a few miles away from Beverly Hills with a paved access road. Their plan was to subdivide it into spacious equestrian estates with a limited number of private owners. After putting a lot of work and money into cleaning up and beautifying the raw land by planting trees, shrubs, and seeding grass to create green meadows, with their building plans carefully worked out and ready for zoning, they ran into a stone wall when they applied to the County of Los Angeles and the City of Beverly Hills for the necessary permits to begin construction.

The county and city wanted to incorporate the valuable stretch of canyon into their long-range plans for creating a greenbelt close to Beverly Hills—that is, when and if ever they scrounged up enough money to do so. Peter was told that under no circumstances could he or anyone else ever expect to be granted building permits to develop the land. After three years of futile waiting and fruitless haggling, Peter and his partner realized that the only alternative was to sell the property to the city, at a price considered fair market value by the city's own estimators. Even though it was a substantial settlement, for Peter and his partner, it was a loss in millions. The city's price was ten times below the going market price. In some consolation, Franklin Canyon is today part of the National Park System and open for public enjoyment.

Next on the agenda for Peter was acquisition of the old Converse Ranch at Santa Paula, a small town near Ventura on the Pacific Coast. There were about four hundred acres of mostly hilly land. When Peter and Didi first took me there to have a look at where we would be living next, I was flabbergasted and said, "What on earth would tempt you to buy this place?" To me, it looked run-down, dusty, and uninviting. The four existing buildings, deserted and partially falling down, did not inspire any confidence. There was one asset, though: the main residence of the Converse family, who had moved to Arizona years before and left behind a house completely furnished, with linen, silver, cutlery, dishes, and heirlooms, even a player piano in the living room with hundreds of rolls of music. The piano was no longer playable; rats had nested among the strings and eaten up the felt pads.

"You just wait and see. I'll make something very special out of this place," Peter said. He had a vision, and in his typical fashion, with his own hands and those of his sons P. J. and Patrick and an ample supply of local laborers, he realized it. In its time, the Converse home must have indeed been a showplace; it was even more so now. Two of the other remaining structures were restored for the help and ranch caretaker to live in. That left only the old barn, a derelict wooden shell of four walls and a leaky roof to be converted into my living quarters. Peter excelled in transforming such a structure into a habitat quite similar to my chalet at Cherokee Lane. He also planted a variety of trees, flowers, and shrubberies, and sodded all the flat land surrounding the houses, thus minimizing the dust clouds blown in by the ocean winds. Planting 25,000 seedling avocado trees and installing an irrigation system was only one of his major projects.

By the time the ranch approached what Peter had visualized, his financial reserves were depleted. Planting the avocado trees, which after five years of growth would provide a substantial cash flow, had been financed by a local bank with a long-term loan of close to a million dollars. In his enthusiasm and pride, Peter had overextended himself. When he fell in arrears with his monthly loan payments, the bank foreclosed and took over the ranch. We had to move out, and Peter was about as low as I had ever seen him, broke and struggling to survive. Not only did he lose the ranch, but he also lost Didi, who hated living under this continual pressure-cooker lifestyle. Their marriage ended in divorce.

Peter moved his office and belongings into a huge army surplus tent on a vacant piece of land he owned outside the town. While living in a neighbor's small guest cottage, he diligently went about pulling himself out of the financial morass by working hard in his construction business. I pursued my film career, even while we were living at the Converse Ranch, commuting to Los Angeles whenever an assignment came up, and wound up living there again. To Peter's credit, he paid off all his debts. He was fortunate in one respect, that Sandy Robertson, a gregarious and willowy long-time friend of his, saw him through one of the most serious double setbacks in his life. For this I thank "Sand Dab" ever so much, as does Peter.

Two years later, by a sheer fluke and dogged persistence, Peter found a ranch to his liking in northern California, located between Santa Rosa and Calistoga in the Napa Valley wine country. Surrounding the home were four hundred acres of partly forested terrain with lots of open meadows and a man-made lake, well suited for the comfort of his sizable collection of exotic animals of mostly African origin. Collecting animals had been one of Peter's primary avocations ever since he was a young boy, and somehow he always managed to take his private zoo along with him wherever he went, from Franklin Canyon to Santa Paula and, lastly, to Santa Rosa. Some of his animals are among those listed and protected as endangered species. It was bruited about that the ranch had belonged to a mysterious owner who was suspected of being a drug dealer on a major scale. When the law began to close in on him, he left his secluded ranch in a hurry, destination unknown, never to return. He has since been caught, convicted, and sentenced to a long residency at San Quentin. The ranch had been left in the hands of a local attorney, whom Peter dealt with but never met in person. The entire transaction was handled by phone, fax, and letters.

While not much attention had been paid to the land itself, there was a smallish but comfortable ranch home and an adjoining guest house with a swimming pool, ready for immediate occupancy. Peter and Sandy succeeded in transforming the property into a veritable Garden of Eden, far superior to the Converse Ranch. This is where Peter lives now, with his private preserve of close to three hundred fifty animals, scattered over grassy fields and wooded hills. Wandering around the property, one can see zebras, scimitar oryx, addax, eland, bongos, kangaroos, giraffes, exotic birds, and other species too numerous to mention—but no carnivores. The place is not open to the public, except for special tours by advance appointment. Visitors are taken around in safari-type vehicles, accompanied by a knowledgeable guide.

One might assume that this is the place where Peter will stay forever. Peter recently married Nancy Schofield, a zoologist, formerly second in charge of the San Francisco Zoo, and they live there happily. But knowing Peter as I do, I can never predict what will be next on his agenda. Once a job is done—and superlatively—another challenge might beckon.

It is part of Peter's inexhaustible energy and vision.

MORE FAMILY MATTERS

During my time spent with Peter in San Francisco and Los Angeles, letters from Sinnie arrived regularly. Some of them were funny and cheerful, others despondent and sad. She commiserated with me about Peter's multiple problems and bad luck when she heard about the Santa Paula fiasco and breakup with Didi, whom both of us loved.

She also kept me up to date with news about Mark, informing me that Mark had returned after a stay of some years in Hawaii. After graduating from Hollywood High, Mark had enrolled at the California College of Arts and Crafts in Oakland for two semesters and then went to the University of Hawaii in Honolulu. He tried his hand at various jobs in Honolulu, such as painting historical murals for government buildings, designing logos, and finding other artistic assignments. In partnership with a lady friend, a schoolteacher, they launched a magazine called *Talk Story Illustrated*, which was meant to entertain and enlighten young students past ten years of age. Mark was assistant editor and art director, contributing some of his own avant-garde cartoon-style drawings. After five issues, the magazine folded, deeply in debt and with stacks of leftover magazines piled up in his friend's garage. He then worked as a bellhop at the Sheraton Waikiki, thinking of it as a possible entrée into the hotel business. But it did not work out because Mark's back was in poor shape and the job was physically strenuous. Somewhat disheartened but undaunted in spirit, as he always seemed to be, he returned to Coronado and moved in with Sinnie into a spacious two-bedroom apartment.

One of Sinnie's letters contained the astounding news item that she was about to get married again and wondered what I thought of that, as though I were the one to grant her permission. Of course, I was delighted for her sake and wished her well with all my heart.

Her suitor and prospective husband was Captain Douglas Cordiner, U.S. Navy, retired, of North Carolina. He had courted her when she was a debutante in Coronado, at just about the time I showed up. In fact, when he heard of our engagement he made a desperate last-ditch effort to curry her favor. He rented a single-engine plane and circled the admiral's residence, towing a streaming banner that spelled "SINNIE, WILL YOU MARRY ME?" It spelled the end of this romantic interlude, and the rejected Romeo also received a stern reprimand from the admiral. Decades later, when he found out that Sinnie was divorced and available, he contacted her by letter, followed by a flood of long-distance calls and more fervent missives, culminating in a marriage proposal. In all those years they had not seen each other, not until Sinnie, reminiscent of an old-fashioned mail-order bride, arrived at Highland, North Carolina, with a prepaid plane ticket. Within a week they spoke their marriage vows, administered by a local clergyman and attended by only one of Captain Cordiner's two daughters, the other having apparently formed an instant enmity toward Sinnie, considering her an interloper.

The rest of their love story is like a Gothic horror tale played out against the foreboding background of an isolated, weathered country house in need of repair and a new coat of paint. Sinnie found out she had married a schizophrenic under medical care. His sudden mood changes, from pleasant and amiable Southern gentleman to abusive tyrant, terrified her. He kept a loaded rifle next to his chair and threatened to shoot himself and take her with him during his bouts of temporary insanity. Shocked and bewildered, she consulted his doctor and stuck it out it for a few weeks, hoping that more intensive medical treatment might alleviate the situation. Unfortunately, this did not happen. Disconsolate, she returned to Coronado to move back in with Mark, who was a tower of strength for her, for which I cannot be thankful enough.

While contemplating the necessary steps to initiate divorce proceedings, she received a telegram informing her that her husband had passed away suddenly, and would she, as his widow, attend to the funeral arrangements and all other pertinent details. Captain Cordiner had put a gun to his mouth and blown out his brains. In his will he left her his house and material possessions, with the exception of some items specifically willed to his two daughters. The house and furniture were sold, and she qualified for a modest pension as a naval officer's widow, enough to support her frugally, with occasional financial help from me.

Fate was not kind to Sinnie. In her last years, beset with terminal cancer, she flatly refused to undergo any kind of medical treatment, insisting on letting nature take its course. For the final six months of her life, she was a recluse, not wanting even her closest friends to see her decaying body and ravaged face. Mark and the attending day nurse were the only ones who had access to her. When Mark informed me that it might be only a matter of a few days before she succumbed, I told him I wanted very much to be with him. I did not even suggest seeing Sinnie, which I knew would only embarrass her. In fact, when he mentioned that I might be coming, she implored him not to let me see her in her present condition, by then living on painkillers in a semiconscious daze.

At daybreak the next morning, Mark called to tell me that it was over and that I could come now, which I did. Sinnie had died in her sleep with Mark sitting next to her bed. His mother's death affected him deeply, and I was glad to be there with him, helping to make all the necessary arrangements according to Sinnie's wishes. She wanted to be cremated and the urn with her ashes placed in the family crypt next to her father and mother at the Naval Academy Cemetery at Annapolis. There was not to be a memorial service nor any kind of gathering of friends for an informal wake. I stayed with Mark for a few weeks, which was soothing for both of us. A decent, honest, and compassionate man, he made me proud of having him as my son. His one misfortune was that he found it difficult to translate his artistic talent and integrity into a steady source of income. I realized that in many ways, Mark and I were much alike, except that I had had better luck in life and was in a position to use and capitalize on the breaks coming my way.

By then the grim reaper had made deep inroads into my family. My mother died unexpectedly after a bout with double pneumonia. I treasure my memory of her as an unselfish giver of herself and of her total devotion to her children and husband. Erna, my youngest sister, died of natural causes. She had admirably overcome her handicap of being retarded, as judged by normal standards, and proved that such a person can have a fruitful and productive life. Surprisingly, in her will, she left me and my sisters equal amounts of money that she had squirreled away in a secret savings account.

Elsa was the next to pass away. In the late 1950s, she had come to America with her husband, Ernst Moz, and settled down near Reno, Nevada, where they opened a sport shop. With the proliferation of ski resorts in the Lake Tahoe area, this gambit paid off. Elsa and her daughter Anne came to visit Sinnie and me frequently, and it was always a joy to have them with us. Then, on New Year's Eve of 1967, I received a call from one of Elsa's closest friends in Reno. She said that Elsa was very ill and asked me to come immediately since Elsa was estranged from her husband, who lived elsewhere. Getting on the next plane to Reno, I went straight to the hospital and was told she had advanced leukemia and a life expectancy of possibly six months. This was shattering to all of us who dearly loved Elsa, and especially to Anne. I brought them to Los Angeles, and they stayed with us in our home on Wetherly Drive.

The hospital at UCLA took care of Elsa in an inspiring professional and personal way. She was under constant observation by a group of young doctors with uncommon medical dedication and appreciation of her cheery, uncomplaining nature, always hopeful for things to get better. She passed the Reno doctor's six-month prognostication by an additional six months. When she had to be hospitalized, I spent every free hour I had with her. I watched the agony of her increasing pain until one day I said to the visiting chief of the cancer unit, taking him aside out of my sister's hearing, "Please, sir, for God's sake, enough is enough. Relieve the poor girl of her misery, with her body functions and mental capacity visibly falling apart and beyond any hope of improvement." Without any further words, her life-supporting maze of wires and tubes was disconnected. Her eyes closed. I sat next to her bed and silently held her hand. After a while, with one single deep sigh, she quietly expired. It was all so surprisingly peaceful and gave me a feeling of immense relief that her suffering was over. It made my sadness easier to bear.

Elsa's estranged husband and many of her friends, who had come all the way from Reno, attended her funeral services. Ernst eventually took her ashes to Salzburg to be placed in our family grave, just big enough to hold six urns. He also looked after Anne, their daughter, who today is a happily married mother with two darling daughters, Rosella and Michelle, living in California.

The death that hit me hardest was my father's. He had been ailing for a long time with emphysema and a lack of circulation in his legs, which led to the doctor's decision to amputate his gangrenous left leg above the knee. For a man of eighty-four, this was a major surgical procedure. Nelly, who had looked after mother and Erna during their illnesses, had to cope with our father's protracted hospitalization. I had a cable from her urging me to come to Salzburg quickly if I wished to see my father still alive. I booked a seat on the next flight to Vienna, arriving there the following day. I rented a car at the airport and drove hurriedly to Salzburg, arriving at Nelly's apartment late in the evening. She told me our father had died the day before.

The next morning, one of those hazy grey Salzburg days with a fine drizzle falling, Nelly and I went to the crematorium at Salzburg's ornate Central Friedhof cemetery, where we were met by a tall, gaunt, elderly functionary in a black military-cut greatcoat down to his ankles, a formal two-pointed shako on his head, and a tall staff with an ornamented brass top in his right hand. Resplendent as this outfit may have been when new, it was by now threadbare, stained, and shabby. He told us that everything was in readiness for cremation, unless I wished to view my father in his coffin. In that case, they would need some time to make him presentable. The very thought of putting pancake makeup, rouge, and lipstick on my father's face was an indignity I wished to spare him. "No, thank you," I said, declining the well-meant offer.

The trolley with my father's coffin was rolled into sight and placed in front of the iron doors leading into the cremation chamber. After a short prayer and benediction by an attending priest, the heavy doors of the oven swung open; mechanically the coffin rolled slowly into it, and the doors closed with a harsh metallic clang. Nelly and I made no attempt to hold back tears and clung to each other wordlessly. Nelly had been absolutely heroic in seeing him through the last months of his suffering. Since she was emotionally drained and physically spent, I suggested she pack a small bag and that we take off in my rental car and go somewhere, anywhere, just to get her away for a few days from this environment.

We drove out of the city, heading toward Vienna through Austria's picturesque wine country along the Danube. We stopped every night at a different village in small country inns along the road, liberally imbibing Bacchus's finest offerings, right from their source in the surrounding vineyards. We cried and laughed intermittently, ate, drank, reminisced, and slightly tipsy, fell into bed for a long night's blessed sleep. It was the best thing we could have done to ease us over the initial shock that now both of our parents and two sisters were gone, aware that we were two parentless, aging orphans. I left for home with a great emptiness in my heart.

YUGOSLAVIA ON MY MIND

On a strong impulse, in the spring of 1976, I decided to travel to Yugoslavia and revisit Tešanj, the place where I was born, and other towns I had known during my early years. Of course, the political situation had changed radically. After World War II, Josip Broz Tito, a Croatian revolutionary resistance fighter, succeeded miraculously in uniting all the region's centuries-long-feuding nationalities and religions (Serbs, Croats, Slovenes, Bosnians, Moslems, Macedonians, and Montenegrins) and numerous other minorities, under the umbrella of one ruling government. He named it the Socialist Federal Republic of Yugoslavia, and took over as its head of state, elevating himself to the rank of Marshal Tito. A Russian-trained communist, Tito naturally attempted to remake his country in the image of Stalin's Russia. Heavily subsidized and armed by the

Soviet Union, Yugoslavia became one of its satellites. Then in 1948, Moscow's Communist Information Bureau expelled Yugoslavia from the USSR, branding it a "revisionist nation," contradictory to Marxist doctrines. This sudden break drew Yugoslavia closer to other European nations and opened the door to tourists and trade agreements with other countries.

I made an appointment with Tugomir Dzalto, the head of Yugoslavia's consulate in San Francisco, to ask him what I might expect as a tourist who had been born in Yugoslavia but was now an American citizen. Also, as a photographer, I wanted to know what restrictions there would be. He said that he would gladly issue the required visa and that I had nothing to fear. He assured me that I would be welcomed with open arms and could travel freely. I could photograph anything I wished, with the exception of military installations and strategic bridges, all well marked with the warning sign of a red circle around a camera with a line through it. Dzalto offered to write a letter of introduction to his home office in Belgrade, requesting that they assist me in any way they could.

Nelly and I had planned for years to make such a sentimental journey together. She still spoke Serbo-Croatian fluently, while I was limited to a few stock phrases and catch words, insufficient to carry on a conversation. I suggested she meet me at the venerable Hotel Europa in Sarajevo, and she answered promptly that she was ready and delighted at the prospect of the trip we had long dreamed about. I booked a seat on a charter flight on Yugoslav Airlines from Los Angeles to Belgrade. With passengers packed in tightly and minimal creature comforts, it was a long and arduous flight, but not enough to diminish my enthusiasm.

Arriving at the Belgrade Airport in July 1976 and going through passport control and custom clearance, I was surprised by the efficiency of the proceedings. What struck me, however, was the noticeable, large presence of military personnel. I was met by a representative of the Yugoslav Tourist Office and taken to the newly built Hotel Yugoslavia, an impressive structure in modern style. It was listed as a luxury hotel, as indeed it was, if somewhat frugal in style and decor, but certainly first-rate in accommodations and service.

Belgrade as a city could not match the sightseeing attractions offered by Vienna, Munich, Paris, London, or other European capitals. Throughout its turbulent history it has been repeatedly set on fire, ransacked, and plundered by invaders, among them Attila the Hun with his wild horsemen. But nothing could compare with the aerial blitz unleashed by Hitler's

Luftwaffe. Within an hour the city was left smoking and in shambles. Historians tell us that at least forty times the city has had to be rebuilt from the ashes and rubble of devastation.

While still showing the telltale marks of destruction, Belgrade appeared to be a thoroughly modern city with wide, tree-shaded boulevards. Most of the damaged historical edifices had either been or were in the process of restoration. Huge, residential high-rise complexes formed the "New City," designated as rental units for lower income workers. I was amazed to see displays in shop windows of a variety of consumer goods, including clothing, cosmetics, TVs, electronic gadgets, washing machines and dryers, sports equipment, and toys for children. Food stalls overflowed with a surfeit of victuals and spirits. Sidewalk cafés and restaurants were crowded with people, mirroring the gridlocked automobiles in the main thoroughfares. People were neatly dressed, some quite fashionably, with loving attention paid to children. There were no beggars or homeless on the streets as far as I could detect. To me it was far different from what I had expected to find in a communist-oriented country. Its citizens were free to travel and could not be denied a passport as long as the applicant did not have a criminal record. However, in talking to many people, I found that a democracy Yugoslavia was not, nor a paradise to live in. How could it be under Marshal Tito's dictatorship?

Before leaving Belgrade, I checked in with the Yugoslav State Department, presenting my letter of introduction, and they, in turn, provided me with another letter to bail me out should I encounter any difficulties. With a rental car and sufficient gasoline coupons to see me through for a while, I headed for Sarajevo, about a five-hour drive away. I was looking forward to seeing the countryside and stopping over at frequent resting places along the road.

As planned, Nelly was waiting for me at the Europa. I had not seen her since our father's funeral, which had been some years before. It was indeed a happy reunion, and Nelly turned out to be a splendid traveling companion and indispensable interpreter. We stayed in Sarajevo for eight days, strolling about that fascinating city with its flavor of the Ottoman Orient mixed with a liberal touch of Western culture and a predominantly Moslem population. For a photographer, the opportunities and inspirations were boundless.

The next stop, Zenica, the town where we had lived as children, was in some ways disappointing. Our apartment above the post office no longer existed. It, as well as the railroad station, had been leveled by bombs during the last days of World War II. My old friend Art Devlin of Lake Placid, New York, a national ski jumping champion and Olympian, told me that he had been the bombardier on that mission. Munich, his flight crew's primary target, was socked in, so they took out Zenica's railroad station and post office as secondary strategic targets. They had done a good job; there was nothing left. However, the Catholic church where I had done my penance serving as an altar boy and the adjoining school were undamaged. Nelly could not resist the urge to sit down and play the church organ, remembering her first lessons in her musical education.

We set out to explore the possibility of finding someone still alive who had served under my father in the post office. Luck was with us as our search led us to an elderly lady, in good health and with sharp mind, who had been my father's Morse code telegraph clerk. We brought her a box of chocolates and encouraged her to ramble on with her memories. She spoke very highly of our father as a man and as an understanding superior. When Nelly asked her casually whether she saw any resemblance between me and my father, she squinted at me and said, "Oh yes, there is, but he is not anywhere near as handsome as his father was." Take that, Otto Lang, I said to myself.

Tešanj, the next town on our list, where we four children had been born in our grandparents' home, was a pleasant surprise. It had hardly changed at all. Having always been a Moslem stronghold, it was still. To find our old homestead was no problem; we instinctively walked up to it on a rough cobblestone footpath. It was exactly as both Nelly and I remembered it. Looking over a white picket fence, we saw the main house with the living quarters and next to it the cook house with the dining room. A few steps away was the infamous woodshed, where I was taken occasionally to receive mild corporal punishment for naughty behavior. Across the front yard stretched clotheslines hung with an assortment of garments. A group of five children were playing on the lawn with a stout woman in peasant garb overseeing their activities. It was an unforgettable tableau. Nelly and I were asked to come in and were offered freshly brewed Turkish coffee, poured into small porcelain cups from a diminutive long-handled brass pitcher. We were served a lump of sugar to be put into the mouth, the hot brew to be slurped over it.

With this mission completed, Nelly and I took off and roamed the country in every direction, stopping at random for the night. It was a rewarding and extraordinary journey ending on the Dalmatian Riviera, a coastline of singular beauty. I put Nelly on a coastal steamer at Dubrovnik to connect at Fiume with a train to Salzburg.

On my return to America I wrote a full-page piece, "There Is Hope for Yugoslavia," for the political section of the *San Diego Union*, and sorted out the wealth of photographs I had taken to prepare a traveling one-man photography show. It was subsequently bought *in toto* by the Yugoslavian government. After my first return visit to Yugoslavia in more than fifty years, and seeing the country with eyes different from those of a ten-year-old boy, I was so taken by its scenic beauty, cities and villages, hard-working people, and immense untapped natural resources, that I seriously contemplated doing a book of photographs on Yugoslavia. It would be coffee-table size in format with approximately 175 photographs. I visualized an introduction by a Yugoslav author, someone like Ivo Andrić, a Nobel Prize winner whose book *The Bridge on the Drina* I have reread many times. He would capture from his native point of view Yugoslavia's torturous evolution. To do such a book, I would have to make another lengthy journey to compile all the material I needed, which I did.

With the Winter Olympics scheduled to be held at Sarajevo in February 1984, the thought occurred to me that it would be the perfect time to have a book on the market. I approached the Yugoslav Olympic Organizing Committee with a proposal to present each official and competitor with a gift copy of the book as a memento. They sparked to the idea and told me to prepare a dummy copy to show them, and then we would settle the financial arrangements for having such a book printed. This meant I would have to make yet another trip to Sarajevo to include winter scenes.

Coincidentally, I had an assignment from *Ski* magazine to write a piece on my advance impressions of the venues for the Olympic Alpine skiing competitions and my general evaluation of Yugoslavia's ability to stage such a major event. As a reporter, I was an invited guest of the government and treated accordingly, under the guidance of Pavle Lukač, the press and public relations chief for the Winter Games. He was short, chubby, and fun to be with—also a workaholic and dynamo. He took me by helicopter over the mountains, showing me the downhill and slalom courses at Jahorina (for the women) and Bjelašnica (for the men). Later I skied these runs. I found the terrain adequate but falling somewhat short of the ultimate technical challenge, compared with that of previous Olympic sites. Nevertheless, in summing up my observations for *Ski*, I wrote, "In my opinion, the Yugoslavs will not only pull it off, but they will pull off the 1984 Winter Olympics in a style to make their nation proud."

When the Yugoslav delegation came to Los Angeles for meetings with Juan Samerang and other high officials of the Olympic organization, in connection with the upcoming Summer Olympics in Los Angeles, I managed to spirit them away for a luncheon at Dorris Johnson's home, which she so generously improvised on the shortest of notice. The Yugoslavs had looked forward to being invited to a private home to see how Americans lived. They could not have chosen a nicer one with a more gracious hostess. When I showed them the dummy copy I had prepared, they oohed and aahed enthusiastically, but when it came to the question of who was going to pay for the printing, they hemmed and hawed, finally saying, "So sorry, we can't do it. We are over our heads in debt." Thus a book conceived with the best of intentions died aborning.

The Sarajevo Olympics were a huge success in spite of unexpected setbacks caused by inclement weather. For Americans, it was considerably sweetened by Bill Johnson's winning the gold medal in the men's downhill and Debbie Armstrong's winning the gold in the women's giant slalom. To put the icing on the cake, the Mahre twins, Steve and Phil, took gold and silver medals in the men's slalom. Only ten years later, most of the splendid facilities built for the Olympics were bombed to smithereens by the fighting factions of Serbs, Croats, and Muslims trying to carve up Bosnia and Herzegovina among themselves.

FOND MEMORIES

One of my happiest memories is my association with the 1984 Summer Olympics held at Los Angeles. Peter Ueberroth, an acknowledged organizational genius, had initiated a novel program of forming a group of volunteer envoys to take care of each participating team. I was given a choice between Yugoslavia and Austria. Aware of my deficiency in Serbo-Croatian, I opted for Austria. As senior member of the group, I was given the distinction of being "envoy at large," meaning that I could spread myself around and have access to every venue.

As the athletes gathered, I was on duty at the UCLA compound of the Olympic Village set aside for athletes and their coaching staff. Most afternoons I was driven by a chauffeur (also a volunteer) to the Rose Bowl to be one of the hosts in the VIP tent to greet arriving dignitaries from FIFA, the worldwide governing body of soccer under its long-lived President João Havelange of Brazil. A sumptuous buffet dinner was served before the game started, and although the best seats were reserved for them to watch the game, there were spare seats available for us hosts. It made a long day for my old bones from early morning breakfast meetings until close to midnight when I got home and into bed.

The Los Angeles Olympics were considered one of the most successful ever held, despite predictions of crippling traffic tie-ups on LA's lifeline freeways and terrorist sabotage. Every event went off on time like a Swiss cuckoo clock. Even the last-minute decision of the Russian team not to participate did not dent the festive ambiance and wholehearted enthusiasm of millions of spectators. The opening and closing ceremonies filled the LA Coliseum to overflowing and, with a liberal dose of Hollywood glitz, were stupendous in scope and presentation. Contrary to dire projections of an astronomical deficit, the LA Olympics ended up with an astounding fiscal surplus, thanks to Ueberroth's astute management.

I have other fond memories of my later years. I remember with nostalgia another journey with Nelly and her closest friend, Traude Beigl. Both widowed, they had developed one of those rare friendships based on love and respect. They lived separately but saw each other practically every day and shared many interests in art, literature, and nature's beauty. We took off from Salzburg in Traude's Mercedes Benz, put at her disposal because she had worked many years for the Mercedes company, and headed at a leisurely pace toward Salonika in northeastern Greece. From there we branched out in various directions. We wanted to visit Meteora, with its incredible monasteries plastered like swallows' nests onto high rocky outcroppings. I also took a side trip alone to Mount Athos at the end of the Acte Peninsula with its many monasteries. Women were not allowed to set foot on this hallowed soil and, therefore, it was strictly a men's world of monks living in relative isolation, dedicated to work and prayer. I stayed overnight and spent a few days at one of these monasteries (Iveron); it gave me a spiritual lift to see how contentedly these monks lived, cut off from most of the comforts of the so-called civilized world. In a lengthy piece, "Pilgrimage to Mount Athos," published in the *San Diego Union*, I wrote in more detail about this experience.

Back home again, I received a letter from Traude, informing me that Nelly was not well. She had been diagnosed with advanced cancer, caused by her life-long habit of smoking, which was kept secret from her since it had progressed beyond the possibility of a cure. After arriving in Salzburg and seeing Nelly, I had a feeling that she knew the score. She kept up a cheerful front, grande dame that she always was, and continued smoking. Sadly realizing that it would be the last time I would see her, I left for home only at her insistence. She died shortly after my visit. Traude had her ashes laid to rest next to our parents and two sisters. I was grateful to have had this journey with Nelly. I missed her, as well as her masterfully written letters, very much. At present, Traude and I correspond with each other frequently, and she keeps me informed by newspaper clippings about the annual Salzburg Festival, which has grown into a world-renowned event with an enormous variety of musical and theatrical offerings.

In the past few years, memories flood my mind and my cup runneth over. I have been honored lately with testimonial dinners, plaques, scrolls, and lifetime achievement awards far beyond my expectations. One was a week-long affair held at Sun Valley in February 1993 to honor Friedl Pfeifer and me as former directors of the ski school, now in the able hands of Rainer Kolb with more than two hundred instructors at peak season. It was a poignant reunion with so many of my old friends, including Kathleen Mortimer-Harriman, Clarita Heath, Gretchen and Don Fraser, Wayne and Sandy Poulsen, former ski school instructors and perennial guests of Sun Valley, and of course, June and my old buddy Friedl, with his inamorata and right-hand girl, Sharon Crose, at his side. I was also proud to have been invited to show a selection of my photographs (hung by that irrepressible impresario Floyd McCracken) in a corner of the Harriman Room, adjoining the lobby of the lodge with a view onto the ice rink.

Seeing the large oil painting of Averell Harriman's handsome likeness hanging over the fireplace took me through the many years of Sun Valley, from the "Golden Years" with Pat Rogers as majordomo, ruling over his wintry domain with a firm but also most giving hand to the days of Bill Janss, the new owner and builder at heart who transformed Sun Valley into a real village community with permanent residents. As a dedicated skier of championship caliber, Janss immeasurably improved the existing lifts and runs and added new ones on Baldy Mountain. The resort's current owners, Earl and Carol Holding, learned to ski from scratch—painfully at times—to better understand and serve the needs of Sun Valley skiers and summer guests. They are a casual, unassuming, family-oriented couple, with a captivating charm and friendliness behind their outer shield of privacy. Standing in line at the ski lift, patiently waiting their turn, they would never give one the impression that they are the owners of Sun Valley. And what a stupendous job they have done in preserving the old and at the same time upscaling the place. Deliberately and at their own pace, they have made Sun Valley into one of the world's great winter and summer resorts. The new day lodge at the foot of Mount Baldy's Warm Springs run is an architectural showplace, as is the most recently inaugurated day lodge on Seattle Ridge at the top of Baldy. They installed the necessary equipment to "snow in" all the runs of this unique mountain with man-made snow, so the resort is no longer at the mercy of nature's whims. With all these improvements, I wonder what could be next in Earl's and Carol's fertile minds for the future. I remember a sunny day not so long ago riding the lift up to the top of Baldy Mountain with Dick and Lili Zanuck, ahead of us their two young sons, already expert skiers, musing with some satisfaction that in a small measure I had been a part of the growth of this splendid ski resort and remembering also how well it had served me.

Two of the most frequent questions I am asked are, "Which is your favorite ski resort?" and "What do you consider your personal best in films?" As to question number one, I would say it depends on the continent. In Europe, it is the trio of St. Anton, Zürs, and Lech; In America, it is the triumvirate of Sun Valley, Idaho; Vail, Colorado; and Deer Valley, Utah.

In answer to the second question, I would answer without much hesitation that my favorite is the ABC-TV special "Beethoven—Ordeal and Triumph." Although I cannot read a note of music or play an instrument, I am a devoted music lover. Why John Secondari and Jean Rogers, his wife, the creators and producers of the series *Saga of Western Man*, of which "Beethoven" was a part, zeroed in on me as director, based only on the recommendation of their ace cameraman Bill Hartigan, with whom I'd worked on a military training film, puzzles me to this day. To work with Rogers and Secondari (author of *Three Coins in the Fountain*), Bill Hartigan, Margot Winchester, and their regular staff was a godsend. The task of capturing Beethoven's life and music on film was daunting and scary. Working with the Boston Symphony Orchestra under Erich Leinsdorf to record some of Beethoven's music in its acoustically perfect hall was another one of the highlights of my entire career in films. Added to this was the inspired playing of Beethoven's piano sonatas and concertos by Claude Frank, portraying the composer.

We shot most of the film in Germany and Austria, in places and lodgings where Beethoven had lived and composed. Somehow in the end, all the pieces fitted together. I must have been in some kind of a special trance that I had never experienced before. Of course, without the help of everyone involved, including the team of editors who bailed me out in some critical situations, it would have never been the film it turned out to be. Beethoven's triumphant music and the personal tragedy of his becoming stone deaf transcended television. It garnered uncommon critical praise and somehow touched viewers not even steeped in classical music. I treasure the select comments from some of our nation's newspapers. This came from the *Hollywood Reporter.*

> It is a tribute to director Otto Lang that this deeply moving study of the life of Ludwig van Beethoven comes off . . . thanks to fine direction and magnificent use of low key and back lighting, the show is a winner. . . . Lang's direction stands out. The man wields a camera like an artist with a paint brush, making the program as pictorially beautiful as Beethoven's lighter music, as visually somber as the composer's stirring works. A tremendous asset to the TV industry.

The Associated Press said that it was "an awesome demonstration of television versatility." The *Evening Star* in Washington, D. C., added that it was "a stunning, beautiful, moving documentary, as charged with drama as any work of fiction." The *Detroit Free Press* called it "an hour of pure treasure for eye and ear." And, among others, the *Houston Chronicle* offered more praise, describing my effort as, "The inspiring story of a man's triumph over tragedy lit up the television screens on Wednesday night . . . . a brilliant hour . . . one of television's highest achievements . . . a feast for the eyes and ears."

Epilogue

A SUMMING UP

It is the spring of 1994. I am now eighty-six years old and have lived for the past seven years with June Campbell in her home perched on a high bluff in West Seattle, overlooking Alki Beach and the waters of Puget Sound. From here we can look past Bainbridge Island onto the whole stretch of the Olympic Peninsula, with its spectacular mountain range dominating the horizon. The daily sight of this panorama, with its constantly changing moods, is wondrous.

On a clear day, when I turn the corner driving on Admiral Way toward downtown Seattle, Mount Rainier fairly jumps into view in its full majesty, near enough to reach for it. I have not yet become jaded by the surprise of its impact, and it never fails to give me a jolt of acute pleasure, feeling that I have finally come home. The restless bird of passage—with his plumage considerably tattered—has settled down and come to roost. After all, it was at Mount Rainier's Paradise Inn that my career in America had its beginnings in 1936. I can count on a host of touchingly loyal friends from those days (Ancient Skiers, Ski For All, and others) who have welcomed me home.

There is something else that drew me to Seattle. While teaching there in 1936, I met a lovely young lady named June Gestner briefly at Mount Baker, and then saw her again at Paradise Inn. From these very first encounters I was attracted by her. Close to nineteen years old at the time, she was beautiful, poised, and rather shy, with a captivating smile, dark hair, and hazel eyes. June loved skiing, not only for the jolly companionship of like-minded young people, but also for the opportunity for her to go off alone on long cross-country treks, cutting with her skis into the pristine snow of forests and meadows. That closeness to nature has stayed with her to this day, as has her love for animals.

Our initial acquaintance developed into an innocent flirtation, with neither one of us ready for a deeper commitment. I had my hands full building a career and June was going to college to study art. Even in high school she had shown a pronounced talent as a painter, inherited from and encouraged by her mother, who had been painting for many years with commendable results. On one of my regular trips through Seattle commuting between Rainier and Baker, June invited me to meet her mother and have lunch at their home in West Seattle. It was a delightful interlude, and I enjoyed meeting Mrs. Gestner, rightly touted as a superior cook and gracious hostess. She had passed on her good looks to June, and had taught her to go by her values pertaining to life in general and human beings specifically. She had infused her with a strict ethical code, without turning her into a prude. Parting from Mrs. Gestner, after expressing my thanks for a delectable meal, I said quite spontaneously, "I want you to know, Mrs. Gestner, if June ever learns to cook as you do, I shall try to woo her into marrying me." It never came to that, and our paths diverged. After the winter season ended I went off to California, and when I returned the following winter, I was married to Sinclair Gannon. Naturally, this changed the relationship between June and me, but we kept in touch through postcards, occasional phone calls, little mementos, and a few rare and brief encounters.

June had been awarded a scholarship as an art student to the University of Colorado in Colorado Springs. She married Joe Campbell, a gifted painter, and they moved to Texas to build a life of their own. Following the untimely death of her husband after thirty-four years of wedlock, June moved back to Seattle with two dogs and three cats to be near her brother Don and sister Mildred. Her main concern was to find a temporary place to settle down with her pets until she found a house suited to her needs, which is the home she still lives in now. By accident, coincidence, or twist of fate, we met again in San Francisco, where I had come on a short business trip from Los Angeles.

She asked me to meet her in the lobby of a hotel off Union Square, where she was staying while visiting a friend. After calling her room, I waited for her to come down. When the door of the elevator opened and she stepped out, I was taken aback at how lovely she looked, even though many years had passed. We moved across the lobby to a small bar, sat down, and began to talk as though we had seen each other only a few weeks before. Then we strolled over to a French bistro on Polk Street for lunch with a glass of wine to supplement the restaurant's cassoulet, a *spécialité de la maison.* Since it was a sunny day, we decided to take a boat cruise past the island of Alcatraz and under the huge span of the Golden Gate Bridge out into the open sea, before returning to have dinner at Fisherman's Wharf. By the time I escorted her back to her hotel, the old rapport of our younger years, more than half a century past, had been fully reestablished. Before we parted in the lobby, I asked June would it be all right if I came to visit her in Seattle.

"That would be nice," she said. "I have a big house with a guest room and you are welcome to use it." A few weeks later, I flew up to Seattle to visit her over a weekend, arriving during one of the city's patented rainy spells. Both of us had miserable colds, with our noses dripping to match the rain outside.

As it happened in the well-known stage play *The Man Who Came to Dinner* (starring the contrary Monty Wooley on Broadway), who stayed on and on, I, too, stayed on and on, even longer than he—seven years later I am still here with June. We help and consult each other in solving problems and share many things, such as music, books, long walks through the woods of Lincoln and Schmitz Parks, the magic of the Olympic Rain Forest, trips to the San Juan Islands and Victoria, British Columbia, in addition to partaking of a plethora of cultural events offered by the fair city of Seattle. We relish the comforts and privacy of the house we live in, surrounded by trees, blooming shrubs, and a profusion of rhododendrons, daffodils, and tulips of all colors. We watch as the swallows have returned to occupy and refurbish their old nests under the eaves, and a pair of newborn squirrels test out their lightning-fast reflexes among the branches of a lilac tree. To my pleasant surprise, I found out that June is an excellent cook—like her mother—and between the two of us we can come up with a superior Chinese stir-fry dinner.

June's appreciation of my writing and encouragement to keep going, in addition to her providing me with the coziest of writer's dens, has been instrumental in my finishing this book, which I began to write long before I moved to Seattle. Initially it was instigated by my two sons and grandsons, and also by Dale, Didi, and her children. Tentatively at first, I began to put down on paper some of the family chronicles and happenings in my life. Once I got past the opening sentence, written in longhand, I actually began to enjoy it. "Scratch," the cat, last of June's original Texas immigrants, often keeps me company while I write, following the strokes of my pen with her nose or else tiptoeing gingerly over the mess of papers scattered around my desk, carefully sorting and pushing them out of her way.

Although this book has had a protracted gestation period, it reminds me of a letter an editor at Henry Holt and Company once wrote to me. "It does not matter how long it takes to write a book," he said. "What matters is how good it is." There is, however, a statement by Ludwig van Beethoven etched more deeply in my mind. I discovered it and put it at the end of the film I directed about his turbulent life. He said, *Only life is short. Art is eternal.*

Courtesy of Hofburg Museum, Vienna

Otto Lang.
Photo by Sue Ellison, Seattle, 1994

.....is a vivid account of an interesting life, highly readable and very gentlemanly. Lang tells his story adeptly, almost gossip-free. That's surely one reason that a dedicated ski instructor got at far in Hollywood as he did.

Chris Goodrich
"Book Review," *Los Angeles Times*

Reading this book is a marvelous vicarious journey through the 20th century.

Barbara McLloyd Michael,
"The Book Monger," Seattle, WA

It takes a good storyteller to be a good film director and Otto Lang spins a fascinating tale about great skiers and actors. Students of both cinema and skiing history will find much to enjoy here.

Seth Masia,
Ski **magazine, NY**

A wonderful, wonderful book.

Leeroy Sopper, former Manager
University Book Store, Seattle WA

It's amazing, it's amusing....

Mort Lund, Editor
Journal of the International Skiing History Association **magazine, Accord, NY**

"You are a great communicator...while reading your adventures I had the feeling I was right there with you, sharing the poignant love story with your wife, the Who's Who power brokers of this world, the many fascinating people, places and events.

Charles Engel, Senior Vice President
Universal Television Co., CA

Otto Lang's life is the stuff that movies are made of. Even at 463 pages, it almost seems too short to encompass it's 86-year-old author's life.....

John Hartl
***Seattle Times* movie critic**

"Your book is a treasure and I will savor it for a long time."

David Brown, President, Manhattan Project, Ltd., NY.

....A Knockout....Pure and simple! I couldn't put it down!

John Jay, Pioneer ski film presenter and author,
Rancho Santa Fe, CA

A Bird of Paradise is filled with stories about skiing and films. It is an enjoyable, engaging and worthwhile read..!..

Ted Elrick,
***Directors Guild of America* magazine, Los Angeles, CA**

"His 86 years have been crowded with large roles: American ski legend, Hollywood producer and director, gifted photographer, world traveler, noted journalist and book author."

Adam Worcester, Editor
West Seattle Herald

"This is a superb book! I might even say a classic of its kind."

James Laughlin,
Founder of New Directions Publishing Co., NY